MW01074407

# THE
# JASTA PILOTS

## NORMAN FRANKS, FRANK BAILEY
## AND RICK DUIVEN

GRUB STREET · LONDON

Published by
Grub Street
The Basement
10 Chivalry Road
London SW11 1HT


Copyright © 1996 Grub Street, London
Text copyright © 1996 Norman Franks, Frank Bailey and Richard Duiven

**British Library Cataloguing in Publication Data**
Franks, Norman L.R. (Norman Leslie Robert), 1940–
The Jasta Pilots: detailed listings and histories, Aug 1916 – Nov 1918
1. Germany, Luftwaffe  2. Fighter pilots – Germany
3. World War, 1914–18 – Aerial operations, German
I. Title  II. Bailey, Frank W.  III. Duiven, Rick
940.4'4'943

**ISBN 1 898697 47 7**

All rights reserved. No part of this publication may be reproduced,
stored in a retrieval system, or transmitted in any form or by any means,
electronic, mechanical, photocopying, or otherwise, without the prior
permission of the copyright owner.

Typeset by Pearl Graphics, Hemel Hempstead
Printed and bound by Biddles Ltd, Guildford and King's Lynn

Printed in the United States of America

# Contents

ACKNOWLEDGEMENTS iv

INTRODUCTION 1

GLOSSARY 2

THE JASTA AIRFIELDS 6

THE JASTA AND MARINE JASTA HISTORIES 13

THE JASTA PILOTS 89

THE MARINE JASTA PILOTS 307

JAGDGESCHWADER AND JAGDGRUPPE
   FORMATIONS 319

JASTA COLOURS 324

FIGHTER 'G' NUMBERS 335

JASTA PILOT CASUALTIES 345

A–Z LIST OF GERMAN FIGHTER ACES 358

# Acknowledgements

This book is an attempt to create a database of information for the many WWI aviation enthusiasts and would-be historians. However, it is acknowledged that with the passage of time, lost information and many conflicting reports, it is impossible for it to be a definitive study, but it is a start.

In compiling this information, the authors wish to thank a number of friends and colleagues who have helped with information and/or photographs: George Williams, Neal O'Connor, Paul Leaman and *Cross & Cockade International*, Tony Svensen, Dan-San Abbott, Jeffrey Sands (whom we also forgot to thank for his help with *Above the Lines*), Peter Kilduff, Nick Mladenoff, Chaz Bowyer and the late Ben Chamberlain. Other photos are from the authors' collections.

We would also like to thank Keith Rennels for photographic help, Tony Svensen for his excellent map of the German airfields in France and Belgium, Robert Franks for his map of the German Armees, and Greg VanWyngarden for his marvellous side-view drawings as well as photographs from his own collection.

Our gratitude also extends to Ronda Rennels for computer expertise and to John Davies of Grub Street publishers, who allows us to indulge our hobbies under the guise of historians and authors. Also to Heather, Dolly and Lin, who help us in so many different ways. And finally to a very few we would say this: Those who can, try, while those who can't, criticise!

# Introduction

Following the success of *Above the Lines**, which covers the aces of the German Air Service and German Marine pilots of WWI, it seemed a logical progression that a full list of all pilots who served in a German Jasta, from their formation in the late summer of 1916 until the end of the Great War, be created. Much of the basic work had already been undertaken by Rick Duiven from his personal interest in the men who had served in each Jasta. From this material, taken from many sources, came the idea of listing all pilots in an alphabetical format so that enthusiasts of WWI aviation as well as historians of that conflict could have as full an A–Z list of these pilots as was possible.

The obvious offshoots of this task were to list, where appropriate, victories claimed by, for the want of a better phrase, the non-aces, that is, those pilots who achieved between one and four confirmed victories, and also to list where known some of these pilots' unconfirmed claims. Therefore this book has to be read in conjunction with *Above the Lines*, for although the aces are named here in the full A–Z listing, their biographies and victory claims are not, as they already appear in some detail in the aces book. It also seemed appropriate to provide an alphabetical list of all German fighter aces, rather than the more usual list by victory number.

In order to give further coverage of the Jasta pilots, more detailed Jasta histories appear in this volume — although shortened versions appeared in *Above the Lines* — and these have also been enhanced with a full list of Jasta Staffelführers and bases. In addition there is also a list of airfields used by the Jastas and Marine Feld Jastas, not only on the Western Front, but also in Italy and Macedonia. To complement the Western Front airfields, our colleague Tony 'Pys' Svensen, in Norway, has provided an excellent map showing the majority of these airfield locations. There is also a map showing the various German Army fronts to which the Jastas were attached, produced by Robert Franks.

Progressing further, it seemed prudent to show which Jastas were grouped together to form the five permanent Jagdgeschwadern and the numerous, less permanent Jagdgruppen, together with their leaders. These were very fluid formations and the units within each Jagdgruppe could change almost daily. However, the main information is here. In addition, a full list of German fighter pilot casualties seemed desirable and there is also a list of RFC/RAF 'G' numbers, pertaining to just fighter aeroplanes. As there are still a number of obvious and less obvious anomalies with this list, some additional 'captured' aeroplanes are noted, although many are not covered by any form of 'G' serials or listing.

Finally there is an attempt to describe and show something of the markings carried by the aircraft of the various Jastas. This is by no means definitive, and probably never will be. Much has been lost to knowledge or memory over the years, and black and white photographs do little to help answer questions of colour. The most obvious and famous colour problem was the engine cowling of the Fokker Triplane flown by Werner Voss. For years it was thought to be black or dark green, until it became clear that it had been chrome yellow! This was due to the way some colours were reproduced on photographic paper of the period.

In the main there was a scheme adopted to identify each Jasta; the famous red-painted machines of Richthofen's Jasta 11, for instance, or the broad black and white bands around the fuselages of Jasta 26's machines. However, any number of pilots carried very individual markings which did not comply with the overall Jasta scheme, while to add to the confusion, some pilots when moving to another unit took their machine with them and may not have changed its colouring. Greg VanWyngarden has made a valiant attempt at depicting as many of the Jasta colourings as are known at this time.

What we hope to have achieved is the most complete record of information about the German Jasta pilots of WWI. It is by no means complete or definitive but it is a basis for further research, and at least the most informative collection of data on this subject in one book.

Norman Franks, Surrey, England; Frank W Bailey, New Jersey, USA; Rick Duiven, California, USA

* The third in a series of Grub Street publications covering the air aces of WWI: *Above the Trenches* (Shores, Franks and Guest, 1990), *Over the Front* (Franks and Bailey, 1992) and *Above the Lines* (Franks, Bailey and Guest, 1993).

# Glossary and Abbreviations

## Ranks

| | | Equivalent |
|---|---|---|
| Fähnr | Fähnrich | Officer Cadet |
| Fw | Feldwebel | Sergeant |
| FwLtn | Feldwebel-Leutnant | Sgt-Major-Lt (wartime) |
| Flg | Flieger | Private |
| Flgmt | Flugmaat | Aviation Petty Officer |
| Flgmstr | Flugmeister | Naval aviation airman |
| Flgobmatr | Flugobermatrose | Aviation Senior Rating |
| Flgomt | Flugobermeister | Aviation Chief Mate |
| Gen | General | Lieutenant General |
| Gen.Ltn | Generalleutnant | Major General |
| Gen.Maj | Generalmajor | Brigadier General |
| Gen.Ob | General-Oberst | General |
| Gefr | Gefreiter | Lance Corporal |
| Hptm | Hauptmann | Captain |
| Ltn | Leutnant | Second Lieutenant |
| Ltn d L | Leutnant der Landwehr | ??? |
| Ltn d R | Leutnant der Reserve | 2nd Lt of the Reserve |
| Ltn z S | Leutnant zur See | Naval Second Lieutenant |
| Maj | Major | Major |
| Obflgmstr | Oberflugmeister | Naval Aviation Snr NCO |
| Oblt | Oberleutnant | First Lieutenant |
| Oblt z S | Oberleutnant zur See | Naval First Lieutenant |
| Obst | Oberst | Colonel |
| ObstLtn | Oberstleutnant | Lieutenant Colonel |
| OfStv | Offizierstellvertreter | Warrant Officer |
| Sgt | Senior Unteroffizier | Sergeant |
| Uffz | Unteroffizier | Corporal |
| Vfw | Vizefeldwebel | Sergeant-Major |
| Vzflgmstr | Vizeflugmeister | Aviation Chief Petty Officer |

## Abbreviations

| | | |
|---|---|---|
| AFP | Armee Flug Park | Aviation supply depot |
| Bogohl | Bombengeschwader | Bombing unit |
| EK I/II | Eisenkreuz I/II Klasse | Iron Cross 1st & 2nd Class |
| FA | Flieger Abteilung | Flying unit/section |
| FAA | Flieger Abteilung Artillerie | Flying unit — artillery |
| FEA | Flieger Ersatz Abteilung | Aviation replacement unit |
| FFA | Feldflieger Abteilung | Field Aviation unit |
| Fr | Freiherr | Baron |
| Gruja | Führer der Jagdgruppe | Leader of a Jagdgruppe |
| Idflieg | Inspektion der Fliegertruppen | Inspectorate of aviation |
| JsSch | Jastaschule | Fighter pilot school |
| JB | Jasta Boelcke | formally Jasta 2 |
| JG | Jagdgeschwader | Permanent Group of Jastas |
| JGr | Jagdgruppe | Temporary Group of Jastas |
| Kasta | Kampfstaffel | Fighting section |
| Kek | Kampfeinsitzerkommando | Group of fighting planes |
| Kest | Kampfeinsitzer Staffel | Home Defence squadron |
| KG | Kampfgeschwader | Bombing unit/squadron |
| Kofl | Kommandeur de Flieger | CO of Armee aviation |
| LFA | Land-Flieger Abteilung | Naval landplane unit |

| | | |
|---|---|---|
| MFJ | Marine Feld-Jasta | Marine Jasta |
| MLS | Marine Land Staffel | Unit operating on land |
| OzbV | Offizier zur besonderen Verwendung | Adjutant |
| Ritter | Ritter | Knight |
| Rittm | Rittmeister | Cavalry Captain |
| SchSt | Schlachtstaffel | ???? |
| SFS I | Seefrontstaffel I — Neümunster | |
| SFS II | Seefrontstaffel II — Zeebrugge | |
| SS | Schutzstaffel/Schusta | Ground support unit |
| Stofl | Stabsoffizier der Flieger | Staff Officer for Aviation |
| Stv | Stellevertreter | Second-in-command |
| zlg/zlgzw | zur landung gezwungen | forced to land* |

## Other Abbreviations

| | |
|---|---|
| C&C | Cross & Cockade Journal |
| CO | Commanding Officer |
| DOI | Died of Injuries |
| DOW | Died of Wounds |
| EA | Enemy Aircraft |
| EOW | End of War |
| IIC | Injured in Crash |
| INJ | Injured |
| INT | Interned |
| KIA | Killed in Action |
| KIAcc | Killed in Accident |
| KIC | Killed in Crash |
| NO | Nachrichten Offizier |
| OTF | Over the Front Journal |
| POW | Prisoner of War |
| Trans | Transferred |
| u/c | unconfirmed |
| WIA | Wounded in Action |

Explanatory note: In the A–Z pilot listings, a date shown in brackets — e.g. (Aug 1917) — indicates an approximate date.

---

* Where a hostile aeroplane was seen to land inside its own lines and apparently relatively undamaged. These were not generally included in a pilot's victory score unless the machine was subsequently seen to be set on fire, or destroyed by artillery fire.

In cases where a victory was claimed, but not confirmed, a '–' appears in the pilots' victory lists where otherwise a number would be shown.

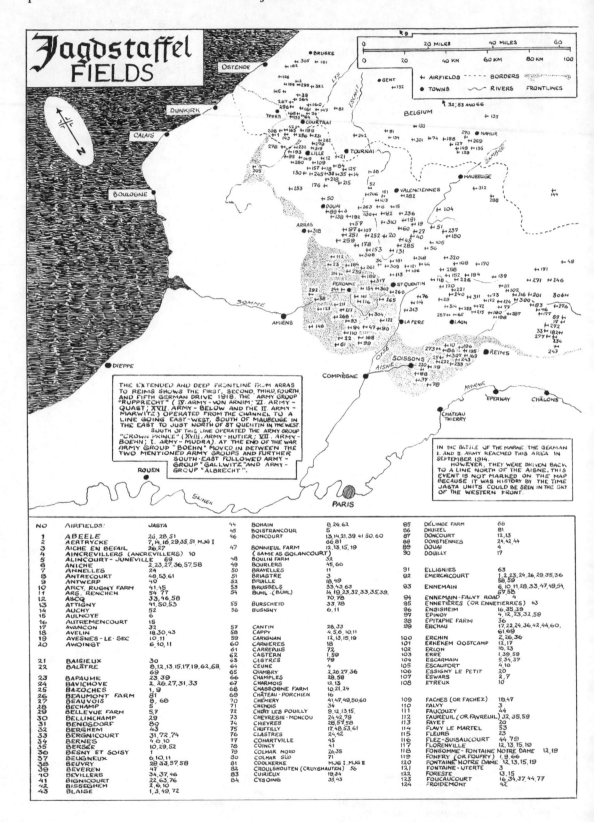

| NO | AIRFIELDS: | JASTA |
|----|-----------|-------|
| 1 | ABEELE | 26, 28, 51 |
| 2 | AERTRYCKE | 7, 14, 16, 29, 35, 51, MJG I |
| 3 | AICHE EN BEFAIL | 26, 27 |
| 4 | AINCREVILLERS (ANCREVILLERS) | 10 |
| 5 | ALINCOURT- JUNEVILLE | 69 |
| 6 | ANICHE | 2, 23, 27, 36, 57, 58 |
| 7 | ANNELLES | 24 |
| 8 | ANTRECOURT | 48, 53, 61 |
| 9 | ANTWERP | 40 |
| 10 | ARCY, RUGNY FARM | 41, 45 |
| 11 | ARS. RENCHEN | 54, 77 |
| 12 | ASCQ | 33, 46, 58 |
| 13 | ATTIGNY | 41, 50, 53 |
| 14 | AUCHY | 52 |
| 15 | AULNOYE | 6 |
| 16 | AUTREMENCOURT | 15 |
| 17 | AVANCON | 32 |
| 18 | AVELIN | 18, 30, 43 |
| 19 | AVESNES- LE- SEC | 10, 11 |
| 20 | AWOINGT | 6, 10, 11 |
| 21 | BAISIEUX | |
| 22 | BALÂTRE | 8, 12, 13, 15, 17, 19, 62, 68, 69 |
| 23 | BAPAUME | 23, 39 |
| 24 | BAVICHOVE | 2, 26, 27, 31, 33 |
| 25 | BAZOCHES | 1, 9 |
| 26 | BEAUMONT FARM | 81 |
| 27 | BEAUVOIS | 8, 68 |
| 28 | BECHAMP | 3 |
| 29 | BELLEVUE FARM | 5, 7 |
| 30 | BELLINCHAMP | 29 |
| 31 | BENSDORF | 89 |
| 32 | BERGHEM | |
| 33 | BERGNICOURT | 31, 72, 74 |
| 34 | BERNES | 4, 6, 10 |
| 35 | BERSÉE | 10, 29, 52 |
| 36 | BESNY ET SOISY | 1 |
| 37 | BEUGNEUX | 6, 10, 11 |
| 38 | BEUVRY | 28, 33, 57, 58 |
| 39 | BEVEREN | 47 |
| 40 | BEVILLERS | 34, 37, 46 |
| 41 | BIGNICOURT | 22, 63, 76 |
| 42 | BISSEGHEM | 2, 6, 10 |
| 43 | BLAISE | 1, 3, 49, 72 |
| 44 | BOHAIN | 8, 26, 62 |
| 45 | BOISTRANCOUR | 5 |
| 46 | BONCOURT | 13, 14, 21, 39 41 50, 60 66, 81 |
| 47 | BONNIEUL FARM (SAME AS GOLANCOURT) | 12, 13, 15, 19 |
| 48 | BOULIN FARM | 32 |
| 49 | BOURLERS | 45, 66 |
| 50 | BRAVELLES | 11 |
| 51 | BRIASTRE | 3 |
| 52 | BRULLE | 18, 49 |
| 53 | BRUSSELS | 33, 43, 63 |
| 54 | BUHL (BUHL) | 14, 19, 23, 32, 33, 35, 39, 70, 78 |
| 55 | BURSCHEID | 33, 78 |
| 56 | BUSIGNY | 6, 11 |
| 57 | CANTIN | 28, 33 |
| 58 | CAPPY | 4, 5, 6, 10, 11 |
| 59 | CARIGNAN | 12, 13, 15, 19 |
| 60 | CARNIERES | 18 |
| 61 | CARREPUIS | 72 |
| 62 | CASTERN | 1, 59 |
| 63 | CASTRES | 79 |
| 64 | CEUNE | 4 |
| 65 | CHAMBRY | 2, 26, 27, 36 |
| 66 | CHAMPLES | 28, 58 |
| 67 | CHARMOIS | 12, 13 |
| 68 | CHASSOGNE FARM | 10, 21, 24 |
| 69 | CHÂTEAU - PORCHIEN | 16 |
| 70 | CHEMERY | 41, 47, 49, 50, 60 |
| 71 | CHEROIS | 34 |
| 72 | CHÉRY LES POUILLY | 9, 12, 13, 15, |
| 73 | CHEVRESIS -MONCOU | 24, 42, 79 |
| 74 | CHIEVRES | 28, 57, 58 |
| 75 | CHUFFILLY | 17, 48, 53, 61 |
| 76 | CLASTRES | 24, 42 |
| 77 | COHARTVILLE | 45 |
| 78 | COINCY | 41 |
| 79 | COLMAR NORD | 26, 35 |
| 80 | COLMAR SÜD | 71 |
| 81 | COOLKERKE | MJG I, MJG II |
| 82 | CROULSHOUTEN (CRUYSHAUTEN) | 56 |
| 83 | CUIRIEUX | 18, 84 |
| 84 | CYSOING | 33, 43 |
| 85 | DÉLINGE FARM | 68 |
| 86 | DHUIZEL | 81 |
| 87 | DONCOURT | 12, 13 |
| 88 | DONSTIENNES | 24, 42, 44 |
| 89 | DOUAI | 4 |
| 90 | DOUILLY | 17 |
| 91 | ELLIGNIES | 63 |
| 92 | EMERCHICOURT | 1, 2, 23, 24, 26, 29, 35, 36 58, 59 |
| 93 | ENNEMAIN | 6, 10, 11, 28, 33, 47, 49, 54, 57, 58 |
| 94 | ENNEMAIN-FALVY ROAD | 4 |
| 95 | ENNETIÈRES (OR ENNETIERRES) | 63 |
| 96 | ENSISHEIM | 16, 35, 39 |
| 97 | EPINOY | 4, 12, 23, 32, 58 |
| 98 | EPITAPHE FARM | 36 |
| 99 | ERCHAU | 17, 22, 24, 36, 42, 44, 60, 61, 69 |
| 100 | ERCHIN | 2, 26, 36 |
| 101 | ERKÉKEM OOSTCAMP | 12, 17 |
| 102 | ERLON | 16, 23 |
| 103 | ERRE | 1, 39, 59 |
| 104 | ESCARMAIN | 5, 34, 37 |
| 105 | ESCAUFORT | 4, 10 |
| 106 | ESSIGNY LE PETIT | 20 |
| 107 | ESWARS | 2, 7 |
| 108 | ETREUX | 10 |
| 109 | FACHES (OR FACHEZ) | 18, 47 |
| 110 | FALVY | 3 |
| 111 | FAUCOUZY | 44 |
| 112 | FAUREUIL (OR FAVREUIL) | 32, 35, 59 |
| 113 | FAYET | 20 |
| 114 | FLAVY LE MARTEL | 53 |
| 115 | FLEURS | 23 |
| 116 | FLEZ-SUISAUCOURT | 44, 79 |
| 117 | FLORENVILLE | 12, 13, 15, 19 |
| 118 | FONSOMME- FONTAINE NOTRE DAME | 12, 19 |
| 119 | FONFRY (OR FOUFRY) | 1, 9, 66 |
| 120 | FONTAINE NOTRE DAME | 12, 13, 15, 19 |
| 121 | FONTAINE- UTERTE | 3 |
| 122 | FORESTE | 13, 15 |
| 123 | FOUCAUCOURT | 16, 34, 37, 44, 77 |
| 124 | FROIDEMONT | 42 |

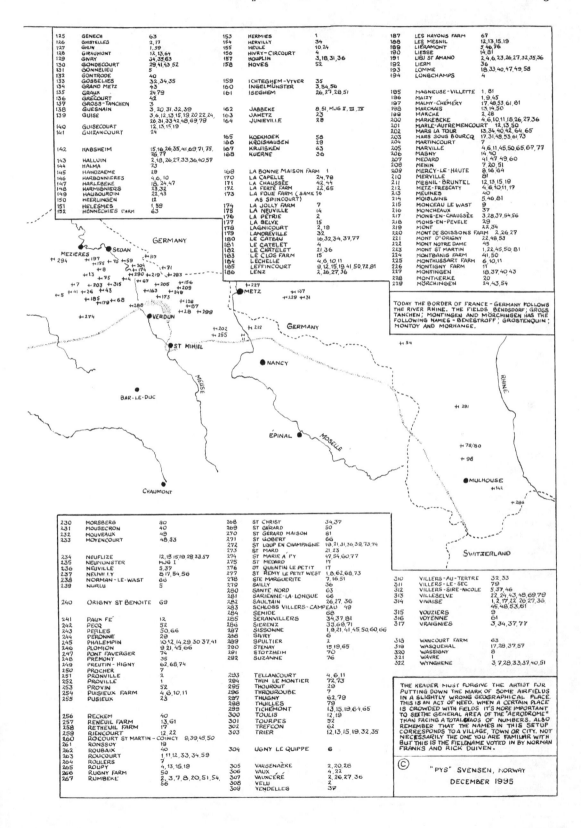

| | | |
|---|---|---|
| 125 | GENECH | 63 |
| 126 | GHISTELLES | 2,17 |
| 127 | GHLIN | 1,59 |
| 128 | GIRAUMONT | 12,13,64 |
| 129 | GIVRY | 34,35,63 |
| 130 | GONDECOURT | 29,41,43,52 |
| 131 | GONNELIEU | 5 |
| 132 | GONTRODE | 40 |
| 133 | GOSSELIES | 32,34,35 |
| 134 | GRAND METZ | 43 |
| 135 | GRAUX | 24,79 |
| 136 | GRECOURT | 42 |
| 137 | GROSS-TANCHEN | 3 |
| 138 | GUESNAIN | 3,20,31,32,39 |
| 139 | GUISE | 3,6,12,13,15,19,20,22,24, 26,31,33,42,48,69,79 |
| 140 | GUISECOURT | 12,13,15,19 |
| 141 | GUIZANCOURT | 24 |
| 142 | HABSHEIM | 15,16,26,35,41,69,71,75, 76,77 |
| 143 | HALLUIN | 2,18,26,27,33,36,40,59 |
| 144 | HALMA | 73 |
| 145 | HANDZAEME | 29 |
| 146 | HARBONNIERES | 4,6,10 |
| 147 | HARLEBEKE | 18,24,47 |
| 148 | HARMIGNIERS | 23,32 |
| 149 | HAUBOURDIN | 22,43 |
| 150 | HEERLINGEN | 12 |
| 151 | HELESMES | 1,59 |
| 152 | HENNECHIES FARM | 63 |
| 153 | HERMIES | 1 |
| 154 | HERVILLY | 34 |
| 155 | HEULE | 10,24 |
| 156 | HIVRY-CIRCOURT | 4 |
| 157 | HOUPLIN | 3,18,31,36 |
| 158 | HOVES | 52 |
| 159 | ICHTEGHEM-VYVER | 35 |
| 160 | INGELMUNSTER | 3,54,56 |
| 161 | ISEGHEM | 26,27,28,51 |
| 162 | JABBEKE | 8,51,MJG II, III ,IV |
| 163 | JAMETZ | 23 |
| 164 | JUNIEVILLE | 28 |
| 165 | KOEKHOEK | 58 |
| 166 | KROISHAUSEN | 29 |
| 167 | KRUISKEN | 63 |
| 168 | KUERNE | 36 |
| 169 | LA BONNE MAISON FARM | 1 |
| 170 | LA CAPELLE | 24,78 |
| 171 | LA CHAUSSEE | 42,44 |
| 172 | LA FERTE FARM | 22,65 |
| 173 | LA FOLIE FARM (SAME 16 AS SPINCOURT) | |
| 174 | LA JOLLY FARM | 7 |
| 175 | LA NEUVILLE | 14 |
| 176 | LA PETRIE | 2 |
| 177 | LA SELVE | 15 |
| 178 | LAGNICOURT | 2,18 |
| 179 | LANDREVILLE | 32 |
| 180 | LE CATEAU | 16,32,34,37,77 |
| 181 | LE CATELET | 4 |
| 182 | LE CHATELET | 21,36 |
| 183 | LE CLOSS FARM | 15 |
| 184 | LECHELLE | 4,6,10,11 |
| 185 | LEFFINCOURT | 9,12,15,19,41,50,72,81 |
| 186 | LENZ | 2,26,27,36 |
| 187 | LES HAYONS FARM | 67 |
| 188 | LES MESNIL | 12,13,15,19 |
| 189 | LIERAMONT | 5,46,76 |
| 190 | LIESSE | 14,81 |
| 191 | LIEU ST AMAND | 2,4,6,23,26,27,32,35,36 |
| 192 | LIERM | 36 |
| 193 | LOMME | 18,33,40,47,49,58 |
| 194 | LONGCHAMPS | 4 |
| 195 | MAGNEUSE-VILLETTE | 1, 81 |
| 196 | MAIZY | 1,9,45 |
| 197 | MALMY-CHEMERY | 17,48,53,61,81 |
| 198 | MARCHAIS | 13,14,50 |
| 199 | MARCKE | 2, 28 |
| 200 | MARKEBEKE | 4,6,10,11,18,26,27,36 |
| 201 | MARLE-AUTREMENCOURT | 12,13,50 |
| 202 | MARS LA TOUR | 13,34,40,42,64,65 |
| 203 | MARS SOUS BOURCQ | 17,31,48,53,61,73 |
| 204 | MARTINCOURT | 7 |
| 205 | MARVILLE | 4,6,11,45,50,65,67,77 |
| 206 | MASNY | 14,40 |
| 207 | MEDARD | 41,47,49,60 |
| 208 | MENIN | 7,20,51 |
| 209 | MERCY-LE-HAUTE | 8,16,64 |
| 210 | MERVILLE | 81 |
| 211 | MESNIL-BRUNTEL | 12,13,15,19 |
| 212 | METZ-FRESCATY | 4,6,10,11,17 |
| 213 | MEUNES | 40 |
| 214 | MOIOLAINS | 5,46,81 |
| 215 | MONCEAU LE WAST | 9 |
| 216 | MONCHEAUX | 37 |
| 217 | MONS-EN-CHAUSSEE | 3,28,37,54,56 |
| 218 | MONS-EN-PEVELE | 29 |
| 219 | MONT | 22,34 |
| 220 | MONT DE SOISSONS FARM | 2,26,27 |
| 221 | MONT D'ORIGNY | 22,48,53 |
| 222 | MONT NOTRE DAME | 45 |
| 223 | MONT ST MARTIN | 1,22,45,50,81 |
| 224 | MONTBANIS FARM | 41,50 |
| 225 | MONTHUSSART FARM | 6,10,11 |
| 226 | MONTIGNY FARM | 11 |
| 227 | MONTINGEN | 18,37,40,43 |
| 228 | MONTKERKE | 20 |
| 229 | MÖRCHINGEN | 24,43,54 |

TODAY THE BORDER OF FRANCE - GERMANY FOLLOWS THE RIVER RHINE. THE FIELDS BENSDORF; GROSS TANCHEN; MONTINGEN AND MÖRCHINGEN HAS THE FOLLOWING NAMES - BENESTROFF; GROSTENQUIN; MONTOY AND MORHANGE.

| | | |
|---|---|---|
| 230 | MORSBERG | 80 |
| 231 | MOUSECRON | 40 |
| 232 | MOUVEAUX | 49 |
| 233 | MOYENCOURT | 48,83 |
| 234 | NEUFLIZE | 12,13,15,19,28,33,57 |
| 235 | NEUMUNSTER | MJG I |
| 236 | NEUVILLE | 5,37 |
| 237 | NEUVILLY | 8,17,54,56 |
| 238 | NORMAN-LE-WAST | 66 |
| 239 | NURLU | 5 |
| 240 | ORIGNY ST BENOITE | 69 |
| 241 | PAUX FE | 12 |
| 242 | PECQ | 52 |
| 243 | PERLES | 50,66 |
| 244 | PERONNE | 28 |
| 245 | PHALEMPIN | 10,12,14,29,30,37,41 |
| 246 | PLOMION | 9,21,45,66 |
| 247 | PONT FAVERGER | 74 |
| 248 | PREMONT | 35 |
| 249 | PREUTIN-HIGNY | 62,68,74 |
| 250 | PROCHER | 7 |
| 251 | PRONVILLE | 7 |
| 252 | PROVILLE | 1 |
| 253 | PROVIN | 52 |
| 254 | PUISIEUX FARM | 4,6,10,11 |
| 255 | PUSIEUX | 23 |
| 256 | RECKEM | 40 |
| 257 | RENEUIL FARM | 13,61 |
| 258 | RETHEUIL FARM | 9,21,45,66 |
| 259 | RIENCOURT | 12,22 |
| 260 | ROICOURT ST MARTIN - COINCY | 9,39,45,50 |
| 261 | RONSSOY | 19 |
| 262 | ROUBAIX | 40 |
| 263 | ROUCOURT | 1,11,12,33,34,59 |
| 264 | ROULERS | 7 |
| 265 | ROUPY | 4,13,15,19 |
| 266 | RUGNY FARM | 50 |
| 267 | RUMBEKE | 2,3,7,8,20,51,54, 56 |
| 268 | ST CHRIST | 34,37 |
| 269 | ST GERARD | 50 |
| 270 | ST GERARD MAISON | 81 |
| 271 | ST GOBERT | 66 |
| 272 | ST LOUP EN CHAMPAGNE | 19,21,31,36,38,73,74 |
| 273 | ST MARD | 23,23 |
| 274 | ST MARIE A' PY | 47,54,60,77 |
| 275 | ST MEDARD | 17 |
| 276 | ST QUENTIN LE PETIT | 17 |
| 277 | ST REMY LE PETIT WEST | 1,8,62,68,73 |
| 278 | STE MARGUERITE | 7,16,51 |
| 279 | SAILLY | 36 |
| 280 | SANTE NORD | 63 |
| 281 | SARIENNE-LA-LONGUE | 66 |
| 282 | SAULTAIN | 26,27,36 |
| 283 | SCHLOSS VILLERS-CAMPEAU | 49 |
| 284 | SEMIDE | 68 |
| 285 | SERANVILLERS | 34,37,81 |
| 286 | SIERENZ | 33,69,71 |
| 287 | SISSONNE | 1,9,21,41,45,50,60,66 |
| 288 | SIVRY | 6 |
| 289 | SPULTIER | 2 |
| 290 | STENAY | 15,19,65 |
| 291 | STOTZHEIM | 70 |
| 292 | SUZANNE | 76 |
| 293 | TELLANCOURT | 4,6,11 |
| 294 | THIN LE MONTIER | 72,73 |
| 295 | THOUROUT | 29 |
| 296 | THROUROUBE | 7 |
| 297 | THUGNY | 62,79 |
| 298 | THUILLES | 79 |
| 299 | TICHEMONT | 13,15,19,64,65 |
| 300 | TOULIS | 12,19 |
| 301 | TOURPES | 52 |
| 302 | TREFCON | 62 |
| 303 | TRIER | 12,13,15,19,32,35 |
| 304 | UGNY LE QUIPPE | 6 |
| 305 | VAKSENAERE | 2,20,28 |
| 306 | VAUX | 4,22 |
| 307 | VAUXCERE | 2,26,27,36 |
| 308 | VELU | 2 |
| 309 | YENDELLES | 37 |
| 310 | VILLERS-AU-TERTRE | 32,33 |
| 311 | VILLERS-LE-SEC | 79 |
| 312 | VILLERS-SIRE-NICOLE | 5,37,46 |
| 313 | VILLESELVE | 22,24,43,48,69,79 |
| 314 | VIVAISE | 1,2,17,22,26,27,36, 45,48,53,61 |
| 315 | VOUZIERS | 9 |
| 316 | VOYENNE | 61 |
| 317 | VRAIGNIES | 3,34,37,77 |
| 318 | WANCOURT FARM | 63 |
| 319 | WASQUEHAL | 17,28,37,57 |
| 320 | WASSIGNY | 8 |
| 321 | WAVRE | 7 |
| 322 | WYNGHENE | 3,7,28,33,37,40,51 |

THE READER MUST FORGIVE THE ARTIST FOR PUTTING DOWN THE MARK OF SOME AIRFIELDS IN A SLIGHTLY WRONG GEOGRAPHICAL PLACE. THIS IS AN ACT OF NEED. WHEN A CERTAIN PLACE IS CROWDED WITH FIELDS IT'S MORE IMPORTANT TO SEE THE GENERAL AREA OF THE "AERODROME" THAN FACING A TOTAL CHAOS OF NUMBERS. ALSO REMEMBER THAT THE NAMES IN THIS SET UP CORRESPONDS TO A VILLAGE, TOWN OR CITY, NOT NECESSARILY THE ONE YOU ARE FAMILIAR WITH BUT THIS IS THE FIELDNAME VOTED IN BY NORMAN FRANKS AND RICK DUIVEN.

© "PYS" SVENSEN, NORWAY
DECEMBER 1995

# The Jasta Airfields
# – Western Front 1916-1918

| Airfield | Armee | Used by Jasta: |
|---|---|---|
| Abeele, SW Poperinghe | 4 | 26, 28, 51 |
| Aertrycke, SW Brugge | 4 | 7, 14, 16, 29, 35, 51 |
| Aische-en-Befail | 17 | 26, 27 |
| Allincourt-Juniville | 1 | 69 |
| Ancrevillers | 5 | 10 |
| Aniche | 17 | 2, 23, 27, 36, 57, 58 |
| Annelles, E Rethel | 1 | 24 |
| Antrecourt, Attigny | 3 | 48, 53, 61 |
| Antwerp | 4 | 40 |
| Arcy, Rugny Ferme | 7 | 41, 45 |
| Ars, Kenchen | 3 | 54, 77 |
| Ascq, E Lille | 6 | 33, 46, 58 |
| Attigny | 3 | 41, 50, 53 |
| Auchy | 6 | 52 |
| Aulnoye | 4 | 6 |
| Autremencourt | 7 | 15 |
| Avançon | 1 | 32 |
| Avelin, E Seclin | 6 | 18, 30, 43 |
| Avesnes-le-Sec, Cambrai | 2 | 10, 11 |
| Awoingt, Cambrai | 2 | 6, 10, 11 |
| | | |
| Baisieux, W Albert | 6 | 30 |
| Balâtre, E Roye | 18 | 8, 12, 13, 15, 17, 19, 62, 68, 69 |
| Bapaume | 17 | 23, 39 |
| Bavichove, N Courtrai | 4 | 2, 26, 27, 31, 33 |
| Bazoches | 7 | 1, 9 |
| Beaumont Ferme | 3 | 81 |
| Beauvois, E Cambrai | 18 | 8, 68 |
| Bechamp, Verdun | 5 | 5 |
| Bellevue Ferme, Senon | 5 | 5, 7 |
| Bellincamps | 6 | 29 |
| Bensdorf | A | 80 |
| Berghem, Brussels | 6 | 43 |
| Bergnicourt, Rethel | 1 | 31, 72, 74 |
| Bernes | 2 | 4, 6, 10 |
| Bersée, NW Douai | 6 | 10, 29, 52 |
| Besny-Soisy | 1 | 1 |
| Beugneux | 7 | 6, 10, 11 |
| Beuvry | 17 | 28, 33, 57, 58 |
| Beveren | 4 | 47 |
| Bévillers, E Cambrai | 2 | 34, 37, 46 |
| Bignicourt | 1 | 22, 63, 76 |
| Bisseghem, Courtrai | 4 | 2, 6, 40 |
| Blaise | 3 | 1, 3, 49, 72 |
| Bohain | 6/18 | 8, 26, 62 |
| Boistrancourt | 2 | 5 |
| Boncourt | 7 | 13, 14, 21, 39, 41, 50, 60, 66, 81 |
| Bonneuil Ferme | 18 | 12, 13, 15, 19 |
| Boulin Ferme | 5 | 32 |
| Bourlers | 7 | 45, 66 |
| Brayelles, Douai | 6 | 11 |
| Briastre | 2 | 3 |
| Bruille, E Douai | 17 | 18, 49 |
| Brussels | 6/17 | 33, 43, 63 |

| Airfield | Armee | Used by Jasta: |
|---|---|---|
| Bühl, nr Saarburg | A | 14, 19, 23, 32, 33, 35, 39, 70, 78 |
| Burscheid | A | 33, 78 |
| Busigny | 2 | 6, 11 |
| | | |
| Cantin | 17 | 28, 33 |
| Cappy, Somme | 2 | 4, 5, 6, 10, 11 |
| Carignan | 5 | 12, 13, 15, 19 |
| Carnières, E Cambrai | 6 | 18 |
| Carrepuis | 18 | 72, |
| Castern | 17 | 1, 59 |
| Castres | 18 | 79 |
| Ceune, Courtrai | 4 | 4 |
| Chambry, Laon | 7/17 | 2, 26, 27, 36 |
| Champles, SE Waterloo | 17 | 28, 58 |
| Charmois, S Stenay | 5 | 12, 13 |
| Chassogne Ferme, Stenay/Verdun | 5 | 10, 21, 24 |
| Château-Porcien, Champagne | 1 | 16 |
| Chéméry | 3 | 41, 47, 49, 50, 60 |
| Chenois, N Verdun | 5 | 34 |
| Chéry-les-Pouilly | 7/9 | 9, 12, 13, 15, 19, 32 |
| Chévresis-Monceau | 18 | 24, 42, 79 |
| Chièvres | 17 | 28, 57, 58 |
| Chuffilly | 3 | 17, 48, 53, 61 |
| Clastres | 18 | 24, 42 |
| Cohartville | 7 | 45 |
| Coincy | 7 | 41 |
| Colmar Nord | B | 26, 35 |
| Colmar Sud | B | 71 |
| Croulshouten | 4 | 56 |
| Cuirieux, Laon | 7 | 19, 34 |
| Cysoing | 6/17 | 33, 43 |
| | | |
| Délinge Ferme | 18 | 68 |
| Dhuizel | 7 | 81 |
| Doncourt | C | 12, 13 |
| Donstiennes | 18 | 24, 42, 44 |
| Douai | 6 | 4 |
| Douilly | 18 | 17 |
| | | |
| Ellignies | 6 | 63 |
| Emerchicourt, S Aniche | 2/17 | 1, 2, 23, 24, 26, 29, 35, 36, 58, 59 |
| Ennemain, N Nesle | 2/18 | 6, 10, 11, 28, 33, 47, 49, 54, 57, 58 |
| Ennetières | 6 | 63 |
| Ensisheim | B | 16, 35, 39 |
| Epinoy, NW Cambrai | 17 | 4, 12, 23, 32, 59 |
| Epitaphe Ferme | 7 | 36 |
| Ercheu | 18 | 17, 22, 24, 36, 42, 44, 60, 61, 69 |
| Erchin | 17 | 2, 26, 36 |
| Erkeghem, Oostcamp, S Brugge | 4 | 12, 17 |
| Erlon, Marle | 7 | 16, 23 |
| Erre, Somain | 17 | 1, 39, 59 |
| Escarmain, Capelle | 2 | 5, 34, 37 |
| Escaufort, Busigny | 2 | 4, 10 |
| Essigny-le-Petit, St Quentin | 2 | 20 |
| Eswars, Meuse | 1 | 2, 7 |
| Etreux, Guise | 7 | 10 |
| | | |
| Faches, Lille | 6 | 18, 47 |
| Falvy, Peronne | 2, | 3 |
| Faucouzy | 18 | 44 |
| Favreuil, Bapaume | 17 | 32, 35, 59 |

| Airfield | Armee | Used by Jasta: |
|---|---|---|
| Fayet | 2 | 20 |
| Flavy-le-Martel | 18 | 53 |
| Fleurs | 2 | 23, |
| Flez-Suisaucourt, N Nesle | 18 | 44, 79 |
| Florenville | 5 | 12, 13, 15, 19 |
| Fonfomme, Fontaine Notre Dame | 18 | 12, 19 |
| Fonfry, N Fère-en-Tardenois | 7 | 1, 9, 66 |
| Fontaine Notre Dame | 18 | 12, 13, 15, 19 |
| Fontaine-Uterte, NE St Quentin | 2 | 3 |
| Foreste | 18 | 13, 15 |
| Foucaucourt, N Chaulnes | 2/18 | 16, 34, 37, 44, 77 |
| Froidmont, SW Tournai | 7 | 42 |
| | | |
| Genech, SW Lille | 6 | 63 |
| Ghistelles, Ostende | 4 | 2, 17 |
| Ghlin, Mons | 17 | 1, 59 |
| Giraumont | C | 12, 13, 64 |
| Givry, N Mons | 2/18 | 34, 35, 63 |
| Gondecourt, Lille | 2/6 | 29, 41, 43, 52 |
| Gonnelieu, Cambrai | 1 | 5 |
| Gontrode, SE Ghent | 4 | 40 |
| Gosselies, Charleroi | 2 | 32, 34, 35 |
| Grand Metz, nr Denze | 6 | 43 |
| Graux | 18 | 24, 79 |
| Grécourt | 18 | 42 |
| Gross-Tanchen, Mörchingen | 19 | 3 |
| Guesnain, Douai | 6/17 | 3, 20, 31, 32, 39 |
| Guise, St Quentin | 2/6/18/19 | 3, 6, 12, 13, 15, 19, 20, 22, 24, 26, 31, 33, 42, 48, 69, 79 |
| Guisecourt | 18 | 12, 13, 15, 19 |
| Guizancourt | 18 | 24 |
| | | |
| Habsheim | B | 15, 16, 26, 35, 41, 69, 71, 75, 76, 77 |
| Halluin, N Lille | 4 | 2, 18, 26, 27, 33, 36, 40, 57 |
| Halma, Rochefort | 1 | 73 |
| Handzaeme | 4 | 29 |
| Harbonnières | 2 | 4, 6, 10 |
| Harlebeke, NE Courtrai | 4 | 18, 24, 47 |
| Harmigniers | 2 | 23, 32 |
| Haubourdin, Lille | 2 | 22, 43 |
| Heerlingen | A | 12 |
| Helesmes, N Denain | 17 | 1, 59 |
| Hennieches Ferme | 18 | 63 |
| Hermies, Cambrai | 1 | 1 |
| Hervilly, Roisel | 2 | 34 |
| Heule, Courtrai | 4 | 10, 24 |
| Hivry-Circourt, Verdun | 5 | 4 |
| Houplin, S Lille | 6 | 3, 18, 31, 36 |
| Hove | 6 | 52 |
| | | |
| Ichteghem-Vyver | 4 | 35 |
| Ingelmünster, E Roulers | 4 | 3, 54, 56 |
| Iseghem, SE Roulers | 4 | 26, 27, 28, 51 |
| | | |
| Jabbeke, SW Brugge | 4 | 8, 51 |
| Jametz | 5 | 23 |
| Juniville | 1/3 | 29 |
| | | |
| Koekhoek, nr Menin | 4 | 58 |
| Kroishouten | 4 | 29 |
| Kruisken | 6 | 63 |
| Kuerne | 4 | 36 |

| Airfield | Armee | Used by Jasta: |
|---|---|---|
| La Bonne Maison Ferme | 7 | 1 |
| La Capelle | 18 | 24, 79 |
| La Chaussée | 18 | 42, 44 |
| La Ferté Ferme | C/18 | 22, 65 |
| La Folie Ferme, Spincourt | 5 | 16 |
| Lagnicourt | 1 | 2, 19 |
| La Jolly Ferme, Stenay | 5 | 7 |
| La Neuville | 5 | 14 |
| Landréville | 5 | 32 |
| La Petrie | 2 | 2 |
| La Selve | 7 | 15 |
| Le Cateau | 2 | 16, 32, 34, 37, 77 |
| Le Catelet | 2 | 4 |
| Le Châtelet, Neuflize | 1 | 21, 36 |
| Léchelle, S Bertincourt | 2 | 4, 6, 10, 11 |
| Le Clos Ferme, Boncourt | 7 | 15 |
| Leffincourt | 3 | 9, 12, 15, 19, 41, 50, 72, 81 |
| Le Mesnil, nr Nesle | 18 | 12, 13, 15, 19 |
| Lens, Mons | 17 | 2, 26, 27, 36 |
| Les Hayons Ferme | 5 | 67 |
| Liéramont | 2 | 5, 46, 76 |
| Liesse | 7 | 14, 81 |
| Lieu St Armand | 17 | 2, 4, 6, 23, 26, 27, 32, 35, 36 |
| Lirm | 17 | 36 |
| Lomme, Lille | 4/6 | 18, 33, 40, 47, 49, 58 |
| Longchamps, Guise | 7 | 4 |
| Lothringen | A | 32 |
| | | |
| Magneuse-Villette, nr Fismes | 7 | 1, 81 |
| Maizy, N Fismes | 7 | 1, 9, 45 |
| Malmy-Cheméry, Sedan | 3 | 17, 48, 53, 61, 81 |
| Marchais | 5/7 | 13, 14, 50 |
| Marcke, Courtrai | 4 | 2, 28 |
| Marckebeke, Courtrai | 4 | 4, 6, 10, 11, 18, 26, 27, 36 |
| Marle-Autremencourt | 7 | 12, 13, 50 |
| Mars-la-Tour | C/5 | 13, 34, 40, 42, 64, 65 |
| Mars-sous-Bourcq | 3 | 17, 31, 48, 53, 61, 73 |
| Martincourt | 5 | 7 |
| Marville | 5/18 | 4, 6, 11, 45, 50, 65, 67, 77 |
| Masny | 17 | 14, 40 |
| Medard | 18 | 41, 47, 49, 60 |
| Menin | 4 | 7, 20, 51 |
| Mercy-le-Haute | 5 | 8, 16, 64 |
| Merville | 3 | 81 |
| Mesnil-Bruntel | 2 | 12, 13, 15, 19 |
| Metz-Frescaty | A/C/5 | 4, 6, 10, 11, 17 |
| Meuines, Courtrai | 4 | 40 |
| Moislains | 2 | 5, 46, 81 |
| Moncheaux, N Douai | 6 | 37 |
| Mons-en-Chaussée | 2 | 3, 28, 37, 54, 56 |
| Mons-en-Pevelle | 6 | 29 |
| Mont, NE Verdun | 5 | 22, 34 |
| Mont Notre Dame | 7 | 45 |
| Mont St Martin | 7 | 1, 22, 45, 50, 81 |
| Montbanis Ferme | 7 | 41, 50 |
| Montceau-le-Wast | 7 | 9 |
| Mont d'Origny | 18 | 22, 48, 53 |
| Monthussart Ferme | 7 | 6, 10, 11 |
| Montigny Ferme | 2 | 11 |
| Möntingen, Metz | A/19 | 18, 37, 40, 43 |

| Airfield | Armee | Used by Jasta: |
|---|---|---|
| Montkerke, Brugge | 4 | 20 |
| Mont Soissons Ferme | 7 | 2, 26, 27 |
| Monveaux | 4/6 | 49 |
| Mörchingen, Metz | A | 24, 43, 54 |
| Morsberg | 19 | 80 |
| Mousecron | 4 | 40 |
| Moyencourt | 18 | 48, 53 |
| Neuflize | 1 | 12, 13, 15, 19, 28, 33, 57 |
| Neuville | 2 | 5, 37 |
| Neuvilly, Le Cateau | 2 | 8, 17, 54, 56 |
| Norman-le-West | 7 | 66 |
| Nurlu, NE Moislains | 2 | 5 |
| Origny St Benoite | 18 | 69 |
| Paux FQ, Laon | 7 | 12 |
| Pecq, E Roubaix | 6 | 52 |
| Perles | 7 | 50, 66 |
| Péronne | 2 | 29 |
| Phalempin, W Douai | 2/6 | 10, 12, 14, 29, 30, 37, 41 |
| Plomion, SE Vervins | 7 | 9, 21, 45, 66 |
| Pont Faverger | 1 | 74 |
| Premont, S Le Cateau | 2 | 35 |
| Prentin-Higny, SE Longuyon | 5 | 62, 68, 74 |
| Procher | 4 | 7 |
| Pronville, nr Quéant | 1/2 | 2 |
| Proville, Cambrai | 1 | 1 |
| Provin, N Lens | 6 | 52 |
| Puisieux Ferme, Laon | 7 | 4, 6, 10, 11 |
| Pusieux, Mars-la-Tour | C | 23 |
| Reckem, SE Menin | 4 | 40 |
| Reneuil Ferme | 7/9 | 13, 61 |
| Retheuil Ferme, Bohain | 2/18 | 17 |
| Riencourt, Arras | 1/6 | 12, 22 |
| Rocourt St Martin, Coincy | 7 | 9, 39, 45, 5, |
| Ronssoy, SE Epehy | 1 | 19 |
| Roubaix | 4 | 40 |
| Roucourt, Bohain | 6/17 | 1, 11, 12, 33, 34, 59 |
| Roulers | 4 | 7 |
| Roupy, Somme | 2/18 | 4, 13, 15, 19 |
| Rugny Ferme | 7 | 50 |
| Rumbeke, Roulers | 4 | 2, 3, 7, 8, 20, 51, 54, 56 |
| St Christ, Somme | 2 | 34, 37 |
| St Gérard | 18 | 50 |
| St Gérard Maison | 3 | 81 |
| St Gobert | 7 | 66 |
| St Loup, Champagne | 1 | 19, 21, 31, 36, 39, 73, 74 |
| St Mard | 7 | 21, 23 |
| St Marguerite | 4 | 7, 16, 51 |
| St Marie-à-Py, Vouziers | 3 | 47, 54, 60, 77 |
| St Medard, Neufchâteau | 3 | 17 |
| St Quentin-le-Petit | 7/1 | 17 |
| St Rémy-le-Petit West, N Reims | 1/3 | 1, 8, 62, 68, 73 |
| Sailly | 4 | 36 |
| Sante Nord | 6 | 63 |
| Sarienne-la-Longue | 7 | 66 |
| Saultain | 17 | 26, 27, 36 |
| Schloss Villers-Campeau | 6 | 49 |
| Sémide | 5 | 68 |
| Seranvillers | 2 | 34, 37, 81 |

| Airfield | Armee | Used by Jasta: |
|---|---|---|
| Sierenz, Mülhausen | A/B | 33, 69, 71 |
| Sissone | 7 | 1, 9, 21, 41, 45, 50, 60, 66 |
| Sivry | 5 | 6 |
| Spultier, Vawre | 17 | 2 |
| Stenay | 5 | 15, 19, 65 |
| Stotzheim | A | 70 |
| Strasse Ennemain-Falvy | 2 | 4 |
| Suzanne, Somme | 2 | 76 |
| | | |
| Tellancourt | 5 | 4, 6, 11 |
| Thin-le-Montier, Charleville | 1 | 72, 73 |
| Thourout | 4 | 29 |
| Thouroube, E Roulers | 4 | 7 |
| Thugny, Rethel | 18 | 62, 79 |
| Thuilles | 18 | 79 |
| Tichémont Castle | C | 13, 15, 19, 64, 65 |
| Toulis | 7 | 12, 19 |
| Tourpes | 6 | 52 |
| Trefcon | 18 | 62 |
| Trier | 2/5 | 12, 13, 15, 19, 32, 35 |
| | | |
| Ugny-l'Equipée, Somme, N Ham | 2 | 6 |
| | | |
| Varsenaere, Brugge | 4 | 2, 20, 28 |
| Vaux, Somme | 2 | 4, 22 |
| Vauxcère | 7 | 2, 26, 27, 36 |
| Vélu | 1 | 2 |
| Vendelles | 2 | 37 |
| Villers-au-Tertre | 4/6/17 | 32, 33 |
| Villers-le-Sec | 18 | 79 |
| Villers-sur-Nicole | 2 | 5, 37, 46 |
| Villeselve, NW Chauny | 18 | 22, 24, 43, 48, 69, 79 |
| Vivaise | 7/9 | 1, 2, 17, 22, 26, 27, 36, 45, 48, 53, 61 |
| Vouziers | 3 | 9 |
| Voyenne, nr Marle | 7 | 61 |
| Vraignes, nr Péronne | 2 | 3, 34, 37, 77 |
| | | |
| Wancourt Ferme | 18 | 63 |
| Wasquehal, Lille | 4/6 | 17, 28, 37, 57 |
| Wassigny | 18 | 8 |
| Wavre | 17 | 1 |
| Wynghene (Winghene) | 4 | 3, 7, 28, 33, 37, 40, 51 |

## MARINE JASTA BASES

| | | | | | |
|---|---|---|---|---|---|
| Aertrycke, SW Brugge | 4 | I | Jabbeke, SW Brugge | 4 | II, III, IV |
| Coolkerke, N Brugge | 4 | I, II | Neumünster, NW Brugge | 4 | I, V |

## JASTA BASES, ITALY

| | | | | | |
|---|---|---|---|---|---|
| Aviano | 14 | I | San Fior | 14 | 1, 39 |
| Campoformidi | 14 | 1, 39 | San Giacomo | 14 | 39 |
| Cervada | 14 | 39 | Udine | 14 | 31 |
| Possanerlo | 14 | I | Veldes | 14 | 1 |
| Roveredo | 14 | 39 | | | |

## JASTA BASES, MACEDONIA

| | | | | | |
|---|---|---|---|---|---|
| Hudova | 1B† | 38 | Mravinca | 1B† | 38 |
| Kalkova | 11 | 25, 38 | Prilip | 11 | 25 |
| Kanatlarci | 11 | 25 | | | |

## JASTA BASES, TURKEY

| | | | | |
|---|---|---|---|---|
| Derra | 55, (1F) | | Djenin | 55, (1F) |

† 1st Bulgarian Army.

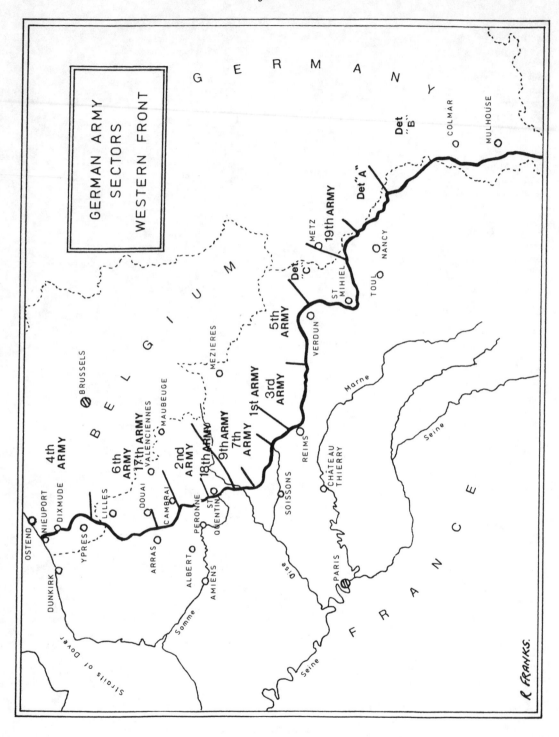

GERMAN ARMY
SECTORS
WESTERN FRONT

GERMANY

BELGIUM

FRANCE

COLMAR
MULHOUSE

Det "B"

Det "A"

19th ARMY

METZ

Det "C"

TOUL
NANCY

ST MIHIEL

VERDUN

5th ARMY

3rd ARMY

MEZIERES

1st ARMY

Marne

Seine

BRUSSELS

7th ARMY

9th ARMY

18th ARMY

2nd ARMY

REIMS

VALENCIENNES

MAUBEUGE

17th ARMY

6th ARMY

4th ARMY

CHÂTEAU
THIERRY

SOISSONS

Oise

LILLE

DOUAI

CAMBRAI

ST QUENTIN

PERONNE

NIEUPORT

DIXMUDE

YPRES

ARRAS

ALBERT

AMIENS

Somme

OSTEND

DUNKIRK

Straits of Dover

Oise

PARIS

Seine

R FRANKS.

# The Jasta and Marine Jasta Histories

## ROYAL PRUSSIAN JAGDSTAFFEL 1

Created on 22 August 1916, from Kommandeur der Flieger 1 (Kofl 1) by Chef des Feldflieger West von Nr.22429 Fl. Hauptmann Martin Zander (two victories) the commander of Kampfeinsitzer Kommando Nord (KEK Nord) was assigned as Commanding Officer, and the other personnel were drawn from Flieger Ersatz Abteilung 7 (FEA7), KEK Nord, and from the various Flieger Abteilung of the 1 Armee. Jasta 1 was based at Bertincourt. On 24 August Offizierstellvertreter Leopold Reimann was the first pilot to score a victory. Leutnant Kurt Wintgens gained his 18th victory on 24 September, and became the first pilot in Jasta 1 to register five victories with the unit. On 10 November Hauptmann Zander was sent to Jastaschule II at Nivelles, and Oberleutnant Hans Kummetz, of Jasta 8, was designated as the new Commanding Officer, reporting on the 18th. On 1 April the Jasta was transferred to the 7 Armee sector. Oberleutnant Kummetz, who had gained six victories, was transferred to Jastaschule I at Valenciennes, on 12 September 1917, and the following day Oberleutnant Otto Deindl, from Jasta 35b, assumed command. On 21 September Jasta 1 departed for Italy. Oberleutnant Deindl was wounded in combat on 18 November, and on the 20th Hans Kummetz returned as his replacement. Oberleutnant Kummetz remained in command until 11 January 1918, when he was killed in combat, after attaining his seventh victory a few days earlier. Leutnant Armbrecht, from Jasta 1, assumed temporary command on 12 January, until replaced by Oberleutnant Walter Korte on 20 January. Korte was transferred to Jasta 72 on 7 March, and Leutnant Armbrecht again assumed command. The Jasta returned to the Western Front during March assigned to the 3 Armee until 7 June, when reassigned to the 7 Armee. On 13 August a move was made to the 17 Armee sector where it remained for the rest of the war. On 23 August Leutnant Armbrecht was replaced by Oberleutnant Bruno von Voigt, from FEA 6, who was transferred to command of Jasta 66 on 3 September. Oberleutnant Kurt von Döring (nine victories) of Jasta 66 became the last Commanding Officer of the Jasta. Jasta 1 had claimed 138 victories, 107 of which were confirmed, while suffering the loss of 12 pilots killed in action, one killed in an accident, one taken prisoner, and four wounded. The unit was demobilised 12 December 1918, at FEA11 Gandau, near Breslau.

| Commanding Officers | | Posted to: |
|---|---|---|
| Hptm Martin Zander | 22 Aug 1916 – 10 Nov 1916 | JsSch I |
| Oblt Erich Hahn | 10 Nov 1916 – 18 Nov 1916 | Acting |
| Oblt Hans Kummetz | 18 Nov 1916 – 12 Sep 1917 | JsSch II |
| Oblt Otto Deindl | 13 Sep 1917 – 19 Nov 1917 | WIA |
| Oblt Hans Kummetz | 20 Nov 1917 – 11 Jan 1918 | KIA |
| Ltn Armbrecht | 12 Jan 1918 – 19 Jan 1918 | Acting |
| Oblt Walter Korte | 20 Jan 1918 – 7 Mar 1918 | J72 |
| Ltn Armbrecht | 8 Mar 1918 – 23 Aug 1918 | Idflieg |
| Oblt Bruno von Voigt | 26 Aug 1918 – 3 Sep 1918 | CO Jasta 66 |
| Oblt Kurt von Döring | 3 Sep 1918 – 11 Nov 1918 | |

### Pilots credited with victories

| | | | |
|---|---|---|---|
| Ltn Hans von Keudell* | 11(12) | Vfw Kister | 2 |
| Oblt Hans Kummetz* | 7 | OfStv Münnichow | 2(3) |
| Vfw Paul Bona | 6 | Uffz Schneider | 2 |
| Vfw Georg Staudacher | 6 | Ltn Ernst Fr von Stenglin | 2 |
| Ltn Kurt Wintgens* | 6(19) | OfStv Alfred Behling | 1 |
| Ltn Raven von Barnekow | 6(11) | Vfw Walter Dittrich | 1 |
| Vfw Gustav Borm | 5 | Oblt Erich Hahn | 1(5) |
| OfStv Wilhelm Cymera* | 5 | Ltn Walter Höhndorf | 1(12) |
| Ltn Herbert Schröder | 5 | Vfw Kurt Jentsch | 1(7) |
| Ltn Hans von Freden | 4(16) | OfStv Karl Lang | 1 |
| Ltn Gustav Leffers* | 4(9) | Ltn Friedrich Liebig | 1 |
| Ltn Werner Zech | 3 | Ltn Franz Ray | 1(17) |
| Hptm Martin Zander | 3(5) | OfStv Leopold Reimann | 1(5) |
| Ltn Armbrecht | 2 | OfStv Karl Stiller | 1 |
| Vfw Belz | 2 | Uffz Weidemann | 1 |
| Ltn Bussmann | 2 | Ltn Weingarten | 1 |
| Rittm Kurt von Döring | 3(11) | Ltn Zilcher | 1 |
| Ltn Erwin Härtl | 2 | Unknown | 4 |
| * Killed in action (and throughout) | | | |

|  | **Airfields occupied** |  |
| Location | Inclusive Dates | Armee |
|---|---|---|
| Bertincourt | 22 Aug 1916 – 22 Sep 1916 | 1 |
| Hermies | 23 Sep 1916 – 26 Oct 1916 | 1 |
| Proville | 27 Oct 1916 – 22 Mar 1917 | 1 |
| Besny-Soisy | 23 Mar 1917 – 31 Mar 1917 | 1 |
| Vivaise | 1 Apr 1917 – 21 Sep 1917 | 7 |
| Veldes (Italy) | Sep 1917 – 2 Nov 1917 | 14 |
| Campoformidi (Italy) | 3 Nov 1917 – 10 Nov 1917 | 14 |
| Aviano (Italy) | 11 Nov 1917 – 15 Nov 1917 | 14 |
| Possanerlo (Italy) | 16 Nov 1917 – 22 Dec 1917 | 14 |
| San Fior (Italy) | 23 Dec 1917 – 13 Mar 1918 | 14 |
| Blaise Mar | 1918 – 30 May 1918 | 3 |
| St Rémy, West | 31 May 1918 – 7 Jun 1918 | 3 |
| La Bonne Maison | 8 Jun 1918 – 12 Jun 1918 | 7 |
| Mont St Martin | 13 Jun 1918 – 26 Jun 1918 | 7 |
| Magneuse-Villette | 27 Jun 1918 – 10 Jul 1918 | 7 |
| Fonfry | 11 Jul 1918 – 19 Jul 1918 | 7 |
| Bazoches | 20 Jul 1918 – 26 Jul 1918 | 7 |
| Maizy | 27 Jul 1918 – 31 Jul 1918 | 7 |
| Sissone | 1 Aug 1918 – 12 Aug 1918 | 7 |
| Emerchicourt | 13 Aug 1918 – 24 Aug 1918 | 17 |
| Roucourt | 25 Aug 1918 – 1 Sep 1918 | 17 |
| Erre-Somain | 2 Sep 1918 – 26 Sep 1918 | 17 |
| Helesmes-Denain | 27 Sep 1918 – 11 Oct 1918 | 17 |
| Ghlin Mons | 12 Oct 1918 – 17 Oct 1918 | 17 |
| Castern | 18 Oct 1918 – 9 Nov 1918 | 17 |
| Wavre | 10 Nov 1918 – 11 Nov 1918 | 17 |

## ROYAL PRUSSIAN JAGDSTAFFEL 2 (Boelcke)

Created 10 August 1916, from FEA7 in accordance with Chef des Feldflieger West von Nr.22429 Fl. Stationed in the 1 Armee sector, it was commanded by Hauptmann Oswald Boelcke who had been credited with 19 victories at this time. The first aircraft were received on 1 September, two Fokker DIIIs from Armee Flugpark 1 (AFP1), and an Albatros DII from Jasta 1. Boelcke scored the unit's first victory, his 20th, on 2 September, and on the 14th became the first pilot to score five victories with the Jasta. Hauptmann Boelcke was killed in an accident, two days after he had scored his 40th victory, on 28 October. The aircraft of Leutnant Erwin Böhme, of Jasta 2, collided in mid-air with Boelcke's, causing him to fall to his death. Böhme survived the collision. Oberleutnant Karl Bodenschatz, the Offizier zur besonderen Verwendung (OzbV) for Jasta 2 assumed temporary command until Oberleutnant Stefan Kirmaier (three victories) took over on 30 October. Kirmaier was killed during combat on 22 November, after having scored his 11th victory two days prior, and Hauptmann Franz Walz (six victories) arrived from Jasta 19 on 29 November to take command. Jasta 2 was re-named Jasta Boelcke, in honour of its first leader, on 17 December. The Jasta's 100th victory was claimed during February 1917, probably on the 25th by Leutnant Werner Voss for his 8th claim. On the 27th the Jasta commenced operations on both the 1 Armee and 2 Armee Fronts. Then on 9 June 1917, Hauptmann Walz was transferred to the command of Jasta 34, and Leutnant Otto Bernert (seven victories) of Jasta 6, was assigned as the new commander. The Jasta moved to the 2 Armee on 1 August, and on to the Flanders Area with the 4 Armee on 7 August. Bernert departed 18 August, with Leutnant Erwin Böhme (13 victories) from Jasta 29, succeeding him as Commanding Officer. After Böhme was killed during combat on 29 November, immediately after having downed his 24th enemy aircraft, Leutnant Freiherr Eberhard von Gudenberg, OzbV, assumed temporary command, until the arrival of Leutnant Walter von Bülow-Bothkamp (28 victories) from Jasta 36 on 13 December. Von Bülow's term as commander was short as he fell in combat on 6 January 1918. Leutnant Max von Müller (36 victories) was assigned as temporary commander until he was killed in combat on 9 January. Another temporary commander, Leutnant Theodor Cammann (one victory), led the unit until Leutnant Otto Höhne (6 victories), of Jasta 59, arrived on 26 January. The Jasta's 200th victory was scored during February 1918, probably on the 26th by Leutnant Richard Plange for his third claim. Jasta Boelcke became a part of Jagdgeschwader III, with Jastas 26, 27 and 36, on 16 February at the airfield at Marcke. JG III was commanded by Hauptmann Bruno Loerzer, who had been credited with 22 victories at this time. Höhne, who had not added to his score, was transferred on 20 February, and Leutnant Karl Bolle (five victories) arrived from Jasta 28w to assume command, which he held until the end of the war. A move was made on 21 May to the 7 Armee Sector, then JGIII was assigned to the 17 Armee, and on 27 September, the unit scored its 300th victory. Jasta 2 was credited with the destruction of 333 aircraft and three balloons while suffering 44 casualties (31 killed in action, nine wounded in action, two prisoner of war, and two in flying accidents).

## Commanding Officers

| | | |
|---|---|---|
| Hptm Oswald Boelcke | 30 Aug 1916 – 28 Oct 1916 | KIAcc |
| Oblt Stefan Kirmaier | 30 Oct 1916 – 22 Nov 1916 | KIA |
| Oblt Karl Bodenschatz | 22 Nov 1916 – 29 Nov 1916 | Acting |
| Hptm Franz Walz | 29 Nov 1916 – 9 Jun 1917 | CO Jasta 34 |
| Ltn Otto Bernert | 9 Jun 1917 – 18 Aug 1917 | FEA 9 |
| Ltn Erwin Böhme | 18 Aug 1917 – 29 Nov 1917 | KIA |
| Ltn Eberhard von Gudenberg | 29 Nov 1917 – 13 Dec 1917 | Acting |
| Ltn Walter von Bülow | 13 Dec 1917 – 6 Jan 1918 | KIA |
| Ltn Max von Müller | 6 Jan 1918 – 9 Jan 1918 | KIA |
| Ltn Theodor Cammann | 11 Jan 1918 – 26 Jan 1918 | Acting |
| Ltn Otto Höhne | 26 Jan 1918 – 20 Feb 1918 | Jastaschule I |
| Ltn Karl Bolle | 20 Feb 1918 – 4 Sep 1918 | Leave |
| Ltn Otto Löffler | 4 Sep 1918 – 18 Sep 1918 | Acting |
| Ltn Karl Bolle | 18 Sep 1918 – 11 Nov 1918 | |

## Pilots credited with victories

| | | | |
|---|---|---|---|
| Ltn Paul Bäumer | 40(43) | Ltn Wilhelm Pappenmeyer* | 4 |
| Ltn Karl Bolle | 31(35) | OfStv Leopold Reimann* | 4(5) |
| Ltn Werner Voss* | 28(48) | Ltn Hans Reimann* | 3(4) |
| Ltn Erwin Böhme* | 22(24) | Oblt Adolf von Tutschek* | 3(27) |
| Hptm Oswald Boelcke* | 21(40) | Ltn Paul Blunck | 2(3) |
| Oblt Otto Bernert | 17(27) | Ltn Diether Collin | 2(13) |
| Ltn Ernst Bormann | 16 | Ltn Johann Heemsoth | 2 |
| Ltn Manfred von Richthofen* | 16(80) | Ltn Fritz Heinz* | 2 |
| Ltn Otto Löffler | 15 | Uffz Paul Keusen* | 2 |
| Ltn Max von Müller* | 12(36) | Ltn Hans Wortmann* | 2 |
| Ltn Hermann Frommherz | 10(32) | Ltn Theodor Cammann | 1(12) |
| Ltn Alfred Lindenberger | 9(12) | Oblt R von Greisheim | 1 |
| Oblt Stefan Kirmaier* | 8(11) | Ltn Fritz Hoffmann* | 1 |
| Ltn Karl Gallwitz | 8(10) | Maat Gustav Kinkle* | 1 |
| Ltn Richard Plange* | 7 | Ltn Walter Lange* | 1 |
| Ltn Gerhard Bassenge | 7 | Ltn Schlack | 1 |
| Ltn Erich König* | 6 | Ltn Paul Schröder | 1 |
| Ltn Otto Höhne | 6 | Ltn Wilhelm Suer | 1 |
| Ltn Hans Imelmann* | 6 | Hptm Franz Walz | 1(7) |
| Ltn Hermann Vallendor | 6 | Ltn Johannes Wintrath* | 1 |
| Uffz Karl Fervers | 4 | Jagdstaffel | 1 |
| Ltn Friedrich Kempf | 4 | | |

## Airfields occupied

| Location | Inclusive Dates | Armee |
|---|---|---|
| Bertincourt | 10 Aug 1916 – 26 Aug 1916 | 1 |
| Vélu | 27 Aug 1916 – 21 Sep 1916 | 1 |
| Lagnicourt | 22 Sep 1916 – 4 Dec 1916 | 1 |
| Pronville | 5 Dec 1916 – 13 Mar 1917 | 1 |
| Eswars | 14 Mar 1917 – 22 Mar 1917 | 1 |
| Pronville | 23 Mar 1917 – 31 Jul 1917 | 1 |
| La Petrie | 1 Aug 1917 – 6 Aug 1917 | 2 |
| Bisseghem | 7 Aug 1917 – 11 Aug 1917 | 4 |
| Ghistelles | 12 Aug 1917 – 26 Aug 1917 | 4 |
| Varsenaere | 27 Aug 1917 – 30 Sep 1917 | 4 |
| Rumbeke | 1 Oct 1917 – 12 Nov 1917 | 4 |
| Bavichove | 13 Nov 1917 – 15 Feb 1918 | 4 |
| Marcke | 16 Feb 1918 – 14 Mar 1918 | 4 |
| Erchin | 15 Mar 1918 – 14 Apr 1918 | 17 |
| Halluin | 15 Apr 1918 – 20 May 1918 | 4 |
| Vivaise | 21 May 1918 – 5 Jun 1918 | 7 |
| Mont Soissons Ferme | 6 Jun 1918 – 17 Jul 1918 | 7 |
| Vauxcère | 18 Jul 1918 – 29 Jun 1918 | 7 |
| Chambry | 30 Jun 1918 – 24 Aug 1918 | 7 |
| Emerchicourt | 25 Aug 1918 – 26 Sep 1918 | 17 |
| Lieu St Armand | 27 Sep 1918 – 29 Sep 1918 | 17 |

| | | |
|---|---|---|
| Spultier, Wavre | 30 Sep 1918 – 9 Oct 1918 | 17 |
| Lens, Mons | 10 Oct 1918 – 8 Nov 1918 | 17 |
| Aniche | 9 Nov 1918 – 11 Nov 1918 | 17 |

## ROYAL PRUSSIAN JAGDSTAFFEL 3

This unit was created on 10 August 1916, from FEA5, as authorised by the Chef des Feldflieger West von Nr.22429 Fl. It was mobilised on 1 September at Vraignes, near Péronne, in the 2 Armee Sector under the command of Oberleutnant Hermann Kohze, from Kampfgeschwader 4, (KG4). The unit was equipped with the Halberstadt DIII. Leutnant Albert Krönig scored the first victory for the unit on 22 September. Leutnant Alfred Mohr gained his fifth victory on 19 March 1917, becoming the first pilot to achieve that total with the Jasta. On 21 March Jasta 3 was transferred to the 6 Armee Sector, where it remained until sent to the 4 Armee Sector on 12 July. Jasta 3 was assigned to the 2 Armee on 13 March 1918, until 11 April when it went back to the 4 Armee in Flanders. 6 June saw the unit with the 2 Armee, then on 9 July a move was made to the 3 Armee where it remained until it was assigned to the 19 Armee on 8 September. On 4 September 1918, Hauptmann Kohze gave up his dual role as CO of Jasta 3 and Jagdgruppe 9 and became the full-time commander of Jagdgruppe 9. Leutnant Georg Weiner (four victories) of Kest 3, took over Jasta 3 for the rest of the war. Jasta 3 was credited with at least 87 confirmed victories while suffering the loss of 16 pilots killed, one taken prisoner, four killed in accidents, plus two wounded.

### Commanding Officers

| | | |
|---|---|---|
| Oblt Hermann Kohze | 1 Sep 1916 – 5 Sep 1918 | CO JGr9 |
| Ltn Georg Weiner | 5 Sep 1918 – 11 Nov 1918 | |

### Pilots credited with victories

| | | | |
|---|---|---|---|
| Ltn Karl Menckhoff | 20(39) | Gefr Meyer | 2 |
| Ltn Julius Schmidt | 14(15) | Vfw Ludwig Weber | 2 |
| Ltn Georg Schlenker | 7(14) | Ltn Ernst Bauer | 1 |
| Ltn Alfred Mohr* | 6 | Vfw Glasemann | 2 |
| Ltn Georg Weiner | 5(9) | Vfw Emil Eisenhuth* | 1 |
| Ltn Kurt Wissemann* | 5 | Ltn Kurt Haber | 1(5) |
| Ltn Joachim von Busse | 4(11) | Oblt Jermann Kohze | 1 |
| Ltn Franz Bacher | 3 | Ltn Albert Krönig* | 1 |
| Uffz Wilhelm Reiss* | 3 | Uffz Rudolf Kühne | 1 |
| Uffz Karl Steudel* | 3 | Vfw Mühlhausen | 1 |
| Vfw Rudolf Eck | 2 | Ltn Stobel | 1 |
| | | Uffz Tönjes | 1 |

### Airfields occupied

| Location | Inclusive Dates | Armee |
|---|---|---|
| Braunschweig | 10 Aug 1918 – 1 Sep 1916 | FEA5 |
| Vraignes | 1 Sep 1916 – 4 Nov 1916 | 2 |
| Fontaine-Uterte | 5 Nov 1916 – 20 Mar 1917 | 2 |
| Guesnain | 21 Mar 1917 – 11 Jul 1917 | 6 |
| Houplin | 12 Jul 1917 – 19 Jul 1917 | 6 |
| Rumbeke | 20 Jul 1917 – 16 Sep 1917 | 4 |
| Guise | 17 Sep 1917 – 19 Sep 1917 | 2 |
| Rumbeke | 20 Sep 1917 – 16 Oct 1917 | 4 |
| Wynghene | 17 Oct 1917 – 12 Mar 1918 | 4 |
| Briastre | 13 Mar 1918 – 23 Mar 1918 | 2 |
| Mons-en-Chaussée | 24 Mar 1918 – 10 Apr 1918 | 2 |
| Ingelmünster | 11 Apr 1918 – 3 May 1918 | 4 |
| Rumbeke | 4 May 1918 – 5 Jun 1918 | 4 |
| Falvy-Péronne | 6 Jun 1918 – 8 Jul 1918 | 2 |
| Blaise | 9 Jul 1918 – 7 Sep 1918 | 3 |
| Gross-Tanchen, Mörchingen | 8 Sep 1918 – 11 Nov 1918 | 19 |

## ROYAL PRUSSIAN JAGDSTAFFEL 4

Jasta 4 was created on 25 August 1916, from KEK Vaux, authorised by Kriegs Ministerium von 31.8.16 Nr.929.16.g.A.7.L., and commenced operations immediately from Roupy, in the 2 Armee Sector. The first Commanding Officer was Oberleutnant Hans-Joachim Buddecke (seven victories). Leutnant Otto

Bernert gained the Jasta's first victory on 6 September, and the first pilot to gain five victories with the Jasta was Leutnant Wilhelm Frankel on 10 October, as his 13th. Buddecke raised his score to ten and was transferred to Turkey on 14 December. Oberleutnant Kurt von Döring was named as his replacement. On 21 December the Jasta was sent to the 5 Armee on the Verdun Front. Later, on 10 February 1917, it returned to the 2 Armee Sector. Then on 24 February they moved to the 6 Armee area until 31 May when the Jasta was sent to the 4 Armee in the Flanders region. On 5 July Jasta 4 was assigned to Jagdgeschwader I, along with Jastas 6, 10 and 11, under the command of Rittmeister Manfred von Richthofen. On 21 November JGI returned to the 2 Armee, and on 7 December Oberleutnant von Döring was promoted to Rittmeister. About two months later, on 22 February 1918, von Döring, who had by now scored nine victories, was named commander of Jagdgruppe 4, and command of Jasta 4 passed to Leutnant Kurt Wüsthoff (26 victories). The Jasta's 100th victory came on 1 April, Leutnant Eugen Siempelkamp downing his first enemy aircraft, a Sopwith Camel, south-east of Fouilloy. Wüsthoff was transferred to Inspektion der Fliegertruppe (Idflieg) on 4 May and was temporarily replaced by Leutnant Victor von Rautter (three victories) until 20 May when Leutnant Ernst Udet (23 victories) arrived from Jasta 11. Also on this date JGI moved to the 7 Armee Sector. Udet was shot down in flames during combat with a two-seater on 29 June, but saved himself by jumping in a parachute, but he was injured on landing. In his absence Leutnant Egon Koepsch (two victories) headed the Jasta for four weeks while Udet was on leave. Jasta 4 gained its 150th victory on 17 July, and moved to the 2 Armee Sector on 8 August. Leutnant Ernst Udet was promoted to Oberleutnant on 14 September, and on the 27th Jasta 4 was assigned to Armee-Abteilung 'C'. They departed there on 9 October for the 5 Armee Front where they spent the rest of the war. On 22 October Udet was called to Berlin and Leutnant Heinrich Maushake (six victories) took temporary command, but on 3 November he was severely wounded in combat, and Leutnant Wolfram von Richthofen (seven victories) assumed command of the Jasta in the air, while Leutnant Egon Koepsch was the acting Commanding Officer. Jasta 4 was credited with 192 confirmed victories for the loss of 11 pilots killed, two shot down and taken prisoner, and nine wounded.

## Commanding Officers

| | | |
|---|---|---|
| Oblt Hans Buddecke | 25 Aug 1916 – 14 Dec 1916 | Turkey |
| Rittm Kurt von Döring | 14 Dec 1916 – 22 Feb 1918 | CO JGr4 |
| Ltn Kurt Wüsthoff | 22 Feb 1918 – 4 May 1918 | Idflieg |
| Ltn Victor von Rautter | 4 May 1918 – 20 May 1918 | Acting |
| Ltn Ernst Udet | 20 May 1918 – 29 Jun 1918 | WIA |
| Ltn Egon Koepsch | 29 Jun 1918 – 19 Sep 1918 | Acting |
| Oblt Ernst Udet | 19 Sep 1918 – 22 Oct 1918 | Berlin |
| Ltn Heinrich Maushake | 22 Oct 1918 – 3 Nov 1918 | WIA |
| Ltn Egon Koepsch | 3 Nov 1918 – 11 Nov 1918 | Acting |

## Pilots credited with victories

| | | | |
|---|---|---|---|
| Oblt Ernst Udet | 39(62) | Ltn Joachim von Winterfeld* | 2 |
| Ltn Kurt Wüsthoff | 27 | Ltn Fritz Anders | 1(7) |
| Ltn Hans Klein | 16(22) | Ltn Hermann Bahlmann | 1 |
| Ltn Victor von Rautter* | 15 | OfStv Behling | 1 |
| Ltn Wilhelm Frankl* | 11(20) | Ltn Geppert | 1 |
| Ltn Heinrich Drekmann* | 10(11) | Ltn Heinz Graf von Gluckewski- | |
| Rittm Kurt von Döring | 9(11) | Kwilicki | 1 |
| Ltn Egon Koepsch | 9 | Ltn Gisbert Groos | 1 |
| Ltn Heinrich Maushake | 6 | Ltn Adolf Hildebrandt | 1 |
| Ltn Otto Bernert | 6(27) | Ltn Kralewski* | 1 |
| Oblt Oskar Frhr v Boenigk | 5(26) | Ltn Richard Krüger* | 1 |
| Ltn Alfred Hübner* | 4 | Ltn Hans Malchow | 1 |
| Oblt Hans Buddecke* | 3(12) | Vfw Otto Marquardt | 1 |
| Vfw Ernst Clausnitzer | 3 | Ltn Reinhardt | 1 |
| Ltn Karl Meyer | 3 | Sgt Otto Schmultzer* | 1 |
| Oblt Rudolf Berthold | 2(44) | Ltn Wilhelm Schultze* | 1 |
| Ltn Fedor Hübner | 2 | Ltn Eugen Siempelkamp | 1(5) |
| Ltn Johann Jessen | 2 | Ltn Wilde | 1 |
| Vfw Linus Patermann | 2 | | |
| (Buddecke killed with Jasta 18.) | | | |

## Airfields occupied

| Location | Inclusive Dates | Armee |
|---|---|---|
| Vaux | 25 Aug 1916 – 31 Aug 1916 | |
| Roupy | 1 Sep 1916 – 11 Dec 1916 | 2 |
| Hivry-Circourt | 12 Dec 1916 – 9 Feb 1917 | 5 |
| Le Catelet | 10 Feb 1917 – 23 Feb 1917 | 2 |

| | | |
|---|---|---|
| Douai | 24 Feb 1917 – 31 May 1917 | 6 |
| Ceune-Courtrai | 1 Jun 1917 – 1 Jul 1917 | 4 |
| Marckebeke | 2 Jul 1917 – 20 Nov 1917 | 4 |
| Lieu St Armand | 21 Nov 1917 – 25 Mar 1918 | 2 |
| Lechelle | 26 Mar 1918 – 2 Apr 1918 | 2 |
| Harbonnières | 3 Apr 1918 – 11 Apr 1918 | 2 |
| Cappy | 12 Apr 1918 – 19 May 1918 | 2 |
| Longchamps, Guise | 20 May 1918 – 25 May 1918 | 7 |
| Puisieux Ferme, Laon | 26 May 1918 – 30 May 1918 | 7 |
| Beugneux | 31 May 1918 – 17 Jul 1918 | 7 |
| Monthussart Ferme | 18 Jul 1918 – 29 Jul 1918 | 7 |
| Puisieux Ferme, Laon | 30 Jul 1918 – 9 Aug 1918 | 7 |
| Ennemain, Falvy | 10 Aug 1918 – 11 Aug 1918 | 2 |
| Bernes | 11 Aug 1918 – 30 Aug 1918 | 2 |
| Busigny-Escaufourt | 30 Aug 1918 – 27 Sep 1918 | 2 |
| Metz-Frescaty | 28 Sep 1918 – 8 Oct 1918 | C |
| Marville | 9 Oct 1918 – 6 Nov 1918 | 5 |
| Tellancourt | 7 Nov 1918 – 11 Nov 1918 | 5 |

# ROYAL PRUSSIAN JAGDSTAFFEL 5

Created by Feldflugchef v.15.1.16- Nr. 10083 Fl, on 21 January 1916 as Kdo des Kampfgeschwader 1, this unit became Jasta 5 pursuant to Kriegs Ministerium von 31.8.16- Nr.929.16.g.A.7.L. on 10.8.16 at Bechamp, 5 Armee, on the Verdun Front from KEK Staffel A, under the command of Oberleutnant Hans Berr (two victories). The unit's first victory was registered on 26 August by Vizefeldwebel Hans Müller as his fifth claim. On 26 September a move was made to Bellevue Ferme, near Senon, and on the 29th the Jasta was sent to the 1 Armee on the Somme Front. On 26 October Oberleutnant Hans Berr became the first pilot to register five victories with Jasta 5. The Jasta moved to the 2 Armee Sector on 11 March 1917, and remained with this armee until the end of the war. Oberleutnant Berr, who had brought his score to ten, was killed in combat with an FE2d from 57 Sqn, RFC, at 0810 hours north of Noyelles, on 6 April, when he collided in mid-air with Vizefeldwebel Paul Hoppe. The following day command of Jasta 5 was assumed by Hauptmann Hans Hünerbein, from Jasta 8, who, unfortunately, was killed at Boistrancourt, while testing S.S.W. DI 3761/16 on 4 May. Leutnant Kurt Schneider (12 victories) took command and the commander's jinx continued as he was severely wounded in combat on 5 June, after having raised his score to 15. Oberleutnant Richard Flashar (one victory) arrived from KG2 to assume command on 10 June. Jasta 5 gained its 100th victory in August 1917. Leutnant Wilhelm Lehmann (two victories) assumed command of Jasta 5, on 12 May; however, after adding two more victories to his score, he was killed in combat on 26 June. Oberleutnant Otto Schmidt (ten victories) arrived on 3 July to take over until the end of the war. The 200th victory was claimed in August 1918, and the 251st on 4 November. Jasta 5 was given credit for at least 253 confirmed victories, the third highest of the Jastas, for the loss of 19 pilots killed, two captured, three killed and one injured in accidents, and eight wounded, one pilot twice, while one was saved by parachute descent.

## Commanding Officers

| | | |
|---|---|---|
| Oblt Hans Berr | 21 Aug 1916 – 2 Jan 1917 | Leave |
| Ltn Ludwig Dornheim | 2 Jan 1917 – 5 Feb 1917 | Acting |
| Oblt Hans Berr | 5 Feb 1917 – 6 Apr 1917 | KIA |
| Hptm Hans von Hünerbein | 7 Apr 1917 – 4 May 1917 | KIAcc |
| Ltn Kurt Schneider | 6 May 1917 – 5 Jun 1917 | WIA |
| Oblt Richard Flashar | 10 Jun 1917 – 31 Dec 1917 | Leave |
| Ltn Wilhelm Lehmann | 31 Dec 1917 – 14 Jan 1918 | Acting |
| Oblt Richard Flashar | 14 Jan 1918 – 12 May 1918 | CO JGr2 |
| Ltn Wilhelm Lehmann | 12 May 1918 – 26 Jun 1918 | KIA |
| Oblt Otto Schmidt | 3 Jul 1918 – 11 Nov 1918 | |

## Pilots credited with victories

| | | | |
|---|---|---|---|
| Ltn Fritz Rumey* | 45 | Oblt Hans Berr* | 8(10) |
| Ltn Otto Könnecke | 33(35) | Uffz Karl Treiber | 7 |
| Ltn Josef Mai | 30 | OfStv Hans Müller | 8(11) |
| Ltn Heinrich Gontermann | 17(39) | Ltn Werner Voss* | 6(48) |
| Ltn Kurt Schneider | 15 | Ltn Rudolf Matthaei | 6(10) |
| OfStv Edmund Nathanael* | 15 | Ltn Wilhelm Lehmann* | 4 |
| Ltn Renatus Theiller* | 10(11) | Ltn Hans Schlömer* | 4 |
| Oblt Otto Schmidt | 9(19) | Uffz Paul Bäumer | 3(43) |

| | | | | |
|---|---|---|---|---|
| Vfw Dilcher | 3 | | Vfw Cremer | 1 |
| Uffz Leicht | 3 | | Oblt Richard Flashar | 1(2) |
| Vfw Ernst Büssing | 2(3) | | Ltn Hans von Hippel | 1(2) |
| Ltn Dahlmann | 2 | | Bfw Kurt Kressner | 1 |
| Ltn Ludwig Dornheim | 2 | | Ltn Rudolf Nebel | 1 |
| Ltn Walter Hoffmann | 2 | | Ltn Niesen | 1 |
| Vfw Paul Hoppe | 2 | | Ltn Alhard Scheck* | 1 |
| Ltn Fritz Oppenhorst | 2 | | OfStv Alfred Sturm | 1 |
| Ltn Kurt Schuhmann* | 2 | | Vfw Artur Weber | 1 |
| Ltn Vollbracht | 2 | | Ltn Wolf | 1(2) |
| OfStv Karl Bey* | 1 | | | |

### Airfields occupied

| Location | Inclusive Dates | Armee |
|---|---|---|
| Bechamp | 21 Aug 1916 – 25 Sep 1916 | 5 |
| Bellevue Ferme, Senon | 26 Sep 1916 – 29 Sep 1916 | 5 |
| Gonnelieu | 30 Sep 1916 – 10 Mar 1917 | 1 |
| Boistrancourt | 11 Mar 1917 – 21 Mar 1918 | 2 |
| Cappy-sur-Somme | 23 Apr 1918 – May 1918 | 2 |
| Villers-sur-Nicole | May 1918 – 4 Nov 1918 | 2 |
| Cyembloux, Charleroi | 5 Nov 1918 – 11 Nov 1918 | 2 |

# ROYAL PRUSSIAN JAGDSTAFFEL 6

Created in the field 25 August 1916, by Kriegs Ministerium von 31.8.16- Nr.929.16 g.A.7.L. u. AOK 5 v. 25.8.16 Ia. 2394, from Fokkerstaffel Sivry, under the command of Rittmeister Josef Wulff from KG5. Due to enemy artillery fire a move was made from Sivry to Jametz still in the 5 Armee Sector. Then on 30 September Jasta 6 was transferred to the 2 Armee. The first pilot to register a victory with the Jasta was Vizefeldwebel Christian Kress on 20 October. On 20 March 1917, a move was made to the 4 Armee Sector. Then on 5 July Jasta 6 was assigned to Jagdgeschwader I, with Jastas 4, 10 and 11, under the command of Rittmeister Manfred von Richthofen. Rittmeister Wulff, who had scored twice, was assigned to Stofl Heimat on 1 May 1917, and command of the Jasta passed to Leutnant Otto Bernert (23 victories) from Jasta Boelcke, but on 9 June, after having scored three more victories, he returned to Jasta Boelcke as Commanding Officer, and command of Jasta 5 passed to Oberleutnant Eduard Dostler (eight victories) from Jasta 34. Vizefeldwebel Fritz Krebs became the Jasta's first pilot to gain five victories on 17 June. Oberleutnant Dostler, who had raised his score to 26, was killed in combat with a RE8 on 21 August near Ypern, and the next day Leutnant Hans Adam (12 victories) assumed command. The bad luck of the commanding officers continued and on 15 November Adam, who had scored his 21st victory on 6 November, was killed north-west of Kortewilde at 0920 hours flying Albatros DV 5222/17. Oberleutnant Wilhelm Reinhard (six victories) from Jasta 11 took over command, and the Jasta moved to the 2 Armee Front on 21 November. On 6 April 1918, the Jasta registered its 100th victory. Hauptmann Reinhard was assigned as commander of Jagdgeschwader I following the death of Rittmeister Manfred von Richthofen on 21 April 1918, and Leutnant Johann Janzen (four victories) assumed command of Jasta 6. By 16 May Jasta 6 had been re-equipped with the Fokker DVII, and on 21 May the unit moved to the 7 Armee Sector. Janzen was shot down and taken prisoner on 9 June after having scored his 13th victory two days before. Another Jasta 6 pilot, Leutnant Hans Kirschstein (24 victories), took over command, and added three more to his score, but on 16 July he and Leutnant Johannes Markgraf were killed in an accident flying a Hannover CLIII at Magneux, near Fismes. The command of Jasta 6 passed to Leutnant Paul Wenzel (six victories). Jasta 6 was equipped with the Fokker DVIII monoplane on 5 August, and on 10 August the unit moved to the 2 Armee Sector. Wenzel was severely wounded on 11 August, after gaining his tenth victory two days earlier. Leutnant Richard Wenzl (six victories) took over the reins of the Jasta. The Fokker DVIIIs were grounded by Kogenluft on 19 August and Jasta 6 was re-equipped with the Fokker DVII. On 1 September Leutnant Ulrich Neckel (24 victories) from Jasta 19 reported to take command until the end of the war. JGI was moved from the 2 Armee to Armee-Abteilung 'C' on 27 September, remaining until 8 October when it was assigned to the 5 Armee Front for the rest of the war. Jasta 6 received credit for at least 201 victories, while suffering the loss of ten pilots killed, two killed and four injured in accidents, three taken prisoner, and nine wounded.

### Commanding Officers

| | | |
|---|---|---|
| Rittm Josef Wulff | 28 Aug 1916 – 1 May 1917 | Stofl Heimat |
| Ltn Otto Bernert | 1 May 1917 – 9 Jun 1917 | CO J2 |
| Oblt Eduard Dostler | 11 Jun 1917 – 21 Aug 1917 | KIA |

| Ltn Hans Adam | 22 Aug 1917 – 15 Nov 1917 | KIA |
| Oblt Wilhelm Reinhard | 26 Nov 1917 – 22 Apr 1918 | CO JGI |
| Ltn Johann Janzen | 28 Apr 1918 – 9 Jun 1918 | POW |
| Ltn Hans Kirschstein | 10 Jun 1918 – 16 Jul 1918 | Injured† |
| Ltn Paul Wenzel | 19 Jul 1918 – 11 Aug 1918 | WIA |
| Ltn Richard Wenzl | 11 Aug 1918 – 1 Sep 1918 | |
| Ltn Ulrich Neckel | 1 Sep 1918 – 11 Nov 1918 | |

† Died of injuries in hospital 16 July 1918.

## Pilots credited with victories

| | | | | |
|---|---|---|---|---|
| Ltn Hans Kirschstein | 27 | | Lt Friedrich Mallinckrodt | 2(6) |
| Ltn Hans von Adam* | 18(21) | | Ltn Matzdorf | 2 |
| Oblt Eduard von Dostler* | 18(26) | | Ltn Friedrich Noltenius | 2(21) |
| Ltn Franz Hemer | 18 | | Ltn Leopold von Raffay | 2 |
| Ltn Johann Janzen | 12(13) | | Uffz Hans Reimers* | 2 |
| Ltn Richard Wenzl | 12 | | Ltn Fritz Schliewen | 2 |
| Ltn Paul Wenzel | 10(12) | | Ltn Karl Stock | 2(3) |
| Vfw Fritz Krebs* | 8 | | Ltn Robert Tüxen | 2 |
| Ltn Moritz Bretschneider-Bodemer* | 6 | | Rittm Josef Wulff | 2 |
| Ltn Ulrich Neckel | 6(30) | | Vfw Fritz Bachmann* | 1 |
| Hptm Wilhelm Reinhard | 6(20) | | Ltn Otto Brieten-Landenberg | 1(5) |
| Ltn Kurt Küppers | 5(6) | | Ltn Johann Czermak | 1 |
| Ltn Karl Deilmann | 4(6) | | Vfw Häusler | 1 |
| Ltn Otto Bernert | 3(27) | | Vfw Heinrich Küllmer | 1(3) |
| Ltn Emil Rolff | 3 | | Ltn Fritz Loerzer | 1(11) |
| FwLtn Fritz Schubert | 3 | | Ltn Roland Nauck | 1 |
| Ltn Martin Skowronski | 3 | | Ltn Werner Nöldecke | 1 |
| Ltn Walter Stock | 3 | | Ltn Max Pollandt | 1 |
| Ltn Karl Galetsky | 2(3) | | Ltn Erich Reiher* | 1 |
| Vfw Karl Holler | 2 | | Ltn Rieth | 1 |
| Vfw Christian Kress* | 2(4) | | Vfw Gottfried Stumpf | 1 |

## Airfields occupied

| Location | Inclusive Dates | Armee |
|---|---|---|
| Sivry | 25 Aug 1916 – 23 Sep 1916 | 5 |
| Jametz | 23 Sep 1916 – 29 Sep 1916 | 5 |
| Ugny l'Equipée, Ham | 30 Sep 1916 – 19 Mar 1917 | 2 |
| Aulnoye | 20 Mar 1917 – 9 Jun 1917 | 4 |
| Bisseghem-Courtrai | 10 Jun 1917 – 1 Jul 1917 | 4 |
| Marckebeke | 2 Jul 1917 – 20 Nov 1917 | 4 |
| Lieu St Armand | 21 Nov 1917 – 24 Nov 1917 | 2 |
| Bouchain | 25 Nov 1917 – 20 Mar 1918 | 2 |
| Awoingt | 21 Mar 1918 – 26 Mar 1918 | 2 |
| Lechelle | 27 Mar 1918 – 3 Apr 1918 | 2 |
| Harbonnières, Proyart | 3 Apr 1918 – 11 Apr 1918 | 2 |
| Cappy | 12 Apr 1918 – 13 Apr 1918 | 2 |
| Lomme, Lille | 14 Apr 1918 – 20 May 1918 | 6 |
| Guise | 21 May 1918 – 26 May 1918 | 7 |
| Puisieux Ferme | 26 May 1918 – 31 May 1918 | 7 |
| Begneux | 31 May 1918 – 18 Jul 1918 | 7 |
| Monthussart Ferme | 18 Jul 1918 – 29 Jul 1918 | 7 |
| Puisieux Ferme | 30 Jul 1918 – 10 Aug 1918 | 7 |
| Ennemain | 10 Aug 1918 – 11 Aug 1918 | 2 |
| Bernes | 11 Aug 1918 – 30 Aug 1918 | 2 |
| N Busigny | 30 Aug 1918 – 27 Sep 1918 | 2 |
| Metz-Frescaty | 28 Sep 1918 – 8 Oct 1918 | C |
| Marville | 9 Oct 1918 – 6 Nov 1918 | 5 |
| Tellancourt | 7 Nov 1918 – 11 Nov 1918 | 5 |

# ROYAL PRUSSIAN JAGDSTAFFEL 7

Jasta 7 was created in the field on 23 August 1916, pursuant to Kriegs Ministerium von 31.8.16 Nr.929.16.g.A.7.L. u. AOK 5 v. 25.8.16 In. 2394, and was mobilised on 21 September at Martincourt, from the personnel of the Fokkerstaffel by the 34th Infantry Division, in the 5 Armee Sector. The first Commanding Officer was Oberleutnant Fritz von Bronsart-Schellendorf, from the above unit. Leutnant

Hermann Kunz gained the first victory for the Jasta on 23 October. On 14 February 1917, Vizefeldwebel Friedrich Manschott gained his fifth victory, the first ace in the unit. When von Bronsart-Schellendorf was killed in combat on 21 July, he had been credited with one victory. His successor was Leutnant Josef Jacobs (five victories) from Jasta 22, who commanded Jasta 7 for the rest of the war. In August 1917 the Jasta moved to the 4 Armee Sector where it remained until the end of the war. On 6 May 1918, the Jasta was based at St Marguerite, and was flying both the Fokker VII and DrI. The Jasta gained its 100th victory on 16 September 1918. Jasta 7 was credited with at least 126 victories while losing 11 pilots killed in combat, two killed in flying accidents, and twelve wounded (one twice).

## Commanding Officers

| | | |
|---|---|---|
| Oblt Fritz von Bronsart-Schellendorf | 11 Aug 1916 – 21 Jul 1918 | KIA |
| Lt Josef Jacobs | 5 Aug 1918 – 11 Nov 1918 | |

## Pilots credited with victories

| | | | |
|---|---|---|---|
| Ltn Josef Jacobs | 43(48) | Vfw Otto Sowa | 2(4) |
| Obflugm Kurt Schönfelder* | 13 | Ltn Otto Schmidt | 2(19) |
| Vfw Friedrich Manschott* | 11(12) | Vfw Ulbrich | 2 |
| Vfw Paul Hüttenrauch | 8 | Ltn Oliver Fr von Beaulieu-Marconnay | 1(26) |
| Ltn Paul Billik | 4(31) | Oblt Fritz von Bronsart-Schellendorf* | 1 |
| Ltn Paul Lotz | 4(10) | Ltn Max Hillmann* | 1 |
| Ltn Karl Degelow | 3(30) | Ltn Johannes Kintzelmann | 1 |
| Uffz August Eigenbrodt | 3 | Ltn Friedrich Kresse* | 1 |
| Ltn Hermann Kunz | 3(6) | Vfw Lieber | 1 |
| Ltn Georg Meyer | 3(24) | Ltn Martin Möbius* | 1(2) |
| Uffz Max Mertens* | 3 | Uffz Peisker | 1 |
| Ltn Willi Nebgen* | 3 | Uffz Reuss | 1 |
| Vfw Otto Schramm* | 3 | Ltn Schäfer | 1 |
| Vfw Hans Horst | 2(4) | Vfw Schendel | 1 |
| Vfw Friedrich Saurwein | 2 | Vfw Franz Schmitt | 1(3) |

## Airfields occupied

| Location | Inclusive Dates | Armee |
|---|---|---|
| Martincourt | 22 Aug 1916 – 28 Sep 1918 | 5 |
| Bellevue Ferme, Senon | 29 Sep 1916 – 19 Oct 1916 | 5 |
| La Jolly Ferme, Stenay | 20 Oct 1916 – 1 Nov 1916 | 5 |
| Procher | 2 Nov 1916 – 4 May 1917 | 5 |
| Eswars | 5 May 1917 – 5 Jun 1917 | 6 |
| Thouroube, Roulers | 6 Jun 1917 – 21 Aug 1917 | 4 |
| Wynghene | 22 Aug 1917 – 14 Sep 1917 | 4 |
| Aertrycke | 15 Sep 1917 – 1 Mar 1918 | 4 |
| Rumbeke | 1 Mar 1918 – 14 Mar 1918 | 4 |
| Roulers | 14 Mar 1918 – 29 Mar 1918 | 4 |
| St Marguerite | 29 Mar 1918 – 1 Oct 1918 | 4 |
| Menin | 1 Oct 1918 – 11 Nov 1918 | 4 |

# ROYAL PRUSSIAN JAGDSTAFFEL 8

Jasta 8 was created on 10 September 1916, through FEA 10 in the field by Chef des Feldflieger West von Nr.24281 Fl. Personnel came from FA6, FA(A)213, FA40 and FA33. The Commanding Officer was Hauptmann Gustav Stenzel (two victories) from Kampfstaffel 'Vardar'. The first flights took place on the 15th from the airfield at Rumbeke, 4 Armee Sector. The Jasta's first victory came on 1 October, by Vizefeldwebel Alfred Ulmer who also became the first ace on 24 January 1917. Hauptmann Stenzel was killed in combat 28 July, near Rumbeke, after having scored his fourth victory on 7 June. The new Commanding Officer, Hauptmann Constantin von Bentheim, reported on 9 August. On 20 November the Jasta was sent to the 2 Armee Front, and a few weeks later on 15 December was assigned to the 18 Armee. Hauptmann von Bentheim was assigned to Jagdgruppe 1 on 1 April 1918, and Leutnant Werner Junck (one victory) assumed command of Jasta 8. On 6 July Junck was wounded and Leutnant de la Camp assumed temporary command, as the unit moved to the 1 Armee Sector. Leutnant Junck returned on 12 August and retained command until the end of the war. The Jasta moved to the 5 Armee Front and remained there until the end of the war. Jasta 8 was credited with at least 95 victories while losing four pilots killed, eight wounded (two more than once) and one killed in an accident.

## Commanding Officers

| | | |
|---|---|---|
| Hptm Gustav Stenzel | 23 Sep 1916 – 28 Jul 1917 | KIA |
| Hptm Constantin von Bentheim | 9 Aug 1917 – 1 Apr 1918 | CO JGr1 |
| Ltn Werner Junck | 1 Apr 1918 – 6 Jul 1918 | WIA |
| Ltn Joachim de la Camp | 6 Jul 1918 – 12 Aug 1918 | Acting |
| Ltn Werner Junck | 12 Aug 1918 – 11 Nov 1918 | |

## Pilots credited with victories

| | | | |
|---|---|---|---|
| Ltn Walter Göttsch | 17(20) | Vfw Peter Glasmacher* | 2 |
| Vfw Rudolf Franke | 15 | Vfw Hans Körner | 2(7) |
| Ltn Wilhelm Seitz | 11(16) | Hptm Gustav Stenzel* | 2(4) |
| Ltn Rudolf Wendelmuth | 10(14) | Vfw Weber | 2 |
| Oblt Konrad Mettlich* | 6 | Oblt Rudolf Frhr von Esebeck | 1 |
| Ltn Werner Junck | 5 | Ltn Gröpler | 1 |
| Ltn Alfred Ulmer* | 5 | Vfw Hoppe | 1 |
| Vfw August Jühe | 4 | Hptm Hans von Hüberbein | 1 |
| Ltn Alfred Träger | 3 | Uffz Matthias Meinberg | 1 |
| Oblt Bruno von Voigt | 3 | Vfw Weichel | 1 |
| Jasta | 2 | | |

## Airfields occupied

| Location | Inclusive Dates | Armee |
|---|---|---|
| Rumbeke | 12 Sep 1916 – 30 Sep 1917 | 4 |
| Jabbeke-Brügge | 30 Sep 1917 – 19 Nov 1917 | 4 |
| Neuvilly, Le Cateau | 20 Nov 1917 – 14 Dec 1917 | 2 |
| Wassigny | 15 Dec 1917 – 21 Mar 1918 | 18 |
| Bohain | 21 Mar 1918 – 24 Mar 1918 | 18 |
| Beauvois | 24 Mar 1918 – 27 Mar 1918 | 18 |
| Balâtre-Roye | 27 Mar 1918 – 5 Jul 1918 | 18 |
| St Rémy | 6 Jul 1918 – 14 Sep 1918 | 1 |
| Mercy-le-Haute | 15 Sep 1918 – 11 Nov 1918 | 5 |

# ROYAL PRUSSIAN JAGDSTAFFEL 9

Originally formed on 1 June 1916, as an Armeestaffel des AOK3, at Vouziers, under the command of Oberleutnant Ascheberg, and equipped with Fokker EIII and EIV aircraft. It transformed into Jasta 9 pursuant to orders issued by Kriegs Ministerium von Nr. 269. 10.16.A.7.L. 28.9.16, and was mobilised on 5 October 1916, remaining in the 3 Armee Sector under the command of Oberleutnant Kurt Student (three victories). On 22 October the first victory was gained for the Jasta by Leutnant Adolf Frey. In early 1917 the Albatros DII arrived, and on 21 January Leutnant Hartmuth Baldamus became the first pilot to register five victories with the unit. Oberleutnant Student, who had raised his score to six, was transferred to Idflieg on 14 March 1918, and was replaced at the head of Jasta 9 by a Jasta 26 pilot, Leutnant Walter Blume (six victories). He held the command to the war's end. During May the Jasta moved to the 7 Armee Sector, where they remained for the rest of the war. During the summer months it was equipped with the Fokker DVII. Leutnant Walter Blume was credited with the Jasta's 100th victory on 14 September. The Jasta was demobilised 15 January 1919. Jasta 9 was credited with at least 107 confirmed victories while losing 13 pilots in combat (two in a mid-air collision during combat), five killed and three injured in accidents, and three wounded in action.

## Commanding Officers

| | | |
|---|---|---|
| Oblt Kurt Student | 5 Oct 1916 – 14 Mar 1918 | Idflieg |
| Ltn Walter Blume | 14 Mar 1918 – 11 Nov 1918 | |

## Pilots credited with victories

| | | | |
|---|---|---|---|
| Ltn Walter Blume | 22(28) | Ltn Werner Peckmann | 3 |
| Ltn Hartmuth Baldamus* | 13(18) | Ltn Herbert Rolle | 3 |
| Ltn Fritz Pütter | 10(25) | Vfw Schneck | 3 |
| Ltn Erich Thomas | 8(10) | Ltn Heinrich Hentzen | 2 |
| Ltn Hermann Pfeiffer* | 7(11) | Ltn Hospelt | 2 |
| Ltn Heinrich Kroll | 5(33) | Ltn Bernard Linke-Schlucknier | 2 |
| Ltn Otto von Breiten-Landenberg | 4(5) | Vfw Schlemmel | 2 |
| Vfw Karl Strünkelnberg | 4(5) | Ltn Bitsch | 1 |
| Oblt Kurt Student | 3(6) | Ltn Franz Büchner | 1(40) |
| Ltn Adolf Frey* | 3 | Ltn Friedrich v Hartmann* | 1 |

| | | | |
|---|---|---|---|
| Ltn Johannes Hentschel | 1 | Vfw Heinrich Kramer | 1(4) |
| Gefr Herrmann | 1 | Ltn Werner Marwitz | 1 |
| Ltn Paul Jäger* | 1 | Ltn Kurt Müller | 1(2) |
| OfStv Hans Knaak* | 1 | Uffz Arno Ulbricht* | 1 |

## Airfields occupied

| Location | Inclusive Dates | Armee |
|---|---|---|
| Leffincourt | 5 Oct 1916 – 23 Mar 1918 | 3 |
| Chéry-les-Pouilly | 24 Mar 1918 – 6 Jun 1918 | 7 |
| Montceau-le-Wast | 6 Jun 1918 – 11 Jul 1918 | 7 |
| Fonfry | 11 Jul 1918 – 20 Jul 1918 | 7 |
| Rocourt St Martin | 20 Jul 1918 – 23 Jul 1918 | 7 |
| Bazoches | 23 Jul 1918 – 26 Jul 1918 | 7 |
| Maizy | 27 Jul 1918 – 31 Jul 1918 | 7 |
| Sissone | 1 Aug 1918 – 11 Oct 1918 | 7 |
| Plounion | 11 Oct 1918 – 11 Nov 1918 | 7 |

# ROYAL PRUSSIAN JAGDSTAFFEL 10

Created from Kampfeinsitzer Kommando 3 on 28 September 1916, at Phalempin, near Lille, in accordance with Kriegs Ministerium von Nr.269. 10.16.A.7.L. through Kommandeur der Flieger 6, it commenced operations on 6 October. It was equipped with four Fokker EIII, one Fokker EI, two Fokker DII, one Halberstadt DII and two Albatros DIIs. The first Commanding Officer was Oberleutnant Ludwig Linck from FA18, who was shot down in flames and killed in combat with FE8s of 40 Sqn and FE2bs of 25 Sqn, RFC, over Carvin on 22 October. Oberleutnant Karl Rummelspacher succeeded him as commander. On 28 October the Jasta was sent to the 5 Armee Sector. Offizierstellvertreter Paul Aue registered the first confirmed victory for Jasta 10 on 25 March 1917. Oberleutnant Rummelspacher was transferred to Idflieg on 18 June 1917, and command of Jasta 10 passed to Leutnant Albert Dossenbach (14 victories) from Jasta 36, but he was killed in combat with DH4s of 57 Sqn, RFC, over Frezenberg on 3 July. Oberleutnant Ernst Freiherr von Althaus (eight victories) from Jasta 14 took over command of the Jasta. On 5 July Jasta 10 joined Jastas 4, 6 and 11 in the formation of Jagdgeschwader I at Marcke, 4 Armee Sector, under the command of Rittmeister Manfred von Richthofen. Von Althaus was sent to Jagdstaffel-schule II on 30 July and Leutnant Werner Voss (34 victories), from Jasta 14, assumed command and became the first pilot to score five times with the Jasta. Almost two months later, on 23 September, Voss, who had raised his score to 48, was killed during combat with a flight from 56 Sqn, RFC, near Frezenberg. Oberleutnant Ernst Weigand (two victories) was named the new commander; however, two days later he was shot down in flames and killed at 1740 hours near Nachtegaal, during combat with 56 Sqn, RFC. Then on 27 September, Leutnant Hans Klein (16 victories) from Jasta 4 was named Commanding Officer. JGI was sent to the 2 Armee Front on 27 November. Klein was wounded, while flying Pfalz DIII 4283/17 at 1300 hours on 19 February 1918, and the next day Leutnant Erich Löwenhardt (ten victories) took over command. JGI moved to the 7 Armee on 20 May. On 30 June the Jasta's 100th victory was reported. Jasta 10 moved back to the 2 Armee on 10 August, the day Löwenhardt, who had a score now of 54, was killed as the result of a mid-air collision with Leutnant Wentz, of Jasta 11, over Chaulnes on 10 August. He jumped but his parachute failed to open. Leutnant Alois Heldmann (nine victories) then took command of Jasta 10 until Leutnant Arthur Laumann (23 victories), from Jasta 66, arrived on 13 August and took command for the rest of the war. After the St Mihiel offensive was over JGI moved to the Armee-Abteilung 'C' Sector for a few days, then made a final move to the 5 Armee Front on 8 October. Jasta 10 received credit for at least 151 confirmed victories as well as ten that are questionable. In attaining this respectable score there were at least 20 pilots killed in combat, four taken prisoner, ten wounded and one killed in an accident. One pilot was saved by taking to a parachute after colliding with an American-flown Spad.

## Commanding Officers

| | | |
|---|---|---|
| Oblt Ludwig Linck | 21 Sep 1916 – 22 Oct 1916 | KIA |
| Oblt Karl Rummelspacher | 23 Oct 1916 – 18 Jun 1917 | Idflieg |
| Ltn Albert Dossenbach | 21 Jun 1917 – 3 Jul 1917 | KIA |
| Oblt Ernst Frhr v Althaus | 6 Jul 1917 – 30 Jul 1917 | JsSchII |
| Ltn Werner Voss | 30 Jul 1917 – 23 Sep 1917 | KIA |
| Oblt Ernst Weigand | 24 Sep 1917 – 25 Sep 1917 | KIA |
| Ltn Max Kühn | 26 Sep 1917 – 26 Sep 1917 | Acting |
| Ltn Hans Klein | 27 Sep 1917 – 19 Feb 1918 | WIA |
| Ltn Erich Löwenhardt | 20 Feb 1918 – 10 Aug 1918 | KIA |

| Ltn Alois Heldmann | 10 Aug 1918 – 13 Aug 1918 | Acting |
| Ltn Arthur Laumann | 13 Aug 1918 – 11 Nov 1918 | |

## Pilots credited with victories

| | | | |
|---|---|---|---|
| Ltn Erich Löwenhardt* | 54 | Ltn Johannes Ohlrau | 2 |
| Ltn Friedrich Friedrichs* | 21 | Oblt Ernst Weigand | 2 |
| Ltn Alois Heldmann | 15 | Oblt Ernst Frhr von Althaus | 1(9) |
| Ltn Werner Voss* | 14(48) | Ltn Gustav Bellen | 1 |
| Ltn Justus Grasmann | 10 | Ltn Fritz Bohlein* | 1 |
| OfStv Paul Aue | 7(10) | Ltn Albert Dossenbach* | 1(15) |
| Ltn Hans Klein | 6(22) | Ltn Max Kühn | 1(3) |
| Vfw Fritz Schumacher | 5 | Gefr Ludwig Möller* | 1 |
| Ltn Wilhelm Kohlbach | 3(5) | Ltn Heinrich Otto | 1 |
| Uffz Hermann Brettle | 2 | Vfw Wawzin | 1 |
| Ltn Arthur Laumann | 2(28) | Ltn Hans Weiss | 1(16) |

## Airfields occupied

| Location | Inclusive Dates | Armee |
|---|---|---|
| Phalempin | 28 Sep 1916 – 27 Oct 1916 | 6 |
| Jametz, Stenay | 28 Oct 1916 – 12 Dec 1916 | 5 |
| Ancrevillers | 12 Dec 1916 – | 5 |
| Leffincourt | – 1 May 1917 | 3 |
| Bersée, Douai | 2 May 1917 – 24 May 1917 | 6 |
| Heul, Courtrai | 25 May 1917 – 2 Jul 1917 | 4 |
| Marckebeke | 2 Jul 1917 – 21 Nov 1917 | 4 |
| Iwuy | 21 Nov 1917 – 20 Mar 1918 | 2 |
| Awoingt | 20 Mar 1918 – 27 Mar 1918 | 2 |
| Lechelle | 27 Mar 1918 – 3 Apr 1918 | 2 |
| Harbonnières, Proyart | 3 Apr 1918 – 12 Apr 1918 | 2 |
| Cappy | 12 Apr 1918 – 13 Apr 1918 | 2 |
| Lomme, Lille | 14 Apr 1918 – 21 May 1918 | 6 |
| Etreux, Guise | 21 May 1918 – 26 May 1918 | 7 |
| Puisieux Ferme, Laon | 26 May 1918 – 31 May 1918 | 7 |
| Rugny Ferme, Beugneux | 31 May 1918 – 18 Jul 1918 | 7 |
| Monthussart Ferme | 18 Jul 1918 – 29 Jul 1918 | 7 |
| Puisieux Ferme | 29 Jul 1918 – 10 Aug 1918 | 7 |
| Ennemain, Falvy | 10 Aug 1918 – 11 Aug 1918 | 2 |
| Bernes | 12 Aug 1918 – 30 Aug 1918 | 2 |
| Escaufourt | 30 Aug 1918 – 20 Sep 1918 | 2 |
| Metz-Frescaty | 25 Sep 1918 – 8 Oct 1918 | C |
| Marville | 9 Oct 1918 – 6 Nov 1918 | 5 |
| Tellancourt | 7 Nov 1918 – 11 Nov 1918 | 5 |

# ROYAL PRUSSIAN JAGDSTAFFEL 11

Created 28 September 1916, through Kommandeur der Flieger 6, in accordance with Kriegs Ministerium von Nr.269.10.16.A.7.L. They became operational on 10 October 1916, in the 6 Armee Sector. The first Commanding Officer was Oberleutnant Rudolf Emil Lang, but he was transferred to command of Jasta 28 on 14 January 1917, and the following day Leutnant Manfred von Richthofen (16 victories), from Jasta Boelcke, assumed command. Richthofen was the first pilot to score on 23 January and to gain five victories with the unit, and he led Jasta 11 until 25 June when he was appointed as Commanding Officer of Jagdgeschwader I (Jastas 4, 6, 10 and 11). Jasta 11 was transferred to the 4 Armee Sector, in Flanders, on 10 June. Leutnant Kurt Wolff (31 victories), a former Jasta 11 pilot who had been sent to command Jasta 29 on 2 May, returned to head the Jasta on 2 July. After adding two more to his score, Wolff was killed during combat on 15 September during a fight with 10 Squadron, RNAS. Leutnant Gisbert-Wilhelm Groos (six victories) took over temporary command until Leutnant Lothar von Richthofen assumed command on 25 September. On 22 November, the Jasta moved to the 2 Armee Front. Lothar was wounded on 13 March 1918, and there were several temporary commanders until he returned on 19 July to again take over. In the meantime, Jasta 11 had been assigned to the 7 Armee on 21 May, remaining there until 10 August when it returned to the 2 Armee Sector. Lothar von Richthofen was again wounded on 13 August and command passed to Oberleutnant Erich Rüdiger von Wedel (nine victories) who held it until the end of the war. After the St Mihiel offensive, JGI was moved to the Armee-Abteilung 'C' Sector on 28 September, until 8 October when it was reassigned to the 5 Armee Front for the rest of the war. Jasta 11 was credited with a total of 350 victories, which includes those of the commanding officers of Jagdgeschwader I (Manfred von Richthofen (27), Wilhelm Reinhard (8) and Hermann Göring (1)). However, 17 pilots were killed in action, two taken prisoner, 19 wounded, and two killed in accidents.

## Commanding Officers

| | | |
|---|---|---|
| Oblt Rudolf Emil Lang | 11 Oct 1916 – 14 Jan 1917 | CO J28 |
| Ltn Manfred von Richthofen | 15 Jan 1917 – 1 May 1917 | Leave |
| Ltn Lothar von Richthofen | 1 May 1917 – 13 May 1917 | WIA |
| Ltn Karl Allmenröder | 13 May 1917 – 15 Jun 1917 | Acting |
| Oblt Manfred von Richthofen | 15 Jun 1917 – 26 Jun 1917 | CO JGI |
| Ltn Karl Allmenröder | 26 Jun 1917 – 27 Jun 1917 | KIA |
| Ltn Kurt Wolff | 28 Jun 1917 – 11 Jul 1917 | WIA |
| Oblt Wilhelm Reinhard | 11 Jul 1917 – 4 Sep 1917 | WIA |
| Ltn Gisbert-Wilhelm Groos | 4 Sep 1917 – 11 Sep 1917 | Acting |
| Oblt Kurt Wolff | 11 Sep 1917 – 15 Sep 1917 | KIA |
| Ltn Gisbert-Wilhelm Groos | 15 Sep 1917 – 25 Sep 1917 | Acting |
| Ltn Lothar von Richthofen | 25 Sep 1917 – 19 Jan 1918 | Leave |
| Ltn Hans-Georg von der Osten | 19 Jan 1918 – 16 Feb 1918 | Acting |
| Ltn Lothar von Richthofen | 16 Feb 1918 – 13 Mar 1918 | WIA |
| Ltn Otto von Breiten-Landenberg | 13 Mar 1918 – 25 Mar 1918 | Acting |
| Ltn Ernst Udet | 25 Mar 1918 – 8 Apr 1918 | Acting |
| Ltn Hans Weiss | 8 Apr 1918 – 2 May 1918 | KIA |
| Ltn Eberhard Mohnicke | 2 May 1918 – 19 Jul 1918 | Acting |
| Ltn Lothar von Richthofen | 19 Jul 1918 – 26 Jul 1918 | JGI |
| Oblt Erich Rüdiger v Wedel | 26 Jul 1918 – 14 Aug 1918 | Acting |
| Ltn Eberhardt Mohnicke | 14 Aug 1918 – 26 Aug 1918 | Leave |
| Ltn Wolfram von Richthofen | 26 Aug 1918 – 30 Aug 1918 | Idflieg |
| Oblt Erich Rüdiger v Wedel | 31 Aug 1918 – 2 Sep 1918 | JGI |
| Ltn Eberhard Mohnicke | 2 Sep 1918 – 4 Sep 1918 | Acting |
| Oblt Erich Rüdiger v Wedel | 4 Sep 1918 – 22 Oct 1918 | JGI |
| Ltn Egon Koepsch | 22 Oct 1918 – 4 Nov 1918 | Acting |
| Oblt Erich Rüdiger v Wedel | 4 Nov 1918 – 11 Nov 1918 | |

## Pilots credited with victories

| | | | |
|---|---|---|---|
| Rittm M von Richthofen* | 64(80) | Ltn Siegfried Gussmann | 4(5) |
| Ltn Lothar von Richthofen | 40 | Ltn Julius Schulte-Frohlinde | 4 |
| Ltn Kurt Wolff* | 31(33) | Ltn Eberhard Stapenhörst | 4 |
| Ltn Karl Allmenröder* | 30 | Ltn Otto Brauneck | 3(10) |
| Ltn Karl-Emil Schäfer* | 22(30) | Ltn Friedrich von Köckeritz | 3 |
| Hptm Wilhelm Reinhard | 14(20) | Ltn Otto Maashoff | 3 |
| Oblt Erich von Wedel | 13 | Ltn Karl von Schönebeck | 3(8) |
| Vfw Sebastian Festner* | 12 | Ltn Ernst Udet | 3(62) |
| Vfw Willi Gabriel | 10 | Ltn Wilhelm Bockelmann | 2(3) |
| Ltn Hans Joachim Wolff* | 10 | Ltn Hans Hintsch* | 2(3) |
| Ltn Werner Steinhuser* | 9(10) | Ltn Constantin Krefft* | 2 |
| Ltn Eberhardt Mohnicke | 8(9) | Ltn Karl Meyer | 2(4) |
| Ltn Wolfram von Richthofen | 8 | Vfw Franz Müller* | 2 |
| Ltn Gisbert-W Groos | 6 | Vfw Alfred Niemz | 2(4) |
| Ltn Erich Just | 6 | Ltn Wilhelm Allmenröder | 1(2) |
| Ltn Friedrich Noltenius | 6 | Oblt Hermann Göring | 1(22) |
| Ltn Alfred Niederhoff* | 5(7) | Vfw Josef Lautenschlager* | 1 |
| Ltn Hans-G von der Osten | 5 | Ltn Georg Simon | 1 |
| Ltn Edgar Scholtz* | 5(6) | Ltn Richard Wenzl | 1(12) |
| Ltn Hans Weiss* | 5(16) | | |

Evidently some of the above claims were not confirmed as the totals are more than 350.

## Airfields occupied

| Location | Inclusive Dates | Armee |
|---|---|---|
| | 5 Oct 1916 – 11 Oct 1916 | AOK6 |
| Brayelles-Douai | 11 Oct 1916 – 13 Apr 1917 | 6 |
| Roucourt, Bohain | 13 Apr 1917 – 9 Jun 1917 | 6 |
| Harlebeke, Bavichove | 10 Jun 1917 – 1 Jul 1917 | 4 |
| Marckebeke, Courtrai | 2 Jul 1917 – 22 Nov 1917 | 4 |
| Avesnes-le-Sec, Cambrai | 22 Nov 1917 – 19 Mar 1918 | 2 |
| Awoingt, Cambrai | 20 Mar 1918 – 25 Mar 1918 | 2 |
| Lechelle | 26 Mar 1918 – 11 Apr 1918 | 2 |
| Cappy | 12 Apr 1918 – 20 May 1918 | 2 |
| Guise | 21 May 1918 – 26 May 1918 | 7 |

| Puisieux Ferme, Laon | 27 May 1918 – 31 May 1918 | 7 |
| Begneux | 1 Jun 1918 – 18 Jul 1918 | 7 |
| Monthussart Ferme | 19 Jul 1918 – 31 Jul 1918 | 7 |
| Puisieux Ferme | 1 Aug 1918 – 10 Aug 1918 | 7 |
| Ennemain | 10 Aug 1918 – 12 Aug 1918 | 2 |
| Montigny Ferme | 13 Aug 1918 – 30 Aug 1918 | 2 |
| Busigny | 31 Aug 1918 – 27 Sep 1918 | 2 |
| Metz-Frescaty | 28 Sep 1918 – 8 Oct 1918 | C |
| Marville | 9 Oct 1918 – 6 Nov 1918 | 5 |
| Tellancourt | 7 Nov 1918 – 11 Nov 1918 | 5 |

## ROYAL PRUSSIAN JAGDSTAFFEL 12

Jasta 12 was created 28 September 1916, by Kriegs Ministerium von Nr.269.10.16.A.7.L., from Fokker-staffel West, in the 7 Armee Sector at Vaux, near Laon. The first Commanding Officer was Oblt Erich Hönemanns, then Hauptmann Paul Hennig von Osterroht from Kampfstaffel 1. The Jasta moved to the 1 Armee area on 1 November, and on 28 November was assigned to the 6 Armee. The first victory came on 4 December by Leutnant Otto Splitgerber, who downed a FE2b over Farbus. Then on 23 December the Jasta moved to the Armee-Abteilung 'A' Sector. A short time later, on 19 February 1917, it moved back to the 1 Armee, and here Leutnant Adolf Schulte became the unit's first ace on 24 March. On 12 April Jasta 12 was reassigned to the 6 Armee Front. Hauptmann von Osterroht, who had scored seven times, was killed in action 23 April and replaced at the head of Jasta 12 by Oberleutnant Adolf von Tutschek (three victories) from Jasta Boelcke. Von Tutschek was wounded in combat 11 August, and temporary command of Jasta 12 passed to Leutnant Victor Schobinger (two victories). During October he scored the Jasta's 100th victory. Schobinger, who had a score of eight, was wounded on 15 November, and was replaced by Oberleutnant Paul Blumenbach. When Jagdgeschwader II was formed on 2 February 1918, in the 7 Armee Sector at Toulis, under the command of Hauptmann Adolf von Tutschek, Jasta 12 became a part of it along with Jastas 13, 15 and 19. After von Tutschek was killed in action 15 March, command of JGII went to Hauptmann Rudolf Berthold. Oberleutnant Blumenbach, with a score of two, was transferred to the command of Jasta 31 on 18 May, and Leutnant Robert Hildebrandt (four victories), from Jasta 13, took over. A move was made to the 18 Armee area on 19 March, then on 12 June a transfer came to the 2 Armee, then on 12 July another move to the 3 Armee. On 13 July Leutnant Hildebrandt was reassigned as Commanding Officer of Jasta 69, and Leutnant Hermann Becker (11 victories) assumed command of Jasta 12 for the rest of the war. Another move came on 24 July to the 9 Armee area. Then due to the heavy fighting in the 18 Armee Sector the Jasta was sent there on 10 August, but was moved back to the 1 Armee again on 28 August. After Hauptmann Berthold had been wounded on 10 August, command of JGII passed to Oberleutnant Oskar von Boenigk. Just before the St Mihiel operation JGII moved to the Armee-Abteilung 'C' area where it remained until 28 September. From there a move was made to the 5 Armee Sector where they scored their 150th victory during October and where they were when the war ended. Jasta 12 was credited with at least 156 victories, of which three were balloons. There were 26 casualties, 17 killed in combat, eight wounded and one taken prisoner.

### Commanding Officers

| Oblt Erich Hönemanns | 8 Oct 1916 – 26 Nov 1916 | CO J22 |
| Hptm Paul von Osterroht | 26 Nov 1916 – 23 Apr 1917 | KIA |
| Oblt Adolf von Tutschek | 30 Apr 1917 – 25 May 1917 | Leave |
| Ltn Friedrich Roth | 25 May 1917 – 24 Jun 1917 | Acting |
| Oblt Adolf von Tutschek | 24 Jun 1917 – 11 Aug 1917 | WIA |
| Ltn Otto von Nostitz | 11 Aug 1917 – 13 Aug 1917 | Acting |
| Ltn Victor Schobinger | 13 Aug 1917 – 15 Nov 1917 | Acting |
| Ltn Otto von Nostitz | 16 Nov 1917 – 17 Dec 1917 | Acting |
| Oblt Paul Blumenbach | 17 Dec 1917 – 18 May 1918 | CO J31 |
| Ltn Robert Hildebrandt | 18 May 1918 – 13 Jul 1918 | CO J69 |
| Ltn Hermann Becker | 13 Jul 1918 – 11 Nov 1918 | |

### Pilots credited with victories

| | | | |
|---|---|---|---|
| Oblt Adolf von Tutschek | 24(27) | Vfw Otto Klaiber | 5 |
| Ltn Hermann Becker | 23 | Ltn Paul Billik | 4(31) |
| Ltn Ulrich Neckel | 10(30) | Ltn Alfred Greven | 4 |
| Vfw Reinhold Jörke | 9(14) | Vfw Robert Reissinger* | 4 |
| Ltn Adolf Schulte* | 9 | Vfw Otto Rosenfeld | 4(13) |
| Ltn Victor Schobinger | 8 | Vfw Arthur Schorisch | 4 |
| Oblt Paul von Osterroht | 7 | Ltn Bertling | 3 |
| Uffz Friedrich Gille | 6 | Ltn Walter Ewers | 3(8) |

| | | | |
|---|---|---|---|
| Ltn Bernhard Knake* | 3 | Ltn Erkenbrecht | 1 |
| Ltn Otto Splitgerber | 3(6) | Ltn Robert Hildebrandt | 1(6) |
| OfStv Grigo | 2 | Ltn Friedrich Hochstetter | 1 |
| Ltn Koch | 2 | Ltn Paul Hoffmann | 1 |
| Ltn Friedrich Roth | 2 | Ltn Otto von Nostitz | 1 |
| Ltn Karl Schöck* | 2 | Vfw Georg Oefele* | 1 |
| Vfw Wittchen | 2 | Flg Rossbach | 1 |
| Ltn Hans Besser | 1 | Ltn Hans Staats* | 1 |
| Oblt Paul Blumenbach | 1(2) | Ltn Telge | 1 |
| OfStv Dobberahn | 1 | Flg Wilke | 1 |

## Airfields occupied

| Location | Inclusive Dates | Armee |
|---|---|---|
| Vaux, Laon | 28 Sep 1916 – 1 Nov 1916 | 7 |
| Riencourt, Arras | 1 Nov 1916 – 28 Nov 1916 | 1 |
| Riencourt | 28 Nov 1916 – 23 Dec 1916 | 6 |
| Niederum | 23 Dec 1916 – 19 Feb 1917 | A |
| Epinoy | 19 Feb 1917 – 12 Apr 1917 | 1 |
| Roucourt | 12 Apr 1917 – 5 Nov 1917 | 6 |
| Erkeghem | 5 Nov 1917 – 16 Nov 1917 | 4 |
| Phalempin | 16 Nov 1917 – 26 Nov 1917 | 2 |
| Roucourt | 26 Nov 1917 – 2 Feb 1918 | 6 |
| Marle | 2 Feb 1918 – 13 Feb 1918 | 7 |
| Toulis | 13 Feb 1918 – 19 Mar 1918 | 7 |
| Guise | 19 Mar 1918 – 23 Mar 1918 | 18 |
| Roupy | 23 Mar 1918 – 24 Mar 1918 | 18 |
| Guisecourt | 24 Mar 1918 – 28 Mar 1918 | 18 |
| Balâtre | 28 Mar 1918 – 13 Apr 1918 | 18 |
| Bonneuil Ferme | 13 Apr 1918 – 21 Apr 1918 | 18 |
| Le Mesnil, Nesle | 21 Apr 1918 – 12 Jun 1918 | 18 |
| Mesnil-Bruntel | 12 Jun 1918 – 12 Jul 1918 | 2 |
| Leffincourt | 12 Jul 1918 – 24 Jul 1918 | 3 |
| Chéry-les-Pouilly | 24 Jul 1918 – 21 Aug 1918 | 9 |
| Fontaine Notre Dame | 21 Aug 1918 – 28 Aug 1918 | 18 |
| Neuflize | 28 Aug 1918 – 3 Sep 1918 | 1 |
| Doncourt | 3 Sep 1918 – 4 Sep 1918 | C |
| Giraumont | 4 Sep 1918 – 28 Sep 1918 | C |
| Charmois, Stenay | 28 Sep 1918 – 18 Oct 1918 | 5 |
| Carignan | 18 Oct 1918 – 3 Nov 1918 | 5 |
| Florenville | 3 Nov 1918 – 10 Nov 1918 | 5 |
| Trier | 10 Nov 1918 – 11 Nov 1918 | 5 |

# ROYAL PRUSSIAN JAGDSTAFFEL 13

Created on 28 September 1916, in the Armee Abteilung 'C' Sector at Mars-la-Tour, pursuant to Kriegs Ministerium von Nr.269.10.16.A.7.L. and commenced operations on 15 October. The unit was commanded by Oberleutnant Erhard Egerer, from FA3b. However, on 27 December Egerer was sent to Idflieg and was relieved by Oberleutnant Eduard Dostler (one victory) as commander. Dostler registered the first victory for the Jasta on 22 January 1917. On 20 February, Jasta 13 was sent to the 5 Armee area, and Oberleutnant Dostler was transferred to Jasta 34 as its Commanding Officer. It is not known who replaced him and commander of Jasta 13. The first combat casualty was Gefreiter Paul Laukandt, who was killed over Foucaucourt on 15 June. On 29 September 1917, Leutnant Wolfgang Güttler, (four victories) assumed command. Jasta 13 was transferred to the 7 Armee Front on 5 November, and on 2 February 1918, it was assigned to Jagdgeschwader II (Jastas 12, 13, 15, and 19). After Güttler had raised his score to eight, he was killed on 20 February 1918, when he and Vfw Hiob were in a two-seater that crashed a short time after take-off at Reneuil Ferme. The following day Oberleutnant Alex Thomas (one victory) assumed command of Jasta 13. JGII was assigned to the 18 Armee on 19 March. Then on 1 May Oberleutnant Thomas was transferred to Jasta 69 as Commanding Officer, and command of Jasta 13 passed to Leutnant Wilhelm Schwartz (two victories) from Jasta 69. On 12 June JGII was sent to the 2 Armee Sector, and the command jinx held, for on 15 June Schwartz was wounded during a balloon attack, and command of Jasta 13 was taken over by Leutnant Franz Büchner (four victories) until the end of the war. Büchner gained his fifth victory on 28 June and became the first pilot to become an ace with Jasta 13. JGII was assigned to the 3 Armee Sector on 12 July, until 24 July, when it moved to the 9 Armee Front. From there the unit moved back to the 18 Armee Sector on 18 August until 28 August when a move was made to the 1 Armee area. JGII was sent to Armee-Abteilung 'C' on 3 September where they remained until 28 September, when a move was made to the 5 Armee Sector until the war ended. Jasta 13 was credited with at least 109 victories, while losing 12 pilots killed, two taken prisoner, two wounded and one killed in an accident.

## Commanding Officers

| | | |
|---|---|---|
| Oblt Erhard Egerer | 15 Oct 1916 – 27 Dec 1916 | Idflieg |
| Oblt Eduard Dostler | 27 Dec 1916 – 20 Feb 1917 | CO J34 |
| ? | 20 Feb 1917 – 29 Sep 1918 | |
| Ltn Wolfgang Güttler | 29 Sep 1917 – 20 Feb 1918 | KIA |
| Oblt Alex Thomas | 21 Feb 1918 – 1 May 1918 | CO J69 |
| Ltn Wilhelm Schwartz | 1 May 1918 – 15 Jun 1918 | WIA |
| Ltn Franz Büchner | 15 Jun 1918 – 11 Nov 1918 | |

## Pilots credited with victories

| | | | |
|---|---|---|---|
| Ltn Franz Büchner | 39(40) | Ltn de Payrebrune | 1 |
| Vfw Albert Haussmann* | 9(15) | Oblt Eduard von Dostler | 1(26) |
| Ltn Werner Niethammer | 6 | Uffz Johannes Fritzsche | 1(3) |
| Ltn Kurt Hetze | 5 | Ltn Golz | 1 |
| Ltn Wolfgang Güttler | 4(8) | Uffz Goretzky | 1 |
| Ltn Robert Hildebrandt | 4(6) | Ltn Ernst Hencke | 1(2) |
| Ltn Hans Pippart | 4(22) | Uffz Walter Hertzsch* | 1 |
| Ltn Wilhelm Schwartz | 4(8) | Vfw Reinhold Jörke | 1(14) |
| Ltn Grimm | 3 | Ltn Kreuzner | 1 |
| Ltn Félix Büchner | 2 | Uffz Willi Laabs* | 1 |
| Ltn Hans Dannenberg | 2(4) | Vfw Jakob Ledermann | 1 |
| Vfw Paul Hiob | 2 | Vfw Ruckdeschel | 1 |
| Vfw Albert Hurrle* | 2(3) | Ltn Hermann Schmidt | 1(2) |
| Ltn Erich Kämpfe* | 2 | Ltn Schröder | 1 |
| Vfw Heinrich Kramer | 2(4) | Ltn Schärz | 1 |
| Uffz Heinrich Piel* | 2 | Oblt Alex Thomas | 1(2) |
| Vfw Brunnengräber | 2 | | |

## Airfields occupied

| Location | Inclusive Dates | Armee |
|---|---|---|
| Mars-la-Tour | 28 Sep 1916 – 19 Feb 1917 | C |
| ? | 20 Feb 1917 – 5 Mar 1917 | 5 |
| La Selve | 5 Mar 1917 – 1 May 1917 | 7 |
| Le Clos Ferme, Boncourt | 1 May 1917 – 30 Oct 1917 | 7 |
| Marle | 1 Nov 1917 – 22 Nov 1917 | 2 |
| Cambrai | 22 Nov 1917 – 2 Feb 1918 | 2 |
| Reneuil Ferme | 2 Feb 1918 – 12 Feb 1918 | |
| Autremencourt | 12 Feb 1918 – 19 Mar 1918 | 7 |
| Guise | 19 Mar 1918 – 23 Mar 1918 | 18 |
| Roupy | 23 Mar 1918 – 24 Mar 1918 | 18 |
| Guisecourt | 24 Mar 1918 – 28 Mar 1918 | 18 |
| Balâtre | 28 Mar 1918 – 13 Apr 1918 | 18 |
| Boneuil Ferme | 13 Apr 1918 – 21 Apr 1918 | 18 |
| Le Mesnil, Nesle | 21 Apr 1918 – 12 Jun 1918 | 18 |
| Mesnil-Bruntel | 12 Jun 1918 – 13 Jul 1918 | 2 |
| Leffincourt | 13 Jul 1918 – 24 Jul 1918 | 3 |
| Chéry-les-Pouilly | 24 Jul 1918 – 18 Aug 1918 | 9 |
| Foreste | 18 Aug 1918 – 26 Aug 1918 | 18 |
| Fontaine Notre Dame | 26 Aug 1918 – 28 Aug 1918 | 18 |
| Neuflize | 28 Aug 1918 – 3 Sep 1918 | 1 |
| Tichémont | 3 Sep 1918 – 28 Sep 1918 | C |
| Stenay | 28 Sep 1918 – 1 Nov 1918 | 5 |
| Carignan | 1 Nov 1918 – 3 Nov 1918 | 5 |
| Florenville | 3 Nov 1918 – 10 Nov 1918 | 5 |
| Trier | 10 Nov 1918 – 11 Nov 1918 | 5 |

# ROYAL PRUSSIAN JAGDSTAFFEL 14

Jasta 14 was created from Fokkerkampfstaffel Falkenhausen on 28 September 1916, through Armee-Abteilung 'A' as authorized by Kriegs Ministerium von Nr.269. 10.16.A.7.L. und Chef des Feldflieger

West Nr.25367.Fl. Stationed at Bühl, near Saarburg, the first Commanding Officer was Hauptmann Kreig, the commander of Fokkerstaffel Falkenhausen. Kreig was transferred on 14 October and Oberleutnant Rudolf Berthold (eight victories) took command, and the Jasta moved to the 5 Armee Sector. By 18 October the Jasta was equipped with seven Fokker biplanes, one Halberstadt biplane, and two Fokker Es. The first victory was scored on 11 November, by Vizefeldwebel Schuhmann. The first pilot to become an ace with the Jasta was Leutnant Josef Veltjens on 1 June 1917. On 12 August, Berthold, who had added four victories to his total, was named commander of Jasta 18, and Leutnant Walter Höhndorf (12 victories) assumed command of Jasta 14; however, he was killed when the AEG DI he was testing crashed at Ire-le-Sec, on 5 September. Leutnant Hans Werner (two victories) took command for the rest of the war. Jasta 14 was reassigned to the 7 Armee on 5 November until 19 March 1918, when it went to the 17 Armee. On 11 April the Jasta moved to the 6 Armee Front, and it moved to the 4 Armee Front on 3 October. The Jasta's 50th victory came during August 1918. Jasta 14 was credited with at least 57 victories, of which five were balloons, while suffering the loss of eight killed in action, five wounded and three prisoners of war.

## Commanding Officers

| | | |
|---|---|---|
| Hptm Kreig | 28 Sep 1916 – 14 Oct 1916 | |
| Oblt Rudolf Berthold | 14 Oct 1916 – 12 Aug 1917 | CO J18 |
| Ltn Walter Höhndorf | 12 Aug 1917 – 5 Sep 1917 | KIA |
| Ltn Hans Werner | 5 Sep 1917 – 11 Nov 1918 | |

## Pilots credited with victories

| | | | |
|---|---|---|---|
| Ltn Johannes Werner | 6(7) | Ltn Breuer | 1 |
| Vfw Hans Bowski | 5 | Ltn Konrad von Bülow | 1(2) |
| Ltn Herbert Boy | 5 | Ltn Hans Grabe | 1 |
| Vfw Paul Rothe | 5 | Ltn Joachim Huth | 1 |
| Ltn Josef Veltjens | 5(35) | Vfw Heinrich Kramer | 1(4) |
| Oblt Rudolf Berthold | 4(44) | Vfw Mikat | 1 |
| Ltn Konrad Bieler | 4 | Vfw Schuhmann | 1 |
| Vfw Otto Gerbig* | 4 | Vfw Peter Stenzel* | 1 |
| Ltn Josef Schulte | 4 | Ltn von Wulffen | 1 |
| OfStv Hüttner | 3 | Jasta | 1 |
| Ltn Kuen | 2 | | |
| Gerbig killed with Jasta 18. | | | |

## Airfields occupied

| Location | Inclusive Dates | Armee |
|---|---|---|
| Bühl, Saarburg | 28 Sep 1916 – 14 Oct 1916 | A |
| Marchais | 14 Oct 1916 – 27 Apr 1917 | 5 |
| La Neuville | 27 Apr 1917 – May 1917 | 5 |
| Marchais | May 1917 – 5 Nov 1917 | 5 |
| Boncourt | 5 Nov 1917 – 5 Jan 1918 | 7 |
| Liesse | 5 Jan 1918 – 19 Mar 1918 | 7 |
| Masny | 19 Mar 1918 – 11 Apr 1918 | 17 |
| Phalempin | 11 Apr 1918 – 3 Oct 1918 | 6 |
| Aertrycke | 3 Oct 1918 – 11 Nov 1918 | 4 |

# ROYAL PRUSSIAN JAGDSTAFFEL 15

Jasta 15 was created on 28 September 1916, from Kampfeinsitzer Kommando Habsheim, in the Armee-Abteilung 'B' Sector, in accordance with Kriegs Ministerium von Nr.269 10.16.A.7.L. It was formed on 10 October from personnel of Feld Flieger-Abteilung 48 and 68 at Habsheim. The Commanding Officer was Hauptmann Hermann Kropp. Leutnant Kurt Haber scored his fifth victory and the first for Jasta 15 on 12 October. Hauptmann Kropp was transferred to Idflieg on 6 November and Oberleutnant Max Reinhold was then named the commander. Jasta 15 moved to the 7 Armee Front on 2 March 1917, where Leutnant Hans-Olaf Esser became the first combat casualty being killed on 16 April. Oberleutnant Reinhold was killed during combat with three Spads over Lierval at 1930 hours on 24 April, and Leutnant Heinrich Gontermann (17 victories) from Jasta 5 was named as his successor. Leutnant Ernst Udet became the Jasta's first ace on 5 May. Then on 30 October Gontermann, who had raised his score to 39, was killed when his Fokker DrI 115/17 crashed at 1614 hours at La Neuville, during a test flight. He died at 2205 hours in a field hospital at Marle. Leutnant Hans von Budde was designated as the new commander. The Jasta moved to the 2 Armee Front on 1 November, and joined Jastas 12, 13, and 19 in making up the newly created Jagdgeschwader II at Autremencourt, in the 7 Armee Sector, on

12 February 1918, under the command of Hauptmann Adolf von Tutschek (24 victories). Von Budde was transferred to Idflieg on 14 March, and Leutnant August Raben assumed command, and after scoring twice, when he was named Commanding Officer of Jasta 18 on 20 March, and the commander of Jasta 18, Oberleutnant Ernst Turck took over Jasta 15. Von Tutschek was killed during combat with 24 Squadron, RFC, five days after his 27th victory, 15 March, while flying Fokker DrI 404/17. Hauptmann Rudolf Berthold (28 victories) was named to head JGII, which moved to the 18 Armee Sector on 19 March. Turck was transferred to Stofl Heimat on 18 May and Leutnant Josef Veltjens (13 victories) was assigned as Commanding Officer. A move was made to the 2 Armee area on 12 June, and on to the 3 Armee Front on 12 July. JGII departed the 3 Armee on 24 July and settled in the 9 Armee Sector, before moving back to the 18 Armee on 18 August. JGII was assigned to the 1 Armee Front on 28 August, and on 31 August Oberleutnant Oskar von Boenigk (21 victories) was named as Commanding Officer of JGII, after Berthold had been hospitalised. JGII was assigned to Armee-Abteilung 'C' on 3 September until 28 September, when it moved to the 5 Armee Front for the rest of the war. Jasta 15 was credited with at least 150 victories, while losing seven pilots killed in action, two killed and one injured in accidents, two taken prisoner, and three wounded.

## Commanding Officers

| | | |
|---|---|---|
| Oblt Hermann Kropp | 9 Oct 1916 – 6 Nov 1916 | Idflieg |
| Oblt Max Reinhold | 8 Nov 1916 – 26 Apr 1917 | KIA |
| Ltn Heinrich Gontermann | 2 May 1917 – 30 Oct 1917 | KIAcc |
| Ltn Hans von Budde | 13 Nov 1917 – 14 Mar 1918 | Idflieg |
| Ltn August Raben | 14 Mar 1918 – 20 Mar 1918 | CO J18 |
| Oblt Ernst Turck | 24 Mar 1918 – 18 May 1918 | Stofl Heimat |
| Ltn Josef Veltjens | 18 May 1918 – 28 Sep 1918 | Acting CO JGII |
| Ltn Hugo Schäfer | 28 Sep 1918 – 12 Oct 1918 | Acting |
| Ltn Josef Veltjens | 12 Oct 1918 – 11 Nov 1918 | |

## Pilots credited with victories

| | | | | |
|---|---|---|---|---|
| Ltn Georg von Hantelmann | 25 | | OfStv Willy Glinkermann | 2 |
| Ltn Josef Veltjens | 24(35) | | Vfw Albert Haussmann | 2(15) |
| Ltn Heinrich Gontermann | 22(39) | | Ltn Karl Mendel | 2(7) |
| Ltn Johannes Klein | 14(16) | | Ltn Hans Müller | 2(11) |
| Ltn Oliver von Beaulieu-Marconnay | 13(25) | | Fw Kurt Schmückle | 2(6) |
| Ltn Hugo Schäfer | 11 | | Ltn Hans von Budde | 1 |
| Vfw Gustav Klaudat | 6 | | Ltn Kurt Haber | 1(5) |
| Ltn Ernst Udet | 5(62) | | Ltn Hebler | 1(3) |
| Ltn Theodor Weischer | 4 | | Ltn Otto Pfältzer | 1(3) |
| Ltn Otto Förster | 3 | | Ltn Arthur Rahn | 1(6) |
| Ltn Joachim von Ziegesar | 3 | | Ltn Friedrich Weitz | 1(3) |
| Ltn Heinrich Arntzen | 2(11) | | Ltn Hellmuth Wendel | 1 |
| Ltn Hans Borck* | 2 | | | |

## Airfields occupied

| Location | Inclusive Dates | Armee |
|---|---|---|
| Habsheim | 29 Sep 1916 – 2 Mar 1917 | B |
| La Selve | 5 Mar 1917 – 1 May 1917 | 7 |
| Le Clos Ferme, Boncourt | 1 May 1917 – 30 Oct 1917 | 7 |
| Marle | 1 Nov 1917 – 22 Nov 1917 | 2 |
| Cambrai area | 22 Nov 1917 – 12 Feb 1918 | 2 |
| Autremencourt | 12 Feb 1918 – 19 Mar 1918 | 7 |
| Guise | 19 Mar 1918 – 23 Mar 1918 | 18 |
| Roupy | 23 Mar 1918 – 24 Mar 1918 | 18 |
| Guisecourt | 24 Mar 1918 – 28 Mar 1918 | 18 |
| Balâtre | 28 Mar 1918 – 13 Apr 1918 | 18 |
| Boneuil Ferme | 13 Apr 1918 – 21 Apr 1918 | 18 |
| Le Mesnil-Nesle | 21 Apr 1918 – 12 Jun 1918 | 18 |
| Mesnil-Bruntel | 12 Jun 1918 – 12 Jul 1918 | 2 |
| Leffincourt | 12 Jul 1918 – 24 Jul 1918 | 3 |
| Chéry-les-Pouilly | 24 Jul 1918 – 18 Aug 1918 | 9 |
| Foreste | 18 Aug 1918 – 26 Aug 1918 | 18 |
| Fontaine Notre Dame | 26 Aug 1918 – 28 Aug 1918 | 18 |
| Neuflize | 28 Aug 1918 – 3 Sep 1918 | 1 |
| Doncourt | 3 Sep 1918 – 4 Sep 1918 | C |
| Giraumont | 4 Sep 1918 – 13 Sep 1918 | C |
| Tichémont | 13 Sep 1918 – 28 Sep 1918 | C |
| Charmois, Stenay | 28 Sep 1918 – 18 Oct 1918 | 5 |

| | | |
|---|---|---|
| Carignan | 18 Oct 1918 – 3 Nov 1918 | 5 |
| Florenville | 3 Nov 1918– 10 Nov 1918 | 5 |
| Trier | 10 Nov 1918 – 11 Nov 1918 | 5 |

## ROYAL BAVARIAN JAGDSTAFFEL 16

Created in the Armee-Abteilung 'B' Sector from Kampfeinsitzer Kommando Ensisheim, including Bavarian Flieger-Abteilung 9, pursuant to Kommandierenden General der Luftstreitkräfte von 28.10.16 Nr.26441 Fl, with Oberleutnant Paul Kremer assuming command. The first victory was scored on 10 March 1917 by Leutnant Robert Dycke, and Leutnant Fritz Grünzweig became the first combat casualty on 14 April, when he was shot down by Maréchal-des-Logis Robert Harpedanne de Belleville, N 49, at 1100 hours near Elbach, during a balloon attack. On 6 May the unit moved to the 1 Armee Sector. About a month later, on 4 June, Jasta 16 moved to the 5 Armee area. Leutnant Ludwig Hanstein became the Jasta's first ace on 14 July. The Jasta was designated Royal Bavarian Jagdstaffel 16 in accordance with Bavarian Kriegs Ministerium von 17.7.17 Nr. 111847.A. On 12 August the Jasta was operating on the Verdun Front. Oberleutnant Kremer was ordered to FEA1, Schleissheim, on 18 August, and command of Jasta 16b passed to Leutnant Heinrich Geigl (five victories) from Jasta 34b. Geigl, who had just gained his sixth victory, was wounded in action on the 20th, and Leutnant Robert Dycke (one victory) assumed temporary command. Jasta 16b moved to the 7 Armee Sector on 21 October until 23 November when it moved back to the Verdun Front. Leutnant Geigl returned from the hospital on 1 December, and again took command. The Jasta moved to the 4 Armee Front in Flanders, on 7 February 1918, remaining there until 13 March when a move was made to the 2 Armee Front. Leutnant Geigl, who now had 13 victories, was killed in a mid-air collision with an Allied aircraft on 4 April. When the Battle of Armentières was going on the unit moved to the 4 Armee Sector, where it remained for the rest of the war, on 13 April, and Leutnant Friedrich Röth (ten victories) from Jasta 23b assumed command on 29 April. Röth was promoted to Oberleutnant on 19 August, and departed on four weeks' leave, on 9 September, with Leutnant Rudolf Eck assuming temporary command. Jasta 16b was given credit for at least 82 victories of which 24 were balloons, while suffering the loss of seven killed in combat, nine wounded, one taken prisoner, and two killed in accidents.

### Commanding Officers

| | | |
|---|---|---|
| Oblt Paul Kremer | 15 Nov 1916 – 18 Jul 1917 | FEA 1 |
| Ltn Heinrich Geigl | 18 Jul 1917 – 20 Aug 1917 | WIA |
| Ltn Robert Dycke | 20 Aug 1917 – 1 Dec 1917 | Acting |
| Ltn Heinrich Geigl | 1 Dec 1917 – 4 Apr 1918 | KIA |
| Oblt Friedrich Röth | 8 Apr 1918 – 9 Sep 1918 | Leave |
| Ltn Rudolf Eck | 9 Sep 1918 – Oct 1918 | Acting |
| Oblt Friedrich Röth | Oct 1918 – 11 Nov 1918 | |

### Pilots credited with victories

| | | | |
|---|---|---|---|
| Oblt Friedrich Roth | 18(26) | Ltn Theodor Rumpel | 2(5) |
| Ltn Ludwig Hanstein | 10(16) | Oblt Ludwig Cordes* | 1 |
| Ltn Heinrich Geigl* | 8(13) | Lt Rudolf Eck | 1(3) |
| Vfw Fritz Schattaur | 8(9) | Lt August Handl | 1 |
| Ltn Karl Odebrett | 6(21) | Vfw Benedikt Jehle | 1 |
| Uffz Eduard Binge | 4 | Ltn Wilhelm Ott | 1 |
| Vfw Johann Neumaier | 4 | Ltn Friedrich Poesch | 1 |
| Vfw Andreas Triebswetter | 4 | Vfw Hans Schorn* | 1 |
| Ltn Otto Kissenberth | 3(20) | Ltn Wilhelm Schulz | 1(6) |
| Ltn Johann Schäfer | 3 | Vfw Hugo Stöber | 1(3) |
| Ltn Robert Dycke | 2 | Ltn Albrecht Weinschenk | 1 |

### Airfields occupied

| Location | Inclusive Dates | Armee |
|---|---|---|
| Ensisheim | 16 Oct 1916 – 13 Apr 1917 | B |
| Habsheim | 13 Apr 1917 – 6 May 1917 | B |
| Château-Porcien | 7 May 1917 – 4 Jun 1917 | 1 |
| Spincourt | 6 Jun 1917 – 20 Oct 1917 | 5 |
| Erlon | 21 Oct 1917 – 23 Nov 1917 | 7 |
| Mercy-le-Haute | 24 Nov 1917 – 4 Feb 1918 | 5 |
| Aertrycke | 7 Feb 1918 – 14 Mar 1918 | 4 |
| Le Cateau | 15 Mar 1918 – 20 Mar 1918 | 2 |
| Foucaucourt | 21 Mar 1918 – 6 Apr 1918 | 2 |

| | | |
|---|---|---|
| St Marguerite | 13 Apr 1918 – Oct 1918 | 4 |
| Scheldewindeke | Oct 1918 – 11 Nov 1918 | 4 |

## ROYAL PRUSSIAN JAGDSTAFFEL 17

Created 23 October 1916, through the Kdr der Flieg 6 pursuant to Kommandierenden General der Luftstreitkräfte von 23-10-16 Nr.26665 Fl, drawing personnel from Armee Flugpark 5. It became operational on 11 November from Metz-Frescaty airfield, in the Armee-Abteilung 'A' Sector. The first victory credited to the unit was scored by Vizefeldwebel Julius Buckler on 17 December. Vizefeldwebel Adolf Wellhausen became the first combat casualty when severely wounded on 9 February 1917, dying two days later in a hospital. Commanded by Rittmeister Heinz von Brederlow, the unit moved to the 7 Armee Front on 28 February. On 16 April Jasta 17 moved to the 1 Armee Sector, and Vfw Buckler became the first pilot to register five victories with the Jasta. Rittmeister von Brederlow was transferred to Idflieg on 10 May, and command passed to Hauptmann Eberhard von Seel, from Jasta 2, who was killed during combat with a Spad over Montigny on 12 June. Another Jasta 2 pilot, Leutnant Ernst Wendler, assumed command on 19 June, and on the 23rd the Jasta moved to the 4 Armee Sector in Flanders. Leutnant Wendler was wounded on 1 October, and Oberleutnant Rudolf von Esebeck, the CO of Kest 7, took over command of Jasta 17. The unit moved to the 2 Armee Sector on 20 November, until 28 December when a move was made to the 18 Armee. On 27 May 1918, Oberleutnant von Esebeck was killed at 1930 hours during combat with Bréguets over Noyon, and on the 29th Oberleutnant Hermann Pritsch became acting commander until Leutnant Günther Schuster (five victories), from Jasta 29, took over on 12 June. On 10 July, the Jasta was in the 3 Armee Sector. However, on 25 July the unit was assigned to the 9 Armee, then came under the 7 Armee on 18 September, finally being sent to the 3 Armee Front on 25 September for the rest of the war. After Schuster was wounded in action on 1 August, Leutnant Julius Buckler (33 victories) had assumed command and remained in that capacity until the end of the war. Jasta 17 was credited with 101 confirmed victories out of 123 claimed, which included 87 aircraft and 14 balloons. However, there were ten pilots killed in combat, two missing, six wounded, and three injured in accidents.

### Commanding Officers

| | | |
|---|---|---|
| Rittm Heinz von Brederlow | 11 Nov 1916 – 10 May 1917 | Idflieg |
| Hptm Eberhard von Seel | 10 May 1917 – 12 Jun 1917 | KIA |
| Ltn Ernst Wendler | 19 Jun 1917 – 1 Oct 1917 | WIA |
| Oblt Rudolf von Esebeck | 4 Oct 1917 – 27 May 1918 | KIA |
| Oblt Hermann Pritsch | 29 May 1918 – 12 Jun 1918 | Acting |
| Ltn Günther Schuster | 12 Jun 1918 – 1 Aug 1918 | WIA |
| Ltn Julius Buckler | 1 Aug 1918 – 11 Nov 1918 | |

### Pilots credited with victories

| | | | |
|---|---|---|---|
| Ltn Julius Buckler | 35 | Rittm Heinz von Brederlow | 1 |
| Vfw Christian Donhauser | 16 | Ltn Albrecht Crüsemann* | 1 |
| Vfw Georg Strasser | 7 | Ltn Wilhelm Gros* | 1 |
| Ltn Karl Bohny | 6 | Uffz Jakob Jacob | 1 |
| Ltn Alfred Fleischer | 6 | Ltn Kaiser | 1 |
| Vfw Gustav Schneidewind | 4(7) | Ltn Neumann | 1 |
| Ltn Jakob Wolff | 4 | Oblt Wilhelm Pritsch | 1 |
| Ltn Otto Fitzner | 3(9) | OfStv Alfred Schreder* | 1 |
| Ltn Günther Schuster | 3(6) | Vfw Schumann | 1 |
| Ltn Wilhelm Becker | 2 | Ltn Seifert | 1 |
| Ltn Walter Brachwitz* | 2 | Uffz Fritz Wolff | 1 |
| Vfw Adolf Werner | 2 | | |

### Airfields occupied

| Location | Inclusive Dates | Armee |
|---|---|---|
| Metz-Frescaty | 11 Nov 1916 – 1 Mar 1917 | A |
| St Quentin-le-Petit | 1 Mar 1917 – 16 Apr 1917 | 7 |
| St Quentin-le-Petit | 16 Apr 1917 – 24 Jun 1917 | 1 |
| Ghistelles, Ostende | 24 Jun 1917 – 28 Aug 1917 | 4 |
| Wasquehal | 28 Aug 1917 – 6 Nov 1917 | 4 |
| Erkeghem, Brugge | 6 Nov 1917 – 20 Nov 1917 | 4 |
| Neuvilly, Le Cateau | 20 Nov 1917 – 2 Dec 1917 | 2 |
| Retheuil Ferme, Bohain | 2 Dec 1917 – 28 Dec 1917 | 2 |
| Retheuil Ferme, Bohain | 28 Dec 1917 – 26 Mar 1918 | 18 |

| | | |
|---|---|---|
| Douilly | 26 Mar 1918 – 28 Mar 1918 | 18 |
| Balâtre | 28 Mar 1918 – 19 May 1918 | 18 |
| Erchau | 19 May 1918 – 10 Jul 1918 | 18 |
| Mars-sous-Bourcq | 10 Jul 1918 – 25 Jul 1918 | 3 |
| Vivaise | 25 Jul 1918 – 19 Sep 1918 | 9 |
| Vivaise | 19 Sep 1918 – 25 Sep 1918 | 7 |
| Chuffilly | 25 Sep 1918 – 9 Oct 1918 | 3 |
| Malmy-Chéméry | 9 Oct 1918 – 3 Nov 1918 | 3 |
| St Medard, Neufchâteau | 3 Nov 1918 – 11 Nov 1918 | 3 |

## ROYAL PRUSSIAN JAGDSTAFFEL 18

Created 30 October 1916, at Halluin, 4 Armee Sector, ground personnel coming from FEA12, by authority of Kommandierenden General der Luftstreitkräfte von Nr.54427. The Commanding Officer was Oberleutnant Karl von Grieffenhagen, from Jasta 1. The first flight over the Front came on 8 January 1917, and the first victory on 23 January by Leutnant Walter von Bülow-Bothkamp, his sixth. He was also the first pilot to obtain five victories with Jasta 18. Leutnant Josef Flink, flying Albatros DIII 1942/16, was the first combat casualty when he was wounded during combat with FE2bs over Neuve Eglise, on 5 April. Oberleutnant von Grieffenhagen was promoted to Rittmeister on 18 April, and transferred to Kampfeinsitzer-Schule, Paderborn on 12 August. Oberleutnant Rudolf Berthold (12 victories), from Jasta 14, assumed command until he was severely wounded on 10 October, after having raised his score to 27. Oberleutnant Ernst Turck (one victory) took over the unit on 13 October. Turck was transferred to Jasta 15 on 20 March 1918. Leutnant August Raben (two victories), from Jasta 15, assumed command of Jasta 18 until the end of the war. The Jasta moved to the 17 Armee Front on 20 March until 8 April when it moved on to the 6 Armee Sector. On 14 June the unit was stationed in the 19 Armee Sector where it remained for the rest of the war. Jasta 18 was given credit for the destruction of 107 enemy aircraft and five balloons while losing eight pilots killed, eleven wounded and one taken prisoner.

### Commanding Officers

| | | |
|---|---|---|
| Rittm Karl v Grieffenhagen | 1 Nov 1916 – 12 Aug 1917 | Paderborn |
| Oblt Rudolf Berthold | 12 Aug 1917 – 10 Oct 1917 | WIA |
| Oblt Ernst Turck | 10 Oct 1917 – 20 Mar 1918 | Jasta 15 |
| Ltn August Raben | 20 Mar 1918 – 11 Nov 1918 | |

### Pilots credited with victories

| | | | |
|---|---|---|---|
| Oblt Rudolf Berthold | 16(44) | Ltn Josef Flink | 2 |
| Lt Hans Müller | 10(12) | Rittm Karl Grieffenhagen | 2 |
| Lt Walter von Bülow-Bothkamp | 9(28) | Ltn Johannes Klein | 2(16) |
| Ltn Kurt Monnington | 8 | Ltn August Raben | 2(4) |
| Ltn Richard Runge* | 7(8) | Ltn Erich Spindler | 2 |
| OfStv Wilhelm Kühne* | 7 | Ltn Kurt Baier | 1 |
| Ltn Paul Strähle | 7(14) | Gefr Deberitz | 1 |
| Ltn Harold Auffahrt | 5(29) | Ltn Walter Dingel | 1(2) |
| Ltn Karl Mendel* | 5(7) | Oblt Werner Jahns | 1 |
| Ltn Josef Veltjens | 5(35) | Vfw Kammendel | 1 |
| Ltn Ernst Wiessner* | 5 | Ltn Walther Kleffel | 1 |
| Ltn Gustav Nolte* | 3 | Ltn Otto Schöber | 1 |
| OfStv Richard Schleichardt | 3 | Ltn Hans Schultz | 1 |
| Ltn Günther von Büren | 2 | Oblt Ernst Turck | 1 |
| Uffz Flemming | 2 | | |
| Von Bülow-Bothkamp killed with Jasta 2. | | | |

### Airfields occupied

| Location | Inclusive Dates | Armee |
|---|---|---|
| Halluin | 27 Oct 1916 – 12 Jun 1917 | 4 |
| Marckebeke | 13 Jun 1917 – 1 Jul 1917 | 4 |
| Harlebeke | 2 Jul 1917 – 23 Nov 1917 | 4 |
| Houplin | 24 Nov 1917 – 28 Nov 1918 | 6 |
| Avelin | 29 Nov 1917 – 1 Dec 1917 | 6 |
| Carnières | 2 Dec 1917 – 13 Dec 1917 | 6 |
| Avelin | 14 Dec 1917 – 19 Mar 1918 | 6 |
| Bruille | 20 Mar 1918 – 7 Apr 1918 | 17 |
| Avelin | 8 Apr 1918 – 11 Apr 1918 | 6 |
| Faches | 12 Apr 1918 – 30 Apr 1918 | 6 |

| Lomme | 30 Apr 1918 – 13 Jun 1918 | 6 |
| Möntingen, Metz | 14 Jun 1918 – 11 Nov 1918 | 19 |

## ROYAL PRUSSIAN JAGDSTAFFEL 19

Created 25 October 1916 at Armee Flugpark 1, at Ronssoy, near Epehy, pursuant to Kdr Gen der Luftstreitkräfte von Nr.54427. Hauptmann Franz Walz (six victories) from Kampfstaffel 2 was assigned as Commanding Officer. However, he was transferred to the command of Jasta 2 (Boelcke) on 28 November, and command was assumed by Oberleutnant Erich Hahn (one victory) from Jasta 1. On 4 December the Jasta was stationed in the 1 Armee Sector, and on the 20th the first formations were flown. The Jasta was sent to the Armee-Abteilung 'A' area at Bühl, near Saarburg, on 28 December. Another move was made on 19 March 1917, to the 7 Armee Sector. Leutnant Walter Böning was credited with the first victory on 6 April, and on 30 April Oberleutnant Erich Hahn became the first pilot to score five victories, his sixth overall. Leutnant Gerlt was the first combat casualty when wounded on 4 May, near Ausheilung. Hahn was killed in action at 1935 hours north-west of Beine on 4 September, with Leutnant Ernst Hess (14 victories) from Jasta 28 replacing him as Commanding Officer. Hess, who had added three more to his score, was shot down in flames while flying Albatros DVa 5347/17, by Adjutant Albert de Kergolay of N 96, while he was in combat with a Letord three-seater at 1330 hours on 23 December, east of the Fresnes-Modelin Ferme Road. On 4 January 1918, Leutnant Konrad von Bülow (one victory), from Jasta 14, assumed command of Jasta 19. After adding one more to his score, he was sent to Idflieg on 14 February, and Leutnant Walter Göttsch (17 victories) from Jasta 8 took over. On 6 February Jasta 19 was with the 7 Armee, and became a part of Jagdgeschwader II, with Jastas 12, 13, and 15, under the command of Hauptmann Adolf von Tutschek (23 victories) who was killed in action on 15 March, after bringing his score to 27. Hauptmann Rudolf Berthold (28 victories) replaced him at the head of JGII. On 19 March the unit moved to the 18 Armee Sector. The loss of commanding officers continued: on 10 April Göttsch, who had added three more to his score, was flying Fokker DrI 419/17 when killed in combat with a RE8 west of Gentelles. Eight days later Leutnant Hans Pippart (nine victories) from Jasta 13 assumed command. The unit moved to the 18 Armee area on 10 August, the date that Hauptmann Berthold was severely wounded and replaced at the head of JGII by Oberleutnant Oskar Freiherr von Boenigk (20 victories). Leutnant Pippart, who had scored another 13 victories, was shot down in flames on the next day during combat with a Bréguet north-west of Guiscard, he jumped in a parachute which did not open in time and he was killed. His successor, Leutnant Ulrich Neckel (20 victories), arrived from Jasta 12 the same day, but on 1 September, after he had scored three more times, he was reassigned as Commanding Officer of Jasta 6, and Leutnant Oliver Freiherr von Beaulieu-Marconnay (13 victories) from Jasta 15 reported on 4 September, the day after a move was made to the Armee-Abteilung 'C' area, to lead the Jasta. On 28 September JGII moved to the 5 Armee Front for the rest of the war. Von Beaulieu-Marconnay brought his score to 25 before he was severely wounded on 18 October. Leutnant Wilhelm Leusch (three victories) took command the following day until the end of the war. Jasta 19 was credited with at least 93 victories, including ten balloons, while they lost 11 killed, and four wounded in action, one prisoner of war.

### Commanding Officers

| Oblt Franz Walz | 25 Oct 1916 – 28 Nov 1916 | CO J2 |
| Oblt Erich Hahn | 28 Nov 1916 – 4 Sep 1917 | KIA |
| Oblt Eichorn | 4 Sep 1917 – 18 Sep 1917 | Acting |
| Ltn Ernst Hess | 18 Sep 1917 – 23 Dec 1917 | KIA |
| Ltn Gerlt | 24 Dec 1917 – 3 Jan 1918 | Acting |
| Ltn Konrad von Bülow | 4 Jan 1918 – 14 Feb 1918 | Idflieg |
| Ltn Walter Göttsch | 14 Feb 1918 – 10 Apr 1918 | KIA |
| Ltn Arthur Rahn | 10 Apr 1918 – 18 Apr 1918 | Acting |
| Ltn Hans Pippart | 18 Apr 1918 – 11 Aug 1918 | KIA |
| Ltn Ulrich Neckel | 11 Aug 1918 – 1 Sep 1918 | CO J6 |
| Ltn Oliver von Beaulieu-Marconnay | 4 Sep 1918 – 18 Oct 1918 | WIA |
| Ltn Wilhelm Leusch | 19 Oct 1918 – 11 Nov 1918 | |

Von Beaulieu-Marconnay was WIA on 18 October and died of wounds on 26 October 1918.

### Pilots credited with victories

| | | | |
|---|---|---|---|
| Ltn Hans Pippart* | 13(22) | Ltn Arthur Rahn | 5(6) |
| Ltn Oliver von Beaulieu-Marconnay* | 12(25) | Ltn Wilhelm Leusch | 5 |
| Ltn Walter Böning | 6(17) | Ltn Hans Körner | 4(6) |
| Ltn Rudolf Rienau | 6 | Ltn Christian Scheller | 4 |
| Oblt Erich Hahn* | 5(6) | Vfw Richard Schneider | 4 |

| | | | |
|---|---|---|---|
| Ltn Walter Göttsch* | 3(20) | Ltn Konrad von Bülow | 1(2) |
| Ltn Ernst Hess* | 3(17) | Ltn Dotzel | 1 |
| Ltn Max Kliefoth | 3 | Vfw Gerdes | 1 |
| Vfw Martin Mallmann* | 3 | Ltn Gerlt | 1 |
| Ltn Ulrich Neckel | 3(30) | Ltn Jumpelt | 1(2) |
| Ltn Franz Brandt | 2(10) | Vfw Ruppert | 1 |
| Gefr Felder | 2 | Uffz Albert Tybelsky | 1 |
| Ltn Gewert | 2 | Jasta | 1 |

## Airfields occupied

| Location | Inclusive Dates | Armee |
|---|---|---|
| Ronssoy, Epehy | 25 Oct 1916 – 3 Dec 1916 | A |
| Lagnicourt | 4 Dec 1916 – 27 Dec 1916 | 1 |
| Bühl, Saarburg | 28 Dec 1916 – 30 Jun 1917 | A |
| St Loup | 30 Jun 1917 – 2 Feb 1918 | 1 |
| Cuirieux | 2 Feb 1918 – 26 Feb 1918 | 7 |
| Toulis | 26 Feb 1918 – 19 Mar 1918 | 7 |
| Guise | 19 Mar 1918 – 23 Mar 1918 | 18 |
| Roupy | 23 Mar 1918 – 24 Mar 1918 | 18 |
| Guisecourt | 24 Mar 1918 – 28 Mar 1918 | 18 |
| Balâtre | 28 Mar 1918 – 13 Apr 1918 | 18 |
| Bonneuil Ferme | 13 Apr 1918 – 21 Apr 1918 | 18 |
| Le Mesnil-Nesle | 21 Apr 1918 – 12 Jun 1918 | 18 |
| Mesnil-Bruntel | 12 Jun 1918 – 12 Jul 1918 | 2 |
| Leffincourt | 12 Jul 1918 – 24 Jul 1918 | 3 |
| Chéry-les-Pouilly | 24 Jul 1918 – 21 Aug 1918 | 9 |
| Fontaine Notre Dame | 21 Aug 1918 – 28 Aug 1918 | 18 |
| Neuflize | 28 Aug 1918 – 3 Sep 1918 | 1 |
| Tichémont | 3 Sep 1918 – 28 Sep 1918 | C |
| Stenay | 28 Sep 1918 – 1 Nov 1918 | 5 |
| Carignan | 1 Nov 1918 – 3 Nov 1918 | 5 |
| Florenville | 3 Nov 1918 – 10 Nov 1918 | 5 |
| Trier | 10 Nov 1918 – 11 Nov 1918 | 5 |

# ROYAL PRUSSIAN JAGDSTAFFEL 20

Jasta 20 was created pursuant to Kommandierenden General der Luftstreitkräfte von 25.10.16 Nr.26806 at Armee Flugpark 2, on 25 October 1916, in the 2 Armee Sector. The Commanding Officer was Oberleutnant Fritz Heising, from Kampfstaffel 23. The first combat casualty was Leutnant Lothar Erdmann, who was killed near St Quentin on 24 December. On 1 January 1917, the Jasta moved to the 2 Armee area, remaining there until 27 May when it was sent to the 4 Armee in Flanders. Oberleutnant Heising was transferred to Idflieg on 19 October and replaced at the head of Jasta 19 by Leutnant Rudolf Wendelmuth (11 victories) from Jasta 8, but he was killed when he collided in mid-air with Leutnant Wilhelm Schultze of Jasta 4 at 1335 hours over Fontaine Notre Dame. Command of Jasta 20 was assigned to Leutnant Joachim von Busse (four victories) from Jasta 3. The Jasta moved to the 17 Armee on 8 December. It returned to the 4 Armee Front on 9 April for the rest of the war. Leutnant von Busse was wounded in combat on 1 August, and temporary command was assumed by Leutnant von Eckartsberg, until 30 August when Oberleutnant Waldemar von Dazur (four victories) replaced him until von Busse returned. Jasta 20 was credited with at least 64 confirmed victories, while losing 19 pilots killed and 11 wounded in combat, three killed in a bomb raid, four killed and three injured in flying accidents.

## Commanding Officers

| | | |
|---|---|---|
| Oblt Fritz Heising | 25 Oct 1916 – 19 Oct 1917 | Idflieg |
| Ltn Rudolf Wendelmuth | 19 Oct 1917 – 30 Nov 1917 | KIAcc |
| Ltn Joachim von Busse | 15 Dec 1917 – 1 Aug 1918 | WIA |
| Ltn von Eckartsberg | 1 Aug 1918 – 30 Aug 1918 | Acting |
| Ltn Waldemar von Dazur | 30 Aug 1918 – | Acting |
| Ltn Joachim von Busse | – 11 Nov 1918 | |

## Pilots credited with victories

| | | | |
|---|---|---|---|
| Ltn Karl Plauth | 10(17) | Ltn Johannes Gildemeister | 5 |
| Ltn Joachim von Busse | 7(11) | Ltn Waldemar von Dazur | 4 |
| Ltn Raven von Barnekow | 5(11) | Ltn Friedrich Mallinckrodt | 4(6) |

| | | | |
|---|---|---|---|
| Ltn Gerhard Flecken | 3(4) | Ltn Heinrich Kämmerer* | 1 |
| Ltn Bruno Hobein | 3(4) | Vfw Friedrich Matthies | 1 |
| Ltn Rudolf Wendelmuth | 3(14) | Ltn Willi Schunke* | 1 |
| Ltn Gustav Beerendonk | 2 | Ltn Wilhelm Schwartz | 1(8) |
| Ltn von Decker | 2 | Vfw Emil Soltau* | 1(2) |
| Ltn Hubert Helten* | 2 | Ltn Hermann Stutz | 1(6) |
| Ltn Alfred Niederhoff | 2(7) | Ltn Hans Viebig | 1(5) |
| Ltn Otto Creutzmann | 1(8) | Ltn Eberhard Voss | 1 |
| Ltn Franz Götte* | 1 | Ltn Georg Weiner | 1(9) |
| Ltn Hugo Jons* | 1(2) | | |

## Airfields occupied

| Location | Inclusive Dates | Armee |
|---|---|---|
| AFP 2 | 25 Oct 1916 – 31 Dec 1916 | 2 |
| Essigny-le-Petit | 1 Jan 1917 – 10 Jan 1917 | 2 |
| Fayet | 11 Jan 1917 – 8 Feb 1917 | 2 |
| Artemps, Somme | 9 Feb 1917 – 1 Mar 1917 | 2 |
| Guise | 1 Mar 1917 – 27 May 1917 | 2 |
| Montkerke | 27 May 1917 – 31 Aug 1917 | 4 |
| Varsenaere | 31 Aug 1917 – 23 Nov 1917 | 4 |
| Guesnain | 23 Nov 1917 – 9 Apr 1918 | 17 |
| Rumbeke | 9 Apr 1918 – 6 Jun 1918 | 4 |
| Menin | 6 Jun 1918 – 11 Nov 1918 | 4 |

# ROYAL SAXON JAGDSTAFFEL 21

Jasta 21 was created on 25 October 1916, at Armee Flugpark 3, in accordance with Kriegs Ministerium von 29.11.16 Nr. 1145.16.g.A.7.L. On 15 November formation took place at Neuflize and Le Chatelet, and commenced operations on 6 December, under the command of Hauptmann Richard Schlieben from Kampfgeschwader VII. Vizefeldwebel Tuczek was shot down in flames over Berru during combat with a Caudron on 10 February 1917, for the first Jasta combat casualty. The first victory came on 24 March, when Leutnant Matthaei flamed a balloon for his first. Hauptmann Schlieben was sent to Idflieg on 26 May, and was replaced by Oberleutnant Eduard von Schleich (one victory). The Jasta moved to the 5 Armee Sector on 2 July. Von Schleich, who had run his score to 25, was transferred to the command of Jasta 32b on 23 October, with Oberleutnant Oskar von Boenigk (five victories) replacing him in Jasta 21. The designation of the Jasta was changed on 24 December from Royal Prussian Jagdstaffel 21 to Royal Saxon Jagdstaffel 21s, and on the 26th a move was made to the 1 Armee. After about two weeks, on 10 January 1918, Jasta 21s was assigned to the 7 Armee Sector, where it remained for the rest of the war. The Jasta's 100th victory came on 24 July. After Hauptmann Rudolf Berthold, the commander of JGII, with a score of 44, was wounded on 10 August, von Boenigk, who had raised his score to 21, became the head of JGII, and command of the Jasta passed to Leutnant Josef Schulte (four victories) from Jasta 14. Jasta 21s ended the war with at least 141 victories while suffering the loss of eight pilots killed and six wounded (one twice) in action and one taken prisoner.

## Commanding Officers

| | | |
|---|---|---|
| Hptm Richard Schlieben | 15 Nov 1916 – 26 May 1917 | Idflieg |
| Oblt Eduard von Schleich | 26 May 1917 – 23 Oct 1917 | CO J32b |
| Oblt Oskar von Boenigk | 23 Oct 1917 – 27 Aug 1918 | CO JGII |
| Ltn Josef Schulte | 27 Aug 1918 – 11 Nov 1918 | |

## Pilots credited with victories

| | | | |
|---|---|---|---|
| Ltn Karl Thom | 27 | Ltn Rudolf Matthaei | 3(10) |
| Hptm Eduard von Schleich | 26(35) | Ltn Christians | 2 |
| Oblt Oskar von Boenigk | 16(26) | Ltn Julius Keller | 2 |
| Ltn Emil Thuy | 13(35) | Ltn Busso von Albersleben* | 1 |
| Vfw Max Kuhn | 12 | Uffz Becker | 1 |
| Ltn Fritz Höhn | 10(21) | Oblt von Brackel | 1 |
| Ltn Paul Turck | 5(10) | Vfw Eduard Horn* | 1 |
| Uffz Heinrich Haase | 5(6) | Ltn Max Raspe | 1 |
| Uffz Willi Dost | 4 | Sgt Vetter | 1 |
| Vfw Karl Schmückle | 4(6) | Ltn Werner Wagener | 1(5) |
| Ltn Hermann Leptien | 3(7) | Vfw Max Zachmann | 1 |

**Airfields occupied**

| Location | Inclusive Dates | Armee |
|---|---|---|
| AFP3 | 25 Oct 1916 – 15 Nov 1916 | |
| Neuflize, Le Chatelet | 15 Nov 1916 – 1 Jul 1917 | B |
| Chassogne Ferme, Verdun | 1 Jul 1917 – 26 Dec 1917 | 5 |
| St Loup | 26 Dec 1917 – 10 Jan 1918 | 1 |
| St Mard | 10 Jan 1918 – 18 May 1918 | 7 |
| Sissone | 18 May 1918 – 6 Jun 1918 | 7 |
| Boncourt | 6 Jun 1918 – 23 Sep 1918 | 7 |
| Sissonc | 23 Sep 1918 – 11 Oct 1918 | 7 |
| Plomion | 11 Nov 1918 – 11 Nov 1918 | 7 |

# ROYAL SAXON JAGDSTAFFEL 22

Jasta 22 was created in accordance with Kriegs Ministerium von 29.11.16 Nr. 1145.16.g.A.7.L. on 25 October 1916, at Armee Flugpark 7, from FFA 11, FFA29 and FA(A)222. The first Commanding Officer was Oberleutnant Erich Hönmanns from Jasta 12, and on 16 November was at Vaux, near Laon, in the 7 Armee Sector. When the Jasta became operational on 1 December it was equipped with nine Halberstadt DII, and two Albatros DII scouts. Leutnant Josef Jacobs scored the Jasta's first victory, his second on 23 January 1917 by downing a Caudron R4 near Terny-Sorny. Also on this date Leutnant Karl Groterjahn was killed in combat between Trosly and Verneuil, to become the first combat casualty. Jacobs was the first to attain the score of five on 16 April. On 15 May the unit moved to the 5 Armee Sector. Oberleutnant Hönmanns was transferred to Idflieg on 29 June, and replaced by Leutnant Alfred Lenz (one victory) from Jasta 14. Lenz held the command for the rest of the war. The Jasta became the Royal Saxon Jagdstaffel on 24 November. On 19 March 1918 the Jasta was moved to the 18 Armee Front, then moved to the 7 Armee Sector on 12 May. On 8 August the Jasta moved to the 2 Armee Front. A final move was made on 20 August back to the 18 Armee Sector. Jasta 22 was credited with 59 victories, including 11 balloons, while losing five pilots killed and two wounded in action, two taken prisoner, and five killed in accidents, four of which were in mid-air collisions.

**Commanding Officers**

| | | |
|---|---|---|
| Oblt Erich Hönemanns | 26 Nov 1916 – 29 Jun 1917 | Idflieg |
| Ltn Alfred Lenz | 1 Jul 1918 – 11 Nov 1918 | |

**Pilots credited with victories**

| | | | |
|---|---|---|---|
| Vfw Karl Bohnenkamp | 15 | Vfw Friedrich Nüsch | 2 |
| Ltn Josef Jacobs | 5(48) | Ltn Oldenberg | 2 |
| Ltn Alfred Lenz | 5(6) | Ltn Erich Thomas | 2(10) |
| Ltn Siegfried Büttner | 4(13) | Vfw Emil Bergmann | 1 |
| Ltn Ulrich Fischer | 4 | Ltn von Borries | 1 |
| Ltn Diether Collin | 4(13) | Ltn Werner Herwarth | 1 |
| Ltn Konrad Schwartz | 4(5) | Ltn Otto Kunst | 1 |
| Vfw Paul Färber | 2 | Ltn Röhr | 1(2) |
| Ltn Julius Fichter | 2(7) | Vfw Teigeler | 1 |
| Oblt Heinrich Karbe | 2 | | |

**Airfields occupied**

| Location | Inclusive Dates | Armee |
|---|---|---|
| Vaux, Laon | 16 Nov 1916 – 26 Nov 1916 | 7 |
| Riencourt, Arras | 26 Nov 1916 – 15 May 1917 | 1 |
| Mont, Verdun | 15 May 1917 – Jun 1917 | 5 |
| Vivaise | Jun 1917 – Sep 1917 | 7 |
| Mont, Verdun | Sep 1917 – Nov 1917 | 5 |
| Near Soissons | Nov 1917 – 19 Mar 1918 | 1 |
| La Ferté Ferme | 19 Mar 1918 – 23 Mar 1918 | 18 |
| Mont d'Origny | 23 Mar 1918 – 29 Mar 1918 | 18 |
| Villeselve | 29 Mar 1918 – 8 Apr 1918 | 18 |
| Erchu | 8 Apr 1918 – 12 May 1918 | 18 |
| Mont St Martin | 12 May 1918 – 8 Jul 1918 | 7 |
| Bignicourt | 11 Jul 1918 – 8 Aug 1918 | 1 |
| Haubourdin, Lille | 8 Aug 1918 – 19 Aug 1918 | 2 |
| Guise | 20 Aug 1918 – 11 Nov 1918 | 18 |

# ROYAL BAVARIAN JAGDSTAFFEL 23

Created on 25 October 1916, in the Armee-Abteilung von Strantz Sector, at Metz-Frescaty, by Kriegs Ministerium von 29.11.16. Nr.1145.16.g.A.7.L. The first Commanding Officer was Oberleutnant Paul Backhaus from KG 2/12, who was promoted to Hauptmann on 18 November. The Jasta commenced operations from Pusieux, on 1 January 1917, equipped with the Albatros DII. Leutnant Lothar Rehm gained the first victory on 14 February 1917. The Jasta moved to the 7 Armee Sector on 16 April. Leutnant Fritz Mönnich was wounded in combat on 3 May over Coucy le Château, becoming the Jasta's first casualty. The designation of the Jasta changed on 17 July pursuant to Bavarian Kriegs Ministerium von 17.7.17 Nr.111847 A to Royal Bavarian Jagdstaffel 23. The next day the Jasta moved to the 5 Armee Front. On 4 August Hauptmann Backhaus was transferred to Flieger-Abteilung (A)259, and command of Jasta 23b was given to Leutnant Otto Kissenberth (six victories) from Jasta 16b. Kissenberth was the first pilot to achieve five victories with the Jasta, his 11th overall on 22 August. On 6 February 1918 Jasta 23b moved to the 17 Armee area. Leutnant Kissenberth, who now had a score of 20, was severely injured while test flying a captured Sopwith Camel when the motor quit at 40 metres altitude north of Epinoy, at 2130 hours on 29 May. Leutnant Heinrich Seywald was assigned as Commanding Officer, but on 29 June he was wounded in combat, and Leutnant Fritz Krautheim took temporary command until Seywald returned on 19 July and held the position for the rest of the war. Jasta 23b moved to the Armee-Abteilung 'A' Sector on 27 September, and Jagdgeschwader IV was established on 10 October and Jasta 23b became a part of it with Jastas 32b, 34b, and 35b, under the command of Hauptmann Eduard von Schleich for the rest of the war. Jasta 23b was credited with at least 66 victories, of which 12 were balloons, while suffering the loss of 14 pilots killed and nine wounded in action, two taken prisoner, one killed in a flying accident, and one shot down but jumped in a parachute unharmed.

## Commanding Officers

| | | |
|---|---|---|
| Hptm Paul Backhaus | 17 Nov 1916 – 4 Aug 1917 | FA(A)259 |
| Ltn Otto Kissenberth | 4 Aug 1917 – 29 May 1918 | IIc |
| Ltn Heinrich Seywald | 2 Jun 1918 – 29 Jun 1918 | WIA |
| Ltn Fritz Krautheim | 2 Jul 1918 – 19 Jul 1918 | Acting |
| Ltn Heinrich Seywald | 19 Jul 1918 – 11 Nov 1918 | |

## Pilots credited with victories

| | | | |
|---|---|---|---|
| Ltn Otto Kissenberth | 13(20) | Ltn Hubert Eder | 1 |
| Ltn Friedrich Röth | 10(28) | Ltn Johann Janzen | 1(13) |
| Vfw Michael Hutterer | 8 | Ltn Hugo Kaemmel | 1 |
| Ltn Heinrich Seywald | 6 | Ltn Heinrich Kütt* | 1 |
| Vfw Albert Haussmann | 3(15) | Vfw Alois Locher | 1 |
| Ltn Theodor Rumpel | 3(5) | Oblt Josef Mühlfeldt* | 1 |
| Ltn Max Gossner | 2(8) | Ltn Josef Müller | 1 |
| Ltn Otto Hohmuth | 2(4) | Ltn Michael Paulin | 1 |
| Uffz Hans Kleinschred | 2 | Vfw Otto Pelz | 1 |
| Ltn Heinrich Küllmer* | 2(3) | Vfw Lothar Rehm | 1 |
| Hptm Paul Backhaus | 1 | Vfw Friedrich Schattauer | 1(9) |
| Flg Siegfried Braun | 1 | Ltn Heinrich Tammann | 1 |
| Ltn Albert Dietlen | 1(9) | Hptm Eduard von Schleich | 10(35) |

Von Schleich's victories were scored while he commanded Jagdgruppen or JGIV, and are said to have been credited to Jasta 23b, giving the Jasta a score of 76 vice 66.

## Airfields occupied

| Location | Inclusive Dates | Armee |
|---|---|---|
| Armee-Abt. v Strantz | 25 Oct 1916 – 1 Jan 1917 | |
| Pusieux, Mars-la-Tour | 1 Jan 1917 – 14 Apr 1917 | 1 |
| Erlon, Marle | 16 Apr 1917 – 14 Jul 1917 | 7 |
| Jametz | 20 Jul 1917 – 24 Nov 1917 | 5 |
| St Mard | 24 Nov 1917 – 4 Feb 1918 | 7 |
| Aniche | 6 Feb 1918 – 16 Mar 1918 | 17 |
| Emerchicourt | 17 Mar 1918 – 27 Mar 1918 | 17 |
| Bapaume | 27 Mar 1917 – 18 Apr 1918 | 17 |
| Epinoy | 18 Apr 1918 – 27 Aug 1918 | 17 |
| Lieu St Armand | 27 Aug 1918 – 25 Sep 1918 | 17 |
| Bühl | 27 Sep 1918 – 8 Oct 1918 | A |
| Harmigniers | 13 Oct 1918 – 5 Nov 1918 | 2 |
| Fleurs | 5 Nov 1918 – 11 Nov 1918 | 2 |

## ROYAL SAXON JAGDSTAFFEL 24

This Jasta was created by Kriegs Ministerium von 29.11.16 Nr.1145.16. g.A.7.L. on 25 October 1916, in the Armee-Abteilung 'A' Sector at Mörchingen, under the command of Rittmeister Konstantin von Braun from KG 2/11. It was mobilised on 31 December. The first offensive patrol was flown on 14 January 1917, and the first combat casualty occurred on 6 February when Leutnant Georg Ferner was wounded over Pompey; the first victory came on 25 February, Offizierstellvertreter Gottlieb Vothknecht downing a Sopwith two-seater for his first victory. On 16 April the Jasta moved to the 1 Armee Sector. On 12 June the Jasta moved to the 5 Armee Front. Then on 27 June they went to the Flanders area with the 4 Armee. Rittmeister von Braun was transferred to Armee Flugpark 1 on 29 June, and command of Jasta 24 was assumed by Leutnant Heinrich Kroll (five victories) from Jasta 9. A move was made on 23 November to the 2 Armee Front, and on the following day the designation was changed to Royal Saxon Jagdstaffel 24. On 28 December the Jasta moved to the 18 Armee Sector, where it remained for the rest of the war. Jasta 24s was credited with at least 91 victories, including one balloon, for the loss of seven pilots killed and five wounded in action, one taken prisoner, and two killed in accidents.

### Commanding Officers

| | | |
|---|---|---|
| Rittm Konstantin von Braun | 1 Dec 1916 – 29 Jun 1917 | AFP1 |
| Ltn Heinrich Kroll | 29 Jun 1917 – 17 Oct 1917 | Leave |
| Ltn Rudolf Hepp | 17 Oct 1917 – 6 Nov 1917 | Acting |
| Ltn Heinrich Kroll | 6 Nov 1917 – 11 Apr 1918 | Leave |
| Ltn Rudolf Hepp | 11 Apr 1918 – 2 May 1918 | Acting |
| Ltn Heinrich Kroll | 2 May 1918 – 14 Aug 1918 | WIA |
| ? | 14 Aug 1918 – 21 Aug 1918 | Acting |
| Oblt Hasso von Wedel | 21 Aug 1918 – 11 Nov 1918 | |

### Pilots credited with victories

| | | | |
|---|---|---|---|
| Ltn Heinrich Kroll | 28(33) | Ltn Stickforth | 2 |
| OfStv Friedrich Altemeier | 21 | OfStv Gottlieb Vothknecht | 2 |
| Ltn Fritz Thiede | 5(8) | OfStv Anton Dierle* | 1 |
| Vfw Kurt Ungewitter | 5(7) | OfStv Paul Felsmann | 1(2) |
| Ltn Wolfgang Güttler | 4(8) | Ltn Rudolf Hepp | 1 |
| Uffz Kurt Reinhold | 4 | Ltn Leppin | 1 |
| Vfw Max Wackwitz | 4 | Ltn Kurt Müller | 1(2) |
| Oblt Hasso von Wedel | 3(5) | Vfw Josef Oehler* | 1(2) |
| Ltn Otto Brandes | 2 | Vfw Alfons Schymik* | 1 |
| Ltn Gebhardt Salzwedel | 2 | Ltn Karl Seifert | 1 |
| | | Ltn Alwin Thurm | 1(5) |

### Airfields occupied

| Location | Inclusive Dates | Armee |
|---|---|---|
| Mörchingen | 25 Oct 1916 – 15 Apr 1917 | A |
| Annelles-Rethel | 16 Apr 1917 – 11 Jun 1917 | 1 |
| Chassogne Ferme | 12 Jun 1917 – 26 Jun 1917 | 5 |
| Heule | 27 Jun 1917 – 8 Sep 1917 | 4 |
| Harlebeke | 8 Sep 1917 – 22 Nov 1917 | 4 |
| Emerchicourt | 23 Nov 1917 – 27 Dec 1917 | 2 |
| Guise | 28 Dec 1917 – 20 Mar 1918 | 18 |
| Pleine Selve | 20 Mar 1918 – 27 Mar 1918 | 18 |
| Villeselve | 27 Mar 1918 – 8 Apr 1918 | 18 |
| Ercheu | 8 Apr 1918 – 11 Aug 1918 | 18 |
| Guizancourt | 11 Aug 1918 – 15 Aug 1918 | 18 |
| Clastres | 15 Aug 1918 – 27 Aug 1918 | 18 |
| Chevresis-Moncou | 27 Aug 1918 – 5 Sep 1918 | 18 |
| Guise | 5 Sep 1918 – 12 Oct 1918 | 18 |
| La Chapelle | 12 Oct 1918 – 20 Oct 1918 | 18 |
| Donstiennes | 20 Oct 1918 – 8 Nov 1918 | 18 |
| Graux | 8 Nov 1918 – 11 Nov 1918 | 18 |

## ROYAL PRUSSIAN JAGDSTAFFEL 25

Created 28 November 1916, through Kommandeur der Flieger, 11 Armee, at Prilip, on the Macedonian Front, pursuant to Kriegs Ministerium von Nr.1425.16.g.A.7.L., and was mobilised on 1 December, under the command of Oberleutnant Friedrich-Karl Burckhardt of Feld Flieger Abteilung 30, and equipped with the Halberstadt DII. The Jasta's first victory came on 10 December, Leutnant Bodo von Lyncker scoring his first victory. Von Lyncker was also the first combat casualty, colliding in mid-air with an enemy Nieuport south of Gjevgjeli, on 18 February. On 13 March 1917, the Jasta moved to Kanatlarci, where Leutnant Otto Brauneck, who came to the Jasta with one claim, became the first ace by downing his sixth victory on 31 March. Oberleutnant Burckhardt was promoted to Hauptmann on 1 December 1917, and on 1 February 1918 was transferred to the Western Front to command Kest 2, at Saarbrücken. Command of Jasta 25 was assumed by Leutnant Renatus Heydacker (two victories) from Jasta 38 until the end of the war. Jasta 25 was credited with the destruction of at least 54 enemy aircraft including eight balloons, while losing only two pilots killed in combat, one killed and two injured in flying accidents.

## Commanding Officers

| | | |
|---|---|---|
| Hptm Friedrich-Karl Burckhardt | 2 Dec 1916 – 1 Feb 1918 | Kest 2 |
| Lt Renatus Heydacker | 5 Feb 1918 – 11 Nov 1918 | |

## Pilots credited with victories

| | | | |
|---|---|---|---|
| Ltn Gerhard Fieseler | 19 | Ltn Bodo von Lyncker* | 2 |
| Vfw Reinhard Treptow | 6 | Vfw Erich Schütze | 2(5) |
| Ltn Otto Brauneck* | 5(9) | Uffz Eggebrecht | 1 |
| Hptm Friedrich Burckhardt | 5 | Ltn Fritz Köhler | 1 |
| Vfw Anton Bauhofer | 4 | Vfw Otto Könnecke | 1(35) |
| Vfw Ernst Meyer | 3 | Vfw Heinrich Schott* | 1 |
| Ltn Gustav Rose | 3 | Vfw Strey | 1 |
| Lt Otto Brauneck killed while with Jasta 11. | | | |

## Airfields occupied

| Location | Inclusive Dates | Armee |
|---|---|---|
| Prilip | 28 Nov 1916 – 13 Mar 1917 | 11 |
| Kanatlarci, Macedonia | 13 Mar 1917 – 1 Jun 1918 | 11 |
| Kalkova | 1 Jun 1918 – 11 Nov 1918 | 11 |

# ROYAL PRUSSIAN JAGDSTAFFEL 26

This Jasta was created by Kriegs Ministerium von Nr.1426.16g.A.7.L. on 14 December 1916, through Kommandeur der Flieger 9, at FEA9 at Darmstadt. After formation it was sent to Colmar Nord, in the Armee-Abteilung 'B' Sector. Oberleutnant Bruno Loerzer (two victories), from Jasta 17, assumed command on 21 January 1917, and the first front flight took place on 27 January. On 25 February the first Jasta victory was scored by Leutnant Friedrich Weitz, his second. Weitz was also the first combat casualty when severely wounded near Ammerzweiler, while inspecting Nieuport XVII #2341 of his victim, Lieutenant Maus, N 49, on 11 March, dying of his wounds on 12 March. On 12 April a move was made to the 2 Armee Front, then on 6 June they went north to the Flanders Sector and the 4 Armee. The first pilot to gain five victories with the unit was Oberleutnant Loerzer on 21 August, although his claim of 6 March was not confirmed until December. On 21 February 1918, Jagdgeschwader III, consisting of Jastas Boelcke, 26, 27, and 36, was created and Oberleutnant Loerzer (17 victories) was named commander. Command of Jasta 26 was assumed by his brother, Leutnant Fritz Loerzer (six victories) from Jasta 63. The unit moved to the 17 Armee Sector on 13 March, then back to the 4 Armee on 11 April. As aerial activity was increasing in the 7 Armee area, JGIII was sent there on 24 May. Leutnant Fritz Loerzer was shot down and taken prisoner on 12 June, and Leutnant Franz Brandt (five victories) assumed command for the rest of the war. On 25 August JGIII moved to the 17 Armee Sector where it remained to the end of hostilities. At the war's end Jasta 26 had been credited with at least 180 victories, of which four were balloons, while losing five killed and 11 wounded in action, a prisoner of war, three forced to land after combats, and one injured in a parachute jump.

## Commanding Officers

| | | |
|---|---|---|
| Oblt Bruno Loerzer | 21 Jan 1917 – 21 Feb 1918 | CO JGIII |
| Ltn Fritz Loerzer | 21 Feb 1918 – 12 Jun 1918 | POW |
| Ltn Bollmann | 12 Jun 1918 – 27 Jun 1918 | Acting |
| Ltn Franz Brandt | 27 Jun 1918 – 22 Aug 1918 | Leave |
| Ltn Helmut Lange | 22 Aug 1918 – 12 Sep 1918 | Acting |
| Ltn Franz Brandt | 12 Sep 1918 – 11 Nov 1918 | |

## Pilots credited with victories

| | | | |
|---|---|---|---|
| Vfw Otto Fruhner | 27 | Ltn Karl Wewer* | 3 |
| Oblt Bruno Loerzer | 24(44) | Ltn Werner Dahm | 2(4) |
| Vfw Erich Buder | 12 | Ltn Ehlers | 2 |
| Vfw Otto Esswein* | 12 | Ltn Macard | 2 |
| Vfw Christel Mesch | 12(13) | OfStv Rudolf Weckbrodt* | 2(3) |
| Ltn Xavier Dannhuber | 10(11) | Ltn Friedrich Weitz | 2 |
| Ltn Fritz Loerzer | 10(11) | Ltn Maximilian Ziegler | 2 |
| Vfw Fritz Classen | 9(10) | Vfw Fritz Beckhardt | 1 |
| Ltn Helmut Lange | 7 | Oblt Theodor Dahlmann | 1(7) |
| Ltn Fritz Reimer | 7 | Ltn Heinrich Drekmann | 1(11) |
| Ltn Walter Blume | 6(28) | Ltn Gantermann | 1 |
| Ltn Franz Brandt | 5(10) | OfStv Fritz Kublum | 1 |
| Ltn Hermann Göring | 4(22) | Uffz Friedrich Neubauer | 1 |
| OfStv Fritz Kosmahl* | 4(9) | Vfw Herbert Werner | 1 |
| Ltn Hans Auer | 3(5) | | |

If the victories scored by Hptm Bruno Loerzer (22) while CO of JGIII and those of Oblt Theodor Dahlmann (4) of JGIII staff are counted in, Jasta 26 would have a score of 206.

## Airfields occupied

| Location | Inclusive Dates | Armee |
|---|---|---|
| Darmstadt | 14 Dec 1916 – 20 Jan 1917 | FEA9 |
| Colmar Nord | 20 Jan 1917 – 2 Mar 1917 | B |
| Habsheim | 2 Mar 1917 – 12 Apr 1917 | B |
| Guise-Ost | 16 Apr 1917 – 23 Apr 1917 | 2 |
| Bohain-Nord | 23 Apr 1917 – 6 Jun 1917 | 2 |
| Iseghem | 8 Jun 1917 – 10 Sep 1917 | 4 |
| Abeele | 11 Sep 1917 – 1 Nov 1917 | 4 |
| Bavichove | 2 Nov 1917 – 10 Feb 1918 | 4 |
| Marckebeke | 11 Feb 1918 – 12 Mar 1918 | 4 |
| Erchin | 13 Mar 1918 – 10 Apr 1918 | 17 |
| Halluin-Ost | 11 Apr 1918 – 23 May 1918 | 4 |
| Vivaise | 24 May 1918 – 7 Jun 1918 | 7 |
| Mont Soissons Ferme | 8 Jun 1918 – 18 Jul 1918 | 7 |
| Vauxcère | 19 Jul 1918 – 30 Jul 1918 | 7 |
| Chambry | 31 Jul 1918 – 24 Aug 1918 | 7 |
| Emerchicourt | 25 Aug 1918 – 26 Sep 1918 | 17 |
| Lieu St Armand | 27 Sep 1918 – 29 Sep 1918 | 17 |
| Soultain | 30 Sep 1918 – 12 Oct 1918 | 17 |
| Lenz | 13 Oct 1918 – 4 Nov 1918 | 17 |
| Aische-en-Befail | 5 Nov 1918 – 11 Nov 1918 | 17 |

# ROYAL PRUSSIAN JAGDSTAFFEL 27

Created 5 February 1917, through Kommandeur der Flieger 9, by Kriegs Ministerium von Nr.1425.16.g.A.7.L. It was formed at Ghistelles, in the 4 Armee area, and commanded by Leutnant Hans von Keudell (11 victories), who on 15 February, flying Albatros DIII 2017/16, downed his 12th victory over Vlamertinghe, and the first for the Jasta. Later, during combat with a Nieuport two-seater over Boesinghe, at 1700 hours, he was severely wounded and died of his wounds. He was replaced at the head of the unit by Leutnant Philipp Wieland, who returned to his former unit on 17 May, and command was taken over by Leutnant Hermann Göring (seven victories) from Jasta 26. Göring was promoted to Oberleutnant on 19 August and also became the first pilot to attain five victories when he downed his 12th on 25 August. When Jagdgeschwader III was created under the command of Oberleutnant Bruno Loerzer on 21 February 1918, Jasta 27 was assigned with Jasta Boelcke, 26 and 36. A move was made to the 7 Armee Front on 21 May. Oberleutnant Hermann Göring, who had raised his score to 21, was named commander of JGI on 28 July, and command of Jasta 27 was given to Leutnant Hermann Frommherz (10 victories) from Jasta Boelcke, and he held it for the rest of the war. JGIII moved to the 17 Armee on 24 August, and during mid-September the unit scored its 100th victory. Leutnant Frommherz made the last war flight on 10 November. Jasta 27 was credited with at least 134 victories, including six balloons, while suffering the loss of 11 killed and six wounded in combat, one taken prisoner, and three killed and four injured in accidents.

## Commanding Officers

| | | |
|---|---|---|
| Ltn Hans von Keudell | 12 Feb 1917 – 15 Feb 1917 | KIA |
| Ltn Philipp Wieland | 22 Feb 1917 – 17 May 1917 | J8 |
| Oblt Hermann Göring | 17 May 1917 – 28 Jul 1918 | CO JGI |
| Ltn Hermann Frommherz | 29 Jul 1918 – 11 Nov 1918 | |

## Pilots credited with victories

| | | | |
|---|---|---|---|
| Ltn Hermann Frommherz | 22(32) | Ltn Stoltenhoff | 3 |
| OfStv Rudolf Klimke | 15(17) | Ltn Fritz Berkemeyer* | 2(4) |
| Ltn Wilhelm Neuenhofen | 15 | Uffz Jahnke | 2 |
| Oblt Hermann Göring | 14(22) | Vfw Alfred Muth* | 2 |
| Ltn Friedrich Noltenius | 13(21) | Ltn Willi Rosenstein | 2(9) |
| Vfw Willi Kampe* | 8 | Oblt Maximilian v Förster* | 1 |
| Vfw Albert Lux | 8 | Ltn Gröning | 1 |
| Ltn Helmut Dilthey | 6(7) | Vfw Jumpelt | 1(2) |
| Sgt Willy Kahle | 6 | Oblt Hans von Keudell* | 1(12) |
| Vfw Max Krauss* | 4 | OfStv Klein | 1(2) |
| Ltn Ludwig Luer | 4(6) | Ltn Hellmuth Roer* | 1 |
| Ltn Franz Brandt | 3(10) | Ltn Willisch | 1 |

## Airfields occupied

| Location | Inclusive Dates | Armee |
|---|---|---|
| Ghistelles | 5 Feb 1917 – 15 Jun 1917 | 4 |
| Iseghem | 16 Jun 1917 – 31 Oct 1917 | 4 |
| Bavichove | 1 Nov 1917 – 12 Feb 1918 | 4 |
| Marckebeke | 13 Feb 1918 – 14 Apr 1918 | 4 |
| Halluin | 15 Apr 1918 – 20 May 1918 | 4 |
| Vivaise | 21 May 1918 – 2 Jun 1918 | 7 |
| Mont Soissons Ferme | 3 Jun 1918 – 17 Jul 1918 | 7 |
| Vauxcère | 18 Jul 1918 – 29 Jul 1918 | 7 |
| Chambry | 30 Jul 1918 – 22 Sep 1918 | 7 |
| Lieu St Armand | 23 Sep 1918 – 29 Sep 1918 | 17 |
| Lenz, Mons | 30 Sep 1918 – 6 Nov 1918 | 17 |
| Aische-en-Befail | 7 Nov 1918 – 11 Nov 1918 | 17 |

# ROYAL WÜRTTEMBERG JAGDSTAFFEL 28

This unit was created by Kriegs Ministerium von Nr.1425.16.g.A.7.L. on 14 December 1916, through Kommandeur der Flieger 10, Böblingen. Oberleutnant Rudolf Lang, from Jasta 11, assumed command on 20 January 1917, and on 24 January the Jasta was in the 4 Armee Sector of the Flanders Front. On 23 March the Jasta was sent to the 6 Armee area, and the first offensive patrol took place on 2 April. Offizierstellvertreter Max Müller scored the Jasta's first victory, his sixth, on 7 April. Oberleutnant Lang was transferred to FEA1, Schleissheim, on 27 April, and Leutnant Karl-Emil Schäfer (23 victories) from Jasta 11, assumed command. Leutnant Alexander Kutscher, flying Albatros DIII 771/17, became the first combat casualty when killed in combat with a Nieuport between Poperinghe and Elverdinghe, on 1 May. Max Müller was the first pilot to achieve five victories with Jasta 28 on 12 May scoring his tenth. At 1605 hours on 5 June Leutnant Schäfer, who had gained his 30th victory the day before, engaged some FE2ds east of Ypern and was killed. Command of the Jasta passed to Hauptmann Otto Hartmann (two victories) from Jasta 18. On 27 August the Jasta moved back to the 4 Armee Sector. The curse of the commanding officers continued and on 3 September Hartmann, who had increased his score to seven, was killed at 0815 hours near Kortewilde. Oberleutnant Werner Jahns (one victory), from Jasta 18, was assigned as the new commander, but he was killed in combat at 1530 hours south-east of Slype, on 24 September. Leutnant Emil Thuy (15 victories), from Jasta 21, reported on 26 September and took command and held it for the rest of the war. Jasta 28w moved to the 2 Armee Front on 6 June 1918, and about a month later, 8 July, moved on to the 1 Armee. As action picked up on the Somme Front the unit was sent to the 17 Armee where they finished the war. Jasta 28w achieved its 100th victory on 14 October, and may have scored more before the Armistice, while losing nine killed and three wounded in action, one prisoner of war, and one injured in a flying accident.

## Commanding Officers

| | | |
|---|---|---|
| Oblt Rudolf Lang | 20 Jan 1917 – 27 Apr 1917 | FEA1 |
| Ltn Karl-Emil Schäfer | 27 Apr 1917 – 5 Jun 1917 | KIA |
| Hptm Otto Hartmann | 8 Jun 1917 – 3 Sep 1917 | KIA |

| Oblt Werner Jahns | 6 Sep 1917 – 24 Sep 1917 | KIA |
| Ltn Emil Thuy | 26 Sep 1917 – 11 Nov 1918 | |

## Pilots credited with victories

| | | | |
|---|---|---|---|
| Ltn Max von Müller* | 24(36) | Uffz Schaack | 2 |
| Ltn Emil Thuy | 17(32) | Ltn Kurt Wittekind* | 2 |
| Ltn Ernst Hess* | 12(17) | Vfw Karolus Bärenfänger | 1 |
| Ltn Franz Ray | 8(17) | Ltn Friedrich Graepel* | 1 |
| Ltn Karl-Emil Schäfer* | 7(30) | Ltn Waldemar Janssen* | 1 |
| Ltn Karl Bolle | 5(36) | Flg Kuhlmey | 1 |
| Ltn Karl Christ | 5 | Vfw Georg Spadinger | 1 |
| Ltn August Hanko | 5 | Ltn Erich Weiss | 1 |
| Hptm Otto Hartmann* | 5(7) | Oblt Erwin Wenig | 1(4) |
| | | Unknown | 1 |

Lt Max Ritter von Müller killed with Jasta Boelcke.

## Airfields occupied

| Location | Inclusive Dates | Armee |
|---|---|---|
| Böblingen | 14 Dec 1916 – 23 Jan 1917 | FEA10 |
| Marcke, Courtrai | 24 Jan 1917 – 25 Mar 1917 | 4 |
| Wasquehal | 26 Mar 1917 – 26 Aug 1917 | 6 |
| Varsenaere, Brügge | 27 Aug 1917 – 13 Nov 1917 | 4 |
| Jabbeke | 13 Nov 1917 – 25 Nov 1917 | 4 |
| Wynghene | 25 Nov 1917 – 7 Dec 1917 | 4 |
| Varsenaere, Brügge | 7 Dec 1917 – 5 Feb 1918 | 4 |
| Wynghene | 5 Feb 1918 – 1 Mar 1918 | 4 |
| Iseghem | 1 Mar 1918 – 21 Mar 1918 | 4 |
| Abeele | 21 Mar 1918 – 29 Mar 1918 | 4 |
| Iseghem | 29 Mar 1918 – 5 Jun 1918 | 4 |
| Ennemain | 6 Jun 1918 – 7 Jul 1918 | 2 |
| Neuflize | 8 Jul 1918 – 10 Aug 1918 | 1 |
| Mons-en-Chaussée | 11 Aug 1918 – 12 Aug 1918 | 2 |
| Neuflize | 13 Aug 1918 – 24 Aug 1918 | 1 |
| Cantin | 25 Aug 1918 – 30 Sep 1918 | 17 |
| Beuvry | 1 Oct 1918 – 12 Oct 1918 | 17 |
| Chièvres | 13 Oct 1918 – 3 Nov 1918 | 17 |
| Champles, Waterloo | 4 Nov 1918 – 11 Nov 1918 | 17 |

# ROYAL PRUSSIAN JAGDSTAFFEL 29

This Jasta was established by K.M.v. Nr.1425.16.g.A.7.L. on 28 December 1916, through FEA5 Hannover, under the command of Hauptmann Hermann Palmer. Leutnant Ludwig Dornheim (two victories), from Jasta 5, relieved Palmer as Commanding Officer on 2 February 1917, and on 13 February the unit left Hannover and proceeded to the 3 Armee Sector. After about a month here they moved to the 1 Armee Front. Leutnant Wilhelm Allmenröder scored the first victory for the unit on 16 March. Vizefeldwebel Karl Möwe was the first combat casualty when killed between Auberive and St Souplet, on 11 April. Then on 29 April Leutnant Dornheim was killed in combat at 1500 hours over Beine. Leutnant Kurt Wolff (29 victories), from Jasta 11, became the new Commanding Officer. The Jasta moved again on 22 June to the 6 Armee Sector, and on 2 July Wolff, who had added two more to his score, was transferred to the command of Jasta 11, and Leutnant Erwin Böhme (12 victories) from the Jastaschule, Valenciennes, succeeded him in command. Another move was made to the 4 Armee Sector on 18 July, and a month later Böhme was transferred to the command of Jasta Boelcke. Oberleutnant Otto Schmidt (six victories), from Jasta 32b, assumed command of Jasta 29. On 18 October Schmidt was severely wounded at 1405 hours by ground fire during a balloon attack, and the following day Oberleutnant Harald Auffahrt (five victories) took over command. Leutnant Fritz Kieckhäfer became the first pilot to achieve five victories with the Jasta on 24 October. On 28 November Jasta 29 moved to the 2 Armee Front, and on 14 December was assigned to the 6 Armee, and finished the year with 35 confirmed victories. Jasta 29 remained with the 6 Armee. When, on 28 September 1918, Oberleutnant Auffahrt was named Commanding Officer of Jagdgruppe 3 the Jasta moved to the 4 Armee Sector. Leutnant Hans Holthusen (two victories), from Jasta 30, took command. Jasta 29 was credited with at least 96 confirmed victories while losing 13 killed and 12 wounded in action, one prisoner of war, and two killed plus one injured in flying accidents.

## Commanding Officers

| | | |
|---|---|---|
| Hptm Hermann Palmer | 31 Jan 1917 – 5 Feb 1917 | Grufı 9 |
| Ltn Ludwig Dornheim | 5 Feb 1917 – 29 Apr 1917 | KIA |
| Ltn Kurt Wolff | 6 May 1917 – 2 Jul 1917 | CO J11 |
| Ltn Erwin Böhme | 2 Jul 1917 – 18 Aug 1917 | CO J2 |
| Oblt Otto Schmidt | 19 Aug 1917 – 18 Oct 1917 | WIA |
| Oblt Harald Auffahrt | 19 Oct 1917 – 28 Sep 1918 | CO JGr3 |
| Ltn Hans Holthusen | 28 Sep 1918 – 11 Nov 1918 | |

## Pilots credited with victories

| | | | |
|---|---|---|---|
| Oblt Harald Auffahrt | 24(29) | Vfw Eugen Weiss | 2 |
| Vfw Karl Pech* | 9 | Oblt Kurt Wolff* | 2(33) |
| Ltn Fritz Kieckhäfer | 7(8) | Ltn Wilhelm Allmenröder | 1(2) |
| Ltn August Burkard | 6 | Ltn Erwin Böhme* | 1(24) |
| Uffz Siegfried Westphal | 6 | Ltn Clauss | 1 |
| OfStv Karl Gregor | 4 | Oblt Theodor Dahlmann | 1(6) |
| Oblt Otto Schmidt | 4(19) | Ltn Siegfried von Lieres | 1 |
| Ltn Hellmuth Contag | 3(4) | Vfw Karl Möwe* | 1 |
| Vfw Hans Fritsche | 3 | Ltn Günther Pastor | 1 |
| Ltn Günther Schuster | 3(6) | Vfw Kurt Petzina | 1(2) |
| Vfw Gilbert Wagner* | 3(4) | Ltn Karl Pokrantz* | 1(2) |
| Vfw Misch | 2 | Ltn Franz Schmitt | 1(3) |
| Ltn Heinrich Nebelthau | 2 | Uffz Paul Schönfelder* | 1 |
| Ltn Eugen Siempelkamp | 2(5) | Vfw Gustav Wackwitz | 1 |
| Ltn Friedrich Weber | 2 | | |

Oblt Kurt Wolff was killed with Jasta 11. Ltn Erwin Böhme was killed with Jasta Boelcke.

## Airfields occupied

| Location | Inclusive Dates | Armee |
|---|---|---|
| Juniville | 15 Feb 1917 – 15 Apr 1917 | 3 |
| Juniville | 16 Apr 1917 – 21 Jun 1917 | 1 |
| Mons-en-Pevelle | 22 Jun 1917 – 27 Jun 1917 | 6 |
| Bersée | 28 Jun 1917 – 17 Jul 1917 | 6 |
| Handzaeme | 18 Jul 1917 – 31 Jul 1917 | 4 |
| Thourout | 1 Aug 1917 – 13 Sep 1917 | 4 |
| Aertrycke | 14 Sep 1917 – 27 Nov 1917 | 4 |
| Emerchicourt | 28 Nov 1917 – 13 Dec 1917 | 2 |
| Bellincamps | 14 Dec 1917 – 30 Mar 1918 | 6 |
| Phalempin | 31 Mar 1918 – 12 Apr 1918 | 6 |
| Gondecourt | 13 Apr 1918 – 17 Aug 1918 | 6 |
| Bellincamps | 18 Aug 1918 – 28 Sep 1918 | 6 |
| Krouishouten | 29 Sep 1918 – 5 Oct 1918 | 4 |
| Aertrycke | 6 Oct 1918 – 11 Nov 1918 | 4 |

# ROYAL PRUSSIAN JAGDSTAFFEL 30

This Jasta was created 14 December 1916, through FEA 11, Breslau, pursuant to Kriegs Ministerium von Nr.1425.16.g.A.7.L., and was mobilised on 21 January 1917, at Phalempin, 6 Armee Sector, as authorised by OHL Ic 44332 op v. 14.1.17. The first Commanding Officer was Oberleutnant Hans Bethge (three victories) of Jasta 1, who was also the first pilot to score with the Jasta. He downed a Nieuport for his fourth victory on 28 March at 1024 hours, west of Bouvines. The first casualty was Gefreiter Heinrich Schneider who was flying Halberstadt DIII 234/16 when he was hit by AA fire over Ploegsteert Wald and forced to come down in Allied territory where he was taken prisoner on 15 February. From Phalempin, the Jasta operated at various times over the 4 Armee and 17 Armee in addition to the 6 Armee. Oberleutnant Bethge, now with 20 victories, flying Pfalz DIIIa 5888/17, was killed in combat with some DH4s south-west of Roulers at 1130 hours, on 17 March 1918. Command of the Jasta passed to Oberleutnant Kurt Preissler, of Jasta 30. Preissler was transferred to JGII on 16 April and Oberleutnant Hans-Georg von der Marwitz (six victories) took over until wounded, then Oberleutnant Richard Flashar, commander of Jagdgruppe 3, took command between 21 and 31 June, then Leutnant Kurt Müller (one victory), from Jasta 24s, took over until Leutnant von der Marwitz returned from hospital on 25 July, and Leutnant Müller was transferred and given command of Jasta 72s. Von der Marwitz departed on 14 days' leave on 1 August, leaving Leutnant Hans Holthusen (two victories) in command. After von der Marwitz returned from leave he was promoted to Oberleutnant on 28 August.

Jasta 30 was credited with 63 victories, including four balloons, while suffering the loss of 12 killed and two wounded in action, five prisoners of war, plus three killed and one injured in accidents.

## Commanding Officers

| | | |
|---|---|---|
| Oblt Hans Bethge | 15 Jan 1917 – 10 Nov 1917 | Leave |
| Oblt Kurt Preissler | 10 Nov 1917 – 10 Dec 1917 | Acting |
| Oblt Hans Bethge | 10 Dec 1917 – 15 Jan 1918 | Leave |
| Oblt Kurt Preissler | 15 Jan 1918 – 29 Jan 1918 | Acting |
| Oblt Hans Bethge | 19 Jan 1918 – 17 Mar 1918 | KIA |
| Oblt Kurt Preissler | 19 Mar 1918 – 16 Apr 1918 | JGII |
| Ltn Hans-Georg v d Marwitz | 17 Apr 1918 – 17 Jun 1918 | WIA |
| Ltn Hans Eggers | 17 Jun 1918 – 21 Jun 1918 | Acting |
| Oblt Richard Flashar | 21 Jun 1918 – 1 Jul 1918 | CO JGr3 |
| Ltn Kurt Müller | 1 Jul 1918 – 25 Jul 1918 | Acting |
| Ltn Hans-Georg v d Marwitz | 25 Jul 1918 – 1 Aug 1918 | Leave |
| Ltn Hans Holthusen | 1 Aug 1918 – 14 Aug 1918 | Acting |
| Oblt Hans-Georg v d Marwitz | 15 Aug 1918 – 11 Nov 1918 | |

## Pilots credited with victories

| | | | |
|---|---|---|---|
| Oblt Hans Bethge* | 17(20) | Ltn Hans Holthusen | 2 |
| Oblt Hans-Georg v d Marwitz | 14(15) | Uffz Emil Liebert* | 2 |
| Ltn Joachim von Bertrab | 5 | Ltn Reinhold Maier* | 2 |
| Ltn Hans Oberländer | 5(6) | Ltn Gustav Nernst* | 2(3) |
| Vfw Josef Heiligers* | 4 | Ltn Friedrich Bieling | 1 |
| Ltn Otto Fuchs | 3 | Ltn Hans Buddecke* | 1(13) |
| Uffz Josef Funk | 3 | Ltn Otto Franke* | 1 |
| Ltn Paul Erbguth | 2 | Ltn Kurt Katzenstein | 1 |

## Airfields occupied

| Location | Inclusive Dates | Armee |
|---|---|---|
| Breslau | 14 Dec 1916 – 25 Jan 1917 | FEA11 |
| Phalempin | 25 Jan 1917 – 9 Aug 1918 | 6 |
| Moislains | 9 Aug 1918 – 10 Aug 1918 | 6 |
| Phalempin | 10 Aug 1918 – 19 Aug 1918 | 6 |
| Avelin | 19 Aug 1918 – 30 Sep 1918 | 6 |
| Baisieux | 30 Sep 1918 – 15 Oct 1918 | 6 |
| Avaing | 15 Oct 1918 – 11 Nov 1918 | 6 |

According to Kofl 6 reports Jasta 30 was with the 6 Armee during its whole existence and in some cases operated over the fronts of various armees in the area. All victories and casualties are also shown in Kofl 6 reports.

# ROYAL PRUSSIAN JAGDSTAFFEL 31

Jasta 31 was created on 14 December 1916, at FEA11, Breslau, pursuant to Kriegs Ministerium von Nr.1425.16.g.A.7.L., and was mobilised on 5 February 1917, under the command of Leutnant Werner Albert (one victory) from KG2. The Jasta commmenced operations in the 3 Armee Sector, with Lt Albert scoring the first victory on 9 March. The first casualty came on 19 April: Leutnant Paul Herrmann was killed in combat with a Spad over Bois Malval. Leutnant Albert was killed during combat with a Spad over Vaudesincourt on 10 May, and command of the unit was assumed by Oberleutnant Günther Viehweger, from Jasta 17. Viehweger was transferred to Idflieg on 6 September, and Leutnant Werner Zech, from Jasta 1, took command before Jasta 31 was sent to the Italian Front on 11 September. On 11 January 1918, Kummetz was killed in combat and Oberleutnant Walter Korte took over for the rest of the time in Italy. After 14 victories and four casualties Jasta 31 started its trip back to the Western Front on 9 March 1918. On 31 March Leutnant Zech was promoted to Oberleutnant. Zech was transferred to Idflieg on 18 May, and Oberleutnant Paul Blumenbach (one victory), from Jasta 12, became the new Commanding Officer. After Blumenbach assumed command of Jagdgruppe 1 on 2 October, Hauptmann Eduard Seldner, from Jasta 57, commanded Jasta 31 for the rest of the war. On 26 October, Leutnant Garsztka became the first pilot to score five victories with the Jasta. Jasta 31 was credited with the destruction of at least 36 enemy aircraft, including five balloons, while losing nine killed and six wounded in combat, two killed and two injured in flying accidents.

## Commanding Officers

| | | |
|---|---|---|
| Ltn Werner Albert | 5 Feb 1917 – 10 May 1917 | KIA |
| Oblt Günther Viehweger | 15 May 1917 – 6 Sep 1917 | Idflieg |
| Oblt Werner Zech | 10 Sep 1917 – 18 May 1918 | Idflieg |

| Oblt Paul Blumenbach | 18 May 1918 – 2 Oct 1918 | CO JGr1 |
| Hptm Eduard Seldner | 2 Oct 1918 – 11 Nov 1918 | |

### Pilots credited with victories

| | | | |
|---|---|---|---|
| Ltn Sylvester Garsztka | 6 | Ltn Addix | 1 |
| Ltn Alwin Thurm* | 4(5) | Ltn Hencke | 1(2) |
| Ltn Werner Albert* | 3(4) | Ltn Holle | 1 |
| Vfw Amschel | 3 | Ltn Hugo Jöns | 1(2) |
| Vfw Kaspar Rahier* | 3 | Ltn Bernhard Lauscher | 1 |
| Oblt Paul Blumenbach | 2(3) | Ltn Mayer | 1 |
| Uffz Brüngel | 2 | Vfw Ernst Oppermann* | 1 |
| Vfw Fritz Jacobsen | 2(8) | Ltn Richard Wenzl | 1(11) |
| Ltn Kosslick | 2(3) | Ltn Wittenhagen | 1 |

Vfw Ernst Oppermann WIA 28 November 1917, DOW 28 December 1917.

### Airfields occupied

| Location | Inclusive Dates | Armee |
|---|---|---|
| Breslau | 14 Dec 1916 – 7 Feb 1917 | FEA11 |
| Mars-sous-Bourcq | 8 Feb 1917 – 23 Jun 1917 | 3 |
| Guesnain, Douai | 23 Jun 1917 – 12 Jul 1917 | 6 |
| Houplin | 12 Jul 1917 – 15 Jul 1917 | 6 |
| Bavichove | 15 Jul 1917 – 1 Sep 1917 | 4 |
| Auritz/Veldes am See | 20 Sep 1917 – 2 Nov 1917 | 14 |
| Udine | 2 Nov 1917 – 14 Nov 1917 | 14 |
| Aviano | 14 Sep 1917 – 19 Nov 1917 | 14 |
| San Giacomo, Vittorio | 19 Nov 1917 – 2 Jan 1918 | 14 |
| St Flor | 2 Jan 1918 – 13 Mar 1918 | 14 |
| Bergnicourt | 28 Mar 1918 – 30 Mar 1918 | 1 |
| St Loup | 30 Mar 1918 – 1 Sep 1918 | 1 |
| Guise | 1 Sep 1918 – 11 Nov 1918 | 1 |

## ROYAL BAVARIAN JAGDSTAFFEL 32

This Jasta was authorised by Kriegs Ministerium von Nr.1425.16.g.A.7.L. at FEA9, Darmstadt. Formation took place on 22 February 1917, in the Armee-Abteilung 'A' Sector, under the command of Oberleutnant Heinrich Schwandner from Schutzstaffel 27. The first Roland DII aircraft were received on 4 March, and the first offensive patrol came five days later. The first casualties occurred during a combat on 16 March: Schwandner was shot down in flames at 1030 hours over Athienville, probably by Lt Albert Deullin, N 73, and Leutnant Lothar von Hausen was killed at 1025 hours north of Hoeville, probably by Capitaine Georges Guynemer. During April the Jasta was assigned to the 7 Armee, and Oberleutnant Bartholomäus Schröder, from AFP A, assumed command on 3 April. During the month of June the unit was transferred to the 1 Armee Sector, and on 28 June Schröder was transferred to AFP1. Oberleutnant Otto Schmidt (five victories), from Jasta 7, arrived on 30 June to take over command, and the Jasta was sent to the 5 Armee Front. The unit's first victory was scored by Oberleutnant Otto Schmidt, his third, on 6 July. In accordance with Bavarian Kriegs Ministerium von 17.7.17 Nr.111847A, Jasta 32 was designated a Bavarian unit on 17 July. Oberleutnant Schmidt, who had added two to his score, but was not a Bavarian, was transferred to the command of Jasta 29 on 19 August, and replaced by Leutnant Hans Auer (three victories) from Jasta 26. During October the unit returned to the 7 Armee area, and on the 19th Auer, who now had five victories, was transferred to FEA1, Schleissheim. Four days later Oberleutnant Eduard von Schleich (25 victories) arrived from Jasta 21 to take command. Leutnant Rudolf Windisch was the first pilot to score five victories, his sixth overall, on 19 November. Von Schleich was transferred to Fliegerschule 1 on 10 January 1918, and Leutnant Johann Czermak (one victory), from Jasta 77b, assumed command of Jasta 23b. Jasta 32b was transferred to the 7 Armee Front on 1 February. Czermak was transferred to FEA1, on 23 July, and Leutnant Emil Koch was named as his replacement. On 29 September the Jasta moved to the Armee-Abteilung 'A' Sector, remaining there until 12 October, when it moved to the 2 Armee Front, staying there for the rest of the war. During October, when Bavarian Jagdgeschwader IV was created, Jasta 32b was assigned with Jastas 23b, 34b and 35b under the command of von Schleich. Leutnant Koch, who now had a score of seven, was wounded by ground fire while on a strafing mission on 24 October. Leutnant Hans Böhning (17 victories), from Jasta 76b, took over as the last commander. Jasta 32(b) scored at least 42 confirmed victories, including four balloons, while losing nine killed and four wounded in action, one taken prisoner, and five killed and two injured in accidents.

### Commanding Officers

| | | |
|---|---|---|
| Oblt Heinrich Schwandner | 23 Feb 1917 – 16 Mar 1917 | KIA |
| Oblt Bartholomäus Schröder | 3 Apr 1917 – 28 Jun 1917 | AFP1 |
| Oblt Otto Schmidt | 30 Jun 1917 – 19 Aug 1918 | CO J29 |
| Ltn Hans Auer | 19 Aug 1917 – 19 Oct 1917 | FEA1 |
| Oblt Eduard von Schleich | 23 Oct 1917 – 10 Jan 1918 | JsSch1 |
| Ltn Johann Czermak | 10 Jan 1918 – 23 Jul 1918 | FEA1 |
| Ltn Emil Koch | 23 Jul 1918 – 24 Oct 1918 | WIA |
| Ltn Hans Böhning | 1 Nov 1918 – 11 Nov 1918 | |

### Pilots credited with victories

| | | | |
|---|---|---|---|
| Ltn Emil Koch | 7 | Ltn Fritz Danker* | 1(2) |
| Ltn Rudolf Windisch | 7(22) | Vfw Josef Kettel | 1 |
| Vfw Otto Stadter | 4 | Ltn Fritz Kieckhäfer | 1(8) |
| Vfw Jakob Landin* | 3 | Oblt Hugo Krauss | 1 |
| Ltn Hans Auer | 2(5) | Vfw Kurt Petzina | 1(2) |
| Vfw Ehrhardt | 2 | Ltn Hans Rolfes | 1(17) |
| Ltn Heinrich Hager | 2 | Ltn Franz Schmidt | 1 |
| Uffz Marchner | 2 | Vfw Franz Tabaka | 1 |
| Oblt Otto Schmidt | 2(19) | Vfw Wiest | 1 |
| Vfw Kurt Starck | 2 | | |

### Airfields occupied

| Location | Inclusive Dates | Armee |
|---|---|---|
| Darmstadt | 14 Dec 1916 – 21 Feb 1917 | FEA9 |
| Destrich, Brülingen | 22 Feb 1917 – Mar 1917 | A |
| Chéry-les-Pouilly | Mar 1917 – Jun 1917 | 7 |
| Avanson | Jun 1917 – 30 Jun 1917 | 1 |
| Landréville | 30 Jun 1917 – 21 Sep 1917 | 5 |
| Boulin Ferme | 21 Sep 1917 – 20 Oct 1917 | 5 |
| Chéry-les-Pouilly | 21 Oct 1917 – 1 Feb 1918 | 7 |
| Guesnain | 1 Feb 1918 – 28 Mar 1918 | 17 |
| Favreuil, Bapaume | 28 Mar 1918 – 18 Apr 1918 | 17 |
| Epinoy | 18 Apr 1918 – 8 Aug 1918 | 17 |
| Villers-au-Tertre | 8 Aug 1918 – 28 Aug 1918 | 17 |
| Villers St Amand | 28 Aug 1918 – 29 Sep 1918 | 17 |
| Bühl | 29 Aug 1918 – 12 Oct 1918 | A |
| Harmigniers | 12 Oct 1918 – 28 Oct 1918 | 2 |
| Gosselies | 28 Oct 1918 – 11 Nov 1918 | 2 |
| Trier | 11 Nov 1918 – | |

# ROYAL PRUSSIAN JAGDSTAFFEL 33

Jasta 33 was established through FEA3, Gotha, by authority of Kriegs Ministerium von Nr.1425.16.g.A.7.L. and was mobilised on 1 March 1917. The first Commanding Officer was Oberleutnant Heinrich Lorenz (one victory) from Jasta 1. The first offensive patrol, in the Armee-Abteilung 'A' Sector, was on 16 March, and the first victory came on 24 April with Oberleutnant Lorenz claiming his second victory. Also, the first combat casualty occurred on 24 April, Unteroffizier Nauczak being severely wounded. A move had been made to the 6 Armee Front on 11 April. Oberleutnant Lorenz was wounded in combat on 15 June, and Leutnant Johann Hesselink (one victory) assumed command of the Jasta until he returned on 14 July. Due to his wounds Lorenz was unable to fly so Hesselink led the Jasta in the air. On 19 September Jasta 33 moved through the 2 Armee Sector and on the 23rd settled in the 4 Armee Sector on the Flanders Front. Jasta 33 moved to the Armee-Abteilung 'A' Sector on 23 January 1918, remaining there until 1 April when it moved to the 6 Armee Front. After a few days, on 26 April the unit moved back to the 4 Armee until 11 June when it was assigned to the 2 Armee. Oberleutnant Lorenz was transferred on 24 June to AFP4 Flugschule and Leutnant Karl von Schönebeck (four victories), from Jasta 59, assumed command for the rest of the war. Another move was made on 7 July to the 1 Armee Sector until 27 August when the Jasta moved to the 17 Armee until the end of the war. The only pilot to score five victories with the Jasta was Vizefeldwebel Emil Schäpe in early October. Jasta 33 was credited with at least 44 victories while losing six killed and seven wounded in action (one pilot twice), and one killed in an accident.

## Commanding Officers

| | | |
|---|---|---|
| Oblt Heinrich Lorenz | 4 Mar 1917 – 15 Jun 1917 | WIA |
| Ltn Johann Hesselink | 18 Jun 1917 – 14 Jul 1918 | Acting |
| Oblt Heinrich Lorenz | 14 Jul 1918 – 24 Jun 1918 | AFP4 |
| Ltn Karl von Schönebeck | 11 Jul 1918 – 11 Nov 1918 | |

## Pilots credited with victories

| | | | |
|---|---|---|---|
| Vfw Emil Schäpe | 17(18) | Vfw Martin Altmaier* | 1 |
| Ltn Karl von Schönebeck | 4(8) | Vfw Franz Eberlein | 1 |
| Oblt Heinrich Lorenz | 4(5) | Ltn Friedrich Ehmann | 1 |
| Vfw Heinrich Gockel | 3 | Ltn Robert Heibert | 1(13) |
| Ltn Fritz Kuke* | 2 | Ltn Johann Hesselink | 1 |
| Uffz Rosenau | 2(3) | Ltn Kurt Jacobs | 1(7) |
| Ltn Richard Ruckel | 2 | Vfw Rebbe | 1 |
| Vfw Fritz Schwarz* | 2 | Ltn Erich Weiss* | 1(2) |
| Ltn Fritz Vossen* | 2 | | |

## Airfields occupied

| Location | Inclusive Dates | Armee |
|---|---|---|
| Gotha | 14 Dec 1916 – 2 Mar 1917 | FEA3 |
| Bühl, Saarburg | 4 Mar 1917 – 11 Apr 1917 | A |
| Villers-au-Tertre | 11 Apr 1917 – 15 Sep 1917 | 6 |
| Guise | 19 Sep 1917 – 20 Sep 1917 | 2 |
| Bavichove | 23 Sep 1917 – 16 Oct 1917 | 4 |
| Wynghene | 17 Oct 1917 – 27 Nov 1917 | 4 |
| Sierenz-Muhlhausen | 10 Dec 1917 – 23 Jan 1918 | A |
| Burscheid | 6 Feb 1918 – 22 Feb 1918 | A |
| Bühl | 22 Feb 1918 – 26 Mar 1918 | A |
| Roucourt | 1 Apr 1918 – 11 Apr 1918 | 6 |
| Ascq | 11 Apr 1918 – 23 Apr 1918 | 6 |
| Lomme-Lille | 23 Apr 1918 – 26 Apr 1918 | 6 |
| Halluin | 26 Apr 1918 – 10 Jun 1918 | 4 |
| Ennemain | 11 Jun 1918 – 6 Jul 1918 | 1 |
| Neuflize | 7 Jul 1918 – 26 Aug 1918 | 1 |
| Cantin | 27 Aug 1918 – 30 Sep 1918 | 17 |
| Beuvry | 30 Sep 1918 – 13 Oct 1918 | 17 |
| Chièvres | 13 Oct 1918 – 4 Nov 1918 | 17 |
| Champles, Waterloo | 4 Nov 1918 – 11 Nov 1918 | 17 |

# ROYAL BAVARIAN JAGDSTAFFEL 34

This unit was created through FEA1, Altenberg, pursuant to Kriegs Ministerium von Nr.1425.16.g.A.7.L. on 20 February 1917. The unit was equipped with the Albatros DIII, and the first Commanding Officer was Oberleutnant Eduard Dostler (two victories) from Jasta 13. The Jasta was sent to the Armee-Abteilung 'C' Sector on 25 February. The first combat casualty was Vizefeldwebel Georg Hentze, who was shot down and taken prisoner on 22 March, and the first victory was scored by Oberleutnant Dostler two days later. Dostler was also the first Jasta 34 pilot to attain five victories with the unit, scoring his seventh overall on 24 May. Dostler, who had added one more to his score, was transferred to the command of Jasta 6 on 9 June, and Hauptmann Franz Walz (seven victories) replaced him until 21 June when Walz was sent to FEA1b, Schleissheim, and Oberleutnant Robert Greim (two victories) assumed command for the rest of the war. Jasta 34 became Bavarian Jagdstaffel 34 on 17 July according to BKM v.17.7.17. Nr.111847-A. On 5 September Jasta 34b was moved to the Verdun front assigned to the 5 Armee, where it remained until 19 October when it moved to the 7 Armee Front. On 22 November the Jasta was sent back to the 5 Armee area and remained there until 16 March 1918. Jasta 34b was assigned to the 2 Armee Sector on 16 March 1918, and remained in this sector for the rest of the war. At this time the Jasta was equipped with the Albatros DV and DVa. On 10 April the first of the new Pfalz DIIIs and Fokker DrIs arrived, but were replaced on 15 June with the Fokker DVII, and during August some Pfalz DXIIs arrrived. When Bavarian Jagdgeschwader IV was created on 6 October Jasta 34b, with Jastas 23b, 32b, and 35b, was assigned under the command of Hauptmann Eduard von Schleich, where it ended the war. Jasta 34b was credited with the destruction of at least 89 enemy aircraft, three of which were balloons, while suffering the loss of ten killed and four wounded in combat, five prisoners of war, two killed and two injured in flying accidents.

## Commanding Officers

| | | |
|---|---|---|
| Oblt Eduard Dostler | 20 Feb 1917 – 10 Jun 1917 | CO J6 |
| Hptm Franz Walz | 10 Jun 1917 – 19 Jun 1917 | FEA1b |
| Oblt Robert von Greim | 19 Jun 1917 – 11 Nov 1918 | |

## Pilots credited with victories

| | | | |
|---|---|---|---|
| Oblt Robert von Greim | 27(28) | Ltn Ludwig Schmid | 2 |
| Vfw Johann Pütz | 7 | Ltn Karl Bauernfeind* | 1 |
| Oblt Eduard von Dostler | 6(26) | Ltn Richard Ernert | 1(2) |
| Ltn Alfons Scheicher | 6 | Oblt Erich Fries | 1 |
| Ltn Heinrich Geigl | 5(13) | Vfw Theodor Himmer | 1(2) |
| Vfw Max Kahlow | 5(6) | Vfw Willy Kempe | 1 |
| Ltn Rudolf Stark | 5(11) | Ltn Hans Kiessling | 1 |
| Ltn August Delling | 5 | Ltn Johann Kithil | 1 |
| Ltn Georg Kröhl | 4 | Vfw Leopold von Raffay | 1(2) |
| Ltn Hans von Adam* | 3(21) | Vfw Max Taucher | 1 |
| Ltn Hans Boes | 2(3) | Uffz Franz Ulm | 1 |
| Vfw Georg Schalk* | 2 | | |

Lt Hans von Adam killed while with Jasta 6.

## Airfields occupied

| Location | Inclusive Dates | Armee |
|---|---|---|
| Altenberg | 20 Feb 1917 – 25 Feb 1917 | FEA1 |
| Mars-la-Tour | 25 Feb 1917 – 5 Sep 1917 | C |
| Mont-Verdun | 5 Sep 1917 – 13 Oct 1917 | 5 |
| Curieux | 13 Oct 1917 – 22 Nov 1917 | 7 |
| Chenois, Virton | 22 Nov 1917 – 15 Mar 1918 | 5 |
| Le Cateau | 16 Mar 1918 – 27 Mar 1918 | 2 |
| Vraignes | 27 Mar 1918 – 12 Apr 1918 | 2 |
| Foucaucourt | 18 Apr 1918 – 31 Jul 1918 | 2 |
| St Christ | 31 Jul 1918 – 11 Aug 1918 | 2 |
| Hervilly | 11 Aug 1918 – 29 Aug 1918 | 2 |
| Seranvillers | 29 Aug 1918 – 4 Sep 1918 | 2 |
| Bévillers | 5 Sep 1918 – 30 Sep 1918 | 2 |
| Ecarmain | 1 Oct 1918 – 7 Oct 1918 | 2 |
| Givry | 7 Oct 1918 – 25 Oct 1918 | 2 |
| Gosselies, Charleroi | 25 Oct 1918 – 11 Nov 1918 | 2 |
| Diedenhöfen | 11 Nov 1918 – | |

# ROYAL BAVARIAN JAGDSTAFFEL 35

Created on 14 December 1916, through FEA6, Grossenhain, as authorised by Kriegs Ministerium von Nr.1425.16.g.A.7.L. Mobilisation started on 7 January 1917, and on 1 March moved to the Western Front, settling in the Armee-Abteilung 'B' Sector on 4 March, when Oberleutnant Herbert Theurich assumed command. The first eight Albatros DIIIs arrived on 14 March from AFP B. Vizefeldwebel Rudolf Nebel became the first combat casualty; he was flying Albatros DIII 2107/16 when shot down by AA fire on 2 April, and taken prisoner. On 14 April Theurich, flying Albatros DIII 2097/16, was shot down in flames over Neubreisach; also on 14 April Vizefeldwebel Gustav Schindler scored the first victory for the Jasta. The following day, 15 March, Oberleutnant Otto Dessloch, from Kofl B, assumed command. On 29 June Dessloch departed on leave and appointed Oberleutnant Otto Deindl as acting CO. Jasta 35 became the Royal Bavarian Jagdstaffel 35 on 17 July in accordance with Bavarian Kriegs Ministerium von 17.7.17 Nr.111847A. On 21 July the unit had moved to the 4 Armee Sector in Flanders. Dessloch returned from leave on 22 July and was transferred to FEA1, Schleissheim, on 24 September and Leutnant Ludwig Hanstein (11 victories), from Jasta 16b, took command. The Jasta was sent to the 2 Armee Front on 30 November, where it finished the year. Jasta 35b was assigned to the 17 Armee area on 7 February 1918, and on 21 March Leutnant Hanstein, who had attained a score of 16, and was the first pilot to attain five victories with the Jasta, was shot down in flames during combat with a two-seater between Noreuil and Vaulx, while flying Albatros DVa 5285/17. Leutnant Otto Fuchs (three victories), from Jasta 77b, arrived on 21 April to assume command, but on 7 June he was transferred back to Jasta 77b as Commanding Officer, and command of Jasta 35b passed to Leutnant Rudolf Stark (six victories) from Jasta 77b, who held it to the end of the war. On 29 September a move was made to the Armee-Abteilung 'A' Sector, until 12 October when the Jasta was sent to the 2 Armee Front and assigned to Bavarian Jagdgeschwader IV along with Jastas 23b, 32b and 34b, under the command of

Hauptmann Eduard von Schleich. It remained with the 2 Armee until the war's end. Jasta 35b was given credit for at least 42 enemy aircraft destroyed while losing six killed and nine wounded in combat, two prisoners of war, and four killed and five injured in accidents.

## Commanding Officers

| | | |
|---|---|---|
| Oblt Herbert Theurich | 4 Mar 1917 – 14 Apr 1917 | KIA |
| Oblt Otto Dessloch | 15 Apr 1917 – 29 Jun 1917 | Leave |
| Oblt Otto Deindl | 29 Jun 1917 – 21 Jul 1917 | Acting |
| Oblt Otto Dessloch | 22 Jul 1917 – 24 Sep 1917 | FEA1 |
| Ltn Ludwig Hanstein | 24 Sep 1917 – 20 Jan 1918 | Leave |
| Oblt Bruno Justinius | 20 Jan 1918 – 30 Jan 1918 | Acting KIA |
| Ltn Franz Diemer | 30 Jan 1918 – 4 Mar 1918 | Acting |
| Ltn Ludwig Hanstein | 4 Mar 1918 – 21 Mar 1918 | KIA |
| Ltn Franz Diemer | 21 Mar 1918 – 21 Apr 1918 | Acting |
| Ltn Otto Fuchs | 21 Apr 1918 – 7 Jul 1918 | CO J77b |
| Ltn Rudolf Stark | 7 Jul 1918 – 28 Jul 1918 | Leave |
| Oblt Gratz | 28 Jul 1918 – 8 Aug 1918 | Acting |
| Ltn Rudolf Stark | 8 Aug 1918 – 11 Nov 1918 | |

## Pilots credited with victories

| | | | |
|---|---|---|---|
| Ltn Ludwig Hanstein* | 5(16) | Vfw Gondermann | 1(3) |
| Ltn Rudolf Stark | 5(11) | Vfw Hofmann | 1 |
| Ltn Karl Hammes | 4 | Oblt Bruno Justinius* | 1 |
| Ltn Wolf v Manteuffel-Szöge* | 3 | Uffz Justus Kaiser* | 1 |
| Ltn Franz Anslinger | 2(3) | Vfw Karl Knocke | 1 |
| Ltn Fritz Berkemeyer | 2(4) | Ltn Rudolf Rath* | 1 |
| Ltn Max Kämmerer | 2 | Vfw Schroth | 1 |
| Ltn Walter Kirchbach | 2 | Uffz Schweppe | 1 |
| Vfw Gustav Schindler | 2 | Uffz Joachim von Stein | 1 |
| Gefr Caspar Schmidt | 2 | Ltn Heinrich Stör | 1 |
| Ltn Friedrich Wendland | 2(4) | Uffz Stumpert | 1 |
| Uffz Emil Barheine | 1 | | |

## Airfields occupied

| Location | Inclusive Dates | Armee |
|---|---|---|
| Grossenhain | 7 Jan 1917 – 1 Mar 1917 | FEA6 |
| Colmar Nord | 4 Mar 1917 – 12 Apr 1917 | B |
| Ensisheim | 12 Apr 1917 – 7 May 1917 | B |
| Habsheim | 7 May 1917 – 21 Jul 1917 | B |
| Ichteghem-Vyver | 21 Jul 1917 – 18 Sep 1917 | 4 |
| Aertrycke | 18 Sep 1917 – 30 Nov 1917 | 4 |
| Premont | 30 Nov 1917 – 7 Feb 1918 | 2 |
| Emerchicourt | 7 Feb 1918 – 28 Mar 1918 | 17 |
| Favreuil, Bapaume | 28 Mar 1918 – 18 Apr 1918 | 17 |
| Epinoy, Cambrai | 18 Apr 1918 – 28 Aug 1918 | 17 |
| Lieu St Armand | 28 Aug 1918 – 29 Sep 1918 | 17 |
| Bühl, Saarburg | 29 Sep 1918 – 12 Oct 1918 | A |
| Givry, Mons | 12 Oct 1918 – 29 Oct 1918 | 2 |
| Gosselies, Charleroi | 29 Oct 1918 – 11 Nov 1918 | 2 |

# ROYAL PRUSSIAN JAGDSTAFFEL 36

This unit was established on 11 January 1917, through FEA11, pursuant to Kriegs Ministerium von Nr.1425.16g.A.7.L, and was activated at FEA13, Breslau on 21 February 1917. The unit was commanded by Leutnant Albert Dossenbach (nine victories), from Jasta 2, and on 1 March was assigned to the 1 Armee Sector. As is fitting, the first victory for the new Jasta was scored by its Commanding Officer, Leutnant Dossenbach, his tenth, on 5 April. Dossenbach was also the first pilot to attain five victories with the Jasta, on 15 April, and on 2 May he was the first combat casualty, being severely wounded during an Allied bomb attack on this airfield. Command of Jasta 36 passed to Leutnant Walter von Bülow-Bothkamp (13 victories) from Jasta 18. By 4 May the Jasta had been equipped with the Albatros DIII. Jasta 36 departed for the 4 Armee Sector in the Flanders area on 18 June, remaining there until 17 September, when it was sent to the 6 Armee Front for three days, then returned to the 4 Armee. Leutnant Walter von Bülow-Bothkamp was reassigned as Commanding Officer of Jasta Boelcke on 13 December, and Leutnant Heinrich Bongartz (26 victories) succeeded him in command. When Jagdgeschwader III was created in February 1918, Jasta 36 was assigned along with Jastas Boelcke, 26 and 27, under the command of Oberleutnant Bruno Loerzer. The Jasta moved again on 13 March 1918, just before the great German Offensive of 21 March, to the 17 Armee Sector, but moved back to the 4 Armee on 17 April. Leutnant Bongartz was severely wounded on 29 April, and command of Jasta 36 passed to Leutnant Richard Plange (seven victories) from Jasta Boelcke. However, on 19 May Plange was killed in combat, and Leutnant Harry von Bülow-Bothkamp, brother of Walter, replaced him as the commander. On 23 May the unit moved to the 7 Armee Front. The 100th victory for Jasta 36 was scored on 15 July. Leutnant Harry von Bülow-Bothkamp was relieved of front line duties on 14 August, because of being the sole surviving son, and was replaced as Commanding Officer by Leutnant Theodor Quandt (eight victories), who held it until the end of the war. Then on 24 August the Jasta moved to the 17 Armee Sector where it remained for the rest of the war. Jasta 36 claimed 156 victories, but was credited with the confirmed destruction of 120 enemy aircraft, of which 11 were balloons, while losing 12 killed and 11 wounded in combat (one of whom died of wounds), one missing, two prisoners of war, and one injured in flying accidents.

## Commanding Officers

| | | |
|---|---|---|
| Ltn Albert Dossenbach | 22 Feb 1917 – 2 May 1917 | WIA/DOW |
| Ltn Walter v Bülow-Bothkamp | 10 May 1917 – 4 Aug 1917 | Leave |
| Ltn Hans Hoyer | 4 Aug 1917 – 21 Aug 1917 | Acting |
| Ltn Walter v Bülow-Bothkamp | 21 Aug 1917 – 29 Oct 1917 | Leave |
| Ltn Hans Hoyer | 29 Oct 1917 – 7 Nov 1917 | Acting |
| Ltn Walter v Bülow Bothkamp | 7 Nov 1917 – 13 Dec 1918 | CO J Boelcke |
| Ltn Heinrich Bongartz | 13 Dec 1917 – 31 Dec 1917 | Leave |
| Ltn Hans Gottfried v Haebler | 1 Jan 1918 – 21 Jan 1918 | Acting |
| Ltn Heinrich Bongartz | 21 Jan 1918 – 30 Mar 1918 | WIA |
| Ltn Harry v Bülow-Bothkamp | 30 Mar 1918 – 13 Apr 1918 | Acting |
| Ltn Heinrich Bongartz | 13 Apr 1918 – 29 Apr 1918 | WIA |
| Ltn Richard Plange | 30 Apr 1918 – 19 May 1918 | KIA |
| Ltn Harry v Bülow-Bothkamp | 27 May 1918 – 22 Jun 1918 | Leave |
| Ltn Max Fuhnmann | 22 Jun 1918 – 6 Jul 1918 | Acting |
| Ltn Harry v Bülow-Bothkamp | 6 Jul 1918 – 14 Aug 1918 | Leave |
| Ltn Max Fuhrmann | 14 Aug 1918 – 21 Aug 1918 | Acting |
| Ltn Theodor Quandt | 21 Aug 1918 – 11 Nov 1918 | |

## Pilots credited with victories

| | | | |
|---|---|---|---|
| Ltn Heinrich Bongartz | 33 | Ltn Gustav Wandelt* | 2 |
| Ltn Walter von Bülow* | 15(28) | Ltn Willi Daugs | 1(2) |
| Ltn Theodor Quandt | 15 | Ltn Gutsche | 1 |
| Ltn Hans von Haebler* | 8 | Vfw Walter Hoffmann* | 1(3) |
| Ltn Hans Hoyer* | 8 | Ltn Edwin Kreuzer | 1(2) |
| Ltn Harry von Bülow | 6 | Vfw Mayer | 1 |
| Vfw Alfred Hübner | 6 | Vfw Hans Mitzkeit | 1(2) |
| Ltn Kurt Jacob | 6(7) | Flg Möhring | 1 |
| Ltn Albert Dossenbach* | 5(15) | Uffz Reinhold Neumann* | 1 |
| Ltn Hans Böhning | 4(17) | Ltn Egon Patzer | 1(2) |
| Vfw Wilhelm Skworz* | 2 | Ltn Otto Steger | 1(2) |

Ltn Walter von Bülow-Bothkamp killed with Jasta Boelcke. Ltn Albert Dossenbach killed with Jasta 10.

## Airfields occupied

| Location | Inclusive Dates | Armee |
|---|---|---|
| Breslau | 11 Jan 1917 – 24 Feb 1917 | FEA11 |
| Rethel | 24 Feb 1917 – 1 Mar 1917 | AFP3 |
| Le Chatelet | 1 Mar 1917 – 16 Apr 1917 | 3 |
| St Loup | 4 May 1917 – 18 Jun 1917 | 1 |
| Sailly | 19 Jun 1917 – 25 Jun 1917 | 4 |
| Marckebeke | 26 Jun 1917 – 2 Jul 1917 | 4 |
| Kuerne | 3 Jul 1917 – 17 Sep 1917 | 4 |
| Houplin | 18 Sep 1917 – 21 Sep 1917 | 6 |
| Kuerne | 22 Sep 1917 – 13 Mar 1918 | 4 |
| Erchin | 14 Mar 1918 – 16 Apr 1918 | 17 |
| Halluin | 17 Apr 1918 – 22 May 1918 | 4 |
| Vivaise | 23 May 1918 – 6 Jun 1918 | 7 |
| Epitaphe Ferme | 7 Jun 1918 – 18 Jul 1918 | 7 |
| Vauxcère | 19 Jul 1918 – 31 Jul 1918 | 7 |
| Chambry | 1 Aug 1918 – 7 Aug 1918 | 7 |
| Ercheu | 8 Aug 1918 – 10 Aug 1918 | 7 |

| | | |
|---|---|---|
| Chambry | 11 Aug 1918 – 24 Aug 1918 | 7 |
| Emerchicourt | 25 Aug 1918 – 27 Aug 1918 | 17 |
| Aniche | 28 Aug 1918 – 27 Sep 1918 | 17 |
| Lieu St Armand | 28 Sep 1918 – 30 Sep 1918 | 17 |
| Saultain | 1 Oct 1918 – 10 Oct 1918 | 17 |
| Lens, Mons | 11 Oct 1918 – 8 Nov 1918 | 17 |
| Lirm | 9 Nov 1918 – 11 Nov 1918 | 17 |

# ROYAL PRUSSIAN JAGDSTAFFEL 37

Jasta 37 was established 10 January 1917, at FEA8, Graudenz, by authority of Kriegs Ministerium von Nr. 1425.16.g.A.7.L, moving to Möntingen in the Armee-Abteilung 'A' Sector on 10 March under the command of Oberleutnant Kurt Grasshoff from Jasta 15. The first offensive patrol took place on 23 March, and the first victory was scored on 13 April, a balloon flamed by Unteroffizier Simon Ruchser, his first and only kill. Ruchser was severely wounded during the attack. The following day Unteroffizier Hermann Jopp became the first fatality after being shot down in flames by ground fire during a balloon attack near Mont Toulon. On 18 July the Jasta moved to the 4 Armee in Flanders, where it remained until 5 August when a move was made to the 6 Armee Front. Leutnant Ernst Udet was the first pilot to gain five victories with the Jasta by downing his 11th on 24 September. Jasta 37 moved back to the 4 Armee Front on 7 October. Then on 7 November Oberleutnant Grasshoff was appointed commander of Jasta 38, with Leutnant Udet taking command of Jasta 37. The Jasta was transferred to the 2 Armee Front on 15 March 1918, and Leutnant Udet was transferred to the temporary command of Jasta 11 on 24 March, leaving Leutnant Ascan Gustav Gobert in temporary command of Jasta 37. Udet's transfer became permanent on 5 April, and on 16 April Gobert was transferred to AFP 2, with Leutnant Georg Meyer (four victories), from Jasta 7, assuming command of the Jasta until the end of the war. Jasta 37 was credited with at least 74 victories, of which 13 were balloons, while losing seven pilots killed and three wounded in combat, three prisoners of war, and two killed in flying accidents.

## Commanding Officers

| | | |
|---|---|---|
| Oblt Kurt Grasshoff | 10 Mar 1917 – 7 Nov 1917 | CO J38 |
| Ltn Ernst Udet | 7 Nov 1917 – 24 Mar 1918 | CO J11 |
| Ltn Ascan Gustav Gobert | 24 Mar 1918 – 16 Apr 1918 | AFP2 |
| Ltn Georg Meyer | 16 Apr 1918 – 11 Nov 1918 | |

## Pilots credited with victories

| | | | |
|---|---|---|---|
| Ltn Georg Meyer | 20(24) | Vfw Robert Wirth | 2(4) |
| Ltn Ernst Udet | 14(62) | OfStv Fahlke | 1 |
| Ltn Heinrich Henkel | 8 | Ltn Theodor Himmer | 1(2) |
| Ltn Albert Hets* | 6 | Vfw Walter Horn* | 1 |
| Ltn Hans Waldhausen | 6 | Uffz Karl Klein* | 1 |
| Ltn Fritz Blume | 4 | Ltn Mappes | 1 |
| Vfw Ernst Hamster | 3 | Uffz Simon Ruchser | 1 |
| Vfw Baerwald | 2 | Ltn Schöbel | 1 |
| Uffz Gengelin | 2 | Vfw Kurt Schulz | 1 |

## Airfields occupied

| Location | Inclusive Dates | Armee |
|---|---|---|
| Graudenz | 10 Jan 1917 – 10 Mar 1917 | FEA8 |
| Möntingen, Metz | 10 Mar 1917 – 18 Jul 1917 | A |
| Wasquehal | 18 Jul 1917 – 5 Aug 1917 | 4 |
| Phalempin | 5 Aug 1917 – 7 Oct 1917 | 6 |
| Wynghene | 7 Oct 1917 – 15 Mar 1918 | 4 |
| Le Cateau | 15 Mar 1918 – 25 Mar 1918 | 2 |
| Mons-en-Chaussée | 25 Mar 1918 – 11 Apr 1918 | 2 |
| Vraignes | 11 Apr 1918 – 22 Apr 1918 | 2 |
| Foucaucourt | 22 Apr 1918 – 27 Jul 1918 | 2 |
| St Christ | 27 Jul 1918 – 11 Aug 1918 | 2 |
| Vendelles | 11 Aug 1918 – 29 Aug 1918 | 2 |
| Seranvillers | 29 Aug 1918 – 3 Sep 1918 | 2 |
| Bevillers | 3 Sep 1918 – 30 Sep 1918 | 2 |
| Neuville | 30 Sep 1918 – 7 Oct 1918 | 2 |
| Escarmain, Capelle | 7 Oct 1918 – 10 Oct 1918 | 2 |
| Villers-sur-Nicole | 10 Oct 1918 – 11 Nov 1918 | 2 |

## ROYAL PRUSSIAN JAGDSTAFFEL 38

This unit was created through AOK Schultz, by authority of Kriegs Ministerium von Nr.1263.16.A.7.L. on 30 June 1917. It was made up from single-seater pilots from Flg.Abt. 30 and Kampfgeschwader 1, designated as Jagdstaffel 'Vardar' and assigned to the Bulgarian 1 Armee. On 1 July the unit was designated as Jagdstaffel 38. The first Commanding Officer was Oberleutnant Rudolf Böhm, from KG1; however, he contracted malaria on 3 October and temporary command of Jasta 38 passed to Leutnant Renatus Heydacker. Leutnant Theodor Siebold became the first combat casualty on 1 October, being killed over Matnica. The first victory scored for the unit was by Leutnant Heydacker on 29 October, his first. Böhm was transferred to Idflieg on 6 November and command of the Jasta was given to Oberleutnant Kurt Grasshoff, from Jasta 37. Grasshoff was severely wounded during combat with four enemy scouts over Predejci, on 12 June 1918, later dying of these wounds. Leutnant Fritz Thiede (five victories), from Jasta 24s, took over the Jasta for the rest of the war. Jasta 38 was given credit for 18 enemy aircraft destroyed, including two balloons, while suffering the loss of four pilots killed and one wounded in action, and one killed and one injured in flying accidents.

### Commanding Officers

| | | |
|---|---|---|
| Oblt Rudolf Böhm | 8 Jun 1917 – 3 Oct 1917 | Hospital |
| Ltn Renatus Heydacker | 3 Oct 1917 – 6 Nov 1917 | Acting |
| Oblt Rudolf Böhm | 6 Nov 1917 – 6 Nov 1917 | Idflieg |
| Oblt Kurt Grasshoff | 6 Nov 1917 – 12 Jun 1918 | KIA |
| Ltn Fritz Thiede | 28 Jun 1918 – 11 Nov 1918 | |

### Pilots credited with victories

| | | | |
|---|---|---|---|
| Ltn Otto Splitgerber* | 3(6) | Ltn Wilhelm Frickart | 1(12) |
| Ltn Fritz Thiede | 3(8) | Ltn Hösch | 1 |
| Vfw Gnädig | 3 | Ltn Kirscht | 1 |
| Vfw Erich Dürre* | 2 | Vfw Lage | 1 |
| Ltn Renatus Heydacker | 2 | Vfw Meissner | 1(2) |

### Airfields occupied

| Location | Inclusive Dates | Armee |
|---|---|---|
| Mravinca | 30 Jun 1917 – 12 Jul 1918 | 1 Bulgarian |
| Hudova | 12 Jul 1917 – 9 Apr 1918 | 1 Bulgarian |
| Kalkova | 9 Apr 1918 – 11 Nov 1918 | 11 |

## ROYAL PRUSSIAN JAGDSTAFFEL 39

This Jasta was formed through FEA 5, Hannover, on 30 June 1917, in conformance with Kriegs Ministerium von Nr. 1263.6.17.A.7.L. It was assigned to the Armee-Abteilung 'B' Sector on 15 August, under the command of Leutnant August Raben, from Jasta 36. The first flight over the front took place on 26 August, then on 15 September the Jasta departed for the Isonzo Front in Italy, arriving later in the month. The first victory was scored, fittingly enough, by its Commanding Officer on 26 September, also Raben's first. Raben, who later commanded Jasta 18, was also the first combat casualty, being severely wounded by flak on 17 November, and temporary command of the Jasta passed to Leutnant Franz Kerssenbrock (two victories). The first pilot to achieve five victories with the Jasta was Vizefeldwebel Bernhardt Ultsch on 23 November, his eighth. Von Kerssenbrock was killed in combat over Conegliano, on 3 December, and the following day Oberleutnant Josef Loeser, from Jasta 1, assumed command. Loeser, who by now had a score of two, was wounded in combat on 4 February 1918, and Leutnant Johann Hesselink (one victory) took command for the rest of the war. Jasta 39, after having scored 41 times in Italy, returned to the Western Front during March and scored 27 more victories before the end of the war. Jasta 39 received credit for the destruction of 68 enemy aircraft, including 14 balloons, while losing seven killed and five wounded in combat, one captured, and one killed in an accident.

### Commanding Officers

| | | |
|---|---|---|
| Ltn August Raben | 2 Aug 1917 – 17 Nov 1917 | WIA |
| Ltn Franz von Kerssenbrock | 17 Nov 1917 – 3 Dec 1917 | KIA |
| Oblt Josef Loeser | 4 Dec 1917 – 4 Feb 1918 | WIA |
| Ltn Johann Hesselink | 4 Feb 1918 – 11 Nov 1918 | |

### Pilots credited with victories

| | | | |
|---|---|---|---|
| Uffz Franz Nülle | 11 | Ltn Busch | 1 |
| Vfw Ludwig Gaim | 5 | Uffz Dierenfeld | 1 |
| Vfw Wilhelm Hippert | 5(8) | Ltn Gunther Keitsch | 1(3) |
| Ltn Wilhelm Sommer | 5 | Uffz Krüchelsdorf | 1 |
| Vfw Bernhardt Ultsch | 5(12) | Ltn Erwin Kreuzer | 1(2) |
| OfStv Reinhold Jörke | 4(14) | Ltn Langen | 1 |
| Ltn Werner Wagener | 3(5) | Oblt Wolfgang Plüschow | 1 |
| Ltn Rudolf Bertelsmeier | 3(4) | Vfw Alfred Ruesche | 1 |
| Ltn Eduard Hannemann | 3 | Uffz Ruppert | 1 |
| Vfw Alfred Müller | 3 | Vfw Willy Schmidt | 1 |
| Ltn Franz v Kerssenbrock* | 2(4) | Vfw Fritz Schröder* | 1 |
| Oblt Josef Loeser | 2 | Ltn G Schröder | 1 |
| Ltn August Raben | 2(4) | Vfw Fritz Zogmann | 1 |
| Vfw Karl Überschaer* | 2 | | |

### Airfields occupied

| Location | Inclusive Dates | Armee |
|---|---|---|
| Hannover | 30 Jun 1917 – 15 Aug 1917 | FEA5 |
| Ensisheim | 15 Aug 1917 – 15 Sep 1917 | B |
| Campoformidi, Italy | 20 Sep 1917 – 13 Nov 1917 | 14 |
| San Giacomo, Italy | 13 Nov 1917 – 16 Nov 1917 | 14 |
| Roveredo, Italy | 16 Nov 1917 – 18 Nov 1917 | 14 |
| Cervada, Italy | 18 Nov 1917 – 11 Dec 1917 | 14 |
| San Fior, Italy | 11 Dec 1917 – 13 Mar 1918 | 14 |
| St Loup | 28 Mar 1918 – 27 Jun 1918 | 1 |
| Boncourt | 28 Jun 1918 – 4 Aug 1918 | 7 |
| Guesnain | 5 Aug 1918 – 13 Aug 1918 | 17 |
| Bapaume | 13 Aug 1918 – 25 Aug 1918 | 17 |
| Rocourt | 25 Aug 1918 – 1 Sep 1918 | 17 |
| Erre-Somain | 1 Sep 1918 – 26 Sep 1918 | 17 |
| Bühl, Saarburg | 27 Sep 1918 – 11 Nov 1918 | A |

## ROYAL SAXON JAGDSTAFFEL 40

This unit was created 30 June 1917, in accordance with Kriegs Ministerium von Nr.1263.16.17.A.7.L, through FEA 6, Grossenhain, and was formed 15 August 1917. It moved to the Armee-Abteilung 'A' Sector on 18 August, under the command of Oberleutnant Eilers. Another move on 14 September to the Armee-Abteilung 'C' Front, where Leutnant Karl Meierdirks scored the first victory on 25 September, also his first. Also on the 25th, Vizefeldwebel Ludwig Hilz became the first combat casualty when wounded by ground fire. Jasta 40s finished the year with three victories and the loss of two pilots. On 15 March 1918 a move was made to the 17 Armee Sector. Then on 24 April a move to the 4 Armee in Flanders, where Jasta 40s remained for the rest of the war. On 14 April Oberleutnant Eilers was transferred and Leutnant Helmut Dilthey (six victories), from Jasta 27, took command, but on 9 July he was killed in action and command passed to Leutnant Carl Degelow (four victories), from Jasta 7, who had arrived at Jasta 40s on 16 May. Degelow held command until the end of the war. Jasta 40s received credit for at least 54 enemy aircraft destroyed, of which three were balloons, while suffering the loss of five killed and six wounded in combat, and one killed in an accident.

### Commanding Officers

| | | |
|---|---|---|
| Oblt Eilers | 15 Aug 1917 – 14 Apr 1918 | Idflieg |
| Ltn Helmut Dilthey | 14 Apr 1918 – 9 Jul 1918 | KIA |
| Ltn Carl Degelow | 11 Jul 1918 – 11 Nov 1918 | |

### Pilots credited with victories

| | | | |
|---|---|---|---|
| Ltn Carl Degelow | 26(30) | Vfw Rausch | 2 |
| Ltn Hermann Gilly | 7 | Ltn Adolf Auer | 1 |
| Ltn Willy Rosenstein | 6(9) | Ltn Helmut Dilthey | 1(7) |
| Vfw Paul Groll* | 3(4) | Ltn Martin Langer | 1 |
| Ltn Alfred King | 3(4) | Ltn Karl Meierdirks | 1(2) |
| Ltn Hans Jeschonnek | 2 | Unknown | 1 |

| Location | Airfields occupied Inclusive Dates | Armee |
|---|---|---|
| Grossenhain | 30 Jun 1917 – 18 Aug 1917 | FEA8 |
| Möntingen-Metz | 18 Aug 1917 – 14 Sep 1917 | A |
| Mars-la-Tour | 14 Sep 1918 – 15 Mar 1918 | C |
| Masny | 15 Mar 1918 – 6 Apr 1918 | 17 |
| Roubaix | 6 Apr 1918 – 5 May 1918 | 4 |
| Mousecron | 5 May 1918 – 6 Jun 1918 | 4 |
| Lomme | 6 Jun 1918 – 24 Aug 1918 | 4 |
| Halluin-Lille | 24 Aug 1918 – 9 Sep 1918 | 4 |
| Reckem | 9 Sep 1918 – 28 Sep 1918 | 4 |
| Bisseghem | 28 Sep 1918 – 8 Oct 1918 | 4 |
| Meuines, Courtrai | 8 Oct 1918 – 10 Oct 1918 | 4 |
| Wynghene | 10 Oct 1918 – 22 Oct 1918 | 4 |
| Gontrode | 22 Oct 1918 – 5 Nov 1918 | 4 |
| Antwerp | 5 Nov 1918 – 11 Nov 1918 | 4 |

# ROYAL PRUSSIAN JAGDSTAFFEL 41

Jasta 41 came into being on 18 June 1917, as authorised by Kriegs Ministerium von Nr.744.17.g.A.7.L, through FEA 4, Posen. Assigned to Armee-Abteilung 'B' on 5 August, under the command of Oberleutnant Maximilian Ziegler genannt Stege, who was killed at the airfield at Ensisheim on 3 September, the same day the first victory for the unit was gained by Leutnant Walter Kypke, also his first. Leutnant Georg Schlenker (seven victories), from Jasta 3, reported to take command on 6 September. Vizefeldwebel Otto Rosenfeld was the first combat casualty. He was shot down during a balloon attack near Lepuix, and taken prisoner, on 29 December; he later escaped and returned to the Jasta. Leutnant Schlenker became the first pilot to achieve five victories with Jasta 41 on 24 February 1918. The Jasta moved to the 6 Armee Sector on 20 March, and then was transferred to the 7 Armee Front on 6 June. Leutnant Schlenker who now had a score of 14, was severely wounded in combat on 30 September. Leutnant Fritz Höhn (18 victories), the acting commander of Jasta 60, reported to assume command of the Jasta; however, three days later he was killed during combat over St Martin l'Heureux. Leutnant Helmut Brünig (seven victories) from Jasta 50 took command until the end of the war. Jasta 41 was credited with at least 73 victories, including ten balloons, while losing ten killed and three wounded in combat, one taken prisoner, and two killed in flying accidents.

## Commanding Officers

| | | |
|---|---|---|
| Oblt Maximilian Ziegler gen. Stege | 1 Aug 1917 – 3 Sep 1917 | KIAcc |
| Ltn Georg Schlenker | 6 Sep 1917 – 30 Sep 1918 | WIA |
| Ltn Fritz Höhn | 30 Sep 1918 – 3 Oct 1918 | KIA |
| Ltn Helmut Brünig | 3 Oct 1918 – 11 Nov 1918 | |

## Pilots credited with victories

| | | | |
|---|---|---|---|
| Vfw Josef Schwendemann | 17 | Vfw Iversen | 1 |
| Ltn Hans Weiss | 10(16) | Ltn Kollatz | 1 |
| Vfw Otto Rosenfeld* | 9(13) | Ltn Georg Michaelis* | 1 |
| Ltn Georg Schlenker | 7(14) | Vfw Ludwig Reimann | 1(2) |
| Ltn Albert Dietlen | 5(9) | Vfw Hermann Reisch* | 1 |
| Ltn Walter Kypke | 4(9) | Ltn Franz Schleiff | 1(12) |
| Ltn Erich Raabe | 4 | Ltn Josef Strauch | 1 |
| Ltn Fritz Höhn | 3(21) | Vfw Weimar | 1(3) |
| Ltn Wilhelm Schulz | 3(6) | Unknown | 1 |
| Vfw Bochmann | 1 | Unknown | 1 |

## Airfields occupied

| Location | Inclusive Dates | Armee |
|---|---|---|
| Posen | 18 Jun 1917 – 5 Aug 1917 | FEA4 |
| Habsheim | 5 Aug 1917 – 20 Mar 1918 | B |
| Phalempin | 21 Mar 1918 – 13 Apr 1918 | 6 |
| Gondecourt | 13 Apr 1918 – 5 Jun 1918 | 6 |
| Arcy, Rugny Ferme | 6 Jun 1918 – 5 Jul 1918 | 7 |
| Coincy | 5 Jul 1918 – 20 Jul 1918 | 7 |
| Montbanis Ferme | 20 Jul 1918 – 23 Jul 1918 | 7 |
| Sissone | 23 Jul 1918 – 5 Aug 1918 | 7 |
| Boncourt | 5 Aug 1918 – 22 Sep 1918 | 7 |

| Leffincourt | 23 Sep 1918 – 27 Sep 1918 | 3 |
| Attigny | 27 Sep 1918 – 8 Oct 1918 | 3 |
| Chéméry | 8 Oct 1918 – 20 Oct 1918 | 3 |
| Medard | 20 Oct 1918 – 11 Nov 1918 | 18 |

## ROYAL PRUSSIAN JAGDSTAFFEL 42

Created through FEA 3, Gotha, by authority of Kriegs Ministerium von Nr. 744.17.g.A.7.L on 6 December 1917, Jasta 42 was assigned to Armee-Abteilung 'C' on 19 December, under the command of Leutnant Karl Odebrett (seven victories). The first combat casualty occurred as Vizefeldwebel Ernst Höfer was wounded on 5 February 1918, and the first Jasta victory was scored on 17 February, by Unteroffizier Freter, his first. Then on 23 March the Jasta departed for the 7 Armee Sector, remaining there until 16 April, then moving on to the 18 Armee Sector, where they were at the end of the war. Odebrett was the first pilot to attain five victories with Jasta 42 on 4 May, his own 12th. Also, Odebrett was one of the very few officers to head a Jasta from the time of its inception to the end of the war, with only a short time off for leave. Jasta 42 received credit for the destruction of at least 27 victories, suffering the loss of four pilots killed and one wounded in action plus one prisoner of war.

### Commanding Officers

| Ltn Karl Odebrett | 15 Dec 1917 – 8 Jul 1918 | Leave |
| Ltn Stickforth | 8 Jul 1918 – 29 Jul 1918 | Acting |
| Ltn Karl Odebrett | 29 Jul 1918 – 11 Nov 1918 | |

### Pilots credited with victories

| Ltn Karl Odebrett | 9(16) | Uffz Zell | 2 |
| Vfw Walter Beyer | 4 | Vfw Gondermann | 1(2) |
| Uffz Lohrmann | 3 | Ltn Fritz Imme | 1 |
| Vfw Willy Schmelter | 3 | Vfw Gustak Kowallik | 1 |
| Uffz Freter | 2 | Vfw Heinz Stock | 1 |

### Airfields occupied

| Location | Inclusive Dates | Armee |
| --- | --- | --- |
| Gotha | 6 Dec 1917 – 19 Dec 1917 | FEA3 |
| Mars-la-Tour | 19 Dec 1917 – 23 Mar 1918 | C |
| Froidmont | 26 Mar 1918 – 16 Apr 1918 | 7 |
| Ercheu | 17 Apr 1918 – 29 May 1918 | 18 |
| Grécourt | 30 May 1918 – 15 Aug 1918 | 18 |
| Clastres | 16 Aug 1918 – Sep 1918 | 18 |
| Parpeville | Sep 1918 – Sep 1918 | 18 |
| Le Brule | Sep 1918 – Oct 1918 | 18 |
| Bois St Dénis | Oct 1918 – Oct 1918 | 18 |
| Thuilles | Oct 1918 – 11 Nov 1918 | 18 |

## ROYAL PRUSSIAN JAGDSTAFFEL 43

This Jasta was authorised by Kriegs Ministerium von Nr. 744.17.g.A.7.L on 6 December 1917, through FEA 4, Posen, and was assigned to the Armee-Abteilung 'A' Sector. The Commanding Officer was Leutnant Wilhelm Flecken (three victories), from Jasta 20. The first offensive patrol took place on 21 January 1918. Then on 2 February the front of Armee-Abteilung 'A' was split and Jasta 43, remaining at the same airfield, came under the 19 Armee. Leutnant Niebecker was the first pilot to score, gaining his second victory, the Jasta's first, on 11 February. The Jasta departed the 19 Armee on 29 March and arrived at its destination in the 6 Armee on 3 April. Leutnant Flecken was transferred to AFP F, Palestine, during May, and Oberleutnant Adolf Gutknecht (one victory), from Jasta 33, assumed command. On 8 August, Gutknecht became the first pilot to score five victories with Jasta 43. When Gutknecht became ill and was admitted to the hospital on 2 November, Leutnant Guido Schobinger assumed temporary command to the end of the war. During the latter months the Jasta was known to have been equipped with the Fokker DVII and Pfalz DXII. Jasta 43 received credit for 36 enemy aircraft destroyed, two of which were balloons, while losing six killed and five wounded in combat, one prisoner of war, and two killed in flying accidents.

## Commanding Officers

| | | |
|---|---|---|
| Ltn Wilhelm Flecken | 1 Nov 1917 – 9 Mar 1918 | Leave |
| Ltn Otto Creuzmann | 9 Mar 1918 – 20 Mar 1918 | Acting |
| Ltn Wilhelm Flecken | 20 Mar 1918 – May 1918 | Palestine |
| Oblt Adolf Gutknecht | May 1918 – 2 Nov 1918 | Hospital |
| Ltn Guido Schobinger | 2 Nov 1918 – 11 Nov 1918 | Acting |

## Pilots credited with victories

| | | | |
|---|---|---|---|
| Ltn Josef Raesch | 7 | Vfw Wilhelm Börlinghaus* | 1 |
| Oblt Adolf Gutknecht | 7(8) | Vfw Karl Burberg | 1 |
| Vfw Ernst Wiehle | 5(6) | Ltn Flecken | 1(4) |
| Ltn Otto Creutzmann | 3(8) | Ltn Friedrich Jakobs | 1 |
| Vfw Max Kiep | 3 | Ltn Josef Keller | 1 |
| Vfw Otto Wandelt* | 3 | Ltn Robert Schmidt | 1 |
| Ltn Niebecker | 2(3) | Ltn Guido Schobinger | 1 |
| Uffz Paul Rüggeberg | 2 | Vfw Julius Trotzky* | 1(2) |
| Gefr Walter Blumensaath | 1 | | |

## Airfields occupied

| Location | Inclusive Dates | Armee |
|---|---|---|
| Posen | 6 Dec 1917 – 21 Dec 1917 | FEA4 |
| Möntingen, Metz | 21 Dec 1917 – 2 Feb 1918 | A |
| Möntingen, Metz | 2 Feb 1918 – 9 Mar 1918 | 19 |
| Mörchingen | 9 Mar 1918 – 29 Mar 1918 | 19 |
| Avelin | 3 Apr 1918 – Apr 1918 | 6 |
| Gondecourt | Apr 1918 – 20 May 1918 | 6 |
| Haubourdin, Lille | 20 May 1918 – 22 Aug 1918 | 6 |
| Seclin | 22 Aug 1918 – 8 Oct 1918 | 6 |
| Grand Metz | 8 Oct 1918 – 11 Oct 1918 | 6 |
| Cysoing | 11 Oct 1918 – 9 Nov 1918 | 6 |
| Berghem, Brussels | 9 Nov 1918 – 10 Nov 1918 | 6 |
| Brussels | 10 Nov 1918 – 11 Nov 1918 | 6 |

# ROYAL SAXON JAGDSTAFFEL 44

Created on 11 December 1917, through FEA 6, Grossenhain, pursuant to Kriegs Ministerium von Nr.744.17.g.A.7.L. and mobilized on 23 December under the command of Leutnant Max Raspe (one victory), from Jasta 21. The Jasta was assigned to the 3 Armee Sector on 26 December. On 14 February 1918, Leutnant Raspe was severely injured during a test flight, and the following day temporary command passed to Leutnant Alfred Freytag. The Jasta moved to the 18 Armee Front on 8 March. Unteroffizier Brinkmann was the first combat casualty when shot down and taken prisoner, flying Albatros DVa 6691/17, south of St Quentin, on 18 March. Freytag was credited with the Jasta's first confirmed victory, also his first, on 30 March. Leutnant Raspe was transferred, and Leutnant Paul Lotz (four victories) arrived from Jasta 7 to take command on 10 June. Lotz became the first pilot to attain five victories with Jasta 44, while getting his ninth on 5 October. Lotz was killed during a test flight on 23 October at the airfield at Donstiennes, and Leutnant von Borries, of Jasta 22, was named as his replacement for the rest of the war. The pilots of Jasta 43 managed to down 20 enemy aircraft, of which four were balloons, while losing three pilots killed and two wounded in combat, two taken prisoner, and two killed and one injured in flying accidents.

## Commanding Officers

| | | |
|---|---|---|
| Ltn Max Raspe | 12 Dec 1917 – 14 Feb 1918 | Injured |
| Ltn Albert Freytag | 14 Feb 1918 – 1918 | Acting |
| Ltn Max Raspe | – 10 Jun 1918 | Trans |
| Ltn Paul Lotz | 10 Jun 1918 – 23 Oct 1918 | KIAcc |
| Ltn von Borries | 26 Oct 1918 – 11 Nov 1918 | |

## Pilots credited with victories

| | | | |
|---|---|---|---|
| Ltn Paul Lotz | 6(10) | Vfw Borges | 1 |
| Uffz Bernard Bartels | 5 | Ltn Breidenbach | 1 |
| OfStv Bansmer | 2 | Ltn Alfred Freytag | 1 |
| Vfw Becker | 2 | Uffz Kretschmar | 1 |
| Ltn Walter Balzer* | 1 | | |

### Airfields occupied

| Location | Inclusive Dates | Armee |
|---|---|---|
| Grossenhain | 11 Dec 1917 – 26 Dec 1917 | FEA6 |
| Leffincourt | 26 Dec 1917 – 8 Mar 1918 | 3 |
| Pleine-Selve | 8 Mar 1918 – 8 Apr 1918 | 18 |
| Ercheu | 9 Apr 1918 – 8 Aug 1918 | 18 |
| Foucaucourt | 8 Aug 1918 – 10 Aug 1918 | 18 |
| Flez-Suisaucourt | 10 Aug 1918 – 26 Aug 1918 | 18 |
| Faucouzy | 27 Aug 1918 – 9 Oct 1918 | 18 |
| La Chaussée | 10 Oct 1918 – 18 Oct 1918 | 18 |
| Donstiennes | 19 Oct 1918 – 11 Nov 1918 | 18 |

## ROYAL PRUSSIAN JAGDSTAFFEL 45

Jasta 45 was formed through FEA1, Altenberg, on 11 December 1917, in accordance with Kriegs Ministerium von Nr. 744.17.g.A.7.L. and on 23 December departed for the Front where it settled in the 5 Armee Sector on 25 December. The first and only Commanding Officer was Leutnant Hans-Joachim Rolfes (one victory), from FEA9, who had served with Jasta 32. The first flight over the lines occurred on 9 January 1918, and on the 20th, appropriately, Rolfes gained the first Jasta victory. Unteroffizier Erich Meyer was the first pilot to attain five victories, getting his fifth on 1 June. On 29 September, Leutnant Rolfes, in addition to his command of Jasta 45, was named as commander of Jagdgruppe Ost. During a brief absence for testing new aircraft from 11 October, until 10 November, the Jasta was under the temporary command of Leutnant Lothar Zencominierski. The last offensive patrol occurred on 30 October carried out by Leutnant Gustav Dörr, Leutnant Ulrich Könnemann, and Gefreiter Kruse, at 1650 hours. Leutnant Rolfes was one of the very few pilots to command a Jasta from its inception to the end of the war. Jasta 45 was given credit for at least 113 enemy aircraft destroyed, including 28 balloons, while losing four killed and five wounded in combat, and two injured in flying accidents.

### Commanding Officers

| | | |
|---|---|---|
| Ltn Hans Rolfes | 17 Dec 1917 – 11 Oct 1918 | Testing |
| Ltn Lothar Zencominierski | 11 Oct 1918 – 10 Nov 1918 | Acting |
| Ltn Hans Rolfes | 10 Nov 1918 – 11 Nov 1918 | |

### Pilots credited with victories

| | | | |
|---|---|---|---|
| Ltn Gustav Dörr | 35 | Ltn Krayer | 3 |
| Vfw Karl Schlegel* | 22 | Ltn Lothar Zencominierski | 3 |
| Ltn Hans Rolfes | 16(17) | Vfw Günther Dobberke | 2(8) |
| Ltn Konrad Brendle* | 8 | Ltn Meixner | 2 |
| Uffz Erich Meyer | 5 | Vfw Stein | 2 |
| Gefr Johann Schlimpen* | 5 | Ltn Arno Benzler | 1(9) |
| Ltn Ulrich Könnemann | 4 | Vfw Otto Bieleit | 1(5) |
| Ltn Berling | 3 | Ltn Bleibtreu | 1 |

### Airfields occupied

| Location | Inclusive Dates | Armee |
|---|---|---|
| Altenberg | 11 Dec 1917 – 24 Dec 1917 | FEA1 |
| Marville | 25 Dec 1917 – 25 Mar 1918 | 5 |
| Cohartville | 31 Mar 1918 – 18 Apr 1918 | 7 |
| Vivaise | 18 Apr 1918 – 18 May 1918 | 7 |
| Sissone | 18 May 1918 – 30 May 1918 | 7 |
| Mont St Martin | 30 May 1918 – 3 Jun 1918 | 7 |
| Rocourt, St Martin | 3 Jun 1918 – 6 Jun 1918 | 7 |
| Arcy | 6 Jun 1918 – 19 Jul 1918 | 7 |
| Mont Notre Dame | 19 Jul 1918 – 26 Jul 1918 | 7 |
| Maizy | 26 Jul 1918 – 11 Oct 1918 | 7 |
| Plomion | 11 Oct 1918 – 31 Oct 1918 | 7 |
| Boulers | 31 Oct 1918 – 11 Nov 1918 | 7 |

## ROYAL PRUSSIAN JAGDSTAFFEL 46

This unit was created on 11 December 1917, pursuant to Kriegs Ministerium von Nr.744.17.g.A.7.L., through FEA 8, Graudenz, and activated on 25 December, being assigned to the 6 Armee. Jasta 46 was commanded by Leutnant Rudolf Matthaei (nine victories) from Jasta 5. On 7 February 1918, the Jasta became part of Jagdgruppe Nord with Jastas 18 and 57. The Jasta's first victory came on 16 February, Vizefeldwebel Robert Heibert scoring his second. Vizefeldwebel Artur Weber was killed during combat with a Camel at 1140 hours over Carvin on 21 February, the unit's first combat casualty. Jasta 46 was transferred to the 2 Armee on 12 March, where it remained for the rest of the war. Heibert became the first pilot to attain five victories with Jasta 46 on 23 March. After Leutnant Matthaei, who had added one to his score, was killed in a crash at Liéramont, while testing an aircraft on 17 April, Oberleutnant Josef Loeser reported to replace him as Commanding Officer. Loeser was shot down in flames during combat with RE8s north of Hamel on 3 June and command of the Jasta passed to Leutnant Otto Creutzmann (four victories), from Jasta 43, who held it to the end of the war. The pilots of Jasta 46 were given credit for at least 50 victories, of which 20 were balloons, while losing ten pilots killed and two wounded in action, and one killed in a flying accident.

| Commanding Officers | | |
|---|---|---|
| Ltn Rudolf Matthaei | 25 Dec 1917 – 17 Apr 1918 | KIAcc |
| Oblt Josef Loeser | 23 Apr 1918 – 3 Jun 1918 | KIA |
| Ltn Otto Creutzmann | 5 Jun 1918 – 11 Nov 1918 | |

| Pilots credited with victories | | | |
|---|---|---|---|
| Ltn Oskar Hennrich | 20 | Vfw Kautz | 2 |
| Ltn Robert Heibert | 12(13) | Uffz Frölich | 1 |
| Ltn Helmut Steinbrecher | 5 | Uffz Erich Gürgenz | 1 |
| Ltn Otto Creutzmann | 3(8) | Ltn Rudolf Matthaei | 1(10) |
| Ltn auf den Haar | 3 | Vfw Schneevogel | 1 |

| Airfields occupied | | |
|---|---|---|
| **Location** | **Inclusive Dates** | **Armee** |
| Graudenz | 11 Dec 1917 – 29 Dec 1917 | FEA8 |
| Ascq-Lille | 29 Dec 1917 – 12 Mar 1918 | 6 |
| Bévillers | 12 Mar 1918 – 23 Mar 1918 | 2 |
| Liéramont | 23 Mar 1918 – 31 Jul 1918 | 2 |
| Moislains | 31 Jul 1918 – Oct 1918 | 2 |
| Villers-sur-Nicole | Oct 1918 – 11 Nov 1918 | 2 |

# ROYAL WÜRTTEMBERG JAGDSTAFFEL 47

Created through FEA 10, Böblingen, in accordance with Kriegs Ministerium von Nr. 744.17.g.A.7.L. on 16 December 1917, and activated on 26 December under the command of Leutnant Walter Kypke (six victories), from Kest 5. Kypke would be one of the very few pilots to command a Jasta from the time of its creation to the end of the war. The Jasta was assigned to Jagdgruppe 4, along with Jastas Boelcke, 26, 27 and 36, in the 4 Armee Sector of Flanders. On 3 February 1918, when Jagdgeschwader III was created from the Jastas of JGr4, Jasta 47w was not included and became an independent unit. The first flight over the lines occurred on 6 March, and the first Jasta victory was scored by Vizefeldwebel Friedrich Ehmann, his first, on 11 March. The Jasta was transferred to the 6 Armee Sector on 29 March, and the Jasta's first combat casualty was Vizefeldwebel Erich Kauffmann, who was killed during combat on 22 April. On 5 May Jasta 47w moved back to the 4 Armee, where Vfw Ehmann became the first pilot to attain five victories on 11 May. Then on 30 May the Jasta returned to the 6 Armee Front, from where on 6 June it was transferred to 2 Armee. Then on 9 July another move was made to the 3 Armee, where the Jasta was at the end of the war. Jasta 47w was credited with at least 16 victories, while suffering the loss of three killed and three wounded in combat, one prisoner of war, and one injured in a flying accident.

| Commanding Officer | |
|---|---|
| Ltn Walter Kypke | 26 Dec 1917 – 11 Nov 1918 |

| Pilots credited with victories | | | |
|---|---|---|---|
| Vfw Friedrich Ehmann | 8 | Ltn Hävernik | 2 |
| Ltn Walter Kypke | 3(9) | Ltn Georg Balz | 1 |
| Uffz Gebhardt | 2 | | |

| Airfields occupied | | |
|---|---|---|
| **Location** | **Inclusive Dates** | **Armee** |
| Böblingen | 16 Dec 1917 – 24 Dec 1917 | FEA10 |
| Harlebeke | 29 Dec 1917 – 8 Mar 1918 | 4 |

| Beveren | 9 Mar 1918 – 28 Mar 1918 | 4 |
| Faches | 29 Mar 1918 – 4 May 1918 | 6 |
| Lomme | 5 May 1918 – 30 May 1918 | 4 |
| Faches | 31 May 1918 – 5 Jun 1918 | 6 |
| Ennemain | 6 Jun 1918 – 8 Jul 1918 | 2 |
| St Marie-à-Py | 9 Jul 1918 – 7 Oct 1918 | 3 |
| Chéméry | 8 Oct 1918 – 22 Oct 1918 | 3 |
| Medard | 23 Oct 1918 – 11 Nov 1918 | 18 |

## ROYAL PRUSSIAN JAGDSTAFFEL 48

Authorised by Kriegs Ministerium von Nr.744.16.g.A.7.L., through FEA11 Brieg-Breslau, on 16 December 1917, the Jasta was commanded by Leutnant Kurt Küppers (five victories), from Jasta 6. The Jasta departed for the front on 1 January 1918, arriving at its airfield in the 18 Armee Sector on 5 January, and the first over-the-front flight was made a week later. Leutnant Karl Stock was the first casualty, being killed during combat near Villers-Outreaux, on 3 February. Leutnant Küppers was the first to score for Jasta 48 when he got his sixth on 6 March. On 9 July the unit moved to the 3 Armee Sector, and from there to the 7 Armee on 25 July. Küppers was reassigned to Idflieg on 23 August and Leutnant Walter Stock (three victories) assumed command. Then on 25 September Jasta 48 moved to the 3 Armee where it was when the war ended. The exact number of casualties or victories credited to Jasta 48 is unknown, as no records are available after 31 August 1918; however, it is known that up to that time six victories were scored, while there were five killed and one wounded in combat, one prisoner of war, and two killed in flying accidents.

| Commanding Officers | | |
|---|---|---|
| Ltn Kurt Küppers | 14 Dec 1917 – 23 Aug 1918 | Idflieg |
| Ltn Walter Stock | 23 Aug 1918 – 11 Nov 1918 | |

| Pilots credited with victories | | | |
|---|---|---|---|
| Ltn Kurt Küppers | 1 (6) | Uffz Hellmuth Krätzschmer | 1 |
| Ltn Carl Galetschky | 1 (2) | Vfw Paul Müller | 1 |
| Uffz Karl Heidelberg* | 1 | Ltn Ernst Schulze* | 1 |

| | Airfields occupied | |
|---|---|---|
| **Location** | **Inclusive Dates** | **Armee** |
| Breslau | 16 Dec 1917 – 5 Jan 1918 | FEA11 |
| Guise | 5 Jan 1918 – 20 Mar 1918 | 18 |
| Mont d'Origny | 20 Mar 1918 – 29 Mar 1918 | 18 |
| Villeselve | 29 Mar 1918 – 7 Apr 1918 | 18 |
| Moyencourt | 7 Apr 1918 – 9 Jul 1918 | 18 |
| Mars-sous-Bourcq | 9 Jul 1918 – 25 Jul 1918 | 3 |
| Vivaise | 25 Jul 1918 – 25 Sep 1918 | 7 |
| Chuffilly | 25 Sep 1918 – 9 Oct 1918 | 3 |
| Malmy-Chéméry | 9 Oct 1918 – 3 Nov 1918 | 3 |
| Antrecourt, Attigny | 3 Nov 1918 – 11 Nov 1918 | 3 |

## ROYAL PRUSSIAN JAGDSTAFFEL 49

This Jasta was created through FEA12, Cottbus, as authorised by Kriegs Ministerium von Nr.744.17.g.A.7.L. on 23 December 1917, and Leutnant Franz Ray (nine victories), from Jasta 28w, was named the Commanding Officer, a position he held until the end of the war. The unit was mobilized 9 January 1918, and sent to the 6 Armee Sector. The first flight over the lines came on 17 February, then Flieger Langenheim was wounded in combat on 8 March for the Jasta's first casualty. Fittingly, the first victory was gained by Leutnant Ray, his tenth, on 27 March. On 3 April a move was made to the Flanders area with the 4 Armee. After a few weeks, on 28 May, the Jasta was sent back to the 6 Armee Front. It remained there only eight days before reporting to the 2 Armee Sector, on 6 June. Leutnant Ray became the first pilot to obtain five victories with Jasta 49, his 14th, on 2 July. Then on 8 July the Jasta moved to the 3 Armee Front where it remained for the rest of the war. Leutnant Ray was directed to report to Berlin-Adlershof to test some new type aircraft on 22 October, and temporary command was given to Leutnant Hermann Habich (seven victories). Jasta 49 was given credit for the destruction of at least 28 enemy aircraft, including one balloon, while suffering the loss of one pilot killed and two wounded in combat and one killed in an accident.

### Commanding Officers

| | | |
|---|---|---|
| Ltn Franz Ray | 15 Dec 1917 – 22 Oct 1918 | Testing |
| Ltn Hermann Habich | 22 Oct 1918 – 11 Nov 1918 | Acting |

### Pilots credited with victories

| | | | |
|---|---|---|---|
| Ltn Franz Ray | 8(17) | Vfw Ernst | 1 |
| Ltn Alois Brandenstein | 8 | Gefr Kämmer | 1 |
| Ltn Hermann Habich | 7 | Ltn Thiel | 1 |
| Ltn Felix Bornträger | 2 | | |

### Airfields occupied

| Location | Inclusive Dates | Armee |
|---|---|---|
| Cottbus | 23 Dec 1917 – 12 Jan 1918 | FEA12 |
| Villers Campeau | 13 Jan 1918 – 2 Apr 1918 | 6 |
| Monveaux | 3 Apr 1918 – 27 May 1918 | 4 |
| Lomme | 28 May 1918 – 5 Jun 1918 | 6 |
| Ennemain | 6 Jun 1918 – 7 Jul 1918 | 2 |
| Blaise | 8 Jul 1918 – 6 Oct 1918 | 3 |
| Chémery | 7 Oct 1918 – 21 Oct 1918 | 3 |
| Medard | 22 Oct 1918 – 11 Nov 1918 | 18 |

## ROYAL PRUSSIAN JAGDSTAFFEL 50

Jasta 50 was established through FEA13, Bromberg, by authority of Kriegs Ministerium von Nr.744.17.g.A.7.L., on 23 December 1917, and was equipped with the Albatros DIII. The Jasta was sent to the 7 Armee Sector on 11 January 1918, where the Commanding Officer, Leutnant Heinrich Arntzen (six victories) from Jasta 15, assumed command. The first flight over the Front came on 25 January, the date that Arntzen, most fittingly as commander, scored the Jasta's first victory, his seventh. Vizefeldwebel Josef Kettel became the first casualty being killed during combat with an AWFK8 over La Fère on 29 January. Arntzen also became the first pilot to score five times, when he claimed his 11th on 23 April, but he failed to score again before he was severely wounded by flak over Villosnes, on 27 May. Leutnant Stoltenhoff took temporary command of the unit until the arrival of Leutnant Hans von Freden (four victories) from Jasta 1. Von Freden held this position until the end of the war. Jasta 50 was equipped with the Fokker DVII by 28 August. On 25 September Jasta 50 moved to the 3 Armee Sector, where it remained until 20 October, when it was sent to the 18 Armee Front. Pilots of Jasta 50 received credit for downing at least 46 enemy aircraft, of which 14 were balloons, while losing five killed and one wounded in combat, and three prisoners of war.

### Commanding Officers

| | | |
|---|---|---|
| Ltn Heinrich Arntzen | 13 Jan 1918 – 27 May 1918 | WIA |
| Ltn Stoltenhoff | 27 May 1918 – 17 Jun 1918 | Acting |
| Ltn Hans von Freden | 17 Jun 1918 – 4 Aug 1918 | Leave |
| Ltn Helmut Brünig | 4 Aug 1918 – 6 Sep 1918 | Acting |
| Ltn Hans von Freden | 6 Sep 1918 – 11 Nov 1918 | |

### Pilots credited with victories

| | | | |
|---|---|---|---|
| Ltn Hans von Freden | 16(20) | Uffz Karl Gräper | 1 |
| Ltn Helmut Brünig | 7 | Ltn Rudolf Kommoss* | 1(2) |
| Ltn Heinrich Arntzen | 5(11) | Ltn von Melle | 1 |
| Ltn Maletski | 4 | Gefr Röhr | 1 |
| Ltn Buddeberg | 3 | Uffz Steinsträter | 1 |
| Ltn Gerhard Schulte | 3 | Uffz Vahldieck | 1 |
| Ltn Wilhelm Kohlbach | 2(5) | | |

### Airfields occupied

| Location | Inclusive Dates | Armee |
|---|---|---|
| Bromberg | 22 Dec 1917 – 10 Jan 1918 | FEA13 |
| Autremencourt | 11 Jan 1918 – 14 Mar 1918 | 7 |
| Marchais | 15 Mar 1918 – 29 May 1918 | 7 |
| Mont St Martin | 30 May 1918 – 7 Jun 1918 | 7 |
| Rocourt, St Martin | 8 Jun 1918 – 19 Jul 1918 | 7 |
| Rugny Ferme | 20 Jul 1918 – 22 Jul 1918 | 7 |
| Montbanis Ferme | 23 Jul 1918 – 29 Jul 1918 | 7 |
| Perles | 30 Jul 1918 – 20 Aug 1918 | 7 |

| Sissone | 21 Aug 1918 – 22 Sep 1918 | 7 |
| Boncourt | 23 Sep 1918 – 24 Sep 1918 | 7 |
| Leffincourt | 25 Sep 1918 – 27 Sep 1917 | 3 |
| Attigny | 28 Sep 1918 – 8 Oct 1918 | 3 |
| Chéméry | 9 Oct 1918 – 16 Oct 1918 | 3 |
| Morville | 17 Oct 1918 – 26 Oct 1918 | 18 |
| St Gérard | 27 Oct 1918 – 11 Nov 1918 | 18 |

## ROYAL PRUSSIAN JAGDSTAFFEL 51

This Jasta was created through FEA14, pursuant to Kriegs Ministerium von Nr.744.17.g.A.7.L. on 27 December 1917, under the command of Oberleutnant Hans-Eberhardt Gandert (two victories), who had been Jagdflieger commander on the Eastern Front. On 4 January 1918, the Jasta was assigned to Jagdgruppe Dixmuiden (Jastas 7, 16b and 51) in the 4 Armee Sector. On 1 March, Oberleutnant Gandert was given command of Jagdgruppe 6 in addition to Jasta 51. Leutnant Heinrich Mindner was killed in action 8 March, the first Jasta casualty. The unit's first victory came on 14 March, Unteroffizier Ernst Binkenstein obtaining his first victory. Oberleutnant Gandert was the first pilot to achieve five victories, getting his own eighth on 28 August. Gandert was shot down and wounded during a balloon attack on 29 September, and taken prisoner. Leutnant Karl Plauth (ten victories), from Jasta 20, arrived to take command of Jasta 51 the same day, and held that position until the end of the war. Jasta 51 was credited with at least 24 victories, while losing 12 pilots killed and two wounded in combat, two prisoners of war, and one injured in a flying accident.

### Commanding Officers

| Oblt Hans-Eberhardt Gandert | 27 Dec 1917 – 29 Sep 1918 | POW |
| Ltn Karl Plauth | 29 Sep 1918 – 11 Nov 1918 | |

### Pilots credited with victories

| Karl Plauth | 7(17) | Ltn Feuereissen | 2 |
| Oblt Eberhardt Gandert | 6(8) | Vfw Kurt Beinecke | 1 |
| Ltn Ernst Pabst | 4 | Ltn Karl Berr | 1 |
| Uffz Ernst Binkenstein* | 3 | | |

### Airfields occupied

| Location | Inclusive Dates | Armee |
|---|---|---|
| | 27 Dec 1917 – 4 Jan 1918 | FEA14 |
| Aertrycke | 4 Jan 1918 – 10 Jan 1918 | 4 |
| Wynghene | 10 Jan 1918 – 1 Feb 1918 | 4 |
| Jabbeke | 1 Feb 1918 – 5 Feb 1918 | 4 |
| Aertrycke | 5 Feb 1918 – 1 Mar 1918 | 4 |
| Iseghem | 1 Mar 1918 – 21 Mar 1918 | 4 |
| Abeele | 21 Mar 1918 – 29 Mar 1918 | 4 |
| Iseghem | 29 Mar 1918 – 23 Apr 1918 | 4 |
| St Marguerite | 23 Apr 1918 – 6 Jun 1918 | 4 |
| Rumbeke East | 6 Jun 1918 – 30 Sep 1918 | 4 |
| Menin | 30 Sep 1918 – 11 Nov 1918 | 4 |

## ROYAL PRUSSIAN JAGDSTAFFEL 52

This unit was created on 27 December 1917, through FEA7, Braunschweig, in accordance with Kriegs Ministerium von Nr.744.17.g.A.7.L. under the command of Leutnant Paul Billik (eight victories) from Jasta 7. Jasta 52 was activated on 9 January 1918, and on 14 January was stationed at Pecq, in the 6 Armee Sector. A move was made to Bersée on 7 February. Gefreiter Walther Condereit became the first combat casualty being killed near Lens on 6 March. As it should be, the Commanding Officer, Billik, was the first to score for the Jasta when he got his ninth on 9 March, and by 7 April he became the first pilot to reach five victories with the unit, by scoring his 13th. Leutnant Billik was forced down behind Allied lines and taken prisoner on 10 August, and command of Jasta 52 was assumed by Oberleutnant Beerendonk (one victory), from Jasta 74, for the rest of the war. Jasta 52 had seen action on the 6 Armee Front during their entire time in action, and was given credit for the destruction of at least 43 aircraft, while suffering the loss of eight pilots killed and one wounded in combat, one prisoner of war, and one injured in a flying accident.

## Commanding Officers

| | | |
|---|---|---|
| Ltn Paul Billik | 24 Dec 1917 – 10 Aug 1918 | POW |
| ? | 10 Aug 1918 – 20 Aug 1918 | Acting |
| Oblt Beerendonk | 20 Aug 1918 – 11 Nov 1918 | |

## Pilots credited with victories

| | | | |
|---|---|---|---|
| Ltn Paul Billik | 23(31) | Vfw Rudolf Lander | 1(2) |
| Vfw Hermann Juhnke | 5 | Vfw Michael Lüderitz* | 1(2) |
| Sgt Murat Schumm | 5(7) | Vfw Paul Reimann* | 1 |
| Ltn Kurt Legel* | 2 | Ltn Robert Schwartz | 1 |
| Gefr Anton Wadowski* | 2 | Vfw Otto Sowa | 1(4) |
| Ltn Becker | 1 | Ltn Wilhelm Saint Mont* | 1 |

## Airfields occupied

| Location | Inclusive Dates | Armee |
|---|---|---|
| Braunschweig | 29 Dec 1917 – 13 Jan 1918 | FEA7 |
| Pecq | 14 Jan 1918 – 6 Feb 1918 | 6 |
| Bersée | 7 Feb 1918 – 13 Apr 1918 | 6 |
| Provin | 14 Apr 1918 – 21 Apr 1918 | 6 |
| Gondecourt, Lille | 22 Apr 1918 – 21 Aug 1918 | 6 |
| Bersée | 22 Aug 1918 – 29 Sep 1918 | 6 |
| Auchy | 30 Sep 1918 – 14 Oct 1918 | 6 |
| Tourpes | 15 Oct 1918 – 30 Oct 1918 | 6 |
| Hove | 31 Oct 1918 – 11 Nov 1918 | 6 |

# ROYAL PRUSSIAN JAGDSTAFFEL 53

This Jasta was created through FEA9, Darmstadt, in accordance with Kriegs Ministerium von Nr.744.17.g.A.7.L., on 27 December 1917, under the command of Leutnant Theodor Quandt (eight victories), from Jasta 36. Jasta 53 was activated 7 January 1918, and on 10 January was based at Attigny, in the 3 Armee Sector. The first flight over the Front came on 10 March, but then a move was made to Mont d'Origny on the 18 Armee Front on 18 March. Leutnant Martin Hänichen became the first pilot to score, getting his first victory on 22 March, the date that Gefreiter Ernst Diehl became the first combat casualty when wounded by ground fire. A move was made on 15 July to the 3 Armee Sector. The Jasta was transferred to the 9 Armee area on 25 July. Leutnant Quandt, who had not added to his score, was reassigned as Commanding Officer of Jasta 36 on 23 August, and Leutnant Robert Hildebrandt (five victories), the CO of Jasta 69, was given command of Jasta 53. On 25 September Jasta 53 returned to the 3 Armee Front until the end of the war. When Hildebrandt departed on three weeks' leave, Leutnant Martin Hänichen assumed temporary command until Hildebrandt returned on 22 October to end the war in command. Jasta 53 was given credit for at least 20 enemy aircraft destroyed, while losing one pilot wounded in combat, four prisoners of war, and one killed in a flying accident.

## Commanding Officers

| | | |
|---|---|---|
| Ltn Theodor Quandt | 24 Dec 1917 – 28 Aug 1918 | CO J36 |
| Oblt Robert Hildebrandt | 28 Aug 1918 – 30 Sep 1918 | Leave |
| Ltn Martin Hänichen | 30 Sep 1918 – 22 Oct 1918 | Acting |
| Oblt Robert Hildebrandt | 22 Oct 1918 – 11 Nov 1918 | |

## Pilots credited with victories

| | | | |
|---|---|---|---|
| Vfw Friedrich Poeschke | 8 | Oblt Robert Hildebrandt | 1(6) |
| Ltn Martin Hänichen | 3 | Ltn Otto Steger | 1(2) |
| Ltn Frank Klausenberg | 2 | Uffz Karl Waldherr | 1 |
| Vfw Hermann Korsch | 2 | Vfw Johannes Walter | 1(2) |
| Uffz Konrad Boness | 1 | | |

## Airfields occupied

| Location | Inclusive Dates | Armee |
|---|---|---|
| Darmstadt | 27 Dec 1917 – 9 Jan 1918 | FEA9 |
| Attigny | 10 Jan 1918 – 17 Mar 1918 | 3 |
| Mont d'Origny | 18 Mar 1918 – 28 Mar 1918 | 18 |
| Flavy-le-Martel | 29 Mar 1918 – 5 Apr 1918 | 18 |
| Moyencourt | 6 Apr 1918 – 14 Jul 1918 | 18 |
| Mars-sous-Bourcq | 15 Jul 1918 – 24 Jul 1918 | 3 |
| Vivaise | 25 Jul 1918 – 24 Sep 1918 | 9 |

| Chuffilly | 25 Sep 1918 – 8 Oct 1918 | 3 |
| Malmy, Sedan | 9 Oct 1918 – 1 Nov 1918 | 3 |
| Antrecourt, Attigny | 2 Nov 1918 – 11 Nov 1918 | 3 |

## ROYAL SAXON JAGDSTAFFEL 54

Jasta 54 was created on 1 January 1918, through FEA6, Grossenhain, by authority of Kriegs Ministerium von Nr.744.17.g.A.7.L., under the command of Leutnant Paul Erbguth (two victories) from Jasta 30. On 19 January the Jasta was assigned to the 2 Armee Sector. Unteroffizier Wilhelm Rincke was killed in combat over Fontaine Notre Dame, on 8 March, thereby being the first casualty from the Jasta 54s. The Jasta's first victory came on 17 March, as Leutnant Matzke gained his first. The unit was reassigned to the 4 Armee Sector in Flanders, on 11 April, and Leutnant Erbguth was transferred to FEA6 on 18 May. He was replaced by Leutnant Ernst Turck, from Jasta 15. The Jasta moved back to the 2 Armee Front on 6 June. Jasta 54s was transferred to the 3 Armee Sector on 10 July, then on to the 19 Armee on 10 August, where they were, under the command of Leutnant von Fichte from Schutzstaffel 16, when the war ended. Jasta 54s was given credit for at least 22 victories, including four balloons, while having three pilots killed in combat and one injured in a flying accident.

### Commanding Officers

| Ltn Paul Erbguth | 28 Dec 1917 – 18 May 1918 |
| Oblt Ernst Turck | 18 May 1918 – |
| Ltn von Fichte | – 11 Nov 1918 |

### Pilots credited with victories

| Ltn Gustav Bürck | 3 | Vfw Kurt Delang | 2(3) |
| Gefr Erich Mix | 3 | Vfw Heinrich Klose | 2 |
| Ltn Seewald | 3 | Ltn Matzke | 1 |
| Gefr August Schwind | 3 | Gefr Pissorowski | 1 |
| OfStv Behncke | 2 | Ltn Helmut Preiss | 1 |
| | | Ltn Vogt | 1 |

### Airfields occupied

| Location | Inclusive Dates | Armee |
| --- | --- | --- |
| Grossenhain | 1 Jan 1918 – 18 Jan 1918 | FEA6 |
| Neuvilly | 19 Jan 1918 – 10 Apr 1918 | 2 |
| Ingelmünster | 11 Apr 1918 – 3 May 1918 | 4 |
| Rumbeke-Ost | 4 May 1918 – 5 Jun 1918 | 4 |
| Ennemain | 6 Jun 1918 – 9 Jul 1918 | 2 |
| Blaise, Vouziers | 10 Jul 1918 – 9 Aug 1918 | 2 |
| Mörchingen | 10 Aug 1918 – | 19 |
| Wallersberg | Aug 1918 – | 19 |
| Ars, Kennchen | – 11 Nov 1918 | 19 |

## ROYAL PRUSSIAN JAGDSTAFFEL 55

This unit was created on 1 January 1918 per order Kriegs Ministerium v. Nr.744.17.g.A.7.L. at FEA2, Schneidemühl; it was mobilized on 25 January, under the command of Leutnant Karl Meierdirks (one victory) from Jasta 40s. Between 15 March and the 31st it travelled to Palestine and set up base at Djenin, Turkey, where it was redesignated Jasta 1 der Heeresgruppe F, in accordance with Kriegs Ministerium v.18.1.18 Nr.335.18.A.7.L.IV.C. The first loss occurred on 3 April, Unteroffizier Kurt Riesmann killed in a crash at Rajak while on a practice flight. The first combat loss occurred on 6 April, Vizefeldwebel Willi Hampel was shot down and taken prisoner at Mulibis. The first victory happened on 25 April with Leutnant Meierdirks scoring his second, an RE8, over Nablus. On 4 May Meierdirks was killed in action over Jericho, his place being temporarily filled by Leutnant Wilhelm Debus of Flieger-Abteilung 300. On 1 June Leutnant Gerhard Wilhelm Flecken (four victories) arrived from Jasta 43 and took command until the end of the war. On 20 September the airfield at Djenin was overrun by the British. They captured all the aircraft and effectively put the unit out of the war. Jasta 55/Jasta 1(F) claimed eight victories, but at a cost of eight pilots killed in action, one killed in a crash, one taken prisoner, and one wounded.

### Commanding Officers

| | | |
|---|---|---|
| Ltn Karl Meierdirks | Jan 1918 – 4 May 1918 | KIA |
| Ltn Wilhelm Debus | 5 May 1918 – 1 Jun 1918 | Acting |
| Ltn Gerhard Wilhelm Flecken | 1 Jun 1918 – EOW | |

### Pilots credited with victories

| | | | |
|---|---|---|---|
| Ltn Hermann Kunz | 3(6) | Ltn Karl Meierdirks* | 1(2) |
| Vfw Gustav Schneidewind | 3(7) | Vfw Weiner | 1 |

### Airfields occupied

| Location | Inclusive Dates | Armee |
|---|---|---|
| Schneidemühl | 1 Jan 1918 – 15 Mar 1918 | FEA3 |
| Djenin | 31 Mar 1918 – 20 Sep 1918 | Turkey |
| Derra | 20 Sep 1918 – 22 Sep 1918 (EOW) | Turkey |

## ROYAL PRUSSIAN JAGDSTAFFEL 56

Created on 20 October 1917 at Geschwader Schule Paderborn pursuant to Kriegs Ministerium von Nr.1744.17.g.A.7.L., it was placed under the command of Leutnant Franz Schleiff (three victories) from Jasta 41. It moved to the Western Front on 14 January settling in the 2 Armee Sector. The first victory belonged to Schleiff who downed an AWFK8 of 35 Squadron, RFC, on 19 February. The first loss occurred on 13 March, Leutnant Walter Bowein being killed over Grevecoeur at 1015 hours. On 27 March Schleiff was severely wounded in action which culminated in the amputation of his left hand. The unit was taken over by Leutnant Rudolph Heins in an acting capacity until Leutnant Diether Collin (six victories) arrived from Jasta 22s on 16 April. Meanwhile Jasta 56 had moved to the 4 Armee Front on 11 April and here it was to see out the war. Leutnant Collin was wounded in action over Bailleul on 13 August and died in hospital that evening. His place was taken by Leutnant Ludwig 'Lutz' Beckmann (seven victories). Jasta 56 was credited with 63 victories, but lost six pilots killed in action, one taken prisoner, one killed in a crash, four wounded, and one more injured in a crash.

### Commanding Officers

| | | |
|---|---|---|
| Ltn Franz Schleiff | 9 Jan 1918 – 27 Mar 1918 | WIA |
| Ltn Rudolph Heins | 27 Mar 1918 – 16 Apr 1918 | Acting |
| Ltn Diether Collin | 16 Apr 1918 – 13 Aug 1918 | KIA |
| Ltn Ludwig Beckmann | 16 Aug 1918 – 11 Nov 1918 | |

### Pilots credited with victories

| | | | |
|---|---|---|---|
| Ltn Franz Piechulek | 12(14) | Ltn Ernst Baumgärtel* | 2 |
| Ltn Franz Schleiff | 9(12) | Uffz Dannemann | 2 |
| Ltn Ludwig Beckmann | 8 | Ltn Kohlpoth | 2 |
| Ltn Diether Collin* | 7(13) | Ltn Wilhelm Oberstadt | 2(3) |
| Ltn Rudolf Heins | 4 | Vfw Weimar | 2(3) |
| Uffz Ludwig Jeckert | 4 | Uffz Gullmann | 1 |
| Vfw Krebs | 3 | Uffz Kaleta | 1(2) |
| Ltn Schramm | 3 | | |

### Airfields occupied

| Location | Inclusive Dates | Armee |
|---|---|---|
| Paderborn | 1 Jan 1918 – 13 Jan 1918 | GwSch |
| Neuvilly | 14 Jan 1918 – 25 Mar 1918 | 2 |
| Mons-en-Chaussée | 26 Mar 1918 – 10 Apr 1918 | 2 |
| Ingelmünster | 11 Apr 1918 – 4 May 1918 | 4 |
| Rumbeke Ost | 5 May 1918 – 29 Sep 1918 | 4 |
| Croulshouten | 30 Sep 1918 – 11 Nov 1918 | 4 |

## ROYAL PRUSSIAN JAGDSTAFFEL 57

This unit was formed on 6 January 1918 at Flieger-Beobachter-Schule Königsberg, by order Kriegs Ministerium von Nr.1744.17.g.A.7.L., and placed under the command of Leutnant Paul Strähle (seven victories) from Jasta 18. It left for the front on 15 January arriving in the 6 Armee Sector on the 24th. The first victory occurred on 11 March, Leutnant Hans Viebig shooting down an RE8 over Arleux at 1615 hours. Two days later Leutnant Werner Haffner was killed over Auchy-La Bassée at 1330 hours as the unit's first loss. Jasta 57 moved to the 4 Armee on 23 April. A further move was made on 6 June, this time to the 2 Armee Then on 8 July the Jasta moved to the 1 Armee, returning to the 17 Armee on 21 August. Strähle was wounded in action on 27 September, his place as CO temporarily taken by Leutnant Johannes Jensen and then Leutnant Blum, until 12 October, when he returned to lead the unit to the end. Jasta 57 finished the war in the 17 Armee Sector, and was demobilised at Bonn. Jasta 57 received credit for at least 33 confirmed victories, at a loss of five pilots killed, one taken prisoner, four wounded, and two injured in crashes.

### Commanding Officers

| | | |
|---|---|---|
| Ltn Paul Strähle | 1 Jan 1918 – 27 Sep 1918 | WIA |
| Ltn Johannes Jensen | 27 Sep 1918 – 9 Oct 1918 | Acting |
| Ltn Blum | 9 Oct 1918 – 12 Oct 1918 | Acting |
| Ltn Paul Strähle | 12 Oct 1918 – 11 Nov 1918 | |

### Pilots credited with victories

| | | | |
|---|---|---|---|
| Ltn Paul Strähle | 8(14) | Gefr Hechler | 2 |
| Ltn Johann Jensen | 6 | Uffz Tracinski | 2 |
| Ltn Hans Viebig | 4(5) | Vfw Emil Hanzog* | 1 |
| Vfw Knobel | 3 | Uffz Meyer | 1 |
| Vfw Otto Wieprich | 3(4) | Gefr Sielemann | 1 |
| Ltn Blum | 2(3) | | |

### Airfields occupied

| Location | Inclusive Dates | Armee |
|---|---|---|
| Königsberg | 6 Jan 1918 – 15 Jan 1918 | Pil/Obs/Sch |
| Wasquehal | 24 Jan 1918 – 23 Apr 1918 | 6 |
| Halluin, SE Reckem | 23 Apr 1918 – 6 Jun 1918 | 4 |
| Ennemain, South | 6 Jun 1918 – 11 Jun 1918 | 2 |
| Ennemain, South | 11 Jun 1918 – 8 Jul 1918 | 18 |
| Neuflize | 8 Jul 1918 – 21 Aug 1918 | 1 |
| Aniche | 21 Aug 1918 – 30 Sep 1918 | 17 |
| Beuvry | 30 Sep 1918 – 12 Oct 1918 | 17 |
| Chièvres | 12 Oct 1918 – 4 Nov 1918 | 17 |
| Champles, SE Waterloo | 4 Nov 1918 – 11 Nov 1918 | 17 |

## ROYAL PRUSSIAN JAGDSTAFFEL 58

Jasta 58 was formed on 6 January 1918 at Flieger-Beobachter-Schule Thorn, pursuant to order Kriegs Ministerium von Nr.744.17.g.A.7.L., and placed under the command of Oberleutnant Hermann Martini (one victory) who reported from Jasta 12 on 28 January. The unit moved to the 2 Armee Front on 25 January. On 1 February they transferred to the 17 Armee Sector. The unit's first loss occurred on 15 March when Vizefeldwebel August Wagner was killed in action over Ecourt. On 2 April the unit transferred to the 6 Armee Front, and the first victory was finally gained on 11 April, by Leutnant Spille who downed a Sopwith Camel at 1450 hours over Sailly-sur-Lys. Martini was replaced as CO on 4 April by Leutnant Albert Dietlen (seven victories) of Jasta 41. He was killed in action eight days later and Leutnant Wendland filled in until Martini could return on the 17th. The unit moved to the 4 Armee on 24 April, and made a further move to 2 Armee on 6 June. Jasta 58 moved to the 1 Armee Sector on 7 July, and then to 17 Armee on 19 August, where it saw out the war. Martini finished the war as the unit's CO, but occasionally moved to AFP2 for brief stays. During his absence temporary commanders included Leutnant Stoltenhoff (three victories) from Jasta 27, Leutnant Martin Demisch (ten victories), and Leutnant Wendland (one victory). On 12 November, Jasta 58 turned in eight Fokker DVIIs at Nievilles and entrained to Paderborn for demobilisation. Jasta 58 pilots were credited with 24 victories, but lost five pilots killed in action, two wounded, and one injured in a crash-landing.

### Commanding Officers

| | | |
|---|---|---|
| Oblt Hermann Martini | 28 Jan 1918 – 4 Apr 1918 | JGr 3 |
| Ltn Albert Dietlen | 4 Apr 1918 – 12 Apr 1918 | KIA |
| Ltn Wendland | 12 Apr 1918 – 17 Apr 1918 | J58 |
| Oblt Hermann Martini | 17 Apr 1918 – 24 Apr 1918 | AFP2 |
| Ltn Wendland | 24 Apr 1918 – 7 May 1918 | Acting |
| Ltn Stoltenhoff | 7 May 1918 – 20 May 1918 | Acting |
| Ltn Martin Demisch | 20 May 1918 – 4 Jun 1918 | Acting |
| Oblt Hermann Martini | 4 Jun 1918 – 10 Jun 1918 | AFP2 |
| Ltn Wendland | 10 Jun 1918 – 22 Jul 1918 | Acting |
| Oblt Hermann Martini | 22 Jul 1918 – 11 Nov 1918 | |

### Pilots credited with victories

| | | | |
|---|---|---|---|
| Ltn Martin Demisch | 10 | Uffz Baumert | 1 |
| Vfw Jeep | 3 | Vfw Dünnhaupt | 1 |
| Ltn Spille | 3 | Uffz de Ray | 1 |
| Ltn Albert Dietlen* | 2(9) | Vfw Max Schnell* | 1 |
| Uffz Kurt Pietzsch | 2 | | |

### Airfields occupied

| Location | Inclusive Dates | Armee |
|---|---|---|
| Thorn | 6 Jan 1918 – 25 Jan 1918 | Pil/Obs/Sch |
| Emerchicourt, North | 25 Jan 1918 – 1 Feb 1918 | 2 |
| Emerchicourt, North | 1 Feb 1918 – 16 Mar 1918 | 17 |
| Aniche, NE | 16 Mar 1918 – 2 Apr 1918 | 17 |
| Ascq, Lille | 2 Apr 1918 – 22 Apr 1918 | 6 |
| Lomme, Lille | 22 Apr 1918 – 24 Apr 1918 | 6 |
| Koekhoek, near Menin | 24 Apr 1918 – 6 Jun 1918 | 4 |
| Ennemain | 6 Jun 1918 – 7 Jul 1918 | 2 |
| Neuflize | 7 Jul 1918 – 19 Aug 1918 | 1 |
| Aniche | 19 Aug 1918 – 1 Oct 1918 | 17 |
| Beuvry | 1 Oct 1918 – 14 Oct 1918 | 17 |
| Chièvres | 14 Oct 1918 – 4 Nov 1918 | 17 |
| Champles, SE Waterloo | 4 Nov 1918 – 12 Nov 1918 | 17 |

## ROYAL PRUSSIAN JAGDSTAFFEL 59

Jasta 59 was formed at Flieger-Beobachter-Schule Schwerin, on 6 January 1918, pursuant to order Kriegs Ministerium von Nr.744.17.g.A.7.L., and placed under the command of Leutnant Otto Walter Höhne (six victories), who reported in from hospital having recovered from wounds received while serving with Jasta 1. The unit moved to the 17 Armee Sector on 24 January and Höhne left to command Jasta 2 two days later, command passing to Oberleutnant Hans-Helmut von Boddien of Jasta 11. The unit's first victory was claimed by Leutnant Karl Hertz on 10 March, downing a Sopwith Camel at 0730 hours over Sains-lez-Marquion. Jasta 59 was to spend the entire war on the 17 Armee Front. The unit's first loss occurred on 9 May, the above-mentioned Leutnant Hertz being killed over Thilloy at 1415 hours. Von Boddien was wounded in combat on 27 September, and command of the Jasta was assumed by Oberleutnant Fritz Krafft (two victories) of Jasta 59. Jasta 59 was credited with 20 victories, but lost three pilots killed in action, one killed in a crash, and two more wounded in action.

### Commanding Officers

| | | |
|---|---|---|
| Ltn Otto Walter Höhne | 27 Dec 1917 – 26 Jan 1918 | CO J2 |
| Oblt Hans-Helmut von Boddien | 29 Jan 1918 – 27 Sep 1918 | WIA |
| Oblt Fritz Krafft | 28 Sep 1918 – 11 Nov 1918 | |

### Pilots credited with victories

| | | | |
|---|---|---|---|
| Oblt Hans-Helmut v Boddien | 5 | Ltn Lehmann | 1 |
| Ltn Karl Hertz* | 3 | OfStv Münnichow | 1(3) |
| Ltn Hinneberg | 2 | Flg Alfred Rüdiger | 1 |
| Oblt Fritz Krafft | 2 | Ltn Oskar Scherf | 1 |
| Vfw Fritz Senf | 2 | Ltn Karl August von Schönebeck | 1(8) |
| Lt Hans Jebens* | 1 | | |

### Airfields occupied

| Location | Inclusive Dates | Armee |
|---|---|---|
| Schwerin | 6 Jan 1918 – 24 Jan 1918 | Pil/Obs/Sch |
| Emerchicourt | 24 Jan 1918 – 28 Mar 1918 | 17 |
| Favreuil | 28 Mar 1918 – 18 Apr 1918 | 17 |
| Epinoy | 18 Apr 1918 – 8 Aug 1918 | 17 |
| Roucourt | 8 Aug 1918 – 1 Sep 1918 | 17 |
| Erre, Somain | 1 Sep 1918 – 26 Sep 1918 | 17 |
| Helesmes, Denain | 26 Sep 1918 – 11 Oct 1918 | 17 |
| Ghlin, Mons | 11 Oct 1918 – 17 Oct 1918 | 17 |
| Castern | 18 Oct 1918 – 11 Nov 1918 | 17 |

## ROYAL PRUSSIAN JAGDSTAFFEL 60

Jasta 60 was created on 11 January 1918 at the Flieger-Beobachter-Schule at Jüterbog by order Kriegs Ministerium von Nr.744.17.g.A.7.L., and was placed under the command of Oberleutnant von Rudno-Rudzinski of Jasta 17. It moved to the Front on 24 January to the airfield in the 7 Armee Sector. The first victory came on 18 March when Unteroffizier Hess claimed a Spad. The first loss occurred on 11 April, Unteroffizier Georg Storr being killed over Mortiers near Laon. Oberleutnant Rudno-Rudzinski was shot down and taken prisoner on 26 May, his place as commander being taken by Leutnant Arno Benzler (four victories) from Jasta 45. Except for a brief leave Benzler was to remain in command until the end of the war. The Jasta moved to the 3 Armee Front on 23 September, where it remained until 22 October when it moved to the 18 Armee, where it ended the war. Jasta 60 was credited with at least 56 victories, but lost five pilots killed in action, three taken prisoner, four wounded in action, and another injured in a crash.

### Commanding Officers

| | | |
|---|---|---|
| Oblt von Rudno-Rudzinski | 5 Jan 1918 – 26 May 1918 | POW |
| Ltn Arno Benzler | 27 May 1918 – 8 Sep 1918 | Leave |
| Ltn Fritz Höhn (acting) | 8 Sep 1918 – 1 Oct 1918 | CO J41 |
| Ltn Arno Benzler | 1 Oct 1918 – 11 Nov 1918 | |

### Pilots credited with victories

| | | | |
|---|---|---|---|
| Vfw Arthur Korff | 8 | Uffz Hess | 3 |
| Uffz Wilhelm Zorn | 8 | Uffz Heinrich Pfaffenritter* | 3 |
| Ltn Günther Dobberke | 7(8) | Ltn Wilhelm Müller | 2 |
| Ltn Fritz Höhn* | 6(20) | Uffz Karl Hofmann* | 1 |
| Ltn Arno Benzler | 5(9) | Vfw Mack | 1 |
| Ltn Karl Ritscherle | 5(8) | Vfw Paul Völker* | 1 |
| Uffz Ernst Bielefeld* | 4 | Ltn Wolff | 1 |
| | | Vfw Zimmermann | 1 |

### Airfields occupied

| Location | Inclusive Dates | Armee |
|---|---|---|
| Jüterbog | 11 Jan 1918 – 24 Jan 1918 | Pil/Obs/Sch |
| Ercheu | 24 Jan 1918 – 27 May 1918 | 7 |
| Sissone | 27 May 1918 – 6 Jun 1918 | 7 |
| Boncourt | 6 Jun 1918 – 23 Sep 1918 | 7 |
| St Marie | 23 Sep 1918 – 7 Oct 1918 | 3 |
| Chéméry | 7 Oct 1918 – 22 Oct 1918 | 3 |
| Medard | 22 Oct 1918 – 11 Nov 1918 | 18 |

## ROYAL PRUSSIAN JAGDSTAFFEL 61

Jasta 61 was formed on 11 January 1918 at Flieger-Beobachter-Schule Köln, by order Kriegs Ministerium von Nr.744.17.g.A.7.L., and placed under the command of Oberleutnant Maximilian Edler von Daniels who reported from Kest 3. It moved to the front on 23 January, taking up residence at an airfield in the 7 Armee Sector. The first loss occurred on 10 February, Leutnant Georg Ferner being killed in a crash at Voyenne during a test flight of a Pfalz DIIIa. The first combat-induced loss happened on 5 March: Vizefeldwebel Kurt Jentsch was shot down in a Pfalz DIIIa by Bréguets. He came down in the German lines near Chavignon but returned safely to the unit. The first victory was recorded on 12 April by Offizierstellvertreter Johann Kopka, as his second, after he downed a Spad two-seater over Juvigny. The unit transferred to the 18 Armee on 18 April. Oberleutnant von Daniels was killed in action over Avricourt on 7 June, command passing to Leutnant Siegfried Büttner (three victories) of Jasta 22s. He was to remain in command to the end of the war. Jasta 61 successively moved to 3 Armee on 12 July, 9 Armee on 26 July, 7 Armee on 18 September, and back to 3 Armee on 25 September, where it finished the war. The unit was credited with at least 28 confirmed victories at a cost of four pilots killed in action, two killed in crashes, two taken prisoner, one wounded, and one lightly injured in a crash-landing.

### Commanding Officers

| | | |
|---|---|---|
| Oblt Maximilian Edler von Daniels | 11 Jan 1918 – 7 Jun 1918 | KIA |
| Ltn Siegfried Büttner | 8 Jun 1918 – 11 Nov 1918 | |

### Pilots credited with victories

| | | | |
|---|---|---|---|
| Ltn Siegfried Büttner | 10(13) | Oblt Maximilian v Daniels* | 1 |
| Ltn Johann Kopka | 4(5) | Uffz Henkel | 1 |
| Ltn Gustav Wember | 4 | Uffz Walter Höhne | 1 |
| Vfw Hermann Behrends | 3 | Vfw Langjahr | 1 |
| Vfw Rothe | 3 | | |

### Airfields occupied

| Location | Inclusive Dates | Armee |
|---|---|---|
| | | Pil/Obs/Sch |
| Köln | 11 Jan 1918 – 23 Jan 1918 | |
| Voyenne, Marle | 23 Jan 1918 – 10 Mar 1918 | 7 |
| Vivaise | 10 Mar 1918 – 18 Apr 1918 | 7 |
| Ercheu | 18 Apr 1918 – 12 Jul 1918 | 18 |
| Mars-sous-Bourcq | 12 Jul 1918 – 26 Jul 1918 | 3 |
| Reneuil Ferme | 26 Jul 1918 – 18 Sep 1918 | 9 |
| Reneuil Ferme | 18 Sep 1918 – 25 Sep 1918 | 7 |
| Chuffilly | 25 Sep 1918 – 9 Oct 1918 | 3 |
| Malmy-Chéméry, Sedan | 9 Oct 1918 – 3 Nov 1918 | 3 |
| Antrecourt, Attigny | 3 Nov 1918 – 11 Nov 1918 | 3 |

## ROYAL PRUSSIAN JAGDSTAFFEL 62

Jasta 62 was created on 16 January 1918 at Flieger-Beobachter-Schule West at Diest, by order Kriegs Ministerium von Nr.744.17.g.A.7.L., under the command of Leutnant Ludwig Luer (four victories) who reported from Jasta 27. It moved to the front on the 26th settling in the 1 Armee Sector. It shifted to the 18 Armee on 16 March. The first loss occurred six days later when Leutnant Zwiters was shot down by flak while flying an Albatros DVa and taken prisoner north-west of Ham. The unit's first victory was claimed on 31 March by Leutnant Tönjes who nailed an SE5a over Montdidier. Jasta 62 moved to the 1 Armee Front on 5 July and two days later Leutnant Luer was posted and command of the Jasta was given to Leutnant Max Näther (eight victories). He was to remain in command, except for leave in August, until the end of the war. Its final move occurred on 14 September to the 5 Armee Front. Jasta 62 was credited with 48 victories but lost three pilots killed in action, two taken prisoner and two more wounded.

### Commanding Officers

| | | |
|---|---|---|
| Ltn Ludwig Luer | 15 Jan 1918 – 22 May 1918 | Hospital |
| Ltn Tönjes | 22 May 1918 – 1 Jul 1918 | Acting |
| Ltn Ludwig Luer | 1 Jul 1918 – 7 Jul 1918 | Posted |
| Ltn Max Näther | 7 Jul 1918 – 28 Jul 1918 | Leave |
| Ltn Hagen | 28 Jul 1918 – 21 Aug 1918 | Acting |
| Ltn Tönjes | 21 Aug 1918 – 6 Sep 1918 | Acting |
| Ltn Max Näther | 6 Sep 1918 – 11 Nov 1918 | |

### Pilots credited with victories

| | | | |
|---|---|---|---|
| Ltn Max Näther | 26 | Ltn Breidenbach | 1 |
| Uffz Friedrich Engler* | 4 | Vfw Ernst Busch* | 1 |
| OfStv Otto Sporbert | 4 | Uffz Hösrich | 1 |
| Vfw Karl Gerster | 2 | Flg Otto Müller | 1 |
| Ltn Hagen | 2 | Uffz Rozmiarek | 1 |
| Ltn Ludwig Luer | 2(6) | Vfw Stadley | 1 |
| Ltn Adomeit | 1 | Ltn Tönjes | 1 |

### Airfields occupied

| Location | Inclusive Dates | Armee |
|---|---|---|
| | | Pil/Obs/Sch |
| Diest | 16 Jan 1918 – 25 Jan 1918 | |
| Thugny near Rethel | 26 Jan 1918 – 16 Mar 1918 | 1 |
| Bohain | 16 Mar 1918 – 26 Mar 1918 | 18 |
| Trefcon | 26 Mar 1918 – 29 Mar 1918 | 18 |
| Balâtre, Roye | 29 Mar 1918 – 5 Jul 1918 | 18 |
| St Rémy | 5 Jul 1918 – 14 Sep 1918 | 1 |
| Preutin-Higny, SE Longuyon | 14 Sep 1918 – 11 Nov 1918 | 5 |

## ROYAL PRUSSIAN JAGDSTAFFEL 63

This unit was formed on 16 January 1918 at the Flieger-Beobachter-Schule Warschau, pursuant to order Kriegs Ministerium von Nr.744.17.g.A.7.L., under the command of Leutnant Fritz Loerzer (seven victories) who reported from Jasta 26. On 1 February it moved to the 18 Armee Sector. Loerzer returned to Jasta 26 on 21 February, command going to Leutnant Hermann Leptien (three victories) of Jasta 21, who would command until the end of the war. The first victory was acquired on 24 February by Unteroffizier Jon Santjer who downed a Bristol F2b south-east of Ham as his second victory. The first losses occurred on 31 March, both Unteroffizier Rupert Merkle and Santjer being killed over Hainvillers, and Vizefeldwebel Friedrich Neubauer was killed over Rollot. On 6 July came a move to 1 Armee, then a move to 6 Armee occurred on 12 August, where it saw out the war. Jasta 63 was credited with at least 17 confirmed victories at a cost of seven pilots killed in action and one killed in a crash while on a test flight.

### Commanding Officers

| | | |
|---|---|---|
| Ltn Fritz Loerzer | 9 Jan 1918 – 21 Feb 1918 | CO J26 |
| Ltn Hermann Leptien | 21 Feb 1918 – 11 Nov 1918 | |

### Pilots credited with victories

| | | | |
|---|---|---|---|
| Ltn Martin Johns | 7 | Vfw Friedrich Neubauer* | 2(3) |
| Ltn Hermann Leptien | 4(7) | Vfw Kettelhack | 1 |
| Vfw Mack | 2 | Uffz Jon Santjer* | 1(2) |

### Airfields occupied

| Location | Inclusive Dates | Armee |
|---|---|---|
| Warschau | 16 Jan 1918 – 1 Feb 1918 | Pil/Obs/Sch |
| Grivy | 1 Feb 1918 – 15 Mar 1918 | 18 |
| Hennieches Ferme | 16 Mar 1918 – 25 Mar 1918 | 18 |
| Wancourt Ferme | 26 Mar 1918 – 5 Jul 1918 | 18 |
| Bignicourt | 6 Jul 1918 – 11 Aug 1918 | 1 |
| Sante Nord | 12 Aug 1918 – 18 Aug 1918 | 6 |
| Ennetières | 18 Aug 1918 – 19 Sep 1918 | 6 |
| Genech | 20 Sep 1918 – 20 Oct 1918 | 6 |
| Ellignies | 20 Oct 1918 – 30 Oct 1918 | 6 |
| Kruisken | 31 Oct 1918 – 9 Nov 1918 | 6 |
| Brussels | 9 Nov 1918 – 11 Nov 1918 | 6 |

## ROYAL WÜRTTEMBERG JAGDSTAFFEL 64

Jasta 64w was formed at FEA 10, Böblingen, on 17 January 1918 by order Kriegs Ministerium von Nr.744.17.g.A.7.L., under the command of Leutnant August Hanko (five victories) who reported from Jasta 28w. It became operational on 5 February, in the 5 Armee Sector. On 22 March it moved to Armee-Abteilung 'C', and suffered its first loss five days later when Offizierstellvertreter Schüschke was shot down and taken prisoner in Pfalz DIIIa 8078/17. He ran out of fuel and was forced to land in the French lines. The first victory was claimed by Leutnant Friedrich Hengst on 7 May, when he shot down Captain James Norman Hall of the 94th Squadron, USAS, at 0950 hours over Vieville en Haye. Hall was wounded in the action and taken prisoner. On 7 July Hanko was removed to hospital due to sickness and was replaced by Leutnant Eugen Siempelkamp (three victories) from Jasta 29. On 14 September Siempelkamp was wounded and sent to hospital. His place as CO was taken by Leutnant Hengst, who led the unit to the end. Jasta 64w was credited with at least 20 confirmed victories, 15 of these coming in the last three months of the war, when it was out-fitted with Fokker DVIIs. These came at a cost of three pilots killed in action, three taken prisoner, and another wounded.

### Commanding Officers

| | | |
|---|---|---|
| Ltn August Hanko | 27 Jan 1918 – 7 Jul 1918 | Leave |
| Ltn Eugen Siempelkamp | 25 Jul 1918 – 14 Sep 1918 | WIA |
| Ltn Friedrich Hengst | 14 Sep 1918 – 11 Nov 1918 | |

### Pilots credited with victories

| | | | |
|---|---|---|---|
| Vfw Albert Bader | 4 | Vfw Trautmann | 2 |
| Ltn Friedrich Hengst | 4(5) | Sgt Gustav Otto Albrecht* | 1 |
| Ltn Leibfried | 3 | Uffz Rudolf Lochner | 1 |

| Sgt Beschow | 2 | Flg Oltzeschner | 1 |
| Ltn Eugen Siempelkamp | 2(5) | | |

| | **Airfields occupied** | |
| **Location** | **Inclusive Dates** | **Armee** |
| Böblingen | 17 Jan 1918 – 5 Feb 1918 | FEA10 |
| Mercy le Haute | 5 Feb 1918 – 22 Mar 1918 | 5 |
| Mars-la-Tour | 22 Mar 1918 – 14 Sep 1918 | C |
| Giraumont | 14 Sep 1918 – 9 Oct 1918 | C |
| Tichémont | 9 Oct 1918 – 11 Nov 1918 | C |

## ROYAL PRUSSIAN JAGDSTAFFEL 65

Jasta 65 was formed on 23 January 1918 by order Kriegs Ministerium von Nr. 744.17.g.A.7.L., under the command of Leutnant Helmuth Contag (three victories) who reported from Jasta 29. It moved to the 5 Armee Front on 6 February, and scored its first victories on the 26th, Gefreiter Rudolf Kassner downing two balloons over Bethelainville at 1700 hours. The first loss occurred on 5 March, Gefreiter Lothmann being shot down and taken prisoner. The next day Contag was killed in action over Beaufort near Stenay at 1730 hours, his place as commander being taken by Leutnant Arno Benzler (one victory) from Jasta 45. His stay was short, transferring to the command of Jasta 60 on 19 March, command of Jasta 69 passing to Leutnant Otto Fitzner (three victories) from Jasta 17, who served until the end. Leutnant Wilhelm Frickart served as acting commander, once when Fitzner was lightly wounded and again when he took a short leave. Jasta 65 moved to Armee-Abteilung 'C' on 6 May. Jasta 65 went to the 5 Armee on 16 September; it remained there until 8 October at which time it returned to Armee-Abteilung 'C'. The unit was credited with at least 34 confirmed victories, but lost six pilots killed in action, two taken prisoner, and three wounded in action.

| | **Commanding Officers** | |
| Ltn Helmuth Contag | 2 Feb 1918 – 6 Mar 1918 | KIA |
| Ltn Arno Benzler | 7 Mar 1918 – 19 Mar 1918 | CO Jasta 60 |
| Ltn Otto Fitzner | 19 Mar 1918 – 25 Aug 1918 | WIA |
| Ltn Wilhelm Frickart | 25 Aug 1918 – 31 Aug 1918 | Acting |
| Ltn Otto Fitzner | 31 Aug 1918 – 8 Sep 1918 | Leave |
| Ltn William Frickart | 8 Sep 1918 – 20 Oct 1918 | Acting |
| Ltn Otto Fitzner | 20 Oct 1918 – 11 Nov 1918 | |

| | **Pilots credited with victories** | | |
| Vfw Josef Hohly | 7 | Ltn Arno Benzler | 2(9) |
| Ltn Otto Fitzner | 6(9) | Ltn Otto Weisshaar | 2 |
| Ltn Wilhelm Frickart | 4(10) | Ltn Helmuth Contag* | 1(4) |
| Uffz Rudolf Kassner* | 4 | Uffz Wilhelm Hofacker* | 1 |
| OfStv Tiedje | 3 | Ltn Rudolf Neitzer* | 1 |
| Uffz Alfred Bäder | 2 | Ltn Heinrich Zempel | 1 |

| | **Airfields occupied** | |
| **Location** | **Inclusive Dates** | **Armee** |
| | 23 Jan 1918 – 5 Feb 1918 | FEA7 |
| Stenay | 6 Feb 1918 – 4 May 1918 | 5 |
| Mars-la-Tour | 6 May 1918 – 15 Sep 1918 | C |
| Marville | 16 Sep 1918 – 7 Oct 1918 | 5 |
| La Ferté | 8 Oct 1918 – 20 Oct 1918 | C |
| Tichémont | 20 Oct 1918 – 11 Nov 1918 | C |

## ROYAL PRUSSIAN JAGDSTAFFEL 66

This unit was formed at FEA 5, Hannover on 27 January 1918, by order Kriegs Ministerium Nr.744.17.g.A.7.L., under the command of Leutnant Rudolf Windisch (eight victories) who reported from Jasta 50. It moved to the 7 Armee Front on 12 February, where it was to remain for the duration of the war. The first victory was claimed on 15 March by Leutnant Windisch who downed a Spad over Vitry-Reims as his ninth. The first loss happened three days later, Unteroffizier Kurt Straube being killed over Aquilcourt. Leutnant Windisch was shot down over Couvrelles and taken prisoner on 27 May. He was later to die in captivity. His place as CO was taken by Leutnant Wilhelm Schulz (four victories) who reported from Jasta 41 on the 28th. Schulz was shot down and taken prisoner on 25 June, his place as CO being taken by Leutnant Lambert Schütt, who had scored his only victory on 28 June. Schütt was, in turn, killed in action on 15 July over the Marne, command passing to Leutnant Konrad Schwartz (four victories) of Jasta 22s. He lasted but four days before being severely wounded and taken prisoner and later dying in captivity on 24 August. Command then passed to Leutnant Arthur Laumann, who was to score 24 of his 26 victories with the unit. He moved to the command of Jasta 10 on 14 August and Leutnant Paul Turck (five victories) arrived from Jasta 21 to assume command. Turck was posted on 3 September and command was assumed by Leutnant Fritz Höhn (12 victories) of Jasta 81. He lasted less than a week before being posted to the command of Jasta 60, and Hauptmann Bruno von Voigt (three victories) of Jasta 1 arrived to take command. He remained for almost three weeks before being posted, and the final commander was Leutnant Werner Preuss, who scored all 22 of his victories with Jasta 66. The unit was demobilised on 28 November. Jasta 66 scored its 50th victory on 18 July, Laumann downing a Spad over Festigny, and was to score 98 confirmed victories in all, the last coming on 29 October when Preuss dropped a Salmson 2A2 over Fay-le-Sec-Ferme. These victories came at a price of five pilots killed and five taken prisoner. Two of these (Schwartz and Windisch) were to die in captivity.

## Commanding Officers

| | | |
|---|---|---|
| Ltn Rudolf Windisch | 18 Jan 1918 – 27 May 1918 | KIA |
| Ltn Wilhelm Schulz | 28 May 1918 – 25 Jun 1918 | POW |
| Ltn Lambert Schütt | 26 Jun 1918 – 15 Jul 1918 | KIA |
| Ltn Konrad Schwartz | 16 Jul 1918 – 20 Jul 1918 | WIA, POW |
| Ltn Arthur Laumann | 21 Jul 1918 – 14 Aug 1918 | CO Jasta 10 |
| Ltn Paul Turck | 14 Aug 1918 – 3 Sep 1918 | Posted |
| Ltn Fritz Höhn | 3 Sep 1918 – 8 Sep 1918 | CO Jasta 60 |
| Hptm Bruno von Voigt | 8 Sep 1918 – 21 Sep 1918 | Posted |
| Ltn Werner Preuss | 21 Sep 1918 – 11 Nov 1918 | |

## Pilots credited with victories

| | | | |
|---|---|---|---|
| Ltn Arthur Laumann | 23(28) | Uffz Otto Stockmann | 2 |
| Ltn Werner Preuss | 22 | Gefr Bergmann | 1 |
| Ltn Rudolf Windisch* | 14(22) | Uffz Berner | 1 |
| Vfw Erich Sonneck | 6 | Flg Eyssler | 1 |
| Ltn Paul Turck | 5(10) | Vfw Gondermann | 1(3) |
| Vfw Otto Bieleit | 4(5) | Uffz Oskar Henschler | 1(2) |
| OfStv Heinrich Hünninghaus | 4 | Ltn Kummerfeld | 1 |
| Sgt Dittberner | 2 | Vfw Walter Schäfer* | 1(2) |
| Uffz Goerner | 2 | Ltn Lambert Schütt* | 1 |
| Vfw Willy Peters | 2 | Ltn Konrad Schwartz* | 1(5) |
| Ltn Wilhelm Schulz | 2(6) | Uffz Kurt Straube* | 1 |

## Airfields occupied

| Location | Inclusive Dates | Armee |
|---|---|---|
| Hannover | 27 Jan 1918 – 12 Feb 1918 | FEA5 |
| St Gobert | 12 Feb 1918 – 4 Mar 1918 | 7 |
| Norman-le-West | 5 Mar 1918 – 30 May 1918 | 7 |
| Foulfry | 31 May 1918 – 19 Jul 1918 | 7 |
| Perles | 20 Jul 1918 – 29 Jul 1918 | 7 |
| Sissone | 30 Jul 1918 – 20 Aug 1918 | 7 |
| Boncourt | 21 Aug 1918 – 8 Oct 1918 | 7 |
| Plomion | 9 Oct 1918 – 3 Nov 1918 | 7 |
| Bourlers | 4 Nov 1918 – 6 Nov 1918 | 7 |
| Sarienne-la-Longue | 9 Nov 1918 – 11 Nov 1918 | 7 |
| Demobilised | 28 Nov 1918 | |

## ROYAL PRUSSIAN JAGDSTAFFEL 67

Jasta 67 was formed on 27 January 1918 at FEA 9, Darmstadt, by order Kriegs Ministerium Nr.744.17.g.A.7.L., under the command of Leutnant Julius Fichter (three victories) who reported from Jasta 22s. He was to remain as CO until the end, except for a brief leave in June, when his place was taken by Leutnant Egon Grund. It left for the Front on 5 February, arriving in the 5 Armee Sector on 8 February. The first victory belonged to Fichter who claimed a Spad XIII at 1015 hours over Tahure on 13 March. The first loss occurred exactly two months later, Leutnant Albert Wunsch wounded in action and transported to hospital. On 31 October it was forced back to Les Hayons Ferme, where it saw out the war. Jasta 69 was demobilised in December 1918 at FEA8, Graudenz. The unit accounted for at least 34 victories, although the last four are lacking in details, occurring after 3 October. These were gained at a cost of one pilot killed in action, two taken prisoner, and one wounded. Fichter died of influenza on 13 December 1918 at Graudnitz.

### Commanding Officers

| | | |
|---|---|---|
| Ltn Julius Fichter | 27 Jan 1918 – 3 Jun 1918 | Leave |
| Ltn Egon Grund | 3 Jun 1918 – 27 Jun 1918 | Acting |
| Ltn Julius Fichter | 27 Jun 1918 – 11 Nov 1918 | |

### Pilots credited with victories

| | | | |
|---|---|---|---|
| Uffz Hans Heinrich Marwede | 5 | Vfw Alfred Auersbach | 2 |
| Vfw Richard Rübe | 5 | Ltn Christiansen | 2 |
| Vfw Thilo Boelcke* | 4 | OfStv Hasenpusch | 2 |
| Ltn Julius Fichter | 4(7) | Ltn Hans Quartier | 2 |
| Uffz Baumgarten | 3 | Gefr Hamann | 1 |
| Vfw Hans Brzenk | 3 | Ltn Alfred Wünsch | 1 |

### Airfields occupied

| Location | Inclusive Dates | Armee |
|---|---|---|
| Darmstadt | 27 Jan 1918 – 5 Feb 1918 | FEA9 |
| Marville | 8 Feb 1918 – 31 Oct 1918 | 5 |
| Les Hayons Ferme | 31 Oct 1918 – 11 Nov 1918 | 5 |

## ROYAL PRUSSIAN JAGDSTAFFEL 68

Jasta 68 was formed in accordance with Kriegs Ministerium von Nr.744.17 g.A.7.L., on 18 January 1918 at FEA3, Gotha, under the command of Leutnant Fritz Pütter, who reported from Jasta 9 with ten confirmed victories. On 19 February it established itself at Délinge Ferme in the 18 Armee. The first victory occurred on 18 March, when Leutnant Pütter downed an English two-seater over Beaurevoir. Its first losses occurred four days later as Flieger Erwin Tresenreuter was shot down in flames in an Albatros DVa west of Ham, but managed to return to the unit; Vizefeldwebel Dettmering I (one of two pilots with the same surname) was also shot down at the same location and taken prisoner. Jasta 68 moved to the 1 Armee on 5 July, then to 5 Armee on 13 September. They were demobilised on 6 December 1918. Pütter was severely wounded in action on 16 July, and died on 10 August. His place as CO was initially taken by Leutnant Paul Schwirzke of Jasta 68, until permanently replaced by Leutnant Rudolf Otto of Jasta 74, who arrived with two confirmed victories. The unit accounted for at least 43 confirmed victories, at a cost of eight pilots killed, one taken prisoner and three more wounded in action.

### Commanding Officers

| | | |
|---|---|---|
| Ltn Fritz Pütter | 3 Feb 1918 – 22 Jun 1918 | Leave |
| Ltn Paul Schwirzke | 22 Jun 1918 – 14 Jul 1918 | Acting |
| Ltn Fritz Pütter | 14 Jul 1918 – 16 Jul 1918 | WIA |
| Ltn Paul Schwirzke | 16 Jul 1918 – 9 Aug 1918 | Acting |
| Ltn Rudolf Otto | 9 Aug 1918 – 11 Nov 1918 | |

### Pilots credited with victories

| | | | |
|---|---|---|---|
| Ltn Fritz Pütter* | 16(26) | Vfw Huar | 3 |
| Ltn Wilhelm Anton Seitz | 5(16) | Ltn Rudolf Otto | 3(5) |
| Vfw Wilhelm Stör | 5 | Ltn Hebler | 2(3) |
| Ltn Paul Schwirzke | 4 | Uffz Erwin Tresenreuter* | 1 |
| Vfw Dettmering II | 3 | Vfw Johann Wieland* | 1 |

### Airfields occupied

| Location | Inclusive Dates | Armee |
|---|---|---|
| Gotha | 18 Jan 1918 – 19 Feb 1918 | FEA3 |
| Délinge Ferme | 19 Feb 1918 – 24 Mar 1918 | 18 |
| Beauvois | 25 Mar 1918 – 27 Mar 1918 | 18 |
| Balâtre, E. Roye | 28 Mar 1918 – 4 Jul 1918 | 18 |
| St Rémy, West | 5 Jul 1918 – 12 Sep 1918 | 1 |
| Sémide | 13 Sep 1918 – 14 Sep 1918 | 5 |
| Preutin | 15 Sep 1918 – 11 Nov 1918 | 5 |
| Demobilised | 6 Dec 1918 | |

## ROYAL PRUSSIAN JAGDSTAFFEL 69

Jasta 69 was formed on 1 February 1918 at FEA4, Posen, by order Kriegs Ministerium Nr.744.17.g.A.7.L., under the command of Leutnant Wilhelm Schwartz (one victory) from Jasta 43. It moved to the 18 Armee on 21 February. The first victory was scored on 23 March by Vizefeldwebel Scheuren who downed a Bristol F2b over Roye at 1157 hours. On the same date, Unteroffizier Max Rentsch was killed in a crash-landing at Mont Origny at 1120 hours. The first combat-related loss occurred on 6 April, Sergeant Pfänder wounded in action and transported to hospital. The unit remained in the 18 Armee until 6 July. On 1 May Leutnant Schwartz was swapped as CO with Oberleutnant Alex Thomas (one victory) of Jasta 13. On 7 July Jasta 69 relocated to the 1 Armee. Thomas went on leave on 15 July, his place being taken by Oberleutnant Robert Hildebrandt (five victories) of Jasta 12. On 20 August Jasta 69 move to Armee-Abteilung 'B'. Thomas returned on 6 September and led the unit to the end of the war, Hildebrandt being transferred to the command of Jasta 53. Jasta 69 was credited with at least 15 confirmed victories at a cost of one pilot killed in action, three taken prisoner, one wounded, two killed in crashes and another injured in a crash.

### Commanding Officers

| | | |
|---|---|---|
| Ltn Wilhelm Schwartz | 1 Feb 1918 – 1 May 1918 | CO J13 |
| Oblt Alex Thomas | 1 May 1918 – 15 Jul 1918 | Leave |
| Oblt Robert Hildebrandt | 15 Jul 1918 – 27 Aug 1918 | CO J53 |
| Oblt Alex Thomas | 6 Sep 1918 – 11 Nov 1918 | |

### Pilots credited with victories

| | | | |
|---|---|---|---|
| Sgt Pfänder | 3 | Vfw Scheuren | 1 |
| Uffz Johannes Fritzsche | 2(3) | Ltn Schmidt | 1(2) |
| Ltn Rudolf Abt | 1 | Gefr Schubert | 1 |
| Uffz Christel Elfers | 1 | Ltn Wilhelm Schwartz | 1(8) |
| Ltn Elting | 1 | Uffz Stehling | 1 |
| Ltn Sarnighausen | 1 | Ltn Vogel | 1 |

### Airfields occupied

| Location | Inclusive Dates | Armee |
|---|---|---|
| Posen | 1 Feb 1918 – 21 Feb 1918 | FEA4 |
| Guise | 21 Feb 1918 – 7 Mar 1918 | 18 |
| Origny St Benoite | 8 Mar 1918 – 25 Mar 1918 | 18 |
| Villeselve | 26 Mar 1918 – 6 Apr 1918 | 18 |
| Ercheu | 6 Apr 1918 – 18 May 1918 | 18 |
| Balâtre | 19 May 1918 – 6 Jul 1918 | 18 |
| Allincourt-Juniville | 7 Jul 1918 – 19 Aug 1918 | 1 |
| Habsheim | 20 Aug 1918 – 25 Aug 1918 | B |
| Sierenz | 26 Aug 1918 – 17 Sep 1918 | B |
| Habsheim | 18 Sep 1918 – 11 Nov 1918 | B |

## ROYAL PRUSSIAN JAGDSTAFFEL 70

This unit was formed on 6 February, 1918 at FEA 11, Brieg, pursuant to Kriegs Ministerium von Nr.744.17..g.A.7.L., under the command of Oberleutnant Hans Schlieter, who reported from Jasta 30. He was to score three confirmed while being the only commander Jasta 70 was to have. On 22 February the unit settled in the Armee-Abteilung 'A' Sector, where they remained until the war ended, and were demobilised there on 6 December 1918. The unit's first victories and first loss both occurred on 2 May. Oberleutnant Schlieter downed a Spad single-seater west of Badonviller as his first victory and Vizefeldwebel Friedrich Megerle also downed his first, an AR2, over Manonviller. Unfortunately, Megerle was wounded in this combat and was transferred to hospital. He returned to the unit in mid-summer, only to be killed in action on 10 July, his ammunition self-igniting. He parachuted from 900 metres but it failed to hold. Jasta 70 was credited with at least 14 confirmed victories, but lost two pilots killed and another two wounded.

### Commanding Officer

| | |
|---|---|
| Oblt Hans Schlieter | 6 Feb 1918 – 11 Nov 1918 |

### Pilots credited with victories

| | | | |
|---|---|---|---|
| Oblt Hans Schlieter | 3 | Ltn Anton Stephan | 2 |
| Vfw Heinrich Krüger* | 2 | Vfw Krist | 1 |

| Vfw Lemke | 2 | Vfw Friedrich Megerle* | 1 |
| Ltn Sauermann | 2 | Sgt Metzger | 1 |

### Airfields occupied

| Location | Inclusive Dates | Armee |
|---|---|---|
| Brieg | 6 Feb 1918 – 22 Feb 1918 | FEA 11 |
| Bühl by Saarburg | 22 Feb 1918 – 25 Aug 1918 | A |
| Stotzheim | 25 Aug 1918 – 11 Nov 1918 | A |
| Demobilised | 6 Dec 1918 | |

## ROYAL PRUSSIAN JAGDSTAFFEL 71

Jasta 71 was formed on 6 February 1918 at FEA13, Bromberg, as authorised by Kriegs Ministerium von 744.17.g.A.7.L., under the command of Leutnant Hermann Stutz who reported from Jasta 20 with two confirmed victories and was to remain its only commander. On 17 February it left for the Front arriving on 21 February in Armee-Abteilung 'B' Sector. It was to spend the entire war in this sector. Its first victory occurred on 10 May, Unteroffizier Hans von Goessel downing an AR2 over Glocker Wald as his first victory. The first loss for the unit occurred on 23 May, Unteroffizier Richard Jentzsch killed over Habsheim. The unit had ten confirmed victories at the cost of four pilots killed in action, one wounded, and one reported missing in action and probably taken prisoner.

### Commanding Officer

| Ltn Hermann Stutz | 6 Feb 1918 – 11 Nov 1918 |
|---|---|

### Pilots credited with victories

| Ltn Hermann Stutz | 4(6) | Uffz Hans von Gössel | 1 |
| Vfw Karl Schmelcher | 1(2) | Vfw Rüttgers | 1 |
| Gefr Johann Diebold | 1 | Gefr Viktor | 1 |

### Airfields occupied

| Location | Inclusive Dates | Armee |
|---|---|---|
| Bromberg | 6 Feb 1918 – 17 Feb 1918 | FEA13 |
| Colmar South | 21 Feb 1918 – 27 Mar 1918 | B |
| Habsheim | 27 Mar 1918 – 3 Jun 1918 | B |
| Sierenz | 3 Jun 1918 – 24 Jun 1918 | B |
| Habsheim | 24 Jun 1918 – 11 Nov 1918 | |

## ROYAL SAXON JADGSTAFFEL 72

Jasta 72s was formed in accordance with Kriegs Ministerium von Nr. 744.17.g.A.7.L. on 11 February 1918 at FEA6, Grossenhain, under the command of Leutnant Karl Menckhoff, 20 victories, from Jasta 3. It became operational on 20 February, arriving in the 3 Armee Sector on 2 March. Another move was made to the 18 Armee Front on 28 March. The first victory was scored on 1 April, by Menckhoff, his 21st. The first loss occurred on 16 June, Leutnant Hansjörg von Dechend killed in action at 1100 hours over Moulin-sous-Touvent. On 7 July the unit moved to the 1 Armee Front. After scoring a total of 39 victories, Menckhoff was shot down and taken prisoner near Château Thiérry on 25 July. His place was taken by Leutnant Kurt Müller (two victories) of Jasta 30. On 23 October Müller was transferred to FEA 6, command passing to Leutnant Gustav Frädrich (five victories). Jasta 72 ended the war in the 1 Armee Sector. Its 50th victory was scored by Leutnant Herbert Mahn on 10 October. Jasta 72s was credited with at least 58 confirmed victories, at a cost of two pilots killed, one taken prisoner, one wounded and one lightly injured in a crash-landing.

### Commanding Officers

| Ltn Karl Menckhoff | 11 Feb 1918 – 25 Jul 1918 | POW |
| Ltn Kurt Müller | 25 Jul 1918 – 23 Oct 1918 | FEA6 |
| Ltn Gustav Frädrich | 23 Oct 1918 – 11 Nov 1918 | |

### Pilots credited with victories

| Ltn Karl Menckhoff | 19(39) | Ltn Hansjörg von Dechend | 3 |
| Ltn Herbert Mahn | 9 | Uffz Paul Knopf | 3 |
| Vfw Karl Arnold | 6 | Ltn Grosse | 2 |

| Ltn Gustav Frädrich | 5(6) | Ltn Gottfried Clausnitzer | I |
| Ltn Ernst Schulz | 4 | Ltn Schmid zur Nedden | I |
| Ltn Gerold Tschentschel | 4(5) | Ltn Porak | I |

### Airfields occupied

| Location | Inclusive Dates | Armee |
| --- | --- | --- |
| Grossenhain | 11 Feb 1918 – 20 Feb 1918 | FEA6 |
| Blaise | 2 Mar 1918 – 8 Mar 1918 | 3 |
| Leffincourt | 8 Mar 1918 – 28 Mar 1918 | 3 |
| Carrepuis | 28 Mar 1918 – 7 Jul 1918 | 18 |
| Bergnicourt, Rethel | 7 Jul 1918 – 10 Oct 1918 | I |
| Thin-le-Montier | 10 Oct 1918 – 11 Nov 1918 | I |

## ROYAL PRUSSIAN JAGDSTAFFEL 73

Jasta 73 was formed on 11 February 1918 at FEA 14, Halle an der Salle, as authorised by Kriegs Ministerium von Nr.744.17.g.A.7.L. under the command of Leutnant Fritz Gerhard Anders from Jasta 4 (one victory). It moved to the Front on 9 March taking up residence in the 3 Armee Sector. Its first loss came on 21 March, Flieger Franz Matuszewsky being shot down in flames over Nauroy. On 21 May it moved to the 1 Armee Front, where it remained for the rest of the war. Finally the Jasta reported its initial victory on 30 May, Vizefeldwebel Fritz John Jacobsen downing his fifth victory, an AR2 over Auberive. Leutnant Anders was lightly wounded in action on 15 October and was transferred to Jastaschule II, his place being taken by Leutnant Wilhelm Schwartz (six victories) reporting in from FEA14. Jasta 73 was the premier night-fighter unit of the Jagdstaffeln, scoring at least seven of its 29 confirmed victories at night. Leutnant Anders was the first night-fighter ace. These victories came at the loss of three pilots killed and one, Anders, wounded.

### Commanding Officers

| Ltn Fritz Gerhard Anders | 11 Feb 1918 – 18 Oct 1918 |
| --- | --- |
| Ltn Wilhelm Schwartz | 18 Oct 1918 – 11 Nov 1918 |

### Pilots credited with victories

| Ltn Franz Kirchfeld | 8 | Vfw Harling | I |
| --- | --- | --- | --- |
| Ltn Fritz Gerhard Anders | 6(7) | Vfw Hermann | I |
| Ltn Fritz John Jacobsen | 6(8) | Ltn Hübner | I |
| OfStv Werner Schluckebier | 3 | Vfw Rudolf Nebel | I |
| Ltn Wilhelm Schwartz | 2(8) | | |

### Airfields occupied

| Location | Inclusive Dates | Armee |
| --- | --- | --- |
| Halle an der Salle | 11 Feb 1918 – 9 Mar 1918 | FEA14 |
| Mars-sous-Bourcq | 9 Mar 1918 – 21 May 1918 | 3 |
| St Rémy-le-Petit | 21 May 1918 – 14 Sep 1918 | I |
| St Loup-en-Champagne | 14 Sep 1918 – 11 Oct 1918 | I |
| Thin-le-Montier | 11 Oct 1918 – 6 Nov 1918 | I |
| Halma, Rochefort | 8 Nov 1918 – 11 Nov 1918 | I |

## ROYAL PRUSSIAN JAGDSTAFFEL 74

This Jasta was created on 16 February 1918 at FEA1, Altenburg, pursuant to Kriegs Ministerium von Nr.744.17.g.A.7.L., under the command of Oberleutnant Theodor Cammann, two victories, who arrived from Jasta Boelcke. It became operational on 5 March operating in the 1 Armee Sector. The first victory was scored by Cammann on 3 April as he downed a Spad XIII over Mourmelon. The first loss was Leutnant Günther Keitsch, who was killed over Reims in an Albatros DVa on 29 May. Cammann took leave on 14 July, his place being taken by Oberleutnant Beerendonk (acting). Cammann was lightly wounded in action on 22 August, the day after his leave expired, and his place as commander was temporarily taken by Leutnant Neumann of the unit, until Cammann's return on 1 October. On 15 September Jasta 74 moved to the 5 Armee Front, where it was to see out the war. The unit was credited with at least 22 confirmed victories, one of these being a night victory by Cammann on 21 August, at the loss of one pilot killed and one wounded. Another pilot, Leutnant Selzer, was captured on 3 August, but managed to escape that evening and return to the unit.

### Commanding Officers

| | | |
|---|---|---|
| Oblt Theodor Cammann | 5 Mar 1918 – 14 Jul 1918 | Leave |
| Oblt Beerendonk | 14 Jul 1918 – 20 Aug 1918 | Acting |
| Oblt Theodor Cammann | 21 Aug 1918 – 22 Aug 1918 | WIA |
| Ltn Neumann | 23 Aug 1918 – 1 Oct 1918 | Acting |
| Oblt Theodor Camman | 1 Oct 1918 – 11 Nov 1918 | |

### Pilots credited with victories

| | | | |
|---|---|---|---|
| Oblt Theodor Cammann | 10(12) | Oblt Beerendonk | 1 |
| Vfw Wilhelm Hippert | 2(8) | Ltn Richter | 1 |
| Ltn Dangers | 2 | Ltn Selzer | 1 |
| Ltn Günther Keitsch* | 2(3) | Gefr Weidner | 1 |
| Ltn Rudolf Otto | 2(5) | | |

### Airfields occupied

| Location | Inclusive Dates | Armee |
|---|---|---|
| Altenburg | 16 Feb 1918 – 5 Mar 1918 | FEA1 |
| Bergnicourt, Rethel | 5 Mar 1918 – 30 Mar 1918 | 1 |
| St Loup-en-Champagne | 30 Mar 1918 – 15 Jul 1918 | 1 |
| Pont Faverger | 15 Jul 1918 – 17 Jul 1918 | 1 |
| St Loup-en-Champagne | 17 Jul 1918 – 15 Sep 1918 | 1 |
| Preutin | 15 Sep 1918 – 11 Nov 1918 | 5 |

## ROYAL PRUSSIAN JAGDSTAFFEL 75

Jasta 75 was formed in accordance with Kriegs Ministerium von Nr.744.17.g.A.7.L., on 14 February 1918 at FEA2, Schneidemühl, under the command of Oberleutnant Hasso von Wedel (one victory), who reported from Jasta 14. It moved on 25 February to the Armee-Abteilung TBU Sector, where it remained for the duration of the war. Its first confirmed victory occurred on 16 May, von Wedel downing a balloon at 1615 hours over Mansbach as his second confirmed victory. In turn, he was lightly wounded in action on 28 June and his place as commander was temporarily taken by Leutnant Lothar Häussler. Von Wedel returned on 1 August and led the unit until 23 August when he was transferred to the command of Jasta 24s and Oberleutnant Walther Karjus (one victory) arrived to assume command. The unit was credited with just four confirmed victories, at a loss of one pilot killed, one wounded, and one who died of wounds.

### Commanding Officers

| | | |
|---|---|---|
| Oblt Hasso von Wedel | 21 Feb 1918 – 28 Jun 1918 | WIA |
| Ltn Lothar Häussler | 12 Jul 1918 – 1 Aug 1918 | Acting |
| Oblt Hasso von Wedel | 1 Aug 1918 – 23 Aug 1918 | CO J24s |
| Oblt Walther Karjus | 23 Aug 1918 – 11 Nov 1918 | |

### Pilots credited with victories

| | | | |
|---|---|---|---|
| Ltn Hesse | 1 | Vfw Meinberg | 1(2) |
| Oblt Walther Karjus | 1 | Oblt Hasso von Wedel | 1(5) |

### Airfields occupied

| Location | Inclusive Dates | Armee |
|---|---|---|
| Schneidemühl | 14 Feb 1918 – 25 Feb 1918 | FEA2 |
| Habsheim | 25 Feb 1918 – 11 Nov 1918 | B |

## ROYAL BAVARIAN JAGDSTAFFEL 76

Jasta 76b was created by authorisation of Kriegs Ministerium von Nr.74.17.g.A.7.L., and Bavarian Kriegs Ministerium von 7.9.17 Nr.144592 on 7 September 1917 at FEA1b, Schleissheim, and moved to the Armee-Abteilung TBU Front on 4 November. Its commander was Leutnant Walter Böning who joined the unit from Jasta 19 on 2 November with six victories. He was to garner eleven more victories while leading the unit. The first loss occurred on 23 November, Unteroffizier Eduard Feig killed in a crash at the airfield at Habsheim. The initial victory belonged to Leutnant Hans Böhning (not to be confused with Ltn Walter Böning) when he downed a Sopwith at Hagenbach on 1 December. The initial combat loss occurred on 12 December, Leutnant Wilhelm Kolb killed in action over Habsheim at 1630 hours in Albatros DVa 5294/17. The unit moved to the 2 Armee Sector on 18 March. Böning was wounded in action on 31 May, his place being taken by Leutnant Ludwig Schmid of Jasta 34b. He, in turn, was wounded on 16 July, and Jasta 76b was then placed under the command of Oberleutnant Amandus Rostock of Jasta 77b. On 10 July the Jasta moved to the 1 Armee area, and to Armee-Abteilung TBU on 19 August. The unit was credited with at least 20 confirmed victories at a cost of six pilots killed in action, another six wounded, three taken prisoner and one killed in a crash.

### Commanding Officers

| | |
|---|---|
| Ltn Walter Böning | 2 Nov 1917 – 31 May 1918 |
| Ltn Ludwig Schmid | 23 Jun 1918 – 16 Jul 1918 |
| Oblt Amandus Rostock | 16 Jul 1918 – 11 Nov 1918 |

### Pilots credited with victories

| | | | |
|---|---|---|---|
| Ltn Walter Böning | 11(17) | Uffz Hapf | 1 |
| Uffz Walther | 2 | Vfw Karl Koller | 1 |
| Ltn Hans Böhning | 1(16) | Vfw Georg Markert* | 1 |
| Uffz Diem | 1 | Ltn Max Schick | 1 |
| Ltn Dumler | 1 | | |

### Airfields occupied

| Location | Inclusive Dates | Armee |
|---|---|---|
| Schleissheim | 7 Sep 1917 – 4 Nov 1917 | FEA1b |
| Habsheim | 4 Nov 1917 – 18 Mar 1918 | B |
| Liéramont | 18 Mar 1918 – 15 Apr 1918 | 2 |
| Suzanne | 15 Apr 1918 – 10 Jul 1918 | 2 |
| Bignicourt | 10 Jul 1918 – 19 Aug 1918 | 1 |
| Habsheim | 19 Aug 1918 – 11 Nov 1918 | B |

## ROYAL BAVARIAN JAGDSTAFFEL 77

The unit was created pursuant to Kriegs Ministerium von Nr.744.17.g.A.7.L. and Bavarian Kriegs Ministerium von 7.9.17 Nr.144592, on 25 November 1917 at FEA1b, Schleissheim, under the command of Oberleutnant Otto Deindl of Jasta 1. It moved to the Western Front on 2 December, arriving in the Armee-Abteilung TBU Sector, where Leutnant Walter Ewers claimed the unit's first two victories on 4 January, his own fourth and fifth. Deindl was transferred to Jastaschule II on 19 January and Ewers took command. The first loss occurred on 16 January; Vizefeldwebel Otto Küpfel crashed and was hospitalised. On 27 March the Jasta moved to the 2 Armee Front. Ewers was killed in action on 15 May, his place being temporarily taken by Oberleutnant Amandus Rostock until he was wounded on 27 May, command going to Leutnant Rudolf Stark of Jasta 34b. Stark was transferred to command Jasta 35b on 14 June, his place being taken by Leutnant Otto Fuchs of Jasta 35b. Rostock resumed command on 21 June, and on 10 July the unit moved to the 3 Armee Front. On 10 July Rostock was transferred to the command of Jasta 76b and Leutnant Max Gossner (six victories) arrived from Jasta 16b to lead the unit until the end of the war. He was to score two more victories with Jasta 77b, to bring his total up to eight confirmed. On 9 August, the unit moved to the 19 Armee area, and on 14 September the unit transferred to the 5 Armee Sector, where it saw out the war. The unit was credited with at least 28 confirmed victories at the cost of four pilots killed in action, three wounded, one taken prisoner, one killed and two injured in crashes.

### Commanding Officers

| | | |
|---|---|---|
| Oblt Otto Deindl | 1 Dec 1917 – 19 Jan 1918 | JsSchII |
| Ltn Walter Ewers | 19 Jan 1918 – 14 Mar 1918 | Leave |
| Ltn Otto Fuchs | 14 Mar 1918 – 25 Apr 1918 | Acting |
| Oblt Walter Ewers | 25 Apr 1918 – 15 May 1918 | KIA |
| Oblt Amandus Rostock | 16 May 1918 – 27 May 1918 | Acting |
| Ltn Rudolf Stark | 28 May 1918 – 14 Jun 1918 | CO J35b |
| Ltn Otto Fuchs | 15 Jun 1918 – 21 Jun 1918 | FlgSch4 |
| Oblt Amandus Rostock | 21 Jun 1918 – 16 Jul 1918 | Acting |
| Ltn Max Gossner | 16 Jul 1918 – 11 Nov 1918 | |

### Pilots credited with victories

| | | | |
|---|---|---|---|
| Ltn Max Gossner | 6(8) | Oblt Amandus Rostock | 2 |
| Oblt Walter Ewers* | 5(8) | Vfw Otto Agne | 1 |
| Vfw Robert Mossbacher | 3 | Ltn Rudolf Fuchs | 1 |
| OfStv Bernhardt Ultsch | 3(10) | Ltn Ludwig Laveuve | 1 |
| Ltn Alexander Hellwig | 2(4) | Vfw Jacob Pollinger | 1 |

| Uffz Georg Sandleitner | I | Ltn Rudolf Stark | I(II) |
| Uffz Robert Schwarz* | I | | |

| | **Airfields occupied** | |
| **Location** | **Inclusive Dates** | **Armee** |
| Schleissheim | 25 Nov 1917 – 2 Dec 1917 | FEA1b |
| Habsheim | 2 Dec 1917 – 27 Mar 1918 | B |
| Le Cateau | 27 Mar 1918 – 2 Apr 1918 | 2 |
| Vraignes | 3 Apr 1918 – 23 Apr 1918 | 2 |
| Foucaucourt | 23 Apr 1918 – 9 Jul 1918 | 2 |
| St Marie, Vouziers | 10 Jul 1918 – 9 Aug 1918 | 3 |
| Ars, Kenchen | 9 Aug 1918 – 14 Sep 1918 | 19 |
| Marville | 14 Sep 1918 – 11 Nov 1918 | 5 |

## ROYAL BAVARIAN JAGDSTAFFEL 78

The unit was created on 8 December 1917 at FEA1b, Schleissheim, in accordance with Kriegs Ministerium von Nr.744.17.g.A.7.L. and Bavarian Kriegs Ministerium von 7.9.17 Nr.144592, under the command of Leutnant Robert Dycke from Jasta 16b (two victories). On 17 December the unit was sent to Armee Abteilung TCU, and relocated to Armee Abteilung TAU on 28 January 1918, where it saw out the war. The first loss occurred on 17 February, Leutnant Friedrich Poesch killed in a crash in Albatros DIII(OAW) 5120/17 on the airfield at Bursheid while taking off at 0930 hours. The unit's first victory was claimed by Vizefeldwebel Karl Kallmünzer as he downed a Spad XII over Parry Wood at 1515 hours on 27 May. Dycke was severely wounded in action on 30 July, his place temporarily taken by Oberleutnant Reinhold Ritter von Benz. He, in turn, was killed in action on 13 August, command going to Leutnant Gerhard Ungewitter and then Leutnant Hans Jungwirth. Finally, Oberleutnant Ludwig Schmid arrived from Jasta Boelcke and assumed permanent command from 9 October until the end of the war. The unit had no 'aces', but was credited with eleven confirmed victories for the loss of two pilots killed in action, three wounded, and one killed in a crash.

| | **Commanding Officers** | |
| Ltn Robert Dycke | 8 Dec 1917 – 30 Jul 1918 | WIA |
| Oblt Reinhold Ritter von Benz | 30 Jul 1918 – 13 Aug 1918 | KIA |
| Ltn Gerhard Ungewitter | 13 Aug 1918 – 14 Sep 1918 | Acting |
| Ltn Hans Jungwirth | 14 Sep 1918 – 9 Oct 1918 | Acting |
| Oblt Ludwig Schmid | 9 Oct 1918 – 11 Nov 1918 | |

| | **Pilots credited with victories** | | |
| OfStv Eduard Prime | 3 | Ltn Lidl | I |
| Vfw Karl Kallmünzer* | 2 | Vfw Ludwig Reimann | I(2) |
| Oblt Reinhold von Benz | I | Ltn Richard Schmidt | I |
| Ltn Hans Jungwirth | I | Ltn Gerhard Ungewitter | I |

| | **Airfields occupied** | |
| **Location** | **Inclusive Dates** | **Armee** |
| Schleissheim | 8 Dec 1917 – 1917 Dec 1917 | FEA1b |
| Mars-la-Tour (?) | 17 Dec 1917 – 1928 Jan 1918 | C |
| Burscheid | 28 Jan 1918 – 1928 Mar 1918 | A |
| Bühl, Saarburg | 28 Mar 1918 – 1911 Nov 1918 | A |

## ROYAL BAVARIAN JAGDSTAFFEL 79

The unit was created by authority of Kriegs Ministerium von Nr.744.17.g.A.7.L. and Bavarian Kriegs Ministerium von 7.9.17 Nr.144592 on 28 January 1918 at FEA1b, Schleissheim under the command of Leutnant Xaver Dannhuber, from Jasta 26. It became operational in the 3 Armee, but on 14 March transferred to the 18 Armee and became a permanent member of Jagdgruppe 12 (Jasta 24s, 42, 44s, 79b), under the command of Leutnant Heinrich Kroll, the CO of Jasta 24s. The first loss occurred on 11 February, Dannhuber himself severely injured when he crashed on a practice flight in a Pfalz DIIIa, his place being taken by Leutnant Hans Böhning. Böhning was to score the unit's first victory, on 22 March, as he brought down an SE5 at Vermand. The first combat loss occurred two days later, Gefreiter Linus Luger wounded in air combat and sent to hospital. Böhning was wounded in action on 20 September, and his place was temporarily taken by Leutnant Roman Schneider, until Dannhuber returned from hospital on 10 October to lead the unit until the end of the war. Jasta 79b had at least 28 confirmed victories, but at a cost of eight pilots killed in action, 13 wounded, five taken prisoner, plus three killed and two injured in accidents.

### Commanding Officers

| | | |
|---|---|---|
| Ltn Xaver Dannhuber | 28 Jan 1918 – 11 Feb 1918 | Injured |
| Ltn Hans Böhning | 12 Feb 1918 – 1 Jul 1918 | Leave |
| Ltn Roman Schneider | 1 Jul 1918 – 31 Jul 1918 | Acting |
| Ltn Hans Böhning | 31 Jul 1918 – 20 Sep 1918 | WIA |
| Ltn Roman Schneider | 20 Sep 1918 – 10 Oct 1918 | Acting |
| Ltn Xaver Dannhuber | 10 Oct 1918 – 11 Nov 1918 | |

### Pilots credited with victories

| | | | |
|---|---|---|---|
| Ltn Hans Böhning | 12(17) | Ltn Fritz Edler von Braun | 2 |
| Ltn Roman Schneider | 5 | Ltn Xaver Dannhuber | 1(11) |
| Ltn Wilhelm Buchstett | 2 | Ltn Erich Stahl | 1 |
| Ltn Alexander Hellwig | 2(4) | Ltn Hofmann | 1(2) |
| Uffz Johann Schmidt | 2 | Flg Leonard Kormann* | 1 |

### Airfields occupied

| Location | Inclusive Dates | Armee |
|---|---|---|
| Schleissheim | 7 Nov 1917 – 2 Feb 1918 | FEA1b |
| Thugny, Rethel | 2 Feb 1918 – 13 Mar 1918 | 3 |
| Villers-le-Sec | 14 Mar 1918 – 24 Mar 1918 | 18 |
| Villesleve | 25 Mar 1918 – 9 Aug 1918 | 18 |
| Flez-Suisaucourt | 10 Aug 1918 – 16 Aug 1918 | 18 |
| Castres | 17 Aug 1918 – 25 Aug 1918 | 18 |
| Chévresis-Monceau | 26 Aug 1918 – 5 Sep 1918 | 18 |
| Guise, East | 6 Sep 1918 – 8 Oct 1918 | 18 |
| La Capelle | 9 Oct 1918 – 28 Oct 1918 | 18 |
| Thuilles | 29 Oct 1918 – 8 Nov 1918 | 18 |
| Graux | 8 Nov 1918 – 11 Nov 1918 | 18 |

## ROYAL BAVARIAN JAGDSTAFFEL 80

Jasta 80b was created on 15 February 1918, at FEA2b, Fürth, pursuant to Kriegs Ministerium von Nr.744.14.g.A.7.L. Oberleutnant Erwin Wenig reported in as Commanding Officer on 25 February, and two days later the unit left for the Front, taking up station in the 19 Armee, where the unit stayed to the end of hostilities. The first serious loss occurred on 25 March; Vizefeldwebel Karl Behringer was severely wounded in combat at 1710 hours over Embercourt. He would die of his wounds on 18 May at Duss. The first victory was scored on 3 May by Oberleutnant Wenig as his second. The unit would record 15 confirmed victories with the loss of five pilots killed, four wounded, two injured in crashes, and one taken prisoner.

### Commanding Officers

| | | |
|---|---|---|
| Oblt Erwin Wenig | 25 Feb 1918 – 14 Aug 1918 | Leave |
| Oblt Gottlieb Rassberger | 14 Aug 1918 – 6 Sep 1918 | Acting |
| Oblt Erwin Wenig | 6 Sep 1918 – 11 Nov 1918 | |

### Pilots credited with victories

| | | | |
|---|---|---|---|
| Ltn Kurt Seit | 5 | Ltn Karl Romeis | 2 |
| Oblt Gottlieb Rassberger | 4 | Ltn Josef Filbig | 1 |
| Oblt Erwin Wenig | 3(4) | | |

### Airfields occupied

| Location | Inclusive Dates | Armee |
|---|---|---|
| Fürth | 15 Feb 1918 – 27 Feb 1918 | FEA2b |
| Morsberg | 27 Feb 1918 – 11 Feb 1918 | 19 |

## ROYAL PRUSSIAN JAGDSTAFFEL 81

Jasta 81 was formed at Brest-Litovsk on 15 June 1917 as Jagdflieger Ober-Ost pursuant to Ober Ost Nr.4685.Ib. 17,4578. Ib 17, 4988 Ib.17 – u. Kriegs Ministerium von 24.9.17 Nr.453.9.17.A.7.L., under the command of Rittmeister Josef Wulff. The pilots comprising the unit came from the fighter pilots and single-seater pilots serving with the various Flieger Abteilungen on the Eastern Front. On 4 July the unit began operations under the control of the KuK 2 Armee. Its first victory in the East occurred on 6 July, Vizefeldwebel Klüpfel downing a Farman over Mlynowcze. Its first loss happened on 18 July, Vizefeldwebel Kunze shot down and taken POW by the Russians. It moved on 16 August serving first with the 8 Armee and later with the Sudarmee. On 24 September 1917 it was officially designated Royal Prussian Jagdstaffel 81. On 30 March 1918 it transferred to the Western Front, taking up residence in the 7 Armee. Leutnant Herbert Wilhelm Franz Knappe reported in on 7 April 1918 to take command. Its first victory on the Western Front occurred on 27 May, Vizefeldwebel Nagler downing a Spad over Trigny as his initial victory. It remained in the 7 Armee for the next six months. On 20 August it shifted to the 2 Armee Front. On 25 August Leutnant Knappe had been severely wounded and his place as CO was temporarily taken by Leutnant Wanjek. Jasta 81 returned to the 7 Armee on 29 August, Leutnant Fritz Höhn arrived as CO on 1 September, but was shortly transferred to command Jasta 60. Leutnant Wilhelm Pritsch from Jasta 17 arrived on 3 September and he was to lead the unit until the end. On 25 September the unit moved to the 3 Armee Sector. Jasta 81 was demobilised on 30 November 1918 at Frankfurt an der Oder. The unit is credited with at least 41 confirmed victories, six on the Eastern Front and 35 on the Western Front. Its losses amounted to five pilots killed in action, two more killed in crashes, six taken prisoner, one wounded in action and two more injured in crashes.

## Commanding Officers

| | | |
|---|---|---|
| Rttm Josef Wulff | 30 Jun 1917 – 7 Apr 1918 | AFP7 |
| Ltn Herbert Knappe | 8 Apr 1918 – 24 Aug 1918 | WIA |
| Ltn Wanjek | 25 Aug 1918 – 1 Sep 1918 | Acting |
| Ltn Fritz Höhn | 1 Sep 1918 – 3 Sep 1918 | CO J60 |
| Oblt Wilhelm Pritsch | 3 Sep 1918 – 11 Nov 1918 | |

## Pilots credited with victories

| | | | |
|---|---|---|---|
| Vzw Dietrich Averes | 10 | Ltn Fritz Höhn* | 2(20) |
| Vfw Alfons Nagler | 10 | Vfw Hans Horst | 2(4) |
| Ltn Herbert Knappe | 8(9) | Vfw Gilardom | 1 |
| Vfw Otto Klüpfel | 3 | Ltn Martin Schoen* | 1 |
| OfStv Reinhold Luedecke | 3(4) | Vfw Friedrich Tenge | 1 |
| Ltn Fritz Höhn was KIA with Jasta 41. | | | |

## Airfields occupied

| Location | Inclusive Dates | Armee |
|---|---|---|
| Formed at Brest-Litovsk as | | |
| Jagdflieger Ober-Ost | 15 Jun 1917 – 4 Jul 1917 | |
| Kniaze | 4 Jul 1917 – 16 Aug 1917 | KuK 2 Armee |
| Mitau | 16 Aug 1917 – 10 Sep 1917 | 8 |
| Mitau | 10 Sep 1917 – 30 Mar 1918 | Sudarmee |
| Liesse | 30 Mar 1918 – 30 May 1918 | 7 |
| Mont St Martin | 30 May 1918 – 27 Jun 1918 | 7 |
| Magneux | 27 Jun 1918 – 28 Jul 1918 | 7 |
| Dhuizel | 28 Jul 1918 – 30 Jul 1918 | 7 |
| Boncourt | 30 Jul 1918 – 16 Aug 1918 | 7 |
| Moislains | 20 Aug 1918 – 26 Aug 1918 | 2 |
| Seranvillers | 26 Aug 1918 – 28 Aug 1918 | 2 |
| Boncourt | 29 Aug 1918 – 24 Sep 1918 | 7 |
| Leffincourt | 25 Sep 1918 – 28 Sep 1918 | 3 |
| Beaumont Ferme | 28 Sep 1918 – 9 Oct 1918 | 3 |
| Malmy-Cheméry | 11 Oct 1918 – 19 Oct 1918 | 3 |
| Merville | 21 Oct 1918 – 26 Oct 1918 | 3 |
| St Gerard Maison | 26 Oct 1918 – 11 Nov 1918 | 3 |

# ROYAL PRUSSIAN JAGDSTAFFEL 82

This unit was created pursuant to Idflieg.v.10.18.16 In.Nr.4357. Kr. und Kriegs Ministerium v.5.9.16 Nr.941.16.g.A.7.L. as Kampfeinsitzer-Staffel 2, with pilots assigned from Kampfeinsitzer-Staffel 1, on 10 August 1916. Later during November 1918, in accordance with Kriegs Ministerium v.29.10.18 – Nr.21370.18.A.7.L.IV.C, Kest 2 was redesignated as Jagdstaffel 82. No information is currently available concerning the activities or commanders of this unit. Kest 2 is thought to have scored at least six victories.

**Pilots credited with victories**

| | | | |
|---|---|---|---|
| Ltn Mittermayr | 2 | Vfw Schönfeldt | 1 |
| Ltn Sauermann | 2 | Vfw Handrock | 1 |

## ROYAL PRUSSIAN JAGDSTAFFEL 83

This Jasta was created as Kampfeinsitzer-Staffel 3 on 14 July 1916, pursuant to Idflieg v.10.8.16 In.Nr.4357. Kr.- und Kriegs Ministerium v.5.9.16 Nr.941.16.g.A.7.L.. Pilots were assigned from Kampfeinsitzer-Staffel 1; it is not known who commanded the unit at this time. Mobilised 19 April 1917, the unit was based at Mörchingen, in the Armee-Abteilung TAU Sector, and on 30 April made its first flight on this front. Oberleutnant Maximilian Edler von Daniels, from Jasta 23, was named as Commanding Officer on 11 August. Five months later, on 11 January 1918, von Daniels was transferred to the command of Jasta 61, and command of Kest 3 was assumed by Leutnant Georg Weiner, who held this position until 4 September when he was reassigned as Commanding Officer of Jasta 3. It is not known who replaced him. Kest 3 became Jasta 83 during November, in accordance with Kriegs Ministerium von 29.10.18. Nr.21370.18.A.7.L.IV.C. Kest 3/Jasta 83 was credited with the destruction of at least nine enemy aircraft, while losing two pilots killed and two wounded in combat.

### Commanding Officers

| | | |
|---|---|---|
| Unknown | 14 Jul 1916 – 11 Aug 1917 | |
| Oblt Maximilian von Daniels | 11 Aug 1917 – 11 Jan 1918 | CO J61 |
| Ltn Georg Weiner | 11 Jan 1918 – 4 Sep 1918 | CO J3 |
| Unknown | 4 Sep 1918 – 11 Nov 1918 | |

### Pilots credited with victories

| | | | |
|---|---|---|---|
| Ltn Georg Weiner | 3(9) | OfStv Grünewald | 1 |
| Flg Bünning | 2 | Uffz Krause | 1 |
| Sgt Hoffmann | 2 | | |

### Airfields occupied

| Location | Inclusive Dates | Armee |
|---|---|---|
| Created | 14 Jul 1916 – | |
| Mörchingen | 19 Apr 1917 – | A |
| Mörchingen | – 11 Nov 1918 | 19 |

## ROYAL WÜRTTEMBERG JAGDSTAFFEL 84

This Jasta was created from Württemberg Kampfeinsitzer-Staffel 4a and 4b. (W) Kest 4 was established on 7 August 1916, at FEA 10, in accordance with Idflieg.v.In.Nr.4249. Kr.- und Kriegs Ministerium v.5.9.16.941.16.g.A.7.L.; the unit was split becoming Kest 4a and Kest 4b on 15 April 1917. Pursuant to Kriegs Ministerium v.29.10.18 Nr.21370.18.A.7.L.IV.C. Kest 4a and 4b became Jagdstaffel 84w. No information is currently available on the activities of this unit. It is known, however, that Kest 4a had at least one victory and Kest 4b at least five victories.

### Commanding Officers

| | |
|---|---|
| Hptm Friedrich Karl Burckhardt (Kest4) | 10 Aug 1916 – 28 Nov 1916 |
| Hptm Claus von Werder (Kest4a) | – 25 Feb 1918 |
| Hptm Friedrich Karl Burckhardt (Kest4a) | 25 Feb 1918 – |
| Ltn Karl Stehle (Kest4b) | 3 Sep 1917 – 21 Sep 1917 |
| Ltn Friedrich Karl Weber (Kest4b) | (Nov 1917) – |
| Ltn Karl Haustein (Kest4b) | (Aug 1918) – (Oct 1918) |

### Pilots credited with victories

| Kest 4a | | Kest 4b | |
|---|---|---|---|
| Vfw Gustav Nestler | 1 | Ltn Heinrich Büssing | 1(2) |
| | | Vfw Heppner | 1 |
| | | Vfw Ludwig Hilz | 1(2) |
| | | OfStv Pohlmann | 1 |
| | | Vfw Weber | 1(3) |

## ROYAL PRUSSIAN JAGDSTAFFEL 85

Created as Kampfeinsitzer-Staffel 5 on 1 August 1916, at FEA5, by Kriegs Ministerium v.5.9.16. Nr.941.16.g.A.7.L., and was mobilised on 19 April 1917. Kest 5 transformed into Jagdstaffel 85 during November 1918, in accordance with Kriegs Ministerium v.29.10.18. Nr.21370.18.A.7.L.IV.C. No information is currently available regarding activities at this time, although it is known that Kest 5 was credited with at least four victories.

| | Commanding Officers | |
|---|---|---|
| Ltn Walter Kypke J41 | 27 Oct 1917 – 16 Dec 1917 | J47w |

| Pilots credited with victories | | | |
|---|---|---|---|
| Vfw Heidfeld | 1 | Ltn Franz Piechulek | 1(14) |
| Ltn Walter Kypke | 1(9) | Vfw Hans von Puttkamer | 1 |

## ROYAL PRUSSIAN JAGDSTAFFEL 86

This Jasta was originally established as Kampfeinsitzer-Staffel 6 at FEA7, pursuant to Kriegs Ministerium v.5.9.16. Nr.941.16.g.A.7.L. on 1 August 1916, and was mobilised 1 March 1918. Then Kriegs Ministerium v.29.10.18 Nr.21370.18.A.7.L.IV.C. established Jagdstaffel 86, to be staffed and equipped by personnel and materiel from Kest 6. No information is currently available on the activities of this unit.

| | Commanding Officers | |
|---|---|---|
| Ltn Karl Stehle J4 | 31 Mar 1917 – 3 Sep 1917 | Kest4b |

## ROYAL PRUSSIAN JAGDSTAFFEL 87

This unit was created as Kampfeinsitzer-Staffel 7, at FEA5, in accordance with Kommando der Flieger Ersatz Abteilung v.14.12.16 – Ia. Nr.235551 – u. Kriegs Ministerium v.28.12.16 Nr.1425.16. It was activated 18 April 1917. Kest 7 evolved into Jagdstaffel 87 pursuant to Kriegs Ministerium v. 29.10.18 Nr.21370.18.A.7.L.IV.C, during November 1918. No information is available concerning activities, although there were at least three victories credited to Kest 7.

| | Commanding Officers | |
|---|---|---|
| Oblt Rudolf Frhr von Esebeck J8 | Jun 1917 – 4 Oct 1917 | J17 |

| Pilots credited with victories | | | |
|---|---|---|---|
| Ltn Karl Bohny | 2(7) | Vfw Karl Bücker | 1(3) |

## ROYAL PRUSSIAN JADGSTAFFEL 88

In accordance with L.M.v.23.12.16 Nr.1425.16.A.7.L. Württemberg Kampfeinsitzer-Staffel 8 was created at FEA10, on 19 February 1917, and was activated on 1 April 1917, and operated until 1 January 1918. It is known that Kest 8 operated in the 4 Armee Sector from 8 April 1917 to 10 November 1917. Kest 8w is known to have scored at least once. Kest 8 became Jagdstaffel 88 during November 1918, in accordance with Kriegs Ministerium v.29.10.18 Nr.21370.18.A.7.L.IV.C.. No information is currently available on activities of this unit.

| | Commanding Officers |
|---|---|
| Oblt Gustav Brockmann | (Feb 1918) – |

## ROYAL PRUSSIAN JAGDSTAFFEL 89

Created on 20 February 1917, as Kampfeinsitzer-Staffel 9 at FEA9, pursuant to Kommando der Flieger Ersatz Abteilung v.14.12.16-Ia. Nr.235551 – v.28.12.16 Nr.1425.16.A.7.L. and activated 21 February 1917. During November 1918, Kest 9 transformed into Jagdstaffel 89 pursuant to Kriegs Ministerium v.29.10.18 Nr.21370.18.A.&.L.IV.C. No information is currently available on commanders or activities.

## ROYAL PRUSSIAN JAGDSTAFFEL 90

This Jasta was created from Kampfeinsitzer-Staffel 1a and 1b, which were formed from Kampfeinsitzer-Staffel 1 on 15 April 1917, in accordance with Idflieg.v.10.8.16-Ia.Nr.4357.Kr. – und Kriegs Ministerium v.5.9.16 Nr.941.16.g.A.7.L. Jagdstaffel 90 was created through Kriegs Ministerium v.29.10.18 Nr.21370.18.A.7.L.IV.C. from personnel and equipment from Kests 1a and 1b. No information is currently available on activities, although it is thought that Kest 1a scored at least three times and Kest 1b twice.

### Commanding Officers

| | |
|---|---|
| Oblt Rudolf Nebel (Kest 1a) | May 1918 – Oct 1918 |
| Hptm Willi Weber (Kest 1b) | (Apr 1918) – (Jul 1918) |

### Pilots credited with victories

| Kest 1a | | Kest 1b | |
|---|---|---|---|
| Vfw Karl Bücker | 1(3) | Ltn Blunck | 1(3) |
| Vfw Heinrich Forstmann | 1 | Ltn Willy Rosenstein | 1(9) |
| Oblt Rudolf Nebel | 1(2) | | |

## ROYAL BAVARIAN JAGDSTAFFEL SCHONGER

Jagdstaffel Schonger is a relatively unknown unit, as it never saw active service in the war. It was formed on 29 October 1918 at FEA 1b, Schleissheim under the command of Oberleutnant Rudolf Schonger, the former OzbV of Jasta 23b. Its pilots comprised Ltn Karolus Bärenfänger (one victory), Ltn Blank, Vfw Knerr, Ltn Marx, Ltn Friedrich Schönmann, and Ltn Gottfried Stumpf (one victory). Ltn Kamm was appointed as OzbV. The war ended before they could take the field, and as such, they were demobilised at FEA1b on 25 November 1918.

## MARINE-FELDJAGDSTAFFEL Nr.I

Marine-Feldjagdstaffel Nr.I was formed on 1 February 1917 at Neumünster from Sonderkommando Sachsenberg and elements of Marine-Feldflieger Abteilung II, under the command of Leutnant zur See Gotthard Sachsenberg. Its first victory was scored on 7 February by Vizeflugmeister Wirtz at Roxem over a Sopwith 1½ Strutter from the 5th Wing of the RNAS. It suffered its first loss on 24 April, the aforementioned Vizeflugmeister Josef Wirtz killed in combat over Becelaere at 0815 hours in Albatros DIII 2281/16. On 19 October 1917, it combined with Marine-Feldjagdstaffel Nr.II to become the Marine Jagdgruppe. After the formation of Marine-Feldjagdstaffel Nr.IV and Nr.V on 1 September, Sachsenberg became the CO of the Marine Jagdgeschwader, and Leutnant zur See Philip Becht (one victory) arrived from SEE II to command MFJ Nr.I on 2 September 1918. It scored its 100th victory on 28 October 1918, a DH9 claimed by Sachsenberg over Deinze as his 30th victory. MFJ Nr.I ended the war with at least 104 victories at the cost of 15 pilots killed, and 18 pilots either wounded or injured in the air or on the ground in bomb raids.

### Commanding Officers

| | | |
|---|---|---|
| Oblt von Santen | Nov 1916 – 1 Feb 1917 | MFAII |
| Ltn Gotthard Sachsenberg | 1 Feb 1917 – 2 Sep 1918 | CO MJGI |
| Ltn z S Philip Becht | 2 Sep 1918 – 11 Nov 1918 | |

### Pilots credited with victories

| | | | |
|---|---|---|---|
| Ltn Gotthard Sachsenberg | 31 | Vzflgmstr Willy Thöne | 5 |
| Ltn Bertram Heinrich* | 12 | Flgmstr Brenner | 4 |
| Ltn Theodor Osterkamp | 6(32) | Ltn z S Philip Becht | 3(4) |
| Ltn Heinrich Wessels* | 6 | Ltn Freymadl | 3 |

| | | | | |
|---|---|---|---|---|
| Vzflgmstr Hermann Hackbusch | 3 | Ltn Kurt Crüger* | 1 |
| Flgmstr Künstler | 3 | Ltn Friedrich von Gotz* | 1 |
| Flgmstr Wagner | 3 | Flgmt Kritz Kühn* | 1 |
| Ltn Tinschert | 3 | Ltn Wilhelm Mattheus | 1 |
| Vzflgmstr Josef Wirtz | 3 | Obflgmstr Karl Meyer | 1(8) |
| Flgmstr Ottomar Häggenmiller* | 2 | Flgmt Nake | 1 |
| Ltn Rohé | 2 | Flgmt Reiss | 1 |
| Ltn Gerhard Schultze* | 2 | Vzflgmstr Horst Sawatski | 1 |
| Ltn Werner Bastian* | 1 | Ltn Schuster | 1 |
| Flgmt Borschert | 1 | Ltn Karl-Heinrich Voss* | 1 |
| Vzflgmstr Bottler | 1 | | |

Flgmstr Ottomar Häggenmiller was KIA with MFJII.

| **Airfields occupied** | | |
|---|---|---|
| Location | Inclusive Dates | Armee |
| Neumünster | 1 Feb 1917 – 15 Apr 1917 | 4 |
| Aertrycke | 15 Apr 1917 – 10 Sep 1917 | 4 |
| Coolkerke | 10 Sep 1917 – 11 Nov 1918 | 4 |

## MARINE-FELDJAGDSTAFFEL Nr.II

Marine-Feldjagdstaffel Nr.II was formed on 19 October 1917 at Coolkerke with Pfalz Scouts under the command of Oberleutnant Reusch. Ltn Theodor Osterkamp from MFJ Nr.I took over on 2 March 1918. It scored its first victory on 28 January 1918, as Flugmaat Groth nailed a Spad VII over Westende-Bad. On 5 September 1918 Osterkamp took over the Marine Jagdgeschwader and Leutnant zur See Max Stinsky from the Marine Land Staffel Neumünster II became the acting CO. It finished the war with at least 75 victories at a loss of eleven pilots killed, one taken prisoner, and four either wounded or injured in crashes.

| **Commanding Officers** | | |
|---|---|---|
| Oblt Reusch | 19 Oct 1917 – 2 Mar 1918 | Leave |
| Ltn Theodor Osterkamp | 2 Mar 1918 – 17 Mar 1918 | Acting |
| Oblt Reusch | 17 Mar 1918 – 21 Mar 1918 | CO SchStI |
| Ltn Theodor Osterkamp | 21 Mar 1918 – 5 Sep 1918 | |
| Ltn z S Max Stinsky | 5 Sep 1918 – 15 Sep 1918 | Acting |
| Ltn Theodor Osterkamp | 15 Sep 1918 – 11 Nov 1918 | |

| **Pilots credited with victories** | | | |
|---|---|---|---|
| Ltn Theodor Osterkamp | 26(32) | Flgmt Eduard Blaass | 1(5) |
| Vzflgmstr Alexandre Zenses | 19 | Flgmt Groth | 1 |
| Vzflgmstr Karl Scharon | 8 | Flgmt Held | 1(2) |
| Flgomt Kulbe | 3(4) | Flgmt Illig | 1 |
| Flgmstr Carl Kuring | 3 | Flgmt Mayer | 1(4) |
| Vzflgmstr Bottler | 2(3) | Ltn Merz | 1 |
| Flgmt Stucke | 2 | Flgmstr Alfons Nitzsche* | 1 |
| Ltn Brockhoff | 2(4) | Ltn z S Max Stinsky* | 1(2) |
| Ltn Hermann Bargmann* | 1 | Ltn Weinert | 1 |

Ltn z S Max Stinsky was KIA with MFJIV. Ltn z S Hermann Bargmann was KIA with MFJIII.

| **Airfields occupied** | | |
|---|---|---|
| Location | Inclusive Dates | Armee |
| Coolkerke | 6 Oct 1917 – 3 Apr 1918 | 4 |
| Jabbeke | 3 Apr 1918 – 11 Nov 1918 | 4 |

## MARINE-FELDJAGDSTAFFEL Nr.III

Marine-Feldjagdstaffel Nr.III was formed at Jabbeke on 23 June 1918 under the command of Leutnant zur See Brockhoff with personnel seconded from both MFJ Nr.I and MFJ Nr.II. It immediately became part of the Marine Jagdgruppe under Sachsenberg. The first victory was scored on 30 June 1918 as Flugmaat Hans Goerth splashed a DH4 into the sea off Mariakerke at 2040 hours. They remained at Jabbeke under the command of Brockhoff until the end of the war, scoring at least 18 confirmed victories.

These came at the price of one pilot killed, one wounded in action, and one wounded by a bomb splinter during a raid on Jabbeke airfield.

| Commanding Officers | |
| --- | --- |
| Ltn z S Brockhoff | 23 Jun 1918 – 11 Nov 1918 |

| Pilots credited with victories | | | |
| --- | --- | --- | --- |
| Vzflgmstr Hans Goerth | 7 | Flgmt Held | 1(2) |
| Flgmt Eduard Blaas | 4(5) | Flgomt Ludewig | 1 |
| Ltn z S Brockhoff | 2(4) | Vzflgmstr Franz Mayer | 1(4) |
| Ltn Fischer | 1 | Flgmt Pfeiffer | 1 |

| | Airfields occupied | |
| --- | --- | --- |
| **Location** | **Inclusive Dates** | **Armee** |
| Jabbeke | 23 Jun 1918 – 11 Nov 1918 | 4 |

## MARINE-FELDJAGDSTAFFEL Nr.IV

Marine-Feldjagdstaffel Nr.IV was formed on 1 September 1918 when the Marine Land Staffel Neumünster II was broken up to form both MFJ Nr.IV and MFJ Nr.V. MFJ Nr.IV was placed under the command of Leutnant zur See Poss and was stationed at Neumünster. Poss accounted for the first victory when he downed a Sopwith Camel on 15 September 1918 over Zeebrugge. He was shot down and taken POW on 15 October 1918 and the unit was handed over to Leutnant zur See Eberhard Krantz. MFJ Nr.IV scored at least 22 victories, including one balloon, with the loss of three pilots killed in action, one (Poss) taken prisoner, and two wounded during an enemy bombing on Jabbeke airfield.

| Commanding Officers | | |
| --- | --- | --- |
| Ltn z S Reinhold Poss | 1 Sep 1918 – 15 Oct 1918 | POW |
| Ltn z S Wilhelm | 16 Oct 1918 – 11 Nov 1918 | |

| Pilots credited with victories | | | |
| --- | --- | --- | --- |
| Flgmstr Gerhard Hubrich | 8(12) | Flgmt Wasserthal | 2 |
| Ltn z S Reinhold Poss | 6(11) | Ltn z S Wilhelm | 2 |
| Flgmstr Albin Bühl | 3(6) | Ltn Hoffknecht | 1 |

| | Airfields occupied | |
| --- | --- | --- |
| **Location** | **Inclusive Dates** | **Armee** |
| Jabbeke | 1 Sep 1918 – 11 Nov 1918 | 4 |

## MARINE-FELDJAGDSTAFFEL Nr.V

Marine-Feldjagdstaffel Nr.V was formed on 1 September 1918 under the command of Leutnant zur See Paul Achilles as part of the break-up of MLS Neumünster. It remained stationed at Neumünster until the end of the war. When MFJ Nr.IV and MFJ Nr.V were formed, they joined the other three Marine-Feldjagdstaffeln to form the Marine Jagdgeschwader under the command of Sachsenberg. The first victory was scored on 5 September 1918 by Flugmaat Karl Engelfried who downed a 219 Squadron, RAF, DH9 over Knocke. The unit was credited with at least 15 confirmed victories at the cost of two pilots killed, one interned in Holland and one other wounded in action.

| Commanding Officers | |
| --- | --- |
| Ltn z S Paul Achilles | 1 Sep 1918 – 11 Nov 1918 |

| Pilots credited with victories | | | |
| --- | --- | --- | --- |
| Ltn z S Paul Achilles | 6(8) | Flgmt Karl Kutschke | 4(5) |
| Flgmt Karl Engelfried | 5(6) | Flgmt Christian Kairies | 1(7) |

| | Airfields occupied | |
| --- | --- | --- |
| **Location** | **Inclusive Dates** | **Armee** |
| Neumünster | 1 Sep 1918 – 11 Nov 1918 | 4 |

## MARINE LAND STAFFEL NEUMÜNSTER II

Seefrontstaffeln I and II (SEE I and SEE II) were vastly different units. SEE I, or Seeflugstation Flanders I, was formed at the beginning of the war, and operated seaplanes over the North Sea. SEE II, or Marine Land Staffel Neumünster II, was formed on 1 October 1917 as a single-seater unit to protect the seaplanes operating in the area. By 8 October it had 15 Albatros DIII scouts on charge, and was operating from Neumünster under the command of Leutnant zur See Hans Rolshoven. Its first loss occurred on 8 November 1917, Leutnant zur See Ritter shot down west of Dunkirk. Its first victory was scored on 19 December, by Flugmeister Albin Bühl, who shot down a Handley Page bomber at 1335 hours near Ostende. Rolshoven was killed in an accident at Zeebrugge in a Pfalz DIII at 1830 hours on 6 May 1918. His place as CO was assumed by Leutnant zur See Reinhold Poss. He, in turn, was transferred to the command of MFJ Nr.IV on 1 September 1918, command passing to Leutnant zur See Eberhard Krantz. Two weeks later SEE II was disbanded and the personnel and aircraft were used to create MFJ Nr.IV and MFJ Nr.V. The unit was credited with at least 31 confirmed victories, for the loss of three pilots killed in action, two more killed in accidents, two taken prisoner, and four wounded in action.

### Commanding Officers

| | | |
|---|---|---|
| Ltn z S Hans Rolshoven | 1 Oct 1917 – 6 May 1918 | KIAcc |
| Ltn z S Reinhold Poss | 7 May 1918 – 1 Sep 1918 | MFJIV |
| Ltn z S Eberhard Krantz | 1 Sep 1918 – 15 Sep 1918 | |

### Pilots credited with victories

| | | | |
|---|---|---|---|
| Flgmt Christian Kairies | 6(7) | Ltn z S Spies | 2 |
| Ltn z S Reinhold Poss | 5(11) | Ltn z S Philip Becht | 1(4) |
| Flgomt Gerhard Hubrich | 4(12) | Vzflgmstr Bieber | 1(2) |
| Flgmt Albin Bühl | 3(6) | Flgmt Karl Engelfried | 1(6) |
| Ltn z S Paul Achilles | 2(8) | Ltn z S Eberhard Krantz | 1(2) |
| Oblt Clements Kähler | 2 | Ltn z S Hans Rolshoven* | 1(2) |
| Ltn z s Theodor Lodemann | 2 | Ltn z S Max Stinsky | 1 |

### Airfields occupied

| Location | Inclusive Dates | Armee |
|---|---|---|
| Neumünster | 1 Oct 1917 – 15 Sep 1918 | 4 |

# THE

# JASTA PILOTS

**IMPORTANT NOTE REGARDING UMLAUTS IN PILOT NAMES**

Throughout the A–Z Listings in this book the authors have assumed the unwritten 'e' after the umlaut and the reader will find the entries positioned accordingly.

**ABT, Rudolf    Ltn d R**
J69                    – 21 Apr 1918    1  POW
Victories:      1.        21 Apr 1918    Spad XI            1230            SW Anezy

**ACH,    Ltn d R**
J35b      (Oct 1918) – 11 Nov 1918    –

**ADAM, Hans Ritter von    Ltn d L**
FAA2b                                    J34      2 Mar 1917 – 4 Jul 1917        3
AFPC              – 1 Mar 1917    –      J6        5 Jul 1917 – 15 Nov 1917    18  KIA
Biography & Victories: See *Above the Lines*.

**ADDIX,    Ltn**
J31                    – 26 Oct 1917    1  WIA
Victories:      1.        26 Oct 1917    Caproni                          E Grudenka

**ADOMEIT,    Ltn d R**
J10      3 Aug 1918 – 21 Sep 1918    –      J62      21 Sep 1918 – 11 Nov 1918    1
Joined Jasta 10 from Jastaschule I.
Victories:      1.        30 Oct 1918    Spad                            Brieulles

**ÄCKERLE, Otto    Ltn d R**
J47w      4 May 1918 – 11 May 1918    –  KIA
Born 12 May 1894, Biberach, Württemberg. Joined Jasta 47w from Jastaschule I. Killed over Deulemont, flying Pfalz DIIIa 5916/17.

**AGNE, Otto    Vfw**
FAA289b  15 Apr 1918 –            –      AFP19              – 26 Oct 1918    –
J77b      6 Aug 1918 – 26 Sep 1918    1      J80b      27 Oct 1918 – 11 Nov 1918    –
Awarded Bavarian Silver Bravery Medal for service with Bavarian Infantry Rgt No 2, on 22 May 1917. Joined Air Service 24 August 1917. Promoted to Vizefeldwebel in July 1918.
Victories:      1.        26 Sep 1918    DH9                1730          Grossprunach

**ALBERT, Werner    Ltn d R**
KG2/11                                    CO J31      5 Feb 1917 – 10 May 1917    4  KIA
Born 30 March 1885, Düsseldorf. Served with Field Artillery Regiment 14 'Grossherzog'. Transferred to aviation in January 1915. Killed during combat with a Spad by Vaudesincourt.
Victories:      1.        9 Mar 1917    Balloon                        Somme-Suippes
              2.        6 Apr 1917    Spad                          Mars-sous-Bourq
              3.        15 Apr 1917    Spad                          Nauroy
              4.        26 Apr 1917    Spad                          Nauroy

**ALBRECHT, Otto    Sgt**
J64w      Sep 1918 – 5 Nov 1918    1  KIA
Born 16 June 1894, Neplecken-Fischhausen, Ost-Prussen. Collided with a Bréguet during combat between Marcheville and Champlon.
Victories:      1.        5 Nov 1918    Bréguet                        Champlon

**ALBRECHT,    Uffz**
J80b      25 Jul 1918 – 11 Nov 1918    –
Joined Jasta 80b from Jastaschule II.

**ALLMENRÖDER, Karl    Ltn**
FA227  29 Mar 1916 –            –      J11      10 Nov 1916 – 27 Jun 1917    30  KIA
Biography & Victories: See *Above the Lines*.

**ALLMENRÖDER, Wilhelm    Ltn**
FA227                          –
J29      16 Feb 1917 – 30 Apr 1917    1      J11      30 Apr 1917 – 24 May 1917    1  WIA
Born 1 August 1894. Joined Jasta 29 from Jastaschule I. Awarded Iron Cross 1st Class on 21 March 1917.

Severely wounded in combat over Fonciers flying Albatros DIII 776/17. Died 30 July 1969, Prien, Germany.

Victories:      1.        16 Mar 1917        Balloon              0930            Moiremont            (a)
                2.        11 May 1917        BF2b                 1715            Beaumont
(a) French 30th Balloon Company, the observer, Adj Bry, made a safe parachute jump.

### ALTEMEIER, Friedrich      OfStv
FA67      21 Jul 1916 – –                          J24s      1 Dec 1916 – 11 Nov 1918      21
J14       25 Oct 1916 – 30 Nov 1916    –
Biography & Victories: See *Above the Lines*.

### ALTENBURG, Kurt      Ltn
J36       13 Jun 1918 – 1918            –          FA3       1918 –                         –
Infantry Regiment 19. Leutnant on 30 March 1916. Joined Jasta 36 from Jastaschule II.

### ALTHAUS, Ernst Fr von      Oblt
FA23      20 Sep 1915 – Apr 1916        – WIA      J10        6 Jul 1917 – 30 Jul 1917      1
KekV      – 1 Sep 1916                  8          JsSchII    31 Jul 1917 –                 –
J4        1 Sep 1916 – 4 Mar 1917       – WIA      Infantry   – 15 Oct 1918                 – POW
J14       Mar 1917 – 5 Jul 1917         –
Biography & Victories: See *Above the Lines*.

### ALTMAIER, Martin      OfStv
J33       (May 1917) – 12 Jun 1917      1  KIA
Born 5 November 1890, Trier. Killed in action at 1210 hours N Monchy-le-Preux, while flying Albatros DIII 2146/16.
Victories:      1.        27 May 1917        SE5                  0735            NE Corbenhem          (a)
(a) Possibly SE5 A8905, No 56 Sqn, RFC, 2/Lt G A Lloyd (POW).

### ALVERSLEBEN, Busso von      Ltn
J4        Jul 1917 – 27 Nov 1917        –          J21s      27 Nov 1917 – 14 Jun 1918      1  WIA
Born 21 April 1898, Wittenmoor. Severely wounded during a balloon attack near Villers-Cotterets, came down in Allied lines and taken prisoner, died of wounds 15 June 1918.
Victories:      1.        14 Jun 1918        Balloon              1800            Crépy-en-Valois

### AMANN,      Ltn
J2        – 1 Dec 1916                  – POW

### AMSCHL,      Vfw
FA290b    10 Feb 1917 – 9 Jul 1917      –          J79b      2 Feb 1918 – 11 Apr 1918      –
J31       10 Sep 1917 – 2 Feb 1918      3          J31       11 Apr 1918 – 11 Nov 1918     –
Born 29 February 1890, Pliesdorf Oberpfalz. Served with Field Artillery Regiment 10 from 22 October 1912 to 1 April 1913. Beobachterschule (Observer school) 1 April 1915, at Schleissheim. 'Emil' Badge on 18 May 1917. Iron Cross 2nd Class on 19 May 1917. Jastaschule I on 9 July 1917. Bavarian MVII K1 mit Schwerten on 11 August 1917. Joined Jasta 31 from Jastaschule I. Iron Cross 1st Class on 21 December 1917. Oester. Tapferkeit Medaille on 31 December 1917.
Victories:      1.        7 Nov 1917         Savoia Pomilio                       NW Sacile
                2.        13 Dec 1917        Camel                                N Crespano
                –         30 Dec 1917        Caproni                              Conegliano
                3.        25 Jan 1918        Camel                                Zenon
                –         6 Sep 1918         DH9                                  Noyon

### ANDERS, Fritz Gerhard      Ltn d R
SchSt8                                               J73       11 Feb 1918 – 13 Oct 1918      6
J35       Mar 1917 – 1 Jun 1917         –          JsSchII   13 Oct 1918 – 11 Nov 1918      –
J4        2 Jun 1917 – 11 Feb 1918      1
Biography & Victories: See *Above the Lines*.

### ANDERS,      Flg
J45       10 Jun 1918 – 14 Sep 1918     –          FEA6      14 Sep 1918 –                  –
Injured in a landing accident on 19 August 1918.

### ANDRE,      Ltn
J18       14 Jun 1918 –                 –

## ANDREAS,   Ltn
J18        13 Jun 1917 – 8 Jul 1917      –
Hospitalised on 8 July 1917.

## ANGELKORTE,   Vfw
J72s       8 Mar 1918 – 11 Nov 1918      –
Joined Jasta 72s from Jastaschule I.

## ANGERMUND, Walter    Oblt
J76b       3 Apr 1918 – 23 May 1918    – WIA
Wounded during combat with SE5s at 0950.

## ANNACK,    Ltn d R
J50        Jan 1918 – 14 Feb 1918     –              J66        14 Feb 1918 –                –
Served with Field Artillery Regiment 12.

## ANSLINGER, Franz     Ltn d R
| | | | | | | | |
|---|---|---|---|---|---|---|---|
| KG3/15 | 13 Oct 1915 – 10 Mar 1916 | – | | JsSch | 1 Sep 1917 – 4 Oct 1917 | – |
| KG/5/14 | 10 Mar 1916 – | – | | AFP2 | 4 Oct 1917 – 21 Jan 1918 | – |
| AFP6 | 30 Sep 1916 – 11 Oct 1916 | – | | J56 | 21 Jan 1918 – 25 Apr 1918 | – |
| J11 | 14 Oct 1916 – 6 Mar 1917 | – | | FEA13 | 25 Apr 1918 – 10 Jun 1918 | – |
| J35 | 6 Mar 1917 – 1 Sep 1917 | 2 | | Kest 4b | 10 Jun 1918 – 11 Nov 1918 | – |

Born 1 May 1887, Freiburg im Breisgau, Baden. Enlisted 6 November 1914, 4th Grenadier Regiment zur Fuss. Promoted Unteroffizier 22 March 1915. Transferred to aviation and FEA9 on 26 June 1915, for pilot's training. Promoted Vizefeldwebel 8 March 1916, and to Leutnant on 25 August 1916. Awarded EK II and EK I. Awarded Baden Ritterkreuz II Klasse mit Schwerten des Ordens vom Zähringer Löwen on 17 May 1918.

| Victories: | 1. | Date and unit unknown | | | | |
|---|---|---|---|---|---|---|
| | 2. | 20 May 1917 | Spad | | Hochstadt | (a) |
| | 3. | 24 May 1917 | Spad | | E Obertraubach | (b) |
| | – | 13 Aug 1917 | Caudron R4 | 1945 | Houthulsterwald | |

(a) Possibly Adj Isnard, N 82, KIA, Spad #1325.
(b) Possibly Lt Rigoulot, N 92, (see OTF Vol 4, No 4, pg 309).

## ANSLINGER, Leopold    Ltn
FA54                                   4         FA 242                                  2
FA24                                   4         Kest 9
Biography & Victories: See *Above the Lines*.

## ARMBRECHT,    Ltn
J1         (Sep 1917) – 17 Aug 1918   2         Idflieg    17 Aug 1918 –                –
Commanded Jasta 1 from 12 January 1918 to 17 August 1918.

| Victories: | 1. | 6 Sep 1917 | DD | 0715 | Mont St Martin |
|---|---|---|---|---|---|
| | 2. | 16 Nov 1917 | Balloon | | Treviso |

## ARNIM, Joachim von    Ltn d R
FAA207                                 –         J2         27 Aug 1916 – 28 Aug 1916   – KIA
Born 8 July 1894, Pensiz Gotlitz. Served in 19th Hussar Regiment. Killed over Le Transloy, possibly by Lt Albert Ball, No 60 Sqn, RFC.

## ARNOLD, Karl    Vfw
J72        8 Mar 1918 – 11 Nov 1918    6
Biography & Victories: See *Above the Lines*.

## ARNTZEN, Heinrich    Ltn d R
FFA34                                  –         J15                    – 23 Dec 1917    2
FFA2                                   4         CO J50     13 Jan 1918 – 27 May 1918   5 WIA
Biography & Victories: See *Above the Lines*.

## ARTMANN, Ludwig    Uffz
J76b       14 Apr 1918 – 12 Jul 1918   – KIA
Born 2 May 1897, Straubing. Killed at 2100 hours near Bignicourt airfield.

## AUE, Paul    OfStv
KG5/30                                    1              J10        10 Oct 1916 – 11 Nov 1918    9
Biography & Victories: See *Above the Lines.*

## AUER, Adolf    Ltn d R
AFP4      22 Jul 1918  – 1 Aug 1918       –              J40s       15 Aug 1918 – 28 Oct 1918    1   WIA
JsSchI    2 Aug 1918 – 14 Aug 1918        –
Born 7 June 1897, Cannstaat. Volunteered 1 October 1914, assigned to Machine-gun Section 9. Promoted
to Gefreiter on 21 December 1914. Awarded the Bravery Medal of the Grand Duchy of Hessia on 17
November 1915. Awarded EK II on 4 August 1916. Promoted to Vizefeldwebel 14 August 1916; Leutnant
d R on 9 December 1916. Assigned to FEA10, Böblingen, 15 December 1917, as a student pilot. Awarded
EKI. Flying Fokker DVII 4043/18 (G/2/27) when wounded in combat with Captain F O Soden of No 41
Sqn, RAF, on SE5a F5545, and forced to land inside Allied lines at Ooteghem. Died 28 January 1986,
Munich.

Victories:      1.          23 Oct 1918       BF2b                            Dutch Border       (a)
                –           25 Oct 1918       EA
(a) Jasta 40s 50th victory, probably E2470, No 20 Sqn, RAF, Lt H L Fennel and Sgt G Aitken (see *OTF* Vol 2, No 4,
pg 379).

## AUER, Hans    Ltn d R
FA9b                                      –              J26        Feb 1917 – 18 Aug 1917       3
J16       1 Nov 1916 – 15 Jan 1917        –              J32b       19 Aug 1917 – 19 Oct 1917    2
FAA296   15 Jan 1917 – Feb 1917           –              FEA1b      19 Oct 1917 –                –
Biography & Victories: See *Above the Lines.*

## AUERSBACH, Alfred    Vfw
J67       23 Mar 1918 – 11 Nov 1918       2
Victories:      1.          16 May 1918       AR2
                2.          22 Jun 1918       Balloon                         Montzéville

## AUFFARTH, Günther    Ltn
J29       10 Nov 1917 – 2 Jan 1918        – KIA
Born 28 June 1894, Marlenwerber. Joined Jasta 29 from Jastaschule I. Shot down in flames by a Camel at
1210 hours over St Auguste.

## AUFFARTH, Harald    Oblt
FFA27                                     –              J29        20 Oct 1917 – 28 Sep 1918    24
FAA266                                    –              CO JGr3    28 Sep 1918 – 11 Nov 1918    –
J18       Sep 1917 – 20 Oct 1917          5
Biography & Victories: See *Above the Lines.*

## AUGST, Otto    OfStv
J12       8 Oct 1916 – 15 Nov 1916        – WIA

## AVERES, Dietrich    Vfw ObOst
          15 Jun 1917 – 5 Mar 1918        1              J81        22 May 1918 – 11 Nov 1918    9
J74       5 Mar 1918 – 22 May 1918        –
Biography & Victories: See *Above the Lines.*

## BACHEM,    Ltn
J44s                – 2 Oct 1918          – WIA

## BACHER, Franz    Ltn
FAA224   24 Apr 1917 –                    –              J3         Oct 1917 – 11 Nov 1918       3
Württemberg Knight's Cross of the Military Merit Order on 27 Sept 1917.
Victories:      1.          19 May 1918       DH9             2030            Zillebeke
                –           11 Jun 1918       SE5a
                2.          14 Sep 1918       Spad            1815            S Thiaucourt
                –           26 Sep 1918       DH9             1715            Buch
                3.          5 Oct 1918        DH9a                            Leitzweiler

## BACHMANN, Fritz    Vfw
J6        (Sep 1917) – 21 Oct 1917        1 KIA
Born 23 February 1893, Neukirchen. Killed at 1120 hours east of Ypern.

| Victories: | – | 17 Sep 1917 | Sopwith | 0720 | Zillebeke See |
| | 1. | 20 Sep 1917 | Balloon | 1400 | Kemmel |

## BACKHAUS, Paul    Hptm

| FFA27 | 1 Aug 1914 – Nov 1914 | – | | CO J23 | 17 Nov 1916 – 4 Aug 1917 | 1 |
| FFA39 | Nov 1914 – Aug 1915 | – | | CO FAA259 | 4 Aug 1917 – 11 Nov 1918 | – |
| CO KG 2/12 | Aug 1915 – 17 Nov 1916 | – | | | | |

Born 11 October 1899, Köln. Entered military service 20 Feb 1908, assigned to Infantry Regiment 53. Named Fähnrich on 18 Oct 1908. Promoted Leutnant 18 August 1909. Entered aviation 1 August 1913. Pilot's Badge 16 April 1914. Awarded EK I on 18 April 1915. Promoted Oberleutnant 27 January 1917. Promoted to Hauptmann 18 November 1917. Knight's Cross 1st Class with Swords of the Württemberg Friedrich Order on 20 Feb 1918. Attained rank of Generalmajor in Luftwaffe during WWII on 1 April 1944. Died 23 December 1960, Paderborn.

| Victories: | 1. | 21 May 1917 | Spad | 1900 | Aizy |

## BADER, Albert    Vfw

| J64w | 1918 – 11 Nov 1918 | 4 |

Württemberg Wilhelm's Cross with Swords. Württemberg Merit Cross with Swords on 1 Nov 1918.

| Victories: | 1. | 4 Sep 1918 | Balloon | 1335 | Mandres |
| | 2. | 12 Sep 1918 | Bréguet | | Friauville |
| | 3. | 29 Sep 1918 | Spad | 1720 | SW Chambley |
| | 4. | 2 Nov 1918 | Spad | | Amanweiler |

## BÄDER, Alfred    Uffz

| J65 | 31 Aug 1918 – 11 Nov 1918 | 2 |

Joined Jasta 65 from Jastaschule II.

| Victories: | 1. | 2 Oct 1918 | Salmson | | Gercourt |
| | 2. | 8 Nov 1918 | Salmson | | Buzy |

## BÄNKER,    Ltn

| J10 | – |

## BÄR, Friedrich    Uffz

| J81 | – 29 Jun 1918 | – KIA |

Born 29 November 1891, Simmozheim. Killed over Reims, during combat with a Spad.

## BÄRENFÄNGER, Karolus    Vfw

| J28w | – 15 Nov 1917 | 1 | | Jasta | | |
| J76b | 15 Nov 1917 – 21 Jun 1918 | – | | Schonger | 29 Oct 1918 – 11 Nov 1918 | – |
| FEA1 | 21 Jun 1918 – | | | | | |

| Victories: | 1. | 25 May 1917 | Sopwith 2 | 1205 | Langemarck | (a) |

(a) Probably #3963, 2/Lts J Johnstone & T S Miller, 45 Sqn, RFC POWs.

## BÄRWALD,    Vfw

| J37 | (Sep 1917) – (Oct 1917) | 2 |

| Victories: | 1. | 25 Sep 1917 | DH5 | 1830 | Monchy |
| | 2. | 17 Oct 1917 | Camel | 0930 | Tolhoek |

## BÄUMER, Paul    Ltn d R

| FA7 | 26 Mar 1917 – | – | | Hosp | 29 May 1918 – | – |
| JB | 28 Jun 1917 – 30 Jun 1917 | – | | JB | 4 Sep 1918 – 12 Oct 1918 | 40 |
| J5 | 30 Jun 1917 – 15 Aug 1917 | 3 | | Idflieg | 12 Oct 1918 – | – |
| JB | 15 Aug 1917 – 29 May 1918 | – INJ | | | | |

Biography & Victories: See *Above the Lines*.

## BAHLMANN, Hermann    Ltn d R

| J4 | 26 Oct 1918 – 11 Nov 1918 | 1 |

| Victories: | 1. | 5 Nov 1918 | DH4 | 1030 | Dun-sur-Meuse |

Last victory scored by Jasta 4.

## BAHR, Erich    Ltn d R

| J11 | 27 Nov 1917 – 6 Mar 1918 | – KIA |

Born 30 September 1893, Beuthen. Killed at 1040 hours between Atricourt and Nauroy, flying Fokker Dr I 106/17.

## BAHREN, Gustav    Ltn d R

| | | | | | |
|---|---|---|---|---|---|
| J10 | (30 Oct 1918) | POW | | | POW #10086 A |

## BAIER, Eberhard    Ltn

| | | | | | |
|---|---|---|---|---|---|
| FA68 | 1916 – 1916 | – | | J16b | 31 Oct 1917 – 11 Nov 1918    – |
| J15 | 24 Oct 1916 – 31 Oct 1917 | – | | | |

Born 20 August 1895, Frankfurt/Main. Entered military service 3 August 1914, Field Artillery Regiment Nr.3, 1914-16. Promoted Leutnant 18 August 1915, wef 10 August 1914. Promoted to Oberleutnant 27 March 1918. CO Stukageschwader 162; CO LG2, 1939 and StG.1 1939-40. Attained rank of Generalleutnant in Luftwaffe during WWII on 1 March 1945. Died 21 February 1983, Wiesbaden.

## BAIER, Kurt    Ltn

| | | | | | |
|---|---|---|---|---|---|
| J15 | – 20 Mar 1918 | – | | J18 | 20 Mar 1918    –                    1 |
| Victories: | 1. | 28 May 1918 | BF2b | 1120 | La Gorgue |

## BAIERLEIN, Anton    Vfw

| | |
|---|---|
| J11 | 26 Nov 1916 – (Mar 1917)    – |

Flew with FA2b before joining Jasta 11. Transferred to FEA1b, Schleissheim.

## BALCKE, Eduard    Ltn

| | |
|---|---|
| J52 | 11 Jul 1918 – 11 Nov 1918    – |

Joined Jasta 52 from Jastaschule I.

## BALDAMUS, Hartmut    Ltn

| | | | | | |
|---|---|---|---|---|---|
| FFA20 | 20 Mar 1915 – | 5 | | J9 | Nov 1916 – 14 Apr 1917    13 KIA |
| J5 | 27 Aug 1916 – Nov 1916 | – | | | |

Biography & Victories: See *Above the Lines*.

## BALLY, Alfred    Ltn

| | |
|---|---|
| J52 | 9 Jan 1918 – 24 Sep 1918    – |

Served as OzbV for Jasta 52.

## BALZ, Georg Helmuth    Ltn d R

| | | |
|---|---|---|
| J47w | 3 Jun 1918 – | 1 |

Joined Jasta 47w from FEA9.

| | | | | |
|---|---|---|---|---|
| Victories: | 1. | 5 Jul 1918 | Camel | E Vaux-sur-Somme |

## BALZAR, Walter    Ltn d R

| | | |
|---|---|---|
| J44s | – 10 Jun 1918 | 2 KIA |

Born 17 August 1896, Königsberg. Served with 33rd Fusiliers Regiment. His body found in his badly smashed aircraft on 23/24 June 1918.

| | | | | |
|---|---|---|---|---|
| Victories: | 1. | 29 Mar 1918 | 2-seater | 1750 | Noyon |
| | – | 17 May 1918 | Spad | 1150 | Montdidier |
| | 2. | 10 Jun 1918 | Spad | 1725 | Ressons-sur-Matz |

## BALZAR,    Ltn

| | |
|---|---|
| J43 | 27 Oct 1918 – 11 Nov 1918    – |

## BANNENBERG,    Uffz

| | |
|---|---|
| J7 | 1917 – 11 Nov 1918    – |

## BANSMER,    OfStv

| | | |
|---|---|---|
| J44s | – 11 Nov 1918 | 2 |

| | | | | |
|---|---|---|---|---|
| Victories: | 1. | 22 Jul 1918 | BF2b | 1820 | S Sailly |
| | 2. | 24 Sep 1918 | Spad XI | 1050 | SW Attigny |

## BANSMER,    OfStv

| | | | | | |
|---|---|---|---|---|---|
| Kest 5 | – 15 Jan 1918 | – | | Kest 5 | 31 Jan 1918 –                    – |
| J47w | 15 Jan 1918 – 31 Jan 1918 | – | | | |

PROBABLY THE SAME AS ABOVE

## BARHEINE, Emil    Uffz

| | | | | | |
|---|---|---|---|---|---|
| J18 | 3 Jan 1917 – 12 Jan 1917 | – | | J35b | 5 May 1917 – 20 Oct 1917    1 WIA |
| J16 | 4 May 1917 – 5 May 1917 | – | | J35b | 4 Nov 1917 –                    – |

Served with KG 3/16 prior to joining Jasta 18. Transferred to Jasta Warschule on 12 Jan 1917. Made a forced landing at AFP4 on 10 Sep 1917, flying Albatros DV 4448/17. Wounded in the right foot NW Roulers, and forced to land on 20 October 1917, hospitalised, but returned to unit.

Victories: 1. 27 May 1917 Caudron 2000 SW Wattweiler

## BARNEKOW, Raven Fr von  Ltn

| | | | | | | |
|---|---|---|---|---|---|---|
| J4 | Sep 1917 – Dec 1917 | – | J11 | 15 Aug 1918 – 23 Aug 1918 | – | WIA |
| J11 | Dec 1917 – Feb 1918 | – | J20 | – 15 Sep 1918 | – | |
| J4 | Feb 1918 – 10 Mar 1918 | – | J1 | 16 Sep 1918 – 11 Nov 1918 | 6 | |
| J20 | 10 Mar 1918 – 15 Aug 1918 | 5 | | | | |

Biography & Victories: See *Above the Lines*.

## BARTELS, Bernard  Uffz

| | | | | |
|---|---|---|---|---|
| FAA223 | – | J44s | Sep 1918 – 11 Nov 1918 | 5 |

Biography & Victories: See *Above the Lines*.

## BARTH, Adam  Vfw

| | | | | | | |
|---|---|---|---|---|---|---|
| FA13 | – 21 Sep 1916 | – | J10 | 21 Sep 1916 – 30 Jan 1918 | 1 | KIA |

Born 31 March 1897, Weinheim, Baden. Awarded EK II and EK I. Awarded Baden Silberne Militärische Karl-Friedrich Verdeinstmedaille on 2 March 1918. Killed over Anneux, flying Albatros DV 4565/17.

Victories: – 25 Mar 1917 Nieuport S Esnes
1. 5 Dec 1917 BF2b 1120 N Cambrai

See *OTF* Vol 4, No 4, pg 310.

## BARTH, Friedrich  Uffz

| | | | | |
|---|---|---|---|---|
| J18 | 7 May 1918 – 16 May 1918 | – | Hosp | 25 May 1918 – |
| J34b | 16 May 1918 – 25 May 1918 | – | | |

Joined Jasta 18 from Jastaschule I. Hospitalised with malaria.

## BARTH, Karl  Ltn

| | | |
|---|---|---|
| J34b | 1 Aug 1918 – 11 Nov 1918 | – |

Joined Jasta 34b from Jastaschule I.

## BARTH, Oskar  Ltn

| | | | | | |
|---|---|---|---|---|---|
| FEA10 | | – | Kest 8 | 23 Jul 1918 – 5 Sep 1918 | – |
| FAA213 | 5 Apr 1917 – | – | FEA | | |
| J10 | 22 Jul 1917 – Sep 1917 | – | Idflieg | – 11 Nov 1918 | – |
| Kest 4a | 26 Sep 1917 – 23 Jul 1918 | – | | | |

Born Stuttgart, 1914 (W) Feldartillerie Regiment König Karl Nr 13 as an Unteroffizier. Promoted Leutnant 29 June 1916. Pilot's Badge 20 May 1917. Saxon Knight's Cross 2nd Class with Swords of the Albert Order 9 June 1917. Württemberg Gold Military Merit Medal on 14 July 1917. Awarded EK I on 28 August 1917.

## BARTH,  Ltn

| | | | |
|---|---|---|---|
| J7 | 24 Jun 1918 – 31 Jul 1918 | – | WIA |

Severely wounded in the head.

## BASSENGE, Gerhard  Ltn

| | | | | | | |
|---|---|---|---|---|---|---|
| Kasta 39 | 1916 – | – | Hosp | 6 Nov 1917 – | – | |
| J5 | Apr 1917 – 2 May 1917 | – | JB | – 11 Nov 1918 | 5 | |
| JB | 2 May 1917 – 6 Nov 1917 | 2 | INJ | | | |

Biography & Victories: See *Above the Lines*.

## BASTGEN,  Ltn

| | | | |
|---|---|---|---|
| J30 | 26 Jan 1918 – 16 Feb 1918 | – | POW |

Joined Jasta 30 from Jastaschule II. Forced to land behind Allied lines SE Bailleul, by a SE5, flying Albatros DV 4422/17 (G.134) with a yellow fuselage and a black diagonal line. Credited to Lt P Clayson, No 1 Sqn, RFC.

## BATHE,  Vfw

| | | | | |
|---|---|---|---|---|
| J81 | – 5 Mar 1918 | – | J74 | 5 Mar 1918 – 11 Nov 1918 – |

## BAUER, Alfred  Ltn d R

| | | | |
|---|---|---|---|
| J17 | 7 Sep 1917 – 16 Sep 1917 | – | KIA |

Born 22 April 1896, Mannheim. Served in Infantry Regiment 81. Killed between Menin and Houthem at 1940 hours in Albatros D III (G.71) possibly by Lt Chidlaw Roberts, No 60 Sqn, RFC.

**BAUER, Ernst    Ltn**
J3          Apr 1917 – 24 May 1917    1   KIA
Born 5 February 1897, Rostock. Served in Field Artillery Regiment 2. Killed near Villers-les-Cagnicourt, flying Albatros DIII 2216/16.

| Victories: | 1. | 13 Apr 1917 | FE2b | 1915 | La Bassée |
|---|---|---|---|---|---|

**BAUER, Josef    Uffz**
J76b       25 Jul 1918 –              –
Joined Jasta 76b from Jastaschule II.

**BAUER, Max    Gefr**
J23b   23 Apr 1918    – 11 Nov 1918    –
Joined Jasta 23b from Jastaschule I. Wounded in action 3 June 1918, returned from hospital 20 June 1918. Wounded when shot down in flames during combat with a Dolphin on 11 August 1918, jumped in a parachute landing safely. Probably downed by Lt C V Gardener, 19 Sqn, RAF.

**BAUER, Michael    Vfw**
J67      20 Mar 1918 – 6 Aug 1918    –          J23b      6 Aug 1918 – 11 Nov 1918    –

**BAUER, Theodor    Gefr**
J28w               – 28 May 1918    –          J34b      28 May 1918 – 30 May 1918    – KIA
Born 28 July 1893, Nürnberg. Served in Reserve Division 15. Shot down in flames E Albert.

**BAUER,    Ltn**
J1                                    –

**BAUERNFEIND, Karl    Ltn**
J34b    8 May 1918 – 19 May 1918    – WIA    J34b      17 Jul 1918 – 22 Sep 1918    1   KIA
Born 1 July 1897, Wiesau. Field Artillery Regiment 3. Severely wounded over Proyart, flying Pfalz DIIIa 8023/17, hospitalised, and returned to Jasta 17 July 1918. Killed near Demicourt, SW Cambrai, probably by 1/Lt G A Vaughn, 17th Pursuit Sqn, USAS.

| Victories: | 1. | 8 Aug 1918 | DH9 | 1255 | NW Proyart |
|---|---|---|---|---|---|

**BAUERHIN,    Vfw**
J40    27 Jul 1917 –               –

**BAUHOFER, Anton    Vfw**
J15               – 12 Apr 1917    –          Kest 4a    13 Jul 1918 – 11 Nov 1918    –
J25      12 Apr 1917 – 13 Jul 1918    4
Born 25 January 1892, Munich. Volunteered for military service 25 March 1915. Awarded Iron Cross 2nd and 1st Class. Oester. Silbern Tapferkeit Medaille. Bulgarian Tapferkeit Kreuz II Klasse and III Klasse.

| Victories: | 1. | 29 Apr 1917 | Nieuport | 0820 | Tepavci |
|---|---|---|---|---|---|
| | 2. | 16 Oct 1917 | AR2 | | Caniste |
| | zlg | 28 Feb 1918 | 2-seater | | |
| | 3. | 18 Mar 1918 | Balloon | 1400 | Opticar |
| | 4. | 4 May 1918 | AR2 | | Sudohol-Rajah |

**BAUM,    Ltn d R**
J79b    1 Jun 1918 – 3 Jun 1918    – POW
Joined Jasta 79b from Jastaschule II. Shot down over Montdidier in a Pfalz DIII.

**BAUMERT,    Uffz**
J58    22 Sep 1918 – 11 Nov 1918    1

| Victories: | 1. | 28 Oct 1918 | DH9 | 1245 | Mons |
|---|---|---|---|---|---|

**BAUMGÄRTEL, Ernst    Ltn d R**
J56    16 Jun 1918 – 4 Oct 1918    2 KIA
Born 13 January 1894, Lengenfeld. Shot down during combat in a Fokker DVII and jumped in his parachute over Gheluve, dead when found.

| Victories: | 1. | 15 Aug 1918 | Camel | 0935 | Poelcapelle |
|---|---|---|---|---|---|
| | 2. | 28 Sep 1918 | SE5a | 1240 | Ypern |

**BAÜMGARTNER, Robert    Ltn d R**
J23    28 Oct 1918 – 11 Nov 1918    –
Joined Jasta 23b from Jastaschule II.

**BAUMGART,     Uffz**

| | | | | | | |
|---|---|---|---|---|---|---|
| J3 | | – 24 Jan 1917 | – | J28 | 24 Jan 1917 – | – |

**BAUMGARTEN,     Uffz**

| | | | |
|---|---|---|---|
| J67 | 23 May 1918 – 11 Nov 1918 | 3 | |

Joined Jasta 67 from Jastaschule II.

| Victories: | 1. | 5 Jul 1918 | Caudron R11 | |
|---|---|---|---|---|
| | 2. | 2 Sep 1918 | Balloon | |
| | 3. | 4 Sep 1918 | Balloon | Ansauville |

**BAUR, Karl Emil     Ltn d R**

| | | |
|---|---|---|
| J3 | Mar 1917 – 19 May 1917 | – KIA |

Born 3 June 1895, Itzehoe. Served in Reserve Infantry Regiment 214. Killed flying Albatros DIII 2139/16 at 2000 hours over Guesnain airfield.

**BAUROSE,     Vfw**

| | | | | | |
|---|---|---|---|---|---|
| J20 | (Apr 1917) – 6 Feb 1918 | – | J71 | 6 Feb 1918 – 11 Nov 1918 | – |

**BAUSNER,     Vfw**

| | |
|---|---|
| J10 | – Jul 1917     – |

**BEAULIEU-MARCONNAY, Heinz Fr von     Ltn**

| | | |
|---|---|---|
| J65 | 27 Aug 1918 – 9 Nov 1918 | – POW |

Served with 10th Uhlan Rgt. Joined Jasta 65 from AFPC. Awarded EK I. Shot down near Verdun, in Fokker DVII 4635/18, the famous 'U 10' now in the Smithsonian Museum. POW #10259 A.

**BEAULIEU-MARCONNAY, Oliver Fr von     Ltn**

| | | | | | |
|---|---|---|---|---|---|
| J18 | 1 Dec 1917 – 20 Mar 1918 | – | CO J19 | 2 Sep 1918 – 18 Oct 1918 | 12 WIA |
| J15 | 20 Mar 1918 – 2 Sep 1918 | 13 | | | |

Biography & Victories: See *Above the Lines*.

**BECKER, Friedrich     Uffz**

| | | |
|---|---|---|
| J20 | 8 Dec 1917 – 10 Dec 1917 | – KIAcc |

Born 9 July 1894, Remschield. Joined Jasta 20 from Jastaschule I. Collided in mid-air with Vfw Gustav Beerendonk over Guesnain airfield; both killed.

**BECKER, Hermann     Ltn d R**

| | | | | | |
|---|---|---|---|---|---|
| FA2 | 1916 – | – | SS11 | | – |
| FA57 | | – | J12 | May 1917 – 11 Nov 1918 | 23 |

Biography & Victories: See *Above the Lines*.

**BECKER, Karl     Ltn d L**

| | | |
|---|---|---|
| J61 | – 6 Jun 1918 | – KIA |

Born 7 March 1894, Florsheim. Shot down in flames by Spads over Fretoy.

**BECKER, Konrad     Gefr**

| | | |
|---|---|---|
| J48 | 1 May 1918 – 26 Aug 1918 | – KIA |

Born 30 January 1892, Stacha. Joined Jasta 48 from AFP18. Shot down over Fins.

**BECKER, Wilhelm     Ltn**

| | | |
|---|---|---|
| J17 | 17 Jun 1917 – 26 Aug 1918 | 2 |

Joined Jasta 17 from AFP1. Transferred to Beobachterschule on 26 August 1918.

| Victories: | 1. | 17 Aug 1917 | Sopwith | 2125 | NE Cortemarck |
|---|---|---|---|---|---|
| | 2. | 1 Apr 1918 | AR2 | 0840 | Mesnil |

**BECKER,     Ltn d R**

| | | | | | |
|---|---|---|---|---|---|
| J12 | – 6 Dec 1917 | – | JsSchII | May 1918 – | – |
| J43 | 6 Dec 1917 – May 1918 | – | J52 | 9 Jun 1918 – 11 Nov 1918 | 1 |

| Victories: | 1. | 8 Jul 1918 | Camel | 0850 | Meurchin |
|---|---|---|---|---|---|

**BECKER,     Gefr**

| | | |
|---|---|---|
| J20 | 10 Aug 1917 – 19 Sep 1917 | – POW |

**BECKER,     Uffz**

| | | |
|---|---|---|
| J21 | 1917 – | 1 |

| Victories: | 1. | 22 Sep 1917 | Caudron | 1140 | Bethelainville |
|---|---|---|---|---|---|

## BECKER,    Ltn
J26                                    –
OzbV for Jasta 26, dates unknown.

## BECKER, von    Ltn
JB                    – 1918          –

## BECKER,    Vfw
J44s                  – 1918          2
Victories:      1.      30 Mar 1918      RE8                1035        S Chauny
                2.      24 Sep 1918      2-seater           1725        Metz-en-Couture

## BECKHARDT, Fritz    Vfw
SS11                  – (Feb 1918)     –              Kest 2     (Apr 1918) –              –
J26         (Feb 1918) – (Apr 1918)    1
Victories:      –       23 Mar 1918      SE5a                           Cherzey
                1.      11 Apr 1918      RE8                1750        N Arras

## BECKMANN, Ludwig    Ltn d R
J6          Dec 1917 – 21 Feb 1918     –              J56    11 Mar 1918 – 11 Nov 1918    8
J48         21 Feb 1918 – 11 Mar 1918  –
Biography & Victories: See *Above the Lines*.

## BEERENDONK, Gustav    Gefr
J10         21 Sep 1916 – (Jan 1917)   –              J20    7 Jun 1917 – 10 Dec 1917    2    KIAcc
Born 20 December 1892, Osnabruck. Flew with KG 7/41 before Joining Jasta 10. Lightly wounded in
action 16 October 1916. Joined Jasta 20 from Jastaschule I. Lightly wounded during a bombing attack on
the Varsenaere airfield by Allied planes, on 3 September 1917. Killed in a collision with Uffz Friedrich
Becker over the Guesnain airfield on 10 December 1917.
Victories:      1.      17 Jul 1917      Camel              1930        Nieuport
                2.      17 Aug 1917      Camel              1215        N Dixmuiden          (a)
(a) Possibly N6334, Naval 6, F/S/Lt Strathy.

## BEERENDONCK,    Oblt
J74         14 Jul 1918 – 20 Aug 1918  1              CO J52  20 Aug 1918 – 11 Nov 1918    –
Acting CO Jasta 74 from 14 July 1918 to 20 August 1918.
Victories:      1.      22 Jul 1918      Spad               1745        Belval

## BEGER,    Uffz
J58         15 Jul 1918 – 11 Nov 1918  –
Hospitalised from 9 Aug to 19 Sep 1918.

## BEHLING, Alfred    OfStv
J4          Sep 1916 –                 –              J1     (Feb 1917) – 11 Mar 1917    1    KIA
Born 18 December 1891, Politz. Killed between Biefvillers and Bihucourt.
Victories:      1.      13 Feb 1917      Morane             1635        Le Transloy

## BEHNEKE,    OfStv
J54s        19 Jan 1918 –              2
Victories:      1.      30 Mar 1918      2-seater           0945        Villers-Bretonneux
                2.      18 May 1918      BF2b               0840        Ypern

## BEHRENDS, Hermann    Vfw
J61         24 Feb 1918 –              3
Victories:      zlg     22 Mar 1918      Spad                           Roye
                1.      3 May 1918       Spad               1215        E Beaucourt
                2.      29 Aug 1918      Balloon
                3.      29 Aug 1918      Balloon

## BEHRENDT,    Ltn
J77b        22 Sep 1918 – 11 Nov 1918  –
OzbV for Jasta 77b.

## BEHRINGER, Karl    Vfw
J80b        19 Mar 1918 – 23 Mar 1918  – WIA

Born 3 December 1896, Tiessendorf. Joined Jasta 80b from Jastaschule I. Wounded at 1710 near Embercourt. Died of wounds 18 May 1918.

## BEINECKE, Kurt    Vfw
J51            – 24 Jul 1918    1  KIA
Born 26 August 1897, Gronau.

| Victories: | 1. | 26 Jun 1918 | Balloon | 1650 | NW Poperinghe |
|---|---|---|---|---|---|

## BEISSEL, Joachim Graf von    Vfw
KG5/25                                    1              Kest                                          –
J22        Jan 1917 – May 1917        –

| Victories: | 1. | Date unknown | | | |
|---|---|---|---|---|---|

## BELITZ,    OfStv
J69            – 14 Aug 1918    –  INJ

## BELLEN, Gustav    Ltn d R
J10      11 Aug 1917 – 11 Oct 1917    1  WIA
Born 26 October 1892. Flying Pfalz DIIIa 8169/17 when wounded. Transferred out of aviation after wound. Died 20 January 1965.

| Victories: | 1. | 21 Sep 1917 | Balloon | 1445 | Elverdinghe | (a) |
|---|---|---|---|---|---|---|

(a) 47-11-2 (BMS 167/D).

## BELTZIG,    Flg
J56        7 Jul 1918 – 11 Nov 1918    –
Joined Jasta 56 from Jastaschule I.

## BELZ,    Vfw
J1          (Jul 1918) – 2 Oct 1918    2
POW. Shot down near Tilloy, flying Fokker D VII 5301/18 (G/1/17) and taken prisoner. Probably by a No 54 Sqn, RAF patrol.

| Victories: | 1. | 19 Jul 1918 | Spad 2 | 1340 | S Billy |
|---|---|---|---|---|---|
| | 2. | 22 Sep 1918 | RE8 | 0855 | Cambrai |

## BENDER, Julius    Ltn d R
J10      9 May 1918 – 30 May 1918    –        J25      23 Jul 1918 – 11 Nov 1918    –
J4      30 May 1918 – 16 Jul 1918    –  WIA
Born 30 August 1893, Michelfeld, Baden. Enlisted 1 August 1914, Infantry. Promoted to Leutnant d R on 18 February 1917. Assigned FEA11 on 3 September 1917, for pilot training. To AFP 'A' on 9 January 1918. To Jastaschule I on 22 January 1918. Made a parachute jump from Fokker DVII 2063/18 at 1930 on 16 July 1918, landed safely. OzbV for Jasta 25, from 23 Jul 1918. Awarded Baden Orden vom Zähringer Löwen on 27 July 1918. Died 19 January 1966, Karlsruhe, Germany (see *OTF* Vol 4, No 4, pg 311).

## BENDER,    Ltn
J12        20 Nov 1916 –

## BENDER,    Ltn
J75                              –

## BENGESSER, Karl    Uffz
J34b        28 Oct 1918 – 11 Nov 1918    –
Joined Jasta 34b from Jastaschule II.

## BENNINGHOFF, Bernhard    Ltn d R
J54        19 Jan 1918 – 27 Feb 1918    –  KIAcc
Born 29 September 1893, Bruckhausen. Killed at Neuvilly airfield.

## BENTHEIM, Constantin von    Hptm
CO JGr15    26 Aug 1917 – 30 Sep 1917    –        CO JGr2  15 Dec 1917 – 28 Dec 1917    –
CO JGr4    30 Sep 1917 – 30 Nov 1917    –        CO JGr1  28 Dec 1917 – 2 Oct 1918    –
CO JGr
Etreux        9 Dec 1917 – 15 Dec 1917    –
Commanded Jasta 8 from 9 August 1917 to 1 April 1918, in addition to the above assignments.

## BENZ, Reinhold Ritter von     Oblt
J78b     27 Apr 1918 – 13 Aug 1918    1   KIA
Born 12 September 1893, Neu-Ulm. Awarded Bavarian Knight's Cross of the Military Max-Josef Order on 28 Sept 1915 for service in Infantry Regiment 17. Joined Air Service on 15 Oct 1917. Commanded Jasta 78b from 30 July 1918 to 13 August 1918. Known to have flown Albatros DVa 6924/17 in Jasta 78b. Killed during combat with DH4s/DH9s over Mondonwald, flying Fokker DVII 4461/18.

| Victories: | 1. | 13 Jul 1918 | Salmson | 1910 | SE Manonviller |
|---|---|---|---|---|---|

## BENZIER, Hermann     Vfw
J30      8 Jul 1918 – 7 Aug 1918     –   INJ
Joined Jasta 30 from AFP 6. Injured during a landing accident.

## BENZLER, Arno     Ltn
| J32b | 14 Feb 1917 – 22 Dec 1917 | – | | J45 | 18 Mar 1918 – 27 May 1918 | 1 |
| J45 | 22 Dec 1917 – 7 Mar 1918 | – | | CO J60 | 27 May 1918 – 11 Nov 1918 | 5 |
| CO J65 | 7 Mar 1918 – 18 Mar 1918 | 2 | | | | |

Biography & Victories: See *Above the Lines*.

## BENZLER,     Gefr
J75                                   –

## BERKLING,     Uffz
J22           – 25 Mar 1917    –  WIA

## BERGMANN, Emil     OfStv
J22s            – 23 Aug 1918    1   KIAcc
Born 21 January 1888, Frankenthal. Crashed into telephone cable on landing at Flavy-le-Martel airfield.

| Victories: | 1. | 1 Apr 1918 | Sopwith 2 | 1145 | Domfront |
|---|---|---|---|---|---|

## BERGMANN, Ludwig     Vfw
J79b            – 20 Jun 1918    –   KIA
Born 1 April 1895, Murnau. Killed in combat with AR2s at 1912 hours near Autheuil.

## BERGMANN,     Gefr
J66             – 22 Jul 1918    1   POW

| Victories: | 1. | 17 Jul 1918 | Bréguet | 1030 | Dormans |
|---|---|---|---|---|---|

## BERGNER,     Ltn
J15           – 20 Mar 1918    –       J18     20 Mar 1918 –        –

## BERKEMEYER, Fritz     Ltn d R
J35             – 19 Aug 1917    2       J27     19 Aug 1917 – 29 Oct 1917     2   KIA
Born 17 June 1897, Dortmund. Forced to land 28 July 1917, and damaged Albatros DIII 2069/16, unharmed. Shot down in flames and killed over Zandvoorde.

| Victories: | 1. | 9 Aug 1917 | DH4 | 2005 | S Stadenberg | (a) |
|---|---|---|---|---|---|---|
| | 2. | 13 Aug 1917 | RE8 | 0930 | Ramskapelle | |
| | 3. | 15 Sep 1917 | Sopwith | 1938 | NW Wervicq | |
| | 4. | 21 Oct 1917 | Sopwith | 1555 | S Rumbeke | (b) |

(a) Probably 2/Lt H E Biederman and Lt A Calder, No 57 Sqn, RFC, KIA.
(b) Probably 2/Lt F L Yeoman, 84 Sqn, RFC.

## BERKLING,     Ltn
J22       1917 – 25 Apr 1918    –       J68     25 Apr 1918 – 11 Nov 1918    –
Wounded in action 23 March 1917.

## BERLING,     Ltn
J45     Aug 1918 – 11 Nov 1918    3

| Victories: | 1. | 29 Aug 1918 | Spad | | Fismes |
|---|---|---|---|---|---|
| | 2. | 4 Sep 1918 | Balloon | 1930 | Mont Notre Dame |
| | 3. | 6 Sep 1918 | Balloon | 1645 | Magneux |

## BERNEIS, Benno     Ltn d R
J9              – 8 Aug 1916    –   KIA
Born 9 May 1893, Furth. Killed near St Souplet.

## BERNER,     Ltn
| | | | | | |
|---|---|---|---|---|---|
| J15 | | – 20 Mar 1918 | – | J18 | 20 Mar 1918 – |

## BERNER,     Uffz
J66         1918 – 1
Victories:     1.        18 Jul 1918        Bréguet XIV

## BERNERT, Fritz Otto     Oblt
| | | | | | | |
|---|---|---|---|---|---|---|
| FFA27 | | – | | JB | 1 Mar 1917 – 30 Apr 1917 | 17 |
| FFA71 | | – | | CO J6 | 1 May 1917 – 9 Jun 1917 | 3 |
| KekV | 1916 – 31 Aug 1916 | 1 | | CO JB | 9 Jun 1917 – 18 Aug 1917 | – WIA |
| J4 | 1 Sep 1916 – 1 Mar 1917 | 6 | | | | |

Biography & Victories: See *Above the Lines.*

## BERNHÖRSTER, Anton     Vfw
J61             – 21 Aug 1918    – KIA
Killed during combat with No 3 Sqn, RAF, flying Fokker D VII 2184/18 (G/3/12). Credited to Lt G R
Riley on Camel F5938

## BERNSMANN, Hermann     Vfw
J29     16 Aug 1918 – 30 Sep 1918    – KIAcc
Born 10 August 1896, Ahans. Joined Jasta 29 from Jastaschule II. Killed during take-off at Marckebeke
airfield.

## BERR, Hans     Oblt
| | | | | | |
|---|---|---|---|---|---|
| CO KekA | | – 21 Aug 1916 | 2 | CO J5 | 21 Aug 1916 – 6 Apr 1917 | 8 KIA |

Biography & Victories: See *Above the Lines.*

## BERR, Carl     Ltn d R
| | | | | | | |
|---|---|---|---|---|---|---|
| FAA233 | 1917 – 1918 | – | | J51 | – 8 Oct 1918 | 1 INJ |

Was at FEA5 Hannover, during April 1917. Shot down during combat, jumped in parachute but injured
his foot on landing.
Victories:     1.        8 Oct 1918        Camel                NW Roulers

## BERS,     Ltn
J12     23 Sep 1918 – 11 Nov 1918    –
Joined Jasta 12 from Jastaschule I.

## BERTELSMEIER, Rudolf     Ltn d R
| | | | | | | |
|---|---|---|---|---|---|---|
| FA1 | | – Oct 1917 | 1 | J39 | Oct 1917 – 8 Dec 1917 | 3 POW |

Flying an Albatros DV when shot down at 1500 hours at Valstagna.
| Victories: | 1. | 7 Sep 1917 | Balloon | | Sakow-Schusna |
|---|---|---|---|---|---|
| | 2. | 25 Oct 1917 | Voisin | | Kolovrat |
| | 3. | 20 Nov 1917 | SALM | | Il Montello |
| | 4. | 22 Nov 1917 | Hanriot | 1530 | De Ros |
| | zlg | 24 Nov 1917 | Hanriot | | W Montebelluna |

## BERTHOLD, Rudolf     Hptm
| | | | | | | |
|---|---|---|---|---|---|---|
| FAA23 | | | | CO J14 | 14 Oct 1916 – 12 Aug 1917 | 4 |
| KekV | – 1 Sep 1916 | 6 | INJ | CO J18 | 12 Aug 1917 – 10 Oct 1917 | 16 WIA |
| CO J4 | 1 Sep 1916 – 14 Oct 1916 | 2 | | CO JGII | Mar 1918 – 10 Aug 1918 | 16 WIA |

Biography & Victories: See *Above the Lines.*

## BERTLING,     Ltn
J12     (Sep 1918) – 11 Nov 1918    3
| Victories: | 1. | 30 Oct 1918 | Spad | | |
|---|---|---|---|---|---|
| | 2. | 31 Oct 1918 | Spad | 1630 | Villers-devant-Dun |
| | 3. | 3 Nov 1918 | Spad | 1625 | Beaumont |

## BERTRAB, Joachim von     Ltn
| | | | | |
|---|---|---|---|---|
| FA71 | | J30 | 6 Mar 1917 – 12 Aug 1917 | 5 POW |

Biography & Victories: See *Above the Lines.*

**BESCHOW,    Sgt**

| | | | | | | |
|---|---|---|---|---|---|---|
| J6 | 23 Sep 1917 – 20 Apr 1918 | – | | J64w | 20 Jun 1918 – 11 Nov 1918 | 2 |
| AFPC | 20 Apr 1918 – 20 Jun 1918 | – | | | | |

Wounded in action 10 March 1918.

| Victories: | 1. | 11 Aug 1918 | Spad | 1050 | S Beney |
|---|---|---|---|---|---|
| | 2. | 12 Sep 1918 | Salmson | | Broussey |

---

**BESEMÜLLER, Adolf    Vfw**

| | | | |
|---|---|---|---|
| J8 | – 13 Mar 1918 | – | WIA |

Born 9 September 1892, Luchow. Severely wounded in the stomach over Ramecourt; died of wounds 14 March 1918, at Lesdins.

---

**BESSER, Hans    Ltn d R**

| | | |
|---|---|---|
| J12 | (Aug 1918) – 11 Nov 1918 | 1 |

| Victories: | 1. | 18 Sep 1918 | Bréguet | 1730 | W Conflans |
|---|---|---|---|---|---|
| | – | 26 Sep 1918 | DH4 | | Landres |

---

**BETHGE, Hans    Oblt**

| | | | | | | |
|---|---|---|---|---|---|---|
| KG1 | | – | | J1 | 23 Aug 1916 – 14 Jan 1917 | 3 |
| KekB | 4 Aug 1916 – 23 Aug 1916 | – | | CO J30 | 15 Jan 1917 – 17 Mar 1918 | 17 KIA |

Biography & Victories: See *Above the Lines*.

---

**BEY, Karl    OfStv**

| | | | |
|---|---|---|---|
| J5 | (Sep 1917) – 23 Nov 1917 | 1 | KIA |

Born 17 April 1888, Altkirch. Killed over Anneux, near Cambrai.

| Victories: | 1. | 17 Oct 1917 | BF2b | 1140 | SW Cambrai |
|---|---|---|---|---|---|

---

**BEYER, Bruno    Uffz**

| | | | | | | |
|---|---|---|---|---|---|---|
| J9 | – 18 Jan 1917 | – | | FAA235 | 9 Jul 1917 – 7 Aug 1917 | – KIA |
| J30 | 18 Jan 1917 – 9 Jul 1917 | | | | | |

Born 6 Oct 1894, Bomberg. Killed at Agnes-le-Dulsans.

---

**BEYER, Walter    OfStv**

| | | | | | | |
|---|---|---|---|---|---|---|
| J66 | 27 Jan 1918 – (Mar 1918) | – | | J24 | 8 Jul 1918 – 29 Jul 1918 | – |
| J42 | – 8 Jul 1918 | 3 | | J42 | 29 Jul 1918 – | 1 |

| Victories: | 1. | 6 May 1918 | Sopwith 2 | 1815 | Domfront |
|---|---|---|---|---|---|
| | 2. | 18 May 1918 | Sopwith 2 | | Pierrepont |
| | 3. | 3 Jun 1918 | AR 2 | | |
| | 4. | 21 Aug 1918 | Spad | 1140 | N Gury |

---

**BEYSCHLAG, Karl    Ltn d R**

| | | |
|---|---|---|
| J35b | 17 Mar 1918 – 11 Nov 1918 | – |

Joined Jasta 35b from Jastaschule I. Crashed his aircraft into a hangar at Emerchicourt, on 21 March 1918; he was not hurt. Shot down during combat with four SE5s on 11 Apr 1918, forced to land near St Martin unharmed. His aircraft was destroyed by British artillery fire. Awarded Bavarian Militär-Verdeinstkreuz 4. Klasse mit Schwerten on 9 July 1918. Hospitalised from 5 Sep 1918 to 6 Oct 1918.

---

**BIEBER,    Ltn d R**

| | | |
|---|---|---|
| J65 | 13 Jun 1918 – 11 Nov 1918 | – |

Joined Jasta 65 from Jastaschule II. Awarded EK I

---

**BIEBER-PALUBIZKI,    von Ltn**

| | |
|---|---|
| J10 | – (Jul 1917) |

---

**BIEBERSTEIN, (see also ROGALLA von BIEBERSTEIN)**
**Hans Joachim    Ltn d R**

| | | | |
|---|---|---|---|
| J3 | – 6 May 1918 | – | KIAcc |

Born 20 March 1895, Schweidnitz. Lieb Hussaren Regiment 1. Killed in accident 6 May 1918 at Rumbeke airfield, at 1735 hours during a practice flight.

---

**BIECK,    Ltn d R**

| | | | |
|---|---|---|---|
| J36 | 2 May 1918 – 30 May 1918 | – | POW |

Joined Jasta 36 from Jastaschule I. Shot down near Morcourt.

**BIEGE,     Gefr**
J51         Aug 1918 –                     –

---

**BIEHL,     Gefr**
J59                  – 14 Aug 1918    – WIA

---

**BIELEFELD, Ernst     Uffz**
J60              – 23 Jun 1918    4  KIA
Born 17 December 1896, Megiko. Killed over Reims.
Victories:      1.       11 Apr 1918         Sopwith
                2.       2 Jun 1918          Spad                            La Ferté
                3.       4 Jun 1918          2-seater        1830            St Imoges
                4.       4 Jun 1918          Spad            1835            St Imoges

---

**BIELEIT, Otto     Vfw**
J45       22 Aug 1918 – 4 Sep 1918    1           J66       4 Sep 1918 – 11 Nov 1918    4
Biography & Victories: See *Above the Lines*.

---

**BIELER, Erich     Flg**
J30       16 Aug 1918 – 11 Nov 1918    –
Joined Jasta 30 from Jastaschule I.

---

**BIELER, Konrad     Ltn**
J14       (Oct 1917) – 4 Feb 1918    4  WIA
Severely wounded.
Victories:      1.       26 Oct 1917         Sopwith 2                       Vendresse
                2.       27 Oct 1917         Caudron R4                      Pargny
                3.       2 Feb 1918          Bréguet                         Avançon
                4.       4 Feb 1918          Sopwith 2                       Pontavert

---

**BIELER,     Ltn**
JB        1 Apr 1917 – 15 Apr 1917    –
Served as OzbV for Jasta Boelcke.

---

**BIELING, Friedrich     Ltn**
J30       24 Aug 1918 – 11 Nov 1918    1
Victories:      1.       22 Sep 1918         Camel           0820            Ploegsteertwald

---

**BIENEN,     Oblt**
J38         Jul 1918 –                     –

---

**BIESEL,     Vfw**
J59         Feb 1918 –                     –

---

**BIEWERS,     Uffz**
J10       24 Apr 1918 – 12 Jul 1918    –           AFP7       12 Jul 1918 –                     –

---

**BIGALK,     Ltn**
J29       6 Sep 1917 – 30 Oct 1917                J14                  – 3 May 1918    – INJ
Reported to Jasta 29 from Jastaschule I. Transferred to Flieger-Beobachter-Schule, Thorn, 30 Oct 1917.
Severely injured in an accident.

---

**BILKE,     Oblt**
J41       Sep 1917 – Mar 1918    –
Served as OzbV for Jasta 41.

---

**BILLIAN, Erwin     Flg**
J47w                  – 11 Oct 1918    – Died
Born 5 August 1899, Karlsruhe. Died in hospital.

---

**BILLIK, Paul     Ltn d R**
SS4       Jan 1917 – 26 Mar 1917    –           J7        6 Jul 1917 – 24 Dec 1917    4
J12       26 Mar 1917 – 6 Jul 1917    12          J52       24 Dec 1917 – 10 Aug 1918    15 POW

Biography & Victories: See *Above the Lines*.

## BINDER, Vfw
J50                    – 11 Nov 1918

## BINGE, Eduard    Uffz
J16b    13 May 1918 – 11 Nov 1918    4
Born 11 February 1893.

| Victories: | | | | | |
|---|---|---|---|---|---|
| | 1. | 19 May 1918 | Balloon | 1830 | SE Furnes |
| | 2. | 19 May 1918 | Camel | 1835 | SW Dixmuiden |
| | 3. | 13 Aug 1918 | BF2b | 1945 | Armentières |
| | 4. | 28 Sep 1918 | SE5a | | |

## BINKENSTEIN, Ernst    Uffz
J51    (Jan 1918) – 24 Aug 1918    3    KIA
Born 20 October 1897, Leipzig. Shot down in flames over Ploegsteertwald.

| Victories: | | | | | |
|---|---|---|---|---|---|
| | 1. | 14 Mar 1918 | Balloon | 1630 | Ypern |
| | 2. | 1 Aug 1918 | DH9 | 0945 | NW Menin |
| | 3. | 7 Aug 1918 | DH9 | 0825 | Le Petit Mortier |

## BISCHOFF,    Uffz
J78b    6 Sep 1918 –                    –
Joined Jasta 78b from Jastaschule I.

## BITSCH,    Ltn
J9    (Apr 1918) – 28 May 1918    1    WIA
Severely wounded near Chiry.

| Victories: | | | | | |
|---|---|---|---|---|---|
| | 1. | 21 Apr 1918 | Spad | 1725 | l'Ecouvillon |

## BLANK,    Ltn
Schonger 29 Oct 1918 – 11 Nov 1918

## BLENDINGER,    Ltn
J78b    1 Nov 1918 – 11 Nov 1918    –

## BLEIBTREU,    Ltn
J45                    1918    1

| Victories: | | | | | |
|---|---|---|---|---|---|
| | 1. | 16 Mar 1918 | Spad | 1730 | Maasbogen |
| | zlg | 4 Sep 1918 | Bréguet | | Condé-sur-Aisne |

## BLEINES,    Oblt
J1                    –
Served as OzbV for Jasta 1.

## BLOCK,    Ltn d R
J6    20 Sep 1918 – 11 Nov 1918    –
Joined Jasta 6 from Jastaschule I.

## BLÜMENER, Kurt    Gefr
J6    21 Jul 1918 – 8 Sep 1918    –    KIA
Born 10 February 1894, Berlin. Shot down in flames in a Fokker D VII during combat over Beaurevoir, jumped in parachute, but it didn't open.

## BLUM,    Ltn d R
Ltn d R                    – 28 Feb 1918    1        J57    28 Feb 1918 – 11 Nov 1918    2
Acting CO Jasta 57 from 9 to 12 October 1918.

| Victories: | | | | | |
|---|---|---|---|---|---|
| | 1. | 20 Jul 1917 | Sopwith | | NW Slype |
| | – | 19 May 1918 | DH9 | | Iseghem |
| | – | 19 May 1918 | DH9 | | Iseghem |
| | 2. | 25 Aug 1918 | DH9 | | Haucourt |
| | 3. | 27 Aug 1918 | Camel | 0910 | Bullecourt |
| | – | 27 Aug 1918 | RE8 | | Gemelincourt |

## BLUME, Fritz    Ltn d R
FAA270    Apr 1917 – Jun 1917    –        J37    20 Sep 1918 – 11 Nov 1918    4
RHBZ 3    – 20 Sep 1918    –

Born 2 September 1893, Hannover. Volunteered 1 Oct 1913 in Fusielier Rgt 73, 6 Komp. Transferred to aviation Aug 1915. Emil Abzeichen 21 May 1916. Awarded EK II and then EK I on 24 Sep 1916. Promoted Leutnant d R on 18 June 1915. OzbV for Jasta 37.

| Victories: | 1. | 1 Oct 1918 | BF2b | 0915 | SE Haussy |
|---|---|---|---|---|---|
| | 2. | 10 Oct 1918 | Balloon | 1645 | N Cambrai |
| | 3. | 14 Oct 1918 | Scout | 0930 | N Neuville |
| | 4. | 30 Oct 1918 | EA | | |

## BLUME, Walter    Ltn d R

| FA65 | 18 Jun 1916 – | | – | FEA13 | 19 Dec 1917 – Feb 1918 | – |
|---|---|---|---|---|---|---|
| FAA280 | | | – | J26 | Feb 1918 – 13 Mar 1918 | – |
| J26 | 20 Jan 1917 – 29 Nov 1917 | 6 | WIA | J9 | 14 Mar 1918 – 11 Nov 1918 | 22 |

Biography & Victories: See *Above the Lines.*

## BLUMENBACH, Paul    Oblt

| J12 | 16 Nov 1917 – 15 May 1918 | 1 | CO JGr1 | 2 Oct 1918 – 11 Nov 1918 | – |
|---|---|---|---|---|---|
| CO J31 | 18 May 1918 – 2 Oct 1918 | 2 | | | |

Joined Jasta 12 from Jastaschule I. Commanded Jasta 12 from March 1918 to 15 May 1918.

| Victories | 1. | 27 Feb 1918 | Spad XI | | Essigny-le-Grand |
|---|---|---|---|---|---|
| | 2. | 15 Jul 1918 | AR2 | 0750 | SE Prosnes |
| | 3. | 6 Sep 1918 | Dolphin | 0950 | N St Quentin |

## BLUMENSAATH, Walter    Gefr

| J43 | 29 Jun 1918 – 11 Nov 1918 | 1 |
|---|---|---|

Joined Jasta 43 from Jastaschule I.

| Victories: | 1. | 31 Jul 1918 | SE5a | 2000 | SW La Bassée |
|---|---|---|---|---|---|

## BLUMENTHAL, Ewald    Ltn

| FAA203 | – 1918 | – | JB | 1918 – 1918 | – |
|---|---|---|---|---|---|

## BLUMENTHAL, Fritz    OfStv

| J53 | 23 Jan 1918 – 12 Aug 1918 | – | POW |
|---|---|---|---|

Brought down in a Fokker D VII 817/18 'Nickchen IV' (G/5 Bde/20), probably by Capt R M Foster, No 209 Sqn, RAF, and Capt F R McCall, No 41 Sqn, in Camel C61 and SE5a E4018 respectively.

## BLUMFEBAUER, H.    Ltn d R

| J12 | – |
|---|---|

## BLUNCK, Paul    Ltn d R

| J29 | 19 Jul 1917 – 28 Aug 1917 | – | Kest 1b | May 1918 – Oct 1918 | 1 |
|---|---|---|---|---|---|
| AFP4 | 28 Aug 1917 – | | JB | Oct 1918 – 11 Nov 1918 | 2 |

Joined Jasta 29 from AFP 6. Hospitalised 24 August 1917. Awarded EK I. Awarded Baden Ritterkreuz II Klasse des Ordens vom Zähringer Löwen on 18 September 1918.

| Victories: | 1. | 31 May 1918 | DH4 | | SW Karlsruhe | (a) |
|---|---|---|---|---|---|---|
| | 2. | 29 Oct 1918 | Camel | | Valenciennes | |
| | 3. | 30 Oct 1918 | DH9 | | Fayet | |

(a) No 55 Sqn, IAF.

## BLUNK,    Ltn

| J12 | 31 Aug 1917 – | – |
|---|---|---|

## BOCHMANN,    Vfw

| J41 | – 1918 | 1 |
|---|---|---|

| Victories: | 1. | 12 Aug 1918 | Bréguet |
|---|---|---|---|

## BOCK, Herbert    Ltn

| J12 | 6 Jan 1918 – (Sep 1918) | – |
|---|---|---|

## BOCKELMANN, Wilhelm    Ltn d R

| J11 | 3 May 1917 – 3 Sep 1917 | 2 | WIA |
|---|---|---|---|

Severely wounded at 1430 hours near Bousbecque, probably by a patrol from No 1 Sqn, RNAS

| Victories: | 1. | 28 Jul 1917 | Caudron | 1720 | Merckem |
|---|---|---|---|---|---|
| | 2. | 13 Aug 1917 | DH4 | 0920 | E Gent |

**BOCKSTEGERS,      Uffz**
J10                      – 15 Dec 1917    –  INJ
Severely injured during a test flight; died of injuries 18 December 1917.

**BOCKSTROH, Wilhelm      Sgt**
J52         2 Sep 1918 – 11 Nov 1918    –
Joined Jasta 52 from Jastaschule I.

**BODDIEN, Hans-Helmut von      Oblt**
J11         24 Jun 1917 – 29 Jan 1918    –              J59       29 Jan 1918 – 27 Sep 1918      5   WIA
Biography & Victories: See *Above the Lines*.

**BODENSCHATZ, Karl      Oblt**
FA3b       2 Oct 1916 – 7 Nov 1916    –                JGI       1 Jul 1917 – 11 Nov 1918      –
J2         8 Nov 1916 – 1 Jul 1917    –
Born 10 December 1890, Rehau/Ober-Franken. Entered military service 27 July 1910, with 8th Bavarian
Infantry Regiment. Promoted Leutnant 28 Oct 1912, to rank from 28 October 1910. Promoted
Oberleutnant 16 March 1916. Acting CO Jasta 2 from 22 to 29 November 1916. Served as OzbV for
Jasta 2 from 8 Nov 1916 to 1 July 1917. Served as Adjutant for Jagdgeschwader I. Promoted Hauptmann
18 Oct 1918. Awarded Eiserne Kreuz I Klasse Bavarian Militär-Verdeinstkreuz 4 Klasse Baden Orden
vom Zähringer Löwen, Ritterkreuz mit Schwerten. Türkische Eiserner Halbmond. Held rank of General
der Flieger in Luftwaffe during WWII from 1 July 1941. Deutsches Kreuz in Silber on 15 June 1942.
Died 25 August 1979, Erlangen. (Obituary in *C&C* Vol 21, No 1, pg 93.)

**BÖDINGHAUS,      Uffz**
J61         21 Jul 1918 – 22 Aug 1918    –
POW Joined Jasta 61 from Jastaschule I. Shot down and taken prisoner near Ribécourt in Pfalz D XII
1460/18.

**BÖHM, Rudolf      Hptm**
KG1                                –              Idflieg    6 Nov 1917 –                 –
CO J38      8 Jun 1917 – 6 Nov 1917    –
Hospitalised on 3 October 1917.

**BÖHM,      Vfw**
J5         (Oct 1918) – 11 Nov 1918    –

**BÖHME, Erwin      Ltn d R**
KG2/10                  8 Sep 1916    1              J29       2 Jul 1917 – 18 Aug 1917      1
J2         8 Sep 1916 – 1 Jul 1917    11             JB        18 Aug 1917 – 29 Nov 1917    11  KIA
Biography & Victories: See *Above the Lines*.

**BÖHME, Max      Ltn**
J5         15 Nov 1916 – 4 Mar 1917    –  POW
Shot down behind Allied lines after combat with FE2bs and DH2s near Tilloy-les-Hermaville, and taken
prisoner, flying Albatros DII 910/16 '8' (G.14). By Lt Pearson, 29 Sqn and Lts Graham & Boddy, No
11 Sqn, RFC.

**BÖHNE, Jupp      Uffz**
J7         (Mar 1918) – 11 Nov 1918    –

**BÖHNING, Hans      Lt d R**
FAA290   26 Apr 1917 – 3 Jul 1917    –              J76b      6 Nov 1917 – 20 Feb 1918      1
J36         3 Jul 1917 – 6 Nov 1917    4              CO J79b  20 Feb 1918 – 20 Sep 1918    12  WIA
Biography & Victories: See *Above the Lines*.

**BÖHREN, Gustav      Ltn d R**
J10         11 Sep 1918 – 18 Oct 1918    –  POW
Joined Jasta 10 from Jastaschule I. Shot down and taken prisoner over Sommerance, on 18 October
1918. POW #10086 A

**BÖHRINGER,      Oblt**
J57         6 Jan 1918 – 17 Apr 1918    –
Served as OzbV for Jasta 57.

**BOELCKE, Oswald    Hptm**

FA13                                                    J2        30 Aug 1916 – 28 Oct 1916    21 KIA
FA62                    – 30 Aug 1916    19
Biography & Victories: See *Above the Lines*.

---

**BOELCKE, Thilo    Vfw**

J67        23 Mar 1918 – 20 Aug 1918    4  KIA
Born 16 September 1896, Wittomin. Flying Albatros DVa 6591/17 when killed by protective fire of the French 85th Balloon Company, while attacking it at Montzéville.

| Victories: | 1. | 16 May 1918 | AR2 | 1945 | Avocourt |
|---|---|---|---|---|---|
| | 2. | 16 Aug 1918 | Spad 2 | | |
| | 3. | 19 Aug 1918 | Balloon | | Thierville |
| | 4. | 20 Aug 1918 | Balloon | 1730 | Montzéville |

---

**BÖMER,    Ltn d R**

J35b        22 Apr 1918    –    –
Crashed his Albatros DVa 7188/17 into a Roland DVIa during take-off on 1 June 1918; he was not harmed. Awarded Bavarian Militär-Verdeinstkreuz 4 Klasse mit Kröne und Schwerten on 12 July 1918.

---

**BOENIGK, Oskar Fr von    Oblt**

KG4/19    Mar 1916 –            –        CO J21   31 Oct 1917 – 27 Aug 1918    16
G6/32                          –        CO JGII 27 Aug 1918 – 11 Nov 1918    5
J4        24 Jun 1917 – 31 Oct 1917    5
Biography & Victories: See *Above the Lines*.

---

**BÖNING, Walter    Ltn d R**

FA6    26 May 1916 – Oct 1916        –        CO J76b   5 Oct 1917 – 31 May 1918    11 WIA
J19    26 Nov 1916 – 5 Oct 1917    6        CO J32b   1 Nov 1918 – 11 Nov 1918    –
Biography & Victories: See *Above the Lines*.

---

**BÖNINGER,    Ltn**

J71        1 Oct 1918 – 11 Nov 1918    –

---

**BÖRLINGHAUS, Wilhelm    Vfw**

J43        6 Dec 1917 – 8 May 1918    2  WIA
Born 22 July 1896, Saarburg. Shot down over Ypres, died of wounds.

| Victories: | 1. | 24 Mar 1918 | Caudron | 1745 | Champenoux |
|---|---|---|---|---|---|
| | 2. | 7 May 1918 | SE5a | 1705 | St Jean |

---

**BÖRNER, Walter    Ltn d R**

J27    10 Dec 1917 – 12 Dec 1917    – KIA
Born 21 May 1896, Berlin. Served in Reserve Jaeger Battalion 26. Joined Jasta 27 from Jastaschule II. Killed over Boesinghe, on an Albatros DV (G.98); probably downed by Lt Wigg of 65 Sqn, RFC.

---

**BOES, Hans    Ltn**

J34b        15 Jun 1918 – 11 Nov 1918    2
Joined Jasta 34b from Jastaschule I.

| Victories: | 1. | Date and unit unknown | | | | |
|---|---|---|---|---|---|---|
| | 2. | 17 Sep 1918 | SE5a | 1000 | W Cambrai | (a) |
| | 3. | 23 Oct 1918 | RE8 | 0900 | | |

(a) 80th victory credited to Jasta 34b.

---

**BÖTZOW, Fritz    Ltn d R**

J55        (Jan 1918) – 28 Apr 1918    – KIA
Born 31 March 1891, Berlin. Killed over Nablus.

---

**BÖVING, Heinrich    Ltn d R**

J9        – 1 Aug 1918    – INJ
Born 29 December 1890, Artern. Served with Reserve Hussar Regiment 2. Served as OzbV for Jasta 9. Crashed near Sissone; died in hospital.

---

**BOHLEIN, Franz    Ltn d R**

J10        (Feb 1918) – 16 Mar 1918    1  KIA
Born 13 January 1897, Bamberg. Killed at 1100 hours over Marcq.

| Victories: | 1. | 12 Mar 1918 | Balloon | 1945 | Lacouture |
|---|---|---|---|---|---|

**BOHLEN,**    **Vfw**
FA209A                        Kest 8            – 11 Nov 1918   –

---

**BOHNENBERGER, Karl**    **Sgt**
J60         – 10 Oct 1918   – KIAcc
Born 11 February 1891, Geisberg. Collided during take-off with Vfw Pfaffenritter over St Juvin; both killed.

---

**BOHNENKAMP, Karl**    **Vfw**
FFA39      May 1915 – Aug 1916     –         J22      25 Jul 1917 – 11 Nov 1918    15
FAA208    Feb 1917 –            –
Biography & Victories: See *Above the Lines*.

---

**BOHNER,**    **Flg**
J43     22 Jan 1918 –           –

---

**BOHNERT,**    **Ltn**
J43     16 Feb 1918 – 4 Jun 1918    – WIA

---

**BOHNY, Karl**    **Ltn d R**
J5          1917 – 1917        –         J17      18 Jan 1918 – 11 Nov 1918    6
Kest7    (Aug 1917) – 18 Jan 1918    2
Biography & Victories: See *Above the Lines*.

---

**BOIT, Georg**    **Flg**
J51         – 12 Mar 1918   – KIA
Born 27 September 1898, Berlin. Shot down in flames over Zandvoorde.

---

**BOLDT, Walter**    **Ltn**
J52     28 Jul 1918 – 11 Nov 1918    –
Joined Jasta 52 from Jastaschule I. Shot down during combat and forced to land between the lines on 22 Aug 1918; not harmed.

---

**BOLDT,**    **Vfw**
J24     30 Jun 1917 – 4 Aug 1917    –        J73           5 Mar 1918    –
J31     4 Aug 1917 – 5 Mar 1918    –
Victories:      –      27 Jul 1917      Sop Tripe      2040      N Menin      (a)
(a) N 5492, also claimed and awarded to Ltn von Schönebeck of Jasta 11.

---

**BOLKENIUS,**    **Uffz**
Kest 7        – 30 Sep 1917   – INJ

---

**BOLLE, Karl**    **Rittm**
KG4/23          1917       –        CO JB     20 Feb 1918 – 11 Nov 1918    31
J28w     Apr 1917 – 20 Feb 1918    5
Biography & Victories: See *Above the Lines*.

---

**BOLLE, Hermann**    **Ltn**
JB        – 18 Jul 1918   – WIA

---

**BOLLEMANN,**    **Vfw**
J60        – 11 Nov 1918    –

---

**BOLLMANN,**    **Ltn d R**
J26     17 Apr 1918 – 11 Nov 1918    –
Joined Jasta 26 from AFP 17. Acting CO Jasta 26 from 12 to 27 June 1917.

---

**BONA, Paul**    **Vfw**
J2        – 13 Oct 1916    –         J1      Dec 1916 – 6 Jun 1917    6 KIA
AFP1    13 Oct 1916 –          –
Biography & Victories: See *Above the Lines*.

---

**BONESS, Konrad**    **Uffz**
J53     17 Aug 1918 – 11 Nov 1918    1

Joined Jasta 53 from Jastaschule II.

| Victories: | 1. | 28 Sep 1918 | Spad | 1150 | Somme-Py |

---

## BONGARTZ, Heinrich    Ltn d R

| FA5 | | – | Hosp | 13 Jul 1917 – 13 Sep 1917 | – |
| KG5/27 | | – | J36 | 13 Sep 1917 – 29 Apr 1918 | 22 WIA |
| J36 | 11 Mar 1917 – 13 Jul 1917 | 11 WIA | | | |

Biography & Victories: See *Above the Lines*.

---

## BONICK,    Gefr
J81                                          –

---

## BORCHERT,    Vfw
J21        Sep 1917 –                        –

---

## BORCHMANN,    Ltn
J17        30 May 1918 –                      –

Served as OzbV for Jasta 17.

---

## BORCK, Hans Joachim    Ltn d R
J15            – 11 Aug 1918    2    KIA

Born 29 June 1893, Ranbolv. Shot down in flames over Rethonvillers.

| Victories: | 1. | 25 Jun 1918 | Bréguet | 1900 | S Rony-le-Grand |
| | 2. | 10 Aug 1918 | SE5a | 1200 | N Roye |

---

## BORDFELD, Walter    Ltn d R

| J10 | 21 Sep 1916 – | – | J11 | – 18 Jun 1917 | – KIA |

Born 12 October 1896, Brakel. Killed over Zandvoorde.

---

## BORGES,    Ltn
J22        May 1918 –                         –

---

## BORGES,    Vfw
J44s           1918           1
| Victories: | 1. | 8 Aug 1918 | SE5a | 1940 | Chaulnes |

---

## BORK, Gustav    Ltn
J15                                          –

---

## BORM, Gastav    Uffz
J1        (Aug 1918) – 11 Nov 1918    5

Biography & Victories: See *Above the Lines*.

---

## BORMANN, Ernst    Ltn d R

| FA42 | 8 Jan 1918 – | – | JB | 4 May 1918 – 11 Nov 1918 | 16 |
| J12 | – 4 May 1918 | – | | | |

Biography & Victories: See *Above the Lines*.

---

## BORNTRÄGER, Felix    Ltn
J49            1918          2
| Victories: | 1. | 30 Jun 1918 | Spad | 1105 | Auchin-Fermé |
| | 2. | 7 Sep 1918 | Bréguet | 1130 | Aubérive |

---

## BORRIES, von    Ltn d R

| J22s | (Aug 1917) – 23 Oct 1918 | 1 | J44s | 23 Oct 1918 – 11 Nov 1918 | – |

CO Jasta 44s from 26 Oct 1918.

| Victories: | – | 18 May 1918 | Spad VII | | |
| | 1. | 18 May 1918 | Spad | 1105 | S Mailly |

---

## BOSSE, (BUSSE)    Ltn
J28w           1918                           –

---

## BOUILLON,    Ltn d R

| J4 | (Aug 1917) – 29 Nov 1917 | – | APF4 | 29 Nov 1917 – | – |

| Victories: | 1. | Date and unit unknown | | | |

**BOUXIER, Josef    Uffz**
J23b    1 Jun 1918 – 12 Jul 1918    –         FEA1b    12 Jul 1918 –              –
Joined Jasta 23b from Jastaschule I.

---

**BOWIEN, Walter    Ltn d R**
J56    9 Feb 1918 – 13 Mar 1918    – KIA
Born 18 September 1895, Mohrungen. Joined Jasta 56 from Jastaschule II. Killed in action at 1015 hours over Crévccoeur.

---

**BOWSKI, Hans    Vfw**
J14    (May 1917) – 3 Sep 1917    5 WIA    J51        Jan 1918 –              –
Biography & Victories: See *Above the Lines*.

---

**BOY, Herbert    Ltn d R**
SchSt30                                         J14    (Dec 1917) – 7 Oct 1918    5 POW
Biography & Victories: See *Above the Lines*.

---

**BRAASCH, Ernst    Ltn d R**
J68    5 Apr 1918 – 11 Apr 1918    – KIA
Born 26 March 1895, Niedernbodeleben. Killed over Aubervillers.

---

**BRAATSCH,    Ltn**
J28w                    1918         –

---

**BRACHWITZ, Walter    Ltn d R**
J17    8 Jul 1917 – 1 Dec 1917    2 WIA
Born 17 February 1894, Göttingen. Joined Jasta 17 from AFP4. Died of wounds on 23 December 1917.
Victories:    1.        19 Aug 1917    BF2b        0750        Oudenberghe
              2.        27 Oct 1917    Camel        1235        W Acheville

---

**BRACKEL, von    Oblt**
J21s        1918 –                    1
Victories:    1.        1 Jun 1918    Bréguet                    Priez

---

**BRAKE, F.    Gefr**
SS37                            1        J26            – 11 Nov 1918    –
Victories:    1.    Date unknown

---

**BRANDENBURG, Max    Vfw**
J29    8 Dec 1917 – 28 Dec 1917    POW
Reported to Jasta 29 from Jastaschule II. Shot down near Le Transloy by AA fire while flying Pfalz DIII 4020/17 (G.116).

---

**BRANDENSTEIN, Aloys Fr von    Ltn d R**
J49    Apr 1918 – 11 Nov 1918    8
Biography & Victories: See *Above the Lines*.

---

**BRANDES, Otto    Ltn d R**
J15    – 12 Feb 1918    –        J24s    12 Feb 1918 – 11 Nov 1918    2
Lightly wounded in action 25 October 1918, at 1235 hours over Etreux-Fesmoy.
Victories:    1.        12 Aug 1918    SE5        1810        NW Roye        (a)
              2.        23 Aug 1918    Spad        1005        Blérancourt
              –        1 Oct 1918    SE5        1125        N St Quentin
(a) Probably Lt H M Wood, 40 Sqn, RAF.

---

**BRANDT, Franz    Ltn d R**
KG3/14    Jul 1916 – Sep 1916    –        J27    31 Dec 1917 – 27 Jun 1918    3
SS2        1916 – 1917    –        CO J26    27 Jun 1918 – 11 Nov 1918    5
J19    2 Feb 1917 – Sep 1917    2
Biography & Victories: See *Above the Lines*.

---

**BRANDT, Kurt    Gefr**
J51    – 16 Sep 1918    – KIA
Born 9 October 1896, Leipzig. Flying a Fokker DVII when killed over Quesnoy. Credited to Captain R L Manuel, N2 Sqn, AFC, in SE5a C1948.

## BRAUNMÜLLER, Georg    Vfw
J11        16 Jan 1917 – 1 Mar 1917      –              AFP6      1 Mar 1917 –              –

## BRAUN, Fritz Edler von     Ltn
J79b        Apr 1918 – 2 May 1918      – WIA              15 Jul 1918 –              2
Wounded in action 2 May 1918, hospitalised, returned to unit 15 July 1918.
Victories:      1.        Sep 1918
                2.        25 Sep 1918        BF2b              1825              Villers Guislain

## BRAUN, Hans     Ltn d R
J34b        10 Sep 1918 – 9 Oct 1918      – KIA
Born 26 October 1886, Munich. Joined Jasta 34b from AFP2. Killed during combat in a collision with
Uffz Ulm near Croix Fonsommé, at 1100 hours.

## BRAUN, Johann     Sgt
J69              – 17 Jun 1918      – KIAcc
Born 2 February 1892, Trier. Collided with Gefr Stehling in mid-air over Assainvillers.

## BRAUN, Konstantin von     Rittm
KG 2/11              – 1 Dec 1916      –        CO JGr5    8 Mar 1918 – 22 Oct 1918      –
CO J24      1 Dec 1916 – 29 Jun 1917      –        CO JGrA    22 Oct 1918 – 11 Nov 1918      –
AFP1        29 Jun 1917 –              –
CO JGr
von Braun      Aug 1917 – Nov 1917      –

## BRAUN, Siegfried     Flg
J23b        27 Jun 1918 – 16 Sep 1918      1 KIA
Born 15 June 1898, Aitrang. Joined Jasta 23b from Jastaschule I. Shot down in flames in his Pfalz DXII
at 1850 hours over Cantin, jumped in parachute but it was also flamed.
Victories:      1.        15 Sep 1918        Camel              1815              Ecoust St Mein

## BRAUN, Walter     Ltn d R
FA1b              – 1916      –        FEA1b      4 Jan 1917 –              –
J1        (Dec 1916) – 4 Jan 1917      –

## BRAUN, Walter     Ltn d R
J20        7 Aug 1917 – 19 Dec 1917      – WIA
Born 3 March 1889, Ludwigsburg. Württemberg Gold Military Merit Medal on 5 December 1917.
Severely wounded at 1405 hours over Faumont; died of wounds 20 Dec 1917.

## BRAUNECK, Otto     Ltn d R
FFA69              4        J11      20 Apr 1917 – 26 Jul 1917      3 KIA
J25        14 Jan 1917 – 10 Apr 1917      3
Biography & Victories: See *Above the Lines*.

## BRECHT, Kurt     Ltn d R
J36        20 Nov 1917 – 29 Jan 1918      – KIA
Born 28 November 1890, Neuhaus. Cuirassier Regiment Nr.3. Leutnant on 28 October 1914. Killed over
Passchendaele.

## BREDERLOW, Heinz Fr von     Rttm
KG4/21              1916      –        J17      21 Jun 1917 – 5 Jul 1917      –
CO J17      11 Nov 1916 – 10 May 1917      1        Idflieg      5 Jul 1917 –              –
Idflieg      10 May 1917 –              –        CO JGr11    19 May 1918 – 11 Nov 1918      –
Served with KG 4/21 prior to joining Jasta 17. Served as OzbV for Jasta 17, 21 June 1917 to 5 July 1917.
Victories:      1.        16 Apr 1917        Caudron              1030              Génicourt
                –        3 Sep 1918        Spad              XIII Soissons

## BREDOW,     Vfw
J14              –

## BREETSCH,    Vfw
J28w                                    –

---

## BREIDENBACH,    Ltn
J44s                    1918          1
Victories:      1.      16 Sep 1918      BF2b              0850          Roupy

---

## BREIDENBACH,    Ltn
J62      13 Aug 1918 – 11 Nov 1918    1
Victories:      1.      26 Sep 1918      Balloon            1535          Thienville

---

## BREIDT, Heinrich    Ltn
J13              – 24 Oct 1917    – KIA
Killed over Chevregny, on 24 October 1917.

---

## BREITENBACH, Bruno    Ltn
J16      3 Jan 1917 – 4 Aug 1917    –              FEA1b    4 Aug 1917                –

---

## BREITEN-LANDENBERG, Otto von    Ltn
J9      Apr 1917 – Dec 1917      4        J6      25 Mar 1918 – 26 Apr 1918    –
J6      Dec 1917 – 16 Mar 1918    1        Idflieg    26 Apr 1918 –              –
J11      16 Mar 1918 – 25 Mar 1918    –
Biography & Victories: See *Above the Lines*.

---

## BREITUNG,    Vfw
J41              – 9 Jan 1918      –                      4 Apr 1918 –              –
J56      9 Jan 1918 – 4 Apr 1918    – AFP2

---

## BRENDLE, Konrad    Ltn d R
J17      27 Sep 1917 – 25 Dec 1917    –        J45      25 Dec 1917 – 2 Sep 1918    9    KIA
Biography & Victories: See *Above the Lines*.

---

## BRENIG,    Ltn
J24s      22 Mar 1918 – 11 Nov 1918    –
Served as OzbV for Jagdgruppe 12.

---

## BRETSCHNEIDER-BODEMER, Moritz-Waldemar    Ltn d R
J6      19 Apr 1918 – 18 Jul 1918    6    KIA
Biography & Victories: See *Above the Lines*.

---

## BRETTEL, Hermann    Uffz
J10      (Jun 1917) – 15 Aug 1917    2    WIA
Wounded at 1920 hours near Moorslede.
Victories:      1.      7 Jun 1917      Spad VII          0720          S Rumbeke        (a)
                2.      10 Aug 1918      Spad VII          1625          SW Clerkem        (b)
(a) Probably B3460 of No 23 Sqn, RFC, 2/Lt Count L T B di Balme, POW.
(b) Probably MdL Camus, N 31, MIA.

---

## BREUER,    Ltn
J14      (Apr 1917) – (Sep 1917)    1
Victories:      1.      25 Sep 1917      Rumpf DD

---

## BREUER,    Ltn
J47w      6 May 1918 – 22 May 1918    – WIA      AFP4              – 18 Jul 1918    –
Hosp      22 May 1918 –              –        J47w      18 Jul 1918 –              –
Joined Jasta 47w from Jastaschule I.

---

## BRINKMANN, Hans    Vfw
J21              – 4 May 1917    – KIA
Born 13 August 1896, Barmen. Killed between Berru and Witry-les-Reims.

---

## BRINKMANN,    Gefr
J40      15 Sep 1918 – 12 Oct 1918    –

**BRINKMANN, Uffz**
J44s — 18 Mar 1918 — POW
Came down at Essigny-le-Grand, in Albatros DVa (G.151), probably by Lts E R Varley and H A F Goodison of No 23 Sqn, RFC, on Spad B6835 and B6845 respectively.

**BROBOWSKI, Heinrich Uffz**
J53 4 Aug 1918 — 28 Sep 1918 — POW

**BROCKE, Ltn d R**
J6 17 May 1918 — 30 Jul 1918 — Idflieg 30 Jul 1918 — —

**BROCKHOFF, Ltn**
J25 1917 — —

**BROCKMANN, Gustav Hptm**
CO Kest 8 —
Knight's Cross 2nd Class with Swords of the Württemberg Friedrich Order on 20 Feb 1918.

**BRODERECK, Fritz Sgt**
J42 — 18 May 1918 — KIA
Born 4 March 1890, Sensburg. Downed by a Spad over Pierrepont.

**BRONSART und SCHELLENDORF, Fritz von Oblt**
CO J7 22 Aug 1916 — 21 Jul 1917 1 KIA
Born 12 January 1891, Hannover. Commanded the Fokkerstaffel near the 34th Infantry Division before joining Jasta 7. Shot down in flames at 1945 hours near Praet-Bosch-Wynendaele Beerst road.
Victories: 1. 16 Mar 1917 Balloon 0930 Belleville

**BRUCHHAUSEN, Oblt**
J53 10 Jan 1918 — 11 Nov 1918 —
OzbV for Jasta 53.

**BRUDEL, Ltn**
J15 (Dec 1916) — May 1917 — KIA

**BRÜCHNER, Vfw**
J78b 18 Aug 1918 — 11 Nov 1918 —
Joined Jasta 78b from Jastaschule II.
Victories: — 6 Nov 1918 DH4 1500 St Georg-Ibingen

**BRÜGMANN, Heinrich Ltn**
FAA240 — J30 Mar 1917 — 15 Aug 1917 — WIA
Born 22 October 1896, Gladbach. Severely wounded in combat with Nieuports over Douvrin; died at 1400 in ambulance.

**BRÜNER, Sgt**
J75 1918 1
Victories: zlg 12 Apr 1918 Sopwith 2 Gottesthal

**BRÜNGEL, Uffz**
J31 1918 2
Victories: 1. 16 Sep 1918 Scout 0845 Gricourt
2. 25 Sep 1918 DH9 1805 Busigny

**BRÜNIG, Helmut Ltn d R**
J32 Jan 1918 — 10 Jan 1918 — CO J41 6 Oct 1918 — 11 Nov 1918 —
J50 10 Jan 1918 — 6 Oct 1918 7
Biography & Victories: See *Above the Lines*.

**BRÜNINGHAUS, Kurt Ltn**
J31 — 14 Aug 1918 — KIAcc
Born 4 July 1898, Vollinghausen. At 0930 hours collided with Lt Mayer in mid-air and was killed, who jumped in a parachute and survived.

## BRUMOW,    Ltn
J26                    − 27 Jan 1918

## BRUNEW,    Ltn
J67      21 Aug 1918 − 11 Nov 1918   −

## BRUNNECKER, Bernhard    Sgt
J29        8 Jul 1918 − 11 Nov 1918    2
Promoted to Vfw 22 Sept 1918.

| Victories: | 1. | 22 Jul 1918 | SE5a  | 0942 | Carvin |
|---|---|---|---|---|---|
| | 2. | 4 Nov 1918 | Camel | | |

## BRUNNENGRÄBER, Christian    Vfw
J13        Sep 1917 − 29 Jan 1918    1   KIA
Born 3 July 1892, Rostock. After flaming a balloon, was attacked by Spads and shot down in flames.

| Victories: | 1. | 29 Jan 1918 | Balloon | | Saucy |
|---|---|---|---|---|---|

## BRUNNER,    Uffz
J76b      5 Jul 1918 −

## BRZENK, Hans    Vfw
| J67 | 23 Mar 1918 − 6 Apr 1918 | J67 | 26 Jun 1918 − 11 Oct 1918 |
|---|---|---|---|
| J81 | 6 Apr 1918 − 22 May 1918 | J36 | 11 Oct 1918 − 21 Oct 1918 |
| J74 | 22 May 1918 − 26 Jun 1918 | J67 | 21 Oct 1918 − 11 Nov 1918 |

Born 16 May 1897. Field Artillery Regiment No 20. Joined aviation 1915. It is not known how many of these claims were confirmed.

| Victories: | − | 1918 | Bréguet XIV | | Verdun |
|---|---|---|---|---|---|
| | − | 1918 | Spad | | |
| | 1. | 1918 | Camel | | Tournai |
| | 2. | 1918 | BF2b | | |
| | 3. | 1918 | Sopwith | | |
| | 4. | 1 Sep 1918 | Sopwith | | Arras |
| | 5. | 1919 | DFW CV | | Poland |

## BUCHER, Franz    Vfw
J30      1 May 1917 − 8 Jun 1917    − KIA
Born 28 July 1895, Düsseldorf. Joined Jasta 30 from Jastaschule I. Killed over Wervicq.

## BUCHHOLZ, Ulrich    Ltn
J20      (Mar 1918) − 31 May 1918    − WIA
Promoted Leutnant 27 January 1915. Awarded Eiserne Kreuz I Klasse Hessische Tapferkeitsmedaille. Born 22 December 1893. Luftwaffe General WWII. Died 20 June 1974.

## BUCHSTETT, Wilhelm    Ltn d R
J79b        − 11 Apr 1918    2   POW

| Victories: | 1. | 22 Mar 1918 | SE5a | | Vermand |
|---|---|---|---|---|---|
| | − | 24 Mar 1918 | Sopwith | | Vermand |
| | 2. | 1 Apr 1918 | Spad | | |

## BUCKLER, Julius    Ltn
FFA209              −        J17    11 Nov 1916 − 11 Nov 1918    36
Biography & Victories: See *Above the Lines*.

## BUDDE, Hans Hermann von    Ltn
| J29 | 16 Feb 1917 − 20 May 1917 | − | CO J15 | 17 Jun 1917 − 14 Mar 1918 | 1 |
|---|---|---|---|---|---|
| J15 | 20 May 1917 − 29 May 1917 | − | Idflieg | 14 Mar 1918 − | − |
| J5 | 29 May 1917 − 17 Jun 1917 | − | | | |

OzbV for Jasta 29 from 16 Feb 1917 to 29 Apr 1917. Acting CO Jasta 29; 29 Apr to 2 May 1917.

| Victories: | 1. | 13 Aug 1917 | Caudron | 1115 | Hurtébise-Ferme |
|---|---|---|---|---|---|

## BUDDEBERG,    Ltn d R
J50      Jan 1918 − 11 Nov 1918    3

| Victories: | 1. | 2 Sep 1918 | Spad 2 | 1100 | Braisne |
|---|---|---|---|---|---|

|   |            |        |      |             |   |
|---|------------|--------|------|-------------|---|
| 2. | 6 Sep 1918 | Spad 2 | 1220 | S Soissons |   |
| 3. | 14 Sep 1918 | Spad | 1020 | Révillon |   |

## BUDDECKE, Hans-Joachim          Hptm

| | | | | | | |
|---|---|---|---|---|---|---|
| FA23 | 1915 – | 3 | FA5 | | | 2 |
| FA6 | | 4 | J30 | 15 Feb 1918 – 8 Mar 1918 | 1 | |
| J4 | 25 Aug 1916 – 14 Dec 1916 | 3 | Hptm J18 | 8 Mar 1918 – 10 Mar 1918 | – KIA | |

Biography & Victories: See *Above the Lines*.

## BUDER, Erich     Vfw

J26      25 Jan 1918 – 11 Nov 1918     12
Previously with Jasta 5.
Biography & Victories: See *Above the Lines*.

## BUDER,     Vfw

Kest 4b    Sep 1918 – 11 Nov 1918    2
Victories:        1.        Date and unit unknown
                  2.        16 Aug 1918        DH4

## BÜCHNER, Felix     Ltn d R

J13        (Sep 1918) – 11 Nov 1918    2
Collided with Gefr Michaelis during a combat, jumped in his parachute and landed safely; Michaelis killed.

| Victories: | – | 13 Sep 1918 | Spad | |
|---|---|---|---|---|
| | 1. | 13 Sep 1918 | Spad | Allamont |
| | 2. | 14 Sep 1918 | Caudron R11 | Conflans |

## BÜCHNER, Franz     Ltn

| | | | | | |
|---|---|---|---|---|---|
| FFA270 | 1916 – | – | J13 | 13 Sep 1917 – 11 Nov 1918 | 39 |
| J9 | Mar 1917 – 13 Sep 1917 | – | | | |

Biography & Victories: See *Above the Lines*.

## BÜCKER, Karl     Ltn

| | | | | | |
|---|---|---|---|---|---|
| FFA34 | 15 Nov 1914 – Apr 1915 | – | Kest 8 | 1 Jan 1918 – 17 May 1918 | – |
| FEA1 | Apr 1915 – | – | Kest 1a | 17 May 1918 – 20 Aug 1918 | 1 |
| FAA230 | Jun 1916 – | 1 | Kest 7 | 20 Aug 1918 – 11 Nov 1918 | 1 |
| JSud | | – | | | |

Born 21 June 1892, Vehrte. Enlisted 24 October 1914, assigned to FEA 5. Promoted to Gefreiter on 20 August 1915. Known to have flown Roland D II 2919/17 in FAA 230. Awarded Iron Cross 2nd on 23 July 1916. Qualified for Flugzeug-Führer Abzeichen (Combat Pilot's Badge) on 3 August 1916. Promoted to Unteroffizier on 22 September 1916. Awarded Iron Cross 1st Class on 27 May 1917. Awarded kuk Tapferkeitsmedaille in Silber 2 Klasse on 31 August 1917. Promoted to Vizefeldwebel on 29 November 1917. Held rank of Hauptmann in WWII. Died 5 October 1970, Osnabruck, Germany.

| Victories: | 1. | 16 Jun 1917 | Balloon | Jezierna |
|---|---|---|---|---|
| | 2. | 16 Aug 1918 | DH4 | |
| | 3. | Oct 1918 | EA | |

## BÜLOW-BOTHKAMP, Harry von     Ltn d R

| | | | | | |
|---|---|---|---|---|---|
| FA53 | Dec 1916 – | – | J36 | 7 Sep 1917 – 2 Jan 1918 | 3 |
| FA272 | – | – | JB | 2 Jan 1918 – 11 Mar 1918 | – |
| J18 | | – | J36 | 11 Mar 1918 – 14 Aug 1918 | 3 |

Biography & Victories: See *Above the Lines*.

## BÜLOW-BOTHKAMP, Konrad von     Ltn

| | | | | | |
|---|---|---|---|---|---|
| J18 | 11 Feb 1917 – 16 Sep 1917 | – | CO J19 | 4 Jan 1918 – 10 Feb 1918 | 1 |
| J14 | 16 Sep 1917 – 4 Jan 1918 | 1 | Idflieg | 10 Feb 1918 – | |
| Victories: | 1. | 17 Oct 1917 | Nieuport | Douaumont | |
| | 2. | 3 Feb 1918 | Bréguet | Berru | |

## BÜLOW-BOTHKAMP, Walter von     Ltn

| | | | | | |
|---|---|---|---|---|---|
| FA22 | 1915 – Oct 1915 | 2 | CO J36 | 10 May 1917 – 13 Dec 1917 | 15 |
| FA300 | Oct 1915 – Dec 1916 | 2 | JB | 13 Dec 1917 – 6 Jan 1918 | – KIA |
| J18 | 7 Dec 1916 – 10 May 1917 | 9 | | | |

Biography & Victories: See *Above the Lines*.

## BÜNNING,    Flg

| Kest | 3 Jun 1918 – Sep 1918 | 2 | | J83 | | 1918 – | |
|------|------------------------|---|---|-----|---|---------|---|
| Victories: | 1. | 13 Jun 1918 | Nieuport | 1030 | S Göhn |
| | 2. | 13 Sep 1918 | Spad | | |

## BÜRCK, Gustav    Ltn d R

| J54 | 19 Jan 1918 – | 3 | | | |
|-----|----------------|---|---|---|---|
| Victories: | 1. | 17 Mar 1918 | Camel | 1030 | NE Banteux |
| | 2. | 1 Jun 1918 | RE8 | 2020 | Ypern |
| | 3. | 2 Sep 1918 | Balloon | 1720 | Champenoux |

## BÜREN, Günther von    Ltn

FA31           – 1918           –           J18      (Aug 1918) – 13 Sep 1918    2  WIA

Awarded Saxon Albert Order, Knight 2nd Class with Swords on 12 Jan 1917. Awarded Saxon Knight's Cross of the Military St Henry Order 24 Oct 1918.

| Victories: | 1. | 30 Aug 1918 | DH4 | | Ennerchen | (a) |
|------------|----|-------------|-----|---|-----------|-----|
| | 2. | 14 Sep 1918 | Spad | 0905 | Gorze | (b) |

(a) Possibly A7708, No 55 Sqn, IAF, Lt H Dechler & 2/Lt A S Papworth.
(b) Probably from the 13th Aero Sqn, USAS.

## BÜSGES,    Ltn

J67      23 May 1918 – 11 Nov 1918    –

Joined Jasta 67 from Jastaschule II.

## BÜSSING, Heinrich    Ltn

J5         21 Aug 1916 – 1917          1         Kest 4b     Aug 1917 – 10 May 1918    1  KIAcc

Born 3 March 1893, Stolberg, Sangerhausen. OzbV for Jasta 5. Known to have flown Albatros DIII 2243/16, and 1999/16. Promoted Leutnant 5 June 1917. Awarded Baden Ritterkreuz II Klasse Orden vom Zähringer Löwen mit Schwerten. Knight's Cross 2nd Class with Swords of the Württemberg Friedrich Order on 20 Feb 1918. Eiserne Kreuz I & II Klasse. Killed testing an Albatros DVa, at Feldberg.

| Victories: | – | 20 Oct 1916 | FE2b | | | |
|------------|---|-------------|------|---|---|---|
| | – | 11 Feb 1917 | BE2 | | | |
| | 1. | 15 Feb 1917 | DH2 | 1045 | S Miraumont | (a) |
| | – | 4 Mar 1917 | BE2 | 1720 | Guedencourt | |
| | – | 6 Mar 1917 | FE2d | | S Arras | |
| | 2. | 22 Aug 1917 | Sopwith | | Colmar | (b) |

(a) #7932, No 32 Sqn, RFC, Lt C H March, also the 29th victory for Jasta 5.
(b) Lt Albert Mezergues, CO Escadrille Sop 129; was captured.

## BÜTTNER, Karl Heinrich Otto    Ltn

J2      (Oct 1916) – 16 Nov 1916    –  POW

Flying Albatros DI 391/16 'Bü' when shot down and taken prisoner. Credited to Captain G A Parker and Lt H E Hervey, No 8 Sqn, RFC, as G.1.

## BÜTTNER, Siegfried    Ltn

J22      Aug 1917 – 7 Jun 1918    4         CO J61     7 Jun 1918 – 11 Nov 1918    9

Biography & Victories: See *Above the Lines*.

## BURBERG, Karl    Vfw

J43      16 Aug 1918 – 11 Nov 1918    –

Joined Jasta 43 from Jastaschule I.

| Victories: | 1. | 14 Oct 1918 | SE5a | | |
|------------|----|-------------|------|---|---|

## BURCHARDT, von der    Ltn

J26      Dec 1917 – (Feb 1918)    –

## BURCKHARDT, August    Ltn

J25      Jan 1917 –    –

## BURCKHARDT, Friedrich-Karl    Hptm

| FA14 | Aug 1914 – Dec 1915 | – | FEA10 | – 10 Aug 1918 | – |
|------|----------------------|---|-------|----------------|---|
| FA30 | – 28 Nov 1916 | – | Kest4a | 10 Aug 1918 – | – |
| CO J25 | 28 Nov 1916 – 25 Feb 1918 | 5 | | | |

Biography & Victories: See *Above the Lines*.

---

### BURCKHARDT,    Flg
J62      15 Aug 1918 – 23 Aug 1918    –              AFP1    23 Aug 1918 –                    –

---

### BURGGALLER,    Vfw
J10      10 Sep 1917 – 10 Apr 1918    –              AFP2    10 Apr 1918                      –
Joined Jasta 10 from Jastaschule I.

---

### BURKARD, August    Ltn d R
J29      1 Jun 1918 – 11 Nov 1918    6
Biography & Victories: See *Above the Lines*.

---

### BURKHARDT, Peter
Unit not known           –
Held Eiserne Kreuz I Klasse. Served with JG 77 and JG2 Richthofen during WWII. Died 22 May 1965.

---

### BURNITZ, Rudolf    Uffz
J62      20 May 1918 – 11 Nov 1918    –

---

### BUSCH, Ernst    Vfw
J62      7 Jun 1918 – 28 Jun 1918    1   KIA
Born 21 November 1890, Oberrad. Killed in action over Montigny, on Albatros DV 5255/.
Victories:      1.        27 Jun 1918      Balloon              0953          Sains-en-Amienois

---

### BUSCH, Otto    Uffz
J30      24 Sep 1917 – 8 Dec 1917    –              AFP6    8 Dec 1917 –                    –
Joined Jasta 30 from AFP6.

---

### BUSCH,    Ltn
J11      26 May 1917 – 16 Jul 1917    –             J39      16 Jul 1917 – Oct 1917          1
Victories:      1.        25 Oct 1917      Voisin W                          St Lucia

---

### BUSS,    Ltn
J73      (Aug 1918) – 11 Nov 1918    –

---

### BUSSE, Joachim von    Ltn
FFA12                                –             J3       Aug 1917 – 1 Dec 1917          4
Kasta 22                             –             CO J20   15 Dec 1917 – 11 Nov 1918      7
Biography & Victories: See *Above the Lines*

---

### BUSSMANN,    Ltn d R
J1       (Jun 1917) – 8 Mar 1918    2             J1       26 Mar 1918 – (Jul 1918)        –
J72      8 Mar 1918 – 26 Mar 1918    –
Victories:      1.        23 Jun 1917      Spad                 2115         N La Fère
                zlg       7 Nov 1917      Nieuport             1045         San Pietro
                2.        18 Jul 1918      Spad 2               0810         Lechelle

---

### BUTTLAR, Hans Burkard von    Ltn
J18      15 Jan 1918 – 23 Mar 1918    –             JGII     22 Jul 1918 – 11 Nov 1918       –
JGII     23 Mar 1918 – 22 Jul 1918    –
Adjutant for JGII from 22 July 1918.

---

### CAMMANN, Theodor    Oblt
                                     1             CO J74   16 Feb 1918 – 11 Aug 1918      10
JB       9 Dec 1917 – 16 Feb 1918    1
Biography & Victories: See *Above the Lines*.

---

### CAMP, Joachim de la    Ltn d R
J8       (May 1917) – (Aug 1918)    –

---

### CARL, Ewald    Ltn d R
J51      (Jan 1918) – 30 Jun 1918    –   KIA
Born 2 May 1895, Essen. Killed over Kemmelberg.

## CARLOWITZ, Jürgen Georg von      Ltn
J1        7 Jan 1917 – 13 Feb 1917      –   KIA
Born 11 February 1897, Spandau. Killed during combat with a BE2d from No 9 Sqn, RFC, over Fregicourt, in Albatros DIII 1990/16 (G.10) probably by 2/Lt Stroud & Lt Burcher, No 9 Sqn, RFC, in a BE2c.

## CHELIUS, Maximilian von      Ltn
J2        Aug 1917 – 14 Sep 1917      –   KIA
Born 26 June 1897, Karzin. Served in a Guards Hussar Regiment. Served with FA14 before joining Jasta 2. Shot down in flames near Dixmuiden, flying an Albatros DVa (G.70); possibly by 2/Lts K Park & H Owen, No 48 Sqn, RFC, on BF2b A7227.

## CHRIST, Karl      Ltn d R
| | | | | | |
|---|---|---|---|---|---|
| KG6 | 1916 – | – | KG6/7 | 1917 – Nov 1917 | – |
| KG5 | 1916 – | – | J28w | Dec 1917 – 11 Nov 1918 | 5 |

Biography & Victories: See *Above the Lines*.

## CHRISTIANS,      Ltn
J21        (Sep 1917) – (Sep 1918)      2

| Victories: | 1. | 2 Sep 1918 | Spad | 1210 | NW Fismes |
|---|---|---|---|---|---|
| | 2. | 2 Sep 1918 | Spad | 1740 | E Fismes |

## CHRISTIANS,      Flg
J56        5 Oct 1918 – 11 Nov 1918      –
Joined Jasta 56 from Jastaschule I.

## CHRISTIANSEN, Waldemar      Ltn
J5        – 11 Dec 1917      –      J46      10 Feb 1918 – 21 Apr 1918      –   KIA
Born 13 December 1895, Seegeberg. Killed near Le Forest.

## CHRISTIANSEN,      Vfw
J67        23 Mar 1918 – 11 Nov 1918      2

| Victories: | 1. | 30 Aug 1918 | DH4 | | Latour |
|---|---|---|---|---|---|
| | 2. | 14 Sep 1918 | Balloon | 1630 | Clermont-Verdun |

## CLASSEN, Fritz      Vfw
| | | | | | |
|---|---|---|---|---|---|
| FA221 | 1915 – | 1 | J3 | 6 Jan 1918 – 14 Feb 1918 | – |
| JsSchI | – 5 Jan 1918 | – | J26 | 14 Feb 1918 – 11 Nov 1918 | 10 |

Biography & Victories: See *Above the Lines*.

## CLAUSNITZER, Ernst      Vfw
J4        (Oct 1916) – 16 Jul 1917      3   POW
Departed on a balloon attack and at 1735 hours forced to land SE Poperinghe, after being attacked by Spads; he was flying Albatros DIII 1162/17 (G.56). Downed by 2/Lt D Langlands, No 23 Sqn, RFC.

| Victories: | 1. | 10 Oct 1916 | FE2b | 1650 | Barleux |
|---|---|---|---|---|---|
| | 2. | 23 Jun 1917 | Balloon | 1450 | Ypern |
| | 3. | 7 Jul 1917 | Nieuport | 1430 | Zillebeke |

## CLAUSNITZER, Gottfried      Ltn
J72s        (Jun 1918) – 11 Nov 1918      1

| Victories: | 1. | 2 Sep 1918 | Balloon | | |
|---|---|---|---|---|---|

## CLAUSNITZER, Hubert      Ltn
J72s        11 Sep 1918 – 1 Nov 1918      –      AFP3      1 Nov 1918 –      –
OzbV for Jasta 72b. Lightly wounded in combat 2 September 1918.

## CLAUSS,      Ltn
| | | | | | |
|---|---|---|---|---|---|
| J29 | 13 Jun 1917 – 21 Jun 1917 | – | Kest 1a | – 27 Oct 1917 | – Hosp |
| J29 | – 6 Aug 1917 | – | J29 | 27 Oct 1917 – 17 Dec 1917 | 1 POW |
| FEA5 | 6 Aug 1917 – | | | | |

Shot down over Armentières, during combat with an RE8, flying Albatros DVa 5390/17. Credited to Lt J L M Sandy and Sgt H F Hughes, No 3 Sqn, AFC (G.101).

| Victories: | 1. | 13 Nov 1917 | RE8 | 1515 | W Blankaart See |
|---|---|---|---|---|---|

## CLAUSSEN,   Ltn
J36        30 Sep 1918 – 11 Nov 1918      –
Joined Jasta 36 from Jastaschule I.

## CLEINO,   Ltn
J12        23 Nov 1916 –                    –

## CLEINOW, Kurt    Ltn d R
J31        4 Jun 1918 – 11 Nov 1918      –

## CLEISS, Friedrich    Ltn d R
J33        30 Dec 1916 – 1 Oct 1917      – KIA
Born 3 September 1890, Lorrach, Baden. Enlisted 1 October 1911, Baden Infantry Regiment 170. Promoted Unteroffizier 9 July 1911. Active Reserve status 30 September 1912. Promoted Vizewacht-meister 4 June 1913. Promoted Leutnant d R 18 February 1915. Awarded EK II on 8 July 1915. Assigned to aviation, FEA5, for pilot training on 26 August 1916. Killed over Hooge, on an Albatros D V (G.78), possibly by Capt W A Wright, No 45 Sqn, RFC and Lt Reeder and Cpl Holmes, No 53 Sqn, RFC, in RE8 A3405 (see *OTF*, Vol 4, No 4, pg 311/312).

## COLLIN, Diether    Ltn d R
| | | | | | | | |
|---|---|---|---|---|---|---|---|
| J22 | Nov 1916 – Nov 1916 | – | | J22 | 21 Feb 1917 – 16 Apr 1918 | 4 | |
| JB | Nov 1916 – 21 Feb 1917 | 2 | | J56 | 16 Apr 1918 – 13 Aug 1918 | 7 | WIA |

Biography & Victories: See *Above the Lines*.

## CONDERERT, Walther    Gefr
J52        25 Feb 1918 – 4 Mar 1918      – KIA
Born 14 September 1891, Gumbinnen. Joined Jasta 52 from Jastaschule I. Killed over Lens, at 1525 hours flying Pfalz DIIIa 4236/17, possibly by Capt R J Tipton, No 40 Sqn, RFC, SE5a C5934 (G.146).

## CONRADT, Karl    Uffz
J17        14 Aug 1917 – 26 Aug 1917     – KIA
Born 4 May 1893, Stuttgart. Joined Jasta 17 from AFP4. Killed at 2040 hours between Slype and Vlisseghem.

## CONTA, von    Ltn
| | | | | | |
|---|---|---|---|---|---|
| FA36 | | – | J11 | 21 May 1918 – 29 Jul 1918 | – |
| J11 | Feb 1918 – 29 Apr 1918 | – | Hosp | 29 Jul 1918 – | – |
| Idflieg | 29 Apr 1918 – 21 May 1918 | – | J11 | Aug 1918 – 11 Sep 1918 | – |

Born 1 January 1880. Known to have flown Fokker Dr I 107/17. Posted to Flieger-observer Schule, Juterborg, on 11 Sept 1918.

## CONTAG, Helmuth    Ltn
J29        18 Sep 1917 – 18 Jan 1918    3        CO J65    2 Feb 1918 – 6 Mar 1918    1 KIA
Born 10 February 1896, Angerburg. Joined Jasta 29 from Jastaschule I. Killed over Beaufort at 1730 hours.

| Victories: | 1. | 18 Oct 1917 | Balloon | 1402 | Oostvlederen |
|---|---|---|---|---|---|
| | 2. | 21 Oct 1917 | DH4 | 1240 | NW Middlekerke |
| | 3. | 4 Nov 1917 | SE5 | 1455 | Pervyse |
| | 4. | 5 Mar 1918 | Balloon | 1040 | Bethelainville |

## CORDES, Ludwig    Oblt d R
J16b       18 Feb 1918 – 24 Mar 1918    1 KIA
Born 5 January 1892, Berlin. Served in 5th Field Artillery Regiment. Killed over Fresnes-Peronne.

| Victories: | 1. | 24 Mar 1918 | Camel | | Ablaincourt |
|---|---|---|---|---|---|

## CORTINE,   Vfw
J10                                          –

## CREMER,   Vfw
J5         (Oct 1917) – (Feb 1918)      1

| Victories: | 1. | 29 Nov 1917 | DH4 | | Cauroir |
|---|---|---|---|---|---|

## CREUTZMANN, Otto    Ltn d R

| | | | | | | |
|---|---|---|---|---|---|---|
| KG2 | | – | Kest 4b | Nov 1917 – 20 Feb 1918 | 1 |
| KG4/23 | | – | J43 | 20 Feb 1918 – 13 Jun 1918 | 3 |
| J20 | 6 Feb 1917 – 12 Aug 1917 | 1 | CO J46 | 13 Jun 1918 – 11 Nov 1918 | 3 |
| AFP4 | 12 Aug 1917 – Nov 1917 | – | | | |

Biography & Victories; See *Above the Lines*.

## CROISSANT, Rudolf    Ltn d R

J68      7 May 1918 – 12 Jun 1918      KIA
Born 30 October 1895, Ebensoben. Killed at 1930 hours over Mery, flying Fokker DVII 2062/18. Credited to Captain M LeBlanc-Smith, No 73 Sqn, RAF, on Camel D1794.

## CRÜSEMANN, Albrecht    Ltn

J17      14 May 1917 – 28 Jul 1917      1   KIA
Born 17 July 1896, Heimsen. Served with Infantry Regiment Nr.48. Joined Jasta 17 from AFP1. Killed at 1935 hours near Nieuport.

| Victories: | 1. | 30 May 1917 | Balloon | | Bouvancourt |
|---|---|---|---|---|---|

## CURTISS,    Ltn

J76b      8 Jul 1918 –      –
Joined Jasta 76b from Jastaschule I.

## CYMERA, Wilhelm    OfStv

| | | | | | | |
|---|---|---|---|---|---|---|
| KG1 | 1916 – | – | J1 | Dec 1916 – 9 May 1917 | 5   KIA |

Biography & Victories: See *Above the Lines*.

## CZARNIKOW,    Oblt

J51      (May 1918) – 11 Nov 1918      –
OzbV for Jasta 51. Acting CO Jasta 51 from 29 Sep – 1 Oct 1918.

## CZERMAK, Johann    Ltn d R

| | | | | | |
|---|---|---|---|---|---|
| Kest 4a | 27 May 1917 – 19 Jun 1917 | – | CO J32b | 10 Jan 1918 – 23 Jul 1918 | – |
| J6 | 24 Jun 1917 – 18 Dec 1917 | 1 | FEA1b | 23 Jul 1918 – | – |
| J77b | 30 Dec 1917 – 10 Jan 1918 | | | | |

Reported to Jasta 6 from Jastaschule I. Acting CO Jasta 6 from 15 to 26 Nov 1917.

| Victories: | 1. | 28 Jul 1917 | DH4 | 1850 | NE Courtrai |
|---|---|---|---|---|---|
| | zlg | 14 Aug 1917 | Camel | 1930 | W Langemarck |

## DÄMERICH,    Ltn

J29      15 Feb 1918 – 15 Jun 1918      –      AFP6      15 Jun 1918 –      –
Joined Jasta 29 from Jastaschule I. Injured in a crash-landing on 13 April 1918.

## DÄNKERT, Oskar    Flg

J9      (Dec 1916) – 24 Jul 1917      –   KIA
Born 21 June 1881, Cottbus. Killed at Pont-à-Chin.

## DAHLMANN, Ernst    Vfw

FAA221      –      J5      23 Feb 1917 – 1 Jun 1917      2   KIA
Born 25 October 1890, Hannover. Killed near Gouzeaucourt-Cambrai.

| Victories: | 1. | 6 Mar 1917 | Vickers | | Boucharesnes |
|---|---|---|---|---|---|
| | 2. | 6 May 1917 | Sopwith | | NW Cambrai |

## DAHLMANN, Theodor Hermann    Oblt

| | | | | | |
|---|---|---|---|---|---|
| FAA63 | May 1916 – Oct 1916 | – | FEA13 | | |
| FAA252 | Nov 1916 – Mar 1917 | – | J26 | 21 Feb 1918 – Jul 1918 | 1 |
| J29 | 15 Apr 1917 – 3 Sep 1917 | 1 | Adj JGIII | Jul 1918 – 11 Nov 1918 | 5 |
| AFP12 | 3 Sep 1917 – | – | | | |

Biography & Victories: See *Above the Lines*.

## DAHM, Werner    Ltn

J26      (Jul 1917) – 21 Feb 1918      2      JG III      21 Feb 1918 – 11 Nov 1918      2
Technical Officer for JG III.

| Victories: | 1. | 13 Jul 1917 | Nieuport | 2005 | NE Langemarck | (a) |
|---|---|---|---|---|---|---|

| | | | | | | | |
|---|---|---|---|---|---|---|---|
| 2. | 8 Nov 1917 | BF2b | | 1500 | | N Zillebeke See | |
| 3. | Date and unit unknown | | | | | | |
| 4. | Date and unit unknown | | | | | | |

(a) Probably B3483, No 1 Sqn, RFC, 2/Lt W C Smith, KIA.

## DANIEL, Hermann Alexander    Fw
Kest 4b                        –

Württemberg Wilhelm's Cross with Swords 4 Feb 1918.

## DANIELS, Maximilian Edler von    Oblt
| | | | | | | | |
|---|---|---|---|---|---|---|---|
| J15 | 14 Mar 1917 – 3 Apr 1917 | – | | J83 | 11 Aug 1917 – 11 Jan 1918 | – | |
| 23 | 4 Apr 1917 – 11 Aug 1917 | – | | J61 | 11 Jan 1918 – 7 Jun 1918 | 1 | KIA |

Born 8 December 1888, Sigmaringen. Commanded Kest 3/Jasta 83 from 11 Aug 1917 – 7 June 1918.
Killed near Mesnil St Georges, on 7 June 1918.
Victories:    1.    15 May 1918    Spad

## DANKE,    Gefr
J5                            –

## DANKER, Fritz    Ltn d R
| | | | | |
|---|---|---|---|---|
| FAA293 | – | J32b | 11 Jan 1918 – 17 Apr 1918 | 1    WIA |

Born 1 June 1894, Leipzig. Promoted to Ltn d R 28 January 1918. Shot down at 1820 hours over
Guesnain airfield; died in hospital on 23 April 1918.
Victories:    1.    Unit and date unkown
             2.    23 Feb 1918    RE8    1530    SW Bailleul

## DANNACKER, Richard    Vfw
| | | | | |
|---|---|---|---|---|
| J12 | 8 Oct 1916 – | – | J22 | Feb 1917 –    – |

## DANNEMANN,    Uffz
J56        1 Feb 1918 – 11 Nov 1918    1
Lightly injured 13 June 1918, in an accident.
Victories:    1.    2 Apr 1918    AWFK8    Warfussée
             2.    9 Oct 1918    Bréguet    1615    Ardoye

## DANNENBERG, Hans    Ltn d R
J13                1917        2
Victories:    1.    3 May 1917    Caudron    Septmonts
             2.    24 Jun 1917    Nieuport    Versigny
             3.    Date and unit unknown
             4.    Date and unit unknown

## DANNHUBER, Xaver    Ltn d R
| | | | | | | |
|---|---|---|---|---|---|---|
| KG6 | | – | | J79b | 7 Nov 1917 – 11 Feb 1918 | –    INJ |
| SS25 | | – | | Hosp | 11 Feb 1918 – | |
| J26 | 25 May 1917 – 7 Nov 1917 | 10 | | CO J79b | 9 Oct 1918 – 11 Nov 1918 | 1 |

Biography & Victories: See *Above the Lines*.

## DASSENIES, Emil    Uffz
J13            – 23 Apr 1918    –    KIA
Born 2 August 1895, Tilsit. Killed over Moreuil.

## DAUBE, Erich    Ltn d R
JB        Sep 1917 – 8 Dec 1917    –    KIA
Born 8 November 1890, Valparaiso. Killed near Moorslede.

## DAUGERS,    Ltn
J74            – 11 Nov 1918    2
Victories:    1.    18 Oct 1918    DH4    Esnes
             2.    29 Oct 1918    EA    Vilosnes

## DAUGS, Willi    Ltn d R
| | | | | | |
|---|---|---|---|---|---|
| FA55 | – | – | J36 | 21 Feb 1917 – | 1 |

Promoted Leutnant on 26 August 1916.

Victories:    1.    19 Apr 1917      Morane                          Prosnes
              2.    Date and unit unknown

## DAUPHIN,    Uffz
J79b    (Apr 1918) –              –

## DAVID, Ernst    Vfw
J30    8 Jul 1918 – 7 Aug 1918    – KIAcc
Born 28 March 1892, Plon. Joined Jasta 30 from AFP6. Killed during a test flight of a Roland DVIa near Fleurbaix.

## DAVID,    OfStv
J12    16 Oct 1916 –              –

## DAVID,    FwLtn
Kest 1a    Sep 1918 – Oct 1918    –

## DAWITZ,    Uffz
J29    16 Feb 1917 – 16 Feb 1917    –        J29      19 Feb 1917 – 11 Mar 1917    –
J21    16 Feb 1917 – 19 Feb 1917    –        Kest 3   11 Mar 1917 –                –

## DAZUR, Waldemar Baron von    Oblt
J20    27 Jan 1918 – 11 Nov 1918    4
Born 29 March 1895, Tschachawe. Volunteered as Fahrenjunker 4 Aug 1914, Garde Fusiller Rgt. Transferred to aviation 20 Sep 1917, learned to fly at FEA4, Posen. Lightly injured in an accident 1 August 1918. Promoted Oberleutnant 20 Sep 1918. Lightly wounded on 9 October 1918.

| Victories: | | | | | |
|---|---|---|---|---|---|
| | 1. | 12 Mar 1918 | SE5a | 0710 | NW Queant |
| | 2. | 9 Jul 1918 | Camel | 1030 | Millekrussien |
| | 3. | 20 Jul 1918 | Camel | 1010 | S Houthulsterwald |
| | 4. | 29 Jul 1918 | Camel | 2020 | Lochean |

## DEBERITZ,    Gefr
J18    Oct 1917 – (May 1918)    1
Victories:    1.    22 May 1918    Spad    1105    Fleurbaix    (a)
(a) Probably 1/Lt P F Baer, 103rd Aero Sqn, USAS, Spad XIII #3173.

## DEBUS, Wilhelm    Ltn
J34    22 Feb 1917 – 2 Sep 1917    –        J300     – 5 May 1918                –
Kest 9    2 Sep 1917 –             –        J55      5 May 1918 – 11 Nov 1918    –
Joined Jasta 34b from Jastaschule I. Awarded EK I. Acting CO Jasta 55, 5 May to 1 June 1918.

## DEBUS,    Vfw
J36    11 Jul 1917 – 17 Jul 17    – WIA
Wounded during combat with a Sopwith.

## DECHEND, Hans Jörg von    Ltn
J72s    20 May 1918 – 16 Jun 1918    3 KIA
Born 27 August 1896, Elsenach. Served in Dragoon Regiment 16. Killed at 1100 hours over Moulin-sous-Touvent.

| Victories: | | | | |
|---|---|---|---|---|
| | 1. | 31 May 1918 | Camel | Blangy-Tronville |
| | 2. | 1 Jun 1918 | Bréguet | Soissons |
| | 3. | 2 Jun 1918 | Camel | Fêret de Laigue |

## DECKER, von    Ltn
J18    2 Oct 1917 – 26 Oct 1917    –        J20      26 Oct 1917 – 13 Jul 1918    2 WIA
Lightly wounded 26 June 1918.

| Victories: | | | | | |
|---|---|---|---|---|---|
| | 1. | 25 Apr 1918 | Camel | 1930 | Dickebusch |
| | 2. | 9 Jul 1918 | SE5a | 1030 | S Dickebusch |

## DEGELOW, Carl    Ltn d R
FAA216    1917 –                  1        J7       21 Aug 1917 – 16 May 1918    3
J36    17 Aug 1917 – 21 Aug 1917    –        J40s     16 May 1918 – 11 Nov 1918    26
Biography & Victories: See *Above the Lines*.

**DEGEN, Josef     Vfw**
J6     17 May 1918 – 14 Jun 1918     – POW
Lost his way after taking off from the Flugpark at Valenciennes, and came down in French lines. He later escaped from captivity.

**DEGETAU,     Ltn**
J45     (Mar 1918) –                           –
OzbV for Jasta 45.

**DEHNE, Bruno     Ltn**
J43     26 Jul 1918 – 15 Aug 1918     –          AFP2     15 Aug 1918 –                    –

**DEHNER, Willibald     Ltn d R**
J32b     9 May 1918 – 30 May 1918     – WIA
Born 28 August 1897, Ansbach. Wounded at 0830 hours on Albatros DVa 6511/17; died of wounds 2 June 1918, at Beaulencourt.

**DEILMANN, Karl     Ltn d R**
| | | | | | |
|---|---|---|---|---|---|
| FFA34 | Oct 1914 – | – | BG5/30 | 14 Feb 1916 – 15 Sep 1916 | 2 |
| FFA52 | 1915 – | – | J6 | 15 Sep 1916 – 17 Aug 1917 | 4 |
| FFA58 | 1915 – 1916 | – | FFA244 | Sep 1917 – Oct 1917 | |

Biography & Victories: See *Above the Lines*.

**DEINDL, Otto     Oblt**
| | | | | | |
|---|---|---|---|---|---|
| J26 | – 19 Apr 1917 | – | J1 | 13 Sep 1917 – 18 Nov 1917 | – WIA |
| AFP2 | 19 Apr 1917 – | – | CO J77b | 20 Nov 1917 – 21 Jan 1918 | – |
| J35 | 7 May 1917 – 13 Sep 1917 | – | | | |

Acting CO Jasta 35, 30 June to 20 July 1917. His Albatros DIII 1712/17 badly damaged in combat N Cortemarck and forced to land at 0830 hours; unharmed. Wounded over Treviso. Transferred to the Air Ministry on 21 January 1918.

**DELANG, Kurt     Vfw**
| | | | | | |
|---|---|---|---|---|---|
| J10 | Feb 1918 – 10 Apr 1918 | – | J54s | Apr 1918 – | 2 |
| AFP2 | 10 Apr 1918 – | – | | | |

Died 25 February 1983, Augsberg.
| Victories: | 1. | Date and unit unknown | | | |
|---|---|---|---|---|---|
| | 2. | 26 Jul 1918 | Balloon | 1210 | Suippes |
| | 3. | 13 Sep 1918 | DH4 | 1750 | St Gènèvive |

**DELLING, August     Ltn d R**
| | | | | | |
|---|---|---|---|---|---|
| J34b | 16 Mar 1918 – 3 Aug 1918 | 5 | FEA2b | | – |
| Hosp | 3 Aug 1918 – | – | | | |

Biography & Victories: See *Above the Lines*.

**DEMANDT, Friedrich     Ltn d R**
J10     Oct 1917 – 30 Nov 1917     – KIA
Born 28 August 1892, Rostatt. Killed over Flesquières, at 1600, flying Pfalz DIIIa 4116/17, with a silver body and yellow tail, credited to Lt G E Thompson, No 46 Sqn, RFC, on Camel B3514; (G.93) (see *C&C* Vol 8, No 3, pg 225).

**DEMANT, Fritz     Sgt**
J52     10 Jan 1918 – 26 Apr 1918     – KIA
Born 7 December 1889, Hirschberg. Killed by ground fire over Chémy.

**DEMBOWSKI,     Ltn**
J24s     19 Oct 1917 – 7 Jun 1918     –          KoflH     7 Jun 1918 –                    –
Acting OzbV for Jasta 24s from 14 to 22 March 1918.

**DEMISCH, Martin     Ltn**
J58     21 Feb 1918 – 24 Sep 1918     10 WIA
Biography & Victories: See *Above the Lines*.

**DENKEWITZ, Hans     Ltn**
| | | | | | |
|---|---|---|---|---|---|
| SS7 | | – | FEA13 | 16 Dec 1917 – | – |
| J36 | 18 Mar 1917 – 16 Dec 1917 | – | | | |

Infantry Regiment Nr.44. Promoted Leutnant 18 August 1915.
Victories:        1.        Date and unit unknown

### DENKHARDT, Robert        Ltn d R
J35b        30 Jan 1918 – 10 Feb 1918        – KIAcc
Born 1 December 1891, Munich. Joined Jasta 35b from Jastaschule I. Killed in a crash at 1500 hours near Premont, with Pfalz DIII 4163/17.

### DENKHAUS, Hermann        Vfw
J7                – 6 Jul 1917        – KIA
Born Wanne, 12 September 1892. Killed over Thorout.

### DENNECKE, Matthais        OfStv
J1                –                J18                – 4 Jun 1917        – KIA
Born 4 October 1891, Neuhalbensleben. Killed during combat with a Nieuport over Houthem, possibly the victim of Lt T F Hazell, No 1 Sqn, RFC.

### DE RAY,        Uffz
J58        28 Apr 1918 – 11 Nov 1918        1
Victories:        1.        15 Sep 1918        Camel

### DERLIN, Günther        Ltn d R
J20        Mar 1918 – 6 Jun 1918        – KIA
Born 23 November 1890, Berlin. Killed over Ploegsteertwald.

### DESSLOCH, Otto        Ltn
FEA8b        29 Jan 1915 – 2 Dec 1915        –                CO
FA8b        10 May 1916 – 2 Jun 1916        –                FEA1b        29 Sep 1917 – 8 Dec 1917        –
CO J16        20 Jan 1917 – 14 Apr 1917        –                FlgSch        9 Dec 1917 – 11 Nov 1918        –
CO J35        15 Apr 1917 – 24 Sep 1917        –
Born 11 June 1889, Bamberg/Unterfranken. Bavarian 5th Chevaulegers Rgt from 20 July 1910 to 21 August 1914; wounded in action, hospitalised until 17 October 1914, returned to unit. Promoted Leutnant 28 October 1912. Observer school FEA1, Schleissheim, from 1 December 1914 to 28 Jan 1915. Pilot's training 3 December 1915 to 19 April 1916. AFP Gaede 20 April 1916 to 9 May 1916. Commanded KEK Ensisheim from 30 Jun 1916 to 29 Jan 1917. Reported to Jasta 35 from Kofl B. Commanded Jasta 35, 15 April – 24 Sept 1917. Commanded Fliegerschule 1 & 5 during period 9 Dec 1917 to end of war. Awarded Eiserne Kreuz I Klasse. Bavarian Militär-Verdeinstorden 4 Klasse mit Schwerten und Kröne. Ritterkreuz on 24 June 1940; Eichelasse mit Schwertennlaub on 10 May 1944. Held rank of Generaloberst in the Luftwaffe during WWII, from 1 March 1944. Died 13 May 1977.
Victories:        1.        Date and unit unknown

### DETERMEYER, Josef        Ltn d R
J47w        1 Mar 1918 – 2 May 1918        – INJ
Joined Jasta 47w from Jastaschule I. Shot down in combat at 1505 hours on Pfalz DIII 8338/17 and severely injured in a crash-landing.

### DETTMERING I,        Vfw
J68                – 22 Mar 1918        – POW
Shot down west of Ham in an Albatros DVa and taken POW.

### DETTMERING II,        Vfw
J68                – 11 Nov 1918        3
Victories:        1.        22 Mar 1918        Camel                St Quentin
        2.        31 May 1918        Bréguet                Thennes
        3.        3 Aug 1918        AR2                1025        Reims

### DEUTSCHMANN,        Ltn
J43        22 Jan 1918 –

### DIEBOLD, Johann        Gefr
J71        15 May 1918 – 11 Jul 1918        1 WIA
Severely wounded in combat with Spads near Fontaine, at 1710 hours.
Victories:        1.        25 Jun 1918        Balloon                1625        St Ulrich

**DIECKMANN, Hans    Uffz**
J52    18 Jun 1918 – 6 Sep 1918    –    FEA8    6 Sep 1918 –    –

**DIEHL, Ernst    Gefr**
J13    – 23 Jan 1918    –    J53    23 Jan 1918 – 22 Mar 1918    – POW

**DIEM,    Uffz**
J76b    15 Feb 1918 – 11 Nov 1918    1
Joined Jasta 76b from Jastaschule I.

| Victories: | 1. | 31 May 1918 | Bréguet | | Hangard |
|---|---|---|---|---|---|

**DIEMER, Franz    Ltn d R**
J1    23 Aug 1916 – 3 Dec 1916    –    J35b    12 Dec 1917 – 16 May 1918    –
J16    3 Dec 1916 – 19 Feb 1917    –    Hosp    16 May 1918 –    –
FEA1b    19 Feb 1917 –    –    J35b    15 Jun 1918 –    –
Also known as 'Zeno'. Flew with FA23 prior to joining Jasta 1. Served with Kest GHQ from 1 to 30 June 1916. Served with Kest Kdo 3 from 30 June to 30 July 1916. Served with Bavarian K Gruppe from 30 July to 3 December 1916. Served as OzbV for Jasta 16. Force-landed in Pfalz DIII 4161/17 breaking fuselage, on 30 Jan 1918. Acting CO Jasta 35b from 30 January to 4 March 1918, and 21 March to 13 May 1918. Awarded Iron Cross I Klasse on 22 April 1918. Hospitalised from 18 May 1918 to 15 June 1918. On leave from 22 June 1918 to 13 August 1918.

**DIENER, Ernst    Ltn d R**
J2    27 Aug 1916 – 30 Sep 1916    – KIA
Born 30 December 1895, Kassel. Served in KG6 before joining Jasta 2. Killed during combat with Nieuports near Bapaume, possibly by Lt Albert Ball, No 60 Sqn, RFC.

**DIERENFELD,    Uffz**
J39    – 4 Feb 1918    1 WIA
Severely wounded in combat with Camels.

| Victories: | 1. | 4 Feb 1918 | Camel | 1130 | Susegana |
|---|---|---|---|---|---|

**DIERLE, Anton    OfStv**
J24    21 Dec 1916 – 5 May 1917    1 KIA
Born 15 June 1887, Windschlag, Offenberg, Baden. Twin brother of Johann Dierle. Flew with KG 2/11 before joining Jasta 24. Awarded EK II. Awarded Silberne Karl-Friedrich Verdeinstmedaille on 8 December 1916. Shot down in flames between Betheniville and Pont Faverger, flying Albatros DIII 1963/16 (G.33) jumped from 200 metres; 4th Army AA fire.

| Victories: | 1. | 9 Mar 1917 | Nieuport 17 | 1220 | N Parroy Woods |
|---|---|---|---|---|---|
| | – | 2 May 1917 | Nieuport 17 | 2015 | Prosnes |

(See *OTF* Vol 4, No 4, pg 312.)

**DIERLE, Johann    OfStv**
KG2/11    –    FA7    1 Jul 1917 –    –
J24    17 Feb 1917 – 1 Jul 1917    –    Kest 4b    – 29 Jul 1918    – KIA
Born 15 June 1887, Windschlag, Offenberg, Baden. Twin brother of Anton Dierle. Awarded EKII. Awarded Silberne Karl-Friedrich Verdeinstmedaille on 8 December 1917. Killed over Rotenburg, Schwarzwald (see *OTF* Vol 4, No 4, pg 312).

**DIETERLE, Arthur    Oblt**
J77b    8 Apr 1918 – 18 Apr 1918    –    FEA1b    – 24 Oct 1918    –
J34b    18 Apr 1918 – 25 Apr 1918    – WIA    J34b    24 Oct 1918 – 11 Nov 1918    –
Joined Jasta 77b from Jastaschule II. Wounded over Marcelcave.

**DIETLAND,**
J22    –

**DIETLEN, Albert    Ltn d R**
FFA60    1916 –    1    J41    Oct 1917 – 4 Apr 1918    5
J23    30 Jun 1917 – 20 Aug 1917    1 WIA    CO J58    4 Apr 1918 – 12 Apr 1918    2 KIA
Biography & Victories: See *Above the Lines*.

**DIETRICH, Wilhelm    Vfw**
J1    19 Jan 1917 – 7 May 1917    – KIA

Born 30 October 1890, Magdeburg. Killed in action 7 May 1917 over St Fergeux.

| Victories: | – | 1 May 1917 | Balloon | 1300 | Revillon |
| | – | 1 May 1917 | Balloon | 1300 | Revillon |

## DIEVES, Friedrich Wilhelm     Ltn
J45                – 25 Aug 1918    –  POW
Flying Fokker DVII 4162/18 when shot down.

## DILCHER,     Vfw
J5          Apr 1917 – Apr 1918      3

| Victories: | 1. | 9 May 1917 | Sopwith 2 | 1500 | St Hilaire | (a) |
| | 2. | 26 May 1917 | FE2b | 1545 | Villers Plouich | |
| | 3. | 18 Aug 1917 | DH5 | | Villers Plouich | |

(a) Probably #7803, No 45 Sqn, RFC, Lt W L Mills (P) KIA & 2/AM J W Laughlin WIA/POW.

## DILTHEY, Helmut     Ltn d R

| FA50 | 18 May 1915 – | | – | | J40 | 14 Apr 1918 – 9 Jul 1918 | 1 | KIA |
| J27 | 19 May 1917 – 14 Apr 1918 | 6 | | | | | | |

Biography & Victories: See *Above the Lines*.

## DINGEL, Walter     Ltn

| FA23 | – | | 1 | | J18 | 4 Sep 1917 – 16 Mar 1918 | 1 |
| J19 | 1 Dec 1916 – 29 Jun 1917 | | – | | J15 | 16 Mar 1918 – 11 Nov 1918 | – |
| J14 | 29 Jun 1917 – 4 Sep 1917 | | – | | | | |

On Staff of JG II.

| Victories: | 1. | 2 Jul 1916 | FE | | Vaulx | (a) |
| | 2. | 11 Sep 1917 | DH4 | 1335 | Moorseele | |

(a) With his observer, Ltn Bartsch.

## DINKEL, Friedrich     Ltn

| FEA5 | 4 Aug 1915 – | | – | | J9 | 7 Oct 1916 – 12 Mar 1917 | – |
| AFP3 | | | – | | AFP3 | 12 Mar 1917 – 11 Nov 1917 | – |
| AOK3 | 25 May 1916 – 5 Oct 1916 | | 1 | | | | |

Promoted Leutnant 14 Sept 1914. EK II on 14 March 1915. Pilot's Badge on 20 July 1916. EK I on 9 Sept 1916. Württemberg Gold Military Merit Medal on 9 October 1916. Knight's Cross of the Württemberg Military Merit Order on 20 February 1918. Knight's Cross 2nd Class with Swords of the Württemberg Friedrich Order on 8 Nov 1918.

| Victories: | 1. | 2 Sep 1916 | Caudron | | | |

## DITTBERNER,     Sgt
J66                – 1918      2

| Victories: | 1. | 27 May 1918 | Spad | | Lesges-Couvrelles |
| | 2. | 15 Aug 1918 | Spad | | |

## DITTMANN,     Ltn
J13                – 11 Nov 1918    –
OzbV for Jasta 13.

## DITTRICH, Walter     Vfw
J1          23 Aug 1916 – 18 Jun 1917    1  WIA       J17      11 Nov 1917 –          –
FEA6                – 11 Nov 1917    –

Promoted to Unteroffizier on 1 January 1916. Received his Imperial German Army Pilot's Badge on 13 January 1916. Promoted Vizefeldwebel on 15 June 1916. Flew with FA32 prior to joining Jasta 1. Awards: EKII on 14 Jan 1916; Saxon Silver St Henry Medal on 14 Feb 1917; Saxon Gold St Henry Medal on 24 July 1917; Saxon Albert Order, Knight 2nd Class with Swords.

| Victories: | – | 3 Mar 1917 | Vickers | | Adinfer |
| | 1. | 1 May 1917 | Balloon | 1300 | Revillon |

## DOBBERAHN,     OfStv
J12          14 Nov 1917 – 23 Mar 1918    1  WIA

| Victories: | 1. | 6 Feb 1918 | Camel | | Lecluse |

**DOBBERKE, Günther    Ltn**

| | | | | | | | |
|---|---|---|---|---|---|---|---|
| J45 | Mar 1918 – 27 May 1918 | 1 | | Ltn d R | | | |
| | | | | J60 | 27 May 1918 – 15 Oct 1918 | 7 | INJ |

Biography & Victories: See *Above the Lines*.

**DÖLGER, Alfred    Gefr**

J80b    7 Apr 1918 – 1 Jun 1918    – WIA
Born 11 September 1894. Joined Jasta 80b from Jastaschule I. Wounded during combat with DHs.

**DÖRFLINGER, Joseph    Vfw**

| | | | | | |
|---|---|---|---|---|---|
| J10 | 26 Aug 1918 – 9 Sep 1918 | – | AFPC | – 15 Oct 1918 | – |
| J4 | 9 Sep 1918 – 10 Oct 1918 | – | J64w | 15 Oct 1918 – 11 Nov 1918 | – |

Born Mulhausen, Alsace. Joined Jasta 10 from Jastaschule I. Died 22 October 1970, Milwaukee, Wis., USA.

**DÖRING, Friedrich    Ltn**

| | | | | | |
|---|---|---|---|---|---|
| J13 | – 20 Feb 1917 | – | J34b | 20 Feb 1917 – 6 Nov 1917 | – |

OzbV for Jasta 34b. Awarded EK I. Awarded Flugzeugführer Abzeichen. Transferred to Idflieg 6 Nov 1917.

**DÖRING, Kurt Bertram von    Rittm**

| | | | | | |
|---|---|---|---|---|---|
| FA38 | 1914 – | – | JGr4 | 22 Feb 1918 – 11 Aug 1918 | – |
| FAA227 | 1916 – | – | J66 | 11 Aug 1918 – 24 Aug 1918 | – |
| CO J4 | 14 Dec 1916 – 22 Feb 1918 | 9 | J1 | 3 Sep 1918 – 11 Nov 1918 | 2 |

Biography & Victories: See *Above the Lines*.

**DÖRLE, Albert    Uffz**

| | | | | | |
|---|---|---|---|---|---|
| J1 | (Oct 1916) – (Dec 1916) | – | FEA8 | (Dec 1916) – | – |

**DÖRR, Gustav    Ltn d R**

| | | | | | |
|---|---|---|---|---|---|
| FA68 | | – | FA257 | May 1916 – Jun 1917 | – INJ |
| FA6 | 18 Mar 1916 – May 1916 | – | J45 | Feb 1918 – 11 Nov 1918 | 35 |

Biography & Victories: See *Above the Lines*.

**DÖRR,    Ltn d R**

J50    Oct 1918 – 11 Nov 1918    –
Served in Pionier Kompagnie 341.

**DOMBROWE, Wilhelm    Flg**

J12    Apr 1918 – 28 May 1918    – KIA
Born 27 June 1895, Rossin. Killed near Mesnil.

**DONHAUSER, Hans Christian Friedrich    Ltn**

| | | | | | |
|---|---|---|---|---|---|
| FA10 | | 1 | J17 | Jun 1918 – 11 Nov 1918 | 18 |

Biography & Victories: See *Above the Lines*.

**DORN,    Ltn**

J9    –

**DORNHEIM, Ludwig Fritz    Ltn**

| | | | | | |
|---|---|---|---|---|---|
| J5 | (Oct 1916) – 5 Feb 1917 | 2 | CO J29 | 5 Feb 1917 – 29 Apr 1917 | – KIA |

Born 26 July 1896, Seehausen. Served as OzbV for Jasta 5. Killed over Beine, at 1500 hours, probably by S/Lt René Dorme of N3.

| Victories: | 1. | 16 Oct 1916 | Caudron | | S Le Forest |
|---|---|---|---|---|---|
| | 2. | 26 Dec 1916 | BE2c | 1145 | Wailly |
| | – | 11 Mar 1917 | Gitterrumpf | | |

**DORP, Erich von    Oblt d R**

J16b    13 Sep 1917 – 11 Nov 1918    –
OzbV for Jasta 16b.

**DORRIEN, von    Ltn d R**

| | | | | | |
|---|---|---|---|---|---|
| J11 | 2 Jul 1918 – 25 Jul 1918 | – WIA | J11 | 14 Sep 1918 – 10 Oct 1918 | – |
| Hosp | 25 Jul 1918 – | – | FEA5 | 10 Oct 1918 – | – |

Joined Jasta 11 from Jastaschule I. Rejoined Jasta 11 from hospital.

## DOSSENBACH, Albert      Ltn d R

| | | | | | | |
|---|---|---|---|---|---|---|
| FA22 | Jun 1916 – | 8 | J36 | 22 Feb 1917 – 2 May 1917 | 6 | WIA |
| SS9 | – 31 Dec 1916 | – | J10 | 3 May 1917 – 3 Jul 1917 | 1 | KIA |
| J2 | 31 Dec 1916 – 19 Feb 1917 | – | | | | |

Biography & Victories: See *Above the Lines*.

## DOST, Willy      Uffz

J21      (Aug 1918) – (Oct 1918)      4

| Victories: | | | | | |
|---|---|---|---|---|---|
| | 1. | 11 Aug 1918 | Bréguet | 1325 | E Arcy |
| | 2. | 24 Aug 1918 | Spad | 1835 | NW Soissons |
| | 3. | 6 Sep 1918 | Spad | 2005 | E Braisne |
| | 4. | 3 Oct 1918 | Spad | 0920 | S Pontavert |

## DOSTLER, Eduard Ritter von      Oblt

| | | | | | | |
|---|---|---|---|---|---|---|
| SS27 | 1916 – 15 Jun 1916 | – | CO J34 | 20 Feb 1917 – 9 Jun 1917 | 6 | |
| Kasta 36 | 15 Jun 1916 – 27 Dec 1916 | 1 | CO J6 | 11 Jun 1917 – 21 Aug 1917 | 18 | KIA |
| | | | CO J13 | 27 Dec 1917 – 20 Feb 1918 | 1 | |

Biography & Victories: See *Above the Lines*.

## DOTZEL,      Ltn

| | | | | | |
|---|---|---|---|---|---|
| J19 | 26 Oct 1916 – 10 Jul 1918 | 1 | J15 | 19 Jul 1918 – | – |

Flew with KG3 prior to joining Jasta 19.

| Victories: | 1. | 15 Apr 1917 | Nieuport | La Neuvillette |
|---|---|---|---|---|

## DRALLE,      Vfw

J51      – 1 Aug 1918      – POW

Shot down in vicinity of Linselles.

## DREES, Franz      Ltn

J55      Jan 1918 – 11 Nov 1918      –

Joined Jasta 55 from Jastaschule II.

## DREKMANN, Heinrich      Ltn d R

| | | | | | | |
|---|---|---|---|---|---|---|
| J26 | Aug 1917 – 29 Aug 1917 | 1 | J4 | 29 Aug 1917 – 30 Jul 1918 | 10 | KIA |

Biography & Victories: See *Above the Lines*.

## DRESCHLER,      Vfw

| | | | | | |
|---|---|---|---|---|---|
| J24 | 28 Jun 1917 – 9 Jul 1917 | – | AFPB | 9 Jul 1917 – | – |

Joined Jasta 24 from AFP4.

## DRESSLER, Hugo      Flg

J53      17 Aug 1918 – 11 Nov 1918      –

Joined Jasta 53 from Jastaschule I.

## DREXLER,      Vfw

| | | | | | |
|---|---|---|---|---|---|
| Kest 7 | – 4 Mar 1918 | – | J43 | 4 Mar 1918 – 3 Aug 1918 | – WIA |

## DRUWEN,      Ltn

J15      –

## DUDEL,      OfStv

J57      (Jul 1918) – 11 Nov 1918      –

## DÜNNHAUPT,      Vfw

J58      25 Jul 1918 – 4 Sep 1918      1 WIA

Severely wounded during combat with DH9s and BF2bs.

| Victories: | 1. | 2 Sep 1918 | DH9 | 1845 | Hamel |
|---|---|---|---|---|---|

## DÜRRE, Erich      Vfw

J38      – 18 Jun 1918      2 KIA

Born 15 October 1892, Berlin. Killed over Stojakovo, in combat with a scout.

| Victories: | 1. | 29 Oct 1917 | AWFK8 | E Cerniste |
|---|---|---|---|---|
| | 2. | 28 Nov 1917 | BE2e | Smol |

## DÜRRWÄCHTER, Franz Xavier     Flg
J23b     6 Apr 1918 – 26 Apr 1918    –   KIAcc
Born 29 August 1898, Wurzburg. Killed at 1830 hours during a practice flight at Epinoy airfield.

## DUMLER,     Ltn
J76b     20 Jun 1918 – 11 Nov 1918    1
Joined Jasta 76b from Jastaschule I.

| Victories: | 1. | 30 Oct 1918 | DH4 | | Carspach |
|---|---|---|---|---|---|

## DUNKELBERG, Johann     Ltn d R
J58     28 Mar 1918 – 2 Jun 1918    –   KIA
Born 12 July 1896, Barsinghausen. Joined Jasta 58 from Jastaschule II. Killed over Bailleul.

## DYCKE, Robert     Ltn d R
J16     7 Dec 1916 – 8 Dec 1917    2         CO J78b   8 Dec 1917 – 30 Jul 1918    –   WIA
Born 24 August 1890, Holzheim. Joined military service 1913, 16th Bavarian Infantry Regiment; Gefreiter in 1914 this unit. Promoted Leutnant 14 Mar 1915. Fliegerschule 15 Sep 1915. 15 Feb 1916 to FA7. 15 Mar 1916 to Kagohl 6/33. Iron Cross 2nd Class 14 November 1914; Bavarian Military Cross 4th Class with Swords 15 December 1915; Pilot's Badge 11 October 1916; Iron Cross 1st Class 8 March 1917; Bavarian Military Merit Order 4th Class with Crown and Swords 10 February 1918. Joined Jasta 16 from AFP B. Acting CO Jasta 16b, 22 Aug 1917 to 1 Dec 1917. Over Weilertal was shot down by DH9 in his Albatros DVa 7225/17.

| Victories: | 1. | 10 Mar 1917 | Balloon | | Retzweiler | (a) |
|---|---|---|---|---|---|---|
| | 2. | 17 Oct 1917 | Spad | | Montfaucon | |

(a) French 74th Company.

## DYRBUSCH, Paul     Uffz
J68     11 May 1918 – 10 Oct 1918    –   KIA
Born 26 April 1894, Königshutte. Killed over Preutin.

## EBERLEIN, Franz     Vfw
J33                         1
Lightly wounded in action 7 June 1917.

| Victories: | 1. | 12 Oct 1917 | Spad | 1245 | Westroosebeke |
|---|---|---|---|---|---|

## EBERT, Friedrich     Ltn d R
FAA298     – 1918    –         J23b     13 Jun 1918 – 11 Nov 1918    –
OzbV for Jasta 23b.

## EBERT,     Uffz
J40     (Jul 1918) – (Aug 1918)    –

| Victories: | zlg | 24 Jul 1918 | BF2b | | |
|---|---|---|---|---|---|

## ECK, Rudolf     Ltn
J3     29 Aug 1916 – 13 Dec 1917    2         J16b     2 Jan 1918 – 11 Nov 1918    1
JsSchII     13 Dec 1917 – 2 Jan 1918    –
Wounded in action 20 April 1918, rejoined Jasta 16b on 29 April 1918.

| Victories: | zlg | 14 Feb 1917 | BE | | Clery |
|---|---|---|---|---|---|
| | 1. | 17 Aug 1917 | Spad | 1030 | Ypern |
| | 2. | 18 Oct 1917 | DH5 | 0955 | Wildermann |
| | 3. | 18 May 1918 | BF2b | 0825 | Langemarck |

## ECKARDT,     Ltn
J16                         –

## ECKE, Gustav     Uffz
J54s     19 Jan 1918 – 18 Mar 1918    –   KIA
Born 16 February 1894, Heimstedt. Killed over Busigny.

## ECKENBERG, Wilhelm     Ltn d R
J32     16 Jul 1917 – 7 Jul 1917    –         J29     7 Sep 1917 – 12 Jun 1918    –
OzbV for Jasta 32. Transferred to Flugubungestelle 5, Mouzon, 12 June 1918.

## ECKERT,     Ltn
J26                         –

**ECKERT,   Ltn**

| | | | | | |
|---|---|---|---|---|---|
| FA29 | | – | J48 | 2 Feb 1918 – 11 Nov 1918 | – |

OzbV for Jasta 48.

---

**EDER, Hubert     Ltn d R**

| | | | |
|---|---|---|---|
| J23b | 28 Jun 1918 – 11 Nov 1918 | 1 | |
| Joined Jasta 23b from Jastaschule I. | | | |
| Victories: | 1. | 27 Aug 1918 | RE8 | 2030 | Cagnicourt |

---

**EDZARD,   Ltn**

| | | |
|---|---|---|
| J58 | 10 Aug 1918 – 11 Nov 1918 | – |

---

**EFFERS, Karl W     Ltn**

| | | | | | |
|---|---|---|---|---|---|
| J11 | Jan 1917 – 5 Jun 1918 | – | AFP17 | 5 Jun 1918 – | – |

OzbV for Jasta 11 from 19 Dec 1917 to 13 June 1918.

---

**EGER,   Uffz**

| | | |
|---|---|---|
| J12 | 16 Apr 1918 – | – |

---

**EGERER, Erhard     Oblt**

| | | | | | |
|---|---|---|---|---|---|
| FA3b | – 15 Oct 1916 | – | Idflieg | 27 Dec 1916 – | – |
| CO J13 | 15 Oct 1916 – 27 Dec 1916 | – | | | |

---

**EGGEBRECHT,     Uffz**

| | | | | |
|---|---|---|---|---|
| J25 | | 1 | | |
| Victories: | 1. | 16 Jan 1918 | Balloon | Opticar |

---

**EGGERS, Hans     Ltn**

| | | | | | |
|---|---|---|---|---|---|
| J2 | (Jun 1917) – 1 Oct 1917 | – | J30 | 14 May 1918 – 11 Oct 1918 | – |
| AFP4 | 1 Oct 1917 – | – | BG4 | 11 Oct 1918 – | – |

Acting CO Jasta 30 from 17 June to 1 July 1918, and 1 August to 15 August 1918.

| | | | | |
|---|---|---|---|---|
| Victories: | – | 18 May 1918 | RE8 | Brielen |

---

**EGLE,   Ltn**

| | | | |
|---|---|---|---|
| J45 | 29 Sep 1918 – 21 Oct 1918 | – Hosp | |

OzbV for Jasta 45.

---

**EHLERS,     Ltn d R**

| | | | | | |
|---|---|---|---|---|---|
| J17 | 8 Jul 1917 – 16 Aug 1917 | – WIA | J26 | – 11 Nov 1918 | 2 |

Joined Jasta 17 from AFP4.

| | | | | |
|---|---|---|---|---|
| Victories: | 1. | 2 Sep 1918 | Camel | 1245 | NE Baralle |
| | 2. | 4 Sep 1918 | Camel | 0910 | Palleul |

---

**EHMANN, Friedrich     Ltn**

| | | | | | |
|---|---|---|---|---|---|
| AFP4 | – 23 Sep 1917 | – | AFPB | 19 Oct 1917 – | – |
| J24 | 23 Sep 1917 – 19 Oct 1917 | – | J33 | | 1 |
| Victories: | – | 6 Jan 1918 | Paul Schmitt | | Gottestal |
| | – | 22 Jan 1918 | Balloon | | Lepuix |
| | 1. | 24 Mar 1918 | DH4 | 1315 | Bortenach |

---

**EHMANN, Friedrich     Vfw**

| | | | | | |
|---|---|---|---|---|---|
| Kest5 | 22 Oct 1917 – 25 Dec 1917 | – | J47w | 25 Dec 1917 – 11 Nov 1918 | 8 |

Biography & Victories: See *Above the Lines*.

---

**EHMANN,     Ltn**

| | | |
|---|---|---|
| J26 | – 11 Nov 1918 | – |

---

**EHRHARDT,     Ltn d R**

| | | | | | |
|---|---|---|---|---|---|
| J32b | | 2 | J32b | 22 Oct 1918 – 11 Nov 1918 | – |
| Victories: | 1. | 21 May 1918 | SE5a | | Bullecourt |
| | 2. | 7 Jun 1918 | DH4 | | Abscon |

**EHRLICH,**    **Uffz**
AFP6               –           J30      8 Jul 1918 – 11 Nov 1918    –

**EICHENAUER, Wilhelm**    **Vfw**
J15    10 Oct 1916 – 4 Jun 1917    –   KIA
Born 17 September 1892, Felda. Killed in combat with Spads over Filain, after a balloon attack.

**EICHHORN,**    **Oblt**
J19    2 Jun 1917 – 1 Oct 1917    –       Kest 4a    1 Oct 1917 –          –
Joined Jasta 19 from Jastaschule I. OzbV for Jasta 19. Acting CO Jasta 19 from 4 to 18 Sep 1917.

**EICHHORN,**    **Uffz**
J58    28 Jan 1918 – 21 Aug 1918    –   INJ
Joined Jasta 58 from Jastaschule II. Severely injured, arm amputated.

**EICKHOFF,**    **Flg**
J17       – 14 Aug 1918    –   INJ

**EID, Karl**    **Ltn**
FA67                         J24    1 Dec 1916 – 10 Mar 1917    –

**EIGENBRODT, August**    **Uffz**
J7    (Apr 1918) – 8 Oct 1918    3   WIA

| Victories: | | | | | |
|---|---|---|---|---|---|
| | 1. | 31 May 1918 | Camel | 1830 | Nieppewald |
| | 2. | 17 Jun 1918 | Camel | 0920 | Dickebuschsee |
| | 3. | 8 Oct 1918 | Dolphin | | |

**EILERS,**    **Oblt**
CO J40    27 Jul 1917 – 14 Apr 1918    –

**EIMBECK, Gustav**    **Vfw**
J13       – 18 Jan 1917    –       AFP6    12 Apr 1917 –          –
J30    18 Jan 1917 – 12 Apr 1917    –

**EISELE, Karl**    **Vfw**
J20    15 May 1917 – 1 Nov 1917    –      J43    1 Nov 1917 – 30 Dec 1917    – KIAcc
Born 25 March 1892, Ludwigsburg. Joined Jasta 20 from Jastaschule I. Killed during a test flight over Möntingen airfield.

**EISENHUTH, Emil**    **Vfw**
FAA211                 1      J3    Apr 1917 – 26 Apr 1917    1   KIA
Born 5 April 1891, Hasselfeld. Shot down in flames near Haynecourt, flying Albatros DIII 2207/16, probably by Capt A Ball, No 56 Sqn, RFC.

| Victories: | | | | | |
|---|---|---|---|---|---|
| | 1. | Date and unit unknown | | | |
| | 2. | 3 Apr 1917 | FE2b | 1655 | Hendecourt |

**EISERBECK, Robert**    **Uffz**
J11    (Feb 1918) – 12 Apr 1918    –   KIA
Born 13 May 1896, Grimme. Killed at 1510 hours over Meault.

**EISSFELDT, Hans**    **Uffz**
FAA248      – 1916    –      J10    28 Sep 1916 – 27 Apr 1917    – WIA
Born 28 January 1893. Severely wounded, didn't fly for rest of war. Attained rank of Colonel in Luftwaffe during WWII. Died 10 April 1976, Friedrichshafen.

**EITEL,**    **Gefr**
Kest 8         –

**ELFERS, Christel**    **Uffz**
J69       – 11 Nov 1918    1

| Victories: | | | | | |
|---|---|---|---|---|---|
| | 1. | 27 Oct 1918 | Balloon | | St Cosman |

## ELTING,     Ltn
J69                                              I
Victories    1.        13 Aug 1918     Spad                    1940            Les Petites Loges

---

## EMBERGER, Gebhard     Ltn d R
J29        6 Aug 1917 – 4 Sep 1917     – KIA
Born 12 February 1896, Schmalegg, Ravensburg. Served with Württemberg L.I.R.123. Joined Jasta 29 from Jastaschule I. Shot down in flames over Poelcapelle, at 2006 hours.

---

## EMELE, Andreas     Vfw
J80b       23 Aug 1918 – 28 Oct 1918     – KIA
Born 28 May 1896, Ringingen. Joined Jasta 80b from AFP B. Killed during combat with a DH9 over Fremerchen.

---

## EMMERICH, Fritz     Vfw
J16b       19 Aug 1918 – 11 Nov 1918     –
Victories:                    Prior to joining Jasta 16b
                    1.        Date and unit unknown

---

## EMMERICH, Richard     Ltn d R
J77b       18 Mar 1918 – 22 Mar 1918     –           J76b     22 Mar 1918 – 11 Apr 1918     – KIA
Born 7 February 1892, Mutterstadt. Joined Jasta 77b from Jastaschule II. Killed at 1820 hours W Albert, after combat with a RE8 at 1740 hours, flying Albatros DVa 5726/17.

---

## ENGEL,     Ltn d R
J45        19 Aug 1918 – 22 Aug 1918     – Hosp

---

## ENGEWALD,     Ltn
J19        Sep 1918 – 11 Nov 1918     –
OzbV for Jasta 19.

---

## ENGLER, Friedrich     Uffz
J63              – 19 May 1918     –           J62     19 May 1918 – 3 Sep 1918     4
WIA. Severely wounded during balloon attack.
Victories:    1.        28 Jun 1918     Balloon          0912            Rocquencourt
              2.        1 Jul 1918      Dolphin          1240            Guérbigny
              3.        19 Jul 1918     Balloon          2005            S Louvercy
              4.        25 Jul 1918     Salmson          1145            S Reims
              –         3 Sep 1918      Balloon

---

## ENGLER,     Ltn d R
Kest 4b                                          –

---

## ENTZ, Walter     Ltn d R
J38              – 7 Sep 1917     – INJ
Born 23 November 1890, Schwetz. Severely injured in a landing accident at Kalnkowa; died in hospital.

---

## ERBELDING,     Ltn
J57        17 Apr 1918 – 11 Nov 1918     –
OzbV for Jasta 57.

---

## ERBGUTH, Paul     Ltn
SchSt21          – 1917     –           CO J54     28 Dec 1917 – 18 May 1918     –
J30        10 Mar 1917 – 28 Dec 1917     2
Wounded in leg on 30 Apr 1915, while with Territorial Reserve Infantry Regiment 107. Awarded Saxon Knight's Cross of the Military St Henry Order 2 Dec 1917.
Victories:    1.        26 Apr 1917     BE2e             1828            SE Haisnes
              2.        21 Sep 1917     Camel            1150            S Wevelghem
              –         12 Mar 1918     BF2b                             N Caudry

---

## ERDMANN, Georg     Uffz
J73              – 6 Apr 1918     – KIA
Born 8 March 1894, Landau. Killed between St Marie-à-Py and Somme-Py, at 1930 hours.

**ERDMANN, Lothar    Ltn**
J20        8 Nov 1916 – 24 Dec 1916    – KIA
Born 1 May 1898, Kiel. Killed over St Quentin.

---

**ERICH, Arond    Ltn**
J63                      – 12 Jun 1918    – KIA
Born 22 August 1896, Konstanz. Flying an Albatros DV when killed at 0845 over Tricot. Credited to
Capt M LeBlanc-Smith, No 73 Sqn, RAF, in Camel D1794.

---

**ERICHSON, Paul    Ltn**
J34      27 May 1917 – 2 Jun 1917      –                 J40        4 Jul 1918 – 31 Jul 1918    – WIA
Kest 7    2 Jun 1917 – 13 Dec 1917    – WIA
Joined Jasta 34 from AFP C.

---

**ERKENBRECHT,    Ltn**
J12      30 Jan 1917 – 11 Mar 1917    – WIA

---

**ERLEWEIN, Wilhelm    Ltn d R**
J47w     6 May 1918 – 8 Jun 1918    – KIA
Born 28 March 1891, Schwabisch-Gmund. Killed in a Pfalz DIIIa over Suzanne-Somme.

---

**ERMECKE,    Ltn**
J33                                                      1
Victories:        1.        13 May 1917    Nieuport            0945          SW Baralle          (a)
(a) Probably B1640, No 40 Sqn, RFC, Lt A B Raymond, POW.

---

**ERNERT, Richard    Ltn d L**
J34      21 Feb 1917 – 7 Jul 1917      1            FAA301                                    – KIA
FEA11     7 Jul 1917 –                  –
Born 6 July 1886, Leipzig. Joined Jasta 34 from FEA1. Awarded EKI. Killed 15 Oct 1917, at Abu Sitte.
Victories:        1.        29 Apr 1917    Balloon                         Génicourt
                  2.        Date and unit unknown

---

**ERNST,    Uffz**
J49                      – 11 Nov 1918    1
Victories:        1.        26 Sep 1918    Bréguet             1050          Tahure

---

**ERNST,    Ltn**
J69                      – 12 Jun 1918    – POW
Shot down in Allied lines near Courcelles.

---

**ERNTHALLER, Karl    OfStv**
J1       23 Aug 1916 – 4 Dec 1916    – KIA
Born 23 December 1892, Munich. Served with FA23 before joining Jasta 1. Killed over Proville, due to
wing failure flying Fokker DI 175/16.

---

**ESEBECK, Rudolf Fr von    Hptm**
J8        (Feb 1917) – Jun 1917      1            CO J17    4 Oct 1917 – 27 May 1918    – KIA
CO Kest 7               – 4 Oct 1917    –
Born 8 March 1888, Karlsruhe. Served in Garde-Regiment zu Fuss 2 (2nd Foot Guard Regiment).
Awarded EK I. Killed at 1930 hours over Noyon, in combat with Bréguets.
Victories:        1.        6 Feb 1917    FE2d                1630          SE Gheluvelt

---

**ESSER, Hans-Olaf    Ltn d R**
J15      10 Oct 1916 – 16 Apr 1917    1 KIA
Born 30 August 1894, Gilberfeld. Killed over Winterberge, near Laon.
Victories:        1.        16 Apr 1917    Nieuport                        Laon

---

**ESSER,    Ltn**
J68       7 May 1918 – 11 Nov 1918    –

---

**ESSWEIN, Otto    OfStv**
J26      30 Oct 1917 – 21 Jul 1918    12 KIA
Biography & Victories: See *Above the Lines*.

**ESTENFELDER, Emil    Gefr**
J79b                – 13 Aug 1918     –  WIA

**ETZOLD, Willy    Ltn d R**
J26        8 Dec 1917 – 18 Feb 1918     –  KIA
Born 4 October 1895, Meerane. Served in 107th Infantry Regiment. Joined Jasta 26 from Jastaschule I.
Killed over Houthulsterwald.

**EWERS, Walter    Oblt**
FA26                                  –          J77b    21 Jan 1918 – 15 May 1918    5   KIA
J12     12 Aug 1917 – 21 Jan 1918    3
Biography & Victories: See *Above the Lines*.

**EY, Eduard    Vfw KekM**
J6        10 Sep 1916 – 16 May 1917     –  KIAcc
Born 4 September 1893, Etz. Killed in a SSW DI, at AFP2 Aulnoye.

**EYSSLER,    Flg**
J66                – 11 Nov 1918    1
Victories:        1.        2 Sep 1918        Spad                            N Soissons

**FABRICE, Viktor von    Ltn**
J10        Nov 1916 – Jun 1917     –
Born 13.25 January 1892. Acting CO Jasta 10 during November 1916. Attained rank of Major in the
Luftwaffe during WWII. Died 13.25 September 1974, Paderborn, Germany.

**FÄRBER, John    Ltn d R**
J22s                – 20 Apr 1918     –  KIA
Born 9 September 1896, Bahrenfeld. Killed over Bies.

**FÄRBER, Paul    Vfw**
J22s                – 23 Sep 1918    2  KIA
Born 5 May 1895, Altenwalde. Killed near Sailly.
Victories:        zlg        15 Dec 1917        AR2                            W Craonelle
                  1.        19 Dec 1917        Balloon              1610       Terny-Sorny
                  2.        26 Feb 1918        Balloon

**FAHLKE,    OfStv**
J37                                    1
Victories:        1.        24 Jun 1917        Spad                            SE Kemnat        (a)
(a) S128, Sgt Michel, N 84.

**FAUKL,    Uffz**
J36        17 Aug 1917 –             –
Joined Jasta 36 from AFP4.

**FEIBICKE, Walter    Uffz**
J44s                – 22 Aug 1918     –  KIAcc at Jussy
Born Berlin, 4 November 1893.

**FEIG, Eduard    Uffz**
J76b                – 23 Nov 1917     –  KIAcc
Born 10 February 1884, Wunsiedel. Killed at Habsheim.

**FEIGE, Lothar    Ltn d R**
J10        30 May 1918 – 30 Jun 1918     –  KIA
Born 15 October 1893, Gotha. Killed over Noroy.

**FELDER,    Gefr**
J19        6 May 1918 – 11 Nov 1918    2
Victories:        1.        11 Aug 1918        Bréguet              1955       N Noyon
                  2.        16 Sep 1918        Bréguet              1755       Conflans        (a)
(a) Probably 96th Aero Sqn, USAS.

## FELIX, Paul    Uffz
J15        – 19 Aug 1917    – KIA over Boncourt.
Born in Berlin, 5 March 1894.

## FELSMANN, Paul    OfStv
| | | | | | | |
|---|---|---|---|---|---|---|
| KG2/11 | | | 1 | Kest 4b | 27 Jun 1917 – 20 Jul 1918 | – KIA |
| J24 | 6 Jan 1917 – 27 Jun 1917 | 1 | | | | |

Born 10 March 1893, Kerzdorf, Lauban. Killed over Rotenburg, Schwarzwald.
| Victories: | 1. | Date unknown | | | |
|---|---|---|---|---|---|
| | 2. | 24 Apr 1917 | Spad VII | 1012 | Prunay |
| | – | 2 May 1917 | Nieuport 17 | 2015 | Prosnes |

## FERNER, Georg    Ltn d R
| | | | | | | | |
|---|---|---|---|---|---|---|---|
| J14 | | – 4 Dec 1916 | – | J19 | 25 Sep 1917 – 11 Jan 1918 | – |
| J24 | 4 Dec 1916 – 6 Feb 1917 | | – WIA | J61 | 11 Jan 1918 – 10 Feb 1918 | – KIAcc |

Born 24 April 1887, Marienburg. OzbV for Jasta 24 and 61. Severely wounded over Pompey. Joined Jasta 19 from AFP1. Killed during a test flight at Voyenne airfield.

## FERVERS, Karl    Uffz
| | | | |
|---|---|---|---|
| JB | Sep 1918 – 11 Nov 1918 | 4 | |

| Victories: | 1. | 27 Sep 1918 | Camel | Aubenscheul |
|---|---|---|---|---|
| | 2. | 28 Sep 1918 | Camel | Epinoy |
| | 3. | 29 Sep 1918 | BF2b | Cagnoucles |
| | 4. | 8 Oct 1918 | Camel | Cagnoucles |

## FESQ,    Vfw
Kest 1a    (Sep 1918) – Oct 1918    –

## FESTLER, Max    Ltn d R
J11      26 Jul 1918 – 11 Aug 1918    – KIA
Born 5 March 1894, Ulm. Served in Württemberg Field Artillery Regiment 13. Joined Jasta 11 from Jastaschule II. Killed over La Chapelle.

## FESTNER, Sebastian    Vfw
| | | | | | |
|---|---|---|---|---|---|
| FA18 | 10 Sep 1916 – 15 Sep 1916 | – | J11 | 11 Nov 1916 – 25 Apr 1917 | 12 KIA |
| FA5 | 15 Sep 1916 – 11 Nov 1916 | – | | | |

Biography & Victories: See *Above the Lines*.

## FEUEREISSEN,    Ltn d R
| | | | | | | |
|---|---|---|---|---|---|---|
| J51 | (Jan 1918) | – 18 May 1918 | 2 WIA | J51 | Jun 1918 – | |

| Victories: | 1. | 15 May 1918 | BF2b | 2010 | W Langemarck |
|---|---|---|---|---|---|
| | 2. | 8 Jun 1918 | DH4 | 1830 | W Kruisstraat |

## FICHTE, von    Ltn
SS16        –    J54s      – 11 Nov 1918    –
Last Commanding Officer of Jasta 54s.

## FICHTER, Julius    Ltn d R
| | | | | | | |
|---|---|---|---|---|---|---|
| KG5/29 | 9 Jul 1916 – 1 Sep 1916 | – | J22 | 23 Feb 1917 – 26 Jan 1918 | 2 |
| KG5/26 | 1 Sep 1916 – 11 Nov 1916 | 1 | CO J67 | 26 Jan 1918 – 11 Nov 1918 | 4 |

Biography & Victories: See *Above the Lines*.

## FICK, Max    Vfw
| | | | | | | |
|---|---|---|---|---|---|---|
| J29 | 16 Feb 1917 – 16 Feb 1917 | – | J29 | 1 Mar 1917 – 24 Aug 1917 | – |
| J21 | 16 Feb 1917 – 1 Mar 1917 | – | AFP4 | 24 Aug 1917 – | – |

## FIESELER, Gerhard    Ltn d R
| | | | | | | |
|---|---|---|---|---|---|---|
| FAA243 | Oct 1916 – 1916 | – | J25 | May 1917 – 11 Nov 1918 | 19 |
| FA41 | 1916 – | – | | | |

Biography & Victories: See *Above the Lines*.

## FILBIG, Josef    Ltn
J80b     28 Jun 1918 – 29 Oct 1918    1
Joined Jasta 80b from Jastaschule I. Hospitalised 29 Oct 1918.

| Victories: | – | 30 Jul 1918 | 2-seater | | Parroy Wald |
| | 1. | 2 Sep 1918 | Balloon | 1700 | Laronxe |

### FINHOLD, Wilhelm    Ltn d R
J34        21 Feb 1917 – 13 Sep 1917    – KIA

Born 4 August 1895, Koln. Served in Field Artillery Rgt Nr.56. Joined Jasta 34 from FEA1b. Awarded EK I. Killed over Boinvillers.

| Victories: | – | 2 May 1917 | Nieuport | | Ancemont-Génicourt |

### FINSTER, Wolfgang    Ltn
J29        1 Jul 1917 – 5 Sep 1917    –                AFPB    5 Sep 1917 –            –

Joined Jasta 29 from AFP1.

### FIRNSTEIN, Walter    Ltn d R
J7        Sep 1918 – 11 Nov 1918    –

### FISCHER, Martin    Ltn d R
J4        Mar 1918 – 27 Apr 1918    –                J4        26 Aug 1918 –                –
AFP2    27 Apr 1918 –                –                J6                    – 29 Oct 1918    – KIA

Born 16 July 1893, Hamburg. Joined Jasta 4 from Jastaschule I on 26 August 1918. Killed in action over Montfaucon.

### FISCHER, Otto    Gefr
J51        Aug 1918 –                –

### FISCHER, Ulrich    Ltn
FA23        Nov 1916 – Jan 1917    –                J22s        Aug 1917 – 11 Nov 1918        4
FA234        Jan 1917 – Aug 1917    –

Born 3 May 1895. Served as Fahrenjunker in Field Artillery Regiment 20, Posen. Transferred to aviation May 1916. Jastaschule I in Aug 1917. Joined Jasta 22s from Jastaschule I.

| Victories: | 1. | 4 Feb 1918 | Sopwith 2 | 1550 | Sinceny |
| | 2. | 19 Feb 1918 | 2-seater | 1605 | Jouy |
| | 3. | 7 Jun 1918 | Spad 2 | | Estrées-St Dénis |
| | 4. | 1 Oct 1918 | Spad | 1040 | Cerisy |

### FISCHER,    Ltn d R
J24s        11 Aug 1918 – 11 Nov 1918    –

Awarded EKI. Forced to land after combat with a SE5 on 30 October 1918, near Vaqueresse, while flying Fokker DVII (OAW) 4600/18.

### FISCHER,    Gefr
Kest 8        Sep 1918 –                –

### FITZNER, Otto    Ltn d R
J17        8 Jul 1917 – 19 Mar 1918    3                CO J65    19 Mar 1918 – 11 Nov 1918        6

Biography & Victories: See *Above the Lines*.

### FLACH,    Gefr
J81                – 16 Jun 1918    – POW

Shot down in no man's land and captured.

### FLASHAR, Richard    Oblt
KG2                – 1917                1                CO J5    8 Jul 1917 – 18 May 1918        1

Commanded Jagdgruppen 2, 3, and 7 at various times.

| Victories: | 1. | Date and unit unknown | | | |
| | 2. | 19 Sep 1917 | Morane | 1203 | Elincourt |

### FLASSBECK,    Flg
J4        26 Oct 1918 – 11 Nov 1918    –

Joined Jasta 4 from Jastaschule II.

### FLATOW,    Vfw
J45        22 Apr 1917 – 31 May 1918    – WIA                FEA14    25 Aug 1918 –
J45        3 Jul 1918 – 25 Aug 1918    –

Wounded in hand; four weeks' leave.

---

### FLECKEN, Gerhard Wilhelm   Ltn

| | | | | | | |
|---|---|---|---|---|---|---|
| J20 | 25 Oct 1916 – 1 Nov 1917 | 4 | | AFPF | Jun 1918 – Jun 1918 | – |
| CO J43 | 1 Nov 1917 – May 1918 | – | | CO | J55 Jun 1918 – 20 Sep 1918 | – |

Born 29 March 1888, Koln. Served in SS15 and KG7 prior to joining Jasta 20. Acting CO Jasta 20, 2 to 20 Oct 1917.

| Victories: | 1. | 15 Mar 1917 | Caudron | | NE Lassigny | |
|---|---|---|---|---|---|---|
| | zlg | 7 May 1917 | Nieuport | 1200 | Vendeuil | |
| | 2. | 13 Jul 1917 | Pup | 2030 | SE Haan | (a) |
| | 3. | 4 Sep 1917 | Camel | | SW Nieuport | |
| | 4. | 8 May 1918 | DH9 | 2030 | Zillebeke | |

(a) A6240, No 54 Sqn, RFC, Capt F N Hudson, POW.

---

### FLEISCHER, Alfred   Ltn d R

| | | |
|---|---|---|
| J17 | 12 Apr 1918 – 11 Nov 1918 | 6 |

Biography & Victories: See *Above the Lines*.

---

### FLEISCHMANN,   Vfw

| | | |
|---|---|---|
| J81 | – 4 Nov 1917 | – KIAcc |

---

### FLEMMING,   Uffz

| | | | | | | |
|---|---|---|---|---|---|---|
| J8 | 10 Sep 1916 – 27 Oct 1916 | – | | J18 | 27 Oct 1916 – Dec 1917 | 2 |

| Victories: | 1. | 14 Feb 1917 | FE2d | 1700 | Zuidschoote | (a) |
|---|---|---|---|---|---|---|
| | – | 17 Mar 1917 | BE2d | | W Ypern | |
| | 2. | 5 May 1917 | FE2d | | Zillebekesee | (b) |
| | – | 25 May 1917 | Nieuport | | British Lines | |

(a) No 20 Sqn, RFC.
(b) Probably 2/Lt L G Bacon (P) WIA & 2/AM G Worthing (O) KIA, No 20 Sqn, RFC.

---

### FLINK, Josef   Ltn

| | | | |
|---|---|---|---|
| J18 | 11 Feb 1917 – 5 Apr 1917 | 2 | POW |

Forced to land in Allied lines near Neuve Eglise, at 1048 hours after combat with FE2ds, flying Albatros DIII 1942/16 (G.20). Credited to Lt H G White and Pvt T Allum, No 20 Sqn, RFC, in FE2b A6385.

| Victories: | 1. | 4 Mar 1917 | Nieuport | 1720 | NW Ypern |
|---|---|---|---|---|---|
| | 2. | 11 Mar 1917 | Sopwith 2 | 1217 | S Ypern |

---

### FLORIAN, Friedrich Karl   Uffz

| | | | |
|---|---|---|---|
| J51 | – 14 May 1918 | – | POW |

Came down after combat in Allied lines flying Albatros DIII 5161/17 (G/2/9). Possibly the victim of Lts D Latimer and T C Noel of No 20 Sqn, RAF, on BF2b C856.

---

### FÖGE, Wilhelm   Uffz

| | | | |
|---|---|---|---|
| J30 | 17 Oct 1917 – 22 Dec 1917 | – | WIA |

Born 13 January 1890, Rudersdorf. Joined Jasta 30 from Jastaschule I. Severely wounded over Armentières, died in hospital.

---

### FÖRSTER, Maximillian von   Oblt

| | | | |
|---|---|---|---|
| J27 | 7 May 1918 – 17 Jun 1918 | 1 | KIAcc |

Born 8 September 1893, Charlottenberg. Hussar Rgt No 3. Was a passenger in a two-seater piloted by Vfw Wilhelm Schäfer, when both were killed in an accident at Mont de Soissons-Ferme airfield.

| Victories: | 1. | 31 May 1918 | Spad 2 | 1810 | W Soissons |
|---|---|---|---|---|---|

---

### FÖRSTER, Moritz   Vfw

| | | |
|---|---|---|
| J32b | – 27 Jun 1917 | – KIA |

Born 29 October 1890, Eckersbach. Killed at 1000 hours over St Hilaire-le-Petit.

---

### FÖRSTER, Otto Ludwig   Ltn

| | | | | | | |
|---|---|---|---|---|---|---|
| J15 | Sep 1917 – 21 May 1918 | 3 | | J11 | 21 May 1918 – 4 Sep 1918 | |

Born 16 March 1894. OzbV for Jasta 11 from 21 May 1918 to 4 Sep 1918. Transferred to Jastaschule I, 4 Sep 1918.

| Victories: | 1. | 22 Sep 1917 | Balloon | 1825 | W La Fre |
|---|---|---|---|---|---|
| | 2. | 30 Sep 1917 | Spad | 1200 | W Aisne-Staubecken |
| | 3. | 21 Oct 1917 | Balloon | 1830 | S Aisne |

**FÖRTIG, Eugen      Uffz**
J16b      15 Jan 1918 – 27 Jan 1918      – KIAcc
Born 19 April 1894, Watterbach. Killed during a test flight of Pfalz DIII 4034/17 at Mercy-le-Haut airfield.

**FORSTMANN, Hans      Ltn**
J1            – 16 Jun 1917      –            J30      16 Jun 1917 – 2 Jul 1917      – KIA
Born 9 June 1894, Geestemunde. Killed at 1130 hours near the Dourges Canal.

**FORSTMANN, Heinrich      Vfw**
Kest 1a      – 10 Oct 1918      1 KIA

| Victories: | 1. | 7 Sep 1918 | DH4 | 1415 | Münzein |
|---|---|---|---|---|---|

**FORSTMANN,      Uffz**
J50      – 11 Nov 1918      –

**FRÄDRICH, Gustav      Ltn d R**
FA30            – 1917            1            J1      Jan 1918 – 26 Mar 1918      –
J39            – Jan 1918      –            J72      26 Mar 1918 – 11 Nov 1918      5
Biography & Victories: See *Above the Lines*.

**FRANCKE, Kurt      Ltn d R**
JB      Apr 1917 – 20 May 1917      – WIA
Born 8 December 1891, Lissa. Severely wounded during combat with Nieuports in the area of Ecourt St Quentin. Died of wounds 1 June 1917.

**FRANCKE, Rudolf      Ltn**
SS17            –            J8      (May 1917) – 11 Nov 1918      15
Biography & Victories: See *Above the Lines*.

**FRANKE, Otto      Ltn**
J30      30 Jun 1918 – 17 Jul 1918      1 KIA
Born 25 September 1897, Bruckstedt. Joined Jasta 30 from Jastaschule I. Killed near Erquinghem, by ground fire at 1910 hours.

| Victories: | 1. | 17 Jul 1918 | Dolphin | 1900 | Erquinghem |
|---|---|---|---|---|---|

**FRANKE, Paul      Ltn**
J53      24 Sep 1918 – 11 Nov 1918      –
Joined Jasta 53 from Jastaschule I.

**FRANKL, Wilhelm      Ltn d R**
FA40      1915 –            1            J4      1 Sep 1916 – 8 Apr 1917      11 KIA
KekV            – 1 Sep 1916      8
Biography & Victories: See *Above the Lines*.

**FRANZ, Albert      Vfw**
J33            – 4 May 1917      – WIA
Born 25 July 1889, Meseritz. Severely wounded over Erchin-Sailly, flying Albatros DIII 2067/16, died three days later.

| Victories: | – | 23 Apr 1917 | Sopwith 2 | 1700 | Boisleux |
|---|---|---|---|---|---|
|  | – | 30 Apr 1917 | EA | 1320 | Monchy |

**FREDEN, Hans von      Ltn d R**
FA10            – 28 Nov 1917      –            J1      26 Mar 1918 – 20 Jun 1918      –
J1      28 Nov 1917 – 8 Mar 1918      4            J50      20 Jun 1918 –            16
J72      8 Mar 1918 – 26 Mar 1918      –
Biography & Victories: See *Above the Lines*.

**FREITAG, Franz      Ltn**
J53      24 Sep 1918 – 11 Nov 1918      –
Joined Jasta 53 from Jastaschule I.

**FRETER,      Uffz**
J42                  2

| Victories: | 1. | 17 Feb 1918 | Spad | 1325 | Flirey |
|---|---|---|---|---|---|
|  | 2. | 24 Mar 1918 | Spad | 1135 | St Mihiel |

## FREY, Adolf    Ltn d R

J9          – 30 Apr 1917    3   KIA
Born 7 September 1891, Genthin. Killed in combat with a Caudron R4 over Nauroy.

| Victories: | 1. | 22 Oct 1916 | Nieuport | 1300 | Tahure |
|---|---|---|---|---|---|
| | 2. | 19 Apr 1917 | Farman | 1145 | S Moronvillers |
| | 3. | 30 Apr 1917 | Spad | 1115 | Moronvillers |

## FREY, Alfred    Ltn

JB      (Jun 1918) – (Jul 1918)      –

## FREYTAG, Alfred    Ltn d R

| FEA4 | – 28 May 1916 | – | J44 | 17 Dec 1917 – 7 Jun 1918 | 1 |
|---|---|---|---|---|---|
| FA252A | 12 Dec 1916 – | – | AFP17 | 8 Jun 1918 – | – |
| J21s | 10 Jul 1917 – 16 Dec 1917 | – | J23b | 10 Oct 1918 – 11 Nov 1918 | – |

Joined military service 14 Oct 1914, assigned to (W) Grenadier-Regiment König Karl Nr.123. Gefreiter on 24 Feb 1915. Unteroffizier on 14 Mar 1915. Vizefeldwebel on 3 May 1915. Württemberg Silver Military Merit Medal on 3 June 1915. Promoted Leutnant 19 July 1915. Transferred to air service during May 1916. Awarded EK II in May 1916. Württemberg Gold Military Merit Medal on 20 May 1918. Acting CO Jasta 44 from 15 February to 10 June 1918. Ehrenbecher dem Sieger im Luftkampfe on 22 May 1918. Knight's Cross of the Württemberg Military Merit Order on 6 June 1918. Saxon Albert Order Knight 2nd Class with Swords on 25 July 1918. OzbV for Jasta 21s from 10 Oct 1918. Adjutant for JGIV from 10 Oct 1918.

| Victories: | 1. | 30 Mar 1918 | RE8 | 1030 | Chauny |
|---|---|---|---|---|---|

## FRICKART, Wilhelm    Ltn d L

| FA24 | 1917 – | 2 | FA20 | | 1 |
|---|---|---|---|---|---|
| FA242 | 1917 – | 5 | J65 | 19 Aug 1918 – 11 Nov 1918 | 4 |

Biography & Victories: See *Above the Lines*.

## FRIEDRICH, Hans    Ltn

J34b     6 Jun 1918 – 7 Jun 1918     – INJ
Joined Jasta 34b from Jastaschule I. Severely injured in an accident during a test flight at Foucaucourt airfield.

## FRIEDRICHS, Friedrich    Ltn d R

| FAA264 | Jun 1917 – | – | J10 | 11 Jan 1918 – 15 Jul 1918 | 21 KIA |
|---|---|---|---|---|---|

Biography & Victories: See *Above the Lines*.

## FRIES, Erich    Oblt

J34b     14 Aug 1918 – 11 Nov 1918    1
Joined Jasta 34b from Jastaschule I. Shot down in flames 3 October 1918, but landed unharmed.

| Victories: | 1. | 29 Aug 1918 | Camel | | N Estrées |
|---|---|---|---|---|---|

## FRITSCH,    OfStv

J28          –

## FRITSCHE,    Uffz

J41      – 21 Apr 1918    – WIA

## FRITZ,    Flg

J80b     8 Sep 1918 – 11 Nov 1918    –
Joined Jasta 80b from Jastaschule II.

## FRITZSCHE, Hans    Vfw

| J29 | 11 Mar 1917 – 9 Apr 1918 | 3 | Idflieg | 9 Apr 1918 – | – |
|---|---|---|---|---|---|

Came to Jasta 29 from AFP3.

| Victories: | 1. | 12 Aug 1917 | Spad | 1000 | Poelcapelle |
|---|---|---|---|---|---|
| | 2. | 19 Sep 1917 | Sopwith | | Langemarck |
| | 3. | 23 Oct 1917 | RE8 | 1730 | W Dixmuiden |

## FRITZSCHE, Johannes    Uffz

| J69 | Mar 1918 – Jun 1918 | 2 | FEA14 | Jun 1918 – | |
|---|---|---|---|---|---|
| J13 | Jun 1918 – Jun 1918 | 1 | | | |

Born 28 April 1893, Leipzig. Died at Halle, 12 September 1918.

| Victories: | 1. | 23 Mar 1918 | BF2b | 1145 | Roye-Nesle |
| | 2. | 25 Mar 1918 | EA | 1455 | SW Noyon |
| | 3. | 29 Jun 1918 | Bréguet | | |

## FRITZSCHE, Walter     Ltn d R
J65     21 May 1918 – 27 May 1918   –   KIA
Born 29 November 1893, Werbau. Served with Ersatz Infantry Regiment 140. Joined Jasta 65 from Jastaschule II. Awarded EK I. Killed during combat with a Spad over Montsec.

## FRODIEN,     Ltn
J40s     15 Jun 1918 – 11 Nov 1918   –

## FRÖHLICH,     Sgt
J46     Aug 1918 – 11 Nov 1918   1

| Victories: | 1. | 26 Sep 1918 | Balloon | 1745 | Liéramont |
| | – | 9 Oct 1918 | DH4 | | Olonge |

## FROMMHERZ, Hermann     Ltn d R

| KG4/20 | 1 Dec 1915 – 3 Mar 1917 | – | JB | 18 May 1918 – 29 Jul 1918 | 8 |
| JB | 19 Mar 1917 – 24 Oct 1917 | 2 | J27 | 29 Jul 1918 – | 22 |
| Schl | 24 Oct 1917 – 18 May 1918 | | | | |

Biography & Victories: See *Above the Lines*.

## FROWEIN, Hans     Ltn
J12     14 Feb 1917                 –
Also served with FFA12 and FA12. Awarded Knight's Cross with Swords of the Royal Hohenzollern House Order on 23 July 1917.

## FRUHNER, Otto     Ltn

| FA51 | (May 1916) – | – | J26 | 11 Aug 1917 – 11 Nov 1918 | 27 |
| FA20 | 1917 – Jul 1917 | – | | | |

Biography & Victories: See *Above the Lines*.

## FUCHS, Otto     Ltn

| J30 | 5 Jun 1917 – 8 Nov 1917 | 3 | CO J35b | 21 Apr 1918 – 7 Jun 1918 | – |
| FEA1b | 8 Nov 1917 – | – | CO J77b | 7 Jun 1918 – 8 Jul 1918 | – |
| J77b | 30 Nov 1917 – 21 Apr 1918 | – | J77b | 9 Oct 1918 – 11 Nov 1918 | – |

Joined Jasta 30 from Jastaschule I. Joined Jasta 77b from FEA1b. Acting CO Jasta 77b from 14 Mar 1918 to 21 April 1918. Transferred to Fliegerschule 4 on 8 July 1918.

| Victories: | 1. | 21 Jun 1917 | BF2b | 0800 | SE Izel | (a) |
| | 2. | 27 Oct 1917 | Camel | 1047 | Harnes | |
| | 3. | 29 Oct 1917 | Camel | 1105 | S Gavrelle | |

(a) A7139, No 11 Sqn, RFC, 2/Lt D C A MacBrayne (P) KIA, Sgt Mollison (O) POW.

## FUCHS, Rudolf     Ltn d R

| J77b | – 18 May 1918 | – | J77b | 30 Jun 1918 – 11 Nov 1918 | 1 |
| J35b | 18 May 1918 – 30 Jun 1918 | – | | | |

| Victories: | 1. | 25 Sep 1918 | Spad | 0805 | Arnaville |

## FÜGNER, Eberhardt     Ltn d R

| KeKV | – 1916 | – | J4 | 1 Sep 1916 – 19 May 1917 | – | KIA |

Born 30 November 1889, Mansfeld. Severely wounded in action 23 Sept 1916, over Le Mesnil. Killed at 2057 hours over Izel flying Albatros DIII 1969/16.

## FÜRSTNAU, Helmuth     Ltn
J44s     – 17 Aug 1918   –   KIA
Born Zittau, 11 April 1898. Infantry Regt Nr.105. Killed between Bernes and Berlaucourt.

## FUGH,     Ltn d R
J36     22 Sep 1918 – 11 Nov 1918   –

## FUHRMANN, Max     Ltn
J36     20 May 1917 – 11 Nov 1918   –
Field Artillery Regiment 9. Promoted Leutnant 8 May 1915. Joined Jasta 36 from Jastaschule I. Acting CO Jasta 36 from 22 June to 6 July 1918 and 14 to 21 August 1918. OzbV for Jasta 36 from 22 Sept 1918.

**FUNK, Joseph     Vfw**

| | | | | | | |
|---|---|---|---|---|---|---|
| FAA231 | 19 Feb 1917 – | – | | FEA10 | 28 Jun 1918 – 11 Nov 1918 | – |
| J30 | 20 May 1917 – 28 Jun 1918 | 3 | | | | |

Awarded EK II on 1 March 1917. Joined Jasta 30 from AFP6. Awarded EK I on 21 July 1917. Promoted Vizefeldwebel 20 June 1918. Württemberg Gold Military Merit Medal on 10 July 1918.

| Victories: | 1. | 31 May 1917 | Balloon | 1008 | Nieppe | (a) |
|---|---|---|---|---|---|---|
| | 2. | 22 Aug 1917 | Npt XXVII | 0950 | N Meurchin | (b) |
| | 3. | 6 Oct 1917 | Spad VII | 1030 | SE Seclin | (c) |

(a) British balloon 9-6-2.
(b) #B3443, No 40 Sqn, RFC, Lt H A Kennedy.
(c) #B3500, No 19 Sqn, RFC, Lt H R Long.

---

**FURCHTBAR,     Ltn**

| | | | |
|---|---|---|---|
| J52 | 15 Jun 1918 – 2 Jul 1918 | – | WIA |

Joined Jasta 52 from Jastaschule I.

---

**GABRIEL, Walter     Vfw**

| | | | | | | | |
|---|---|---|---|---|---|---|---|
| FA21 | | | 1 | AFP1 | 21 Jul 1917 – | | – |
| J19 | 27 Jun 1917 – 21 Jul 1917 | – | | FAA250 | | – 20 Aug 1917 | – POW |

Reported to Jasta 19 from AFP1. Twin brother to Willi Gabriel (see below).

---

**GABRIEL, Willi     Vfw**

| | | | | | | |
|---|---|---|---|---|---|---|
| FA34 | 1915 – | – | SS15 | 1918 – | | 1 |
| FA21 | 1916 – | – | J11 | 15 Apr 1918 – 22 Aug 1918 | | 10 |
| FA44 | | – | AFP2 | 22 Aug 1918 – | | – |
| FA207 | | – | | | | |

Biography & Victories: See *Above the Lines*.

---

**GACKSTÄTTER, Wilhelm     Ltn d R**

| | | | | | |
|---|---|---|---|---|---|
| FEA10 | 2 Nov 1917 – – | | J51 | 15 Aug 1918 – 18 Aug 1918 | – KIA |
| J12 | – (Jan 1918) | – | | | |

Born 26 December 1893, Kirchberg, Gerabronn. Infanterie Regiment 126. Knight's Cross of the Württemberg Military Merit Order on 15 April 1916. Shot down in flames at 1845 hours over Fletre.

---

**GADE,     Ltn**

| | | |
|---|---|---|
| J5 | 1918 | – |

---

**GAIM, Ludwig     Vfw**

| | | | | | | |
|---|---|---|---|---|---|---|
| FAA293 | – 6 Jan 1917 | – | WIA | J39 | 27 Jun 1917 – 4 Apr 1918 | 5 |

Biography & Victories: See *Above the Lines*.

---

**GALETSCHKY, Carl     Ltn d R**

| | | | | | |
|---|---|---|---|---|---|
| J27 | Feb 1917 – 18 Aug 1917 | – | J48 | 5 Jan 1918 – 11 Nov 1918 | 1 |
| J6 | 18 Aug 1917 – 5 Jan 1918 | 2 | | | |

Born 9 December 1896. Awarded EK II. Died March 1966.

| Victories: | 1. | 19 Sep 1917 | RE8 | 1005 | Houthulst Wald |
|---|---|---|---|---|---|
| | 2. | 7 Oct 1917 | RE8 | 0810 | E Ypern |
| | – | 1 Mar 1918 | Spad | | XIII Francilly |
| | 3. | 3 May 1918 | Spad | 1350 | NE Plessier |

---

**GALLWITZ, Karl     Ltn**

| | | | | | | |
|---|---|---|---|---|---|---|
| FA37 | 1917 | 2 | JB | 24 Aug 1917 – Apr 1918 | 8 | WIA |
| J29 | 13 Aug 1917 – 20 Aug 1917 | – | | | | |

Biography & Victories: See *Above the Lines*.

---

**GANDERT, Hans-Eberhardt     Oblt**

| | | | | | | |
|---|---|---|---|---|---|---|
| FFA31 | 14 Sep 1914 – 25 Jul 1915 | – | FA54 | 7 Jun 1916 – 1916 | | – |
| FA20 | 25 Jul 1915 – 1 Sep 1915 | – | FA24 | 1916 – 1917 | | 2 |
| FFA31 | 1 Sep 1915 – 26 Oct 1915 | – | J51 | 21 Dec 1917 – 29 Sep 1918 | 6 | POW |

Biography & Victories: See *Above the Lines*.

---

**GANTERMANN,     Ltn**

| | | |
|---|---|---|
| J26 | – 11 Nov 1918 | 1 |

| Victories: | 1. | 30 Oct 1918 | Dolphin | Grandglise |
|---|---|---|---|---|

**GANTZ, Helmut       Ltn d R**
J56       12 Aug 1918 – 20 Sep 1918    – WIA
Born 23 July 1893, Thorn. Joined Jasta 56 from Jastaschule I. Severely wounded in combat over Armentières; died in hospital.

**GARSZTKA, Sylvester      Ltn**
J31       Jul 1918 – 2 Oct 1918      6 WIA
New information: Born 31 Dec 1896; KIFA 1919.
Biography & Victories: See *Above the Lines*.

**GASSL,      Uffz**
J35b       7 Aug 1918 – 11 Nov 1918    –
Joined Jasta 35b from Jastaschule II.

**GEBBERT, Max      Ltn**
J32b      15 Nov 1917 – 7 Feb 1918     –              J78b      9 Feb 1918 – 29 May 1918    – INJ
AFP6      7 Feb 1918 – 9 Feb 1918      –
Born 19 November 1896, Erlangen. Died in Erlangen hospital 29 May 1918, with FEA1.

**GEBBERT,      Ltn**
J43                                   –

**GEBHARDT,      Gefr**
J47w      28 Dec 1917 –                 2
Joined Jasta 47w from Jastaschule I.
Victories:      1.       17 Mar 1918     Camel          1230          SW Staden
                2.       20 Apr 1918     SE5a           1840          Vieux Berquin

**GEIGER, Hugo      Ltn d R**
FA46      31 Mar 1917 – 12 Jun 1917    –              J34b      1 Jul 1917 – 21 Aug 1917    – KIA
JsSch     23 Jun 1917 – 30 Jun 1917    –
Born 1 July 1892, Bishofswiesen. Entered military service as a Leutnant 27 November 1914, 1st Bavarian Field Artillery Regiment. Awarded Bavarian Militär-Verdeinst Orden 4th Klasse on 17 April 1915. Awarded EKI on 9 November 1915. Transferred to aviation 10 August 1916, trained as an observer. December 1916, commenced pilot's training. Transferred to AFP6 on 25 March 1917. Recommended for Bavarian Flugzeugführer Abzeichen on 3 May 1917. Known to have flown Albatros D III 2063/16; Albatros D III 2094/17; Albatros D III 634/17; Albatros D V 2219/17. Killed N Verdun, Höhe 326, probably by Sous-Lieutenant Robert de Bonnefoy, N84 (see *C&C* GB Vol 13, No 3).

**GEIGL, Heinrich-Georg      Ltn d R**
KG6/36                                               CO J16b 18 Aug 1917 – 4 Apr 1918     8 KIA
J34b      26 Feb 1917 – 17 Aug 1917    5
Biography & Victories: See *Above the Lines*.

**GEISELER, Heinz      Ltn**
J20       27 Nov 1916 – 27 Jul 1917    –              J46       10 Feb 1918 – 1918          –
J33       27 Jul 1917 – 10 Feb 1918    –              Kest 1a    1918 – 11 Nov 1918         –
Joined Jasta 20 from Jastaschule I.
Victories:     zlg       30 Apr 1917     FE2b           0845          Oppy

**GEIST, Heinrich      Ltn d R**
J9               – 16 Jul 1917     – KIAcc
Born 12 May 1890, Munich. Killed during a test flight south of Vouzires.

**GEISTBECK, Aloys      Ltn**
J32b      15 Nov 1917 – 15 Sep 1918    –              FEA1b     15 Sep 1918 –               –
Severely injured in an accident 29 March 1918.

**GELLENTHIN, Günther      Ltn**
J40       27 Jul 1917 – 21 Jan 1918    – KIA
Born 12 May 1896, Berlin. Killed over Longuyon.

**GELSZ,      Uffz**
SS23                                    –            J59       1 Mar 1918 –
J20              – 1 Mar 1918     –

## GENGELIN, Uffz
J37       – 1918      2

| Victories: | 1. | 8 Aug 1918 | Camel | | |
|---|---|---|---|---|---|
| | 2. | 16 Sep 1918 | Scout | 1540 | NW Cambrai |

## GENTZ, Oblt
J45    6 Jun 1918 – 10 Jun 1918    –
OzbV for Jasta 45.

## GEPPERT, Ltn d R
J4    1 Oct 1918 – 11 Nov 1918    1
Joined Jasta 4 from Jastaschule II.

| Victories: | 1. | 3 Nov 1918 | Spad | 1650 | Stenay |
|---|---|---|---|---|---|

## GERBIG, Otto Vfw
J14    Mar 1917 – 15 Aug 1917   4      J18    12 Aug 1917 – 18 Aug 1917   –
KIA Born 2 April 1894, Erfurt. Mortally wounded at 2045 hours near Passchendaele.

| Victories: | 1. | 17 Mar 1917 | Caudron | 1510 | N Paiss |
|---|---|---|---|---|---|
| | 2. | 14 Apr 1917 | Caudron | | Craonelle |
| | 3. | 2 Jun 1917 | Caudron R4 | | Berry-au-Bac |
| | 4. | 3 Jun 1917 | Sopwith 2 | 1850 | Corbény |

## GERDES, Vfw
J19    16 Mar 1918 –      1

| Victories: | 1. | 31 Mar 1918 | Bréguet | | E Montdidier |
|---|---|---|---|---|---|

## GERICK, Georg Uffz
J75             –

## GERICKE, Ltn
FA32        –       J1    23 Aug 1916 –       –

## GERLT, Ltn
FA9        –       J15    10 Jul 1918 – 11 Nov 1918   –
J19    24 Jan 1917 – 10 Jul 1918   1
Acting CO Jasta 19 at various times: 11 Nov 17 – 8 Dec 17; 29 Dec 17 – 4 Jan 18; 7 Jan 18 – 11 Jan 18; 10 Apr 18 –14 Apr 18; 20 Jun 18 – 11 Jul 18. Severely wounded 4 May 1917, returned to Jasta in autumn of 1917.

| Victories: | 1. | 22 Apr 1917 | Caudron | | St Etienne |
|---|---|---|---|---|---|

## GERSTENBERG, Alfred Oblt
FA69        –       FA3            –
KG2        –       J11    31 Aug 1917 – 20 Oct 1917   – WIA
Born 6 April 1893. Severely wounded at 1200 hours over Wassenmolen. Wound Badge in Black. Awarded Eiserne Kreuz I Klasse. Austro-Hungarian Militär-Verdeinstkreuz 3 Klasse. Promoted Oberleutnant 20 June 1918. Attained rank of Lieutenant General in Luftwaffe during WWII. Died 1959.

## GERSTER, Karl Vfw
J62    21 Feb 1918 – 11 Nov 1918   2
Joined Jasta 62 from Jastaschule II.

| Victories: | 1. | 1 Jul 1918 | Dolphin | 1230 | Saulchoy |
|---|---|---|---|---|---|
| | 2. | 4 Nov 1918 | Bréguet | | Brieulles |

## GEWERT, Ltn
J19    (Sep 1918) – 11 Nov 1918   2

| Victories: | 1. | 13 Sep 1918 | Bréguet | 1720 | Charey |
|---|---|---|---|---|---|
| | 2. | 14 Sep 1918 | Salmson | 1920 | Beney |

## GEYER, Uffz
J76b    25 Jul 1918 –      –
Joined Jasta 76b from Jastaschule II.

## GIEGOLD, Hugo Ltn d R
J23b    9 Nov 1917 – 5 Jan 1918        FEA1b    5 Jan 1918 –

Awarded Knight's Cross with Swords of the Royal Hohenzollern House Order on 1 March 1917. Joined Jasta 23b from Jastaschule I, Schleissheim, as an instructor.

### GILLARDONI, Vfw
J81      – 3 Nov 1917    1   POW

| Victories: | 1. | 24 Aug 1917 | Balloon | | Kakku |

### GILDEMEISTER, Johannes   Ltn d R
J20    14 Jan 1918 – 11 Nov 1918   5
Biography & Victories: See *Above the Lines*.

### GILLE, Friedrich   Uffz
J12    8 Oct 1916 –        6
Biography & Victories: See *Above the Lines*.

### GILLES, Artur   Ltn
J10    22 Oct 1918 – 11 Nov 1918   –
Joined Jasta 10 from Jastaschule II.

### GILLY, Hermann   Ltn d R
FAA204    Nov 1917 – Mar 1918   –      J40    14 Apr 1918 – 11 Nov 1918   7
Biography & Victories: See *Above the Lines*.

### GLÄSER, Ewald   Ltn d R
J31      – 29 Sep 1917   –   KIAcc
Born 27 July 1891, Saarbrücken. Killed over Kuplienek, during test flight.

### GLÄSER, Oblt
J32    24 Feb 1917 – 26 May 1917   –      AFP1    26 May 1917 –

### GLASEMANN, Vfw
J3    (Sep 1918) – 11 Nov 1918   1

| Victories: | 1. | 5 Nov 1918 | DH4 | 1600 | Morsberg |

### GLASMACHER, Peter   Vfw
J8      – 5 May 1917   2   KIA
Born 3 June 1893, Köln. Killed Near St Eloi – Zillebeke See.

| Victories: | – | 16 Nov 1916 | FE2b | | W Ypern | |
| | 1. | 24 Jan 1917 | Bréguet | | Boesinghe | |
| | 2. | 6 Feb 1917 | Nieuport | 1330 | S Bixschoote | (a) |

(a) A6622, No 1 Sqn, RFC, Capt J M E Shephard.

### GLATZ, Uffz
J18      1918    1

| Victories: | 1. | 21 Apr 1918 | Spad | | Froyelles |

### GLINKERMANN, Willy   OfStv
KEKH    1916   –      J15    10 Oct 1916 – 29 May 1917   2   KIA
Killed near Orgeval.

| Victories: | 1. | 17 Mar 1917 | Nieuport | | NW Reims |
| | – | 16 Apr 1917 | Farman | 1040 | Juvincourt |
| | 2. | 22 May 1917 | Spad | | Beaurieux |

### GLÖCKLEN, Hilmar   Ltn
J50    (Jan 1918) – 6 Apr 1918   –      J15    22 Aug 1918 – 11 Nov 1918   –
J21s    6 Apr 1918 – 22 Aug 1918   –
Shot down in flames 16 July 1918, jumped in a parachute breaking right foot on landing.

### GLUCZEWSKI-KWILCKI, Heinz Graf von   Ltn
J4    (Dec 1917) – 11 Nov 1918   2
Born 31 Dec 1895. Served in 3rd Uhlan Guard Regiment.

| Victories: | 1. | 15 May 1918 | Bréguet | 1115 | N Harbonnières |
| | 2. | 26 Sep 1918 | DH9 | 1615 | |

## GNÄDIG, Vfw
J38      1918      3

| Victories: | 1. | 3 Jan 1918 | BE | NW Doiran-See |
|---|---|---|---|---|
| | 2. | 6 Jan 1918 | DD | NW Dorian-See |
| | 3. | 17 Jul 1918 | Nieuport | |

## GNAMM, Walter    Ltn
| FA23 | – | J4 | 1 Sep 1916 – | – |
|---|---|---|---|---|

## GOBERT, Ascan Gustav    Ltn
| J37 | – 16 Apr 1918 – | AFP2 | 16 Apr 1918 – | – |
|---|---|---|---|---|

Acting CO Jasta 37, 24 March – 5 April 1918.

## GOCKEL, Heinrich    Vfw
J33      20 Feb 1918 – 11 Nov 1918      3

Born 20 December 1891, Madfeld. Served with Landwehr Infantry Regiment from 8 August 1914. To FEA8 on 13 July 1916. FAA282 from 18 July 1917 to 20 Feb 1918. Promoted Vizefeldwebel on 11 November 1917. Lightly wounded in action 8 March 1918. Crash-landed in a burning aircraft near Cambrai, on 2 Sep 1918, not harmed. Awards: Iron Cross 2nd Class, 28 November 1914; Iron Cross 1st Class, 3 April 1915; Pilot's Badge 22 September 1917.

| Victories: | 1. | 10 Jun 1918 | Camel | 0745 | Gournay | (a) |
|---|---|---|---|---|---|---|
| | 2. | 29 Aug 1918 | Camel | | Bugnicourt | (b) |
| | 3. | 1 Sep 1918 | Camel | | Quéant | |

(a) Possibly D1963, No 73 Sqn, RAF, Lt B W de Leyson, POW.
(b) Possibly Sgt A C Harbour, No 43 Sqn, RAF, POW.

## GODT,    Uffz
| FA24 | – 21 Sep 1916 – | J10 | 21 Sep 1916 – | – |
|---|---|---|---|---|

## GÖCKEL,
J13      –

## GÖDE,    Ltn
| FAA210 | – 23 Aug 1916 – | J1 | 23 Aug 1916 – | – |
|---|---|---|---|---|

## GÖHLER,    Gefr
J3      – 10 Jul 1918    – INJ

Injured during a test flight of a Pfalz DXII.

## GÖRING, Hermann Wilhelm    Oblt
| FFA25 | 1915 – | 2 | J5 | 20 Oct 1916 – 2 Nov 1916 | – WIA |
|---|---|---|---|---|---|
| KekS | 9 Jul 1916 – 1916 | – | J26 | 15 Feb 1917   17 May 1917 | 4 |
| KekM | 1916 – 1916 | 1 | CO J27 | 17 May 1917 – 8 Jul 1918 | 14 |
| J7 | – 20 Oct 1916 | – | CO JGI | 8 Jul 1918 – 11 Nov 1918 | 1 |

Biography & Victories: See *Above the Lines*.

## GÖRNE, Gottlieb    Ltn d R
J31      – 3 May 1917    – KIA

Born 9 January 1894, Hamburg. Down in flames between Aure and Marvaux.

## GÖRNER,    Uffz
J66      2

| Victories: | 1. | 14 Oct 1918 | Bréguet | S Laon |
|---|---|---|---|---|
| | 2. | 21 Oct 1918 | Bréguet | Itancourt |

## GÖRNHEIMER,    Gefr
J53      5 Oct 1918 – 11 Nov 1918    –

## GÖSSEL, Hans von    Uffz
J71      – 11 Nov 1918   1   Hans

| Victories: | 1. | 9 May 1918 | AR2 | Glückerwald |
|---|---|---|---|---|

**GÖTHE, Friedrich      Vfw**
J52        6 May 1918 – 21 May 1918   – KIAcc
Born 22 October 1888, Kentschen. Killed in a crash-landing near Laventie.

**GÖTTE, Franz      Ltn d R**
J6               – 22 May 1917   –              J20      22 May 1917 – 17 Aug 1917   1   KIA
Killed at 1215 hours over Slype.

| Victories: | 1. | 12 Jul 1917 | Camel | 1155 | Slype |
| | zlg | 26 Jul 1917 | Sopwith | 1900 | Dixmuide |

**GÖTTSCH, Walter      Ltn d R**
| FA33 | 1916 – 10 Sep 1916 | – | Hosp | Nov 1917 | – |
| J8 | 10 Sep 1916 – 3 Feb 1917 | – WIA | J8 | Jan 1918 – 10 Feb 1918 | 15 |
| Hosp | 3 Feb 1917 – | – | CO J19 | 10 Feb 1918 – 10 Apr 1918 | 3   KIA |
| J8 | Apr 1917 – Nov 1917 | 2 WIA | | | |

Biography & Victories: See *Above the Lines.*

**GÖWEN,      Rttm**
J31                             –

**GOLDMANN,      Ltn**
J38               1918             –

**GOLLINZKY,      Vfw**
J25                             –

**GOLZ,      Ltn**
J13        (Dec 1917) –              1

| Victories: | 1. | 29 Dec 1917 | Caudron | Cerny |

**GONDERMANN,      Vfw**
| J35b | (Jun 1917) – (Jan 1918) | 1 | J66 | (Apr 1918) – | 1 |
| J42 | (Jan 1918) – (Apr 1918) | 1 | | | |

Awarded Iron Cross I Class on 26 January 1918.

| Victories: | 1. | 12 Nov 1917 | Camel | 1405 | Houthulst Wald | (a) |
| | 2. | 16 Mar 1918 | AR2 | | | |
| | 3. | 25 Jun 1918 | Spad | | | |

(a) Possibly B2417, No 65 Sqn, RFC, Lt E H Scott, WIA/POW.

**GONTERMANN, Heinrich      Ltn d R**
| FA25 | 1916 – 11 Nov 1916 | – | J15 | 30 Apr 1917 – 30 Oct 1917 | 22 KIAcc |
| J5 | 11 Nov 1916 – 30 Apr 1917 | 17 | | | |

Biography & Victories: See *Above the Lines.*

**GORETSKI,      Uffz**
| J13 | 1917 – 4 Aug 1918 | 1 | J64w | 11 Aug 1918 – 11 Nov 1918 | – |
| J65 | 4 Aug 1918 – 11 Aug 1918 | – | | | |

| Victories: | 1. | 29 Sep 1917 | AR2 | Douaumont |

**GÖRZEL, Heinrich      Flg**
J19        6 May 1918 – 7 May 1918   – POW

**GOSSEN,      Vfw**
| J37 | – 15 May 1918 | – | Eichhorn | 15 Jun 1918 – |
| J65 | 15 May 1918 – 15 Jun 1918 | – | | |

**GOSSNER, Max      Ltn d R**
| Kest 31 | 31 Jun 1916 – | – | J16b | 25 May 1918 – 10 Jul 1918 | – |
| J23b | 30 Sep 1917 – 25 May 1918 | 2 | CO J77b | 10 Jul 1918 – 11 Nov 1918 | 6 |

Biography & Victories: See *Above the Lines.*

## GRABE, Hans    Ltn
J14                – 31 May 1918    1  WIA
Born 4 December 1895, Gorlitz. Served in Field Artillery Rgt Nr.57. Severely wounded, DOW 7 June 1918.

| Victories: | 1. | 28 Mar 1918 | SE5a | 1210 | Gavrelle |
|---|---|---|---|---|---|

## GRÄBER,    Ltn
J62        16 Jan 1918 – 11 Nov 1918    –
OzbV for Jasta 62.

## GRÄPEL, Friedrich    Ltn
J28w              – 4 Jan 1918    1  KIA
Born 31 March 1896, Rudolstadt, Schwarzenburg. Killed at 1130 hours near Becelaere.

| Victories: | 1. | 30 Nov 1917 | RE8 | 1510 | S Pervyse |
|---|---|---|---|---|---|

## GRÄPER, Carl Emil    Uffz
J50              – 8 Aug 1918    1        FEA13    8 Aug 1918 –          –

| Victories: | 1. | 14 Jul 1918 | Nieuport | | Chambry |
|---|---|---|---|---|---|

## GRAF,    Uffz
J31              – 1 Jun 1918    – WIA
Wounded over Laon.

## GRAFE, Winand    Ltn d R
KekN              – 1916    2        J2    27 Aug 1916 – 22 Sep 1916    – KIA
Born 31 October 1893, Elberfeld. Killed during combat with BE12s of 19 Sqn east of Bapaume.

| Victories: | 1. | Date unknown |
|---|---|---|
| | 2. | Date unknown |

## GRAMP, Josef    Ltn
J34b    10 Nov 1917 – 4 Mar 1918    –        FEA1b    4 Mar 1918 –          –
Joined Jasta 34b from Jastaschule I.

## GRAP,    Vfw
J65    2 Feb 1918 – 10 Apr 1918    –
Idflieg    10 Apr 1918 –
Joined Jasta 65 from Jastaschule I.

## GRASSHOFF, Kurt    Oblt
J15    10 Oct 1916 – 10 Jan 1917    –        CO J38    7 Nov 1917 – 12 Jun 1918    – WIA
CO J37    10 Jan 1917 – 7 Nov 1917    –
Born 24 January 1891, Wesel. Severely wounded over Predejci, Macedonia.

## GRASSMANN, Justus    Ltn d R
FA32              –        J10    17 Oct 1917 – 11 Nov 1918    10
Biography & Victories: See *Above the Lines*.

## GRATZ,    Oblt
J35b    13 Oct 1917 – 23 Aug 1918    –
OzbV for Jasta 35b. Awarded Iron Cross I Class on 19 May 1918.

## GRAUBERT,    Oblt
J29    30 Aug 1918 – 11 Nov 1918    –
OzbV for Jasta 29.

## GRAUL,    Ltn d R
J4    3 Aug 1917 – (Sep 1917)    –
Joined Jasta 4 from AFP4.

## GRAWERT, Hans Kurt von    Oblt
J3        1918        –
Also served in FFA7, FFA12, FFA45, FFA74, FA42 & KG4. Awarded Knight's Cross with Swords of the Royal Hohenzollern House Order.

## GREGOR, Karl    OfStv

FAA210  19 May 1916 –                     –           Ltn J29    3 Jul 1918 – 26 Aug 1918    –
J29        23 May 1917 – 27 Jul 1917   4  WIA        Idflieg   26 Aug 1918 –
Joined the Air Service in May 1915. Joined Jasta 29 from AFP1 on 23 May 1917. Severely wounded
27 Jul 1917, left leg amputated. Rejoined Jasta 29 from FEA5 on 3 July 1918. Awarded EKI on 28 Feb
1917. Awarded Knight's Cross of the Royal Hohenzollern House Order. Awarded Goldene Militär-
Verdeinstkreuz on 30 October 1918.

| Victories: | – | | | 1916 | | |
|---|---|---|---|---|---|---|
| | 1. | 29 Jun 1917 | Nieuport | 1910 | SW Fresnoy | (a) |
| | 2. | 22 Jul 1918 | SE5a | 0940 | S Courrières | |
| | 3. | 8 Aug 1918 | DH9 | 1620 | SW Warfussée | (b) |
| | 4. | 5 Oct 1918 | DH9 | | | |

(a) Probably B1677, 29 Sqn RFC, Lt V A Norvill.
(b) Probably D7317, 27 Sqn, RAF.

## GREIBNER,    Ltn

J15             1916 –                    –

## GREIM, Robert Ritter von    Oblt

FFA3b      1915 –                  1        FA46b   22 Feb 1917 –                   –
FAA204                             –        J34b    4 Apr 1917 – 11 Nov 1918    27
Biography & Victories: See *Above the Lines*.

## GREVEN, Alfred    Ltn d R

J12             – 11 Nov 1918    4
Awarded Saxon Albert Order, Knight 2nd Class with Swords 23 May 1917. Awarded Saxon Merit Order
31 Aug 1918. Proposed for Knight's Cross of the Military St Henry Order, but it was not received.

| Victories: | 1. | 18 Sep 1918 | Bréguet | 1730 | SW Conflans |
|---|---|---|---|---|---|
| | 2. | 26 Sep 1918 | DH4 | | Giraumont |
| | 3. | 31 Oct 1918 | Spad | | Villers |
| | 4. | 3 Nov 1918 | Spad | | Pouilly |

## GRIEFFENHAGEN, Karl von    Oblt / Rittm

FA32            – 23 Aug 1916    –           CO J18   31 Oct 1916 – 12 Aug 1917    2
J1         23 Aug 1916 – 31 Oct 1916   –
Born 1 January 1889, Karklaugken (E Prussia). Served in 11th Dragoner Regiment. Flew as an observer
in Festungsfla 5, FA12, FA45 and Kagohl 1. Served with KEK Bertincourt prior to Jasta 1. Promoted
to Rittmeister 18 April 1917. Injured when forced to land after combat 24 April 1917. Awarded the
Knight's Cross with Swords of the Hohenzollern House Order on 1 May 1917. Transferred to command
the Kampfeinsitzer-Schule (Jastaschule II) at Paderborn on 12 August 1917, remained to end of war.

| Victories: | 1. | 25 Jan 1917 | FE2d | | Bousbecque | (a) |
|---|---|---|---|---|---|---|
| | 2. | 17 Mar 1917 | BE2d | 1305 | S Polderhoek | |

(a) A34, Lt S Adler & Lt R W White, No 20 Sqn, RFC.

## GRIESHEIM, R. von    Oblt

JB         (Aug 1918) – 11 Nov 1918    1
Victories:    1.    30 Oct 1918    SE5a                    Fresnes    (a)
(a) Probably Capt A A Callender, No 32 Sqn, RAF. KIA.

## GRIGO,    OfStv

J12        1 Feb 1917 – 8 Jun 1917    2  WIA
Also wounded in combat 26 May 1917.

| Victories: | 1. | 11 Mar 1917 | DH2 | | SE Grévillers | |
|---|---|---|---|---|---|---|
| | zlg | 24 Mar 1917 | FE2b | 1030 | Croiselles | |
| | 2. | 23 Apr 1917 | Pup | 1205 | Neuville | |
| | 3. | 30 May 1918 | Balloon | | Montbré | (a) |

(a) French 59th Balloon Co.

## GRIMM,    Ltn d R

J13             – 11 Nov 1918    3
| Victories: | 1. | 28 Jul 1918 | Spad | 1850 | Chaudun |
|---|---|---|---|---|---|
| | 2. | 12 Sep 1918 | Bréguet | | Thiaucourt |
| | 3. | 14 Sep 1918 | Bréguet | | Conflans |

## GRÖNER, Ferdinand   Ltn d R

| | | | | | | |
|---|---|---|---|---|---|---|
| J14 | 17 Oct 1916 – 15 Dec 1916 | – | | AFPB | 5 Apr 1917 – | – |
| JsSchI | 15 Dec 1916 – 21 Jan 1917 | – | | J16 | 23 Apr 1917 – 20 Jul 1917 | – |
| J26 | 21 Jan 1917 – 5 Apr 1917 | – | | J71 | – 11 Nov 1918 | – |

Transferred to Staffheimat 20 Jul 1917.

## GRÖNING,   Ltn d R

| | | |
|---|---|---|
| J27 | 15 Jul 1918 – 11 Nov 1918 | 1 |

Victories:   1   28 Oct 1918

## GRÖPLER,   Ltn

| | | |
|---|---|---|
| J8 | – 11 Nov 1918 | – |

Victories:   –   9 Oct 1918   EA   1700

## GROLL, Paul   Vfw

| | | | | | | | |
|---|---|---|---|---|---|---|---|
| SS5 | 1917 | 1 | | J40s | (Aug 1918) – 7 Oct 1918 | 3 | KIA |

Born 7 December 1892, Chemnitz. Killed over Ghent.

| Victories: | | | | | | |
|---|---|---|---|---|---|---|
| | 1. | 15 Jun 1917 | Spad | | Cormicy | (a) |
| | 2. | 10 Aug 1918 | SE5a | 1010 | Swartenbrouck | |
| | 3. | 3 Oct 1918 | Spad XIII | | Roulers | |
| | 4. | 7 Oct 1918 | Camel | | | |

(a) With his observer, Vfw Kauffmann.

## GROOS, Gisbert-Wilhelm   Ltn

| | | | | | |
|---|---|---|---|---|---|
| J4 | May 1917 – 24 May 1917 | 1 | | CO | |
| J11 | 24 May 1917 – 14 Sep 1918 | 6 | | JsSchII | 16 Sep 1918 – | – |

Biography & Victories: See *Above the Lines*.

## GROS, Wilhelm Emmanuel   Ltn d R

| | | | |
|---|---|---|---|
| J17 | 11 Nov 1916 – 22 Aug 1917 | 1 | KIA |

Born 6 July 1892, Karlsruhe. Enlisted 19 October 1914. Assigned to FA27 as a mechanical specialist on 11 January 1915. Transferred to FEA5 for pilot's training on 1 June 1915. Promoted Gefreiter on 1 August 1915 and to Unteroffizier on 18 September 1915. Assigned to FAA207 27 October 1915. Qualified for Flugzeugführer Abzeichen on 11 January 1916. Awarded EKII on 29 February 1916. Promoted Vizefeldwebel 13 April 1916. Awarded Baden Silberne Militär-Verdeinstmedaille on 10 June 1916. Promoted Leutnant d R on 28 September 1916. Awarded EKI on 11 October 1916. Awarded Baden Ritterkreuz II Klasse mit Schwerten des Ordens vom Zähringer Löwen on 19 April 1917. Killed at 1105 hours over Vlisseghem.

| Victories: | | | | | |
|---|---|---|---|---|---|
| | 1. | 12 Feb 1917 | Nieuport | | Landremont |
| | – | 13 Apr 1917 | Caudron | | Berry-au-Bac |

(See *OTF* Vol 4, No 4, pg 318.)

## GROSCH, Fritz Walther   Oblt

| | | | | | | |
|---|---|---|---|---|---|---|
| FEA1 | 7 Dec 1914 – 27 Jan 1915 | – | | Gotha | 22 Oct 1916 – 31 Dec 1916 | – |
| FA50 | 28 Jan 1915 – 22 Jun 1916 | – | | ObsSch | 1 Jan 1917 – 12 Dec 1917 | – |
| FA49 | 23 Jun 1916 – 12 Aug 1916 | – | | PilSchs | 13 Dec 1917 – 7 Aug 1918 | – |
| Staff | 13 Aug 1916 – 21 Aug 1916 | – | | J4 | 8 Aug 1918 – 12 Sep 1918 | – |
| FFA254 | 22 Aug 1916 – 21 Oct 1916 | – | | | | |

Born 14 April 1891, Coburg. Entered military service 26 September 1910, assigned to Field Artillery Regiment 40. Reported to Jasta 4 from Jastaschule I. Observer training FEA1. Observer with FA50, FA49 & FAA254. Observerschule Schwerin, 1 Jan 1917. 13 Dec 1917 commenced pilot's training. Joined Jasta 4 from Jastaschule I. Wounded in the arm 24 Aug 1918, landed near Guise. Deutsches Kreuz in Silber on 2 April 1943. Attained rank of Generalleutnant in the Luftwaffe during WWII, from 1 June 1943. Died 22 November 1972, Munich, Germany.

## GROSSE,   Ltn

| | | | | | | |
|---|---|---|---|---|---|---|
| J1 | – 13 Mar 1918 | – | | J76b | 7 Aug 1918 – | – |
| J72s | 13 Mar 1918 – 7 Aug 1918 | 1 | | J72s | – 11 Nov 1918 | 1 |

| Victories: | | | | | |
|---|---|---|---|---|---|
| | 1. | 6 May 1918 | Spad | 1940 | Grivesnes |
| | 2. | 30 Oct 1918 | Spad | | Château-Porcien |

## GROTERJAN, Karl   Ltn d R

| | | | | | |
|---|---|---|---|---|---|
| KG5 | | 3 | | J22 | – 26 Jan 1917 | – | KIA |

Born 18 July 1891, Berlin. Served in Infantry Regiment 52. Promoted Leutnant 18 February 1915. Killed between Trosly and Verneuil.

| Victories: | 1. | Date and unit unknown |
|---|---|---|
| | 2. | Date and unit unknown |
| | 3. | Date and unit unknown |

## GROTHEUS,     Uffz
| J3 | 1918 | – |
|---|---|---|

## GRÜNWALD,     OfStv
| J83 | | 1 | | |
|---|---|---|---|---|
| Victories: | 1. | 15 Aug 1918 | DH4 | Courbesseaux |
| | – | 16 Aug 1918 | DH9 | Buchsweiler |

## GRÜNZWEIG, Fritz     Ltn d R
| FA9b | 16 May 1916 – 20 Aug 1916 | – | FEA1b | 30 Nov 1916 – 8 Feb 1917 | – |
|---|---|---|---|---|---|
| J16 | 1 Nov 1916 – 30 Nov 1916 | – | J16 | 15 Feb 1917 – 14 Apr 1917 | – KIA |

Born 19 September 1892, Ludwigshafen. Attacked a balloon at Ellbach, and was in turn attacked and killed by MdL Robert Harpedanne de Belleville of N49.

## GRÜTER, Richard     Ltn d L
| J17 | 7 Sep 1917 – 1 Apr 1918 | – KIA |
|---|---|---|

Born 13 December 1893, Russland. Served with Grenadier Rgt 89. Joined Jasta 17 from Jastaschule I. Crash-landed after combat on 16 September 1917. Killed over Montdidier.

## GRÜTTNER, Erich     Vfw
| J43 | 8 Nov 1918 – 11 Nov 1918 | – |
|---|---|---|

## GRUND, Egon     Ltn
| FA214A | 7 Dec 1915 | – | FA36 | 12 Jul 1918 – | – |
|---|---|---|---|---|---|
| J67 | 16 May 1918 – 12 Jul 1918 | – | | | |

Born 16 August 1893, Bruchsal, Baden. Enlisted on 1 October 1913, Field Artillery Regiment 50. Promoted Unteroffizier 5 August 1914; Vizefeldwebel on 8 January 1915; Leutnant d R on 22 March 1915. Transferred to FEA1, on 7 August 1915, for observer training. FEA4 from 22 November 1915 to 4 December 1915. Acting CO Jasta 67 from 3 to 27 June 1918. OzbV for Jasta 67. Awarded Baden Ritterkreuz II Klasse mit Schwerten des Ordens vom Zähringer Löwen on 29 August 1918.

## GSCHWENDER,     Ltn
| FA12 | – | J43 | 9 Feb 1918 – | – |
|---|---|---|---|---|

## GUDENBERG, Eberhard Fr von     Ltn
| J29 | 28 May 1917 – 19 Oct 1917 | – | JB | 19 Oct 1917 – 11 Nov 1918 | – |
|---|---|---|---|---|---|

Not a pilot. Joined Jasta 29 from AFP1. OzbV for Jasta 29 and Jasta Boelcke.
Acting CO Jasta B from 29 November 1917 to 13 December 1917.

## GÜLDNER, Hugo     Oblt
| J23b | 25 Mar 1918 – 10 May 1918 | – | AFP12 | 10 May 1918 – | – |
|---|---|---|---|---|---|

Joined Jasta 23b from Jastaschule II.

## GÜNTER,     Ltn
| J8 | – 22 Jan 1918 | – INJ |
|---|---|---|

## GÜNTHER, Wolfgang     Ltn d R
| J2 | 27 Aug 1916 – 20 Dec 1916 | – | J17 | 16 Mar 1917 – 21 May 1917 | – INJ |
|---|---|---|---|---|---|
| FAA205 | 20 Dec 1916 – | – | | | |

## GÜNTHER,     Ltn
| J21s | 1918 |
|---|---|

## GÜRGENZ, Erich     Uffz
| J46 | 10 Feb 1918 – 4 Apr 1918 | 1 KIA |
|---|---|---|

Born 10 September 1885, Berlin. Killed over Liéramont airfield; some sources say that he was the pilot of 'Stropp' the Albatros DVa 7161/17 in the Smithsonian (see WWI Aero No 110, pg 11-19).

| Victories: | 1. | 12 Mar 1918 | SE5a | 1050 | Merckem |
|---|---|---|---|---|---|

## GÜRKE, Wilhelm    Ltn d R

| | | | | | |
|---|---|---|---|---|---|
| FAA263 | | – | J5 | (Feb 1918) – 10 Mar 1918 | – KIA |

Born 11 July 1887, Hochst. Served in Field Artillery Rgt 92. Killed over Honnecourt.

## GÜTTLER, Wolfgang    Ltn

| | | | | | |
|---|---|---|---|---|---|
| FA72 | 1916 – | – | J24s | 10 Mar 1917 – 29 Sep 1917 | 4 |
| FA285A | | – | CO J13 | 29 Sep 1917 – 20 Feb 1918 | 4 KIAcc |

Biography & Victories: See *Above the Lines*

## GÜTTLER,    Ltn

| | | | | | |
|---|---|---|---|---|---|
| J73 | 11 Feb 1918 – 7 Apr 1918 | – | J81 | 7 Apr 1918 – | – |

OzbV for Jasta 81

## GULLMANN,    Uffz

| | | | |
|---|---|---|---|
| J56 | 9 Feb 1918 – (Oct 1918) | 1 | |

Joined Jasta 56 from Jastaschule II.

| Victories: | 1. | 31 Jul 1918 | SE5a | 1015 | SW Armentières |
|---|---|---|---|---|---|

## GUNTRUN,    Ltn

| | | |
|---|---|---|
| J52 | 29 Jun 1918 – 11 Nov 1918 | – |

Joined Jasta 52 from Jastaschule I.

| Victories: | – | 10 Jul 1918 | Camel | | l'Epinette |
|---|---|---|---|---|---|

## GUSSMANN, Siegfried    Ltn d R

| | | | | | |
|---|---|---|---|---|---|
| FA3 | 1917 – | 1 | FEA5 | 26 Apr 1918 – 22 Aug 1918 | – |
| J11 | Nov 1917 – 7 Apr 1918 | 3 | J11 | 22 Aug 1918 – 11 Nov 1918 | 1 |

Biography & Victories: See *Above the Lines*.

## GUTERMUTH, Hans    Ltn d R

| | | |
|---|---|---|
| J5 | (Oct 1916) – 16 Feb 1917 | 2 KIA |

Born 22 August 1893, Aachen. Killed between Gommecourt and Hebuterne, flying an Albatros DIII (G.13), by Sgt Smith & Lt Aldred, No 5 Sqn, RFC, in a BE2c.

| Victories: | 1. | 2 Feb 1917 | DH2 | 1530 | Gommecourt |
|---|---|---|---|---|---|
| | 2. | 14 Feb 1917 | Morane | 1100 | Guedecourt |

## GUTKNECHT, Adolf    Oblt

| | | | | | |
|---|---|---|---|---|---|
| J43 | May 1918 – 2 Nov 1918 | 7 | Hosp | 2 Nov 1918 – 11 Nov 1918 | – |

Biography & Victories: See *Above the Lines*.

## GUTSCHE,    Ltn

| | | |
|---|---|---|
| J36 | 13 Jun 1918 – 13 Aug 1918 | 1 WIA |

Joined Jasta 36 from Jastaschule II. Shot down in flames, jumped in a parachute, landing near Bussny, hospitalised.

| Victories: | 1. | 9 Aug 1918 | Spad | 1915 | Montdidier |
|---|---|---|---|---|---|

## HAAKE, Karl    Ltn d R

| | | | | |
|---|---|---|---|---|
| J43 | 6 Dec 1917 – 26 Sep 1918 | – | IdFlieg | 26 Sep 1918 – |

OzbV for Jasta 43.

## HAAR, auf den    Ltn

| | | |
|---|---|---|
| J46 | Sep 1918 – 11 Nov 1918 | 3 |

| Victories: | – | 5 Sep 1918 | SE5a | 1200 | E Havrincourt | (a) |
|---|---|---|---|---|---|---|
| | – | 5 Sep 1918 | SE5a | 1210 | NE Ribécourt | (a) |
| | 1. | 24 Sep 1918 | Balloon | 1612 | Fins | |
| | 2. | 29 Sep 1918 | SE5a | 1030 | Aubencheul | |
| | 3. | 1 Oct 1918 | Balloon | 1610 | Gouzeaucourt | |

(a) Also claimed by Ltns Meyer and Himmel of Jasta 37.

## HAASE, Heinrich    Uffz

| | | | | | |
|---|---|---|---|---|---|
| SS8 | 1918 | 1 | J21 | 1918 – 10 Oct 1918 | 5 WIA |

Wounded in arm during balloon attack.

Biography & Victories: See *Above the Lines*.

## HAASS,    Vfw

| | | | | | |
|---|---|---|---|---|---|
| AFP1 | – 13 Jun 1917 | – | AFP4 | 3 Sep 1917 – | – |
| J29 | 13 Jun 1917 – 3 Sep 1917 | – | | | |

Severely wounded in the neck 14 August 1917.

---

### HABER, Kurt    Ltn d R

| | | | | | |
|---|---|---|---|---|---|
| FFA6b | 1916 – Aug 1916 | 4 | J3 | 26 Oct 1916 – 20 Dec 1916 | – KIA |
| J15 | Aug 1916 – Oct 1916 | 1 | | | |

Born Beithen, Upper Silesia, 4 July 1895. Killed over Peronne by Charles Nungesser, N65.
Biography & Victories: See *Above the Lines*.

---

### HABICH, Hermann    Ltn

| | | | | | |
|---|---|---|---|---|---|
| FAA47 | 1914 – | – | J49 | Mar 1918 – 11 Nov 1918 | 7 |
| OfStv | | | | | |
| FAA215 | – 1916 | – | | | |

Biography & Victories: See *Above the Lines*.

---

### HAEBLER, Hans Gottfried von    Ltn d R

| | | | | |
|---|---|---|---|---|
| FAA273 | – | J36 | 30 Sep 1917 – 22 Mar 1918 | 8 POW |

Biography & Victories: See *Above the Lines*.

---

### HÄFNER, Erwin    Ltn

| | | | |
|---|---|---|---|
| J22 | – 13 Aug 1918 | – | KIAcc |

Born 25 March 1893, Niebenstein. Killed in mid-air collision with Flg Horstmann at 1100 hours over Balâtre.

---

### HÄGELE, Otto    Uffz

| | | | |
|---|---|---|---|
| J32b | – 4 Nov 1918 | – | KIA |

Born 23 October 1893, Esslingen. Shot down in flames over Le Quesnoy.

---

### HÄNICHEN, Martin    Ltn

| | | | | | |
|---|---|---|---|---|---|
| J13 | – 21 Mar 1918 | – | J53 | 22 Mar 1918 – 11 Nov 1918 | 3 |

Technical Officer for Jasta 53. Acting CO Jasta 53 from 31 August 1918 to 22 October 1918.

| Victories: | 1. | 22 Mar 1918 | BF2b | 1600 | Croix |
|---|---|---|---|---|---|
| | 2. | 6 Sep 1918 | Spad 2 | | Coucy-le-Château |
| | 3. | 6 Sep 1918 | Spad 2 | | Coucy-le-Château |

---

### HÄNISCH, Eberhard    Ltn d R

| | | | |
|---|---|---|---|
| J15 | 10 Oct 1916 – 26 May 1917 | – | KIA |

Born 9 July 1895, Breslau. Also known as 'Puz'. Killed over Chermizy, near Laon.

---

### HÄRTL, Erwin    Ltn d R

| | | | |
|---|---|---|---|
| J1 | 17 Sep 1917 – 27 Nov 1917 | 2 | WIA |

Joined Jasta 1 from FEA1b on 17 September 1917.

| Victories: | 1. | 25 Oct 1917 | Caproni | | E Canale |
|---|---|---|---|---|---|
| | 2. | 7 Nov 1917 | Pomilio | 0900 | NE Cordenus |

---

### HÄUSLER,    Vfw

| | |
|---|---|
| J6 | 1 |

| Victories: | 1. | 25 Mar 1917 | Sopwith 2 | Sablonière |
|---|---|---|---|---|

---

### HÄUSSLER,    Uffz

| | | | |
|---|---|---|---|
| KG3 | | J19 | 26 Oct 1916 – 14 Jan 1917 – |

---

### HÄVERNIK,    Ltn

| | | |
|---|---|---|
| J47w | 14 Jan 1918 – Apr 1918 | 2 |

Joined Jasta 47w from Jastaschule I.

| Victories: | 1. | 12 Apr 1918 | Camel | 1645 | Le Petit Mortier |
|---|---|---|---|---|---|
| | 2. | 17 Apr 1918 | 2-seater | 1200 | S Estaires |

---

### HAFF, Otto    Ltn d R

| | | |
|---|---|---|
| J23b | 28 Sep 1918 – 11 Nov 1918 | – |

Reported from Jastaschule I.

---

### HAFNER, Werner    Ltn d R

| | | | |
|---|---|---|---|
| J57 | 19 Feb 1918 – 13 Mar 1918 | – | KIA |

Born 31 May 1895, Pforzheim, Baden. Joined Jasta 57 from AFP6. Killed over W La Bassée, at 1330 hours, possibly by Capt H W Woollett, No 43 Sqn, RFC.

---

### HAGEN,    Ltn d R

| | | |
|---|---|---|
| J62 | 13 Apr 1918 – 11 Nov 1918 | 2 |

Joined Jasta 62 from Jastaschule I. Acting CO Jasta 62, 28 Jul to 21 Aug 1918.

| Victories: | 1. | 15 Jul 1918 | Balloon | 1455 | Chigny |
|---|---|---|---|---|---|
| | 2. | 10 Oct 1918 | DH4 | 1324 | Haumont |

## HAGER, Heinrich      Ltn d R

| J32b | 5 May 1918 – 5 Sep 1918 | 2 | WIA |

Severely wounded at 1200 hours by explosive bullet in the upper arm.

| Victories: | 1. | 18 May 1918 | Camel | 1110 | Vitry |
|---|---|---|---|---|---|
| | 2. | 29 Aug 1918 | DH4 | 0940 | Monchy-Tilloy |

## HAHN, Erich      Oblt

| KekN | – 23 Aug 1916 | – | CO J19 | 29 Nov 1916 – 4 Sep 1917 | 5 | KIA |
| J1 | 23 Aug 1916 – 29 Nov 1916 | 1 | | | | |

Biography & Victories: See *Above the Lines*.

## HAINZL,      Uffz

| J76b | 29 Jul 1918 – | – |

Joined Jasta 76b from Jastaschule II.

## HAITSCH,      Flg

| J79b | 5 May 1918 – 27 May 1918 | – | WIA |

## HAKE,      Ltn

| J18 | 11 Feb 1917 – 21 Feb 1917 | – | AFP1 | 20 Apr 1917 – | – |
| J36 | 21 Feb 1917 – 20 Apr 1917 | – | | | |

Promoted Leutnant on 27 April 1915.

## HAKENBERG,      Vfw

| J81 | – 5 Mar 1918 | – | ObOst | | |
| | | | J74 | 5 Mar 1918 – 11 Nov 1918 | – |

## HALBHERR,      Gefr

| Kest 8 | (Sep 1918) – | – |

## HAMANN,      Gefr

| J67 | 12 Jul 1918 – 11 Nov 1918 | 1 |
| Victories: | 1. | 1 Aug 1918 | Salmson 2A2/DH4 |

## HAMMES, Karl      Ltn d R

| J35 | 11 Aug 1917 – 9 Sep 1917 | 4 | WIA |

Born 25 March 1896, Zell/Mosel. Volunteered 3 Aug 1914, as Fahrenjunker, Foot Artillery Regiment 9. Transferred to aviation Sept 1916. Served in FAA276 from Apr 1917, awarded EKI here. Jastaschule I in Aug 1917. Shot down by a Camel on 9 Sept 1917, landed and taken to Field Hospital 502, Lichtervelde, his Albatros DV 2336/17 destroyed. Possibly downed by Capt C F Collett, No 70 Sqn, RFC. Vienna opera star post-war but killed in action over Poland in 1939.

| Victories: | 1. | 31 Aug 1917 | Spad | 1910 | W Dixmuide | |
|---|---|---|---|---|---|---|
| | 2. | 1 Sep 1917 | Spad | 0800 | Wervicq | (a) |
| | 3. | 3 Sep 1917 | Triplane | 0955 | Eesen-Zaren | |
| | 4. | 9 Sep 1917 | Camel | 1910 | Stadenberg | (b) |

(a) Possibly 2/Lt E M Sant, No 19 Sqn, RFC, POW.
(b) Possibly D3928, No 70 Sqn, RFC, Lt N C Saward, POW.

## HAMPEL, Willi      OfStv

| J16b | 21 May 1917 – 9 Jan 1918 | – | J55 | 9 Jan 1918 – 6 Apr 1918 | – | POW |

Shot down near Malibis.

## HAMSTER, Ernst      Vfw

| J37 | (Aug 1917) – 26 May 1918 | 3 | J65 | 26 May 1918 – 11 Nov 1918 | – |
| Victories: | 1. | 30 Sep 1917 | RE8 | 1155 | E Tilloy |
| | 2. | 30 Sep 1917 | RE8 | 1205 | SW Fresnes |
| | 3. | 23 Nov 1917 | Camel | 1210 | E Voormzeele |

## HANDL, August      Ltn d R

| J76b | 2 Dec 1917 – 9 Dec 1917 | – | J16b | 9 Dec 1917 – 22 Apr 1918 | 1 | WIA |

Forced to land behind British lines and taken prisoner.

| Victories: | 1. | 24 Mar 1918 | DH4 | | Flaucourt |

## HANKO, August    Ltn d R

| | | | | | | |
|---|---|---|---|---|---|---|
| FFA38 | | – | J28w | 24 Jan 1917 – 24 Jan 1918 | 5 | |
| KG1/2 | | – | CO | | | |
| J20 | 2 Nov 1916 – 24 Jan 1917 | – | J64w | 24 Jan 1918 – 7 Jul 1918 | – | Hosp |

Biography & Victories: See *Above the Lines.*

## HANNEMANN, Eduard    Ltn

| | | | | | |
|---|---|---|---|---|---|
| J39 | – 5 Mar 1918 | 2 | J39 | 30 Apr 1918 – 11 Nov 1918 | 1 |
| J74 | 5 Mar 1918 – 30 Apr 1918 | – | | | |

Victories:
| | | | | |
|---|---|---|---|---|
| 1. | 7 Nov 1917 | Caproni | | Pordenone |
| 2. | 30 Dec 1917 | Caproni | 1240 | Susegana |
| 3. | 4 Jun 1918 | Bréguet | 2030 | Prosnes |

## HANS, Anton    Gefr

Kest 1          – 31 Oct 1916    – Died
Born 13 November 1879, Bihlafingen, Laupheim. Died in hospital, Mannheim.

## HANSEN,    Ltn

J3     26 Aug 1916 – 6 Dec 1916    – WIA

## HANSEN,    Gefr

J26    (Feb 1917) –    –

## HANSEN,    Ltn

J28    (Oct 1917) –    –

## HANSEN,    Vfw

J35    28 May 1917 –    –

## HANSON,    Ltn d R

FEA9          – 21 Jan 1917    –          J26    21 Jan 1917 – Apr 1917    –
OzbV for Jasta 26.

## HANSTEIN, Ludwig    Ltn d R

| | | | | | | |
|---|---|---|---|---|---|---|
| FA9 | May 1916 – 31 Oct 1916 | 1 | CO | | | |
| J16b | 31 Oct 1916 – 25 Sep 1917 | 10 | J35b | 24 Sep 1917 – 21 Mar 1918 | 5 | KIA |

Biography & Victories: See *Above the Lines*.

## HANTELMANN, Georg von    Ltn

J18    6 Feb 1918 – 18 Mar 1918    –          J15    18 Mar 1918 – 11 Nov 1918    25
Biography & Victories: See *Above the Lines*

## HANZOG, Emil    Vfw

J57    Aug 1918 – 23 Oct 1918    1 KIA
Born 12 May 1894, Altenhagen. Downed over Bantigny.
Victories:    1.    3 Oct 1918    Dolphin

## HAPF,    Uffz

J76b    12 Dec 1917 – 20 Apr 1918    1          J80b    27 Jun 1918 – 11 Nov 1918    –
AFP19          – 27 Jun 1918    –
Joined Jasta 76b from Jastaschule I.
Victories:    1.    15 Mar 1918    Spad          Alt-Thann

## HARBERS,    Vfw

J73    11 Feb 1918 – 11 Nov 1918    1
Victories:    1.    27 Oct 1918    Spad          Aisnetel

## HARDEL,    Uffz

J10    24 Aug 1917 – 20 Oct 1917    – WIA
Wounded in action at 1310 hours.

## HARENDT,    Uffz

J19    22 May 1918 – 27 Aug 1918    –          AFP9    27 Aug 1918 –    –

**HARLESS,     Uffz**
J80b     21 Aug 1918 – 11 Nov 1918     –
Joined Jasta 80b from Jastaschule II.

---

**HARLING,     Vfw**
J31                    – 20 Feb 1918     – WIA
Vfw J73     Aug 1918 – 11 Nov 1918     1
Wounded at 1000 hours.
Victories:     1.         27 Oct 1918         Spad                                          Aisnetel

---

**HARNISCH,     Vfw**
J45     29 Sep 1918 – 11 Oct 1918     –
Transferred to Jastaschule I.

---

**HARTL, Hans     Ltn d R**
FA9b                                –                    FEA16     17 Sep 1917 –                    –
J16b     5 Jan 1917 – 17 Sep 1917     –

---

**HARTMANN, August     Ltn**
J30     30 Jun 1918 – 11 Nov 1918     –
Joined Jasta 30 from Jastaschule I. Wounded in combat 10 July 1918.

---

**HARTMANN, Friedrich von     Ltn**
J9                    – 16 Jun 1917     1 KIAcc
Born 19 May 1893, Subtoto. Killed in mid-air collision with Vfw Stemmler over Leffincourt airfield during practice combat.
Victories:     1.         30 Apr 1917         Spad                    0925         SW Nauroy

---

**HARTMANN, Otto     Hptm**
FA48          1916 –                    –                    J18     17 May 1917 – 6 Jun 1917     –
KG3/15     1916 –                    2                    CO
SS3          – 17 May 1917     –                    J28w     6 Jun 1917 – 3 Sep 1917     5 KIA
Biography & Victories: See *Above the Lines*.

---

**HARTMANN,     Oblt**
J6     18 May 1918 – 11 Nov 1918     –

---

**HARTMANN, von     Ltn**
KekJ               – 1916               –                    J4     27 Nov 1917 – (Feb 1918)     –
J11     12 Oct 1916 – 27 Nov 1917     –
OzbV for Jasta 11, 4 Apr – 12 Jul 1917.

---

**HASENPUSCH,     OfStv**
J67     23 Mar 1918 – 11 Nov 1918     2
Victories:     1.         1 Aug 1918         Salmson 2A2
                2.         14 Sep 1918         Bréguet XIV                    Doncourt

---

**HASLBECK, Hans     Uffz**
J32b               – 29 Oct 1918     – KIA
Born 10 January 1898, Munich. Killed at Erquelines.

---

**HASSELMANN, Paul     Ltn d R**
J28w               – 3 Oct 1918     – KIA
Born 7 March 1895, Recklinghausen, Sud Westfalen. Killed over Douai.

---

**HATTENKOFER, Anton     Vfw**
J23b     23 Sep 1918 – 11 Nov 1918     –
Reported from Jastaschule I.

---

**HAUENSPERGER,     Ltn d R**
J32b     17 Oct 1918 – 11 Nov 1918     –

---

**HAUFFE,     Ltn d R**
J9               – 23 May 1918     – INJ
Injured in a landing accident.

**HAUFT,    Ltn**
J35b      23 Aug 1918 – 11 Nov 1918    –
Joined Jasta 35b from AFP3. OzbV for Jasta 35b.

**HAUK, Paul    Gefr**
J48        4 Jun 1918 –                 –
Joined Jasta 48 from Jastaschule I.

**HAUSEN, Lothat Fr von    Ltn**
J32      20 Feb 1917 – 16 Mar 1917    –   POW
Born 16 July 1894, Leipzig. Served in Jäger Battalion 13. Shot down at 1025 hours N Höville, by Capt
Georges Guynemer, and taken prisoner; died of wounds, 15 July 1917.

**HAUSER,    Gefr**
J50        Sep 1918 – 11 Nov 1918     –

**HAUSNER, Franz    Ltn d R**
J23b      23 May 1918 – 27 May 1918    –   KIA
Born 9 September 1893, Friedrichstadt. Reported to Jasta 23b from Jastaschule I. Collided in mid-air
with Ltn Hornfischer over Bourlon Wood.

**HAUSSMANN, Albert    Vfw**
| | | | | | | |
|---|---|---|---|---|---|---|
| KG3/26 | 1916 – | | 1 | J15 | 25 Jun 1917 – (Jun 1918) | 2 |
| SS8 | – 1917 | | – | J13 | (Jun 1918) – 16 Oct 1918 | 9   KIA |
| J23 | 13 Apr 1917 – 25 Jun 1917 | | 3 | | | |

Biography & Victories: See *Above the Lines*.

**HAUSTEIN, Karl    Ltn**
J37                                  –           Kest 4b                              –
Commanded Kest 4b (Aug 1918 – Oct 1918).

**HEBBEN, Victor    OfStv**
FA5          – 21 Sep 1916    –            J10      21 Sep 1916 – 20 Apr 1917    –  WIA

**HEBLER,    Ltn**
J15      (Oct 1917) – 20 Mar 1918    1        J68      10 Jul 1918 – 11 Nov 1918    2
J18      20 Mar 1918 – 10 Jul 1918    –

| Victories: | | | | | |
|---|---|---|---|---|---|
| | 1. | 14 Oct 1917 | Balloon | 1645 | S Staubecken | (a) |
| | 2. | 26 Sep 1918 | Balloon | 1415 | Aubérive | |
| | 3. | 26 Sep 1918 | Balloon | 1415 | Aubérive | |

(a) French 27th Company, Observer Lt Bacquet not harmed.

**HECHLER,    Gefr**
J57      (Jun 1918) – 11 Nov 1918    2

| Victories: | | | | | |
|---|---|---|---|---|---|
| | 1. | 25 Aug 1918 | Dolphin | 1000 | SW Bapaume |
| | 2. | 29 Aug 1918 | Camel | | N Bourlonwald |

**HECHT,    Vfw**
J10        Nov 1917 – 27 Dec 1917    –   POW
Shot down in 5th Brigade Sector, at Estrées-en-Chaussée, while flying Pfalz DIII 1370/17 (G.110), by
2/Lts A.G. Hanna and R.A. Burnand, No 35 Sqn, RFC (who were themselves taken prisoner 31 March 1918).

**HECK, Julius    Uffz**
Kest 5          – 10 Oct 1916    –   KIA
Born 20 February 1891, Stuttgart. Killed near Friburg.

**HECKEL, Friedrich    Uffz**
J16b      6 Apr 1918 – 8 Jun 1918    –   WIA
Born 24 April 1893. Wounded over Houthulst Wald.

**HEDESCHINSKY, Stanislaus    Uffz**
J14          – 18 Sep 1917    –            AFP5          1917 –
J34b      18 Sep 1917 – 1917    –

*Top left*: Jasta Boelcke summer 1918: Ltn Alfred Frey, Ltn Alfred Lindenberger (12), Ltn Otto Löffler (15), Ltn Wilhelm Suer (1), Gefr Mynereck, Ltn Gerhard Bassenge (7), Ltn Eberhard Fr von Gudenberg (OzbV), Ltn Ernst Bormann (16), Ltn Karl Bolle, CO (36), Ltn Hermann Frommherz (32) and Ltn Johann Heemsoth (2).

*Top right*: Jasta Boelcke, 16 August 1918: Gefr Mynereck, Ltn Otto Löffler (15), Ltn Fritz Heinz (2), Ltn Fritz Hoffmann (1), Ltn Eberhard Fr von Gudenberg (stv), Ltn Karl Bolle, CO (36), Oblt von Griesheim (1), Ltn Franz Klausenberg (2), Ltn Gerhard Bassenge (7), Vfw Kurt Jentsch (7) and Ltn Alfred Lindenberger (12).

*Middle left*: Jasta 4, 1917: -?-, Vfw Ernst Clausnitzer (3), --, Oblt Kurt von Döring, CO (11), Ltn Bouillon ? (1), Ltn Busso von Alversleben (1), -?-, Ltn Wilhelm Schultze

(1), -?-, Ltn Hans Klein (22), -?-.

*Middle right*: Jasta 5, spring 1917: rear: -?-, Vfw Josef Mai (30), OfStv Edmund Nathanael (15), Vfw Ernst Dahlmann (2), OfStv Alfred Sturm (1), OfStv Löwensen; front: Hptm Hans von Hünerbein, CO (1), Ltn Heinrich Gontermann (39), Ltn Kurt Schneider (15), Ltn Neisen (1), Ltn Vorländer and Ltn Rudolf Nebel (2).

*Bottom*: Jasta 5, Cappy 1918: Ltn Fritz Oppenhorst (2), Ltn Otto Könnecke (35), Ltn Wilhelm Lehmann (4), Vfw Erich Buder (Jasta 26) (12), Oblt Zettelemayer (JGr Adj), Oblt Richard Flashar, CO and OC JGr2, (2), Ltn Schaumberg (OzbV), Ltn Rath, Ltn Hans Schlömer (4), Ltn Josef Mai (30), Ltn Hans von Hippel (2), Ltn Fritz Rumey (45) and Uffz Vogt.

*Top left*: Jasta 7, November 1917: seated: Ltn Hermann Kunz (6), Ltn Josef Jacobs, CO (48), Ltn Otto Kunst (1); standing: Vfw Swoboda, Ltn Paul Billik (31), Vfw Rudolf Lander (2), Ltn Paul Lotz (10), Ltn Max Hillmann (1), Ltn Mühlen, Obflugm Kurt Schönfelder (13), Ltn Carl Degelow (30) and Vfw Hans Horst (4).

*Top right*: Jasta 7 and guest, 23 January 1918: Uffz Jupp Böhne, Vfw Paul Hüttenrauch (8), Ltn Carl Degelow (30), -?-, FSL H S J E Youens (3 Naval Sqn), Ltn Otto Kunst (1) Obflugm Kurt Schönfelder (13).

*Middle left*: Jasta 9, 1916: front: Oblt Walter Zietlow, Oblt Kurt Student, CO (6), Ltn Prinz Franz von Thurn und Taxis; rear: Ltn Willi Rosenstein (9), Ltn Werner Marwitz (1) Ltn Hartmut Baldamus (18), Ltn Hermann

Pfeiffer (11), Ltn Oskar Dänkert, Ltn Heinrich Kroll (33) and Ltn Graf von der Recke.

*Middle right*: Jasta 10, June 1917: Uffz Hermann Brettel (2), Vfw Burggaller, Vfw Adam Barth (1), -?-, Oblt Ernst Fr von Althaus, CO (9), Ltn Max Kühn (3), Oblt Ernst Weigand (3), -?-, Ltn Erich Löwenhardt (54) and Ltn Alois Heldmann (15).

*Bottom*: Jasta 10 mid-1918: OfStv Paul Aue (10), Vfw Burggaller, Gefr Alfons Nitsche, -?-, Ltn Fritz Friedrichs (21), Ltn Erich Löwenhardt (54), Oblt Hugo Schäfer (OzbV), Ltn Hans Weiss (16) (Jasta 11), Ltn Max Kühn (3), Ltn Alois Heldmann (15), Ltn Justus Grassmann (10).

*Top left*: Jasta 11, 1917: Ltn von Hartmann, Ltn Wolfgang Plüschow (1), Ltn Constantin Krefft (2), Ltn Georg Simon (1), Ltn Kurt Wolff (33), Ltn Karl Effers, Oblt Manfred von Richthofen (80), Ltn Lothar von Richthofen (40), Ltn Hans Hintsch (3), Ltn Otto Brauneck (10), Ltn Matthof and Ltn Karl Allmenröder (30).

*Top right*: Jasta 12 pilots, spring 1917: seated: Oblt Adolf von Tutschek (27) Ltn Bender (?), Vfw Grigo (3), Vfw Arthur Schorisch (4), Ltn Paul Billik (31); standing: Vfw Otto Rosenfeld (13), Ltn Karl Schöck (2), Ltn Friedrich Hochstetter (1), Ltn Oskar Müller (OzbV), Vfw Friedrich Gille (6), Vfw Robert Riessinger (4) and Vfw Reinhold Jörke (13).

*Middle left*: Jasta 12 pilots, August 1918: front: Ltn Hermann Becker, CO (23); l to r: Ltn Alfred Greven (4), Flg Wilke (1), Flg Rossbach (1), Ltn Günther Stölting, Ltn Friedrich Roth (2), Ltn Georg von Wurmb (OzbV rear),

Ltn Ulrich Neckel (30), Ltn Hans Besser (1), Ltn Muhs, Fw Wittchen (2) and Ltn Herbert Bock.

*Middle right*: Jasta 14, April 1917: front l to r: Vfw Hermann Margot, Ltn Gustav Nolte (3), Ltn Friedrich Vonschott; 2nd row: Ltn Otto Krönert, Ltn Otto Weigel, Oblt Rudolf Berthold, CO (44), Ltn Werner Zech (3), Ltn Werner Peckmann (3), Ltn Kuen (2); 3rd row: Ltn Walter Kypke (9), Vfw Gottlieb Vothknecht (2), Ltn Georg Ferner, Ltn Georg Michaelis (1), Ltn Josef Klever, OfStv Hüttner (3), Ltn Breuer (1), Ltn Max Lenz (OzbV) and Uffz Oswald Rottmann.

*Bottom*: Jasta 15, 9 October 1918: Vfw Gustav Klaudat (6), Ltn Hilmar Glöcken, Ltn Joachim von Ziegesar (3), Ltn Josef Veltjens (35), Ltn Georg von Hantelmann (25), Ltn Hugo Schäfer (11) and Vfw Theodor Weischer (4). Celebrating Hantelmann's 20th victory.

*Top*: Jasta 18, March 1918: standing front: Ltn Hermann Margot, Ltn Hugo Schäfer (11), Ltn Hans von Buttlar, Oblt Rudolf Berthold, who'd been wounded on the 7th, Oblt Hans Buddecke (13) who'd come to take over but was killed on the 10th, Ltn Johannes Klein (16), Ltn Arthur Rahn (6); rear: Ltn Georg von Hantelmann (25), Ltn P Lohmann, Ltn Josef Veltjens (sitting) (35), Oblt Ernst Turck (1), Ltn Walter Dingel (2), Ltn Walter Kleffel (1), Vfw Theodor Weischer (4) and Ltn Konrad von Bülow-Bothkamp (2).

*Middle left*: Jasta 18 late August 1918: Uffz Glatz (1), OfStv Wilhelm Kühne (7), Ltn Hans Müller (13), Ltn Kurt Monnington (8), Ltn August Raben, CO (4), Ltn Erich Spindler (2), Ltn Kurt Baier (1), Ltn Heinz Künster (2), Ltn Kandt, OfStv Richard Schleichardt (3) just out of picture. Note ravens on building awning and hand cranked alarm siren on table.

*Middle right*: Jasta 21s, 30 August 1918; front: Oblt von

Kalckreuth (OzbV), Oblt Oskar von Boenigk CO (26), Ltn Fritz Höhn (21); middle: Vfw Karl Schmückle (6), Ltn Christians (2), Ltn Julius Keller (2), -?-; rear: Vfw Heinrich Haase (6), -?-, -?-, Ltn Schlumps, Vfw Karl Thom (27).

*Bottom left*: Jasta 21s and visitors, summer 1918: Ltn Werner Preuss, J66 (22), Ltn Arno Benzler, J60 (9), -?-, Ltn Schlumps (OzbV Gruja), Ltn Julius Keller (2), Ltn Hans Rolfes, OC JGr Ost and J45 (17), Ltn Fritz Höhn (20), Ltn Rupke (Gruppe Adj), Oblt Oskar Fr von Boenigk, CO (26), Ltn Christians (2), Ltn Walter Blume (CO J9) (28), -?-,Oblt von Kalckreuth (OzbV); front: Ltn George Schlenker, CO J41 (14).

*Bottom right*: Jasta 22s, spring 1917: Ltn Stock (3), Ltn Alfred Wunsch (1), Vfw Hoppe, Ltn Rath, Ltn Josef Jacobs (48), Oblt Erich Hönemanns CO, Ltn Diether Collin (13), Ltn Werner Herwarth (1), Ltn Georg Meyer (24), Ltn Röhr (1), Vfw Joachim Graf Fr von Beissel (1), Ltn Ulrich Fischer (4) and Ltn Heinrich Karbe (2).

*Top left*: Jasta 22s, c Aug 1917: Ltn Kurt Monnington (8), Vfw Emil Bergmann (1), Ltn Hans Unger, Ltn Julius Fichter (7), Ltn Söbeck, Vfw Karl Bohnenkamp (15), Ltn Siegfried Büttner (13), Oblt Heinrich Karbe (2), Ltn Alfred Wunsch (1), Ltn Alfred Lenz CO, (6) and Ltn Ulrich Fischer (4).

*Top right*: Jasta 25 pilots, Macedonia: Vfw Gollinzky, Vfw Pinkert, Vfw Anton Bauhofer (4), Uffz Eggebrecht (1), OfStv Reinhard Treptow (6) and Ltn Gerhard Fieseler (19).

*Middle left*: Jasta 26, May 1918: Vfw Erich Buder (12), Vfw Fritz Classen (11), Ltn Fritz Riemer (8), Uffz Fritz Zogmann (1) (left window), Ltn Weiss (OzbV) (left window), Ltn Fritz Loerzer CO (11), Hptm Bruno Loerzer (44) (JGIII), Ltn Otto Marquardt (1), Vfw Herbert Werner (1), Ltn Werner Dahm (4) (right window), Vfw Otto Esswein (12), OfStv Fritz Kublum (1) (right window), Vfw Otto Fruhner (27), Ltn Eckert.

*Middle right*: Jasta 28w, mid 1917: standing: -?-, Ltn Otto Koch (OzbV) and Vfw Kurt Wittekind (2); seated: Vfw Karolus Bärenfänger (1), Ltn August Hanko (5), Oblt Karl Weber, -?-, -?-, Ltn Erich Welss (new OzbV), Ltn Ernst Hess (17), Ltn Emil Lamprecht. The German shepherd belongs to Hanko.

*Bottom*: Jasta 28w, summer 1917: front/seated: Ltn Max von Müller (36), Ltn Franz Ray (17), Ltn August Hanko (5); seated behind: Ltn Karl Bolle (35), Ltn Ernst Hess (17); standing: Vfw Karolus Bärenfänger (1), Vfw Paul Wagner, Ltn Otto Koch (OzbV), Ltn Emil Lamprecht, Oblt Erwin Wenig (4), Hptm Otto Hartmann, CO (7), Ltn Erich Welss (new OzbV), Ltn Kurt Wittekind (2) and Oblt Karl Weber.

*Top left*: Jasta 32b, summer 1917: front: Ltn Wilhelm Eckenberg (OzbV), Ltn Fritz Kieckhäfer (8), Ltn Rudolf Windisch (22), Ltn Hans Rolfes (17); middle: Ltn Kurt Starck (2), Oblt Otto Schmidt CO (20), Ltn Lothar Zencominierski (3), Vfw Franz Tabaka (1); rear: Ltn Richler, Ltn Werner Ulmer, Vfw Kurt Petzinna (2), Vfw Konrad Poralla, Holsmint.

*Top right*: Jasta 37, late 1917: Ltn Ernst Udet, CO (62), Ltn Ascan Gobert (stv), Ltn Krämer, Ltn Karl Haustein, Bitterscha, Vfw Fahlke (1), Ltn Heinrich Zempel (1), Fw Walter Horn (1) and Vfw Bärwald (2).

*Middle*: Jasta 40, and prisoners, 14 July 1918: Ltn Frodian,

Ltn Willi Rosenstein (9), Uffz Ebert, Lt Marshall (85 Sqn RAF), Ltn Hermann Gilly (7), Lt B N Garrett (64 Sqn RAF), Ltn Carl Degelow, CO (30), and Ltn Hans Jeschonneck (2).

*Bottom left*: Jasta 41, early 1918: l to r: Ltn Josef Strauch (1), Ltn Georg Schlenker, CO (14), Ltn Werner Ulmer, Oblt Bilke (OzbV), Vfw Josef Schwendemann (17), Vfw Iversen (1), Vfw Hermann Juhnke (5), Ltn Hans Weiss (16) and Vfw Ludwig Reimann (2).

*Bottom right*: Jasta 54s, 1918. Unteroffizier Erich Mix is third from the left (seated), by one of the unit's Fokker DVIIs.

*Top* : Jasta 56, 25 October 1918: Ltn Ludwig Beckman, CO, (8), -?-, Uffz Dannemann (2), Flg Beltzig, Ltn Schramm (3), Vfw Krebs (3), Flg Christians; front: Uffz Leinegraber.

*Middle left*: Jasta 60, October 1918: Vfw Wunnenberg, Vfw Zimmermann (1), Ltn Günther Dobberke (8), Ltn Schwager, Ltn Arno Benzler, CO (9), Ltn Wolff (1), Ltn Karl Ritscherle (8), Vfw Mack, Vfw Bollemann and Vfw Arthur Korff (8).

*Middle right*: Jasta 65, May 1918: Ltn Otto Fitzner, CO (9), Ltn Wilhelm Frickart (12), Ltn Heinrich Zempel (1), Ltn Bieber, Ltn Heinz Fr von Beaulieu-Marconnay, Ltn Walter Fritzsche, OfStv Tiedje (3), Vfw Josef Hohly (7), Gefr Scheutzel and Ltn Rost (OzbV).

*Bottom left*:Jasta 68, June 1918: Gefr Paul Dyrbusch, Ltn Berkling, Ltn Esser, Ltn Paul Schwirzke (4), Ltn Fritz Pütter, CO (25), Ltn Philipp Kirschenlohr (OzbV), Ltn Rudolf Croissant, Uffz Huar (3) and Ltn Gerhard Hoffmann.

*Bottom right*: JGII at the end of the war; front: Oblt Fritz Krapfenbauer (NO), Ltn Wilhelm Leusch, CO J19 (5), Ltn Josef Veltjens, CO J15 (35), Oblt Oskar Fr von Boenigk, OC JGII (26), Ltn Franz Büchner, CO J13 (40), Ltn Hermann Becker, CO J12 (23), Ltn Hans von Buttlar (Adj), Ltn Walter Dingel (TO); second row: Vfw Hermann Margot, Ltn Krauss, Ltn Gewert (2), Ltn Dittmann, Ltn Werner Niethammer (6), Ltn Joachim von Ziegesar (3), Ltn Hans Besser (1), Ltn Hugo Schäfer (11); third row: Vfw Theodor Weischer (4), Ltn Rudolf Rienau (6), Ltn Koch (2), Ltn Scheller (4); back row: Ltn Siebert, Ltn Telge (1), Ltn Alfred Greven (4), -?-, -?-, -?-, Ltn Bertling (3).

*Top*: Ltn Willy Allmenröder (front), Jasta 29, with Ltns Karl Lanke and Johannes Klein, summer 1917.

*Above left*: Ltn Heinrich Arntzen, gained seven victories with Jastas 15 and 50 in 1917-18, having already scored four with FFA2 in 1916.

*Above centre*: Ltn Raven Fr von Barnekow, scored 11 victories with Jastas 20 and 1, following service with 4 and 11.

*Above right*: Ltn Wilhelm Allmenröder, brother of Karl, who flew with Jastas 29 and 11, gaining two victories.

*Right*: Ltn Franz Anslinger flew with Jastas 11, 35b and 56 and scored three victories.

*Top left*: Ltn Paul Bäumer, Jastas 5 and 2, 43 victories, seen here in front of his Fokker Drl with one of his ground personnel.

*Top right*: Westphalian Ltn Ludwig `Lutz' Beckmann, eight victories with Jasta 56 in 1918.

*Middle left*: Oblt Fritz Otto Bernert scored 27 victories and served with Jastas 4, 2 and 6. Right is Oblt Ernst Fr von Althaus who scored his 9th and final victory commanding Jasta 10 in 1917.

*Above right*: OfStv Alfred Behling, Jasta 1, scored one victory before being killed on 11 March 1917.

*Above left*: Vfw Karl Bey of Jasta 5 with the crew of his one and only victory, an 11 Sqn BF2b; Lts E Scholtz and H C Wookey, 17 October 1917. Bey was killed the following month.

*Top*: Oblt Oswald Boelcke, father of the Jastas.

*Above left*: Ltn Hans Böhning, Jastas 36, 76 and 79, achieving 17 victories.

*Above centre*: Vfw Hans Brzenk flew with Jastas 67, 81, 74, and 36 in 1918.

*Middle right*: Ltn Heinrich Bongartz (right), 33 victories flying with Jasta 36, with Hptm Bruno Loerzer, commander of JG III, 44 victories.

*Right*: Vfw Hans Brinkman, killed 4 May 1917 while with Jasta 21s.

*Top left*: Ltn Julius Buckler, 36 victories, all with Jasta 17, 1916- 18.

*Top centre*: Ltn Hans von Budde, Jastas 29, 5 and then commanded Jasta 15 from October 1917 to March 1918.

*Top right*: Hptm Hans-Joachim Buddecke scored most of his victories over the Balkans but saw action with Jasta 4, 18 and 30, being killed with the latter unit on 10 March 1918.

*Bottom left*: Oblt Theodor Dahlmann scored five of his seven kills while being adjutant of JGIII in 1918. At right JGI's CO, Hermann Göring, 22 victories.

*Bottom right*: Vfw Dilcher, Jasta 5 1917, three victories.

*Top left*: Rittm Kurt-Bertram von Döring, Jasta 4, JGr4, Jastas 66 and 1, scored 11 victories.

*Top right*: Vfw Willy Gabriel (left), Jasta 11, eleven victories 1918, and his twin brother Walter, who served briefly with Jasta 19 in 1917.

*Above left*: Ltn Gustav Frädrich, Jasta 72 (6) seen here putting on his Heinecke parachute harness, July 1918.

*Above right*: Heinrich Gontermann, Jasta 5 and 15, 39 victories; killed in a crash, 30 October 1917, testing a Fokker Triplane.

*Right*: Ltn Sylvester Garsztka, survived the war with six victories with Jasta 31 but died in a crash in 1919.

*Top left*: Hermann Göring, commanding JGI in 1918, previously saw action with Jastas 7, 5, 26 and 27. 22 victories.

*Top right*: Ltn Justus Grassmann, Jasta 10, ten victories.

*Middle left*: Oblt Adolf Gutknecht, commanded Jasta 43 in 1918; eight victories.

*Above*: Killed whilst ground strafing on 16 October 1918, Vfw Albert Haussmann had gained 15 victories, including this Spa 89 French Spad while with Jasta 13.

*Left*: Oblt Erich Hahn, scored six victories with Jastas 1 and 19, but was killed in action on 4 September 1917.

*Top left*: Ltn Heinrich Henkel, Jasta 37 in 1918; eight victories.

*Top right*: Vfw Max Holtzem flew throughout the war, the last year with Jasta 16b.

*Middle left*: Ltn Hans Joachim von Hippel of Jastas 5 and 71, scored four victories but was only credited with two.

*Above*: Vfw Fritz Jacobsen, a pre-war pilot, later served with Jastas 31 and 73, scoring eight victories by the war's end.

*Left*: Vfw Hermann Juhnke, FAA 238 and later with Jasta 52, scored five victories in 1918.

*Top left*: Fw Willy Kahle scored six victories in the last weeks of the war flying with Jasta 27.

*Top right*: Vfw Erich Klutke, Jasta 12, January 1918.

*Middle left*: Ltn Rudolf Klimke, Jasta 27, 17 victories.

*Above*: Vfw Koch, Jasta 17 over the winter of 1917-18.

*Left*: Ltn Emil Koch, Staffelführer Jasta 32b 1918, seven victories.

*Top left*: OfStv Wilhelm Kühne, seven victories with Jasta 18.

*Top centre*: Jasta 18's Ltn Heinz Künster scored two victories in 1918. Note Jasta 18's raven insignia.

*Top right*: Ltn Hermann Kunz, Jasta 7 and Jasta 55, 6 victories.

*Middle left*: Ltn Arthur Laumann, Jastas 66 and 10, 28 victories.

*Middle right*: Ltn Alfred Lenz (6) Jasta 22 and the Iron Knight, Hptm Rudolf Berthold (44), Jastas 4, 14, 18 and JG II.

*Left*: OfStv Jakob Ledermann, Jasta 13, wounded and PoW, 20 August 1918.

*Top*: Hptm Bruno Loerzer (44), Oblt Hermann Göring (22), Oblt Lothar von Richthofen (40), Ltn Hans Kirschstein (27), Oblt Constantine Krefft (2), Ltn Friedrich Mallinckrodt (6), Fw/Ltn Fritz Schubert (3).

*Middle left*: Uffz Rudolf Lochner scored one victory with Jasta 64w; served in the Luftwaffe post war.

*Middle centre*: Ltn Rudolf Matthaei scored nine victories with Jasta 21s, and a tenth as CO of Jasta 46. Killed in a crash 17 April 1918.

*Middle right*: Obflgmt Karl Meyer, eight victories with Seefrontstaffel and MFJ I, 1916-17.

*Left*: Saxon born Ltn zur See Horst Merz flew with MFJII. Later flew the Do.X post war and became an Oberst in the Luftwaffe in WWII.

*Top left*: Uffz Erich Mix scored three kills with Jasta 54s but became an `ace' in WWII. Seen here with his personalised Fokker DVII and ground mechanic in 1918.

*Top right*: Ltn Hans-Karl Müller (right) with Kek Arvillers. Later served with Jasta 5 and brought his score to nine before being badly wounded in December 1916.

*Bottom left*: Ltn Eberhardt Mohnicke of Jasta 11 (right),

nine victories with Manfred von Richthofen, on the occasion of the Baron's 61st victory, 3 September 1917.

*Bottom centre*: Ltn Hans Müller, Jastas 12, 15 and 18; 12 victories in 1918.

*Bottom right*: Vfw Johann Neumaier shot down three aircraft and a balloon while serving with Bavarian Jasta 16 in 1917.

*Top left*: Vfw Alfred Niemz, Jasta 11, 1918.

*Top centre*: Oblt Wolfgang Plüschow, Jasta 11 and 39; note observer badge.

*Top right*: Ltn sur See Reinhold Poss (11) and Obflm Christian Kairies (7) of Seefrontstaffel, 1918.

*Middle left*: Ltn Viktor von Pressentin von Rautter, Jastas 59 and 4, 15 victories. Killed in action 31 May 1918.

*Above*: Ltn Rudolf Rienau, Jasta 19, six victories.

*Left*: Ltn Arthur Rahn of Jastas 19 and 15 was wounded as acting CO of Jasta 19 on 17 July 1918 after six victories.

*Top*: Aces of Jasta 5; -?-, Fritz Rumey (45), Paul Bäumer (43), Josef Mai (30), Otto Könnecke (35), -?-.

*Middle left*: Three Pour le Mérite holders, two being Marine fighter pilots; l to r: Ltn Josef Jacobs (48), Oblt z S Gotthard Sachsenberg (31) and Oblt z S Theodor Osterkamp (32) who also scored kills in WW2.

*Middle right*: Ltn Hans Rolfes, 17 victories, mostly with Jasta 45 in 1918.

*Above*: Ltn Hugo Schäfer, 11 victories with Jasta 15 in 1918.

*Right*: Vfw Emil Schäfer, Jasta 33.

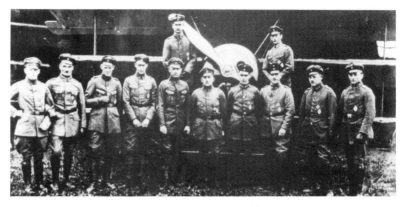

*Top left*: Oblt Franz Schleiff of Jasta 56 had his left hand amputated but had scored 12 victories when this happened on 27 March 1918.

*Top right*: Pilots of Jasta 5, May 1918 at Cappy: Ltn Hans Schlömer (4), Fw Fritz Rumey (45), Hans von Hippel (2), Ltn Fritz Oppenhorst (2), Oblt Zettelmeyer (JGr 2 Adj), Oblt Richard Flashar, CO (2), Ltn Wilhelm Lehmann (4), Ltn Schaumberg (OzbV), Ltn Rath, Uffz Vogt; rear: Fw Josef Mai (30) and Fw Otto Könnecke (35).

*Middle left*: Ltn Julius Schmidt, 15 victories, 14 with Jasta 3.

*Middle right*: Pilots of Jasta 10 in July 1918: Ltn Justus Grassmann (10), Ltn Alois Heldmann (15), Oblt Hugo Schäfer (OzbV), Ltn Erich Löwenhardt (54), Ltn Fritz Friedrichs (21), Ltn Walter Lehmann,  -?-, OfStv Paul Aue (10), Vfw Fritz Schumacher (5), -?-.

*Above*: Oblt Kurt Student, six victories, scored flying Fokker Eindekkers and later as Staffelführer of Jasta 9 in 1917.

*Left*: Ltn Robert Schmidt had a narrow escape on 12 August 1918 while with Jasta 43.  Despite burns to his face he baled out safely whilst using a repaired parachute.

*Top left*: Oblt Ernst Wilhelm Turck, gained one victory with Jasta 18 and later commanded Jastas 15 and 54 in 1918.

*Top right*: Fw Otto Wandelt, Jasta 43, gained three victories before his death in combat, 6 May 1918.

*Middle left*: Jasta 2 pilots, summer 1917, at Proville: front: Ltn Stren, Ltn Rolf Fr von Lersner, Ltn Franz Pernet; middle: Ltn Herwen (guest from K.u.K [Austrian]), Oblt Otto Bernert, CO (27), Ltn Werner Voss (48), (CO Jasta 5), Ltn Raoul Stojsavlesevic (guest from K.u.K., Austrian ace [10], also attached to Jasta 6 in 1917), Ltn

Ernst Wendler; rear: Ltn Friedrich Kempf (4), Ltn Hermann Frommherz (32), Ltn Hans Eggers, Ltn Otto Hunzinger, Oblt Georg Zeumer (4), Oblt Karl Bodenschatz (OzbV), Ltn Gerhard Bassenge (7), Ltn Wilhelm Prien, and Ltn Johannes Wintrath (1).

*Middle right*: Oblt Ernst Udet scored 62 victories with Jastas 15,37,11 and 4.

*Bottom left*: Ltn Weiss flew with Jasta 18 in 1917.

*Bottom right*: Vwf Otto Wieprich, four victories, and Gefr Hitschler, Jasta 57.

*Top left*: Personal marking of Vfw Ludwig Weber of Jasta 3, 1917. His 2236/17 has the name Lulu on its fuselage.

*Top right*: Ltn Hans Schlömer's Albatros DV of Jasta 5, with black fuselage motif with white border. Note streamers attached to tailplane.

*Middle left*: This Fokker DVII was the mount of Ltn Georg Weiner, Staffelführer of Jasta 3 in late 1918.

*Middle right*: Ltn Oskar von Boenigk's Pfalz DIII while with Jasta 4, whose aircraft carried a black spiral band around their fuselages from nose to tail.

*Left*: Paul Bäumer's Eidelweiss-marked Albatros DV, Jasta 5.

*Above*: Although this picture is of Jasta 4, it shows the Fokker Triplane flown by Ltn Hans Kirschstein while with Jasta 6, with black and white stripes to upper and lower surfaces of the top wing as well as to the interplane struts. L to r: Ltn Julius Bender, Ltn Heinrich Maushake (6), Ltn Egon Koepsch (9), Ltn Karl Meyer (4) and Ltn Heinrich Drekmann (11).

*Bottom left*: Vfw Carl Holler's Jasta 6 Albatros DIII No.9, early 1917.

*Top left*: Albatros DVs of Jasta 8 showing the black and white tail markings.

*Top right*: Pfalz DIIIa of Jasta 8, 1918.

*Middle left*: Ltn Alois Heldmann's Jasta 10 Pfalz DIII, June 1917.

*Middle right*: Jasta 10's Pfalz DIIIs, Awoingt, March 1918.

*Bottom left*: Line up of Jasta 12 aircraft showing a mixture of Albatros DV and Fokker DrI Triplanes, Toulis airfield, March 1918.

*Bottom right*: Uffz Heinrich Piel's Jasta 13 Fokker DVII 373/18, with stork insignia and small roundels indicating bullet hole repairs. Piel was killed in this machine on 29 June 1918.

*Right*: Ltn Ludwig Hanstein of Jasta 16b, standing in front of a black fuselaged Albatros Scout showing the black and white comet or shooting star insignia and a white fuselage cross (probably Ltn von Bertrab's machine).

*Top left*: Ltn Robert Dycke (two victories) flew this DV with Jasta 16b.

*Top right*: OfStv Adolf Schreder's white-tailed Albatros DV of Jasta 17 with lightning flash insignia.

*Middle left*: Ltn Günther von Büren (2) with his version of the Jasta 18 raven marking on his Fokker DVII in 1918.

*Middle right*: Fokker Triplanes of Jasta 19. Nearest the camera is Ltn Arthur Rahn's 433/17; April 1918.

*Bottom*: Ltn Fritz Höhn's Jasta 21s Pfalz DIII. Aluminium doped fusclage with red zig-zag markings, red stripes on tail while black stripes appear on the engine area. He carried a black `H' beneath the cockpit. Note unit's black and white stripe behind cockpit.

*Top*: Eduard von Schleich's Albatros DVa with the Bavarian lion insignia used while commanding Jasta 21s. Unit marking of a black and white band encircles the fuselage aft of the cockpit.

*Middle left*: Another Jasta 21s Albatros DV. The black and white fuselage band can just be seen over the right shoulder of Ltn Julius Keller (1) while the tailplane is in a light colour, as is the spinner. The other two pilots are Vfw Karl Schmückle (6) and at right, Vfw Karl Thom (27).

*Middle right*: Albatros DVs of Jasta 23b in March 1918 showing off their white tails; the right-hand machine also has the white line extended across the rear stabilizer.

*Bottom left*: Jasta 27 in 1917. Nearest the camera is Hermann Göring's machine with its white tail and nose; the others carry numbers for personal identification.

*Bottom right*: Ltn Rudolf Klimke's personalised Fokker DVII while with Jasta 27 in 1918, showing his initials 'RK'.

*Top left*: Pfalz DIII of Jasta 30 carrying a large orange and black diamond shape on its fuselage sides. L to r: Ltn Hans Holthusen (2), Ltn Hans-Georg van der Marwitz (14), Oblt Hans Bethge, CO (20), Wels (Ltn Karl Weltz?), Ltn Fr von der Horst, groundcrewman.

*Top right*: Jasta 30's Albatros DIIIs showing individual markings. Third aircraft is 767/17 flown by Ltn Oskar Seitz, with an 'S' on the fuselage aft of the cockpit.

*Middle left*: Close-up of the Oskar Seitz Albatros DIII. In addition to the 'S', the tail fin and rudder have a diamond pattern motif.

*Middle right*: Vfw Kurt Petzinna's Albatros Scout of Jasta 32b. Black tail and spinner, and black `KP' initials on fuselage.

*Bottom left*: Vfw Max Kahlow, Jasta 34b, with his coloured bands around the fuselage aft of the cockpit. Note lozenge fabric to lower wing.

*Bottom right*: Ltn Hans Böhning of Jasta 36, like so many others, carried his initial below the cockpit.

*Top left*: Oblt Kurt Grasshoff, Staffelführer of Jasta 37 in his personally marked Albatros DIII, 1917.

*Top right*: This Jasta 37 Albatros DVa was flown by Ltn Gerhard Schreiber.  Black fuselage and diagonal black and white stripes on tailplane are typical markings under Udet from late 1917.  Personal marking of a white number and white checkerboard on fuselage.

*Middle*: Albatros DVs of Jasta 71, summer 1918.  Note the variations of the Balkenkreuz markings, and striped elevators.

*Bottom left*: A large `M' was carried on Carl Menckhoff's Fokker DVII while CO of Jasta 72.

*Bottom right*: Albatros DVa machines of MFJ II.  No.8 is 1113/17.

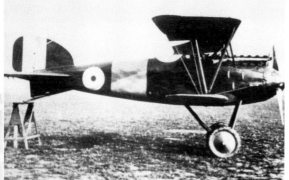

*Top left*: G.1, Albatros DI of Jasta 2, Ltn Karl Büttner, repainted with RFC markings.

*Top right*: G.14, Albatros DII 910/16 shot down 4 March 1917 when flown by Ltn Max Böhme of Jasta 5.

*Middle left*: G.42, Albatros DIII 2015/16, brought down on 4 June 1917, Ltn Georg Simon of Jasta 11 being captured.

*Middle right*: G.56, Albatros DVa, 1162/17, of Jasta 4. Ltn Ernst Clausnitzer was taken prisoner after a combat with a 23 Squadron Spad on 16 July 1917. Taken to England.

*Above*: G.90, Albatros DVa 5253/17, flown by Ltn Hans Sakowsky of Jasta 14 on 13 November 1917.

*Left*: Ltn Ernst Clausnitzer of Jasta 4 had scored three victories before being captured on 16 July 1917.

*Top left*: G.97, Albatros DV 4545/17, Jasta 24s, shot down by AA fire, 7 December 1917; Vfw Max Wackwitz was taken prisoner.

*Top right*: G.110, Pfalz DIII 1370/17 of Jasta 10, flown by Vfw Hecht, shot down by 35 Squadron RFC, 27 December 1917.

*Middle*: G.101, Albatros DV, 5390/17, brought down by 3 AFC Squadron, 17 December 1917. Ltn Clauss of Jasta 29 was taken prisoner. This machine is now in the Australian War Memorial Museum.

*Bottom*: G.125, Fokker Drl Triplane 144/17, Jasta 11, brought down by AA fire on 13 January 1918, with Ltn Eberhard Stapenhörst being taken prisoner.

*Right*: Ltn Hans Fr von Puttkammer, Jasta 3, PoW 19 February 1918 - G.138.

*Top left*: G.141, Pfalz DIII 4184/17 of Jasta 15 in which Vfw Hegeler was brought down on 26 February 1918.

*Top right*: G.144, Albatros DVa brought down by 13 Squadron, 6 March 1918 capturing Ltn Otto Hohmuth of Jasta 23b. The Jasta's tail stripe marking in black and white is clearly shown.

*Middle*: G. 159, Lt W Duncan of 60 Squadron brought down this Albatros DVa 5734/17, on 1 April 1918. Jasta 56's Vfw Weimar was taken into captivity. It was later flown to England.

*Above*: G.158, Fokker DrI Triplane 147/17. Although a Jasta 11 machine it was being flown on 24 March 1918 by Jasta 10's Ltn Keseling who was captured.

*Left*: Ltn Hans von Haebler, Jasta 36; shot down on 22 March, he died of his wounds the next day. His Triplane, 509/17, became G.152.

*Top left*: G/3/4, Pfalz DIIIa 8282/17, flown by Flg Andreas Köhler of Jasta 35b on 24 April 1918, brought down by ground fire.

*Top right*: G/5/13, Pfalz DIIIa 8284/17 of Jasta 77b, forced down on 30 May 1918, putting Vfw Jakob Pollinger into British hands.

*Middle left*: G/2/15, Gefr Reinhold Preiss of Jasta 14, brought down while flying Ltn Hans Werner's Fokker Dr1, 9 June 1918.

*Middle right*: G/5/17, Fokker DVII 2469/18, flown by Kurt Wüsthoff of Jasta 15, brought down by pilots of 24 Squadron RAF, 17 June 1918.
This was Georg Hantelmann's usual machine.

*Above*: G/2/27, Fokker DVII of Jasta 40, shot down by 41 Squadron RAF on 28 October 1918, Leutnant Adolf Auer being captured.

*Left*: Kurt Wüsthoff, Jasta 15, prisoner of war, 17 June 1918.

## HEEMSOTH, Johann    Ltn d R
JB        May 1918 – 11 Nov 1918    2
Awarded Iron Cross 1st Class.

| Victories: | 1. | 2 Jun 1918 | Bréguet | | SW Chévillon |
|---|---|---|---|---|---|
| | 2. | 16 Jun 1918 | DH9 | | S Roye |

## HEGELER,    Vfw
J24s    23 Sep 1917 – 12 Feb 1918    –        J15    12 Feb 1918 – 26 Feb 1918    –  POW
Joined Jasta 24s from AFP4. Shot down behind Allied lines flying Pfalz DIII 4184/17 (G.141), credited to 2/Lt A Cowper, No 24 Sqn, RFC, in SE5a B664.

| Victories: | – | 9 Oct 1917 | Nieuport | 1007 | Gheluwe | (a) |
|---|---|---|---|---|---|---|
| | – | 15 Nov 1917 | SE5 | 1325 | E Zillebeke See | |

(a) Also claimed and awarded to Ltn d R Müller of Jasta 11.

## HEIBERT, Robert    OfStv
FAA207    Oct 1915 –            –        J33    17 Aug 1917 – 17 Dec 1917    1
FAA227        – 17 Aug 1917    –        J46    17 Dec 1917 – 11 Nov 1918    12
Biography & Victories: See *Above the Lines*.

## HEIDELBERG, Karl    Uffz
J48        24 Jan 1918 – 21 Apr 1918    1  KIA
Born 12 February 1896, Imbshausen. Came down near Reims.

| Victories: | – | 16 Mar 1918 | DH4 | 1050 | Escaufourt |
|---|---|---|---|---|---|
| | 1. | 24 Mar 1918 | AR2/Bréguet | | NW Hombleux |

## HEIDELBURG, Viktor    Ltn
J20    27 Jun 1917 – 2 Aug 1917    –
Joined Jasta 20 from Jastaschule I.

## HEIDENFELD,    Uffz
J36        18 Jun 1917            –
Joined Jasta 36 from Jastaschule I.

## HEIDENREICH,    Ltn
J6        17 May 1918 – 30 May 1918    –  POW

## HEIDT,    OfStv
J40        27 Jul 1917 – (Dec 1917)    –

## HEIDFELD,    Uffz
Kest 5        – 15 Jan 1918    –        Kest 5    31 Jan 1918 –            1
J47w    15 Jan 1918 – 31 Jan 1918    –

| Victories: | 1. | 25 Jun 1918 | DH4 | | Offenberg |
|---|---|---|---|---|---|

## HEILIGERS, Josef    Vfw
J30        20 Jan 1917 – 20 Nov 1917    4  KIA
Born 23 April 1894, Aachen. Joined Jasta 30 from AFP6. Killed over Ostricourt, at 1347 hours.

| Victories: | 1. | 7 Jun 1917 | FE2d | 0800 | Koelberg | (a) |
|---|---|---|---|---|---|---|
| | 2. | 24 Jun 1917 | Nieuport | 1940 | S Beaumont | (b) |
| | zlg | 12 Jul 1917 | Martinsyde | 2125 | Annequin | (c) |
| | 3. | 14 Jul 1917 | Martinsyde | 0800 | W Leforest | |
| | 4. | 12 Aug 1917 | Nieuport | 2030 | Courrières | (d) |
| | – | 18 Aug 1917 | BF2b | 0755 | S Lallaing | (e) |

(a) Probably A1957, No 25 Sqn, RFC, 2/Lt G H Pollard/Lt F S Ferrieman.
(b) Probably B1607, No 29 Sqn, RFC, Capt W P Holt.
(c) Probably A1572, No 27 Sqn, RFC, 2/Lt H G Palmer.
(d) Probably A6771, No 40 Sqn, RFC, Lt W D Cullen.
(e) Credited to a Jasta 12 pilot.

## HEINEMANN,    Vfw
FA5b        – 21 Sep 1916    –        J10    21 Sep 1916 –

## HEINRICHS,    Uffz
J18        – 22 Jul 1917    –  WIA
Wounded while escorting Kagohl 3 aircraft.

## HEINS, Rudolph    Ltn d R

J56       1 Feb 1918 – 18 Jun 1918    4  WIA
Joined Jasta 56 from Jastaschule II. Acting CO Jasta 56 from 27 Mar to 16 Apr 1918.

| Victories: | | | | | |
|---|---|---|---|---|---|
| | 1. | 13 Mar 1918 | BF2b | 1015 | Marcoing |
| | 2. | 16 Mar 1918 | DH4 | 1130 | Villeret |
| | 3. | 28 Mar 1918 | Camel | 0925 | Morcourt |
| | 4. | 18 Jun 1918 | Camel | 0915 | NE Dickebusch |

## HEINZ, Fritz    Ltn d R

JB       Aug 1918 – 27 Sep 1918    2  KIA
Born 27 January 1894, Brebach. Killed in action near Awoingt, near Cambrai, probably by Lt I W
Awde, No 56 Sqn, RAF.

| Victories: | | | | | |
|---|---|---|---|---|---|
| | 1. | 26 Aug 1918 | Camel | | Bourlonwald |
| | 2. | 2 Sep 1918 | Camel | | Boiry |

## HEISING, Fritz    Hptm

| | | | | |
|---|---|---|---|---|
| FFA6 | 2 Aug 1914 – 7 Sep 1914 | – | CO | |
| FFA10 | 8 Sep 1914 – 6 Feb 1916 | – | J20 | 17 Nov 1916 – 31 Oct 1917    – |
| CO | | | FlgSch | 1 Nov 1917 – 11 Nov 1918    – |
| KG4/23 | 7 Feb 1916 – 17 Nov 1916 | – | | |

Born 7 August 1888, Nieheim/Kreis Höxter. Entered military service 28 May 1908, Infantry Regiment
15, as a Fahrenjunker. Fähnrich on 20 February 1909. Promoted Leutnant 19 November 1909. Pilot's
training from 1 April 1913 to 1 August 1914. Promoted Oberleutnant 18 September 1915. Commanded
Fliegerschulen at Hamburg, Altenberg & Gohn/Potsdam, from 1 Nov 1917 to end of war. Promoted
Hauptmann 18 October 1918. Attained rank of Generalmajor in Luftwaffe during WWII on 1 November
1944. Died 27 July 1963, Köln.

## HELD,    Ltn

J4       22 Oct 1918 – 11 Nov 1918    –
Joined Jasta 4 from Jastaschule II.

## HELDMANN, Alois    Ltn d R

| | | | | |
|---|---|---|---|---|
| FA57 | Aug 1915 – | – | J10 | 24 Jun 1917 – 11 Nov 1918    15 |
| FA59 | | – | | |

Biography & Victories: See *Above the Lines*.

## HELLER, Otto    Vfw

| | | | | |
|---|---|---|---|---|
| J11 | 20 Apr 1917 – 15 May 1917 | – | J24s | 18 Jul 1917 – 18 Dec 1917    2 |
| FAA238 | 15 May 1917 – | – | J42 | 18 Dec 1917 –    – |
| J20 | 29 Jun 1917 – 18 Jun 1917 | – | J40 | – 6 Jun 1918    – KIA |

Born 2 March 1893, Grunau. Reported to Jasta 20 from Jastaschule I. Shot down in flames at 0845
hours during combat with some SE5s over Warneton.

| Victories: | | | | |
|---|---|---|---|---|
| | – | 11 Sep 1917 | Sopwith | 0955 | Passchendaele |
| | – | 12 Nov 1917 | RE8 | 1250 | W Lille |

## HELLINGER, Horst    Ltn d R

J5       Jun 1917 – 2 Jul 1917    –  WIA
Born 2 August 1889, Leipzig. Served in Reserve Infantry Regiment Nr.133. Severely wounded in a
balloon attack at Heudicourt, by protective fire of KBS12, died of wounds. Albatros DV (G.50).

## HELLMANN,    Gefr

J27       15 Dec 1917 – 29 Jan 1918    –  INJ       Idflieg    29 Jan 1918 –
Injured in an accident during take-off.

## HELLWIG, Alexander    Ltn

J77b       14 Nov 1917 – 8 Jul 1918    2       J79b       8 Jul 1918 –       2
Joined Jasta 77b from Jastaschule II.

| Victories: | | | | | |
|---|---|---|---|---|---|
| | 1. | 8 Mar 1918 | Bréguet | 1630 | Oberaspach |
| | 2. | 28 Jun 1918 | BF2b | | |
| | 3. | 8 Aug 1918 | Camel | 1615 | Lamotte |
| | 4. | 11 Aug 1918 | Spad | 0845 | NW Bus |

## HELLWIG, Eduard August      Gefr
J40s                    – 27 Jun 1918    – WIA
Born 16 April 1894, Grebendorf. Wounded over Ploegsteert Wald; died of wounds.

## HELMIGK, Hans     Ltn
J27        6 Jun 1917 – 22 Mar 1918    –                    Rfla501  22 Mar 1918 –                    –
Injured in an accident on 26 July 1917. Lightly wounded in combat 13 December 1917. Transferred to
Riesen Flugzeug-Abteilung 501.

## HELTEN, Hubert     Ltn d R
J20      15 Jan 1918 – 12 Jun 1918    2  KIA
Born 5 October 1891, Krefeld. Joined Jasta 20 from Jastaschule I. Killed over Bailleul.

| Victories: | 1. | 31 May 1918 | SE5a | 1020 | NE Nieppewald |
|---|---|---|---|---|---|
| | 2. | 9 Jun 1918 | Camel | 0930 | S Ploegsteert |

## HEMER, Franz     Ltn d R
FAA283      1917 –                    –                    J6      10 Sep 1917 – 9 Aug 1918      18 WIA
Biography & Victories: See *Above the Lines*.

## HENCKE, Ernst     Ltn d R
J13        (Jun 1918) –                    1                    J31      (Sep 1918) –                    1

| Victories: | 1. | 9 Jun 1918 | SE5a | | Thiescourt |
|---|---|---|---|---|---|
| | 2. | 3 Sep 1918 | Camel | 2010 | Rony-le-Petit |

## HENGST, Friedrich     Ltn d R
KG3                    –                    J64w      6 Feb 1918 – 11 Nov 1918      4
SchSt3    1 Jan 1917 –                    1
Commanded Jasta 64w from 14 September 1918.
Biography & Victories: See *Above the Lines*.

## HENKE,     Vfw
J24        8 Jul 1917 – 26 Aug 1917    –                    AFP4      26 Aug 1917 –                    –
Reported from AFP4.

## HENKEL, Hans     Ltn
J19        Feb 1917 – Sep 1917    –
Joined Jasta 19 from Jastaschule I. Transferred to Albatros Works.

## HENKEL, Heinrich     Ltn d R
J37        May 1918 – 11 Nov 1918    8
Biography & Victories: See *Above the Lines*.

## HENKEL,     Uffz
J61                                          1
Victories:      1.      16 Aug 1918    Spad

## HENN, Josef     Uffz
J53        23 Jan 1918 – 11 Mar 1918    – KIAcc
Born 18 May 1892, Trier. Joined Jasta 53 from Jastaschule I. Killed in an accident shortly after take-
off near Mesnil, at 1230 hours.

## HENNEBEIL, Wilhelm     Vfw
J12        18 Nov 1916 – 4 Dec 1916    – KIA
Born 6 May 1892, Meschede. Killed S Bailleul during combat with FEs.

## HENNIES,     Uffz
J49                    – 2 Sep 1918    – WIA

## HENNIG, Oskar     Uffz
J10        11 Sep 1918 – 11 Nov 1918    –
Joined Jasta 10 from Jastaschule I.

## HENNIG,     Flg
J19        3 Oct 1918 – 11 Nov 1918    –

**HENNRICH, Oskar    Vfw**

| | | | | | |
|---|---|---|---|---|---|
| FAA273 | Oct 1917 – | – | J46 | 6 May 1918 – 11 Nov 1918 | 20 |

Biography & Victories: See *Above the Lines*.

**HENSCHLER, Oskar R    Uffz**

| | | | | | |
|---|---|---|---|---|---|
| J10 | 2 Aug 1918 – 25 Aug 1918 | – | J66 | 25 Aug 1918 – 11 Nov 1918 | 1 |
| Victories: | 1.    29 Aug 1918 | Spad | | Serches | |

**HENSEL, Ernst    Ltn d R**

| | | | |
|---|---|---|---|
| J62 | 1 Feb 1918 – 3 Apr 1918 | – | WIA |

Born 6 December 1893, Berlin. Severely wounded over Courtemanche, and died of wounds 8 April 1918 in a hospital.

**HENSEL,    Uffz**

| | | |
|---|---|---|
| J35b | 3 Oct 1918 – 11 Nov 1918 | – |

Joined Jasta 35b from Jastaschule I.

**HENTSCHEL, Johannes    Ltn**

| | | | | | |
|---|---|---|---|---|---|
| J9 | – 21 Aug 1918 | – INJ | J9 | 8 Oct 1918 – | 1 |
| Hosp | 21 Aug 1918 – 8 Oct 1918 | – | | | |
| Victories: | 1.    23 Oct 1918 | DH9 | 1710 | W Guise | |

**HENTZE, Georg    Vfw**

| | | | | | |
|---|---|---|---|---|---|
| J12 | – 20 Jan 1917 | – | J34 | 25 Feb 1917 – 22 Mar 1917 | – POW |
| J26 | 20 Jan 1917 – 25 Feb 1917 | – | | | |

**HENTZEN, Heinrich    Ltn d R**

| | | |
|---|---|---|
| J9 | | 2 |
| Victories: | 1.    8 Jul 1918 | Spad |
| | 2.    2 Sep 1918 | Spad    1833    W Terny-Sorny |

**HEPP, Rudolf    Ltn**

| | | | | | |
|---|---|---|---|---|---|
| FA65 | | – | J24s | 1 Dec 1916 – 25 Oct 1918 | – |
| J14 | 25 Oct 1916 – 1 Dec 1916 | – | AFPA | 25 Oct 1918 – 11 Nov 1918 | – |

Acting OzbV for Jasta 24s from 17 September to 11 October 1917. Acting CO Jasta 24s from 17 October to 6 November 1917 and 11 April to 2 May 1918. Forced to land at Leffincourt after combat crashing Albatros DII 1731/16 on 27 April 1917.

| | | | | |
|---|---|---|---|---|
| Victories: | 1.    12 Apr 1918 | Sopwith 2 | 1845 | Ribécourt |

**HEPPERLIN,    Uffz**

| | | |
|---|---|---|
| J76b | 30 Jul 1918 – | – |

Joined Jasta 76b from Jastaschule II.

**HEPPNER,    Vfw**

| | | |
|---|---|---|
| Kest 4b | (Jul 1918) – | 1 |
| Victories: | 1.    20 Jul 18 | DH4    Oberndorf |

**HERBST,    Ltn d R**

| | | |
|---|---|---|
| J50 | 1 Jun 1918 – 11 Nov 1918 | – |

Served in Fusilier Rgt 40. OzbV for Jasta 50.

**HERING,    Vfw**

| | |
|---|---|
| J71 | – |

**HERING, Walter    OfStv**

| | | | |
|---|---|---|---|
| J17 | – 7 Aug 1918 | – | KIAcc |

Born 2 November 1892, Osterode. Killed at Vivaise airfield.

**HERMANN,    Gefr**

| | | |
|---|---|---|
| J9 | | 1 |
| Victories: | 1.    31 Jul 1918 | Spad 2    Ilizy |

**HERMANN,    Vfw**

| | | |
|---|---|---|
| J73 | Sep 1918 – 11 Nov 1918 | 1 |
| Victories: | 1.    27 Oct 1918 | Spad    Aisnetel |

## HEROLD, Andreas   Uffz
J77b   17 May 1918 – 1 Jun 1918   – KIA
Born 15 August 1890, Karbach. Joined Jasta 77b from Jastaschule II. Killed at Foucaucourt, at 2030 hours.

## HERRMANN, Paul   Ltn
J31   – 19 Apr 1917   – KIA
Born 10 November 1891, Hamburg. Killed in combat with a Spad over Bois Malval.

## HERRMANN,   Uffz
J5   1917 –   –
Known to have flown Albatros D II 1740/16.

## HERRMANN,   Fw
J67   11 Sep 1918 – 11 Nov 1918   –

## HERRSCHEL,   Ltn
J72s   11 Feb 1918 – 11 Sep 1918   –   FAA231   –
OzbV for Jasta 72s.

## HERTEL, Christoph   Uffz
J10   – 31 May 1917   – INJ

## HERTEL,   Uffz
J40s   27 Apr 1918 – 11 Nov 1918   –

## HERTRICH,   Ltn
J76b   16 Feb 1918 – 6 Apr 1918   –   J76b   27 Jul 1918 – 4 Sep 1918   –
AFP2   6 Apr 1918 – 27 Jul 1918   –   JsSch5   4 Sep 1918 –   –
Joined Jasta 76b from Jastaschule II on 16 February 1918.

## HERTWIG,   Ltn
J40   27 Jun 1917 – Dec 1917   –

## HERTZ, Karl   Ltn d R
J4   7 Sep 1917 – 26 Jan 1918   –   J59   26 Jan 1918 – 9 May 1918   3 KIA
Born 5 August 1893, Hamburg. Killed at 1415 hours Bapaume-Thilloy.

| Victories: | | | | | |
|---|---|---|---|---|---|
| | – | 17 Sep 1917 | Nieuport | 0340 | W Houthulst Wald |
| | 1. | 10 Mar 1918 | Camel | 0730 | Sains-les-Marquion |
| | 2. | 6 Apr 1918 | Camel | | Lens |
| | 3. | 2 May 1918 | Camel | | Chérisy |

## HERTZSCH, Walter   Uffz
J13   – 25 Jun 1918   1 WIA
Born 15 May 1890, Lembach. WIA and severely injured in a crash-landing at Ennemain airfield, Jasta 28w, died 26 June 1918, at Maréchalpot.

| Victories: | 1. | 11 Jun 1918 | SE5a |
|---|---|---|---|

## HERWARTH, Werner   Ltn d R
FA23   –   Idflieg   (May 1917) –   –
J22   Nov 1916 – (May 1917)   1

| Victories: | 1. | 28 May 1917 | Nieuport | Malmaison |
|---|---|---|---|---|

## HESS, Ernst   Ltn d R
FA9/   FA5   – 21 Sep 1916   –
FA62   1914 –   –   J10   21 Sep 1916 –   –
KekD   1   J28w   12 Jun 1917 – 19 Sep 1917   12
FokStC   1   CO J19   19 Sep 1917 – 23 Dec 1917   3 KIA
Biography & Victories: See *Above the Lines*.

## HESS, Konrad   OfStv
J1   23 Aug 1916 – 8 Feb 1917   – KIAcc
Born 14 Feb 1897, Paderborn. Served in FA32 prior to joining Jasta 1. Killed during a test flight over Golancourt.

## HESS, Paul     Uffz
J42                    – 26 Feb 1918    – KIA
Born 4 November 1892, Markersdorf. Shot down near Pannes.

## HESS, Rudolf Walter     Ltn d R
J35b     16 Oct 1918 – 11 Nov 1918    –
Born Alexandria, Egypt, 26 April 1894. Returned to Germany 1908. 1st Bavarian Infantry Rgt, WIA
France 12 June 1916. 18th Bavarian Regt, Romania; WIA. Commissioned 8 October 1917. EKII
21 April 1915. Joined Jasta 35b from Jastaschule II. Hitler's deputy in Nazi party. POW in England
10 May 1941. Died in Spandau prison, 17 August 1987.

## HESS,     Uffz
J60                                           3
| Victories: | 1. | 18 Mar 1918 | Spad | | |
| | 2. | 21 Apr 1918 | SE5a | | SW Noyon |
| | 3. | 23 Apr 1918 | Bréguet | | Noyon |

## HESSE, Konrad     OfStv
FA23     – 23 Aug 1916    –          J1     23 Aug 1916 –           –

## HESSE,     Ltn
J75                                           1
| Victories: | 1. | 12 Aug 1918 | Spad | | Olenberg |

## HESSELINK, Johann     Ltn
FA57                    –          CO J39    4 Feb 1918 – 11 Nov 1918    –
J33     (May 1917) – 4 Feb 1918    1
Acting commander Jasta 33 from 18 June to 14 July 1917.
| Victories: | – | 25 May 1917 | Spad | 1400 | Quémappe | |
| | 1. | 27 May 1917 | Pup | 0730 | SE Hamblain | (a) |
(a) Possibly A7340, No 66 Sqn, RFC, Lt S S Hume, POW.

## HESSLAUER,     Ltn
J78b                    –

## HESTWIG,     Ltn
J9                    –

## HETS, Albert     Ltn d R
J37     (Jun 1918) – 11 Aug 1918    6  KIA
Biography & Victories: See *Above the Lines*.

## HETZE, Kurt     Ltn d R
J13     Jun 1918 – 13 Sep 1918    5  WIA
Biography & Victories: See *Above the Lines*.

## HEUSSLER,     Vfw
J26     20 Jan 1917 – 22 Feb 1917    –          Kofl2    22 Feb 1917 –           –

## HEYDACKER, Renatus     Ltn
J38     (Nov 1917) – 5 Feb 1918    1          CO J25    5 Feb 1918 – 11 Nov 1918    –
OzbV for Jasta 38.
| Victories: | 1. | 29 Oct 1917 | BE12 | | Hodz-Obasi |
| | 2. | 14 Nov 1917 | BE2e | | Adrian See |

## HEYDE, Günther von der     Ltn
J9                    – 21 Apr 1917    – KIA
Born 26 October 1896, Berlin. Served with Infantry Regiment 160. Shot down in flames during combat
with three Spads at 2000 Hours over Nauroy.

## HEYDE,     Vfw
J50                    – 11 Nov 1918    –

## HILBERER, Fritz     Ltn d R
J13                    – 25 Jun 1918    – KIA
Born 3 November 1893, Breisach. Shot down in flames over Chaulnes.

## HILDEBRANDT, Adolf    Ltn d R
J4        28 Aug 1918 – 11 Nov 1918    1
Joined Jasta 4 from Jastaschule I. Died 27 December 1965, Kassel, Germany.
Victories:    1.        3 Nov 1918        Spad XIII            1645            Woevrewald

## HILDEBRANDT, Robert    Ltn
FA56                                        –            CO J69    15 Jul 1918 – 24 Aug 1918    –
J13        (Feb 1918) – 18 May 1918    4            CO J53    28 Aug 1918 – 11 Nov 1918    1
CO J12    18 May 1918 – 15 Jul 1918    1
Biography & Victories: See *Above the Lines*.

## HILGER,    OfStv
J27        22 Apr 1917 – 31 May 1917    –                        31 May 1917 –
Reported from AFP6. Injured in an accident near Bersée, 2 May 1917, flying Roland DII 2851/16. Transferred to Heimatz.

## HILLERBRAND,    Vfw
J32b            – 30 May 1918    – WIA

## HILLMANN, Max    Ltn d R
J7        Oct 1917 – 26 Feb 1918    – WIA        J7        14 Jun 1918 – 18 Jun 1918    1 KIA
Born 20 October 1896, Charlottenberg. Severely injured in crash-landing after combat with DH4s, returned from hospital 14 June 1918. Shot down in flames over St Marguerite.
Victories:    1.        17 Jun 1918        Camel            0800        Dickebusch See

## HILPERT,    OfStv
J12        10 Nov 1916 –                –

## HILPERT,    Ltn
J77b        11 Dec 1917 – 4 Mar 1918    –            AFPB        4 Mar 1918 –            –
Joined Jasta 77b from Jastaschule II.

## HILSCHER,    Gefr
J81                            –

## HILZ, Ludwig    Vfw
FA9b                                1            J40s            – 25 Sep 1917    – WIA
J16        1 Nov 1916 – 7 Feb 1917    –            FlgSchI            –            –
J31        7 Feb 1917 – (Aug 1917)    –            Kest 4b            – 26 Aug 1918    – KIA
Kest 4b    (Aug 1917) –                1
Wounded during combat with a Caudron, was hit by ground fire.
Victories:    1.        12 Oct 1916        Bréguet 5                    Umkirch
            2.        17 Aug 1917        Sopwith 2                    Hirzfelden        (a)
(a) Probably Adj Maneval (P) & Cpl Gaillard (G) of Escadrille Sop 123.

## HIMMER, Theodor    Vfw
J34b        6 Mar 1917 – 17 Dec 1917    1            J37        (Sep 1918) –            1
Idflieg    17 Dec 1917 –                –
Joined Jasta 34 from FEA1. Awarded EKI.
Victories:    1.        29 Apr 1917        Farman                    Génicourt
            2.        5 Sep 1918        SE5a            1210        NE Ribécourt

## HINKE,    Ltn
JGr7        (Jul 1918) –                –
Staff Jagdgruppe 7.

## HINKY,    Ltn
J44s            – 27 Oct 1918    – WIA

## HINNEBERG,    Ltn
J58        26 Jan 1918 – 11 Nov 1918    2
Victories:    1.        11 Apr 1918        RE8                    Lens
            2.        22 Aug 1918        DH4            1410        Ablainville

## HINTSCH, Hans    Ltn d R
J11        12 Oct 1916 – 24 May 1917   2   KIA
Born 30 March 1894, Bremen. First victory with an unknown unit in 1916. Killed over Izel at 0930 hours flying Albatros DIII 2016/16.

| Victories: | 1. | Date and unit unknown | | | | |
|---|---|---|---|---|---|---|
| | 2. | 13 May 1917 | Nieuport | 2120 | E Fresnes | (a) |
| | 3. | 23 May 1917 | Triplane | 2115 | Carvin | (b) |

(a) Probably A6665, No 29 Sqn, RFC, Sgt W H Dunn, POW.
(b) Probably N5481, No 8 Sqn, RNAS, F/S/Lt H A Pailthorpe, KIA.

## HIOB, Paul    Vfw
J13        – 20 Feb 1918   2   KIAcc
Born 25 February 1895, Benzhausen. Killed over Reneuil Ferme, flying a two-seater with Ltn d R Wolfgang Güttler as passenger.

| Victories: | 1. | 20 Aug 1917 | Spad | | Esnes |
|---|---|---|---|---|---|
| | 2. | 3 Jan 1918 | AR2 | | Aisne-Staubecken |

## HIPPEL, Hans Joachim von    Ltn
FA37      Oct 1917 –                   1          J71    15 Aug 1918 – 11 Nov 1918   –
J5        22 Dec 1917 – 15 Aug 1918    1
Served in Field Artillery Rgt 4. Promoted to Leutnant in May 1915. Transferred to aviation in November 1916. Continued to fly between the wars and flew Ju52s in the Luftwaffe during 1940-41 as an Oberleutnant. Died 6 August 1975, Boppard/Rhine, Germany.

| Victories: | 1. | 30 Oct 1917 | Nieuport 17 | | Russian Lines | (a) |
|---|---|---|---|---|---|---|
| | 2. | 19 Jan 1918 | SE5a | 1000 | W Vendhuille | |
| | – | 22 Aug 1918 | Spad XIII | 0900 | Sennheim | |
| | – | 27 Oct 1918 | Spad | | Hartmannsweiler | |

(a) Ltn König was his observer.

## HIPPERT, Wilhelm    OfStv
FAA227    1917 –                       –          J74    5 Mar 1918 – 11 Nov 1918   3
J39       Oct 1917 – 5 Mar 1918        5
Biography & Victories: See *Above the Lines*.

## HIRSCHFELD,    Oblt
J51                                    –

## HIRSCHFELD,    Ltn d R
J4        Jul 1918 – 28 Aug 1918       –          J81    28 Aug 1918 – 31 Aug 1918  – WIA

## HIRTH,    Ltn
J2        – 20 Oct 1916                –          Idflieg   20 Oct 1916 –

## HITSCHLER,    Uffz
J18       1 Dec 1917 – 28 Jan 1918     –          J57    28 Jan 1918 – 11 Nov 1918  –

## HOBEIN, Bruno Richard Louis    Ltn d R
J3        9 Aug 1917 – 24 Feb 1918     –          JsSchII  2 May 1918 – 2 Jul 1918    –
J20       24 Feb 1918 – 2 May 1918     1          J20      3 Jul 1918 – 24 Sep 1918   2 WIA
Joined Jasta 3 from AFP4.

| Victories: | 1. | Date and unit unknown | | | |
|---|---|---|---|---|---|
| | 2. | 16 Mar 1918 | Camel | 0715 | Neuville |
| | 3. | 2 Sep 1918 | BF2b | 2000 | Gheluvelt |
| | 4. | 5 Sep 1918 | BF2b | 1350 | Espirès |
| | – | 13 Sep 1918 | BF2b | | |
| | – | 13 Sep 1918 | BF2b | | |

## HOCHSTETTER, Friedrich    Ltn d R
J12       31 Mar 1917 –                1
Württemberg Gold Military Merit Medal on 21 December 1917.

| Victories: | 1. | 26 May 1917 | Pup | 0810 | Cagnicourt |
|---|---|---|---|---|---|

## HÖFER, Ernst    Vfw

| | | | | | | |
|---|---|---|---|---|---|---|
| FA20 | | – | AFPC | | – | |
| J23 | 4 Apr 1917 – 14 Jul 1917 | – | J34b | 16 Dec 1917 – 20 Dec 1917 | – | |
| FEA1b | | | J42 | 20 Dec 1917 – 5 Feb 1918 | – | WIA |

## HÖFIG,    Ltn

| | | | |
|---|---|---|---|
| J37 | – 24 Jul 1918 | – | KIA |

## HÖHN, Fritz    Ltn d R

| | | | | | | |
|---|---|---|---|---|---|---|
| FAA227 | | – | CO J60 | 9 Sep 1918 – 29 Sep 1918 | 6 | |
| J21s | (Nov 1917) – 1 Sep 1918 | 10 | CO J41 | 30 Sep 1918 – 3 Oct 1918 | 3 | KIA |
| CO J81 | 1 Sep 1918 – 9 Sep 1918 | 2 | | | | |

Biography & Victories: See *Above the Lines*.

## HÖHNDORF, Walter    Ltn d R

| | | | | | |
|---|---|---|---|---|---|
| FA12 | – 1916 | 2 | J1 | 23 Aug 1916 – 1 Sep 1916 | 1 |
| KekV | – 23 Aug 1916 | 9 | J4 | 1 Sep 1916 – | – |

Biography & Victories: See *Above the Lines*.

## HÖHNDORF,    Uffz

| | | |
|---|---|---|
| J18 | 31 Aug 1917 – Dec 1917 | – |

## HÖHNE, Otto Walter    Ltn d R

| | | | | | |
|---|---|---|---|---|---|
| KekN | – 23 Aug 1916 | – | CO J59 | 27 Dec 1917 – 26 Jan 1917 | – |
| J1 | 23 Aug 1916 – 29 Aug 1916 | – | CO J2 | 26 Jan 1918 – 20 Feb 1918 | – |
| J2 | 29 Aug 1916 – 10 Jan 1917 | 6 WIA | | | |

Biography & Victories: See *Above the Lines*.

## HÖHNE, Walter    Uffz

| | | |
|---|---|---|
| J61 | Apr 1918 – (Jun 1918) | – |
| Victories: | 1.    27 Jun 1918 | Balloon |

## HÖHNE,    Uffz

| | | | |
|---|---|---|---|
| J37 | – 9 May 1918 | – | INJ |

## HÖNLE,    Uffz

| | | |
|---|---|---|
| J26 | Jan 1918 – 27 Jan 1918 | – |

## HÖNEMANNS, Erich    Oblt

| | | | | | |
|---|---|---|---|---|---|
| CO J12 | 8 Oct 1916 – 26 Nov 1916 | – | Idflieg | 29 Jun 1917 – | – |
| CO J22 | 26 Nov 1916 – 29 Jun 1917 | – | | | |

Born 20 November 1887, Hannover. Promoted Oberleutnant 25 February 1915. Held rank of Major d R in WWII, taken prisoner 10 January 1940, sent to England, then Canada. Repatriated 1943. Died 10 April 1969, Köln-Marienberg, Germany.

## HÖRING,    Ltn d R

| | | | | | |
|---|---|---|---|---|---|
| J35 | 25 Feb 1917 – 25 Jul 1917 | – | FEA3 | 25 Jul 1917 – | – |

Joined Jasta 35 from FEA6. OzbV for Jasta 35.

## HÖSRICH,    Uffz

| | | | | |
|---|---|---|---|---|
| J62 | 20 Jul 1918 – 11 Nov 1918 | 1 | | |
| Victories: | 1.    30 Oct 1918 | Spad | | Romagne |

## HÖVELHAUS,    Ltn

| | |
|---|---|
| J33 | – |

Lightly wounded on 12 April 1918.

## HOFACKER, Hans    Ltn d R

| | | | |
|---|---|---|---|
| J33 | 30 Nov 1917 – 30 Nov 1917 | – | WIA |

Born 15 October 1891, Offenberg, Baden. Brother of Wilhelm Hofacker. Assigned to Infantry Rgt 170 on mobilisation. Promoted Leutnant d R 21 October 1914. Served as an observer in FFA43. Awarded EK I on 18 July 1916. Awarded the Baden Ritterkreuz II Klasse mit Schwerten des Ordens vom Zähringer Löwen on 14 October 1916. Wounded over Havrincourt, DOW 1 Dec 1917 (see *OTF*, Vol 4, No 4, pg 319).

**HOFACKER, Wilhelm      Uffz**
J65        23 Feb 1918 – 30 Aug 1918     1   KIA
Born 10 February 1894, Offenberg, Baden. Brother of Hans Hofacker. Joined Jasta 65 from Jastaschule I. Killed in combat with a DH4 near Hermeville.

| Victories: | 1. | 23 Aug 1918 | Caudron | | Gironville | (a) |
|---|---|---|---|---|---|---|

(a) 20th victory for Jasta 65.
(See *OTF*, Vol 4, No 4, pg 319.)

**HOFFMANN, Friedrich      Ltn**
J11        30 May 1918 – 30 Jun 1918     –   KIA
Born 27 July 1896, Gardenheim. Served in Infantry Regiment 116. Killed at 2000 hours over Passy.

**HOFFMANN, Fritz Paul      Ltn d R**
JB        25 Aug 1918 – 29 Sep 1918     1   KIA
Born 5 June 1896, Dronecken. Killed W Cambrai, possibly by 2/Lts N J Nock & W E Grainger, No 10 Sqn, RAF.

| Victories: | 1. | 16 Sep 1918 | BF2b | | SW Cambrai |
|---|---|---|---|---|---|

**HOFFMANN, Gerhard      Ltn d R**
J68        17 Mar 1918 – 9 Oct 1918     –   KIA
Born 6 October 1894, Brostau. Killed over Preutin. Joined Jasta 68 from Jastaschule I.

**HOFFMANN, Kurt      Uffz**
J51              – 24 Jul 1918     –   KIA
Born 14 August 1896, Weimar. Collided with Vfw Beinecke in mid-air during combat over Pont Rouge.

**HOFFMANN, Paul      Ltn d R**
FAA224        – 1918     –        J12     10 Jan 1918 – 1 Apr 1918     1   WIA
Born 3 March 1893, Banth. Wounded over Montdidier, died 2 Apr 1918, in Field Hospital 48.

| Victories: | 1. | 29 Jan 1918 | Camel | 1630 | Méricourt |
|---|---|---|---|---|---|

**HOFFMANN, Walter      Uffz**
J5        Sep 1916 – 22 Feb 1917     2        J36     22 Feb 1917 – 16 Aug 1917     1   KIA
Born 6 January 1896, Sportehnen. Killed near Merkem-Dixmuiden.

| Victories: | 1. | 4 Jan 1917 | ? | | Clery |
|---|---|---|---|---|---|
| | 2. | 24 Jan 1917 | Caudron | | Harbonnières |
| | 3. | 12 Aug 1917 | Rumpf DD | 0850 | Boesinghe |

(See *C&C GB* Vol 20, No 1, pg 38.)

**HOFFMANN,      Uffz**
J1              – 4 May 1918     –        FEA1b     21 Oct 1918 –          –
J77b        4 May 1918 – 21 Oct 1918     –

**HOFFMANN,      Flg**
J24s        11 Jul 1918 – 11 Nov 1918     –
Lightly injured 13 August 1918, in crash-landing.

| Victories: | – | 4 Nov 1918 | BF2b | 1140 | Mormal Woods |
|---|---|---|---|---|---|

**HOFFMANN,      Sgt**
J83              2

| Victories: | 1. | 16 Sep 1918 | Spad | 0740 | SW Frescaty |
|---|---|---|---|---|---|
| | 2. | 5 Oct 1918 | DH9a | | Trippstadt |

**HOFMANN, Karl      Uffz**
J60              – 28 Sep 1918     1   KIA
Born 3 November 1892, Stuttgart. Killed over Argonne Forest.

| Victories: | 1. | 26 Sep 1918 | Spad | 0900 | Massiges |
|---|---|---|---|---|---|

**HOFMANN,      Vfw**
J35b        6 Jun 1918 – 11 Nov 1918     1
Joined Jasta 35b from Jastaschule I.

| Victories: | 1. | 13 Sep 1918 | DH4 | 1050 | Récourt |
|---|---|---|---|---|---|

## HOFMANN, Ltn
J79b                                        1
Victories:      1.        Unknown date and unit
                2.        7 Sep 1918        Spad                      0810                Villequier-Aumont

## HOFMEISTER, Otto    Ltn d R
J79b              – 11 Oct 1918    –  KIAcc
Born 6 September 1895, Munich. Killed during test flight of Pfalz DXII 2581/18 over La Flamangrie.

## HOHENAU, Friedrich-Franz Graf von    Ltn
J11        26 Jun 1918 – 25 Jul 1918    –  WIA
Born 7 July 1896, Dresden. Served in LK Rgt 1. Severely wounded in combat at 1945 hours, died next day (26th) in hospital at Grugny.

## HOHLY, Josef    Vfw
J29        8 Dec 1917 – 8 Feb 1918    –              J65        8 Feb 1918 – 2 Oct 1918        7    WIA
Biography & Victories: See *Above the Lines*.

## HOHMUTH, Otto    Ltn d R
FAA267  11 Apr 1917 – 30 Jun 1917    2              J23b      20 Sep 1917 – 6 Mar 1918        2    POW
J32b      9 Jul 1917 – 20 Sep 1917    –
Born 3 October 1892, Meersburg. Volunteered 23 Aug 1914 assigned to Garde Fuss Artillery Regiment 2, Jüterborg. Transferred to aviation June 1916. Flight training at FEA11 Breslau as Vfw. Jastaschule on 1 July 1917. Forced down intact during combat with a RE8 of No 13 Sqn, RFC, 2/Lt F Belway & 1/AM F Rose, S Feuchy, flying Albatros DV 2359/17 (G.144). EKII on 4 May 1917
Victories:      1.        13 May 1917       Spad                                          Ft Pompelle          (a)
                2.        13 May 1917       Spad                                          Ft Pompelle          (a)
                3.        12 Dec 1917       Caudron              1508                     S Bras
                4.        19 Jan 1918       Balloon              1520                     Belleville
(a) With his observer, Ltn Wagner.

## HOLLE, Ltn
J31              – 27 Sep 1918    1  WIA
Victories:      1.        16 Sep 1918       DH9                  0915                     NE Douchy

## HOLLE, Ltn
J79b              –

## HOLLER, Carl    Vfw
FA71              –                              FA71                                          –
J6        Jan 1917 – May 1917    2
Victories:      zlg       11 Feb 1917       Caudron              1630                     SW Péronne
                1.        19 May 1917       FE2b                 1720                     Villers Guislain
                2.        30 May 1917       Pup                  0810                     Beaurevoir           (a)
(a) Probably B1721, No 54 Sqn, RFC, Lt F W Kantel, POW.

## HOLSMINT,    ?
J32              –

## HOLTHAUS, Friedrich    Ltn d R
J48        1 Jun 1918 – 5 Jun 1918    –  KIA
Born 18 June 1898, Duisburg. Joined Jasta 48 from Jastaschule I. Killed near Moyencourt airfield, ground fire.

## HOLTHUSEN, Hans    Ltn d R
J30        6 Oct 1917 – 29 Sep 1918    2              CO J29   29 Sep 1918 – 11 Nov 1918      –
Joined Jasta 30 from Jastaschule I. Acting CO Jasta 30 from 1 Aug to 14 August 1918.
Victories:      1.        21 May 1918       Camel                1100                     Calonne
                2.        10 Jul 1918       Camel                1109                     Kemmel               (a)
                –        14 Jul 1918       SE5a                 0940                     Merris
(a) Possibly D9500, No 43 Sqn, RAF, Lt C B Ridley.

## HOLTZEM, Max    Vfw
FA9        1914 – Sep 1914    –  Hosp              FEA      18 Aug 1915 – 21 Jul 1916        –
FA34      12 Oct 1914 – 17 Apr 1915    –              J16b     22 Sep 1917 – 11 Nov 1918        –
Born 1 December 1892, Elberfeld. Entered military service 14 October 1913, Flieger Battalion Nr.3.

Earned his Military Pilot's Badge 22 April 1914. Assigned to Pfalz Factory 17 April 1915. Promoted Unteroffizier 27 January 1916; Vizefeldwebel 11 April 1918. Assigned back to Pfalz Factory as a test pilot, 21 July 1916. Awarded Iron Cross 2nd Class 26 January 1918. Awarded Bavarian Military Merit Order with Swords Demobilised 16 December 1918.

Victories:        –        18 Mar 1918        SE5
(See *C&C US*, Vol 12, No 2, pp 169-186; obituary in *C&C* Vol 21, No 2, pg 132.)

## HONIG, Emmerich     Ltn
J14                   – 4 Jun 1918        – KIAcc
Born 11 July 1895, Allenstein, served in Infantry Regiment z Pf 12. Killed in test flight at Phalempin.

## HOPFER,     Ltn
J26                                       –
Joined Jasta 26 from FEA9. OzbV for Jasta 26.

## HOPPE, Paul     Uffz
J5        Oct 1916 – 6 Apr 1917        2 KIA
Born 9 February 1895, Braunschweig. Collided with Oblt Hans Berr during combat with a FE2d over Noyelles, at 0810 hours; killing both. Known to have flown Albatros D III 2241/16.

| Victories: | | | | | |
|---|---|---|---|---|---|
| 1. | 11 Mar 1917 | DH2 | | Bapaume |
| 2. | 25 Mar 1917 | Sopwith 2 | 0920 | W Beugny |

## HOPPE,     Vfw
J8                                   1
| Victories: | 1. | 21 Jul 1918 | Spad | 1925 | Reimser Wald |

## HOPPE,     Vfw
J22        Nov 1916 – (May 1917)        –

## HORN, Eberhard     Ltn
J3        – 10 Jul 1918        – INJ
Injured during a test flight of a Pfalz DXII.

## HORN, Eduard     Vfw
J21        – 4 May 1917        1 KIA
Born 16 May 1890, Rasvitch. Killed between Berru and Witry-les-Reims.
| Victories: | 1. | 12 Apr 1917 | Nieuport 2 | 1100 | S Nauroy |

## HORN, Leohard     Gefr
J16b     6 May 1918 – 8 Jun 1918        – WIA
Wounded over Houthulst Wald.

## HORN, Walter     Fw
J37        – 4 Dec 1917        1 KIA
Born 12 July 1891, Serkowitz. Killed over Wynghene.
| Victories: | 1. | 24 Nov 1917 | RE8 | 0920 | SE St Jean |

## HORNFISCHER, Otto     Ltn d R
J23b     23 May 1918 – 27 May 1918        – KIA
Born 27 April 1898, Weiden. Collided in mid-air with Ltn Hausner over Bourlon.

## HORST, Hans     Vfw
J7        Apr 1917 – May 1918        2        J81        May 1918 – 11 Nov 1918        2

| Victories: | 1. | 14 Aug 1917 | Balloon | | NE Poperinghe |
|---|---|---|---|---|---|
| | 2. | 22 Aug 1917 | Pup | 1845 | Houthulst Wald |
| | zlg | 12 Dec 1917 | Spad | 1615 | S Houthulst Wald |
| | 3. | 28 Jun 1918 | Spad | | Courmes |
| | 4. | 3 Aug 1918 | Spad | | Jonchéry |

## HORST,     Ltn
J26        Feb 1917 – 9 Oct 1917        –        AFP4        9 Oct 1917 –        –

## HORST, Fr von der     Ltn
J30        22 Aug 1917 – 6 May 1918        –        Idflieg        6 May 1918 –        –
Joined Jasta 30 from Jastaschule I.

## HORSTMANN, Hermann    Flg
J22    – 13 Aug 1918  –  KIAcc
Born Meidrich, 24 September 1899. Collided in mid-air with Ltn Hüfner, at 1100 over Balâtre.

## HOSPELT,    Ltn
J9                                                              2
| Victories: | 1. | 16 May 1918 | Bréguet | 1125 | SE Guny |
|---|---|---|---|---|---|
| | 2. | 31 Aug 1918 | Spad | 1841 | E Jurigny |

## HOSRICH,    Uffz
J62    20 Jul 1918 – 11 Nov 1918    1
| Victories: | 1. | 30 Oct 1918 | Spad | | Romagne |
|---|---|---|---|---|---|

## HOWE, Hans    Fw
| FA5b | | – | J11 | 11 Oct 1916 – 17 Feb 1917 | – |
|---|---|---|---|---|---|
| J10 | 21 Sep 1916 – 11 Oct 1916 | – | AFP6 | 17 Feb 1917 – | – |

Also served in KEK 3.

## HOYER, Hans    Ltn d R
| FA10 | | – | J36 | Jul 1917 – 15 Nov 1917 | 8  KIA |
|---|---|---|---|---|---|
| FFA270 | | – | | | |

Biography & Victories: See *Above the Lines.*

## HUAR,    Vfw
J68    18 May 1198 – 26 Sep 1918    3  WIA
| Victories: | 1. | 27 Jun 1918 | Balloon | 1950 | Estrées-St Dénis |
|---|---|---|---|---|---|
| | 2. | 19 Jul 1918 | Balloon | 1435 | Mourmelon-le-Petit |
| | 3. | 2 Sep 1918 | Bréguet | | Reimser Wald |

## HUBNER,    Uffz
J22    2 Feb 1917 –                         –

## HUCHLER, Anton    Flg
J39    – 4 Nov 1917  –  KIA
Born 15 December 1886, Hochdorf, Waldsee. Killed over Cividale, Italy.

## HÜBNER, Alfred    Ltn d R
J4    24 Jun 1917 – 14 Aug 1917    4  KIA
Born 1 September 1894, Dresden. Served in Field Artillery Regiment Nr.12. Killed at 2035 hours over Moorslede, in an Albatros DV with white wings, yellow fuselage and black tail, probably by pilots of No 1 Sqn, RFC.
| Victories: | 1. | 12 Jul 1917 | Triplane | 2120 | Zuidschoote |
|---|---|---|---|---|---|
| | 2. | 31 Jul 1917 | RE8 | 1250 | S Zillebeke See |
| | 3. | 4 Aug 1917 | Caudron | 2055 | Beninghe |
| | 4. | 13 Aug 1917 | Sopwith | 2100 | S St Jean |

(See *C&C* Vol 8 No 3, pg 224.)

## HÜBNER, Alfred    Vfw
J36    14 Feb 1918 – 11 Nov 1918    6
Biography & Victories: See *Above the Lines.*

## HÜBNER, Fedor    Ltn
J4    30 Mar 1918 – 16 May 1918    2  POW
Shot down during combat with Camels at 1615 hours over Corbie, flying Fokker DrI 546/17 (G/5/8), by Capt S T Edwards, Lt M S Taylor, and Lt W R May, No 209 Sqn, RAF, in Camels B7199, D3329 and B6398 respectively.
| Victories: | 1. | 12 Apr 1918 | Spad | 1400 | Bayonvillers |
|---|---|---|---|---|---|
| | 2. | 3 May 1918 | AWFK8 | 1145 | SW Albert |

## HÜBNER,    Vfw
J67    23 Mar 1918 – 11 Nov 1918    –

## HÜBNER,    Ltn
J73    22 Jun 1918 – 11 Nov 1918    1
| Victories: | 1. | 24 Oct 1918 | Salmson | | Asfeld |
|---|---|---|---|---|---|

**HÜLS,    Ltn**
J5           Oct 1918 – 11 Nov 1918    –

---

**HÜNERBEIN, Hans von       Hptm a D**
J8          (Apr 1917) – 7 Apr 1917     1              CO J5     7 Apr 1917 – 4 May 1917    – KIAcc
Born 7 February 1879, Volkershausen. Killed during a test flight of SSW DI 3761/16 at the Boistrancourt
airfield.
Victories:        1.           7 Apr 1917          Nieuport 17                                Becelaere

---

**HÜNNINGHAUS, Heinrich      OfStv**
J66                  – 11 Nov 1918    4
Victories:        1.          6 Jul 1918          Spad 2
                  2.          31 Jul 1918         Spad 2
                  3.          22 Sep 1918         Spad                        Pont Arcy
                  4.          29 Sep 1918         Spad                        N Jouy

---

**HÜTTENRAUCH, Paul      Uffz**
J7          Feb 1918 – 11 Nov 1918    8
Biography & Victories: See *Above the Lines.*

---

**HÜTTERER, Michael      Uffz**
J23          23 May 1918 – 11 Nov 1918    8
Biography & Victories: See *Above the Lines.*

---

**HÜTTNER,      OfStv**
J14          16 Oct 1916 – (Sep 1917)     3
Victories:        1.          11 Feb 1917         Nieuport          1530          Gerden
                  2.          11 Apr 1917         Spad              1145          Berry-au-Bac
                  3.          5 May 1917          Balloon                         Craonne

---

**HÜTTNER,      Gefr**
J76b          23 Feb 1918 – 6 Apr 1918    –              AFP2       6 Apr 1918 –              –
Joined Jasta 76b from Jastaschule II.

---

**HÜTTNER,      Uffz**
J78b          27 Jul 1918 – 24 Aug 1918    –             AFPA       24 Aug 1918 –             –
Joined Jasta 78b from AFP A.

---

**HUGEL, Ludwig      Gefr**
J65          4 Oct 1918 – 28 Oct 1918    – KIA
Born 25 September 1888, Münster. Shot down in flames at 1300 hours during combat with three Spads
NW Pont-à-Mousson.

---

**HUHLE,      Fw**
J36          22 Jun 1918 – 11 Nov 1918    –
Joined Jasta 36 from Jastaschule I.

---

**HUISSEL,      Uffz**
Kest 8          (Sep 1918) –             –

---

**HUMMELL, Hans      Ltn**
J77b          13 Jul 1918 – 2 Aug 1918    –              J49       2 Aug 1918 – 11 Nov 1918    –
Joined Jasta 77b from AFP13.

---

**HUNOLTSTEIN, Gustav Fr von      Ltn**
J32b          16 Sep 1917 – 11 Nov 1918    –
OzbV for Jasta 32b.

---

**HUNZINGER, Otto      Ltn**
J2          (Jun 1917) – 1 Oct 1917    –              AFP4       1 Oct 1917 –              –

---

**HUPFER,      Ltn d R**
J26                  – 11 Nov 1918    –
OzbV for Jasta 26.

---

## HURRLE, Albert    Vfw

| | | | | | |
|---|---|---|---|---|---|
| FAA243 | 1917 | 1 | J13 | Oct 1917 – 30 Jan 1918 | 2    KIA |

Born 13 December 1889, Rastatt, Baden. Killed over Lavergny-Ferme.

| Victories: | 1. | 17 Jun 1917 | Spad | Goldbach | (a) |
|---|---|---|---|---|---|
| | 2. | 26 Sep 1917 | Spad | Pinon | |
| | 3. | 29 Jan 1918 | Caudron | G.4 Remigny | |

(a) Observer was Ltn d R Spieler.
(See *OTF*, Vol 4, No 4, pg 319.)

## HURRLE,    Vfw

| | | | | | |
|---|---|---|---|---|---|
| FFA229 | 1917 – 29 Aug 1917 | – | AFP7 | 5 Dec 1917 – 24 Dec 1917 | – |
| JsSch | 29 Aug 1917 – 17 Sep 1917 | – | J45 | 25 Dec 1917 –   3 Apr 1918 | –    POW |
| J34 | 18 Sep 1917 – 5 Dec 1917 | – | | | |

Served in Infantry. Transferred to aviation in October 1916. AFP10 in July 1917, then to Russia. Shot down by ground fire at 0850 hours near Bailly, on an Albatros DV. (See French VI° Armée Prisoner Interrogation Report.)

## HUSTER,    Uffz

| | |
|---|---|
| J58 | 10 Aug 1918 – 11 Nov 1918    – |

## HUTH, Joachim-Friedrich    Ltn d R

| | |
|---|---|
| J14 | 7 Jun 1917 – 23 Mar 1918    1    WIA |

Born 31 July 1896, Neuhof/Kreis-Osterberg/Sachsen. Entered military service 13 July 1914, Infantry Regiment Nr.58. Promoted Leutnant d R 4 January 1915. Severely wounded, hospitalised until 8 April 1919. Ritterkreuz on 11 September 1940. Attained rank of Generalleutnant in Luftwaffe during WWII, on 1 July 1944. Died 27 March 1962, Koblenz.

| Victories: | 1. | 28 Jan 1918 | Balloon | 1520 | NE Septsaulx |
|---|---|---|---|---|---|

## HUTHMACHER,    Uffz

| | |
|---|---|
| J36 | 16 Sep 1918 – 11 Nov 1918    – |

## IHDE, Rudolf    Flg

| | |
|---|---|
| J10 | 14 Mar 1918 – 18 Mar 1918    –    KIA |

Born 20 October 1895, Waren. Killed at 1120 hours over Anbigny.

## IHLE, Georg    Uffz

| | |
|---|---|
| J52 | 2 Sep 1918 – 11 Nov 1918    – |

Joined Jasta 52 from Jastaschule I.

## IHLE, Max    Ltn d R

| | | | | | |
|---|---|---|---|---|---|
| FEA1 | 27 Dec 1914 – | – | KG6/34 | 1 Apr 1916 – 19 Dec 1916 | – |
| AFP2 | 29 Jul 1915 – | – | J23 | 29 Dec 1916 – 7 May 1917 | – |
| FA1b | 9 Sep 1915 – 3 Mar 1916 | – | AFP C | 8 May 1917 – | – |
| FEA1 | 4 Mar 1916 – 31 Mar 1916 | – | Kest 7 | | – |

Pilot's Badge on 10 July 1915. Promoted Leutnant 23 January 1916. EKII on 27 Jan 1916. Bavarian Military Merit Order 4th Class with Swords on 10 April 1916. EKI 27 January 1917. Knight's Cross 2nd Class with Swords of the Württemberg Friedrich Order on 2 Nov 1917.

## ILLIG,    Ltn

| | |
|---|---|
| J77b | 6 Feb 1918 – 2 Sep 1918    – |

Joined Jasta 77b from Jastaschule I. OzbV for Jasta 77b from 29 Apr to 2 Sep 1918.

## IMELMANN, Hans    Ltn d R

| | | | | | |
|---|---|---|---|---|---|
| Kek M | – Oct 1916 | – | JB | Oct 1916 – 23 Jan 1917 | 6    KIA |

Biography & Victories: See *Above the Lines*.

## IMME, Fritz    Ltn d R

| | | | | | |
|---|---|---|---|---|---|
| J34b | 9 Dec 1917 – 11 Dec 1917 | – | J42 | 11 Dec 1917 – 11 Jun 1918 | 1    KIA |

Born 12 November 1897, Halle. Joined Jasta 34b from Jastaschule I. Killed over Mery.

| Victories: | 1. | 17 May 1918 | Spad | |
|---|---|---|---|---|

## IVERSEN,    Vfw

| | | | | | |
|---|---|---|---|---|---|
| J41 | – 9 Jan 1918 | 1 | J56 | 9 Jan 1918 – 6 Jun 1918 | – |

Sick leave 6 June 1918.

| Victories: | 1. | 6 Dec 1917 | Nieuport | N Fontaine |
|---|---|---|---|---|

## JACOB, Fritz    Uffz
J12        13 Nov 1917 – 24 Jan 1918      – KIA
Born 9 September 1892, Schlesien. Killed over Izel.

## JACOB, Kurt    Ltn
J33        (Jul 1917) – (Jan 1918)     1          J36        2 May 1918 – 18 Jul 1918      6  WIA
Biography & Victories: See *Above the Lines*.

## JACOBS, Josef Carl Peter    Ltn d R
| FFA11/ | | | J12 | Oct 1916 – 26 Nov 1916 | – |
| FSW | – | | J22 | 26 Nov 1916 – 2 Aug 1917 | 3 |
| Kek W | 1 | | CO J7 | 5 Aug 1917 – 11 Nov 1918 | 44 |

Biography & Victories: See *Above the Lines*.

## JACOBSEN, Fritz John    Vfw
| FA1 | May 1915 – | – | J31 | 15 Dec 1916 – 5 Mar 1918 | 2 |
| J17 | 11 Nov 1916 – Dec 1916 | – | J73 | 5 Mar 1918 – 11 Nov 1918 | 6 |
| J9 | Dec 1916 – 15 Dec 1916 | – | | | |

Biography & Victories: See *Above the Lines*.

## JÄGER, Karl    Flg
J31            – 7 Nov 1917      – KIA
Born 27 February 1892, Buschoff. Killed over Cividale.

## JÄGER, Paul    Ltn d R
J9            – 16 Mar 1918    1  KIA
Born 12 June 1892, Ibar. Killed at 1755 hours over Berru.
Victories:    1.        6 Mar 1918      Balloon           0900           Mourmelon-le-Grand

## JÄGER,    Vfw
J20        29 Apr 1917 – 6 May 1917      – INJ
Joined Jasta 20 from AFP2. Severely injured in a landing accident.

## JÄNICKE, Paul    Ltn d R
J22            – 4 Jun 1917      – KIA
Born 19 January 1890, Leipzig, Saxony. Shot down in flames over Vregny, possibly by MdL Paris of N65.

## JÄSCHKE, Alfred    OfStv
J30.        19 Aug 1918 – 28 Oct 1918      – POW
Forced to come down in Allied lines near Tournai, and taken prisoner, flying a Fokker DVII (G/2/28).

## JAGLA,    Vfw
J11        11 May 1918 – 29 Jul 1918      –          AFP7        29 Jul 1918 –              –

## JAHN,    Vfw
Kest 1a    (Sep 1918) – (Oct 1918)      –

## JAHNKE,    Uffz
J9                                    –

## JAHNKE,    Vfw
J21            – 22 Aug 1917      – WIA

## JAHNKE,    Uffz
J27            – 11 Nov 1918    2
Victories:    1.        28 Oct 1918      EA
              2.        30 Oct 1918      Dolphin

## JAHNS, Werner    Oblt
J18        13 Jun 1917 – 4 Sep 1917     1          CO J28     4 Sep 1917 – 24 Sep 1917      – KIA
Born 9 April 1892, Grossjablau-Danzig, West Prussen. Killed at 1530 hours SE Slype.
Victories:    1.        12 Jul 1917      Spad              1515           Quesnoy              (a)
(a) Probably A6633, No 19 Sqn, RFC, Lt D W Weld.

**JAKOB, Uffz**
J17 (Sep 1918) – 11 Nov 1918 1
Victories: 1. 2 Sep 1918 Spad 2 1100 Savigny

**JAKOBOWITZ, Martin Fw**
KG 1/2 – J25 (Apr 1917) – 1
Victories: 1. 29 Apr 1917 Nieuport Skochivir

**JAKOBS, Friedrich Ltn d R**
J43 6 Jul 1918 – 11 Nov 1918 1
Wounded in action 24 July 1918; shot through foot.
Victories: 1. 22 Jul 1918 DH9 0855 Cysoing

**JANDER, Hermann Flg**
J24s 11 Jun 1918 – 23 Aug 1918 – KIA
Born 1 February 1898, Peine. Reported from AFP18. Flying a Fokker DVII when killed in combat with three Spads from Escadrille Spa 86 at 1010 hours south of Blérancourt.

**JANISZEWSKI, Johann Gefr**
J71 – 19 Jun 1918 – J75 19 Jun 1918 – 12 Aug 1918 – KIA
Born 27 May 1895, Siebenschleissen. Killed during combat at 1710 hours over Fontaine; ID card shows he belonged to Jasta 75 from 19 June 1918, and a personal letter written 8 June 1918 was addressed to Jasta 71.

**JANSEN, Ltn**
Kest 8w – 27 May 1917 – WIA

**JANSSEN, Waldemar Ltn d R**
J28w 21 Aug 1917 – 17 Mar 1918 1 KIA
Born 19 January 1890, Wesselburen. Knight's Cross 2nd Class with Swords of the Württemberg Friedrich Order on 20 Feb 1918. Shot down over Roulers, at 1230 hours.
Victories: 1. 22 Oct 1917 Pup W Beerst

**JANZEN, Johann Ltn d R**
KG2/12 Aug 1916 – – CO J4 28 Mar 1918 – 28 Apr 1918 –
J23 28 Nov 1916 – 16 Oct 1917 1 CO J6 28 Apr 1918 – 9 Jun 1918 9 POW
J6 16 Oct 1917 – 28 Mar 1918 3
Biography & Victories: See *Above the Lines*.

**JANZEN, Uffz**
J17 – 25 Sep 1918 – INJ

**JAUCH, Hugo Flg**
J47w – 28 Jun 1918 – KIAcc
Born 2 June 1899, Schwenningen, Rottwell. Killed at Epenancourt-sur-Somme.

**JEBENS, Hans Ltn**
J59 – 27 Sep 1918 1 KIA
Born 30 March 1899, Gustroto. Jumped from his burning plane in a parachute over Bouchain, but 'chute didn't open.
Victories: 1. 24 Sep 1918 BF2b Bantouzelle

**JECKERT, Ludwig Uffz**
J56 12 Jul 1918 – Oct 1918 4 Hosp Oct 1918 – –
Joined Jasta 56 from Jastaschule I.
Victories: 1. 31 Jul 1918 Camel 1845 Hooge
2. 5 Sep 1918 Camel 1825 Lendelede
3. 28 Sep 1918 RE8 0800 Moorslede
4. 29 Sep 1918 RE8 0830 Zonnebeke

**JEDWIEL, Vfw**
J46 10 Feb 1918 – 17 Mar 1918 – WIA

## JEEP,      Vfw

| | | | | J58 | 28 Jan 1918 – 11 Nov 1918 | 3 |
|---|---|---|---|---|---|---|
| J12 | 7 Dec 1917 – 28 Jan 1918 | – | | | | |
| Victories: | 1. | 19 Jul 1918 | Balloon | 0720 | W Livry-Vesle | |
| | 2. | 4 Sep 1918 | DH9 | 1045 | d'Hivergies-Fé | |
| | 3. | 15 Sep 1918 | Balloon | 1305 | Vitry | |

## JEHLE, Benedikt     Vfw

| FAA295 | | | | FEA2 | 8 Jun 1918 – | |
|---|---|---|---|---|---|---|
| J16b | 17 Dec 1917 – 8 Jun 1918 | 1 | | | | |
| Born 18 June 1895. | | | | | | |
| Victories: | 1. | 18 Mar 1918 | Camel | 1120 | Busigny | |

## JENSEN, Johannes     Ltn

J57       (Apr 1918) – 11 Nov 1918      6
Biography & Victories: See *Above the Lines*.

## JENTSCH, Kurt     Uffz

| FA66 | 1916 – 1916 | 3 | J5 | 18 Jan 1918 – 23 Jan 1918 | – |
|---|---|---|---|---|---|
| FA30 | 1916 – 1916 | – | J61 | 23 Jan 1918 – 13 Aug 1918 | – |
| J1 | 19 May 1917 – Aug 1917 | 1 | JB | 13 Aug 1918 – 4 Sep 1918 | – WIA |
| FAA234 | Aug 1917 – | 3 | | | |

Biography & Victories: See *Above the Lines*.

## JENTZSCH, Richard     Vfw

| J47w | 10 Jan 1918 – 23 Apr 1918 | – | J71 | – 23 May 1918 | – KIA |
|---|---|---|---|---|---|
| FEA13 | 23 Apr 1918 – | – | | | |

Born 11 February 1897, Leipzig. Joined Jasta 47w from Jastaschule I. Killed over Habsheim.

## JERRATSCH, Karl     Ltn d R

FAA268                                    Kest 7                    – 24 Oct 1918     – WIA
Born 22 November 1888, Schwerin. Reserve Infantry Regiment 213. Died in hospital at Düsseldorf.

## JESCHONNEK, Hans     Ltn

J40s      22 Apr 1918 – 11 Nov 1918      2
Born 9 April 1899, Hohensalza. Entered military service 10 August 1914, as a Fähnrich in 3rd Niederschleissische Infantry Regiment 50. Promoted Leutnant 26 September 1914. WIA 6 October 1915. Commenced pilot training at AFPs on 19 July 1917. Awarded EKI; Knight's Cross with Swords of the Royal Hohenzollern House Order. Ritterkreuz on 27 October 1939. Generaloberst in WWII on 1 March 1942; Luftwaffe Chief of Staff, from 1 February 1939, until he committed suicide 19 August 1943.

| Victories: | 1. | 11 Jun 1918 | RE8 | 1515 | Vlamertinghe |
|---|---|---|---|---|---|
| | 2. | 18 Oct 1918 | Spad | | Roulers |

## JESSEN, Johannes     Ltn d R

J4        30 May 1918 – 11 Nov 1918      2

| Victories: | 1. | 1 Aug 1918 | Nieuport | 0930 | Cuiry-Housse |
|---|---|---|---|---|---|
| | 2. | 4 Aug 1918 | Spad | 2005 | N Vauxtin |

## JÖNS, Hugo     Ltn d R

| J10 | 21 Sep 1916 – 16 Dec 1916 | – | J31 | 4 Feb 1917 – (Apr 1917) | 1 |
|---|---|---|---|---|---|
| J17 | 16 Dec 1916 – 4 Feb 1917 | – | J20 | 15 Jun 1917 – 23 Sep 1917 | 1 KIA |

Born 31 March 1895, Köln. OzbV for Jasta 10, 21 Sep to 16 Dec 1916. Joined Jasta 20 from Jastaschule I. Acting CO Jasta 10 from 23 Oct to 16 Dec 1916. Killed over Dixmuiden.

| Victories: | 1. | 18 Apr 1917 | Voisin | 0800 | Aubérive | |
|---|---|---|---|---|---|---|
| | 2. | 20 Jul 1917 | Camel | 2010 | NW Wilskerke | (a) |

(a) Probably N6360, No 6 Sqn RNAS, F/Cdr G McLennan.

## JÖRKE, Reinhold     OfStv

| J12 | 27 Feb 1917 – Oct 1917 | 9 | J39 | – 11 Nov 1918 | 4 |
|---|---|---|---|---|---|
| J13 | Oct 1917 – (Mar 1918) | 1 | | | |

Biography & Victories: See *Above the Lines*.

## JÖRSS,     Gefr

J72s      20 May 1918 – 7 Jun 1918      –           AFP18     7 Jun 1918 –

**JOHNS, Martin     Ltn d L**
J63     18 Mar 1918 – 11 Nov 1918     7
Biography & Victories: See *Above the Lines*.

---

**JOPP, Hermann     Uffz**
J37          – 14 Apr 1917     – KIA
Born 2 March 1893, Krauschutz. Shot down in flames by flak during a balloon attack near Mont Toulon.

---

**JOPP, Philipp     Vfw**
J79b          – 2 May 1918     – KIA
Born 11 January 1892, Machtilshausen. Killed over Montdidier at 2000 hours.

---

**JOSCHKOWITZ,     Ltn d R**
J4     18 Sep 1917 – 1 Apr 1918     1          AFP2     1 Apr 1918 –          –
Joined Jasta 4 from Jastaschule 1.

| Victories: | 1. | 26 Sep 1917 | Spad 7 | 1040 | Becelaere |
|---|---|---|---|---|---|

---

**JÜHE, August     Vfw**
J8     (Mar 1918) – 11 Nov 1918     4

| Victories: | 1. | 28 Mar 1918 | Bréguet | | Voyennes |
|---|---|---|---|---|---|
| | 2. | 25 Apr 1918 | Sopwith | 1745 | S Marcelcave |
| | 3. | 12 Aug 1918 | Spad 13 | 1055 | Reims |
| | 4. | 26 Sep 1918 | Spad 13 | 1600 | Etain |

---

**JÜNEMANN,     Vfw**
J67     23 Mar 1918 – 11 Nov 1918     –

---

**JUHNKE, Hermann     Vfw**
FAA238     Jul 1916 –          –          Kest 5          – 4 Mar 1918          –
J41          1917 –                    J52     4 Mar 1918 – 11 Nov 1918     5
Biography & Victories: See *Above the Lines*.

---

**JUMPELT, Walter     Ltn**
J27     20 Apr 1917 – 24 Dec 1917     1          J19     24 Dec 1917 – (Apr 1918)     1
Joined Jasta 27 from Jastaschule I.

| Victories: | 1. | 21 Sep 1917 | DH4 | 0700 | Becelaere |
|---|---|---|---|---|---|
| | 2. | 31 Mar 1918 | Bréguet | | Guérbigny |

---

**JUNCK, Werner     Ltn**
FA33     1916 –          –          J8     (Apr 1917) – 11 Nov 1918     5
Biography & Victories: See *Above the Lines*.

---

**JUNGE, Werner     Ltn**
J9     23 Sep 1916 – 25 Feb 1917     – WIA
Born 20 May 1896, Kiel. Severely wounded at 1640 hours, died next night in hospital at Grandpré.

---

**JUNGSCHERT,     Vfw**
J13          –

---

**JUNGWIRTH, Hans     Ltn**
J78b     28 Jul 1918 – 11 Nov 1918     1
Acting CO Jasta 78b, 14 Sep to 9 Oct 1918.

| Victories: | 1. | 22 Aug 1918 | DH9 | 0905 | Ingweiler | (a) |
|---|---|---|---|---|---|---|

(a) Possibly from No 104 Sqn, IAF.

---

**JUNKER,     Ltn**
J65     2 Feb 1918 – 23 May 1918     –          AFP5     23 May 1918 –          –
Served in Infantry Regiment Nr.18. OzbV for Jasta 65.

---

**JUST, Erich     Ltn d R**
J11     20 Sep 1917 – 11 Nov 1918     6
Biography & Victories: See *Above the Lines*.

---

**JUSTINUS, Bruno     Oblt**
J35b     29 Sep 1917 – 30 Jan 1918     1 KIA
Born 22 August 1892, Beyreuth. Was observer for Ltn Ernst Udet in FAA 206 during Aug 1915. Force-

landed at Coolkerke airfield on 2 October 1917, and damaged his Albatros DV 4603/17; unharmed. Awarded Pilot's Badge on 19 November 1917. Acting CO Jasta 35b 20 to 30 January 1918. Shot down in flames W Forenville at 1420 hours flying Albatros DV 4630/17, possibly by Lt K W Junor, No 56 Sqn, RFC.

| Victories: | 1. | 13 Nov 1917 | Camel | 1655 | Boesinghe |
|---|---|---|---|---|---|

### KADE,    Uffz

J50                              – 19 Jan 1918   – KIAcc
Born 20 March 1892, Ebersbach. Killed during a test flight over La Neuville.

### KÄHLERT,    Uffz

J27        8 Dec 1917 – 12 Dec 1917    – POW
Joined Jasta 27 from Jastaschule I.

### KÄMMEL, Hugo    Ltn d R

| KG6/34 | | | – | FEA13 | | – 10 Sep 1918 | – |
|---|---|---|---|---|---|---|---|
| J23 | 29 Dec 1916 – 19 Sep 1917 | 1 | | Kest 1a | 10 Sep 1918 – | | – |
| StoflH | 19 Sep 1917 – | | – | | | | |

| Victories: | 1. | 16 Mar 1917 | Sopwith | 1255 | Pagny |
|---|---|---|---|---|---|

### KÄMMER,    Gefr

J49                                   1
| Victories: | 1. | 27 Jun 1918 | Salmson | 1050 | Framerville |
|---|---|---|---|---|---|

### KÄMMERER, Heinrich    Ltn d R

J20        3 Mar 1917 – 13 Mar 1918   1 KIA
Born 25 November 1891, Hamburg. Shot down in flames over Sallaumines.

| Victories: | 1. | 19 Mar 1917 | Nieuport | | Flavy-le-Martel |
|---|---|---|---|---|---|

### KÄMMERER, Max    Ltn d R

J35b        5 Oct 1917 – 25 Oct 1918   2        FEA1b   25 Oct 1918 –        –
Reported to Jasta 35b from AFP 4. Awarded Bavarian Militär-Verdeinstkreuz 2 Klasse mit Schwerten on 19 November 1917. Injured in a landing accident on 4 Dec 1917 and hospitalised; returned 7 Jan 1918. Promoted Leutnant d R on 16 February 1918. Had to make forced landings on 9 March 1918 by Fertequenne and on 16 March 1918, by Brancourt. Awarded Iron Cross I Class on 19 March 1918. Awarded Bavarian Militär-Verdeinstkreuz 4 Klasse on 17 July 1918.

| Victories: | 1. | 20 Oct 1917 | Camel | | Oostnieuwkerke |
|---|---|---|---|---|---|
| | 2. | 28 Aug 1918 | DH9 | 0700 | Bévillers |

### KÄMPFE, Erich    Ltn d R

J13        (Jan 1918) – 18 Sep 1918   2 WIA
Born 17 June 1895, Schonheide. Jumped in a parachute but was severely wounded by ground fire on way down; DOW 20 September 1918, in hospital at Metz.

| Victories: | 1. | 3 Jan 1918 | Spad | | S Pargnan |
|---|---|---|---|---|---|
| | 2. | 3 Jan 1918 | Balloon | | NW Pargnan |

### KÄPPELER, Karl    Vfw

FA300                              J55              – 8 May 1918   – KIA
Born 15 April 1892, Hohenzollern. Killed over Djenin.

### KÄSER,    Ltn

J47w        18 Feb 1918 – (Apr 1918)
Assigned to Jasta 47w from Jastaschule I.

### KAHLE, Willy    Fw

J27        29 Jul 1918 – 11 Nov 1918   6
Biography & Victories: See *Above the Lines*.

### KAHLOW, Max    Vfw

FA42        Apr 1917 –            1        J34b        18 Jun 1917 – 11 Nov 1918   5
Biography & Victories: See *Above the Lines*.

## KAIRIS, Vfw
J13      – 9 May 1917    – INJ
Injured in a forced landing.

## KAISER, Justus   Uffz
J35b    21 Sep 1917 – 18 Feb 1918   1   KIA
Born 19 July 1897, Nürnberg. Awarded Bavarian Militär-Verdeinstkreuz 3 Klasse mit Schwerten on 21 October 1917. Shot down in flames near Esquerchin, W Douai, in Albatros DV 4448/17.

| Victories: | 1. | 12 Oct 1917 | Camel | 1220 | SW Courtrai | (a) |

(a) Probably by Capt H B Coomber, No 45 Sqn, RFC, KIA.

## KAISER, Ltn d R
J17      – 11 Nov 1918   1

| Victories: | 1. | 4 Oct 1918 | Spad | St Morel |
| | – | 18 Oct 1918 | Spad | |

## KALKREUTH, von   Oblt
J21s      – 22 Aug 1918   –      JGII    22 Aug 1918 – 11 Nov 1918   –
OzbV for Jasta 21. Served on staff of JGII.

## KALETA, Uffz
J56    12 Feb 1918 – 4 Apr 1918   1      AFP2    4 Apr 1918 –      –
Joined Jasta 56 from Jastaschule II.

| Victories: | 1. | Unknown date and unit | | | |
| | 2. | 28 Mar 1918 | SE5a | 0920 | Chaulnes |

## KALFF, Bruno   Ltn
KG4/22      –      J20    25 Jan 1917 – 27 Jan 1917   – KIA
Born 23 January 1895, Graudenz. Killed near Essigny-le-Petit airfield.

## KALLMÜNZER, Karl   Vfw
SS24      –      J78b    – 12 Aug 1918   1   WIA
Born 28 June 1897, Friedenfels. Severely injured in crash-landing after combat with DH4s over Wasselinheim; died in hospital.

| Victories: | zlg | 27 May 1918 | Spad 2 | 1520 | Parroywald |
| | 1. | 30 Jul 1918 | DH9 | 0840 | Gross Rombach |

## KAMMANDEL, Vfw
| J8 | | – 27 Oct 1916 | – | J18 | 1 Mar 1917 – 12 Aug 1917 | 1 |
| J18 | 27 Oct 1916 – 15 Feb 1917 | | – | J14 | 12 Aug 1917 – | – |
| J27 | 15 Feb 1917 – 1 Mar 1917 | | – | | | |

| Victories: | 1. | 11 Mar 1917 | BE2d | 1435 | NW Armentières |

## KAMPE, Willi   OfStv
J27      – 8 Mar 1918   8   KIA
Lightly wounded in combat 22 January 1918.
Biography & Victories: See *Above the Lines*.

## KAMPE, Ltn
J13    (Sep 1917) – (Sep 1918)    –

## KANDT, Ltn
J18    Aug 1918 – Sep 1918    –

## KARBE, Heinrich   Oblt
J22    Nov 1916 – Mar 1918   2

| Victories: | 1. | 24 Oct 1917 | Spad | 1010 | Malmaison |
| | 2. | 19 Feb 1918 | Spad 2 | | Bruyrès |

## KARG, Franz-Josef   Ltn d R
J23    4 Oct 1917 – 19 Oct 1917   – KIAcc
Born 21 February 1895, München. Joined Jasta 23 from Jastaschule I. Killed at 1530 hours at Jametz airfield.

## KARJUS, Walther    Oblt

| | | | | | |
|---|---|---|---|---|---|
| FAA207 | | – | SS17 | | – |
| J11 | 30 Mar 1918 – 29 May 1918 | – | CO J75 | 21 Aug 1918 – 11 Nov 1918 | 1 |
| AFP2 | 29 May 1918 – | – | | | |

Awarded Knight's Cross with Swords of the Royal Hohenzollern House Order on 26 July 1917. Only had one arm.

| Victories: | 1. | 21 Oct 1918 | DH4 | | Enslingen |
|---|---|---|---|---|---|

## KARLCHER,    Ltn

J51    (Aug 1918) –                    –

## KARSTEN, Albert    Sgt

J48    27 Aug 1918 – 18 Oct 1918    – KIA

Born 14 March 1890, Bevenrode. Joined Jasta 48 from Jastaschule I. Killed near Valenciennes.

## KASSNER, Rudolf    Uffz

| | | | | | | |
|---|---|---|---|---|---|---|
| J29 | 9 Dec 1917 – 8 Feb 1918 | – | J65 | 10 Feb 1918 – 13 Jun 1918 | 4 | WIA |

Born 24 November 1897, Schwachtwalde. Joined Jasta 29 from FEA5. Awarded EKI. Severely wounded during combat with a DH4 over Amanweiler; died of wounds.

| Victories: | 1. | 26 Feb 1918 | Balloon | 1700 | Bethelainville |
|---|---|---|---|---|---|
| | 2. | 26 Feb 1918 | Balloon | 1700 | Bethelainville |
| | 3. | 16 Mar 1918 | Balloon | 1305 | Sivry-la-Perche |
| | 4. | 3 May 1918 | Spad | 2000 | Mort Homme |

## KATHOL, Werner    Ltn d R

J29    26 Jul 1917 – 27 Oct 1917    –    Kest

Joined Jasta 29 from Jastaschule I. Lightly wounded in action 27 July 1917.

## KATZENSTEIN, Kurt    Ltn d R

| | | | | | |
|---|---|---|---|---|---|
| J30 | 11 Aug 1917 – 9 Jan 1918 | – | FEA2 | Mar 1918 – 26 Apr 1918 | – |
| J55 | 9 Jan 1918 – Mar 1918 | – | J30 | 26 Apr 1918 – 11 Nov 1918 | 1 |

Joined Jasta 29 from Jastaschule I.

| Victories: | 1. | 9 Jun 1918 | Camel | 0920 | La Gorgue | (a) |
|---|---|---|---|---|---|---|

(a) Possibly D3348, No 210 Sqn, RAF, Lt W Breckenbridge.

## KATZNER, Jakob    Gefr

J43    19 Aug 1918 – 5 Sep 1918    – KIA

Joined Jasta 43 from Jastaschule I. Body found in his crashed aircraft 16 September 1918.

## KAUFFMANN, Hans Erich    Vfw

J47w    10 Jan 1918 – 21 Apr 1918    – DOW

Born 20 October 1895, Dessau, Sachsen. WIA over Le Petit Mortier-Estaires; died of wounds in Lille, 22 April.

## KAUFMANN,    Ltn

J15                    –

## KAUS, Erich    Ltn

| | | | | | |
|---|---|---|---|---|---|
| AFP6 | – Apr 1917 | – | J30 | 2 Dec 1917 – 31 May 1918 | – WIA |
| J31 | Apr 1917 – Dec 1917 | – | | | |

Wounded in combat with SE5s.

## KAUTZ,    Vfw

J46    – 11 Nov 1918    2

| Victories: | 1. | 3 Aug 1918 | RE8 | | Assevillers |
|---|---|---|---|---|---|
| | 2. | 5 Sep 1918 | Balloon | 1515 | NE Bapaume |

## KAYL, Erich    Ltn d R

J32b    16 Mar 1918 – 23 May 1918    – WIA

Born 28 May 1897, Pauesova. Severely wounded over Vis-en-Artois, at 1145 hours during combat with DH4s and Camels, flying Albatros DVa 7372/17; died of wounds 27 May 1918.

## KEHR, Hans    Vfw

J20    – 17 Mar 1918    – KIA

Born 14 March 1894, Halberstadt. Shot down in flames E of Queant.

## KEITSCH, Günther    Ltn
J39                  – 5 Mar 1918    1           J74        5 Mar 1918 – 29 May 1918    2  KIA
Born 18 January 1895, Kolberg. Shot down in flames over Betheny-Reims, in an Albatros DVa
(G/2/12) probably by Capt P J Clayson, No 1 Sqn, RAF.

| Victories: | 1. | 2 Feb 1918 | Camel | | |
|---|---|---|---|---|---|
| | 2. | 20 Apr 1918 | Nieuport | | Prunay |
| | 3. | 29 May 1918 | Sopwith 2 | | Betheny |

## KELBER, Eugen    Ltn d R
J12      11 Sep 1918 – 13 Sep 1918    – KIA
Born 1 November 1896, Messbach. Killed west of Langeville-Mars-la-Tour, during combat with two
Spads.

## KELLER, Josef    Ltn d R
J43        5 Jun 1918 – 11 Oct 1918    1  INJ
Severely injured in an accident.

| Victories: | 1. | 8 Aug 1918 | SE5a | 1530 | SW Bray-sur-Somme |
|---|---|---|---|---|---|

## KELLER, Julius    Ltn d R
J21s                                   2
Württemberg Gold Military Merit Medal, 25 July 1918.

| Victories: | 1. | 8 Mar 1918 | Morane | 1215 | E Nauroy |
|---|---|---|---|---|---|
| | 2. | 21 Aug 1918 | Spad | 1630 | Soissons |

## KEMPA, Anton    Gefr
J3              – 14 Sep 1918    – POW
POW #30 430.

## KEMPE, Willy    Vfw
FA39                                             J34        15 Jul 1917 – 22 Jul 1917    1  POW
Shot down by ground fire in Allied lines.

| | 1. | 22 Jul 1917 | Caudron | | E Sanzey |
|---|---|---|---|---|---|

## KEMPF, Friedrich Paul    Ltn d R
KG4/20      Jan 1916 –                –          JB         Jan 1918 – 18 Aug 1918    1
JB        4 Apr 1917 – 17 Oct 1917    3          JsSchI     18 Aug 1918 – 11 Nov 1918    –
JsSchI    17 Oct 1917 – Jan 1918     –
Born 9 May 1894, Freiburg, Baden. Enlisted 1 October 1913, Baden Infantry Rgt 113. Promoted
Unteroffizier 3 August 1914. Assigned to FEA3, on 6 May 1915, for pilot's training. Transferred
to Militar-Flieger-Schule on 20 May 1915. Awarded EKII and the Baden Silberne Militär-
Verdeinstmedaille. FEA9 from 29 November 1915 to 4 January 1916. Promoted Vizefeldwebel 17 January
1916. Qualified for his Flugzeugführer Abzeichen on 21 May 1916. Promoted Leutnant d R on
9 September 1916. Awarded EKI; Bulgarian Military Merit Cross 5th Class with War Ribbon on 10
June 1917, kuk Feldpilot Abzeichen on 8 November 1917. Known to have flown Fokker Dr I 213/17.
Awarded Baden Ritterkreuz II Klass mit Schwerten des Ordens vom Zähringer Löwen on 21 February
1918. Died August 1966.

| Victories: | 1. | 29 Apr 1917 | BE2e | 0745 | SW La Pavé | |
|---|---|---|---|---|---|---|
| | 2. | 5 Jun 1917 | Pup | 0840 | Masnières | (a) |
| | 3. | 20 Oct 1917 | Camel | 1220 | Gravenstafel | |
| | 4. | 8 May 1918 | Camel | 1420 | W Steenwerck | |

(a) B1729, No 54 Sqn, RFC, 2/Lt B G Chalmers, POW.
(See *OTF*, Vol 4, No 4, pg 321/322.)

## KEMPTE,    Oblt
J18              – 15 Mar 1918    –

## KERN,    OfStv
FA71                             –          FA300                                   –
J17      11 Nov 1916 – 31 Dec 1916    –

## KERNCHEN, Erwin    Vfw
J25              – 5 Jan 1917    – KIAcc
Born Berlin, 20 January 1895. Crashed between Prbilci and Lurce, Bulgaria.

## KERSSENBROCK, Franz von     Ltn

| | | | | | | |
|---|---|---|---|---|---|---|
| FA1 | 30 Jun 1917 – | | 2 | J39 | – 3 Dec 1917 | 2  KIA |

Born 21 May 1895, Barntrup. Fahrenjunker Kurs Regt 4, on 1 April 1914. Transferred to aviation in June 1915. Trained as an observer, sent to Serbia in Sept 1915. Pilot's training 5 Feb 1917 in Graudenz, and Allstein. Acting CO Jasta 39 from 17 Nov to 3 Dec 1917. Killed over Conegliano, Italy.

| Victories: | 1. | 2 Jul 1917 | Spad | | Werone |
|---|---|---|---|---|---|
| | 2. | 6 Jul 1917 | Voisin | | Wischnew-Süd |
| | 3. | 25 Oct 1917 | Voisin | 0825 | Volarje |
| | 4. | 25 Oct 1917 | Farman | 1520 | Tersimonte |
| | zlg | 7 Nov 1917 | Caproni | | Sacile |

## KERSTING, Max     Ltn d R

| | | | |
|---|---|---|---|
| J48 | 24 Jan 1918 – 3 Feb 1918 | – KIA | |

Born 29 January 1893, Siegen. Joined Jasta 48 from Jastaschule II. Shot down in flames over Aubencheul-aux-Bois, probably by Capt H Maddocks, No 54 Sqn, RFC.

## KERZMANN, Wieand     Ltn d R

| | | | | | |
|---|---|---|---|---|---|
| SS10 | | – | J58 | 9 Feb 1918 – 5 Jun 1918 | – |
| J4 | – 9 Feb 1918 | – | AFP4 | | – |

## KESELING,     Ltn

| | | |
|---|---|---|
| J10 | – 24 Mar 1918 | – POW |

Shot down by AA fire in an Fokker DrI 147/17, a Jasta 11 aircraft (G.158).

## KESSLER,     Ltn

| | | |
|---|---|---|
| J12 | 13 May 1918 – | – |

## KESSLER,

| | | |
|---|---|---|
| Kest 4b | – (Jul 1918) | – |

## KETTEL, Josef     Vfw

| | | | | | | |
|---|---|---|---|---|---|---|
| J32b | – 10 Jan 1918 | 1 | J50 | 10 Jan 1918 – 29 Jan 1918 | – KIA | |

Born 27 May 1897, Ramscheid. Killed in combat with an AWFK8 over La Fre, in Albatros DIII 2370/17 (G.129), by Lt R Fagan and 2/Lt A Matt, No 82 Sqn, RFC.

| Victories: | 1. | 4 Jan 1918 | AR2 | | Pontavert |
|---|---|---|---|---|---|

## KETTELHACK,     Vfw

| | |
|---|---|
| J63 | 1 |

| Victories: | 1. | 9 Aug 1918 | 2-seater | 1900 | Mourmelon-le-Grand |
|---|---|---|---|---|---|

## KEUDELL, Hans von     Ltn

| | | | | | | |
|---|---|---|---|---|---|---|
| FA32 | – 23 Aug 1916 | – | J27 | 12 Feb 1917 – 15 Feb 1917 | 1  KIA | |
| J1 | 23 Aug 1916 – 5 Feb 1917 | 11 | | | | |

Biography & Victories: See *Above the Lines*.

## KEUSEN, Paul     Vfw

| | | |
|---|---|---|
| JB | Sep 1918 – 4 Nov 1918 | 2  KIA |

Born 27 September 1896, Ohlige. Killed near Monbray, probably by Capt R King, No 4 Sqn, AFC.

| Victories: | 1. | 29 Sep 1918 | BF2b | | E Irony | |
|---|---|---|---|---|---|---|
| | 2. | 4 Nov 1918 | BF2b | 1430 | Villerau | (a) |

(a) Possibly Lt F C D Scott & 2/Lt C Rigby, No 62 Sqn, RAF.

## KIECKHAFER, Fritz     Ltn

| | | | | | | |
|---|---|---|---|---|---|---|
| J32 | 11 Jun 1917 – 30 Aug 1917 | 1 | J29 | 30 Aug 1917 – 4 May 1918 | 7  WIA | |

Biography & Victories: See *Above the Lines*.

## KIEL,     Vfw

| | | |
|---|---|---|
| J39 | Jan 1918 – | – |

## KIEL, Emil     Ltn d R

| | | |
|---|---|---|
| J63 | Aug 1918 – 11 Nov 1918 | – |

## KIEP, Max Hermann     Vfw

| | | |
|---|---|---|
| J43 | 22 Feb 1918 – 28 Oct 1918 | 3  KIA |

Born 9 October 1891, Hamburg. EKII in Dec 1914, also awarded EKI. Killed over Mont St Aubert.

| Victories: | 1. | 22 Apr 1918 | AWFK8 | 1330 | Nieppe |
| | 2. | 2 Jun 1918 | SE5a | 1325 | W Merville |
| | – | 27 Jun 1918 | SE5a | 1115 | SW Bethune |
| | 3. | 3 Oct 1918 | DH9 | 1835 | SW Carvin |

## KIESSLING, Hans    Ltn
J34b    5 Dec 1917 – 9 Jan 1918    – WIA    J79b    7 Jul 1918 – 8 Aug 1918    – WIA
J34b    16 Mar 1918 – 7 Jul 1918    1
Joined Jasta 34b from Jastaschule II. Wounded by AA fire over Verdun, flying Pfalz DIII 4031/17 on 9 January 1918. Rejoined Jasta 34b from FEA1b.

| Victories: | 1. | 30 May 1918 | BF2b | 1200 | N Corbie |

## KILIAN, Bernhard    Ltn d R
J21s                – 9 Dec 1917    – KIAcc
Born 19 January 1894, Neideburg. Served in Infantry Regiment 42. Killed at Pauvres airfield.

## KING, Alfred    Oblt
Kasta    25 Sep 1916 –    1    StoflH    24 Jul 1917 –    –
J20    12 May 1917 – 24 Jul 1917    –    Oblt J40    Sep 1917 – 25 Apr 1918    3 WIA
Born 20 May 1897, Stuttgart. Fahrenjunker Infantry Rgt Kaiser Friedrich 125 (7 Württemberg). Wounded in Serbia. Apr 1916 to FEA2, Schneidemuhl. Aug 1916 to KGOHL Muizon. Mid-Sep 1916 to Kampfstaffel 25. Severely injured in a crash 17 Nov 1916. Joined Jasta 20 from Jastaschule I. Joined Jasta 40 from hospital. Awarded Iron Cross II and I Class. Severely wounded during combat with DH9s at 1500 hours 25 Apr 1918. Assigned to Kampfstaffel VII on release from hospital.

| Victories: | 1. | 2 Nov 1916 | Nieuport | | Bouchavesnes | (a) |
| | 2. | 30 Oct 1917 | Nieuport | | Buxières | |
| | 3. | 11 Feb 1918 | Spad | | Pont-à-Mousson | |
| | 4. | 25 Apr 1918 | DH9 | 1500 | Dickebusch | |

(a) With his observer, OfStv Koch.

## KINKEL, Gustav    Flgmt
JB        Dec 1916 – 25 Jan 1917    1 POW
Shot down during combat with a DH2 at 1130 hours NE Moislains, and taken prisoner flying Albatros DIII 1982/16 (G.5), by Lt A E McKay, No 24 Sqn, RFC, in DH2 7884.

| Victories: | 1. | 25 Jan 1917 | FE2b | 1130 | NE Moislains | (a) |

(a) Probably Lts S Alder & R W White, No 20 Sqn, RFC.

## KINTZELMANN, Johannes    Ltn
J7    23 Aug 1916 – 8 Jan 1918    1    Idflieg    8 Jan 1918    –
Served with FA71 and FAA208 before joining Jasta 7. Awarded Saxon Knight's Cross of the Military St Henry Order 11 Nov 1917.

| Victories: | 1. | 27 Dec 1916 | Farman | 1100 | Louvemont |

## KINZIG, Friedrich    Flg
FA301                    J55            – 20 Sep 1918    – KIA
Born 1 April 1897, Nedarhausen. Killed over Djenin.

## KIRCHBACH, Walter    Ltn d R
FAA296                    J35b    6 Mar 1917 – 4 Jul 1917    2 KIAcc
Born 30 October 1893, Frankfurt a.M. Acting CO Jasta 35 on 14-15 April 1917. Forced to make an emergency landing flying Albatros DIII 2071/16 on 7 June 1917. Killed due to wing failure at 1850 hours flying Albatros DIII 2085/16 near Hartwald.

| Victories: | zlg | 14 May 1917 | Farman | | Lusse | |
| | 1. | 24 May 1917 | Nieuport | | S Neideraspach | (a) |
| | 2. | 5 Jun 1917 | Spad | | Gewenheim | |

(a) Probably Caporal Rondot, Escadrille N92.

## KIRCHFELD, Franz    Ltn d R
J73    11 Feb 1918 – 11 Nov 1918    8
Biography & Victories: See *Above the Lines*.

## KIRMAIER, Stefan    Oblt
Kek E        – 8 Sep 1916    3    J2    8 Sep 1916 – 22 Nov 1916    8 KIA
Biography & Victories: See *Above the Lines*.

## KIRSCHENLOHR, Philip     Ltn d R
J67      27 Jan 1918 – 28 Jan 1918      –          J68      28 Jan 1918 – 11 Nov 1918      –
Joined Jasta 67 from FEA9. OzbV for both Jastas 67 and 68.

## KIRSCHSTEIN, Hans     Ltn d R
FA19                              –          FA3                                     –
FA256                             –          J6       13 Mar 1918 – 16 Jul 1918      27 INJ
Biography & Victories: See *Above the Lines*.

## KIRSCHT,     Ltn
J38      Nov 1917 –                      1
Victories:    1.        20 Nov 1917       Nieuport                      W Gjevgjali

## KIRST, Richard     Ltn d R
J10      12 Oct 1918 – 5 Nov 1918      – KIA
Born 15 April 1895, Heinitz. Served in Infantry Regiment 341. Joined Jasta 10 from Jastaschule II.
Killed over Loupoy.

## KISCHKAT,     Vfw
J20                              –

## KISSENBERTH, Otto     Oblt
FA8b             1914 – 21 Mar 1915      – WIA        Ltn d R
FA9b      8 Jul 1915 – 1916             –            J16b      1 Nov 1916 – 4 Aug 1917      3
KekE      1916 – 1 Nov 1916      3                   Oblt CO
                                                     J23b      4 Aug 1917 – 29 May 1918      14 INJ
Biography & Victories: See *Above the Lines*.

## KISTER,     Vfw
J1       (Jul 1918) – 22 Aug 1918      2 WIA
Victories:    1.        18 Jul 1918       Caudron R11            1930         Neuilly
              2.        22 Aug 1918       Bristol F2b            1100         Courcelles

## KITHIL, Johann     Ltn d R
J34b      17 Nov 1917 – 11 Nov 1918      1
Joined Jasta 34b from Jastaschule II. His aircraft carried one white band trimmed in black just aft of
pilot's seat.
Victories:    –        17 Jun 1918       EA
              1.        7 Aug 1918        SE5            1004         Hangard

## KLÄUKER,     Ltn
Kest 1a      (Sep 1918) –                      1

## KLAIBER, Otto     Vfw
FA232                             –          J12      (Sep 1918) – 11 Nov 1918      6
Biography & Victories: See *Above the Lines*.

## KLAMKER,     Ltn
Kest 4b      (Nov 1917) –                      –
OzbV for Kest 4b.

## KLAMT, Rudolf     Uffz
KG2/8                                        Hosp      21 Aug 1918 – 1 Oct 1918      –
J10      12 Aug 1918 – 21 Aug 1918      – WIA        J10       1 Oct 1918 – 11 Nov 1918      –
Born 8 September 1898. During WWII was a Fliegerstabsingenieur (General Officer) in the Luftwaffe.

## KLAUDAT, Gustav     Vfw
J15      (Jul 1918) – 23 Oct 1918      6 WIA
Biography & Victories: See *Above the Lines*.

## KLAUS, Max     Flg
J52      29 Jul 1918 – 11 Nov 1918      –
Joined Jasta 52 from Jastaschule I.

## KLAUSENBERG, Franz    Ltn
| | | | | | | |
|---|---|---|---|---|---|---|
| JB | Aug 1918 – 24 Sep 1918 | – | | J53 | 24 Sep 1918 – 11 Nov 1918 | 2 |

| Victories: | 1. | 2 Oct 1918 | AR2 | 1435 | Liry |
|---|---|---|---|---|---|
| | 2. | 26 Oct 1918 | Bréguet | 1240 | Attigny |

## KLEEGOBERT,    Ltn
| | |
|---|---|
| J37 | – |

## KLEEMANN,    Ltn
| | | | | | |
|---|---|---|---|---|---|
| J5 | (Feb 1917) – 6 May 1917 | – | J15 | 6 May 1917 – | – |

OzbV for both Jasta 5 and 15. Wounded in right upper arm on 3 May 1917.

## KLEFFEL, Walther F    Ltn
| | | | | | | |
|---|---|---|---|---|---|---|
| J18 | 11 Sep 1917 – 2 Oct 1917 | 1 | WIA | J15 | 20 Mar 1918 – | – |

Wounded in combat with DH4s.

| Victories: | 1. | 2 Oct 1917 | DH4 | 1330 | Roulers |
|---|---|---|---|---|---|

## KLIEMENHAGEN, Ernst    Vfw
| | | | |
|---|---|---|---|
| Kest 8w | – 18 May 1917 | – | KIAcc |

Born 17 May 1888, Kassel-Bettenhausen, Hessen. Killed at Neumünster airfield.

## KLEIN, Georg    Ltn
| | | | | | | |
|---|---|---|---|---|---|---|
| FEA6 | 10 Jul 1916 – | | – | J10 | – 22 Feb 1918 | – |
| AFP3 | Mar 1917 – 14 Apr 1917 | | – | FEA10 | 23 Feb 1918 – 6 Apr 1918 | – |
| FFA251 | 15 Apr 1917 – | | – | Kest 4b | 7 Apr 1918 – 11 Nov 1918 | – |
| JsSch1 | 28 Jul 1917 – 19 Nov 1917 | | – | | | |

EKII 23 April 1915. Promoted Leutnant 7 April 1916. Pilot's Badge on 3 June 1917. Awarded EKI. Knight's Cross 2nd Class with Swords of the Württemberg Friedrich Order on 23 Nov 1917. Knight's Cross of the Württemberg Military Merit Order on 8 March 1918.

## KLEIN, Hans    Oblt d R
| | | | | | | | |
|---|---|---|---|---|---|---|---|
| Kek | – 4 Nov 1916 | – | | J10 | 27 Sep 1917 – 19 Feb 1918 | 6 | WIA |
| J4 | 4 Nov 1916 – 13 Jul 1917 | 16 | WIA | Hosp | 19 Feb 1918 – | – | |
| Hosp | 13 Jul 1917 – | | | J10 | 26 Apr 1918 – 11 Nov 1918 | – | |

Biography & Victories: See *Above the Lines*.

## KLEIN, Hermann    Ltn
| | | | |
|---|---|---|---|
| J29 | 13 Feb 1917 – 15 Feb 1917 | – | INJ |

Reported to Jasta 29 from AFP3. Severely injured during a test flight.

## KLEIN, Johannes    Ltn
| | | | | | |
|---|---|---|---|---|---|
| J29 | 11 Feb 1917 1 7 Aug 1917 | 1 | J15 | 20 Mar 1918 – 11 Nov 1918 | 14 |
| J18 | 7 Aug 1917 – 20 Mar 1918 | 2 | | | |

Biography & Victories: See *Above the Lines*.

## KLEIN, K    OfStv
| | | | | | | |
|---|---|---|---|---|---|---|
| J27 | 22 Mar 1917 – 6 Aug 1917 | 2 | AFPS | 6 Aug 1917 | | – |

Joined Jasta 27 from AFP4.

| Victories | 1. | Date and unit unknown | | | | |
|---|---|---|---|---|---|---|
| | 2. | 3 Jun 1917 | Triplane | 1850 | Bousbecque | (a) |

(a) Possibly N6297, 10 Naval Sqn, F/S/Lt N G McNeil.

## KLEIN, Karl    Uffz
| | | | |
|---|---|---|---|
| J37 | – 14 Aug 1918 | – | KIA |

Born 14 August 1890, Gilschbach. Killed over Vendelles.

| Victories: | – | 21 Jun 1918 | BF2b | | Mezières |
|---|---|---|---|---|---|

## KLEIN, Martin    Vfw
| | |
|---|---|
| J5 | Nov 1917 – 18 Feb 1918    – KIA |

Born 12 November 1895, Mannheim. Served with FA57 before Jasta 5. Killed over Beaurevoir. Awarded EKI. Awarded Bavarian Silbern KFMVM on 11 January 1917.

**KLEINDIENST, Fritz     Ltn d R**
J18        18 Nov 1916 – 24 Apr 1917    –   KIA
Born 18 June 1895, Liebenwalde. Shot down in flames at 0920 hours near Korentje, N Comines.

---

**KLEINEBERG,     Gefr**
J20           Mar 1918 – 11 Jun 1918    –   POW

---

**KLEINEBERG,     Gefr**
AFP5            – 17 Mar 1918    –              AFP5     19 Apr 1918 –                          –
J65      17 Mar 1918 – 19 Apr 1918    –

---

**KLEINHEMPEL, Ernst     Ltn d R**
J46             – 30 Jul 1918    –   KIAcc
Born 10 September 1895, Wilkau. Drowned in Somme Canal, near Allaines.

---

**KLEINHENZ, Karl     Ltn**
J11      11 Oct 1916 – 5 Apr 1917     –              AFP6     5 Apr 1917 –                         –
OzbV for Jasta 11.

---

**KLEINSCHRODT, Hans     Uffz**
J64w    29 May 1918 – 3 Aug 1918    –         J23b    3 Aug 1918 – 11 Nov 1918    2
Joined Jasta 64w from Jastaschule II.

| Victories: | 1. | 15 Sep 1918 | Camel | 1815 | Arleux |
| | 2. | 16 Sep 1918 | DH4 | 1130 | Denain |

---

**KLENK,     Ltn**
Kest 1b    (Apr 1918) –                    1

---

**KLEPPER,     Ltn**
J12     23 May 1918 –                      –

---

**KLEVER, Josef     Ltn d R**
J14       (Apr 1917) –              ·           J39             – 3 Sep 1917    –   KIA
Born 2 November 1892, Rheinbohlen. Killed near Wattweiler.

---

**KLIEFOTH, Max     Ltn d R**
J19       1 Aug 1918 – 27 Oct 1918    3   POW
Born 15 January 1896, Wismar. Volunteered 3 Aug 1914, assigned to Field Artillery Regiment 24 from 22 Sep 1914 to April 1918. FEA2 Schneidemühl 1 May 1918 – 28 June 1918. Joined Jasta 19 from Jastaschule I. Crash-landed on airfield after losing propeller on 1 Oct 1918. Shot down by 1/Lt E V Rickenbacker, 94th Aero Sq, AEF, and taken prisoner, at 1640 hours. POW #588A. Died 1949 in Madison, Wisconsin, USA.

| Victories: | 1. | 12 Sep 1918 | Spad 2 | | Thiaucourt |
| | 2. | 13 Sep 1918 | Spad | 1930 | Jaulny |
| | 3. | 14 Sep 1918 | Bréguet | | Conflans |

---

**KLIMKE, Rudolf     Ltn**
FFA55           – 1916    1         KG3/13           – 1917              1
FA50            – 1916    –         J27      12 Sep 1917 – 21 Sep 1918    15 WIA
FA19            – 1917    –
Biography & Victories: See *Above the Lines*.

---

**KLIMSCH, Reinhold     Ltn**
J51           Jan 1918 – 18 May 1918    –   KIAcc
Born 28 April 1897, Charlottenburg. Killed near St Marguerite during a practice flight.

---

**KLINK, Erich     Ltn d R**
J73      22 Jun 1918 – 6 Aug 1918    –         J68    6 Aug 1918 – 18 Oct 1918    –   KIA
Born 12 September 1888, Friedeberg. Shot down near Bantheville.

---

**KLÖTZEL,     Ltn d R**
FAA285          – 1918    –                       10 Jun 1918 – 14 Sep 1918    –
J45      31 Mar 1918 – 23 May 1918    –    Idflieg    14 Sep 1918 –                 –
Joined Jasta 45 from AFP7. OzbV for Jasta 45.

## KLOSE, Heinrich    Vfw
J54s                 2

| Victories: | 1. | 12 Jun 1918 | Salmson | 1840 | Autheuil |
|---|---|---|---|---|---|
| | 2. | 13 Sep 1918 | DH4 | 1750 | Serrières |

## KLOSE,    Ltn
J45                          –

## KLÜPFEL,    Vfw
ObOst/J81 (Jul 1917) –       3      J77b    Dec 1917 – 16 Jan 1918    –    INJ

Hit by ground fire and forced to land, unharmed, on 29 September 1917. Injured in an accident shortly after take-off.

| Victories: | 1. | 6 Jul 1917 | Farman | Mlynowcze |
|---|---|---|---|---|
| | 2. | 6 Jul 1917 | Balloon | S Zborow |
| | zlg | 8 Jul 1917 | Nieuport | Batkow |
| | 3. | 19 Jul 1917 | Balloon | Zborow |

## KLUMPP, Erwin    Ltn d R
FEA10    7 Aug 1916 –         –      JB    8 Jan 1918 – 3 Feb 1918    –    KIAcc
FFA284    4 May 1917 – 20 Dec 1917    –

Born 27 Aug 1891, Stuttgart. (W) Infantry Regiment 125. Vizefeldwebel on 30 April 1912. Offizierstellvertreter on 4 August 1914, to (W) Infantry Regiment 121. Promoted Leutnant on 5 July 1915 back with (W) Infantry Regiment 125. Württemberg Friedrich Order, Knight 2nd Class with Swords on 21 January 1916. Transferred to aviation 7 August 1916. EKI on 15 September 1917. Knight's Cross of the Württemberg Military Merit Order on 27 September 1917. Killed in a landing accident at Thielt airfield.

## KLUTH, Heinrich    Vfw
J29    6 Aug 1918 – 11 Nov 1918    –
Assigned to Jasta 29 from Jastaschule I.

## KLUTKE, Erich    Vfw
J12    8 Oct 1916 –           –

## KNAAK, Hans    OfStv
J9         – 6 Oct 1918    1    KIA
Born 27 December 1892, Neuhof. Killed over Sissone airfield at 1000 hours.

| Victories: | 1. | 6 Sep 1918 | Spad | 1820 | N Soissons |
|---|---|---|---|---|---|

## KNAKE, Bernhard    Ltn d R
J12    13 Jun 1917 – 24 Jul 1917    3    KIAcc
Born 28 July 1889, Münster. Doctor of Philosophy. Joined Jasta 12 from Jastaschule I. Killed near Epinay.

| Victories: | 1. | 27 Jun 1917 | Nieuport | 2000 | Croiselles |
|---|---|---|---|---|---|
| | 2. | 22 Jul 1917 | Camel | 2040 | S Moeuvres |
| | 3. | 23 Jul 1917 | Camel | 1800 | W Hulluch |

## KNAPE,    Ltn
J47w    1 Feb 1918 –           –
Reported to Jasta 47w from Jastaschule I.

## KNAPPE, Herbert Wilhelm Franz    Ltn
FFA21          – 1916        1      J73    11 Feb 1918 – 8 Apr 1918    –
ObOst        – 11 Feb 1918       –     CO J81    8 Apr 1918 – 24 Aug 1918    8    WIA
Biography & Victories: See *Above the Lines*.

## KNAUSS, Karl    Oblt
J34b    30 Oct 1918 – 11 Nov 1918    –
Joined Jasta 34b from Jastaschule II.

## KNERR,    Vfw
J Schonger    29 Oct 1918 – 11 Nov 1918    –

## KNOBEL,    Vfw
J57      (Jul 1918) – 29 Aug 1918    3    WIA
Shot down in flames during combat with a Camel; unharmed.

| Victories: | 1. | 22 Aug 1918 | RE8 | | Achiet-le-Grand |
|---|---|---|---|---|---|
| | 2. | 25 Aug 1918 | Dolphin | 1000 | NE Martinpuich |
| | 3. | 27 Aug 1918 | Camel | 0910 | N Hendecourt |

## KNOCKE, Karl    Vfw
J35b    (Jul 1917) – 20 Jan 1918    1    INJ
Shot down 25 August 1917, near Bovekerke, aircraft smashed, but he was unharmed. Crashed into Gefr Zimmermann at Aertrycke airfield, AFP4, in Albatros DV 4666/17; unharmed, Zimmermann hospitalised on 11 October 1917. Crash-landed Albatros DV 4665/17 on 20 January 1918, after combat with a Spad.

| Victories: | 1. | 27 Oct 1917 | Camel | 1430 | NW Dixmuiden |
|---|---|---|---|---|---|

## KNOPF, Paul    Uffz
J72s    6 Apr 1918 – 1 Jul 1918    3    Hosp    1 Jul 1918 –    –

| Victories: | 1. | 22 Apr 1918 | Bréguet | 1840 | S Montdidier |
|---|---|---|---|---|---|
| | 2. | 6 May 1918 | Spad | 1945 | N Coullemelle |
| | 3. | 1 Jun 1918 | Bréguet | | Soissons |

## KOBETSCH,    Ltn
J46    10 Feb 1918 – 11 Nov 1918    –

## KOBILINSKI, Albrecht von    Ltn
FA20                     J36    20 Feb 1917 – 3 May 1917    – WIA
Promoted Leutnant 19 June 1916. Wounded when a munitions wagon exploded on his airfield.

## KOCH, Emil    Ltn d R
FEA2b    – 29 Dec 1917    –    J32b    29 Dec 1917 – 24 Oct 1918    7    WIA
Biography & Victories: See *Above the Lines*.

## KOCH, Heinrich    Uffz
J36    14 Feb 1918 – 31 May 1918    – KIA
Born 13 November 1891, Elipe. Killed SW of Soissons during combat with a two-seater.

## KOCH, Herbert    Flg
J64w    19 Jun 1918 – 10 Aug 1918    – KIA
Born 1 October 1894, Dresden, Sachsen. Killed over Pont-à-Mousson.

## KOCH, Otto    Ltn
J28w    (Jun 1917) – 1918    –
OzbV for Jasta 28w. Knight's Cross 2nd Class with Swords of the Württemberg Order on 20 Feb 1918.

## KOCH, Wilhelm    Ltn d R
J6    4 Aug 1917 – Jan 1918    –    J55    Jan 1918 – 20 Sep 1918    –
Joined Jasta 6 from AFP4.

## KOCH,    Ltn
J12    11 Nov 1917 – 11 Nov 1918    2
Crashed in a SSW DIII on 16 Aug 1918; not harmed.

| Victories: | 1. | 19 Jan 1918 | Camel | 1145 | E Mauville-Fe |
|---|---|---|---|---|---|
| | 2. | 28 Feb 1918 | SE5a | | St Gobain |
| | – | 14 Aug 1918 | Balloon | 1200 | Marchelepot |

## KOCH,    Flg
J13    23 Sep 1918 – 11 Nov 1918    –
Reported to Jasta 13 from Jastaschule I.

## KOCH,    Vfw
J17    (Nov 1917) – (Mar 1918)    –

## KÖCKERITZ, Friedrich August Fr von    Ltn d R
J11    30 Jul 1918 – 11 Nov 1918    3
Born 9 April 1898. Joined Jasta 11 from Jastaschule I. Died 5 February 1975, Oberkochen, Württemberg.

| Victories: | 1. | 10 Aug 1918 | SE5 | 1215 | |
|---|---|---|---|---|---|
| | 2. | 31 Aug 1918 | Dolphin | 1945 | |
| | 3. | 3 Nov 1918 | Spad | 1550 | |

**KÖCKLER, Wilhelm     Oblt**

| | | | | | | |
|---|---|---|---|---|---|---|
| FFA32 | 27 May 1915 – 11 Dec 1915 | – | | J23b | 4 Dec 1916 – 23 Aug 1917 | – |
| Idflieg | 12 Dec 1915 – 23 Jan 1916 | – | | AFP5 | 23 Aug 1917 – 14 Oct 1917 | – |
| KG4 | 24 Jan 1916 – 4 Dec 1916 | – | | SS9 | 15 Oct 1917 – | – |

Leutnant, (W) Pionier Bataillon Nr 13. Awarded EK II on 13 Sept 1914. Baden Knight 2nd Class with Swords of the Order of the Zähringer Löwen on 10 Jan 1915. Qualified as an observer. Knight 2nd Class with Swords of the Württemberg Friedrich Order on 20 Aug 1915. Promoted Oberleutnant 18 Sept 1915. Observer's Badge on 12 October 1915. OzbV for Jasta 23. EKI on 10 Dec 1916. Knight's Cross of the Württemberg Military Merit Order on 27 January 1917.

**KÖHLER, Andreas     Flg**

| | | | |
|---|---|---|---|
| J35b | 5 Apr 1918 – 25 Apr 1918 | – | POW |

Assigned to Jasta 35b from Jastaschule I. Forced to land after combat near Emerchicourt, on 11 April 1918. Failed to return from a test flight in Pfalz DIIIa 8284/17 (G/3/4), shot down by ground fire in Allied lines near Vimy-Combles.

**KÖHLER, Arthur     Uffz**

| | | | | | |
|---|---|---|---|---|---|
| J23 | 2 Jan 1917 – 15 Jan 1917 | – | | FAA284 | 22 Feb 1917 – | – |
| J26 | 15 Jan 1917 – 22 Feb 1917 | – | | | | |

Served in AFP-Ost prior to Jasta 23.

**KÖHLER, Erich     Vfw**

| | | |
|---|---|---|
| J9 | 23 Sep 1916 – | – |

**KÖHLER, Fritz     Ltn d R**

| | | | | | | |
|---|---|---|---|---|---|---|
| FA48 | 16 Aug 1916 – 1 Aug 1917 | – | | FEA11 | 17 Sep 1918 – 29 Oct 1918 | – |
| J25 | 13 Feb 1918 – | 1 | | Kest 9 | 30 Oct 1918 – 11 Nov 1918 | – |
| J38 | – 16 Sep 1918 | – | | | | |

Born 14 November 1897, Derby, England. Entered military service 14 August 1914, Uhlanen Regiment Nr.19. Reserve Infantry Regiment 119, 10 December 1914. Gefreiter on 12 March 1915. Unteroffizier on 8 May 1915. Vizefeldwebel on 11 May 1915. Promoted Leutnant d R on 9 August 1915. Observerschule on 24 April 1916. Pilot's training from 2 August 1917 to 13 February 1918. Ritterkreuz on 4 November 1941. Attained rank of Generalmajor in the Luftwaffe during WWII, on 1 August 1944. Died 20 February 1949, Ulm-Söflingen.

| Victories: | 1. | 22 May 1918 | AR2 | 0900 | W Prespa-See |
|---|---|---|---|---|---|

**KÖHLER, Karl     Ltn d R**

| | | | |
|---|---|---|---|
| J9 | – 30 May 1918 | – | KIA |

Born 14 February 1896, Dresden. Killed near Chambrey.

**KÖHLER, Ludwig**

| | | |
|---|---|---|
| J22 | (Jul 1917) | – |

**KÖHLER,     Uffz**

| | | | |
|---|---|---|---|
| J56 | 18 May 1918 – 18 Jun 1918 | – | WIA |

Joined Jasta 56 from Jastaschule I.

**KÖNEMANN, Egon     Ltn**

| | | | |
|---|---|---|---|
| JB | Jul 1917 – 22 Aug 1917 | – | KIA |

Born 8 August 1890, Charlottenberg. Killed during combat with Camels over Lombardzyde.

**KÖNIG, Erich     Ltn d R**

| | | | |
|---|---|---|---|
| JB | Oct 1916 – 2 Apr 1917 | 6 | KIA |

Biography & Victories: See *Above the Lines*.

**KÖNIG, Ewald     Ltn d R**

| | | | |
|---|---|---|---|
| J23b | 29 Oct 1917 – 3 May 1918 | – | POW |

Joined Jasta 23b from AFP5. Came down in British lines N of Gonnelieu, flying Pfalz DIIIa 8151/17 (G/1/2); engine trouble.

**KÖNIG, Walter     Uffz**

| | | | |
|---|---|---|---|
| J31 | – 3 Sep 1917 | – | KIA |

Born Dortmund, 19 January 1891. Killed over Tidietelhof.

**KÖNIG,    Uffz**
J36        1 Oct 1917 –                    –
Joined Jasta 36 from Jastaschule I.

---

**KÖNNECKE, Otto      Ltn d R**
J25        3 Dec 1916 –                    2          J5      20 May 1917 – 11 Nov 1918      33
AFP2               – 20 May 1917      –
Biography & Victories: See *Above the Lines*.

---

**KÖNNEMANN, Ulrich      Ltn**
FAA216     Apr 1917 – Dec 1917            –          J45     23 May 1918 – 11 Nov 1918       4
Born 12 December 1897, Wittenburg. Joined Hussar Regiment 15 on 8 August 1914. Transferred to aviation in Dec 1916. Jastaschule in May 1918. Joined Jasta 45 from Jastaschule I.

| Victories: | | | | | |
|---|---|---|---|---|---|
| | 1. | 15 Jul 1918 | Bréguet | 2105 | Conde |
| | 2. | 2 Sep 1918 | Spad XI | 1600 | Magneux |
| | 3. | 14 Sep 1918 | Salmson | 1620 | Fismes |
| | 4. | 30 Oct 1918 | Salmson | 1110 | Froidmont |

---

**KOEPSCH, Egon      Ltn d R**
J4         2 Oct 1917 – 20 Oct 1918       8          J4      4 Nov 1918 – 11 Nov 1918        1
CO J11     20 Oct 1918 – 4 Nov 1918       –
Biography & Victories: See *Above the Lines*.

---

**KÖRNER,    Ltn**
Kest 1a    (Sep 1918) –                   1

---

**KÖRNER, Hans      Ltn**
J8         (Jan 1917) – 15 Feb 1917       1          FAA246   May 1917 – Oct 1917           1
J27        15 Feb 1917 –                  –          J8       Oct 1918 – Dec 1917           1
J8         1 Mar 1917 – May 1917          –          J19      Dec 1917 – 11 Nov 1918        4
Biography & Victories: See *Above the Lines*.

---

**KÖRNER,    Ltn**
J37                                       1
| Victories: | 1. | 1 Oct 1918 | BF2b | 0915 | Haussay |
|---|---|---|---|---|---|

---

**KOHL, Herbert      Ltn**
J34b       16 Mar 1918 – 21 Mar 1918      –  POW
Became disoriented and landed in British lines.

---

**KOHLBACH, Wilhelm      Ltn d R**
J50        (Jun 1918) – 6 Aug 1918        2          J10     17 Aug 1918 – 11 Nov 1918       3
Biography & Victories: See *Above the Lines*.

---

**KOHLPOTH,    Ltn**
J56        3 Jul 1918 – Oct 1918          2  Sick
Joined Jasta 56 from Jastaschule I.

| Victories: | 1. | 29 Sep 1918 | DH9 | 1230 | Beythem |
|---|---|---|---|---|---|
| | 2. | 8 Oct 1918 | Camel | | Ingelmünster |

---

**KOHZE, Hermann      Oblt**
KG4                                                  CO JGr9   Mar 1918 –                    –
CO J3      1 Sep 1916 – 4 Sep 1918        1          CO JGr9   4 Sep 1918 – 11 Nov 1918      –
| Victories: | 1. | 18 Mar 1918 | Bréguet | 1115 | NW Montbréhain |
|---|---|---|---|---|---|
| | – | 18 Jun 1918 | BF2b | | Bray-sur-Somme |
| | – | 14 Sep 1918 | DH9 | | Pont-à-Mousson |

---

**KOLB, Wilhelm      Ltn**
J76b               – 12 Dec 1917      –  KIA
Born 18 June 1895, Munich. Served in Field Artillery Rgt 7. Killed over S Habsheim, at 1630 hours, while flying Albatros DV 5294/17.

---

**KOLLATZ,    Ltn**
J41                                       1
| Victories | 1. | 12 Aug 1918 | Bréguet 14B2 | | |
|---|---|---|---|---|---|

**KOLLER, Karl    Vfw**

| | | | | | | |
|---|---|---|---|---|---|---|
| SS34 | 4 Apr 1916 – 2 May 1917 | – | FA47 | 28 Feb 1918 – 16 Mar 1918 | – | |
| AFP3 | 22 Nov 1917 – 3 Dec 1917 | – | J76b | 3 Apr 1918 – 25 May 1918 | 1 | POW |
| FA273 | 4 Dec 1917 – 27 Feb 1918 | – | | | | |

Born 22 February 1898, Glonn/München. Entered military service 11 August 1914, Bavarian Eisenbahn-Etsatz-Bataillons. 8th Bavarian Infantry Division on 5 November 1914. Commenced pilot's training 16 January 1916. Fliegerschulen 1 & 4 from 3 May 1917 to 22 November 1917. Jastaschule from 17 March 1918 to 2 April 1918. Took off at 2000 hours in Albatros DVa 7221/17 coming down near Hedauville, (G/3/7); downed by 2/Lt A A Leitch, No 65 Sqn, RAF, in Camel D1903. Ritterkreuz on 10 April 1942 Deutsches Kreuz in Gold on 7 February 1944, with the Luftwaffe, WWII. Attained rank of General der Flieger on 1 November 1944.

| Victories: | 1. | 17 May 1918 | DH4 | | NW Mesnil |
|---|---|---|---|---|---|

**KOMMOSS, Rudolf    Ltn**

| | | | | |
|---|---|---|---|---|
| J50 | 22 Dec 1917 – 1 Apr 1918 | 1 | KIA | |

Born 15 May 1895, Alt-Ramten. OzbV for Jasta 50. Killed during a balloon attack by ground fire east of Bouvancourt.

| Victories: | 1. | Date and unit unknown | | | |
|---|---|---|---|---|---|
| | 2. | 24 Mar 1918 | RE8 | 1425 | Quessy |

**KOPKA, Johann    OfStv**

| | | | | | | |
|---|---|---|---|---|---|---|
| FAA262 | – 1918 | 1 | J61 | 24 Feb 1918 – | | 4 |

Biography & Victories: See *Above the Lines*.

**KORFF, Arthur    Ltn**

| | | |
|---|---|---|
| J60 | (Aug 1918) – 11 Nov 1918 | 8 |

Biography & Victories: See *Above the Lines*.

**KORIATH, Gustav    Flg**

| | | | | | | |
|---|---|---|---|---|---|---|
| FA8 | | – | J19 | – 1 Mar 1918 | – | KIAcc |

Born 16 June 1889, Bochum. Killed over airfield at St Loup.

**KORMANN, Bernhard    Flg**

| | | | |
|---|---|---|---|
| J79b | 5 May 1918 – 23 Aug 1918 | 1 | KIA |

Born 28 January 1893, Bertholdshof. Killed at 1200 hours near Fismes, flying Fokker D VII 4284/18 (Works No 2985) (G/3/13) by Lts C Pithey & H Rhodes, No 12 Sqn, RAF, in an RE8.

| Victories: | 1. | 16 Aug 1918 | Spad | 1145 | Coucy-le-Château |
|---|---|---|---|---|---|

**KORSCH, Hermann    Vfw**

| | | |
|---|---|---|
| J53 | 10 May 1918 – 11 Nov 1918 | 2 |

| Victories: | 1. | 22 Aug 1918 | Spad | | Coucy-le-Château |
|---|---|---|---|---|---|
| | 2. | 28 Oct 1918 | Spad | 1655 | Vaubourg |

**KORTE, Walter    Oblt**

| | | | | | | |
|---|---|---|---|---|---|---|
| CO J1 | 20 Jan 1918 – 7 Mar 1918 | – | Idflieg | 18 Jun 1918 – | | – |
| J72s | 7 Mar 1918 – 18 Jun 1918 | – | | | | |

**KORTÜM, Joachim    Ltn**

| | | | | | |
|---|---|---|---|---|---|
| FAA 216 | – 1917 | | FAA 242 | 14 Apr 1918 – 30 Nov 1918 | – |
| J10 | Mar 1918 – 14 Apr 1918 | – | | | |

**KOSMAHL, Fritz    OfStv**

| | | | | | |
|---|---|---|---|---|---|
| FFA22 | | 3 | J26 | 22 Aug 1917 – 22 Sep 1917 | 4    WIA |
| FFA261 | | 2 | | | |

Biography & Victories: See *Above the Lines*.

**KOSSLICK,    Ltn**

| | | | | | | |
|---|---|---|---|---|---|---|
| J31 | (Oct 1917) – 5 Mar 1918 | 2 | FA6 | 1 Aug 1918 – | | – |
| J73 | 5 Mar 1918 – 1 Aug 1918 | – | | | | |

Flew in Turkey with FA6.

| Victories: | 1. | 25 Oct 1917 | SALM | | Rocina |
|---|---|---|---|---|---|
| | 2. | 15 Nov 1917 | Balloon | | NE Treviso |

**KOWALLIK, Gustav    Vfw**
J34b       12 Dec 1917 – 18 Dec 1917    –           J42       18 Dec 1917 –                        1
Assigned to Jasta 34b from AFP5.
Victories:       1.          6 May 1918         AR2                 1810                SE Lassigny

**KRÄTZSCHMER, Hellmuth    Uffz**
J48       29 Dec 1917 – 30 Mar 1918    1   POW
Joined Jasta 48 from Jastaschule I. Crash-landed on 5 March 1918, injured. Flying a Pfalz when wounded
and forced to land near Blérancourt, at 1115.
Victories:       –          1 Mar 1918         Spad XIII                               W St Quentin
                 1.         21 Mar 1918         AWB                                    NW Séraucourt
(See French VI Armée Prisoner Interrogation Report.)

**KRÄMER,    Ltn**
J37                                       –

**KRAFFT, Fritz    Oblt**
JB           – 14 Apr 1918    –           J59       14 Apr 1918 – 11 Nov 1918    2
Assumed acting command of Jasta 59 on 27 September 1918.
Victories:       1.         17 Jun 1918         DH9                 1030                Bapaume
                 2.         24 Sep 1918         SE5a                                   Inchy

**KRAH, Paul    Gefr**
J48       29 Dec 1917 –                    –
Joined Jasta 48 from Jastaschule I.

**KRALEWSKI,    Ltn d R**
J4        (Dec 1916) – (Mar 1917)    1       J62       7 Feb 1918 – 19 May 1918    –
Kest 8    (Mar 1917) – 31 Dec 1917    –       J63      19 May 1918 – 1 Jul 1918    –   KIAcc
J27       31 Dec 1917 – 7 Feb 1918    –
Killed at 2130 hours during a test flight over Wancourt airfield.
Victories:       1.          6 Mar 1917         FE2b                1645                Ransart

**KRAMER, Heinrich    Vfw**
J14       (Apr 1917) – May 1917    1           J13       Aug 1917 –                        2
J9        May 1917 – Aug 1917    1
Victories:       1.         14 Apr 1917         Caudron             1200                Juvigny
                 2.         18 Aug 1917         AR2                 1200                S Avocourt
                 3.         27 Oct 1917         Spad                                   S Fresnes
                 4.         28 Jan 1918         Caudron                                Vendeuil

**KRAMER,    Ltn**
J28w                                      –

**KRANZ, Carl    Ltn d R**
J35b       31 Oct 1918 – 11 Nov 1918    –
Joined Jasta 35b from Jastaschule II.

**KRANZ, Willy    Vfw**
J23       31 May 1917 – 17 Sep 1917    –           J14       17 Sep 1917                        –
Joined Jasta 23 from Jastaschule I.

**KRAPFENBAUER, Fritz    Oblt**
FA6b                                      –           JGII      4 May 1918 – 11 Nov 1918    –
Adjutant for FA6b 16 February to 4 May 1918. Nachrichten Offizier, 4 May to 31 August 1918; JGII
Staff. Acting CO JG II, 25 October to 2 November 1918.

**KRATZER,    Ltn d R**
J32b       18 Oct 1918 – 11 Nov 1918    –

## KRAUSE, Helmut    Gefr
Kest 4a                – 5 Aug 1916      –  KIAcc
Born 11 September 1890, Bedchsteinwalde, Tuchel. Killed at Karlsruhe.

## KRAUSE,    Vfw
J8ob                   – 7 Mar 1918      –  INJ

## KRAUSE,    Uffz
J83/Kest 3                            1
Victories:      1.        5 Sep 1917      Caudron                          Remoncourt

## KRAUSS, Hugo    Oblt
J32b      27 Jun 1918 – 22 Aug 1918   1  KIAcc
Born 28 May 1885, Beyerberg. Served in Infantry Rgt 13. Crashed shortly after take-off at Villers-au-
Tertre airfield.
Victories:      1.        28 Jul 1918      DH4            0845            Croisselles

## KRAUSS, Max    Vfw
J27        20 Apr 1917 – 19 Jan 1918    4  KIA
Born 19 May 1893, Leipzig. Severely wounded in Sept 1914 in infantry. After recuperation he transferred
to aviation in 1915; assigned to FAA225. Awarded Silver St Henry Medal on 21 Feb 1917; Friedrich
August Silver Medal; Friedrich August Bronze Medal; EKI on 31 July 1917. Joined Jasta 27 from
Jastaschule I, Valenciennes. Killed at 1430 over Blankensee, in combat with a two-seater.
Victories:      1.        7 Jul 1917      RE8            1145            NW Ypern
                2.        16 Jul 1917     Sopwith        0810            NE Ypres
                –         24 Jul 1917     Martinsyde     2045            S Passchendaele    (a)
                –         28 Jul 1917     Martinsyde     0745            Staden             (b)
                3.        14 Aug 1917     Balloon        1642            NW Ypern
                –         20 Sep 1917     Spad VII       1815            Hooge
                4.        13 Jan 1918     Spad           1240            SW Gheluve
(a) Also claimed and awarded to Oblt Hermann Göring.
(b) Also claimed and awarded to Ltn Hörauf & OfStv Sättler of FA45.

## KRAUSS,    Ltn
J12        (Sep 1918) – 11 Nov 1918    –

## KRAUSS,    Ltn
J41                    – (Sep 1917)    –

## KRAUT, Richard    Ltn d R
J4        3 Aug 1918 – 25 Oct 1918    1         J66      25 Oct 1918 – 11 Nov 1918    –
Joined Jasta 4 from Jastaschule I.
Victories:      1.        26 Sep 1918     DH9            1715            S Metz

## KRAUTHEIM, Fritz    Ltn
J16b      7 May 1918 – 18 May 1918    –         J23b     18 May 1918 – 11 Nov 1918    –
Acting CO Jasta 23b from 2 July to 19 July 1918.

## KRAYER,    Ltn d R
J10       29 Jul 1918 – 31 Jul 1918    –        J45      13 Aug 1918 – 23 Sep 1918    3  INJ
J6        31 Jul 1918 – 13 Aug 1918    –
Joined Jasta 10 from Jastaschule II. Severely injured in an accident.
Victories:      1.        21 Aug 1918     Spad 2         1150            Rosnay
                2.        2 Sep 1918      Balloon        1555            Reims
                3.        6 Sep 1918      Balloon        1645            Magneux

## KREBS, Fritz    Vfw
J6        (May 1917) – 16 Jul 1917    8  KIA
Biography & Victories: See *Above the Lines*.

## KREBS,    Vfw
J56       9 Sep 1918 – 11 Nov 1918    3
Joined Jasta 56 from Jastaschule I.

| Victories: | 1. | 28 Sep 1918 | Spad | | Kastelhoek | |
| | 2. | 29 Sep 1918 | SE5a | 0815 | Westroosebeke | |
| | 3. | 9 Oct 1918 | Bréguet | 1617 | Ardooye | |

## KREFFT, Constantin    Ltn d R

| FA5b | | – | | JGI | 25 Jun 1917 – 9 Jan 1918 | – |
| J11 | 11 Oct 1916 – 25 Jun 1917 | 2 | | Idflieg | 9 Jan 1918 – | – |

Technical Officer for Jasta 11 and JGI. Injured in a crash-landing 11 August 1917.

| Victories: | 1. | 11 Mar 1917 | FE8 | 1145 | Vimy-Givenchy | |
| | 2. | 2 Apr 1917 | FE2d | 0945 | Courcelles | (a) |

(a) Probably A5151, No 57 Sqn, Capt H Tomlinson & Lt N C Denison.

## KREMER, Paul    Oblt

| KG6/33 | | | | FEA1b | 18 Aug 1917 | – |
| J16 | 15 Nov 1916 – 18 Aug 1917 | | | | | |

Commanded a Fliegerschule.

## KRESS, Christian    Vfw

| Kek M | | – 1916 | | – | J6 | 10 Sep 1916 – 10 Nov 1916 | 2 KIA |

Born 14 November 1890, Geroda. Killed over Nesle, at 1300 hours, probably by Lt Georges Guynemer, N3.

| Victories: | 1. | Date and unit unknown | | | |
| | 2. | Date and unit unknown | | | |
| | 3. | 20 Oct 1916 | Morane | | S Péronne |
| | 4. | 2 Nov 1916 | Voisin | | Chaulnes |

## KRESSE, Friedrich    Ltn d R

| J7 | 24 Jun 1918 – 16 Sep 1918 | 1 WIA |

Born 26 October 1893, Dresden. Served in Grenadier Rgt Nr.101. Severely wounded in combat with Camels of No 209 Sqn, RAF, over Houplines, flying a Fokker DVII (G/1/16), died later as a POW.

| Victories: | 1. | 14 Sep 1918 | RE8 | | SE Ypern |

## KRESSNER, Kurt    Vfw

| J5 | 28 Mar 1918 – 28 Apr 1918 | 1 INJ |
| Victories: | 1. | 25 Apr 1918 | BF2b | | Marcelcave |

## KREUTZER,    Ltn

| J19 | – 12 May 1917 | – WIA |

Severely wounded in the foot during combat with a Spad.

## KREUZER, Edwin    Ltn d R

| J36 | 21 Feb 1917 – 18 Aug 1917 | 1 WIAcc | J74 | 5 Mar 1918 – 11 Nov 1918 | – |
| J39 | (Feb 1918) – 5 Mar 1918 | 1 | | | |

Field Artillery Bttn 240. Leutnant on 30 September 1915. Shot down on 12 July 1917; his plane was destroyed by British artillery, but he was not harmed. Wounded in an accidental firing of machine-guns by Ltn Degelow. Awarded Baden Orden vom Zähringer Löwen on 17 April 1918. Joined Jasta 36 from FEA11.

| Victories: | 1. | 6 Apr 1917 | Caudron | | Berry-au-Bac |
| | 2. | 25 Feb 1918 | Balloon | | Ponzano |

## KREUZNER,    Ltn

| J13 | | | 1 |
| Victories: | 1. | 6 Apr 1917 | Farman | | S Vailly |

## KRICKOW,    Vfw

| J58 | 28 Oct 1918 – 11 Nov 1918 | – |

## KRIEG,    Hptm

| CO J14 | 28 Sep 1916 – 15 Oct 1916 | – |

Commanded Fokkerstaffel Falkenhausen.

## KRIST,    Vfw

| J70 | – 11 Nov 1918 | 1 |
| Victories: | 1. | 25 Sep 1918 | DH4 | | Brumath |

## KROEGER, Uffz
J7 – 1 Jun 1918 – WIA

## KRÖHL, Georg Ltn d R
J34b 6 Sep 1917 – 19 Aug 1918 4 FEA2b 19 Aug 1918 – –
Born 22 October 1896, Ilefeld. In military service before war as a Fähnrich in a Bavarian Infantry Rgt. Promoted Leutnant d R 29 March 1916. Transferred to aviation in 1917, trained at FEA2, Furth, and Nürnberg. Joined Jasta 34b from Jastaschule I. His aircraft carried a red band on fuselage just aft of pilot's seat. Killed 13 September 1925 at Schleissheim.

| Victories: | 1. | 1 Jan 1918 | Spad | | Bois de Cheppy |
|---|---|---|---|---|---|
| | 2. | 4 Apr 1918 | AWFK8 | | Bois de Hamel |
| | – | 12 Jul 1918 | 2-seater | 1140 | E Herville |
| | 3. | 20 Jul 1918 | SE5a | 0830 | Hamel |
| | 4. | 8 Aug 1918 | DH9 | 1255 | SE Morcourt |

## KRÖNERT, Otto Uffz
J14 – 24 Nov 1916 – KIA
Born 7 July 1889, Graudenz. Killed near Château-Salins.

## KRÖNERT, Ltn
J14 Apr 1917 – Sep 1917 –

## KRÖNIG, Albert Ltn d R
J3 26 Aug 1916 – 16 Nov 1916 1 INJ J3 Jan 1918 – 2 Feb 1918 – KIAcc
J27 10 Dec 1917 – Jan 1918 –
Born 10 September 1892, Graudenz. Severely injured 16 November 1916 in a landing accident. Joined Jasta 27 from AFP4. Killed at 1750 hours at Thielt airfield.

| Victories: | 1. | 22 Sep 1916 | Sopwith | 0915 | N Bouchavesnes |
|---|---|---|---|---|---|

## KROLL, Heinrich Claudius Oblt d R
FA17 Apr 1916 – 5 Nov 1916 – J24s 29 Jun 1917 – 14 Aug 1918 28 WIA
J9 5 Nov 1917 – 29 Jun 1917 5
Biography & Victories: See *Above the Lines*.

## KROPP, Hermann Oblt
CO J15 9 Oct 1916 – 8 Nov 1916 – Idflieg 8 Nov 1916 – –

## KRÜCHELSDORF, Uffz
J39 (Jun 1918) – 11 Nov 1918 1

| Victories: | 1. | 6 Nov 1918 | DH9 |
|---|---|---|---|

## KRÜGER, Heinrich Vfw
J70 – 12 Aug 1918 2 KIA
Born 5 May 1896, Dresden. Killed in combat with a DH9 near Grunstadt.

| Victories: | 1. | 27 May 1918 | DH4 | 1320 | Elfringen |
|---|---|---|---|---|---|
| | 2. | 30 Jun 1918 | DH9 | | Schirmeck |

## KRÜGER, Kurt Ltn d R
J55 – 17 Jul 1918 – KIA
Born 30 April 1895, Frankfurt a.M. Killed over Bet-Dedschan.

## KRÜGER, Richard Ltn d R
J4 – 17 Jul 1917 1 DOW
Born 20 January 1892, Schwerin. Served in Infantry Regiment 176. Severely wounded at 1315 hours over Comines, died at 2105 hours in hospital.

| Victories: | 1. | 7 Jul 1917 | Triplane | 1105 | W Wervicq |
|---|---|---|---|---|---|

## KRÜGER, Ltn d R
J4 24 Apr 1918 – 11 May 1918 – AFP2 11 May 1918 – –

## KRUSE, Alfred Uffz
J29 16 Aug 1918 – 11 Nov 1918 –
Joined Jasta 29 from Jastaschule I.

**KRUSE,  Gefr**
J45    28 Aug 1918 –                          –
Joined Jasta 45 from Jastaschule II.

---

**KUBLUM, Fritz    OfStv**
J20      11 Dec 1917 – 30 Mar 1918    –            Idflieg      6 Jul 1918 –              –
J26      30 Mar 1918 – 6 Jul 1918     1
Joined Jasta 20 from Jastaschule I. Hospitalised 10 June 1918.
Victories:    1.      3 Jun 1918      Bréguet            1920            Armentières

---

**KÜFFBERGER, Heinrich    Ltn d R**
J23b              – 9 Jun 1918    – KIA
Born 3 September 1894, Wurzberg. Killed over Phalempin.

---

**KÜGLER, Xaver    Ltn d R**
FAA236                            –          FEA1b    19 Oct 1917 –              –
J23      23 Aug 1917 – 19 Oct 1917    –
OzbV for Jasta 23.

---

**KÜHN, Fritz    Uffz**
J79b      2 May 1918 – 12 Jun 1918    – WIA

---

**KÜHN, Max    Ltn d R**
J10      Jul 1917 – 3 May 1918    1          AFP2      3 May 1918 –              –
Acting CO Jasta 10 from 26 & 27 Sep 1917.
Victories:    1.      Date and unit unknown
              2.      Date and unit unknown
              3.      2 Feb 1918      SE5a            1530            Bouchain

---

**KÜHN,    Ltn**
J28w                            –

---

**KÜHN,    Ltn**
J33          1917 –                  –

---

**KÜHNE, Rudolf    Vfw**
J3        (Oct 1918) – 11 Nov 1918    1
Victories:    1.      5 Oct 1918      DH9                             Ekenbach

---

**KÜHNE, Wilhelm    OfStv**
FA14                            –          J15      Jan 1918 – 20 Mar 1918    –
J29      12 Feb 1917 – 21 Jul 1917    –          J18      20 Mar 1918 – 30 Aug 1918    7   KIA
StoflH    21 Jul 1917 –                 –
Biography & Victories: See *Above the Lines.*

---

**KÜLLMER, Heinrich    Vfw**
J6        8 May 1917 – 2 Aug 1917    1          J23b      24 Sep 1917 – 16 May 1918    2   KIA
J34      2 Aug 1917 – 18 Sep 1917    –
Born 10 May 1896, Cluentel. Lightly wounded 5 June 1917, returned to Jasta 6 on 13 June 1917. Killed
over Sailly.
Victories:    1.      28 Jul 1917      Nieuport          1150            N Terhand
              2.      1 Jan 1918      Spad                             Maasschleife
              3.      18 Feb 1918      Camel                            Bailleul

---

**KUEN, Adolf    Ltn d R**
FAA 103?    15 Jan 1916 – 3 Oct 1916    –          FAA 297    23 Aug 1917 – 10 Aug 1918    –
J14        Feb 1917 – Aug 1917    2
Victories:    1.      3 Feb 1917      Caudron          1525            SW Embermenil
              2.      12 Jul 1917      Caudron                          E Cerny

---

**KÜNSBERG, Rüdiger Fr von    Ltn**
J300                          J55      3 May 1918 – 8 Jun 1918    – KIA
Born 20 February 1898, Munich. Served in Field Artillery Rgt 1. Killed over Tulkern at 0800 hours.

## KÜNSTER, Heinz   Ltn

| | | | | | | |
|---|---|---|---|---|---|---|
| J18 | 7 Jul 1918 – 11 Nov 1918 | 2 | | | | |
| Victories: | 1. | 14 Sep 1918 | Spad XIII | 0915 | Thiaucourt | |
| | 2. | 1 Oct 1918 | Spad | | XIII | |

## KÜPPERS, Kurt   Ltn d R

| | | | | | |
|---|---|---|---|---|---|
| FA45 | 1916 | – | J6 | Oct 1917 – 14 Dec 1917 | 1 |
| J6 | (Mar 1917) – Aug 1917 | 4 | J48 | 14 Dec 1917 – 23 Aug 1918 | 1 |
| KG3/14 | Aug 1917 – Oct 1917 | – | Idflieg | 23 Aug 1918 | – |

Biography & Victories: See *Above the Lines*.

## KÜTT, Heinrich   Ltn d R

| | | | | |
|---|---|---|---|---|
| J23b | 10 Sep 1917 – 7 Jun 1918 | 1 | WIA | |

Born 3 September 1894, Wurzburg. Wounded in action 19 Feb 1918. Severely wounded over Douai, landed at Jasta 30 airfield at Phalempin, died of wounds 9 June 1918.

| | | | | | |
|---|---|---|---|---|---|
| Victories: | 1. | 17 Oct 1917 | Spad | 1500 | Verdun |

## KUHLMEY,   Flg

| | | | | | |
|---|---|---|---|---|---|
| J28w | | 1 | | | |
| Victories: | 1. | 28 May 1918 | SE5a | 0845 | S Dickebuschsee |

## KUHN, Max   Vfw

| | | |
|---|---|---|
| J21s | (Jun 1918) – (Sep 1918) | 12 |

Biography & Victories: See *Above the Lines*.

## KUKE, Fritz   Ltn

| | | | | |
|---|---|---|---|---|
| J33 | – 18 Nov 1917 | 2 | KIAcc | |

Born 14 March 1886, Dirschau. Killed during test flight over Wynghene airfield.

| | | | | | |
|---|---|---|---|---|---|
| Victories: | – | 8 Jul 1917 | Rumpf DD | 2130 | Inchy |
| | 1. | 21 Oct 1917 | Camel | 1415 | NE Ypern |
| | 2. | 27 Oct 1917 | Camel | 1125 | Dadizeele |
| | zlg | 10 Nov 1917 | RE8 | | SW Boesinghe |

## KUMINS,   Ltn

| | | | | | |
|---|---|---|---|---|---|
| J7 | 23 Aug 1916 – 22 Feb 18 | – | Kofl4 | 22 Feb 1918 – | – |

OzbV for Jasta 7.

## KUMMERFELD,   Ltn d R

| | | | | | |
|---|---|---|---|---|---|
| J66 | | 1 | | | |
| Victories: | 1. | 29 Aug 1918 | Spad | | Courvelles |

## KUMMETZ, Hans   Oblt

| | | | | | | |
|---|---|---|---|---|---|---|
| CO J1 | 18 Nov 1916 – 12 Sep 1917 | 6 | CO J1 | 20 Nov 1917 – 11 Jan 1918 | 1 | KIA |
| JsSchII | 12 Sep 1917 – 20 Nov 1917 | – | | | | |

Biography & Victories: See *Above the Lines*.

## KUNST, Otto   Ltn

| | | | | | |
|---|---|---|---|---|---|
| J3 | – Jun 1917 | – | J7 | 2 Aug 1917 – 2 Mar 1918 | – |
| J22 | Jun 1917 – 2 Aug 1917 | 1 | | | |

Transferred to Junkers Flg Wrks.

| | | | | | |
|---|---|---|---|---|---|
| Victories: | 1. | 29 Jun 1917 | Nieuport | 1530 | SW Vailly |

## KUNZ, Hermann   Ltn d R

| | | | | | |
|---|---|---|---|---|---|
| J7 | Aug 1917 – Dec 1917 | 3 | J55 | 3 May 1918 – 20 Sep 1918 | 3 |

Biography & Victories: See *Above the Lines*.

## KUNZE,   Ltn

| | |
|---|---|
| J7 | – |

## KUNZE,   Vfw

| | | |
|---|---|---|
| J81 | – 18 Jul 1917 | – POW |

## KUPFER,   Vfw

| | | |
|---|---|---|
| J38 | (Jul 1918) – | – |

## KURTH, Helmut     Ltn d R

| | | | | | |
|---|---|---|---|---|---|
| FAA208 | | – | J34 | 24 Feb 1917 – 23 May 1917 | – |
| J17 | 11 Nov 1916 – 18 Jan 1917 | – | Kest 6 | 23 May 1917 – | – |
| J26 | 18 Jan 1917 – 24 Feb 1917 | – | | | |

## KUTSCHER, Alexander     Ltn d R

| | | | | | |
|---|---|---|---|---|---|
| FA32 | | – | J28 | – 1 May 1917 | – DOW |
| J5 | 27 Aug 1916 – | – | | | |

Born 27 September 1882, Saarbrucken. Severely wounded over Poperinghe, during combat with a Nieuport, while flying Albatros DIII 771/17 'K' (G.30), landed in Allied lines near Elverdinghe, where he died, the victim of 2/Lt E S T Cole and Lt F Sharpe, No 1 Sqn, RFC, in Nieuport Scouts N1508 and N1550 respectively.

## KUTSCHERA, Wilhelm     Uffz

| | | | |
|---|---|---|---|
| J3 | – 31 May 1918 | – | KIA |

Born 14 September 1895, Furtwangen. Killed by ground fire.

## KUTTER, Otto     Uffz

| | | | |
|---|---|---|---|
| J48 | – 9 May 1918 | – | KIA |

Born 28 December 1893, Egelstal. Killed over Montdidier, by a Spad.

## KYPKE, Walter     Ltn d R

| | | | | | |
|---|---|---|---|---|---|
| FFA2 | 1915 | – | J41 | Sep 1917 – 27 Oct 1917 | 4 |
| FFA57 | 1916 | – | Kest 5 | 27 Oct 1917 – 26 Dec 1917 | 1 |
| Kek A | Feb 1916 – 16 Oct 1916 | 1 | J47w | 26 Dec 1917 – 11 Nov 1918 | 3 |
| J14 | 16 Oct 1916 – Sep 1917 | – | | | |

Biography & Victories: See *Above the Lines*.

## LAABS, Wilhelm     Uffz

| | | | |
|---|---|---|---|
| J13 | – 16 Jul 1918 | 1 | KIAcc |

Born 26 December 1892, Woedtke. Killed shortly after take-off when he jumped from his burning plane.

| Victories: | 1. | 10 Jun 1918 | SE5a | | Château Sorel |
|---|---|---|---|---|---|

## LAAK, Gerhard     Ltn d R

| | | | |
|---|---|---|---|
| J61 | – 17 Mar 1918 | – | KIAcc |

Born 19 September 1896, Mechernich. Killed in an accident shortly after take-off at Vivaise airfield.

## LACH,     Uffz

| | | |
|---|---|---|
| J36 | 14 Aug 1918 – 11 Nov 1918 | – |

## LAGE,     Vfw

| | | | | |
|---|---|---|---|---|
| J38 | | | 1 | |
| Victories: | zlg | 29 Oct 1917 | BE12 | Dojran See |
| | 1. | 28 Nov 1917 | Nieuport | S Stojakovo |

## LAITENBERGER, Robert     Uffz

| | |
|---|---|
| J4 | – |

Born 27 September 1889, Neckarwestheim. Died 2 January 1919, in hospital.

## LAMY,     Ltn

| | |
|---|---|
| J39 | (Jun 1918) – |

OzbV for Jasta 39.

## LAMPRECHT, Emil     Ltn

| | | | | | |
|---|---|---|---|---|---|
| J28 | (Jul 1917) – (Oct 1917) | – | J7 | 14 Mar 1918 – 11 Nov 1918 | – |

Knight's Cross 2nd Class with Swords of the Württemberg Friedrich Order on 6 Sept 1917. OzbV for Jasta 7.

| Victories: | zlg | 27 Jul 1917 | RE8 | 0925 | Ploegsteert Wald |
|---|---|---|---|---|---|

## LANDER, Rudolf     Vfw

| | | | | | | |
|---|---|---|---|---|---|---|
| J22 | (Jan 1917) – 2 Aug 1917 | – | J52 | 9 Jan 1918 – 29 Aug 1918 | 1 | KIAcc |
| J7 | 2 Aug 1917 – 28 Dec 1917 | 1 | | | | |

Born 9 May 1892, Werichanowe. Crash landed on 9 Sept 1917, aircraft destroyed, he was not hurt. Died in a crash at FEA13, Bromberg.

| Victories: | 1. | 10 Dec 1917 | Sopwith 2 | | Ghent |
| | 2. | 17 May 1918 | BF2b | 1945 | Sailly |

## LANDGRAF, Ltn
J20        3 Mar 1917 – 28 Jun 1917    –        Idflieg    28 Jun 1917 –        –

## LANDIN, Jakob    OfStv
J32b        – 27 Feb 1918    3    KIAcc
Born 21 August 1892, Westheim. Crashed at 1730 hours, shortly after take-off at Guesnain airfield.

| Victories: | 1. | 23 Dec 1917 | AR2 | | S Vailly |
| | 2. | 6 Jan 1918 | Nieuport | | W Paissy |
| | 3. | 23 Feb 1918 | RE8 | 1535 | Willerval |

## LANG, Karl    OfStv
J1        19 May 1917 – 1 Jan 1918    1    KIA
Born 24 July 1893, Stockhausen. Shot down in flames and killed during combat with a Sopwith Camel at 1110 hours near Vittorio, Italy.

| Victories: | 1. | 25 Jun 1917 | Spad | 1130 | Chaillevois |
| | zlg | 22 Jul 1917 | Caudron | 1200 | La Fère |

## LANG, Oskar    Ltn d R
| FFA60 | 29 Jul 1915 – 3 Apr 1916 | – | FEA9 | 19 Nov 1916 – 31 Jan 1917 | – |
| FEA9 | 3 Apr 1916 – 12 May 1916 | – | Kest 3 | 31 Jan 1917 – 18 Apr 1917 | – |
| AFP5 | 2 Jun 1916 – 21 Aug 1916 | – | Kest 1b | 18 Apr 1917 – 13 May 1917 | – KIA |
| J5 | 21 Aug 1916 – 19 Nov 1916 | – | | | |

Born 1 June 1895, St Georgen, Baden. Received German Pilot's Licence No 637 on 31 December 1913. Enlisted 3 August 1914, assigned to FEA3, Gotha. Transferred to Fest-Flieger-Abteilung Metz on 6 February 1915. Flugzeugführer Abzeichen on 28 February 1915. AFP5 on 30 March 1915. Promoted Unteroffizier on 28 May 1915. EKII on 4 September 1915. Vizefeldwebel on 15 September 1915. Transferred to Ersatz-Kampf-Einsitzer-Abteilung Köln, 12 May 1916 to 2 June 1916. Awarded Baden Silberne Militär-Verdeinstmedaille on 3 December 1915. Promoted Leutnant d R 20 January 1916. Awarded the Knight's Cross 2nd Class with Swords of the Royal Hohenzollern House Order with Swords on 21 January 1917 (see OTF, Vol 4, No 4, pg 324).

## LANG, Rudolf    Oblt
| CO J11 | 11 Oct 1916 – 14 Jan 1917 | – | FEA1 | 24 Apr 1917 – | – |
| CO J28 | 20 Jan 1917 – 24 Apr 1917 | – | | | |
Assumed command of Bavarian Fliegerschule I on 24 April 1917.

## LANG, Rudolf    Gefr
J78b        – 8 Jul 1918    – WIA
Wounded in bombing raid on his airfield.

## LANGE, Helmut    Ltn
J26        11 Jan 1918 – 11 Nov 1918    9
Biography & Victories: See Above the Lines.

## LANGE, Walter    Ltn d R
J40        27 Jul 1917 – Sep 1917    –        JB        Sep 1917 – 20 Oct 1917    1    KIA
Born 19 January 1894, Richenau. Served with Field Artillery Regiment 12. Killed during combat with Camels at 1220 hours near Passchendaele.

| Victories: | 1. | 20 Sep 1917 | Camel | 1210 | SW Stade | (a) |
(a) Probably F/S/Lt H S Broughall, 10 Sqn, RNAS.

## LANGE,    ?
J13        (Sep 1918) – 11 Nov 1918    –

## LANGEN,    Ltn
| J39 | – 5 Mar 1918 | 1 | J39 | 30 Apr 1918 – | – |
| J74 | 5 Mar 1918 – 30 Apr 1918 | – | | | |
| Victories: | 1. | 4 Jun 1918 | Spad 2 | | Cuchery |

**LANGENBACH,** **Ltn**
J81      – 8 Aug 1918    –        FEA4    8 Aug 1918 –        –

**LANGENBACH,** **Ltn**
J81      – 16 Jun 1918    –   POW (over Mont St. Quentin)

**LANGENHEIM,** **Flg**
J49      – 8 Mar 1918    –   INJ
Severely injured in an accident at his airfield.

**LANGER, Bruno** **Ltn d R**
J3        – 4 Feb 1918    –   KIA
Born 1 March 1889. Served in Jäger Battalion. 5 Shot down in flames over Ypern-Westroosebeke, flying an Albatros DVa (G.131), by Lt H Crompton or 2/Lt H Hegarty, No 60 Sqn, RFC.

**LANGER,** **Vfw**
J26    18 Jan 1917 – 25 May 1917    –

**LANGER, Martin** **Ltn d R**
J40    27 Jul 1917 –              1
Victories:    1.        11 Dec 1917      DH4                     Mamey

**LANGJAHN,** **Ltn**
J61                         1
Victories:    1.        6 Oct 1918       Spad

**LANKE, Karl** **Ltn**
J29    3 Aug 1917 – 3 Sep 1917    –       AFP12    3 Sep 1917 –        –
Assigned to Jasta 29 from AFP6.

**LAPP, Max** **Oblt**
J77b    17 Nov 1917 – 29 Apr 1918    –       J77b    2 Sep 1918 – 22 Sep 1918    –
OzbV for Jasta 77b.

**LAUENSTEIN,** **Ltn**
J39      (Jun 1918) –           –

**LAUKANDT, Paul** **Gefr**
J13        – 15 Jun 1917    –   KIA
Born Tilsit, 24 January 1889. Killed over Foucaucourt.

**LAUMANN, Arthur** **Ltn d R**
FFA265    Mar 1918 – 25 May 1918    –       J10    14 Aug 1918 – 11 Nov 1918    5
J66    25 May 1918 – 14 Aug 1918    23
Biography & Victories: See *Above the Lines*.

**LAUMANN, Richard** **Ltn d R**
J10    24 Apr 1918 – 4 Jul 1918    –       J10    30 Jul 1918 –        –
Idflieg    4 Jul 1918 – 30 Jul 1918    –

**LAURISCH, Hans** **Ltn**
FAA254        – 1917      2       Kest 4b        – 30 Jul 1918    –   INJ
Born 19 November 1897, Charlottenburg. DOW 31 July 1918, Freiburg.
Victories:    1.       27 Jun 1917      Spad                  Berry-au-Bac       (a)
            2.        20 Aug 1917      Spad                  Töter Mann
(a) With Observer, Ltn Thiele.

**LAUSCHER, Bernhard** **Ltn**
J31      (Mar 1918) – 4 Sep 1918    1   INJ
Injured in landing accident.
Victories:    1.       18 Jun 1918      AR2           1020        Hochberg

**LAUTENSCHLAGER, Josef** **Vfw**
J11    14 May 1917 – 29 Oct 1917    1   KIA

Born 12 March 1892, Reifenthal. Killed by mistake by a German two-seater at 1045 hours N Houthulsterwald, flying Fokker DrI 113/17.

| Victories: | 1. | 7 Jul 1917 | Sopwith 2 | 1810 | W Comines |
|---|---|---|---|---|---|

### LAUTZ, Walter    Ltn d R
J20          – 29 Jan 1917    –  WIA
Born 2 January 1888, Westerwaldkries. Served in Infantry Rgt 364. Wounded over Vendhuille, died of wounds in Berlin, on 19 May 1917.

### LAVEUVE, Ludwig    Ltn
J77b     24 Apr 1918 – 18 Oct 1918    1
Joined Jasta 77b from Jastaschule I.

| Victories: | 1. | 1 Jun 1918 | DH | 1100 | Longneau |
|---|---|---|---|---|---|

### LECHNER,    Vfw
J6        14 Aug 1918 – 30 Aug 1918    –          IdFlieg   30 Aug 1918 –          –
Joined Jasta 6 from Jastaschule I. Injured 16 August 1918, during a test flight.

### LEDERMANN, Jakob    OfStv
J13          – 20 Aug 1918    1  POW
Joined Jasta 13 from Jastaschule I. Forced down in Allied lines after combat with Spads.

| Victories: | 1. | 14 Aug 1918 | Scout | 1840 | Chaulnes |
|---|---|---|---|---|---|

### LEFFERS, Gustav    Ltn d R
FA32        – 1916        –          J1      23 Aug 1916 – 27 Dec 1916    4  KIA
KekB/AKN     – 23 Aug 1916    5
Biography & Victories: See *Above the Lines*.

### LEGEL, Kurt    Ltn d R
J52      6 Apr 1918 – 27 Apr 1918    2  KIAcc
Born 16 August 1897, Pegau. Served in Reserve Infantry Rgt Nr.133. Joined Jasta 52 from Jastaschule I. Killed shortly after take-off over Faumont.

| Victories: | 1. | 17 Apr 1918 | Camel | 0720 | Merville |
|---|---|---|---|---|---|
| | 2. | 21 Apr 1918 | SE5a | 1925 | Bailleul |

### LEGRIS,    Ltn
Kest 1b    (Apr 1918) – (Sep 1918)    –

### LEHMANN, Burkhard    Ltn
FA32          – 23 Aug 1916    –          J12      28 Jul 1917 – 5 Aug 1917    –  KIA
J1      23 Aug 1916 – 28 Jul 1917    –
Born 20 March 1894, Halberstadt. Killed in action at 2040 hours near Hendecourt-les-Cagnicourt, on 5 August 1917.

### LEHMANN, Walter    Ltn d R
J10      15 May 1918 – 1 Aug 1918    –  POW
Born 24 January 1895, Eibenstock. Served in Infantry Regiment 139. Awarded: Saxon Knight's Cross of the Military St Henry Order on 18 Aug 1916. Shot down over Fère-en-Tardenois. Attained rank of Oberst (Colonel) in Luftwaffe during WWII. Died 16 August 1976, Wiessee, Germany.

### LEHMANN, Werner    Ltn d R
KEK Voz                    3          J9      23 Sep 1916 – 23 Sep 1916    –  KIAcc
Born 25 April 1894, Berlin. Killed over Somme-Py.

| Victories: | 1. | Date and unit unknown |
|---|---|---|
| | 2. | Date and unit unknown |
| | 3. | Date and unit unknown |

### LEHMANN, Werner    Ltn
J40     Dec 1917 –          –

### LEHMANN, Wilhelm    Ltn
J5      Aug 1917 – 26 Jun 1918    4  KIA
Born 9 July 1892, Forst. Served in Lieb Grenadier Rgt 8. Acting CO Jasta 5 from 31 Dec 1917 to 14 Jan 1918. Commanded Jasta 5, 12 May to 26 June 1918. Killed over Albert, probably by 1/Lt F E Kindley, USAS.

| Victories: | 1. | 6 Sep 1917 | Sopwith 2 | 1405 | Mont St Martin |
|---|---|---|---|---|---|
|  | 2. | 29 Apr 1918 | DH4 |  | N Cachy |
|  | 3. | 21 May 1918 | Camel |  |  |
|  | 4. | 13 Jun 1918 | SE5a |  | Bouzincourt |

## LEHMANN,    Gefr
J5          Oct 1918 – 11 Nov 1918    –

## LEHMANN,    Ltn
J59              – 11 Nov 1918    1

| Victories: | 1. | 24 Sep 1918 | BF2b | Boursies |
|---|---|---|---|---|

## LEHRMUND, Karl    Uffz
J52      17 Sep 1918 – 11 Nov 1918    –
Joined Jasta 52 from Jastaschule I.

## LIEBFRIED,    Ltn
J64w      14 Jun 1918 – 11 Nov 1918    3
Joined Jasta 64w from Jastaschule I.

| Victories: | 1. | 14 Sep 1918 | Salmson | Bland |
|---|---|---|---|---|
|  | 2. | 10 Oct 1918 | DH4 | Beaume-Haiewald |
|  | 3. | 23 Oct 1918 | Bréguet | SE Pagny |

## LEICHT, Fritz    Ltn d R
J31              – 5 Nov 1918    –  KIA
Born 22 May 1896, Graudenz. Killed over Beney.

## LEICHT,    Uffz
J5              – 11 Nov 1918    4

| Victories: | 1. | 26 Aug 1918 | Balloon | 1700 | S Harbonnières |
|---|---|---|---|---|---|
|  | 2. | 20 Sep 1918 | BF2b | 1040 | Croix Fonsommé |
|  | 3. | 24 Sep 1918 | SE5a | 0830 | S Hamel |
|  | 4. | 23 Oct 1918 | BF2b |  |  |

## LEIENDECKER, Heinz    Uffz
J9              – 3 Feb 1918    –  WIA
Lightly wounded in combat S Tahure.

## LEIM, Paul    OfStv
| FFA35 | 5 Aug 1914 – 19 Apr 1915 | – | J300 | 27 Sep 1917 – | – |
|---|---|---|---|---|---|
| FFA14 | 19 Apr 1915 – | – | J55 | 3 May 1918 – 20 Aug 1918 | – |
| J27 | 7 Mar 1917 – 25 May 1917 | – | Ltn Kest |  |  |
| Kest 4b | 24 May 1917 – 27 Sep 1917 | – | 4b/J84 | 20 Aug 1918 – 11 Nov 1918 | – |

Joined Fliegertruppe on 1 June 1913. Commanded Kest 4b/Jasta 84. Awarded: Goldene Militär-Verdeinstkreuz on 3 July 1918; Prussian Crown Order Medal; Württemberg Silver Military Merit Medal; Turkish Silver Liakat Medal.

## LEINEGRABER,    Uffz
| J22s | – 16 Apr 1918 | – | J56 | 16 Apr 1918 – 11 Nov 1918 | – |
|---|---|---|---|---|---|

## LEMKE, Alfred    Gefr
J10              – 3 May 1917    –  POW
Flying Albatros DII 473/16 ran out of fuel and force-landed near Abbeville-Fampoux, at 1600 hours; (G.32).

## LEMKE,    Vfw
J70              – 11 Nov 1918    2

| Victories: | 1. | 16 Aug 1918 | DH4 | Dagsburg |
|---|---|---|---|---|
|  | 2. | 25 Sep 1918 | DH4 | Bergzabern |

## LENZ, Alfred    Ltn d R
| FFA61 | Jun 1915 – | 1 | J14 | 16 Oct 1916 – 1 Jul 1917 | – |
|---|---|---|---|---|---|
| FA23 | Jan 1916 – | – | CO J22 | 1 Jul 1917 – 11 Nov 1918 | 5 |
| J4 | 1 Sep 1916 – 16 Oct 1916 | – |  |  |  |

Biography & Victories: See *Above the Lines*.

**LENZ, Max    Ltn**
J14       (Jan 1917) –          –
OzbV for Jasta 14.

---

**LEONHARD, Franz    Ltn d R**
J34b    17 Nov 1917 – 4 Mar 1918    –          FEA1b    4 Mar 1918 –          –
Assigned to Jasta 34b from Jastaschule I.

---

**LEPPIN,    Ltn d R**
J24s    27 Mar 1918 – 11 Nov 1918    1
Victories:    1.       8 Aug 1918       2-seater          1545       Misery

---

**LEPTIEN, Hermann    Ltn d R**
J21       (Sep 1917) – 21 Feb 1918    3       CO J63    21 Feb 1918 – 11 Nov 1918    4
Biography & Victories: See *Above the Lines*.

---

**LERSNER, Rolf Fr von    Ltn**
JB       (Jun 1917) – Aug 1917       –       KG3       Aug 1917 –          –

---

**LEUSCH, Wilhelm    Ltn**
FFAM       1915 –          –       J13    1 Nov 1916 – Apr 1917       –
Ltn d R                                  J19    Apr 1917 – 11 Nov 1918    5
FFA19       1915 –          –
Biography & Victories: See *Above the Lines*.

---

**LEYH, Erich    Uffz**
J21          – 19 Apr 1917       –       J29    19 Apr 1917 – 26 May 1917    – KIA
Born 27 December 1883, Morbach. Awarded EK II on 21 May 1917. Killed over Caurel.

---

**LIDL,    Ltn d R**
J78b                         1
Victories:    1.       30 Aug 1918       Balloon          1609       Laronxe

---

**LIEBAU, Kurt    Vfw**
J57       Sep 1918 – 1 Nov 1918       –
Served in Infantry on Russian Front. Died 13 May 1983, Milwaukee, Wis., USA.

---

**LIEBER,    Vfw**
J7                         1
Victories:    1.       16 Sep 1918       SE5a          Menin

---

**LIEBERT, Emil    Uffz**
J30    9 Sep 1917 – 3 Jan 1918    2 KIA
Joined Jasta 30 from Jastaschule I. Killed in collision with a German balloon.
Victories:    1.       17 Sep 1917       DH5       0800       N Vitry       (a)
              –       17 Sep 1917       DH5       0810       S Izel       (b)
              2.       3 Jan 1918       Camel       1450       Meurchin
(a) Possibly A9410 of No 41 Sqn, RFC, Lt G C Holman.
(b) Possibly A9409 of No 41 Sqn, RFC, 2/Lt R E Taylor.

---

**LIEBERZ,    Ltn d R**
J35b    23 Apr 1918 – 10 Sep 1918    –          FEA1b    10 Sep 1918 –          –
Joined Jasta 35b from Jastaschule I. Injured in crash-landing a Roland DVIa at Guesnain airfield on
27 May 1918. Crash-landed in Roland DVIa 1215/18 on 16 June 1918, slightly injured. OzbV 30 August
to 13 October 1917 and 11 June 1918 to 7 July 1918.

---

**LIEBIG, Friedrich-Wilhelm    Ltn**
J22       (Jul 1918) – (Oct 1918)       –       J1       Oct 1918 – 11 Nov 1918    1
Victories:    1.       4 Oct 1918       Camel          1150       Cambrai

---

**LIERES und WILKAU, Siegfried von    Ltn**
J14          – 1 Jul 1917       –       AFP4    15 Sep 1917 –
J29    1 Jul 1917 – 15 Sep 1917    1
Wounded in action 4 Sept 1917.
Victories:    1.       21 Aug 1917       RE8          1030       Langemarck

**LIESE, Fritz     Uffz**

J50          (Jan 1918) – 9 Mar 1918     – KIA
Born 16 February 1890, Hergermuhle. Collided with an unknown staffel colleague over Montigny.

---

**LILIENTHAL, Arnold     Uffz**

FAA237                               –                    J17          5 Jun 1918 –                          –
Joined Jasta 17 from AFP18

---

**LIMPERT, Erich     Ltn**

FA56                                 –                    J21          2 Jul 1917 – 27 Jul 1917     – KIA
J18          12 Jun 1917 – 2 Jul 1917    –
Born 10 September 1892, Nürnberg. Shot down in flames over Cheppy Wald.
Victories:          1.          Date and unit unknown, possibly FA56

---

**LINCK, Ludwig Karl Wilhelm     Oblt**

FA18                                 –                    J10          21 Sep 1916 – 22 Oct 1916     – KIA
Born 19 October 1889, Bremen. Commanded Jasta 10 from 21 September to 22 October 1916. Shot
down in flames and killed in combat with FE8s and FE2bs of No 40 and 25 Sqns, RFC, over Carvin.

---

**LINDENBERG, Georg     Flg**

J52          10 Jul 1918 – 10 Aug 1918     – INJ
Joined Jasta 52 from Jastaschule I.

---

**LINDEN, von der     Flg**

J80b          20 Jun 1918 – 20 Jul 1918    –                    AFP19          20 Jul 1918 –                  –
Joined Jasta 80b from Jastaschule II.

---

**LINDENBERGER, Alfred     Ltn**

FA234                                3                    JB          May 1918 – 11 Nov 1918          9
Biography & Victories: See *Above the Lines*.

---

**LINGENFELDER, Rudolf     Uffz**

J16b          9 Dec 1917 – 21 Feb 1918     – KIAcc
Born 1 September 1898, Neustadt. Killed in landing accident at Aertrycke airfield.

---

**LINKE, Bernhard     Ltn**

J43          20 Jul 1918 – 11 Nov 1918     –

---

**LINKE, Richard Paul     Vfw**

FA12                                 –                    J26          18 Jan 1917 – 18 Nov 1917     –
J14          25 Oct 1916 – 1 Dec 1916    –                    AFPB          18 Nov 1917 –                 –
J24          1 Dec 1916 – 18 Jan 1917    –

---

**LINKE,     Oblt**

J18          14 Jul 1917 – 11 Nov 1918     –
OzbV for Jasta 18. Acting CO Jasta 18 from 21 Mar to 14 Apr 1918.

---

**LINKE-SCHLUCKBIER, Bernhard     Ltn**

J9                                   2
Victories:     . 1.          23 Jun 1918          Spad
               2.          15 Jul 1918          Bréguet

---

**LINSINGEN, Hans-Karl von     Ltn**

KG2                                  –                    J59          26 Jan 1918 –                    –
J11          27 Nov 1917 – 24 Jan 1918     – INJ
Born 16 July 1896. Severely injured in a crash in Pfalz DIII 4223/17. Attained rank of Oberst d R during
WWII. Died 13 March 1968.

---

**LISCHKE, Kurt     Hptm**

FA39                                 –                    J6          9 Jul 1917 – 11 Nov 1918     –
Born 10 July 1890. OzbV for Jasta 6. Acting CO Jasta 6 from 6 to 16 Feb 1918.

**LOCHER, Alois    Uffz**

| | | | | | |
|---|---|---|---|---|---|
| FEA1 | 5 May 1915 – 25 Apr 1916 | – | J23b | 30 Dec 1916 – 17 Sep 1917 | 1 |
| AFP | 25 Apr 1916 – 22 Jun 1916 | – | J32b | 17 Sep 1917 – | – |
| Vfw | | | | | |
| FA3b | 23 Jun 1917 – | – | | | |

Pilot's Badge on 11 Oct 1916. Awarded EK II on 29 Oct 1916. Württemberg Silver Military Merit Medal, 7 January 1917. Promoted Vizefeldwebel on 23 May 1917. Awarded EK I on 3 September 1917.

| Victories: | 1. | 20 Aug 1917 | Spad 7 | 1947 | Samogneux |
|---|---|---|---|---|---|

**LOCHNER, Rudolf    Uffz**

| | | |
|---|---|---|
| J64w | (Aug 1918) – 11 Nov 1918 | 1 |

Flügkapitän, Dip Ing., post-war.

| Victories: | 1. | 29 Oct 1918 | Salmson | | St Benoit |
|---|---|---|---|---|---|

**LODEMANN, Ulrich    JsSch I**

| | | | | |
|---|---|---|---|---|
| | – Nov 1917 | – | Kest 4b | Nov 1917 – | – |

**LÖFFLER, Otto    Ltn d R**

| | | |
|---|---|---|
| JB | Dec 1917 – 11 Nov 1918 | 15 |

Biography & Victories: See *Above the Lines*.

**LÖHR,    Uffz**

| | |
|---|---|
| J44s | – 8 Aug 1918    – POW |

Shot down over Proyart, wounded, probably by No. 65 Sqn, RAF.

**LÖRBROCKS,    Oblt**

| | | | | | |
|---|---|---|---|---|---|
| J48 | 19 Dec 1917 – 27 Jan 1918 | – | Idflieg | 27 Jan 1918 – | – |

OzbV for Jasta 48.

**LOERZER, Bruno    Hptm**

| | | | | | |
|---|---|---|---|---|---|
| FFA25 | 2 Aug 1915 – 1 Sep 1915 | – | J5 | 21 Aug 1916 – 11 Nov 1916 | – |
| FA60 | 2 Sep 1915 – 1 Oct 1915 | – | Oblt J17 | 11 Nov 1916 – 18 Jan 1917 | – |
| FFA25 | 2 Oct 1915 – 8 Jan 1916 | – | CO J26 | 21 Jan 1917 – 21 Feb 1918 | 21 |
| FAA203 | 9 Jan 1916 – 3 Apr 1916 | – WIA | Hptm | | |
| Hosp | 3 Apr 1916 – 1916 | – | CO JGIII | 21 Feb 1918 – 11 Nov 1918 | 21 |
| KekJ | 1916 – 21 Aug 1916 | 2 | | | |

Biography & Victories: See *Above the Lines*.

**LOERZER, Fritz    Ltn**

| | | | | | |
|---|---|---|---|---|---|
| | | | J26 | 21 Feb 1917 – 9 Jan 1918 | 6 |
| Kek J | 11 Mar 1916 – 10 Sep 1916 | – | CO J63 | 9 Jan 1918 – 21 Feb 1918 | – |
| Ltn d R | | | CO J26 | 21 Feb 1918 – 12 Jun 1918 | 4 POW |
| J6 | 10 Sep 1916 – 21 Feb 1917 | 1 | | | |

Biography & Victories: See *Above the Lines*.

**LOESER, Josef    Oblt**

| | | | | | |
|---|---|---|---|---|---|
| FA40 | – Dec 1917 | – | CO J39 | 4 Dec 1917 – 4 Feb 1918 | 2 WIA |
| J1 | Dec 1917 – 4 Dec 1917 | – | J46 | 18 Apr 1918 – 3 Jun 1918 | – KIA |

Born 10 May 1889, Rottingen, Bayern. Jastaschule I on 13 Nov 1917. Commanded Jasta 46 from 23 April to 3 June 1918. Shot down in flames N Hamel during combat with RE8s of No 3 Sqn, AFC.

| Victories: | 1. | 11 Jan 1918 | Camel | | Scomigo | (a) |
|---|---|---|---|---|---|---|
| | 2. | 4 Feb 1918 | Camel | 1130 | Barbisano | |

(a) B2436, 45 Sqn, 2/Lt D W Ross, KIA.

**LÖSSL, Ernst Ritter & Edler von    Ltn d R**

| | | | | | |
|---|---|---|---|---|---|
| FA21 | | – | J27 | 15 Feb 1917 – 1 Mar 1917 | – |
| J18 | 18 Nov 1916 – 15 Feb 1917 | – | J18 | 1 Mar 1917 – 23 May 1917 | – WIA |

Born 14 April 1894, Darmstadt. Severely wounded over Becelaere, making a forced landing; died of wounds 24 May 1917.

**LÖWENHARDT, Erich    Oblt**

| | | | | | |
|---|---|---|---|---|---|
| FFA265 | 1916 – | – | Oblt J10 | Mar 1917 – 10 Aug 1918 | 54 KIA |

Biography & Victories: See *Above the Lines*.

## LÖWENSEN, OfStv
J5    (Mar 1917) – (May 1917)    –        J37             –
Awarded EK II & EK I

## LOHMANN, P.    Ltn
J14        – 7 Jun 1917    – WIA    J15    23 Mar 1918 – 11 Nov 1918    –
J18    1 Nov 1917 – 23 Mar 1918    –
Promoted Leutnant 1 Sept 1915. OzbV for Jasta 15. Wound Badge in Black. Eiserne Kreuz I Klassc. Haus-Orden von Hohenzollern, Ritterkreuz mit Schwerten. Sächsische Albrechts-Orden, Ritterkreuz 2 Klasse mit Schwerten.

## LOHRMANN,    Uffz
J42                3

| Victories: | | | | | |
|---|---|---|---|---|---|
| | 1. | 10 Aug 1918 | SE5a | 1125 | Rosières |
| | 2. | 14 Sep 1918 | DH9 | 1532 | W Holnon Wald |
| | 3. | 5 Oct 1918 | SE5a | 1600 | Magny-la-Fosse |

## LOHRMANN,    Uffz
J46    –

## LOIBL, Siegfried    Ltn
J34b    1 Nov 1918 – 11 Nov 1918    –
Assigned to Jasta 34b from Jastaschule I.

## LORBEER, Fritz    Flg
J48        – 23 Sep 1918    –    AFP7    23 Sep 1918 –

## LORENZ, Heinrich    Oblt
KG1        – Dec 1916    1    J33    4 Mar 1917 –        4
J1        Dec 1916 – 4 Mar 1917    –
Biography & Victories: See *Above the Lines*.

## LORENZ, Karl    Ltn d R
FA12                –    J24    1 Dec 1916 – 13 Apr 1917    –
J14    25 Oct 1916 – 1 Dec 1916    –    AFPA    13 Apr 1917 –    –
Eiserne Kreuz I Klasse. Wound Badge in Black. Lübeckisches Hanseatenkreuz. Remained in military service after war. Promoted Hauptmann 1 Nov 1923.

## LORENZEN,    Vfw
J8    –

## LOSCH, Johann    Vfw
J34b    6 Aug 1918 – 11 Nov 1918    –
Assigned to Jasta 34b from AFP3.

## LOSSOW, Waldo Fr von    Ltn
FAA286               –    J77b        – 11 Nov 1918    –
Died 4 July 1968, Ashville, North Carolina, USA.

## LOTHMANN,    Gefr
J65    22 Feb 1918 – 5 Mar 1918    – POW
Joined Jasta 65 from Jastaschule I. Flying Albatros DVa 5695/17 when shot down at 1445 hours SE of Bras, during a balloon attack.

## LOTZ, Paul    Ltn d R
J7    (Oct 1917) – 10 Jun 1918    4    CO J44s    10 Jun 1918 – 23 Oct 1918    6    KIAcc
Biography & Victories: See *Above the Lines*.

## LUDOVICI, Helmo    Ltn d R
J35b    24 Oct 1918 – 11 Nov 1918    –
Joined Jasta 35b from Jastaschule II.

## LUDWIG,    Ltn
J71        – 11 Nov 1918    –

## LUER, Ludwig    Ltn d R

| | | | | | |
|---|---|---|---|---|---|
| J27 | 7 Mar 1917 – 9 Jan 1918 | 4 | Hosp | 22 May 1918 – 1 Jul 1918 | – |
| CO J62 | 9 Jan 1918 – 22 May 1918 | 2 | CO J62 | 1 Jul 1918 – 8 Jul 1918 | – |

Biography & Victories: See *Above the Lines*.

## LÜBBERT, Friedrich-Wilhelm    Ltn

J11    (Oct 1917) – 17 Feb 1918    – WIA

Born 22 February 1898. Wounded during combat with SE5s over Rumilly, at 1230 hours. Died 25 November 1966. (Brother of Hans-Georg.)

## LÜBBERT, Hans-Georg Eduard    Ltn

J11    1 Mar 1917 – 30 Mar 1917    – KIA

Born 29 December 1893, Hamburg. Wounded in action 6 March 1917 over Lens, at 1200 hours. Killed in combat with a Nieuport at 1415 hours, betweeen Bailleul and Thelus. Probably by Captain R Gregory, No 40 Sqn, RFC. (See *C&C* Vol 8, No 3, pg 224.) (Brother of Friedrich-Wilhelm.) (See *OTF* Vol 2, No 3, pg 274.)

## LÜBBERT,    Vfw

J40    (Dec 1917)    –

## LÜDECKE, Günther Hussar    Ltn

J36    29 Oct 1917 – 18 Nov 1917    – INJ

Rgt 17. Promoted Leutnant on 18 June 1915. Assigned to Jasta 36 from Jastaschule I. Injured in an accident during take-off when motor quit.

## LÜDECKE, Reinhold    OfStv

J81    3 Jul 1918 – 11 Nov 1918    3 –

Joined Jasta 81 from Jastaschule II.

| Victories: | 1. | Date and unit unknown | | |
|---|---|---|---|---|
| | 2. | 22 Jul 1918 | Spad | W Chatillon |
| | 3. | 10 Aug 1918 | Spad | Braisne |
| | 4. | 10 Aug 1918 | Spad | Braisne |

## LÜDER,    Ltn

J18    15 Nov 1917 – 15 Feb 1918    –

## LÜDERITZ, Michael    Fw

| | | | | | | |
|---|---|---|---|---|---|---|
| SS4 | – 1917 | 1 | Vfw J52 | 3 Jul 1918 – 13 Jul 1918 | 1 | DOW |

Born 29 September 1891, Kirschrode. Joined Jasta 52 from Jastaschule I. Severely wounded in combat by Neuve Chapelle, died of wounds.

| Victories: | 1. | 10 Sep 1917 | Sopwith | | N Schaapbalie | (a) |
|---|---|---|---|---|---|---|
| | 2. | 8 Jul 1918 | SE5a | 0900 | Bauvin | |

(a) With his observer, Fw Weitz.

## LÜTJOHANN, Walter    Ltn d R

J63    – May 1918    – KIA

Born 14 May 1893, Holtenau. Killed during combat with a Camel E of Amiens.

## LÜTZENDORF,    Sgt

| | | | | | |
|---|---|---|---|---|---|
| J65 | 29 Jul 1918 – 16 Aug 1918 | – | FA31 | 16 Aug 1918 – | – |

## LUFT,    Fw

Kest 8    (Sep 1918)    –

## LUGER, Linus    Gefr

J79b    – 19 Jul 1918    – KIAcc

Born 22 September 1896, Stettin. Wounded in action 24 March 1918. Killed shortly after take-off at 1630 hours in an accident at Erchin.

## LUPP, Karl    Ltn d R

J46    – 12 Apr 1918    – KIA

Born 5 February 1888, Düsseldorf. Killed over Orvillers-la-Boiselle.

## LUTJOHANN, Walter     Ltn
J63                    – 15 May 1918   –  KIA
Killed during combat with a Camel E of Amiens.

## LUTTEROTH, Hans     Ltn
J7              Dec 1917 – 6 Apr 1918   –  KIAcc
Born 2 June 1895, Hagenau. Killed during take-off at Meulebeke.

## LUTZ,     Ltn
J18         4 Sep 1917 – 5 Sep 1917     –

## LUTZ,     Ltn
J28                    – 4 Sep 1917   –  WIA
Hit by AA fire.

## LUX, Albert     Vfw
J27         27 Nov 1917 – 11 Nov 1918    7
Biography & Victories: See *Above the Lines*. (Score now believed to be eight.)

## LUX, Heinrich     Ltn
J75                                    –

## LUX, Jakob     Flg
J1                     – 3 Jul 1918   –  KIA
Born 17 February 1895, Köln. Killed over Anthenay.

## LYNCKER, Bodo Fr von     Ltn
J2                     – 13 Nov 1916   –  INJ        Oblt J25  28 Nov 1916 – 18 Feb 1917    2   KIA
Born 22 October 1894, Berlin. Severely injured in an accident 13 November 1916. Collided during combat
with a Nieuport S Gjevgjeli, killing both.

| Victories: | 1. | 10 Dec 1916 | Nieuport | | Hudova |
|---|---|---|---|---|---|
| | 2. | 18 Feb 1917 | Nieuport | | Gjevgjeli |

## MAASHOFF, Otto     Ltn d R
FEA7    19 Feb 1916 – 18 Jul 1916    –        AFPA      18 Apr 1918 –            –
FA5     18 Jul 1916 – 28 Apr 1917    –        Kest 2      1918 – 21 Jun 1918   –  WIA
J11     28 Apr 1917 – 17 Apr 1918    3
Born Mettmann 3 April 1895. Joined military service 6 August 1914, assigned Hussaren Regiment 11.
Promoted Gefreiter on 6 November 1914. Fusilier Regiment 19 on 1 August 1915. Promoted
Vizefeldwebel on 7 October 1915. Entered aviation 19 February 1916. Promoted Leutnant d R on
6 November 1915. Attained rank of General Ingenieur in Luftwaffe during WWII, on 1 August 1940.
Died 26 October 1941.

| Victories: | 1. | 7 May 1917 | RE8 | 1830 | W Fresnes |
|---|---|---|---|---|---|
| | 2. | 11 May 1917 | BE | 1225 | Willerval |
| | 3. | 24 May 1917 | Sop Tripe | 0902 | N Douai |

## MACK,     Vfw
J60                    – 11 Nov 1918    1
| Victories: | 1. | 3 Sep 1918 | Spad | | |
|---|---|---|---|---|---|

## MACK,     Vfw
J63                                   2
| Victories: | 1. | 2 Sep 1918 | AWFK8 | 1230 | Lomme |
|---|---|---|---|---|---|
| | 2. | 24 Sep 1918 | SE5a | 1800 | S Ypern |

## MADER,     Gefr
Kest 1a    7 Sep 1918 – 11 Nov 1918    –
Joined Kest 1a from Jastaschule II. Known to have flown Albatros DVa 7408/17, and Fokker DVIII
107/18 in Kest 1a.

## MÄURER, Vfw

| | | | | | |
|---|---|---|---|---|---|
| J15 | – 20 Mar 1918 | – | J18 | 20 Mar 1918 – 21 Apr 1918 | – WIA |

Severely wounded.

| Victories: | – | 25 Mar 1918 | Camel |
|---|---|---|---|

## MAHN, Herbert   Ltn d R

| | | | |
|---|---|---|---|
| J72 | 3 Jun 1918 – 11 Nov 1918 | 9 |

Biography & Victories: See *Above the Lines*.

## MAI, Josef   Ltn d R

| | | | | | |
|---|---|---|---|---|---|
| KG5/29 | – 1916 | – | J5 | 17 Apr 1917 – 11 Nov 1918 | 30 |

Biography & Victories: See *Above the Lines*.

## MAIER, Reinhold   Ltn d R

| | | | | | | |
|---|---|---|---|---|---|---|
| FEA2 | 2 May 1917 – | – | FA5 | 23 Oct 1917 – | – |
| FEA10 | – 23 Oct 1917 | – | J30 | 30 Dec 1917 – 19 Oct 1918 | 2 KIA |

Born 2 December 1891, Plochingen. Joined Jasta 30 from Jastaschule I. Wounded in action 28 January 1918. Württemberg Friedrich Order Knight 2nd Class with Swords on 20 February 1918. Killed near Leuze-Ellignies, Belgium.

| Victories: | 1. | 21 Jun 1918 | Balloon | 1630 | Aix Noulette |
|---|---|---|---|---|---|
| | 2. | 24 Jul 1918 | Balloon | 2200 | NW Grénay |

## MAIER, Uffz

| | | | |
|---|---|---|---|
| J8 | – 28 Jan 1918 | – WIA |

## MAIER, Vfw

| | | | |
|---|---|---|---|
| J36 | 22 Feb 1917 – 12 Jul 1917 | 1 WIA |

| Victories: | 1. | 27 May 1917 | Balloon | | S Nauroy | (a) |
|---|---|---|---|---|---|---|

(a) 64th French Balloon Company.

## MAIER, Uffz

| | | | |
|---|---|---|---|
| J46 | (Jun 1918) – 9 Jul 1918 | – WIA |

## MAIER-HAAKE, Ltn

| | | |
|---|---|---|
| J36 | 27 Aug 1918 – 11 Nov 1918 | – |

## MALCHOW, Hans   Ltn

| | | |
|---|---|---|
| J4 | 1 Sep 1916 – Apr 1917 | 1 |

| Victories: | 1. | 4 Apr 1917 | FE2b | 0950 | SW Arras |
|---|---|---|---|---|---|

## MALETSKY, Karl   Ltn d R

| | | | | | |
|---|---|---|---|---|---|
| J10 | 29 Jul 1918 – 17 Aug 1918 | – | J50 | 17 Aug 1918 – 11 Nov 1918 | 4 |

Born 1 September 1895. LF Artillery Regiment 9. Joined Jasta 10 from Jastaschule II.

| Victories: | 1. | 20 Aug 1918 | Balloon | | SW Noyon |
|---|---|---|---|---|---|
| | 2. | 14 Sep 1918 | Spad | 1020 | Révillon |
| | 3. | 26 Sep 1918 | Spad | 1800 | Perthes |
| | 4. | 26 Sep 1918 | Spad | 1810 | Le Mesnil |

## MALLINCKRODT, Friedrich   Ltn

| | | | | | |
|---|---|---|---|---|---|
| KeKS | – 1916 | – | J10 | 1 Jan 1917 – 1 Mar 1917 | – |
| J6 | 10 Sep 1916 – 1 Jan 1917 | 2 | J20 | 1 Mar 1917 – 30 Apr 1917 | 4 WIA |

Biography & Victories: See *Above the Lines*.

## MALLMANN, Martin   Vfw

| | | | | | |
|---|---|---|---|---|---|
| FAA226 | | – | J19 | 6 Jul 1917 – 19 Jan 1918 | 3 KIA |

Born 28 July 1892, Boppard. Killed near Vendetre.

| Victories: | 1. | 3 Sep 1917 | Balloon | Pontavert |
|---|---|---|---|---|
| | 2. | 19 Sep 1917 | Caudron | Villers |
| | 3. | 7 Dec 1917 | Caudron | Berry-au-Bac |
| | zlg | 15 Dec 1917 | AR2 | Craonne |

## MALZ, OfStv

| | |
|---|---|
| J12 | 8 Oct 1916 – |
| | – |

## MALZ, Hans    OfStv
J20      5 May 1917 – 3 Sep 1917    – KIA
Born 2 July 1890, Berlin. Joined Jasta 20 from AFP2. Killed during an enemy bombing attack on the airfield at Varsenaere.

## MANGER, Hermann    Ltn
J56      16 Mar 1918 – 22 Mar 1918    – KIA
Born 15 April 1894, Münsterberg. Joined Jasta 56 from Jastaschule I, Valenciennes. Shot down in flames near Bihecourt, NW Marteville.

## MANGOLD, Fritz    Ltn
J51                                     –

## MANN,    OfStv
J5                                      –

## MANSCHOTT, Friedrich    Vfw
FAA203            – 1916        1        J7        (Jan 1917) – 16 Mar 1917    11 KIA
Biography & Victories: See *Above the Lines*.

## MANTEUFFEL, Eitel-Friedrich Rüdiger von    Ltn

| | | | | | |
|---|---|---|---|---|---|
| School | 5 Feb 1915 – 19 Aug 1915 | – | Staff | 4 Sep 1917 – 24 Sep 1917 | – |
| AFP7 | 20 Aug 1915 – 22 Aug 1915 | – | Kest 9 | 25 Sep 1917 – 16 Oct 1917 | – |
| FFA26 | 23 Aug 1915 – 31 Mar 1916 | – | Kest 1b | 17 Oct 1917 – 7 Nov 1917 | – |
| Misc | 1 Apr 1916 – 28 Jun 1916 | 1 | FEA5 | 8 Nov 1917 – 28 Dec 1917 | – |
| FFA29 | 29 Jun 1916 – 14 Jul 1916 | – | Instr | 29 Dec 1917 – 4 May 1918 | – |
| FFA27 | 15 Jul 1916 – 10 Aug 1916 | – | JGII | 4 May 1918 – 10 Jul 1918 | – |
| Staff | 11 Aug 1916 – 13 Jul 1917 | – | FEADarm | Aug 1918 – 11 Nov 1918 | – |
| J14 | 14 Jul 1917 – 3 Sep 1917 | – | | | |

Born 24 September 1895, Rastatt. Joined military service 22 March 1914, as a Leutnant in Grenadier Regiment 109. Various aviation schools until assigned to AFP7. Pilot for Kampfeinsitzer-Abteilung, Grand Headquarters and in 7 Armee, 1 April 1916 to 28 June 1916. Various staff assignments 11 August 1916 to 14 July 1917. Adjutant for Jagdgeschwader II. Attained rank of Generalmajor in Luftwaffe during WWII on 1 October 1944. Died 31 July 1984, Wiesbaden.

Victories:     1.       22 May 1916      Caudron G.4                      Carlepont        (a)
(a) Probably Sgt Schneider (P) and S/Lt Danne (O), Escadrille C 43, both POWs.

## MANTEUFFEL-SZÖGE, Wolf Baron von    Ltn
J4      1 Sep 1916 – (Mar 1917)    –        J35b    17 Feb 1918 – 8 May 1918    3 KIA
Born 12 March 1895, Capschjoken (Russia). Served in 2nd Uhlan Rgt. Joined Jasta 35b from Jastaschule II. Forced to land after combat with a two-seater near Croiselles, on 11 April 1918. Killed near Biaches-St Vaast, during combat with ten Camels.

| Victories: | 1. | 8 Mar 1918 | SE5a | 1140 | Bourlonwald | (a) |
|---|---|---|---|---|---|---|
| | 2. | 21 Mar 1918 | Camel/Pup | 0900 | N Bapaume | |
| | 3. | 21 Mar 1918 | Camel/Pup | 1620 | Bertincourt | |

(a) Probably 2/Lt R N Topliss, No 64 Sqn, RFC, (WIA/POW).

## MAPPES,    Ltn
J37            – 11 Nov 1918    1
Wounded in action 26 September 1918.

| Victories: | 1. | 10 Oct 1918 | EA | 1700 | NE Denain |
|---|---|---|---|---|---|

## MARCARD,    Ltn
J9                          –        J26      (Jul 1918) – 11 Nov 1918    2

| Victories: | 1. | 8 Jul 1918 | Spad | 1105 | Corcy |
|---|---|---|---|---|---|
| | 2. | 16 Sep 1918 | SE5 | 1800 | Sauchy-Chauchy |

## MARCHNER,    Uffz
J32b      May 1918 – 11 Nov 1918    2

| Victories: | 1. | 28 May 1918 | SE5a | 1245 | NE Pelves |
|---|---|---|---|---|---|
| | 2. | 30 Oct 1918 | | | |

## MARCUS,    Ltn d R
J36    11 Nov 1916 – 21 Jul 1917    –
OzbV for Jasta 17.

## MARCZINKE, Max    Uffz
FAA235                              1            J30    19 Mar 1918 – 30 Mar 1918    – POW
Joined Jasta 30 from Jastaschule II. Shot down over Ploegsteert Wald, flying Pfalz DIII 8078/17.
Victories:    1.        22 Dec 1917    RE8                                    Liévin
Other crew member for first victory was Ltn Hertel.

## MARCZINSKI, Paul    Uffz
J30    5 May 1918 – 22 Jul 1918    – KIA
Born 18 May 1898, Lyck. Joined Jasta 30 from Jastaschule I. Killed near Point Maudit, by Lt G J
Strange, No. 40 Sqn, RAF.

## MARGOT, Hermann    Vfw
FA23                               –            J18    12 Aug 1917 – 16 Mar 1918    –
J4     1 Sep 1916 – 16 Oct 1916    –            J15    16 Mar 1918 – 11 Nov 1918    –
J14    16 Oct 1916 – 12 Aug 1917    –

## MARKERT, Georg    Vfw
J76b    4 May 1918 – 31 May 1918    1 KIA
Born 18 November 1891, Wallnersbach. Joined Jasta 76b from Jastaschule I. Killed in mid-air collision
with Ltn Walter Böning, falling in flames at 1815 hours near Fricourt.
Victories:    1.        30 May 1918    Camel                                  Albert

## MARKGRAF, Johannes    Ltn
J6     11 Jul 1918 – 16 Jul 1918    – KIAcc
Born 15 September 1896, Demmin. Served in Reserve Infantry Regiment 18. Joined Jasta 6 from
Jastaschule II. Killed in an accident in a two-seater at Magneux airfield.

## MARGRAF,    Ltn d R
J35    19 Mar 1917 – 14 Apr 1917    – WIA    J35    31 May 1917 – 13 Sep 1917    –
Reported to Jasta 35 from AFP B. Wounded in action during combat with a Sopwith but made a safe
landing at Colmar Nord airfield. Rejoined Jasta 35 from hospital on 31 May 1917.

## MARKWIRTH, Paul    Fw
J7     – 21 May 1917    – KIAcc
Born 3 March 1887, Pilgramsdorf. Killed while flying Roland DII 993/16 near Erchin airfield.

## MAROCKE, Kurt    Flg
J5     – 1 Oct 1918    – KIA
Born 12 November 1896, Paarbor. Killed near Origny.

## MARQUARDT, Otto    Vfw
J4     Jun 1917 – Aug 1917    1            J26    Aug 1917 – Mar 1918    –
Transferred to Pilot/Observer School, Juterborg.
Victories:    1.        12 Jul 1917    SE5            2105            Zandvoorde

## MARTENS, Arthur    Vfw
J11    6 Aug 1918 – 10 Oct 1918    –            J64w    15 Oct 1918 – 11 Nov 1918    –
Joined Jasta 11 from Jastaschule I.

## MARTENS,    Flg
J65    30 Oct 1918 – 11 Nov 1918    –

## MARTIN,    Ltn
J46    (Jul 1918) – 11 Aug 1918    – WIA

## MARTIN,    Ltn
J76b    4 May 1918 – 5 Aug 1918    –            AFPF    5 Aug 1918 –    –
Joined Jasta 76b from Jastaschule I.

**MARTINI, Hermann    Oblt**

| | | | | | | |
|---|---|---|---|---|---|---|
| FA36 | – 17 Nov 1917 | – | CO J58 | 17 Apr 1918 – 24 Apr 1918 | – |
| J12 | 17 Nov 1917 – 25 Jan 1918 | 1 | AFP2 | 24 Apr 1918 – 4 Jun 1918 | – |
| CO J58 | 25 Jan 1918 – 4 Apr 1918 | – | CO J58 | 4 Jun 1918 – 10 Jun 1918 | – |
| CO | | | AFP2 | 10 Jun 1918 – 22 Jul 1918 | – |
| JGrIII | 4 Apr 1918 – 17 Apr 1918 | – | CO J58 | 22 Jul 1918 – 11 Nov 1918 | – |

Awarded Saxon Knight's Cross of the Military St Henry Order on 6 February 1918; Saxon Merit Order, Knight 2nd Class with Swords on 1 December 1916; Saxon Albert Order, Knight 2nd Class with Swords; Iron Cross II and I Class; Austro-Hungarian Military Merit Cross, 3rd Class with War Decoration; proposed for Bavarian Military Merit Order 4th Class with Swords 10 Oct 1918, but was not received. Promoted Hauptmann on 1 June 1922.

Victories:    –    30 Nov 1917    Scout                    Cambrai

---

**MARWEDE, Hans Heinrich    Uffz**

| | | | |
|---|---|---|---|
| Kest 2 | | J67 | 18 Jun 1918 – 3 Oct 1918    5    POW |

Biography & Victories: See *Above the Lines*.

---

**MARWITZ, Hans-Georg von der    Oblt**

| | | | |
|---|---|---|---|
| KG5 | – 1916 | – | J30    18 Apr 1917 – 11 Nov 1918    15 |
| SS10 | – Feb 1917 | – | |

Biography & Victories: See *Above the Lines*.

---

**MARWITZ, Werner    Ltn**

J9                    – 30 Apr 1917    1    KIA

Born 7 February 1893, Berlin. Killed near Nauroy.

Victories:    1.    19 Apr 1917    Spad            1000    SW Aubérive

---

**MARX, Erich    Oblt**

Kest 1                    – 21 Mar 1917    –    WIA

Born 11 November 1888, Posen. Infantry Rgt 62. Wounded over Mannheim. Died in hospital at Mannheim-Sandhofen.

---

**MARX,    Uffz**

J35b    (Sep 1918) – 11 Nov 1918    –

---

**MARX,    Ltn**

J78b                    – 17 Dec 1917    –    J3    17 Dec 1917 –

Served as OzbV for Jasta 78b.

---

**MARX,    Ltn**

JSchonger    29 Oct 1918 – 11 Nov 1918    –

---

**MASCHINSKY,    Vfw**

J19    26 May 1918 – 7 Jun 1918    –    POW

---

**MASSKOW,    Ltn d R**

J1                    –

OzbV for Jasta 1.

---

**MASSMANN,    Ltn**

J14                    – 22 Dec 1917    –    WIA

---

**MASSOW, von    Ltn**

J3                    –

---

**MATTHAEI, Rudolf    Ltn d R**

| | | | | | |
|---|---|---|---|---|---|
| KG2/9 | 5 Oct 1916 – 25 Oct 1916 | – | J5 | 1 Aug 1917 – 17 Dec 1917 | 6 |
| J21 | 25 Oct 1916 – 1 Aug 1917 | 3 | J46 | 17 Dec 1917 – 17 Apr 1918 | 1    KIAcc |

Biography & Victories: See *Above the Lines*.

---

**MATTHIES,    Ltn**

J4    (May 1918) – 11 May 1918    –    AFP2    11 May 1918 –    –

**MATTHIES, Ltn**

J59 11 Apr 1918 – 12 Apr 1918 – AFP17 12 Apr 1918 – –

**MATTHIES, Friedrich Vfw**

J20 7 Jun 1917 – 3 Sep 1917 1 DOW

Joined Jasta 20 from Jastaschule I. Severely wounded during an enemy bombing attack on the airfield at Varsenaere, on 3 September 1917, died 4 September.

| Victories: | 1. | 28 Jul 1917 | Sopwith | 1725 | Coxyde |

**MATTHIESEN, Max Ltn**

FAA203 – J31 10 Sep 1917 – –
J29 23 Mar 1917 – 10 Sep 1917 –

**MATTHOFF, Ltn**

J11 12 Oct 1916 – Feb 1917 –

**MATUSZEWSKY, Franz Flg**

J73 11 Feb 1918 – 21 Mar 1918 – KIA

Born 25 September 1896, Jawada. Killed near Nauroy, in flames.

**MATZDORF, Ltn**

J6 30 May 1918 – 19 Sep 1918 2

Transferred to Jastaschule II on 19 Sep 1918.

| Victories: | 1. | 17 Jul 1918 | Bréguet | 1035 | Igny-le-Breuil |
| | 2. | 19 Aug 1918 | Camel | 0950 | Beauvais |

**MATZKE, Ltn d R**

J27 8 Jun 1917 – 7 Aug 1917 1 J54 19 Jan 1918 – Mar 1918 –
J40 7 Aug 1917 – 19 Jan 1918 –

Joined Jasta 27 from AFP4.

| Victories: | 1. | 17 Mar 1918 | Camel | 1025 | Lesdain |

**MAUCK, Vfw**

Kest 2 – J67 2 Jun 1918 – 11 Nov 1918 –

**MAUSHAKE, Heinrich Ltn d R**

J4 20 Nov 1917 – 3 Nov 1918 6 WIA

Biography & Victories: See *Above the Lines*.

**MAUTE, Friedrich Flg**

J47w – 24 Jan 1918 – KIA

Born 9 April 1887, Onstmettingen, Bailingen. Killed near Harlebeke.

**MAY, Paul Uffz**

J47w 27 Dec 1917 – 27 Apr 1918 – APF6 27 Apr 1918 – –

Joined Jasta 47w from Jastaschule I.

**MAYER, Josef Gefr**

J32b – 21 Jan 1918 – KIA

Born 3 November 1898, Katzberg. Killed at 1150 hours over Mars-sous-Bourcq.

**MAYER, Vfw**

J9 –

**MAYER, Ltn d R**

J31 – 11 Nov 1918 1

Shot down over St Loup on 14 August 1918, jumped safely in parachute. Lightly wounded in action 14 October 1918.

| Victories: | 1. | 2 Oct 1918 | Camel | 0950 | Homblières |

**MAYER, Flg**

J36 – 5 May 1918 – WIA

**MEEDER, Johann    Uffz**
J23b     14 Jun 1918 – 27 Jun 1918    – WIA
Joined Jasta 23b from Jastaschule I. Wounded while flying a Roland DVIb.

**MEESS,    Ltn**
Kest 4b                                    –

**MEGERLE, Friedrich    Vfw**
J70                – 16 Jul 1918    1  KIA
Born 20 June 1894, Oberehrn. Wounded during combat with an AR2 on 2 May 1918. Killed near Saarburg.

| Victories: | 1. | Date and unit unknown | | |
|---|---|---|---|---|
|  | 2. | 2 May 1918 | AR2 | E Manonville |

**MEHL,    Gefr**
J29     31 Oct 1918   – 11 Nov 1918    –
Reported to Jasta 29 from Jastaschule II.

**MEIER, Stefan    Flg**
J79b                – 5 Jul 1918    – KIAcc
Born 3 November 1896, Altdorf. Killed in an accident during a test flight at 1545 hours 5 July 1918.

**MEIERDIRKS, Karl    Ltn d R**
J12     17 Jul 1917 – 23 Aug 1917    –           J55      Jan 1918 – 4 May 1918    1  KIA
J40     23 Aug 1917 – Jan 1918    1
Born 2 June 1896, Bremen. Commanded Jasta 55 from 1 April 1918 to 4 May 1918. Killed over Jericho.

| Victories: | 1. | 25 Sep 1917 | Bréguet | Mance |
|---|---|---|---|---|
|  | 2. | 25 Apr 1918 | RE8 | Nablus |

**MEINBERG, Matthias    Vfw**
J8                –           J75           – 11 Nov 1918    2

| Victories: | 1. | 3 Jun 1917 | Sopwith 2 | 1645 | Menin | (a) |
|---|---|---|---|---|---|---|
|  | 2. | 1 Nov 1918 | Bréguet |  | Obersulzbach |  |

(a) Probably A1012, No 70 Sqn, RFC, 2/Lt R M Neil & Lt S W Harley, KIA.

**MEINEL, Kurt    Uffz**
J22s                – 17 Jun 1918    – KIA
Born 16 November 1893, Schoeneck. Collided in mid-air with Flieger Moser, over Thiescourt, both killed.

**MEINHARDT, Albert    Uffz**
J21s                – 1 Jan 1918    – KIA
Born 14 October 1894, Güstrow. Killed south of Brimont.

**MEISE,    Ltn**
J10     11 Oct 1918 – 11 Nov 1918    –
Joined Jasta 10 from Jastaschule II.

**MEISS,    Ltn**
SS15                – 25 Jan 1917    1           J20      25 Jan 1917 –           –

| Victories: | 1. | date unknown |
|---|---|---|

**MEIXNER,    Ltn d R**
FAA262                –           J45      19 Aug 1918 – 11 Nov 1918    2

| Victories: | 1. | 2 Sep 1918 | Spad | 1130 | Château de la Malle |
|---|---|---|---|---|---|
|  | 2. | 15 Sep 1918 | Balloon | 1500 | Braisne |

**MELLE, von    Ltn d R**
J50     (Jun 1918) – 11 Nov 1918    1
Served in Field Artillery Regiment 46.

| Victories: | 1. | 3 Oct 1918 | Spad | 1045 | Liry |
|---|---|---|---|---|---|

**MELLENTHIN, Ewald von    Ltn d R**
J3     1 Sep 1916 – 12 Sep 1916    – KIA
Born 17 November 1885, Deffau. Killed over Pozières.

**MENCKHOFF, Carl    Oblt d R**
J3    (Mar 1917) – 11 Feb 1918    20        J72s    11 Feb 1918 – 25 Jul 1918    19 POW
Biography & Victories: See *Above the Lines*.

**MENDEL, Karl Albert    Ltn d R**
J15    (Apr 1917) – 20 Mar 1918    2        J18    20 Mar 1918 – 6 Jun 1918    5 KIA
Biography & Victories: See *Above the Lines*.

**MERK,    Gefr**
J71                             –

**MERKLE, Ruppert    Uffz**
J63                  – 31 Mar 1918    – KIA
Born 15 May 1897, Ludwigshafen. Killed during combat with a Spad over Hainvillers.
Victories:    zlg    31 Mar 1918    Sopwith

**MERTENS, Heinrich    Vfw**
J35    30 Aug 1917 – 4 Sep 1917    – WIA
Joined Jasta 35 from Jastaschule I. Severely wounded, landed near Haewind.

**MERTENS, Max    Uffz**
J7                  – 19 Jun 1918    3 KIA
Born 10 March 1896, Potsdam. Missing in action after a balloon attack on Pfalz DIIIa (G/2Bde/16),
claimed by Capt A H Cobby, No 4 Sqn, AFC, on Camel D1929. Came down in the Nieppe Forest-
Bailleul area.

| Victories: | 1. | 14 May 1918 | Balloon | 1645 | N Ypern |
| | – | 17 Jun 1918 | Dolphin | 1015 | S Dickebuschsee |
| | 2. | 18 Jun 1918 | Camel | 0920 | S Dickebuschsee |
| | 3. | 19 Jun 1918 | Balloon | 1900 | Poperinghe |

**MERZ, Arthur    Ltn d R**
J28w    5 Jul 1918 – 22 Aug 1918    1 WIA
Born 9 January 1896, Neiderstein-Sinsheim, Baden. Joined military service 26 August 1914. Feldartillerie
Rgt Nr.14. Promoted to Unteroffizier on 1 June 1915, and to Vizefeldwebel on 9 September 1915.
Assigned to Balloon Defence Unit #6 on 18 September 1915. Promoted to Leutnant d R on 8 November
1915. Awarded the EKII Klasse 25 November 1915. Transferred to K-Flakbatterie 105 on 8 January
1917. Reported to FEA3 for pilot's training 22 June 1917. Transferred to AFP2, 21 June 1918. Joined
Jasta 28w from AFP2. Wounded at 0830 hours near Ghislain; died of wounds 27 August 1918.

| Victories: | 1. | 15 Aug 1918 | Bréguet | 1125 | Ambonnay |

**MESCH, Christian    Vfw**
J26    28 May 1918 – 11 Nov 1918    12
Biography & Victories: See *Above the Lines*.

**MESSTORF, Ernst    Uffz**
J26                  – 2 May 1918    – KIA
Born 4 July 1874, Hamburg. Shot down in flames south of Armentières.

**METTLICH, Konrad    Oblt z S**
MFJ I    Nov 1916 – Jun 1917    –        J8    Jun 1917 – 13 Mar 1918    6 KIA
Biography & Victories: See *Above the Lines*.

**METZGER,    Sgt**
J70                  – 11 Nov 1918    1
| Victories: | 1. | 16 Sep 1918 | DH9 | | SE Landau |

**METZKE,    Ltn**
J20                             –

**MEYER, August    Uffz**
J34b    4 Apr 1918 – 25 Apr 1918    – KIA
Born 24 April 1895, Diechtach. Joined Jasta 34b from Jastaschule I. Killed at 1810 hours SE Marcelcave.

## MEYER, Erich      Uffz

| | | | | | |
|---|---|---|---|---|---|
| FAA207 | | – | Kest | 6 Oct 1918 – Oct 1918 | – |
| FA26 | | – | Kest 8 | Oct 1918 – 11 Nov 1918 | – |
| J45 | Jan 1918 – 16 Jul 1918 | 5 INJ | | | |

Joined Kest 6 from hospital.

## MEYER, Ernst      Vfw

| | | | | | |
|---|---|---|---|---|---|
| J25 | (Apr) 1917 – 12 Aug 1918 | 3 | J38 | 12 Aug 1918 – 11 Nov 1918 | – |

Known to have flown Halberstadt DII D.820/16.

| Victories: | 1. | 2 May 1917 | Caudron | | Cerna-Bogen |
|---|---|---|---|---|---|
| | 2. | 7 May 1918 | Nieuport | | Poliste |
| | 3. | 22 May 1918 | Nieuport | 0900 | S Tomaros |

## MEYER, Georg      Ltn d R

| | | | | | |
|---|---|---|---|---|---|
| FA69 | 18 Aug 1916 – 1916 | – | J7 | 2 Aug 1917 – 4 Apr 1918 | 3 |
| FFA253 | 1916 – 1917 | 1 | J37 | 4 Apr 1918 – 11 Nov 1918 | 20 |
| J22 | (Mar 1917) – 2 Aug 1917 | – | | | |

Biography & Victories: See *Above the Lines*.

## MEYER, Johann-Paul      Uffz

| | | | |
|---|---|---|---|
| J32 | – 8 May 1918 | – | KIA |

Born 24 June 1891, Viechtach. Killed in action over Roeux.

## MEYER, Karl      Ltn

| | | | | | |
|---|---|---|---|---|---|
| FA201A | 1 Feb 1917 – 14 Jul 1917 | – | J4 | 6 Sep 1917 – 19 Sep 1918 | 3 |
| J11 | 14 Jul 1917 – 6 Sep 1917 | 1 | | | |

Served in 8th Cuirassier Rgt. Wounded in action 17 July 1917, at 2055 hours, near Ypern, possibly by Capt N W Webb, No 70 Sqn, RFC. OzbV for J4. Transferred to Jastaschule II as an instructor 19 September 1918.

| Victories: | 1. | 31 Jul 1917 | RE8 | 1300 | Diemlingseck | (a) |
|---|---|---|---|---|---|---|
| | 2. | 28 Jun 1918 | Spad | 0950 | Corcy | |
| | 3. | 15 Jul 1918 | Spad | 1640 | N Fossoy | |
| | 4. | 18 Jul 1918 | Camel | 0930 | Marsuil | |

(a) RE8 A4724, 'A' Sqn, RFC, Lt J Longton and 2/Lt T L Carson.

## MEYER, Werner      Ltn

| | | | |
|---|---|---|---|
| J34b | 12 Jul 1918 – 20 Jul 1918 | – | DOW |

Born 28 December 1896, Hannover. Served in Infantry Regiment 135. Joined Jasta 34b from Jastaschule II. Severely wounded in action 20 July 1918, east of Hamel, jumped in parachute landing near Cerisy, DOW 21 July.

## MEYER, Wilhelm      Uffz

| | | | |
|---|---|---|---|
| J16b | 15 May 1918 – 30 Jul 1918 | – | WIA |

Wounded over Ypern, 30 July 1918.

## MEYER, Wilhelm      Vfw

| | | | |
|---|---|---|---|
| J47w | 27 Dec 1917 – 24 Sep 1918 | – | POW |

Joined Jasta 47w from Jastaschule I. Flying Fokker DVII 4522 during an attack on a French balloon near Suippes, on 24 September 1918, he was shot down and taken prisoner by defending fire E of Fismes, at 1630 hours.

## MEYER,      Gefr

| | | |
|---|---|---|
| J3 | (Sep 1918) – 11 Nov 1918 | 2 |

| Victories: | 1. | 25 Sep 1918 | DH9a | 1115 | SE Saaralben |
|---|---|---|---|---|---|
| | 2. | 27 Sep 1918 | Spad | 1730 | Champenouxwald |

## MEYER,      Sgt

| | | | |
|---|---|---|---|
| J8 | – 28 Jan 1918 | – | WIA |

## MEYER,      OfStv

| | | |
|---|---|---|
| J27 | 14 Feb 1917 – 2 Jun 1917 | – |

Joined Jasta 27 from Ubungspark Ost. Transferred to Heimatzschutz on 2 June 1917.

## MEYER,      Uffz

| | | |
|---|---|---|
| J35b | 20 Aug 1918 – 11 Nov 1918 | – |

Joined Jasta 35b from Jastaschule I.

## MEYER, Vfw
J38

---

## MEYER, Uffz
J57     22 Feb 1918 – 5 May 1918    1   INJ
Severely injured in an accident.

| Victories: | 1. | 17 Apr 1918 | Camel | 1505 | Hazebrouck |
|---|---|---|---|---|---|

---

## MICHAELIS, Georg   Ltn d R
J14     (Mar 1917) – Sep 1917    –     J41     (Sep 1917) – 8 Feb 1918   1   KIA
Born 9 July 1894, Burghstadt. Killed during combat with a Spad over Füllern.

| Victories: | 1. | 25 Jan 1918 | AR2 | 1235 | S Ammerzweiler |
|---|---|---|---|---|---|

---

## MICHAELIS, Robert   Gefr
J12     8 Oct 1916 – 22 Nov 1916   –   KIA
Born 12 June 1895, Schwerin. Killed W Guedecourt.

---

## MICHAELIS,   Gefr
J13     23 Sep 1918 – 11 Nov 1918   –

---

## MIESEGADES, Hans   Vfw
J3     25 Aug 1916 – 1 Sep 1916   –   KIAcc
Born 24 March 1895, Bremen. Served in KEK Colmar, prior to joining Jasta 3. Killed in accident during test flight of a biplane Fokker.

---

## MIKAT,   Vfw
J14                   1

| Victories: | 1. | 30 Jan 1918 | Spad | 1240 | La Ville-aux-Bois |
|---|---|---|---|---|---|

---

## MILCH, Erhard   Hptm

| | | | | InfRgt 41 | | |
|---|---|---|---|---|---|---|
| FAA205 | 5 Aug 1915 – 27 Aug 1915 | – | | | 23 Apr 1918 – 8 Jun 1918 | – |
| Oblt | | | | ArtRgt273 | | |
| FFA204 | 28 Aug 1915 – 14 Jun 1916 | – | | | 9 Jun 1918 – 18 Jul 1918 | – |
| ArtFlgSch | | | | Kofl17 | 19 Jul 1918 – 19 Sep 1918 | – |
| | 15 Jun 1916 – 3 Jul 1917 | – | | CO | | |
| AFP6 | 4 Jul 1917 – 8 Jul 1917 | – | | FAA204 | 20 Sep 1918 – 30 Sep 1918 | – |
| CO FA5 | 9 Jul 1917 – 29 Jul 1917 | – | | Hptm | | |
| Staff | 30 Jul 1917 – 22 Apr 1918 | – | | CO JGr6 | 1 Oct 1918 – 11 Nov 1918 | – |

Entered military service 24 February 1910 as a Fahrenjunker, Fussartillerie Regiment 1. Fähnrich on 18 October 1910. Commissioned as a Leutnant 18 August 1911. Transferred to aviation 1 July 1915, trained at FEA 1 as an observer. Promoted Oberleutnant 18 August 1915. Promoted Hauptmann 18 October 1918. Commanded Jagdgruppe 6 from 1 October 1918. Awarded the Knight's Cross with Swords of the Hohenzollern House Order. CO FA412, Polish Border, 1919. Promoted Oberst 28 October 1933. Promoted Generalmajor 24 March 1934. Promoted Generalleutnant 28 March 1935. Promoted General der Flieger 30 January 1936. Promoted Generaloberst 1 November 1938. Ritterkreuz on 4 May 1940. Attained rank of Generalfeldmarschall during WWII on 19 July 1940. Died 25 January 1972, Wuppertal, Germany.

---

## MINDNER, Heinrich   Ltn d R
J51     Jan 1918 – 8 Mar 1918   –   KIA
Born 28 May 1898, Breslau. Killed near Rumbeke.

---

## MISCH,   Vfw
J29     9 Apr 1917 – 12 Nov 1917   2
Joined Jasta 29 from AFP3. Transferred to FEA2 Schneidemühl, on 12 November 1917.

| Victories: | 1. | 29 Jul 1917 | Spad VII | 1000 | Poelkapelle | (a) |
|---|---|---|---|---|---|---|
| | 2. | 12 Aug 1917 | Nieuport | 1020 | SW Stadenberg | |

(a) B3531, No 19 Sqn, RFC, Lt F B West, KIA.

---

## MITTERMAYR, Hans   Vfw

| FA11 | | – | | J19 | 28 Nov 1916 – (Oct 1917) | – |
|---|---|---|---|---|---|---|
| J5 | 8 Oct 1916 – 27 Nov 1916 | – | | Kest 4 | 23 May 1917 – 1918 | 2 |

Victories:    1.      21 Oct 1917      DH4                          W St Avol              (a)
              2.       7 Jul 1918      DH4                          Kaiserlauten
(a) #A7583, No 57 Sqn, RFC, 2/Lt Crane (P) POW Lt Engles KIA.

## MITZKEIT, Hans    Vfw
FA206A                              1             AFP4    12 Aug 1917            –
J36       22 Feb 1917 – 12 Aug 1917   1
Other crew member for first victory, Ltn Müller.
Victories:    1.      24 Jan 1917      EA                           Ploegsteert
              2.      15 Apr 1917      Spad                         Thugny                 (a)
(a) Probably #373, Escadrille N 15, Sgt Buisson, POW.

## MIX, Erich    Uffz
J54s      (Jun 1918) – 11 Nov 1918     3
See *Above the Lines* for additional information.

## MÖBIUS, Martin    Ltn d R
FAA211 10 Apr 1917 – 15 Dec 1917    1             J7       18 Jan 1918 – 24 Jan 1918    1   KIA
Born 15 November 1894, Annaberg. Joined FAA211 from AFP6. Wounded in action 22 April 1917.
Awarded the Saxon Knight's Cross of the Military St Henry Order on 22 June 1917, for actions with
FAA211. Awarded Iron Cross 1st Class on 9 November 1917. Transferred on 15 December 1917, to
AFP4, Ghent. Joined Jasta 7 from Jastaschule I. Collided with Lt A W Morey, MC, 60 Sqn, RFC, who
was flying SE5a B4897, over Becelaere, killing both.
Victories:    1.      Date not known
              2.      24 Jan 1918      SE5a               1350         Becelaere

## MÖHRING, Ludwig    Flg
J36       11 Aug 1918 – 21 Oct 1918   1             J27      21 Oct 1918 – 11 Nov 1918    –
Victories:    1.      27 Aug 1918      Camel                        SW Boiry

## MÖLLER, Ludwig    Gefr
J10       10 Jul 1918 – 18 Jul 1918   1   KIA
Born 5 January 1891, Budelsdorf. Joined Jasta 10 from Jastaschule II. Killed near Chaudun.
Victories:    1.      16 Jul 1918      Spad               1355         Oppy

## MÖLLER,    Uffz
J64w      17 Feb 1918 – 11 Nov 1918    –
Joined Jasta 64w from AFP4.

## MÖNNICH, Fritz    Ltn d R
J23       16 Dec 1916 – 7 Jun 1917     –
Served in KG 3/17 prior to joining Jasta 23. Wounded in action over Coucy-le-Château, 3 May 1917.
Awarded EK I on 25 May 1917. Transferred to Fliegerschule Paderborn, 7 June 1917.

## MÖRKE,    Vfw
J21       Sep 1917 –                   –

## MÖWE, Karl    Vfw
J29       16 Feb 1917 – 11 Apr 1917    1   KIA
Born 20 February 1895, Rudau. Reported to Jasta 29 from AFP3. Killed between St Souplet and
Aubérive, possibly by Lt Armand Pinsard, Escadrille N78.
Victories:    1.      17 Mar 1917      Caudron                      Mourmelon              (a)
(a) Probably from Escadrille C47, Sgts Raux & Lethon, KIA.

## MOHNICKE, Eberhardt    Ltn
KG2       1916 –                       –             J11      30 Apr 1917 – 8 Sep 1917    9
Biography & Victories: See *Above the Lines*.

## MOHR, Alfred    Ltn d R
J3        15 Sep 1916 – 1 Apr 1917     6   KIA
Born 20 January 1889, Oberemmel. Was flying Albatros D III 2012/16 (G.18) when he was shot down
near Arras, by 2/Lts Gordon and Baker, No 12 Sqn, RFC.
Biography & Victories: See *Above the Lines*.

**MOHRING, Vfw**

| Kest 1a | – 1 Sep 1918 | – | Kest 4a | – 1 Sep 1918 | – |

**MOLLWEIDE, Ltn d R**

| J17 | – 11 Nov 1918 | – |

**MONNINGTON, Kurt Ltn d R**

| FA62 | – 1917 | – | J18 | 20 Mar 1918 – 11 Nov 1918 | 8 |
| J15 | – 20 Mar 1918 | – |

Biography & Victories: See *Above the Lines*.

**MORHAU, Ltn**

| J30 | 23 Jan 1918 – 10 Feb 1918 | Hosp |

Joined Jasta 30 from Jastaschule I.

**MORZIK, Vfw**

| J6 | – 14 Feb 1917 | – |

**MORZIK, Friedrich Wilhelm 'Fritz' OfStv**

| FlgBn 2 | 1 Jun 1914 – 5 Aug 1914 | – | JsSch | 20 Mar 1917 – 14 May 1917 | – |
| FFA17 | 6 Aug 1914 – 19 Feb 1915 | – | J26 | 15 May 1917 – 3 Jun 1917 | – |
| PilSch | 20 Feb 1915 – 8 May 1915 | – | FEA1 | 4 Jun 1917 – 9 Sep 1917 | – |
| VSPW | 9 May 1915 – 14 Feb 1916 | – | FEA2 | 10 Sep 1917 – 16 Jan 1918 | – |
| FA300 | 15 Feb 1916 – 23 Feb 1917 | – | Kest 5 | 17 Jan 1918 – 23 Apr 1918 | – |
| Idflieg | 24 Feb 1917 – 19 Mar 1917 | – | Kest 8 | 24 Apr 1918 – 11 Nov 1918 | – |

Born 10 December 1891, Passenheim, West Prussia. Entered military service 14 April 1907. Promoted Gefreiter on 11 August 1910. Promoted Unteroffizier on 15 April 1911. Observer with Flieger Bataillon 2 and Feld-Flieger-Abteilung 17. Promoted Sergeant on 15 October 1914. Promoted Vizefeldwebel on 24 December 1914. Promoted Offizierstellvertreter on 12 July 1916. Ritterkreuz on 16 April 1942. Attained rank of Generalmajor in Luftwaffe during WWII on 1 October 1943. Died 17 June 1985, Freudenstadt.

**MOSER, Fritz Flg**

| J22s | – 17 Jun 1918 | – KIA |

Born 13 January 1898, Wolfach. Collided in mid-air with Unteroffizier Meinel, over Thiescourt, both killed.

**MOSER, Robert Oblt**

| J32 | 22 Apr 1918 – 5 May 1918 | – | AFP6 | 5 May 1918 – | – |

**MOSSBACHER, Robert Vfw**

| J77b | 18 Feb 1918 – 11 Nov 1918 | 3 |

Joined Jasta 77b from Jastaschule I. Shot down in flames 26 September 1918, but was able to land safely behind German lines.

| Victories: | zlgzw | 5 Mar 1918 | AR2 | | Sternenberg |
| | – | 9 Mar 1918 | AR2 | | Gildweiler |
| | 1. | 12 Mar 1918 | Spad | | Belfort |
| | 2. | 15 May 1918 | Camel | 0930 | Villers-Bretonneux |
| | – | 4 Jul 1918 | Camel | | |
| | 3. | 12 Sep 1918 | 2-seater | 1255 | Thimmenheim |

**MÜHLEN, Ltn**

| J7 | (Oct 1917) – | – |

**MÜHLEN, von Ltn**

| FA8 | | – | J71 | 6 Feb 1918 – 11 Nov 1918 | – |

Served as OzbV for Jasta 71.

**MÜHLFELDT, Josef Oblt**

| J23b | 27 Jun 1918 – 11 Aug 1918 | 1 DOW |

Born 13 September 1891, Wendelstein. Joined Jasta 23b from Jastaschule I. Severely wounded in combat with a Dolphin on 11 August 1918, died of wounds on 12 August.

| Victories: | 1. | 30 Jul 1918 | RE8 | 1130 | Albert |

## MÜHLHAUSEN,      Vfw
J3                          – 11 Nov 1918    –
Victories        –          22 Oct 1918         DH9a                              Dudweiler
Victory also claimed by Kest 2.

## MÜLLER, Albert      Flg
J75                         – 14 Oct 1918    –
Born 13 November 1898, Ditzenbach-Geislingen. Died because of illness on 14 October 1918.

## MÜLLER, Alfred      Uffz
J7         (Aug 1918) –                      –

## MÜLLER, Alfred      Vfw
J39                         – 11 Nov 1918    3
Victories:       1.         16 Aug 1918         BF2b
                 2.         4 Sep 1918          DH9              1010             Chalmes
                 3.         5 Sep 1918          2-seater         1845             Douai

## MÜLLER, Aristides Fritz      Ltn d R
J36       28 May 1917 – 22 Sep 1918       –
OzbV for Jasta 36. Promoted to Leutnant 2 March 1915. Transferred to Idflieg on 22 September 1918.

## MÜLLER, Franz      Oblt d R
FA18                   – 16 Jul 1917    –              J11      19 Jul 1917 – 27 Oct 1917      2    KIAcc
Born 2 March 1896, Antwerpen. Killed at 0830 hours during a test flight of a Fokker biplane.
Victories:       1.         14 Aug 1917         Sopwith          1735             Bixschoote
                 2.         9 Oct 1917          Nieuport         1430             Gheluwe

## MÜLLER, Gottlob      Ltn
AFP18    11 May 1918 – 6 Jun 1918     –              JsSchII    3 Jul 1918 – 9 Jul 1918       –
FAA290   7 Jun 1918 – 2 Jul 1918      –              J79b       10 Jul 1918 – 11 Nov 1918     –
Born 17 March 1895, Kitzingen, Unterfranken. Assigned to 15th Bavarian Infantry Regiment on
5 August 1914. Appointed Fahrenjunker Unteroffizier 16 Sep 1914. Appointed Fähnrich 12 Nov 1914.
Offizierstellvertreter on 25 May 1915. Promoted Leutnant on 24 June 1915. WIA 8 June 1916,
hospitalised and convalesence to 27 Sep 1917; WIA 26 Oct 1916, hospitalised and convalesence to
27 April 1917. Staff Oberkommando 6 from 28 Apr 1917 to 28 Oct 1918. Various flying schools from
29 Oct 1917 to 11 May 1918. Ritterkreuz on 8 June 1943. Attained rank of Generalleutnant in Luftwaffe
during WWII on 1 Nov 1943. Died 28 April 1945.

## MÜLLER, Hans      Ltn d R
J12                 1917 – 1918            –          J18      20 Mar 1918 – 11 Nov 1918      10
J15                 1918 – 20 Mar 1918     2
Biography & Victories: See *Above the Lines*.

## MÜLLER, Hans-Karl      Ltn
FA3      3 Jan 1915 – 1 May 1915       –              KEKA     28 Jun 1916 – 21 Aug 1916      2
Instr.   1 May 1915 – 20 Feb 1916      –              J5       21 Aug 1916 – 26 Dec 1916      6    WIA
KG2/11   20 Feb 1916 – 28 Jun 1916     1
Biography & Victories: See *Above the Lines*.

## MÜLLER, Hans Rudolf      Ltn d R
J20       (Jun 1918) – 1 Oct 1918      –              J51      1 Oct 1918 – 11 Nov 1918       –
Joined Jasta 20 from Jastaschule I.

## MÜLLER, Heinrich      Vfw
J5        (Oct 1916) – 30 Apr 1917     –              J15      30 Apr 1917 – 25 May 1917      –    KIAcc
Born 6 January 1893, Wolfenbuettel. Killed in accident after take-off at the Mortiers airfield.

## MÜLLER, Heinz      Ltn
J27                         – 8 May 1918    – KIA
Born 11 October 1895, Konstanz. Killed SE Ypern.

**MÜLLER, Hermann    Ltn**
J19       16 May 1918 – 29 Jul 1918      –  INJ
Joined Jasta 19 from Jastaschule II.

---

**MÜLLER, Hugo    Gefr**
J26       11 Dec 1917 –                  –
Joined Jasta 26 from Jastaschule II.

---

**MÜLLER, Josef    Ltn d R**
J29       31 May 1918 – 27 Jun 1918      –  KIA
Born 12 March 1896, Siegen. Reported to Jasta 29 from Jastaschule I. Killed at 1135 hours over Billy, in flames.

---

**MÜLLER, Josef    Ltn d R**
J23b      28 Jun 1918 – 11 Nov 1918      1
Joined Jasta 23b from Jastaschule I. Demobilised on 31 January 1919.

| Victories: | 1. | 31 Jul 1918 | Camel | 1245 | Estevelles |
|---|---|---|---|---|---|

---

**MÜLLER, Kurt    Ltn d R**

| J9 | (Jun 1917) – 2 Oct 1917 | 1 | | CO J30 | 1 Jul 1918 – 25 Jul 1918 | – |
|---|---|---|---|---|---|---|
| J24s | 2 Oct 1917 – 1 Jul 1918 | 1 | | J72s | 25 Jul 1918 – 23 Oct 1918 | – |

Commanded Jasta 72s from 1 August 1918 until transferred to FEA6 on 23 October 1918. Awarded Saxon Ritterkreuz II Klasse mit Schwerten des Albrecht Orden – 20 June 1918; Reuss Ehrenkreuz III Klasse mit Schwerten on 27 June 1918.

| Victories: | 1. | 24 Jun 1917 | Balloon | 2020 | Chaude Fontaine |
|---|---|---|---|---|---|
| | 2. | 15 May 1918 | Spad | 0930 | |

---

**MÜLLER, Max Ritter von    Ltn**

| FA1b | Aug 1914 – 18 Aug 1914 | – | INJ | JB | 1 Sep 1916 – 21 Jan 1917 | 5 | |
|---|---|---|---|---|---|---|---|
| FA1b | – 1916 | – | | J28 | 21 Jan 1917 – 3 Nov 1917 | 24 | |
| KekB | 18 May 1916 – 31 Jul 1916 | – | | JB | 3 Nov 1917 – 9 Jan 1918 | 7 | KIA |
| Kek | 31 Aug 1916 – 10 Aug 1916 | – | | | | | |

Biography & Victories: See *Above the Lines*.

---

**MÜLLER, Oskar    Ltn**
J12       19 Jan 1917 – 3 Jun 1918       –          J31       3 Jun 1918 – 11 Nov 1918   –
OzbV for Jasta 12 and Jasta 31.

---

**MÜLLER, Otto    Flg**
J62       11 Aug 1918 – 11 Nov 1918      1

| Victories: | 1. | 10 Oct 1918 | DH4 | 1324 | Haumont |
|---|---|---|---|---|---|

---

**MÜLLER, Paul    Vfw**
Kest 9                                   –          J48       22 Jan 1918 – (Mar 1918)   1

| Victories: | 1. | 24 Mar 1918 | Bréguet | | SW Remansart |
|---|---|---|---|---|---|

---

**MÜLLER, Wilhelm    Ltn d R**
J60       (Apr 1918) – (Jun 1918)        2

| Victories: | 1. | 7 Apr 1918 | BF2b | | |
|---|---|---|---|---|---|
| | 2. | 23 Jun 1918 | Spad | | Courmont |

---

**MÜLLER,    Vfw**
J5        (Oct 1918) – 11 Nov 1918        –

---

**MÜLLER,    Gefr**
J15       (Dec 1916) –                    –

---

**MÜLLER,    Ltn**
J36                                        –

---

**MÜLLER,    Uffz**
Kest 1a        – Jan 1918        –          J43       Jan 1918 – 21 Apr 1918    –  POW
Shot down inside British lines E Hazebrouck, Albatros DVa (G/2Bde/4).

## MÜLLER,    Ltn
J75                    –

## MÜLLER,    Uffz
J79b          – 1 Apr 1918   – WIA/POW
Wounded during combat and came down in French territory and was taken prisoner.

## MÜNNICHOW,    OfStv

| | | | | | | |
|---|---|---|---|---|---|---|
| J1 | (May 1917) – 26 Jan 1918 | 2 | J59 | 26 Jan 1918 – (Mar 1918) | | 1 |
| Victories: | 1. | 9 May 1917 | Spad | 1910 | Courtecon | |
| | 2. | 25 Oct 1917 | Spad | | Woltschech | |
| | 3. | 25 Mar 1918 | RE8 | | Bapaume | |

## MÜNZ, Albert    Ltn d R

| | | | | | |
|---|---|---|---|---|---|
| FEA7 | – 28 Nov 1915 | – | JsSch | 7 Apr 1917 – | – |
| FFA32 | 28 Nov 1915 – | – | JB | 9 May 1917 – 20 May 1917 | – KIA |
| FEA7 | 30 Oct 1916 – 7 Apr 1917 | – | | | |

Born 5 September 1887, Münzingen. Entered war as a Vizefeldwebel with the 119th Reserve Infantry Regiment. Awarded EK II 11 Sept 1914. Promoted Leutnant on 9 Nov 1914. Awarded EK I on 21 June 1916. Knight's Cross of the Württemberg Military Merit Order on 7 August 1916. Joined Jasta B from Jastaschule I. Killed N Ecourt St Quentin.

## MUHS,    Ltn
J12      Aug 1918 – 10 Aug 1918   – POW
Shot down in French III Armée Sector near Cuvilly, at 1115 hours, flying a Fokker VII.

## MUNZERT, Hermann    Ltn
J59     13 Jun 1918 – 9 Jul 1918   – KIA
Born 2 January 1897, Zweibrucken. Shot down in flames between Willerval and Fampoux.

## MUTH, Alfred    Vfw
J27     20 Apr 1917 – 5 Sep 1917   2 KIA
Born 26 September 1893, Gothen. Joined Jasta 27 from Jastaschule I, Valenciennes. Killed near Moorslede, at 1945 hours.

| Victories: | 1. | 26 Jul 1917 | Sopwith | 2040 | Becelaere | (a) |
|---|---|---|---|---|---|---|
| | 2. | 20 Aug 1917 | DH4 | 1220 | W Becelaere | |

(a) Probably SE5a A8925, Capt P B Prothero, No 56 Sqn, RFC, KIA.

## MUTHS,    Ltn
J28w    (Oct 1917) –        –

## MYNERECK,    Gefr
JB      (Sep 1918) – 11 Nov 1918   –

## MYRRHE,    Gefr
J56    16 Aug 1918 – 11 Nov 1918   –
Joined Jasta 56 from Jastaschule I. On sick leave during October 1918.

## NÄGELE, Heinrich    Uffz
J38        – 24 Jan 1918   – KIA
Born 14 June 1891, Waldshut. Also served in Turkish FA1(?). Killed near Cerniste, Macedonia.

## NÄTHER, Max    Ltn d R
J62    31 Mar 1918 – 11 Nov 1918   26
Biography & Victories: See *Above the Lines*.

## NAGLER, Alfons    Vfw

| | | | | | |
|---|---|---|---|---|---|
| FFA220 | 8 Oct 1915 – 27 Sep 1917 | – | J74 | 5 Mar 1918 – 22 May 1918 | 1 |
| ObOst | – 5 Mar 1918 | – | J81 | 22 May 1918 – 11 Nov 1918 | 9 |

Biography & Victories: See *Above the Lines*.

## NATHANAEL, Edmund    OfStv

| | | | | | |
|---|---|---|---|---|---|
| FFA42 | 1916 – | – | J5 | Mar 1917 – 11 May 1917 | 15 KIA |
| J22 | Dec 1916 – Mar 1917 | – | | | |

Biography & Victories: See *Above the Lines*.

**NAUCK, Roland    Ltn d R**
J6          Oct 1916 – 8 Apr 1917    1  KIA
Born 27 February 1893, Ziersohn. Killed at Villevegne, near St Quentin, flying Albatros DIII 2234/16 (G.21), by Lt de Laage de Meux of N 124.
Victories:          1.          26 Oct 1916          Caudron                              Omiecourt

**NAUCZAK,    Uffz**
J33                – 23 Apr 1917    –  WIA
Severely wounded.

**NAUJOCK, Max    Ltn d R**
J36       1 Jan 1918 – 9 Mar 1918    –  DOW
Born 12 March 1890, Marienburg. Promoted Leutnant 24 Dec 1914. Served in Field Artillery Regiment 73. Joined Jasta 36 from Jastaschule I. Shot through the lungs during combat landing near Roulers, died during transportation to hospital.

**NAUWERCK, Alfred    Vfw**
J57       (Sep 1918) – 23 Oct 1918    –  KIA
Born 2 March 1897, Achern. Killed near Bantigny.

**NEBEL, Rudolf    Ltn**
J5          30 Nov 1916 – 31 Jul 1917    1          Kest 1a    May 1918 – 11 Nov 1918    1
Kest 1b    31 Jul 1917 – May 1918          –
Known to have flown Albatros D III 2231/16 with Jasta 5. Awarded Iron Cross I Class. Commanded Kest 1b from 31 July 1917 to May 1918. Commanded Kest 1a from May 1918 to end of war. Known to have flown Fokker DVII 666/18 while with Kest 1b.
Victories:          1.          26 Apr 1917          FE2b          2005          Joncourt
                    2.           7 Sep 1918          DH4           1426          Niederbronn

**NEBEL, Rudolf    Vfw**
SS23                                            J35       7 Mar 1917 – 2 Apr 1917    –  POW
Hit by Flak and forced to land near Grossen Belchen, flying Albatros DIII 2107/16. Escaped to Switzerland on 5 May 1917, where he was interned.

**NEBEL, Rudolf    Vfw**
J73                – 11 Nov 1918    1
Victories:          1.          21 Aug 1918          Spad          1950          Vaux-Varennes
(Possibly the same pilot who flew with Jasta 35.)

**NEBELTHAU, Heinrich    Ltn**
J29       23 Feb 1918 – 11 Nov 1918    2
Joined Jasta 29 from Jastaschule I.
Victories:          1.          11 Jul 1918          DH9           0915          Marquion
                    2.          31 Jul 1918          BF2b          2010          SW Doulieu

**NEBGEN, Willi    Ltn d R**
J7          14 Jun 1918 – 22 Oct 1918    4  KIA
Born 6 July 1891, Zubenhain. Killed near Nieppe.
Victories:          1.          18 Jun 1918          Camel         1000          N Kemmelberg
                    2.          22 Aug 1918          BF2b          0940          Westroosebeke        (a)
                    3.           2 Sep 1918          AWFK8         1230          Lomme
                    4.          Date and claim unknown
(a) Capt D Latimer and Lt T C Noel, 20 Sqn, D7993.

**NEBL, Josef    Uffz**
J23b       4 Oct 1918 – 30 Oct 1918    –  KIA
Born 5 November 1898, Obersochering.

**NECKEL, Ulrich    Ltn d R**
FA25          1917 –                    –          J13       18 May 1918 – 12 Aug 1918    14
J12       Sep 1917 – 18 May 1918    10          J6          1 Sep 1918 – 11 Nov 1918    6
Biography & Victories: See *Above the Lines*.

**NEETZEL,    Vfw**
J40        Dec 1917 –                          –
_____

**NEHLER,    Ltn**
J38        Jul 1918 –                          –
_____

**NEISEN,    Ltn**
J5         Mar 1917 – May 1917      1
Known to have flown Albatros II 1799/16 with Jasta 5.
Victories:       1.        7 May 1917      FE2b            1140            Inchy-en-Artois
_____

**NEITZER, Rudolf    Ltn**
J65        5 Jul 1918 – 8 Aug 1918    1  KIA
Born 28 July 1898, Krefeld. Joined Jasta 65 from Jastaschule II. Killed over Metz, during combat with
a DH.
Victories:       1.        22 Jul 1918     Balloon          1307            Mandres
_____

**NERNST, Gustav    Ltn**
FA5                                 –           J30        20 Jan 1917 – 21 Apr 1917    – KIA
J10        25 Sep 1916 – 20 Jan 1917    3
Born 25 January 1896, Saarbrücken. Killed during combat with FE2bs and Sopwith Triplanes, near
Arras, while flying Albatros DIII 2147/16 (G.22). Generally credited to FL A R Arnold, 8 Sqn, RNAS,
on Sopwith Triplane N5458 and Lt R G Malcolm and 2/Lt J B Weir, No 20 Sqn, RFC, on FE2b A6375.
Victories:       1.        Date and unit unknown
                 2.        3 Apr 1917      Nieuport         1440            Esquerchin       (a)
                 3.        5 Apr 1917      Sopwith 2        1205            W Rouvroy        (b)
(a) A6674, No 40 Sqn, RFC, 2/Lt S A Sharpe POW.
(b) A1073, No 43 Sqn, RFC, 2/Lt C P Thornton (P) POW & 2/Lt H D Blackburn (O), KIA.
_____

**NESTLER, Gustav    Vfw**
Kest 4a    Sep 1917 – Nov 1917      1
Württemberg Gold Military Merit Medal, 2 Nov 1917.
Victories:       1.        16 Sep 1917     Sopwith 1 1/2                    Bitsch
_____

**NETTE,    Ltn**
J13        23 Sep 1918 – 11 Nov 1918   –
_____

**NETZTHALER,      Gefr**
J80b       26 Sep 1918 – 11 Nov 1918   –
Joined Jasta 80b from AFP C.
_____

**NEU, Edmund    Ltn**
J76b       23 Apr 1918 – 16 Jul 1918    – WIA     J76b    12 Aug 1918 – 11 Nov 1918    –
Joined Jasta 76b from Jastaschule II. Severely wounded by a Spad during a balloon attack.
_____

**NEUBAUER, Friedrich    Uffz**
KG4/19                              1           J63        9 Feb 1918 – 31 Mar 1918    2  KIA
J26        – 9 Feb 1918      1
Born 27 January 1892, Leipzig. Other crew member first victory was Oberleutnant Kohl (2). Killed
during combat with a Spad over Rollot.
Victories:       1.        27 Oct 1917     RE8                             N Zillebekesee
                 2.        15 Dec 1917     RE8              0947            SW Zillebekesee
                 3.        30 Mar 1918     2 seater
                 4.        30 Mar 1918     Spad XI
_____

**NEUBAUER, Kurt    Ltn**
J28w                                            –
Knight's Cross 2nd Class with Swords of the Württemberg Friedrich Order, 20 February 1918.
_____

**NEUENHOFEN, Wilhelm    Ltn d R**
FFA215     1 Jul 1917 – 31 Dec 1917    –           J27        31 Dec 1917 – 11 Nov 1918    15
Biography & Victories: See _Above the Lines._
_____

## NEUGEBAUER, Vfw
J28w 22 Aug 1917 – 20 Aug 1918 – Idflieg 20 Aug 1918 –

## NEUMAIER, Johann Vfw
FA9b – J16b 8 Aug 1917 – 27 Feb 1918 4
Awarded EK II & EK I. Transferred to BMW 27 February 1918.

| Victories: | 1. | 20 Aug 1917 | Spad | Louvemont |
|---|---|---|---|---|
| | 2. | 18 Sep 1917 | Balloon | Ft Belleville |
| | 3. | 10 Dec 1917 | Caudron R4 | Bacherauville |
| | 4. | 13 Dec 1917 | Caudron R4 | Belleville |

## NEUMANN, Franz Flg
J79b – 2 Oct 1918 – WIA
Severely wounded during low-level sortie.

## NEUMANN, Friedrich Uffz
J37 – 1 Jun 1918 – KIA
Born 7 June 1889, Gerbauen. Killed between Etinehem and Péronne.

## NEUMANN, Reinhold Uffz
J36 23 Nov 1917 – 4 Sep 1918 1 WIA
Born 10 December 1891, Bromberg. Joined Jasta 36 from Jastaschule II. Severely wounded in the stomach during combat over Abancourt. Landed safely but died at 2100 hours in the hospital after an operation.

| Victories | 1. | 15 Jul 1918 | Spad | S Dormans |
|---|---|---|---|---|

## NEUMANN, Wilhelm Ltn d R
J40 7 Sep 1917 – 8 Sep 1917 – KIAcc
Born 9 January 1893, Forbach. Reserve Infantry Regiment 16. Killed during a test flight over Möntingen/Metz airfield.

## NEUMANN, Ltn d R
J17 11 Nov 1916 – 25 May 1917 1 J74 3 Jun 1918 – 11 Nov 1918 –
J31 25 May 1917 – 3 Jun 1918 –
Acting CO Jasta 74, 23 Aug 1918 to 1 Oct 1918.

| Victories: | 1. | 25 Mar 1917 | Nieuport | Cormicy |
|---|---|---|---|---|

## NEUMÜLLER, Otto Ltn
J4 (Dec 1916) – (Jan 1917) –

## NICOLAY, Rudolf Ltn d R
J32b 10 Sep 1918 – 11 Nov 1918 –

## NIEBECKER, Ltn d R
FAA211 1 J43 3 Feb 1918 – 7 Mar 1918 2 INJ
Other crew member on first victory Ltn Wedde. Severely injured in a landing accident.

| Victories: | 1. | 15 Sep 1917 | Avro | | Courrières |
|---|---|---|---|---|---|
| | 2. | 11 Feb 1918 | Balloon | 1010 | Minorville |
| | 3. | 20 Feb 1918 | Nieuport | | Château-Salins |

## NIEDERHOFF, Alfred Ltn d R
J20 25 Oct 1916 – 30 Apr 1917 2 J11 30 Apr 1917 – 28 Jul 1917 5 KIA
Biography & Victories: See *Above the Lines*.

## NIEDERMEIER, Ltn
J13 23 Sep 1918 – 11 Nov 1918 –
Joined Jasta 13 from Jastaschule I.

## NIEMCZYK, Flg
J50 Sep 1918 – 11 Nov 1918 –

## NIEMZ, Alfred Vfw
J11 30 Sep 1918 – 11 Nov 1918 2
Born 23 November 1896. Joined Jasta 11 from Jastaschule II. Awarded EKII and EKI

| Victories: | 1. | Date and unit unknown | | |
|---|---|---|---|---|
| | 2. | Date and unit unknown | | |
| | 3. | 10 Oct 1918 | Spad | 1200 |
| | 4. | 4 Nov 1918 | Spad | 1645 |

## NIESS, Adolf     Vfw
J6      23 Sep 1917 – Feb 1918        –

## NIETHAMMER, Werner     Ltn d R
J13                – 11 Nov 1916    6
Biography & Victories: See *Above the Lines*.

## NISCHKE,     Oblt
J21                                    –

## NISSEN, Hans     Ltn d R
J54s      19 Jan 1918 – 16 May 1918    – KIA
Born 7 July 1893, Munfbarup. Killed near Passchendaele.

## NISSEN, Joachim     Ltn d R
J52      18 Feb 1918 – 9 Mar 1918      – WIA
Born 1 June 1893, Swinemunde. Joined Jasta 52 from Jastaschule I. Severely wounded near Malmaison, died of wounds at 2200 hours the same day.

## NITSCHE, Alfons     Gefr
J10      30 Mar 1918 – 12 Jul 1918     –            AFP7       12 Jul 1918 –                  –

## NOACK, Walter     Ltn
J29      5 Jun 1918 – 16 Sep 1918      –
Reported to Jasta 29 from Jastaschule I. Severely wounded 8 July 1918. Transferred to a flying school as an instructor, on 16 September 1918. Awarded Saxon Knight's Cross of the Military St Henry Order on 7 October 1918.

## NÖCKEL, Paul     Uffz
J28w      21 Feb 1918 – 3 May 1918     – INJ
Born 12 January 1894, Oberderschlag. Wounded in action 10 March 1918. Crash-landed after combat on airfield at Marckebeke, Belgium, severely injured, died of injuries.

## NÖLDECKE, Werner     Ltn d R
J6      17 Jun 1918 – 11 Nov 1918    1 INJ
Born 13 July 1893. Injured in an accident on 22 July 1918, remained with Jasta.

| Victories: | 1. | 3 Jul 1918 | Spad | 1910 | Courtieux |
|---|---|---|---|---|---|

## NOLTE, Gustav     Ltn
J14                – 30 Dec 1916    –            J18       30 Dec 1916 – 28 Jul 1917       3 KIA
Born 25 February 1895, Hamburg. Killed at 2100 hours, near Roulers.

| Victories: | 1. | 29 Apr 1917 | FE2d | 1900 | Hooge | |
|---|---|---|---|---|---|---|
| | 2. | 2 Jun 1917 | Pup | 1000 | Coxyde | |
| | 3. | 2 Jun 1917 | Nieuport | 1030 | Thourout | (a) |

(a) Probably B3491, No 1 Sqn, RFC, 2/Lt H E Waters, POW.

## NOLTE, Gustav     Vfw
J36      25 Jun 1918 – 16 Jul 1918     – DOW
Born 16 December 1893, Asfeld. During combat with two two-seaters over Treloup, at 1800 hours, he was wounded in the chest and jumped from his Triplane in a parachute, but died of his wounds.

| Victories: | 1. | Date and unit unknown | | |
|---|---|---|---|---|

## NOLTENIUS, Friedrich     Ltn d R
FAA234      Jun 1918 – Jun 1918        –            J6       22 Sep 1918 – 20 Oct 1918    2
J27      15 Jul 1918 – 22 Sep 1918    13            J11      20 Oct 1918 – 11 Nov 1918    6
Biography & Victories: See *Above the Lines*.

## NOSTITZ, Otto von     Ltn
KG5/27                Oct 1916       –            J12       2 Jun 1917 – Aug 1917          1
Acting CO Jasta 12 from 11 August 1917 to 13 August 1917. Transferred to Jastaschule II, August 1917.

Victories:  1.          Date and unit unknown, probably Kasta 27.
          2.      27 Jun 1917      Nieuport        2000        S Haucour        (a)
(a) Probably B1572, No 29 Sqn, RFC, 2/Lt D Bird, KIA.

## NOTH, George Hermann Paul      Ltn d R
FA38                    –                    JB        Mar 1917 – 19 May 1917    –    POW
Shot down in Albatros D III 796/17 at Gouy-en-Ternois, W Arras; died of wounds as a POW. Downed by Captain W M Fry of No 60 Sqn, RFC, in B1602.

## NOTZKE,    Ltn
J14      (Apr 17) – (Sep 17)          –

## NÜLLE, Hans    Vfw
FA72    23 Mar 1916 – 9 Feb 1917    –        Instr.      Aug 1917 – 5 Apr 1918      –
KG4/23   11 Apr 1917 – 16 Aug 1917   –        J39       28 Apr 1918 – 11 Nov 1918    11
Biography & Victories: See *Above the Lines*.

## NÜSCH, Friedrich    Vfw
J22s                – 1 Oct 1918      2  KIA
Born 11 May 1894, Vaihingen an der Enz.
Victories:  1.        5 Jun 1918        DH9        0905
          2.       30 Sep 1918        Camel       1025        Omissy

## NUSSBAUM, Max    Ltn
J43      6 Oct 1918 – 11 Nov 1918    –

## OBERLÄNDER, Hans    Ltn d R
J30    15 May 1917 – 23 May 1918   6  WIA
Biography & Victories: See *Above the Lines*.

## OBERMEIER,    Ltn
J76b    24 Apr 1918 – 11 May 1918    –  WIA      J76b      22 Jul 1918 –        –
Joined Jasta 76b from Jastaschule I.

## OBERSTADT, Wilhelm    Ltn
J56      5 May 1918 – 10 Jul 1918    3  WIA
Joined Jasta 56 from Jastaschule I. Lightly wounded in action 13 May 1918. Severely wounded in action 10 July 1918.
Victories:  1.      24 Jun 1918        Camel       1020        Polygonwald
          2.      25 Jun 1918        Camel       2045        Wervicq
          3.      29 Jun 1918        SE5a        1045        Poperinghe

## ODEBRETT, Karl    Ltn d L
FA47                – 24 May 1916   1  WIA      J16b     11 Nov 1916 – 7 Sep 1917    6  WIA
FAA215   25 Jul 1916 – 11 Nov 1916    –        J42      6 Dec 1917 – 11 Nov 1918    14
Biography & Victories: See *Above the Lines*.

## OEFELE, Georg    Vfw
FAA287              –                J12       27 Jun 1917 – 22 Jul 1917    1  KIA
Born 29 June 1890, Griesbach. Shot down in flames at 0925 hours over Oppy, during combat with Camels/Pups.
Victories:  1.      14 Jul 1917        FE8         1650        N Boursies

## OEHLER, Karl-Josef    Vfw
FAA257              1                J27       15 Apr 1917 – 21 Apr 1917    1
FA211              –                J24       22 May 1917 – 20 Aug 1917    –  KIA
Born 6 March 1889, Nordrach-Offenburg. Qualified for German Pilot's Licence No.447 on 30 June 1913. First assignment in WWI was to Feld Flieger-Abteilung 52, the designation of which was later changed to Flieger-Abteilung 22. Awarded the Baden Karl-Friedrich Verdeinstmedaille on 23 January 1917. Transferred to Jastaschule I on 21 April 1917. Joined Jasta 24 from AFP1. Killed during combat with a SE5/Triplane over Polderhoek, while flying Albatros DIII 756/17.

| Victories: | 1. | 11 May 1917 | Spad | | Willers Wald | (a) |
| | 2. | 25 Jul 1917 | Sopwith 2 | 0800 | Potyse | |
| | – | 27 Jul 1917 | Sopwith | 2045 | Zonnebeke | (b) |

(a) Shared with his observer, Ltn d R Feldmann.
(b) Credited to Ltn Wever of Jasta 26.

## OERTEL, Kurt    Flg

J20          – 8 Oct 1918     – KIA

Born 17 February 1898, Chemnitz. Killed near Roulers.

## OERTELT, Reinhold    Ltn d R

| KG3 | – | | J19 | 26 Oct 1916 – 7 Jul 1917 | 1 KIA |

Born 18 May 1893, Berlin. Killed near Cauroy, 47th victim of Capitaine Georges Guynemer, Escadrille Spa 3.

| Victories: | zlg | 16 Apr 1917 | Caudron | 1030 | Laneuville |

## OESTERREICH, Albert    Ltn

J11      12 Oct 1916 – 16 Mar 1917    –

Served with KEK III before joining Jasta 11.

## OFFERMANN,    Ltn

| FA18 | – | | J10 | 21 Sep 1916 – (Jul 1917) | – |

## OHLRAU, Johannes    Ltn d R

| FAA252 | – | | J10 | 24 Jun 1917 – Aug 1917 | 1 |
| Victories: | 1. | 17 Aug 1917 | Sopwith | 1015 | Becelaere |

## OLDENBERG,    Ltn

| J22s | Sep 1918 – 11 Nov 1918 | 2 |
| Victories: | 1. | 21 Sep 1918 | DH9 | 1830 | Cambrai |
| | 2. | 23 Sep 1918 | Balloon | 1620 | Attilly |

## OLTZESCHNER,    Flg

J64w    5 May 1918 – 11 Nov 1918    1

Joined Jasta 64w from Jastaschule I.

| Victories: | 1. | 17 Jul 1918 | Spad XIII | 1102 | St Louis Ferme | (a) |

(a) 1/Lt Henry B McClure, 139th Aero Sqn, USAS, POW.

## OPELT,    Flg

J72s    3 Jun 1918 – 11 Nov 1918    –

## OPPEL,    Uffz

J10    (May 1917) –        –

## OPPENHORST, Fritz    Ltn

| J5 | Dec 1917 – 15 Aug 1918 | 2 | J71 | 15 Aug 1918 – 11 Nov 1918 | – |

Held Iron Cross II Class.

| Victories: | 1. | 5 Dec 1917 | BF2b | 1100 | Abancourt |
| | 2. | 18 Mar 1918 | Camel | 1120 | E Awoingt |

## OPPERMANN, Ernst    Vfw

J31          – 28 Nov 1917    1 WIA

Born 25 February 1894, Berlin. Wounded over Udine, died of wounds 28 December 1917.

| Victories: | 1. | 26 Oct 1917 | Caproni | | N Logarsce |

## OSTEN, Hans-Georg von der    Ltn

| FA38 | 1 Aug 1916 – Nov 1916 | – | J4 | 16 Mar 1918 – 28 Mar 1918 | – WIA |
| J11 | 10 Aug 1917 – 16 Mar 1918 | 5 | | | |

Biography & Victories: See *Above the Lines*.

## OSTERREICHER,    Ltn

| J80b | – | | J78b | | – |

## OSTERROHT, Paul Henning Aldabert Theodor von     Hptm

| | | | | | | |
|---|---|---|---|---|---|---|
| BAO | 1914 – 1915 | – | J12 | 12 Oct 1916 – 23 Apr 1917 | 7 | KIA |
| KG1/1 | 1916 – 12 Oct 1916 | – | | | | |

Biography & Victories: See *Above the Lines.*

## OSTROP, Paul     Vfw

JB     (Oct 1916) – 23 Jan 1917    –   KIA

Born 26 June 1892, Duisburg. Killed at 1440 hours near Miraumont, when he had wing failure on his Albatros DII during combat with Lt E C Pashley, 24 Sqn, in DH2 #7930.

## OTT, Wilhelm     Ltn d R

J16b     18 Jul 1918 – 11 Nov 1918    1

| Victories: | 1. | 5 Sep 1918 | Camel | 2010 | Langemarck | (a) |
|---|---|---|---|---|---|---|

(a) 75th victory for Jasta 16b.

## OTTO, Heinrich     Ltn

J10     6 May 1918 – 16 Jun 1918    1

Born 28 March 1894. Severely wounded during balloon attack 6 June 1918. Transferred to Idflieg on 16 June. Knight's Cross 2nd Class with Swords of the Württemberg Friedrich Order 25 July 1918. Served as an Oberstleutnant (LtCol) in the Luftwaffe during WWII. Died December 1975, Germany.

| Victories: | 1. | 6 Jun 1918 | Balloon | 0750 | Villers-Cotterets |
|---|---|---|---|---|---|

## OTTO, Rudolf     Ltn

| | | | | | | |
|---|---|---|---|---|---|---|
| FA283 | (Jun 1917) – 1917 | 1 | J74 | 5 Mar 1918 – 9 Aug 1918 | 2 | |
| ObOst | 1917 – 1918 | – | J68 | 9 Aug 1918 – 11 Nov 1918 | 3 | |

Biography & Victories: See *Above the Lines.*

## OTTOWELL,     Uffz

J33     –

Lightly wounded in action 15 September 1918.

## OVEN, Walter von     Oblt

J73     11 Feb 1918 – 24 Jun 1918    –

Served as OzbV for Jasta 73, 11 Feb 1918 to 27 Apr 1918.

## PABST, Ernst     Ltn d R

J22s     (Oct 1917) – 1 Jan 1918      J51     1 Jan 1918 – 11 Nov 1918    4

Born 31 December 1897, Rheda (Westfalen). Volunteered 17 March 1915. FA92 in January 1917, then to FA39 as an observer. Promoted to Leutnant d R 31 August 1918. Awarded Iron Cross II and I Class.

| Victories: | 1. | 18 Mar 1918 | Nieuport | 1155 | Den Aep |
|---|---|---|---|---|---|
| | 2. | 29 Apr 1918 | DH4 | 1840 | W Sailly |
| | 3. | 3 May 1918 | DH4 | 1930 | N Estaires |
| | 4. | 28 May 1918 | DH4 | 1120 | E Neuf Berquin |

## PABST, Karl     Uffz

J50     – 2 Sep 1918    –   KIA

Born 12 August 1893, Eckertsberga. Flying Fokker DVII 2012 when shot down by AA fire at Charleville, near St Menehould, at 1150 hours.

## PÄGELOW, Wilhelm     Uffz

J53     10 May 1918 – 11 Nov 1918    –

Joined Jasta 53 from Jastaschule II.

## PÄGELOW,     Gefr

J71     – 6 Sep 1918    –   MIA

## PALAND, Ernst     Ltn d R

J20     21 Jan 1918 – 25 Jan 1918    –   WIA

Joined Jasta 20 from Jastaschule I.

## PANNES, Wilhelm     Ltn d R

J46     (Apr 1918) – 29 May 1918    –   KIA

Born 30 August 1898, Krefeld. Shot down in flames over Meault.

## PAPE,     Vfw
J38        (Jul 1918) –              –

---

## PAPENMEYER, Wilhelm      Ltn d R
JB        11 Nov 1917 – 28 Mar 1918     4   KIA
Born 8 December 1895, Hamein. Joined Jasta B from Jastaschule I. Killed over Acheville, flying Fokker
DrI 409/17.

| Victories: | 1. | 18 Nov 1917 | Spad VII | 1100 | NE Langemarck | (a) |
| | 2. | 4 Jan 1918 | SE5a | 1245 | Gheluvelt | (b) |
| | 3. | 24 Feb 1918 | RE8 | 1545 | St Julien | (c) |
| | 4. | 28 Mar 1918 | RE8 | | Arleux | (d) |

(a) Probably #3575, 2/Lt G A Cranswick, No 23 Sqn, RFC, KIA.
(b) Probably C5334, No 60 Sqn, RFC, Capt F H B Selous, MC, KIA.
(c) Probably B5071, No 4 Sqn, RFC, 2/Lts R D White (P) & W A Keeler (O) KIA.
(d) Probably #6571, Lts A D Pope and H S Redpath, No 52 Sqn, RAF, POWs.

---

## PARLOW,     Ltn
J22                                           1

| Victories: | 1. | 16 Apr 1917 | Caudron | | E. Cernay |

---

## PASTOR, Günther      Ltn
J29        6 Jun 1917 – 12 Jul 1917     1   WIA      J11       24 Sep 1917 – 31 Oct 1917     –   KIA
Joined Jasta 29 from AFP1. Severely wounded 12 July 1917, at 2004 hours, forced to land E of Annay,
hospitalised. Killed in Fokker Dr I 121/17 N Moorslede, at 1520 hours. From Frankfurt.

| Victories: | – | 2 Jul 1917 | EA | 1050 | Vimy |
| | 1. | 6 Jul 1917 | AWFK8 | 1545 | W Lens |

---

## PASTOR, Herbert      Ltn
J29        7 Sep 1917 – 28 Sep 1917     –   KIA
Born 5 August 1898, Posen. Served in Foot Artillery Regiment 6. Severely wounded in action 12 July
1917. Killed at 0800 hours W Veldhoek, by Capt J T B McCudden, No 56 Sqn, RFC.

| Victories: | 1. | 6 Jul 1917 | BE | | Lens |

---

## PATERMANN, Linus      Vfw
J4        1916 – 12 Jul 1917     2   KIA
Born 23 September 1894, Strelitz. Killed at 1100 hours, over Gheluvelt.

| Victories: | 1. | 7 Apr 1917 | Nieuport | 1710 | NW Biache | (a) |
| | 2. | 11 Jul 1917 | Sopwith | 2140 | W Houthem | |

(a) A6692, No 29 Sqn, RFC, Capt A Jennings.

---

## PATZER, Egon      Ltn d R
SS27        – 21 Jul 1917     1              J36        21 Jul 1917 – 9 Aug 1918     1   KIA
Born 3 June 1896, Obernik. Promoted to Vizefeldwebel on 3 September 1917. Promoted to Leutnant
d R on 25 June 1918. Shot down near Montfaucon.

| Victories: | 1. | Date and unit unknown, probably Schutzstaffel 27 | | | |
| | 2. | 5 Oct 1917 | DH4 | 1625 | SW Westroosebeke |

---

## PAUL,     Vfw
J18        14 Jan 1917 – 23 Jan 1917     –              J28        24 Jan 1917 –              –

---

## PAULIN, Michael      Ltn d R
FAA289b                                                  J14        30 Aug 1917 – 18 Sep 1917     –
J18        1 Aug 1917 – 30 Aug 1917     –              J23b       18 Sep 1917 – 19 Jun 1918     1
Transferred to FEA1b on 19 June 1918.

| Victories: | 1. | 9 May 1918 | SE5a | 1150 | Monchy |

---

## PAULUS, Alfons      Ltn d R
J21        – 25 May 1917     –   KIA
Born 8 October 1892, Hohn. Killed at 1715 hours near Dontrien, down in flames.

---

## PAYEBRUNE, de      Ltn
J13        (Mar 1917) –                    1

| Victories: | 1. | 18 Mar 1917 | Caudron | | NW Beaurieux |

## PECH, Karl    Vfw
J29        18 Jan 1918 – 19 May 1918    9  KIA
Biography & Victories: See *Above the Lines*.

## PECKMANN,    Ltn
J15                – 29 Apr 1917    – WIA

## PECKMANN, Werner    Ltn d R
J14        (Apr 1917) – (Sep 1917)    –          J9        (Jul 1918) – (Sep 1918)    3
Victories:        1.        31 Jul 1918    Spad XI                    Olizy
                  2.        22 Aug 1918    Spad          1230        Blérancourt
                  3.         4 Sep 1918    Spad          1815        Soissons

## PEISKER,    Uffz
J7                1917 – (Sep 1918)    1
Wounded in action 28 May 1918.
Victories:        1.        16 Sep 1918    SE5a                      Menin

## PELTZER, Peter    Gefr
J5                – 29 Aug 1918    – WIA
Born 29 November 1892, Rhendt. Severely wounded in combat between Biaches and Herbercourt, died 31 August 1918, at Bernes.

## PELTZER,    Gefr
J19        14 Jun 1918 – 30 Jun 1918    –          J13        30 Jun 1918 –          –
Reported to Jasta 19 from AFP18.

## PELZ, Otto    Vfw
J23b        12 May 1917 – 17 Sep 1917    1          J32b        17 Sep 1917 – 3 Dec 1917    – KIA
Born 4 April 1893, Zettitz. Joined Jasta 23 from Jastaschule I. Killed north of Verneuil, probably by Lieutenant Jaille, Spa 75, who claimed an Albatros DV near St Soupir as his second victory this date.
Victories:        1.         6 Sep 1917    Spad          1403        Ornes

## PERNET, Franz    Ltn
JB        (Jun 1917) – 5 Sep 1917    – KIA
Born 23 Apr 1895, Birkenwerder. Served in FA14 prior to Jasta B. Killed at sea near Westende, by 2/Lt K R Park and 2/AM H Lindfield, No 48 Sqn, RFC, in A7182.

## PERTZ, Karl    Ltn d L
J23        15 Dec 1916 – 22 Jan 1917    – KIA
Born 18 January 1881, Dresden. Joined Jasta 23 from FEA7. Killed as he was attacked by two Nieuports while attempting to land at the Pusieux airfield.

## PETER, Albin    Uffz
J14                – 25 Jun 1918    – KIAcc
Born 23 March 1890, Reuss. Killed at Phalempin airfield.

## PETERS, Hans    Ltn d R
J32        31 Mar 1917 – 5 May 1917    –          Kest 3        5 May 1917 –          –

## PETERS, Ludwig    Ltn d R
FA12                –          J24s        1 Dec 1916 – 11 Nov 1918    –

## PETERS, Willy    Vfw
J66                – 16 Jun 1918    2  POW
Shot down during a balloon attack; Sgt Moreaux and Lt Saulnier of Escadrille Spa 53 claimed an EA that had just flamed a balloon this date.
Victories:        1.        27 May 1918    Spad                      Courvelles
                  2.        16 Jun 1918    Balloon                    Villers-Cotterets

## PETERSEN,    Ltn d R
J36        9 Oct 1918 – 11 Nov 1918    –
Joined Jasta 36 from Jastaschule II.

## PETERSSON, Hans     Ltn
J3          26 Aug 1916 – 21 Oct 1916    –  KIA
Born 9 March 1893, Berlin. Served in KEK Colmar, before joining Jasta 3. Killed near Péronne.

## PETZINNA, Kurt     Vfw
J32                    – 19 Aug 1917     1               J29     19 Aug 1917 – 3 Sep 1917     1   KIAcc
Born 8 June 1893, Gelsenkirchen. Crashed during take-off, near Torhut-Revisne.

| Victories: | zlg | 12 Jul 1917 | Spad | | Reims | |
|---|---|---|---|---|---|---|
| | 1. | 16 Jul 1917 | Balloon | 1450 | Mourmelon | |
| | 2. | 26 Aug 1917 | Balloon | 1440 | N Elverdinghe | (a) |

(a) 49 Cié Aérostières, observer, S/Lt Caron, not harmed.

## PETZOLD,     Vfw
J6                    – 28 Jun 1917    –

## PEVELING, Karl     Ltn
J46       10 Feb 1918 – 12 Mar 1918    –  WIA

## PFÄLTZER, Otto     Ltn d R
KekH            1916 – 1916             1          FA220        1917 –                      1
J15       10 Oct 1916 – (May 1917)      1

| Victories: | 1. | 18 Mar 1916 | Farman | Dornbach |
|---|---|---|---|---|
| | 2. | 12 Oct 1916 | Bréguet | Bremgarten |
| | 3. | 22 Jun 1917 | Balloon | |

## PFÄNDER,     Sgt
J69                    – 6 Apr 1918     3  WIA
Severely wounded during combat with a Caudron R9.

| Victories: | 1. | 24 Mar 1918 | BF2b | 1430 | Fréniches | |
|---|---|---|---|---|---|---|
| | 2. | 1 Apr 1918 | AR2 | 1640 | W Ville | |
| | 3. | 3 Apr 1918 | Balloon | 1145 | Ribécourt | (a) |

(a) French 69th Balloon Cié, Sgt C Debas killed.

## PFAFFENRITTER, Heinrich     Uffz
J60                    – 17 Jul 1918     2  WIA     J60      (Sep 1918) – 10 Oct 1918     1   KIAcc
Born 1 April 1897, Nürnberg. Severely wounded during combat with Spads. Involved in a mid-air collision with Sgt Bohnenberger near St Juvin, on 10 October 1918, both killed.

| Victories: | 1. | 17 Jul 1918 | Spad | | Villers Allerand |
|---|---|---|---|---|---|
| | 2. | 17 Jul 1918 | AR2 | | Villers Allerand |
| | 3. | 27 Sep 1918 | Spad | 1820 | Tahure |

## PFEIFFER Hermann     Ltn d R
FFA10     Aug 1915 – Jul 1916       –          J9      5 Oct 1916 – 20 May 1917     11 KIAcc
AOK3      Jul 1916 – 7 Oct 1916      –
Biography & Victories: See *Above the Lines*.

## PFEIFFER, Paul     Vfw
J34       6 Mar 1917 – 30 Apr 1917    –          KG3/16   30 Apr 1917 –
Joined Jasta 34 from FEA1.

## PHILIPP, Alfred     Vfw
J57       14 May 1918 – 17 May 1918   –  KIA
Born 22 November 1891, Chemnitz. Joined Jasta 57 from Jastaschule I. Killed over Somme Valley.

## PHILIPPS, Herwarth     Ltn d R
JB        10 Sep 1916 – 1 Oct 1916    –  KIA
Born 26 July 1895, Kiel. Served with KEK Vaux prior to Jasta B. Killed Beaulincourt, S Bapaume, by AA fire.

## PIECHL, Paul     OfStv
FFA2b     3 Aug 1914 – Oct 1914       –          KEK Ost  6 Aug 1916 – 10 Oct 1916    –
FFA7b     (Jan 1915) – 6 Aug 1916     1          J5       10 Oct 1916 – 20 Oct 1916    –  KIA
Born 4 November 1890, Waakirchen. Awarded Iron Cross 2nd Class on 26 Feb 1915. Bavarian Military Merit Cross 3rd Class with swords on 12 May 1915. Württemberg Silver Military Merit Medal, 15 August 1915. Promoted Vizefeldwebel on 20 August 1915. Eiserne Kreuz I Klasse on 15 April 1916. Bavarian Silver Bravery Medal for actions on 6, 19 and 20 June 1916, with Feldflieger-Abteilung 7b.

Killed near Longueval, in Halberstadt DIII 393/16.

| Victories: | 1. | 28 May 1916 | | | St Eloi | (a) |

(a) Probably Captain E W Barrett, No 29 Sqn, RFC, in DH2 #5946.

---

## PIECHULEK, Franz  Ltn d R

| | | | | | | |
|---|---|---|---|---|---|---|
| Kest 5 | 27 Oct 1917 – 14 Dec 1917 | 1 | | J56 | 9 Jan 1918 – 11 Nov 1918 | 12 |
| J41 | 14 Dec 1917 – 9 Jan 1918 | 1 | | | | |

Biography & Victories: See *Above the Lines*.

---

## PIEL, Heinrich  Uffz

J13      (Jun 1918) – 29 Jun 1918    2  KIA

Born 31 October 1894, Duisdorf. Shot down in flames during combat with Spads over Amiens.

| Victories: | 1. | 9 Jun 1918 | Spad | | Thiescourt |
|---|---|---|---|---|---|
| | 2. | 11 Jun 1918 | Spad | | |

---

## PIEPIORKA, Paul  Ltn

J71      – 20 Jun 1918    – KIA

Born 26 September 1895, Danzig. Killed near Sierenz.

---

## PIETZSCH, Kurt  Uffz

J58      15 Jul 1918 – 11 Nov 1918    2

Wounded during a balloon attack on 15 September, and forced to land.

| Victories: | 1. | 10 Aug 1918 | Balloon | 1825 | Fismes |
|---|---|---|---|---|---|
| | 2. | 15 Sep 1918 | Balloon | 1305 | Wancourt |

---

## PIEZ, Richard  Vfw

Kest 3      – 2 May 1917    – KIA

Born 5 June 1893, Mainz. Killed in combat with a Spad over Gerolen.

---

## PINKERT,  Vfw

| J25 | May 1917 – 12 Aug 1918 | | J38 | 12 Aug 1918 – 11 Nov 1918 |
|---|---|---|---|---|

---

## PIPPART, Hans  Ltn d L

| | | | | | | |
|---|---|---|---|---|---|---|
| FAA220 | 1 Feb 1916 – 18 Apr 1917 | – | | J13 | 4 Dec 1917 – 18 Apr 1918 | 4 |
| Kasta 1 | 18 Apr 1917 – 4 Dec 1917 | 6 | | J19 | 18 Apr 1918 – 11 Aug 1918 | 12 KIA |

Biography & Victories: See *Above the Lines*.

---

## PIRN,  Uffz

J80b      –

---

## PISSOWOTZKY,  Gefr

J54s      (Oct 1918) – 11 Nov 1918    1

| Victories: | 1. | 30 Oct 1918 | Balloon | 1540 | Monsard |
|---|---|---|---|---|---|

---

## PLANGE, Richard  Ltn d R

| J2 | (Sep 1917) – 29 Apr 1918 | 7 | | J36 | 29 Apr 1918 – 19 May 1918 | – KIA |
|---|---|---|---|---|---|---|

Biography & Victories: See *Above the Lines*.

---

## PLAUTH, Karl  Ltn d R

| | | | | | | |
|---|---|---|---|---|---|---|
| FA204 | – 1918 | – | | J51 | 29 Sep 1918 – 11 Nov 1918 | 7 |
| J20 | 14 Jun 1918 – 29 Sep 1918 | 10 | | | | |

Biography & Victories: See *Above the Lines*.

---

## PLEISS, Gotthilf  Ltn d R

J9      – 17 Mar 1918    – POW

Württemberg Gold Military Merit Medal, 6 June 1918. Flying an Albatros when shot down during combat with two Spads.

---

## PLESSEN, Karl von  Ltn

J59      27 Mar 1918 – 16 May 1918    – KIA

Born 3 November 1896, Trechow. Killed over Tilloy.

---

## PLÜSCHOW, Wolfgang  Oblt

| J11 | 12 Oct 1916 – 20 May 1917 | – | | J39 | – 5 Jul 1918 | 1 KIA |
|---|---|---|---|---|---|---|

Born 28 January 1888, München. Served in Infantry Regiment 97. Wounded in combat 7 May 1917.

Qualified as an observer before becoming a pilot. Died 5 July 1918, at Chemnitz.

Victories:       1.          30 Jan 1918          Camel                                    E Spresiano

---

### PLUM, Heinrich      Uffz
J81          Jun 1918 – 4 Jul 1918     – Sick Lv     AFP4        1 Oct 1918 –                     –
J29      19 Aug 1918 – 1 Oct 1918     –
Joined Jasta 29 from AFP6.

---

### POSCHINGER, Wilhelm Ritter von      Ltn
J32b      27 Mar 1917 – 17 Jul 1917     –             FEA1        17 Jul 1917 –                    –
OzbV for Jasta 32b from 27 May 1917.

---

### PODBIEL, Paul      Uffz
J40s                  – 4 Oct 1918     – KIA
Born 3 January 1893, St Piefab. Killed between Menin and Wervicq.

---

### PODDAY,      Ltn
J52      25 Feb 1918 – 11 Nov 1918     –
Joined J52 from Jastaschule II.

---

### POESCH, Friedrich      Ltn
J16b      30 Sep 1917 – 19 Dec 1917     1             J78b      19 Dec 1917 – 17 Feb 1918      – KIAcc
Reported to Jastaschule 6 September 1917. Sent to AFP5 15 September 1917. Joined Jasta 16b from AFP5. Killed in an accident at 0930 hours, at Burschied airfield while flying Albatros DIII (OAW) 5120/17.

Victories:       1.          10 Dec 1917          Spad                                     Champneuville

---

### POESCHKE, Friedrich      Vfw
J53      5 May 1918 – 11 Nov 1918     8
Biography & Victories: See *Above the Lines*.

---

### POHLMANN, Fritz      Uffz
J31                  – 17 Jun 1917     – KIAcc
Born 2 December 1895, Flensburg. Killed during a test flight at airfield Mars-sous-Bourcq.

---

### POHLAMNN,      OfStv
Kest 4b                                1
Victories:       1.          20 Jul 1918          DH4                                      Oberndorf

---

### POCKRANTZ, Karl      Ltn d R
J29      29 Mar 1917 – 15 May 1917     1 KIA
Born 23 September 1892, Bremen. Flew with FA24 prior to joining Jasta 29. Collided with Spad VII S1199 in mid-air S Pont Faverger, both pilots killed. The French pilot was Lt Pollet, Escadrille N102.

Victories:       1.          Date and unit unknown, probably with FA24
                 2.          15 May 1917          Spad VII                                 S Pont Faverger

---

### POLLANDT, Max      Ltn d R
J13      22 Oct 1916 – 29 Dec 1916     –             AFP11      10 Jan 1917 –                     –
J23      29 Dec 1916 – 10 Jan 1917     –             J6         10 Jun 1917 – Jun 1917            1
Served in FA54 before being assigned to Jasta 13.
Victories:       1.          17 Jun 1917          SE5          0955          Deaucamps          (a)
(a) A4862, No 56 Sqn, RFC, 2/Lt H G Spearpoint, POW.

---

### POLLINGER, Jakob      Vfw
J77b      22 May 1918 – 30 May 1918     – POW
Joined Jasta 77b from Jastaschule I. Ran out of fuel and landed in British lines near Bourney, Pfalz DIIIa 8284/17 (G/5Bde/13).

---

### PONATH, Alfred      Ltn d R
J68      22 Jun 1918 – 4 Jul 1918     – KIA
Born 13 July 1890, Hamburg. Killed near Davenescourt.

---

### POPP, Hans      Sgt
J77b      30 Jul 1918 – 17 Sep 1918     – KIA

Born 9 February 1894, Hof. Killed in action at 1655 hours on a Fokker D VII (G/2Bde/22) between Warville and Eply, down in flames. Claimed by Maj K L Caldwell, No 74 Sqn, RAF.

### PORAK, Ltn
| | | | | | |
|---|---|---|---|---|---|
| J72s | 20 May 1918 – 11 Nov 1918 | 1 | | | |
| Victories: | 1. | 21 Aug 1918 | Spad XI | 1035 | Gueux |

### PORALLA, Konrad Vfw
| | | | | |
|---|---|---|---|---|
| J32b | – 23 Aug 1917 – WIA | J45 | 17 Dec 1917 – (Mar 1918) | – |
| J32b | – 17 Dec 1917 – | J81 | (Mar 1918) – 2 May 1918 | – INJ |

Severely wounded over Dannevoux, 23 August 1917. Severely injured 2 May 1918.

### POSCHINGER, Wilhelm Ritter von Ltn
| | | | |
|---|---|---|---|
| J32b | 27 Mar 1917 – 17 Jul 1917 – | FEA1b | 17 Jul 1917 – | – |

### POSSIN, Emil Uffz
| | |
|---|---|
| J53 | 21 Mar 1918 – 12 Aug 1918 – WIA |

Joined Jasta 53 from Jastaschule I.

### PRACLIK, Rudolf Gustav Uffz
| | |
|---|---|
| J5 | (Oct 1918) – 11 Nov 1918 – WIA |

Wounded when shot down in flames during combat with SE5s on 25 October 1918, jumped in parachute and landed safely.

### PRAHLOW, Ltn
| | | | | |
|---|---|---|---|---|
| Kest 3 | – 11 Nov 1918 – | | | |
| Forced to land after a combat on 13 July 1918, unharmed. | | | | |
| Victories: | – | 23 Oct 1918 | DH9 | 1305 Frescaty |

### PRASSE, Ltn d R
| | | | |
|---|---|---|---|
| J26 | Nov 1917 – 15 Jan 1918 – | FEA9 | 15 Jan 1918 – | – |

Trained at Jastaschule I. Severely injured in an accident on 7 December 1917.

### PREHN, Alfred Vfw
| | | | |
|---|---|---|---|
| FA5 | – | J10 | 21 Sep 1916 – 16 Nov 1916 – |
| KEK3 | – 1916 1 | J11 | 16 Nov 1916 – 1 Mar 1917 – |

Transferred to a naval air station on 1 March 1917.
| | | | | | |
|---|---|---|---|---|---|
| Victories: | 1. | 21 Jun 1916 | FE8 | NW Ypres | (a) |

(a) Probably Captain L.H. Sweet, No 29 Sqn, RFC, in FE8 #6378.

### PREISS, Reinhold Gefr
| | |
|---|---|
| J14 | – 9 Jun 1918 – POW |

Shot down and forced to land near Dickebusch, flying Fokker Dr I 583/17. (G/2nd Bde/15), credited to Lt J C Bateman, No 1 Sqn, RAF.

### PREISS, Helmut Uffz
| | | | |
|---|---|---|---|
| J54s | – 16 Jun 1918 1 | J47w | 16 Jun 1918 – – |
| Victories: | 1. | 16 Jun 1918 | DH9 | 2105 Villers-Bretonneux |

### PREISSLER, Kurt Oblt
| | | | |
|---|---|---|---|
| J30 | 22 Oct 1917 – 16 Apr 1918 – | JGr2 | 16 Apr 1918 – – |

Joined Jasta 30 from Jastaschule I. Acting CO Jasta 30 from 10 November 1917 to 10 December 1917, 15 January to 29 January 1918, and 19 March to 16 April 1918.

### PRESSENTIN gen von RAUTTER, Viktor von Ltn
| | | | |
|---|---|---|---|
| J59 | 11 Mar 1918 – 15 Mar 1918 – | J4 | 15 Mar 1918 – 31 May 1918 15 KIA |

Biography & Victories: See *Above the Lines*.

### PREUSS, Karl Uffz
| | |
|---|---|
| J31 | – 27 Jan 1918 – KIA |

Born 13 August 1889, Königsberg. Killed at 1340 hours in an Albatros over Roverode, Italy.

### PREUSS, Werner Ltn d R
| | |
|---|---|
| J66 | – 11 Nov 1918 22 |

Biography & Victories: See *Above the Lines*.

**PREY, Xaver     Gefr**
J35b      16 Jun 1918 – 11 Nov 1918
Severely damaged Fokker DVII 4540/18 in a bad landing on 25 October 1918.

---

**PRIEN, Wilhelm     Ltn d R**
JB        7 Jun 1917 – 30 Aug 1917     –          Kest4b      Sep 1917 – Nov 1917      –
AFP4      30 Aug 1917 –                –
Born 23 December 1891, Hamburg. Joined Jasta B from Jastaschule I.

---

**PRILLWITZ, Ludwig     Flg**
J81              – 2 Sep 1918     – POW
Shot down by AA fire near Bouleuse, French Vème Armée Sector, in a Fokker DVII.

---

**PRIME, Eduard     OfStv**
J78b      18 Jan 1918 – 11 Nov 1918     2
Joined Jasta 78b from Jastaschule I.

| Victories: | | | | | |
|---|---|---|---|---|---|
| – | 12 Jul 1918 | Spad | 1100 | Blamont | |
| 1. | 20 Jul 1198 | DH9 | 0810 | Blaesheim | (a) |
| – | 22 Jul 1918 | DH9 | 1700 | Celleswald | (b) |
| 2. | 22 Aug 1918 | DH9 | 0900 | Zebern | (c) |
| – | 16 Sep 1918 | DH4 | 1330 | Alteckendorf | (d) |
| – | 25 Sep 1918 | DH9a | 1500 | Bühl | (e) |
| zlg | 27 Oct 1918 | Spad | 1700 | Herbéviller | |

(a) No 99 Sqn, IAF, Lt F E Thompson & 2/Lt S C Thornley, D1679.
(b) No 55 Sqn, IAF, 2/Lt G Broadbent & Sgt T Jones.
(c) No 104 Sqn, IAF, Lt Horace P Wells & Lt John T Redfield, DH9 D2917.
(d) No 55 Sqn, IAF, 2/Lt W E Johns & 2/Lt A E Amey
(e) No 110 Sqn, IAF. (See *Above the Lines*, p 235.)

---

**PRINZ,     Vfw**
J40s      14 Jun 1918 – 7 Aug 1918     – WIA
Joined Jasta 40s from Jastaschule I. Injured in a crash-landing after combat.

---

**PRITSCH, Hermann     Oblt**
J17       17 Apr 1918 – 3 Sep 1918     1          CO J81     10 Sep 1918 – 11 Nov 1918      –
Joined Jasta 17 from Jastaschule I. Acting CO of Jasta 17 from 29 May 1918 to 12 June 1918.
Victories:     1.          9 Jun 1918     Sopwith 1 1/2     1220          Montigny

---

**PROBST, Richard     Gefr**
J79b             – 24 Aug 1918     – WIA
Born 12 January 1898, Barnstedt. 164th Infantry Rgt. Severely wounded, died of wounds 21 October 1918.

---

**PROSKE, Paul     Uffz**
J7               – 15 Feb 1918     – WIA
Also wounded on 6 January 1918.

---

**PRÜFER, Ewald     Ltn**
J30       23 Oct 1918 – 11 Nov 1918     –
Joined Jasta 30 from Jastaschule II.

---

**PÜLZER,     Uffz**
J80b                                     –

---

**PÜTTER, Fritz     Ltn d R**
FA251     9 Dec 1916 – 7 Mar 1917     –          J68        3 Feb 1918 – 16 Jul 1918     15 KIA
J9        7 Mar 1917 – 3 Feb 1918     10
Biography & Victories: See *Above the Lines*.

---

**PÜTZ, Johann     Vfw**
J23       12 Dec 1916 – 17 Sep 1917     –          J34b       17 Sep 1917 – Sep 1918     7
Biography & Victories: See *Above the Lines*.

---

**PUTTKAMMER, Hans Fr von     Ltn**
Kest 5    (Nov 1917) – 18 Jan 1918     1          J3         18 Jan 1918 – 19 Feb 1918     – POW

Shot down wounded flying Albatros DVa 4495/17 (G.138). Downed by 2/Lt W H Kent of No 60 Sqn, RFC, in SE5a B4860.

| Victories: | 1. | 22 Nov 1917 | Paul Schmitt | | Dammerkirch |
|---|---|---|---|---|---|

## QUAMBUSCH, Werner    Ltn
J1    (Dec 1916) – 19 Jan 1917    –
Transferred to HlBg 1 19 Jan 1917.

## QUANDT, Theodor    Ltn d R
| FAA270 | 1 Jan 1917 – 1 Apr 1917 | – | J53 | 10 Jan 1918 – 21 Aug 1918 | – |
|---|---|---|---|---|---|
| J36 | 1 Apr 1917 – 24 Dec 1917 | 8 | J36 | 21 Aug 1918 – 11 Nov 1918 | 7 |

Biography & Victories: See *Above the Lines*.

## QUARTIER, Hans    Ltn d R
J67    23 May 1918 – 2 Sep 1918    2  POW
Joined Jasta 67 from AFP5. Flying a Fokker DVII when shot down by AA fire during a balloon attack, 0940 at Crécy-au-Mont.

| Victories: | 1. | 19 Jul 1918 | Balloon | |
|---|---|---|---|---|
| | 2. | 2 Sep 1918 | Balloon | (a) |

(a) French 52nd Balloon Company, S/Lt Gravier made a safe descent by parachute.

## QUAST, Paul    Ltn d R
J63    – 3 Apr 1918    –  KIA
Born 29 October 1894, Friedendorn. Killed over Montdidier.

## QUITTENBAUM, Hilmar    Ltn d R
J28W    – 15 Sep 1918    –  KIA
Born 19 May 1896, Kawentachin, Schwetz. Killed between Arleux and Douai.

## RAAB, Anton 'Toni'    Ltn
J40s    Jul 1918 – Sep 1918    –    JGr6    Sep 1918 –    –
Adjutant for Jagdgruppe 6.

## RAABE, Erich    Ltn d R
J41    (Sep 1917) – 20 Aug 1918    4  WIA    J41    Sep 1918 – 11 Nov 1918    –
Born 4 January 1896, Saarbrücken. Volunteered during August 1914. Wounded in action 30 October 1914. Promoted to Gefreiter on 1 August 1915, Unteroffizier on 29 February 1916, Vizefeldwebel on 11 July 1916, Leutnant on 31 July 1916. Joined Jasta 41 from Jastaschule I. Rejoined Jasta 41 from hospital in Sept 1918. OzbV for Jasta 41. Sometimes credited with six victories.

| Victories: | 1. | 11 Feb 1918 | Balloon | 1715 | Ellbach |
|---|---|---|---|---|---|
| | 2. | 13 Mar 1918 | AR2 | | Dammerkirch |
| | 3. | 7 Jun 1918 | Balloon | | Villers-Cotterets |
| | 4. | 7 Jul 1918 | Balloon | | |

## RABE,    Ltn
FAA223    –    Kofl    2 Aug 1917    –
J27    26 May 1917 – 2 Aug 1917    –
Injured in an accident 12 July 1917.

## RABEN, August    Ltn d R
| SS7 | 25 Jan 1917 – | – | CO J15 | 14 Mar 1918 – 23 Mar 1918 | – |
|---|---|---|---|---|---|
| J36 | 17 Feb 1917 – 1 Aug 1917 | – | CO J18 | 23 Mar 1918 – 20 Aug 1918 | 2 |
| J39 | 2 Aug 1917 – 15 Mar 1918 | 2 | | | |

Born 2 December 1892. Reserve Field Artillery Regiment 55. Promoted Leutnant 24 December 1914. Transferred to Fliegerei 18 April 1916. Joined Jasta 36 from Jastaschule I. Severely wounded in action by AA fire 17 November 1917. Injured in an accident 20 March 1918. Commanded Jagdgruppe 'Raben' from 20 August 1918 to end of war. Awarded the Knight's Cross with Swords of the Royal Hohenzollern House Order, and Iron Cross 2nd and 1st Class.

| Victories: | 1. | 26 Sep 1917 | Caproni | | Lom |
|---|---|---|---|---|---|
| | 2. | 26 Sep 1917 | Caproni | | Lom |
| | 3. | 13 Aug 1918 | DH9 | | Altdorf |
| | 4. | 30 Aug 1918 | DH4 | 1200 | Amannweiler |

## RACZEK, von    Ltn
J11        18 Aug 1918 – 11 Nov 1918    –
Joined Jasta 11 from Jastaschule II. Awarded Eiserne Kreuz I Klasse. Wound badge in black.

## RADEMACHER,    Ltn d R
J10        14 May 1918 – 29 May 1918    –    POW
Shot down flying Albatros DVa (G/2Bde/13).

## RAESCH, Josef    Ltn d R
FA7        Dec 1917 – 6 Jun 1918    –              J43        6 Jun 1918 – 11 Nov 1918    7
Biography & Victories: See *Above the Lines*.

## RAFFAY, Leopold von    Ltn d R
J34        26 Feb 1917 – 11 Jun 1917    1          J6        11 Jun 1917 – 30 Aug 1918    1
Born 27 October 1897. Came to Jasta 34 from FEA1. Severely wounded during combat with FE2ds on
16 June 1917. Severely injured on 30 July 1917, near Puisieux Ferme airfield. Promoted Leutnant 17
April 1918. Transferred to Idflieg, 30 August 1918.

| Victories: | 1. | 23 Apr 1917 | Balloon | 1715 | Belrupt |
|---|---|---|---|---|---|
| | 2. | 16 Jun 1917 | FE2d | 1835 | NE Ypern |

## RAHIER, Kaspar    Vfw
J31        – 19 Nov 1917    3    KIA
Born 17 January 1892, Julich. Killed near Vidor-Piave.

| Victories: | 1. | 18 Aug 1917 | Spad | | SE Bixschoote |
|---|---|---|---|---|---|
| | 2. | 26 Oct 1917 | Caproni | 1445 | Cividale |
| | 3. | 26 Oct 1917 | Hanriot | 1500 | Olizza |

## RAHN, Arthur    Ltn d R
J19        21 Dec 1916 – 20 Oct 1917    3          J15        18 Mar 1918 – 29 Mar 1918    1
J18        20 Oct 1917 – 18 Mar 1918    –          J19        29 Mar 1918 – 17 Jul 1918    2    WIA
Biography & Victories: See: *Above the Lines*.

## RAITHEL, Johann    Ltn
FAA295     2 Dec 1916 – 27 Feb 1917    –          FEA1b     5 Feb 1918 – 9 Mar 1918    –
FEA1b      28 Feb 1917 – 1 Jul 1917    –          FEA2      10 Mar 1918 – 30 Apr 1918    –
FAA291     2 Jul 1917 – 21 Sep 1917    –          FlgSch6   1 May 1918 – 17 Jul 1918    –
J34b       22 Sep 1917 – 10 Oct 1917    –    WIA
Born 11 March 1897, Munich. Entered military service 5 August 1914, assigned to the 1st Bavarian Foot
Artillery Rgt. Wounded in action 29 October 1914, hospitalised until 28 December 1914, rejoined his
unit. Promoted to Gefreiter on 1 May 1915. Transferred to 23rd Bavarian Infantry Rgt as a Fähnrich
on 9 May 1915. Promoted Leutnant on 11 March 1916. Assigned to FEA1b on 4 July 1916. Sent to
FAA295 as an observer on 2 Dec 1916. Assigned to FEA1b on 28 Feb 1917. Ordered to FAA291 as a
pilot on 2 July 1917. Joined Jasta 34b from Jastaschule I. Wounded in action south of Bezonvaux,
hospitalised. Awarded Eiserne Kreuz I Klasse. Bavarian Militär-Verdeinstorden 4 Klasse mit Schwerten.
Wound badge in Matt-Weiss (dull white). Attained rank of Lieutenant General in the Luftwaffe during
WWII. Awarded the Ritterkreuz (Knight's Cross of the Iron Cross) WWII. Died 29 January 1961,
Hamburg.

## RASBERGER, Gottlieb    Oblt
J80b       16 Mar 1918 – 11 Nov 1918    4
Joined Jasta 80b from Jastaschule I. Lightly wounded in action 1 July 1918, hospitalised until 8 July
when he returned to his unit. Acting CO Jasta 80 from 14 August to 6 September 1918.

| Victories: | 1. | 2 Sep 1918 | Balloon | 1520 | Brouville |
|---|---|---|---|---|---|
| | 2. | 14 Sep 1918 | DH9 | 1000 | Pelter |
| | 3. | 14 Sep 1918 | Spad | 1750 | W Vhampenoux |
| | zlg | 26 Sep 1918 | Spad XI | 1630 | Athienville |
| | 4. | 30 Oct 1918 | Spad | 1700 | Bulmont |

## RASPE, Max    Ltn
J21s       – 12 Dec 1917    1          CO J44   12 Dec 1917 – 10 Jun 1918    –
Severely injured during a test flight 14 February 1918.

| Victories: | 1. | 20 Aug 1917 | Nieuport 2 | | Hessen Wood |
|---|---|---|---|---|---|
| | zlg | 7 Sep 1917 | Spad | 1050 | S Malancourt |

**RATH,    Ltn**
J22        Mar 1918 – May 1918        –
Awarded EKI.

---

**RATH, Hans-Joachim    Ltn**
FEA1      7 Jun 1915 – 23 Mar 1916    –        J22s    7 Jan 1917 – 2 Aug 1918    –
KG5       24 Mar 1916 – 12 Dec 1916   –        CO SS5  16 Jun 1918 – 30 Nov 1918  –
AFP7      13 Dec 1916 – 6 Jan 1917    –
Born 11 December 1894, Berlin. Joined the Army 22 March 1914, as a Leutnant in Infantry Rgt 32.
During WWII attained rank of Major General in the Luftwaffe, awarded the Deutsches Kreuz in Gold
and the Ritterkreuz. Died 10 May 1968 in Bad Neuenahr.

---

**RATH, Otto    Ltn**
J22        Nov 1916 – 31 Jul 1917       –        Idflieg    31 Jul 1917 –              –

---

**RATH, Rudolf    Vfw**
J35        9 Mar 1917 – 24 Apr 1917     1   KIA
Born 24 April 1897, Elberfeld. Joined Jasta 35 from FEA6. Killed at 0722 hours, near Hagenbach, flying
Albatros DIII 2120/16.
Victories:        1.        14 Apr 1917        Sopwith 1 1/2                        Schernweiler        (a)
(a) Probably N5117, No 3 Wing, RNAS, F/S/Lt H Edwards (POW) & Gunner Coghlan (KIA).

---

**RAU, Karl    Sgt**
J40s                    – 24 Sep 1918        –   Died
Born 22 October 1892, Heilbronn. Died in hospital.

---

**RAUSCH,    Vfw**
J40s       27 Jul 1917 – 11 Aug 1918    2
Victories:        1.        22 Nov 1917        Balloon                        Haudainville
                  2.        27 Jun 1918        Camel          0935            Bailleul

---

**RAVEN,    Ltn**
J80b       (Aug 1918) – (Sep 1918)

---

**RAY, Franz    Ltn d R**
J1         1 Oct 1916 – 17 Dec 1916     1        J49    15 Dec 1917 – EOW          8
J28w       15 Jan 1917 – 15 Dec 1917    8
Biography & Victories: See *Above the Lines*.

---

**RAY, de    Uffz**
J58        29 Apr 1918 – 11 Nov 1918    1
Victories:        1.        15 Sep 1918        Camel

---

**REBBE,    Vfw**
J33        (May 1918) –                 1
Victories:        1.        3 May 1918        BF2b          1220            W Beaucamps

---

**RECHENDRESS, Heinrich    Uffz**
J56        17 Jun 1918 – 29 Jun 1918    –   KIA
Born 22 September 1891, Berkum. Reported to Jasta 56 from Jastaschule I. Shot down in flames at 2020
near Steenwerck.

---

**RECKE, Graf von der    Ltn**
J9         23 Sep 1916 – (Dec 1916)     –        FAA232

---

**REDLER,    Gefr**
J7                    – 23 Jan 1918      –        J52    23 Jan 1918 –              –

---

**REE, Fritz    Ltn d R**
J68        7 May 1918 – 5 Jun 1918      –   KIA
Born 28 March 1898, Köln. Killed at 1330 hours near Méry, flying Albatros DVa 7296/17.

---

**REHER, Walter    Ltn d R**
J48        28 Jun 1918 – 1 Jul 1918     –   KIAcc
Born 30 May 1892, Schafhaus. Joined Jasta 48 from Jastaschule I. Killed near Moyencourt airfield.

## REHM, Lothar    Ltn
J23         29 Dec 1916 – 15 Jul 1917     1              FEA1b      15 Jul 1917 –
Served in KG6/34 prior to joining Jasta 23. Bavarian Military Merit Order 4th Class with Swords on 9 September 1916. Awarded EKI on 20 Feb 1917

Victories:    1.         14 Feb 1917        Balloon              1545          Gironville           (a)
(a) French 85th Balloon Co, Observer, Adj J M Durnad, WIA.

## REICHENBACH, Walter    Uffz
SS16                              3              J5              – 25 Jul 1917    – KIAcc
Born 19 January 1890, Ribnitz. Other crew member on first two victories, Uffz O Trankner (1) & (2). (Ace Observer.) Other crew member on third victory, Flg Misiak (1). Severely injured in a forced landing near Busigny, died same day.

Victories:    1.         5 May 1917         Nieuport                           Pontavert
              2.         5 May 1917         Caudron                            La Ville-aux-Bois
              3.         10 May 1917        Spad                               Berry-au-Bac

## REICHENBACH,    Vfw
JB           – 8 Oct 1917    – INJ
Severely injured in landing accident.

## REICHERT, Thomas    OfStv
FA26                              –              J12        8 Oct 1916 – Mar 1917    – WIA

## REIFHAÜSER,    Ltn
J1           (Aug 1916) –                –

## REIHER, Erich    Ltn d R
J6           (Jun 1917) – 24 Jun 1917    1    KIA
Born 20 September 1890, Chemnitz. His Albatros DIII was downed by AA fire of the 12th Balloon Section (G.49).

Victories:    1.         20 Jun 1917        Balloon              1800          Bailleul             (a)
(a) (32-6-2) (BM 99/D) 2/Lt W F N Forrest and Capt P G Bateman, both unharmed.

## REIMANN, Hans    Ltn d R
KG2/8        – 1 Sep 1916     1              J2         1 Sep 1916 – 23 Sep 1916    3   KIA
Born 24 June 1894, Minden. Served with KG2/8 prior to joining Jasta 2. Killed in a collision with a Martinsyde, flown by Lt L F Forbes, at 0955 hours over Noreuil.

Victories:    1.         30 Jun 1916        EA                                 Bapaume
              2.         17 Sep 1916        FE2b                 1135          Trescault            (a)
              3.         22 Sep 1916        BE12                               Le Transloy          (b)
              4.         23 Sep 1916        Martinsyde           0950          Bus                  (c)
(a) From No 11 Sqn, RFC.
(b) 6544, No 19 Sqn, RFC, 2/Lt G Hedderwick.
(c) 7480, No 27 Sqn, RFC, 2/Lt O.G. Godfrey, POW/DOW.

## REIMANN, Leopold Rudolf    OfStv
FA32         1916 – 1916      –              J1         23 Aug 1916 – 1 Sep 1916    1
KekB         1916 – 23 Aug 1916    –         J2         1 Sep 1916 – 24 Jan 1917    4   KIAcc
Biography & Victories: See *Above the Lines.*

## REIMANN, Ludwig    Vfw
J41          – 30 Nov 1917    1              J78b       28 Feb 1918 – 11 Nov 1918   1
J77b         30 Nov 1917 – 28 Feb 1918    –

Victories:    1.         18 Oct 1917        Spad                               Aultmunsteroi
              2.         3 Nov 1918         Spad                 1300          Marainville

## REIMANN, Paul    Vfw
J52          1 Feb 1918 – 5 Jun 1918    1    KIA
Born 25 June 1891, Reisse. Killed over Aubers, down in flames.

Victories:    1.         Date and unit unknown
              2.         5 Jun 1918         BF2b                 1835          Epinette

## REIMERS, Hans    Uffz
J6           21 Jul 1918 – 4 Sep 1918    2    WIA
Born 29 October 1894, Hamburg. Severely wounded near Cambrai, 4 September 1918, died of wounds

5 September 1918.

| Victories: | 1. | 8 Aug 1918 | | Bréguet | | 1930 | Bethencourt |
| | 2. | 9 Aug 1918 | DH9 | | 1800 | | Epanancourt |

### REIMERS,    Vfw

| FA67 | | | – | | Idflieg | 8 Jun 1917 – | | – |
| J19 | 24 Jan 1917 – 8 Jun 1917 | | – | | | | | |

### REINHARD, Wilhelm    Hptm

| FAA205 | 1916 – 1916 | | – | | Hptm | | | |
| FA28 | 1916 – 1917 | | – | | CO J6 | 26 Nov 1917 – 22 Apr 1918 | 6 | |
| J11 | 24 Jun 1917 – 26 Nov 1917 | 6 | | | CO JGI | 2 Apr 1918 – 3 Jul 1918 | 8 | KIAcc |

Biography & Victories: See *Above the Lines*.

### REINHARD,    Lt

| J4 | | – 9 Aug 1918 | | – | WIA |

### REINHARD,    Uffz

| J76b | 5 Jul 1918 – | | – |

Joined Jasta 76b from Jastaschule I.

### REINHARDT,    Ltn d R

| J4 | 22 Jul 1918 – 11 Nov 1918 | 1 |

Wounded in action 9 August 1918, over Tincourt, forced to land. Returned to Jasta 4 after hospitalisation.

| Victories: | 1. | 3 Nov 1918 | Spad | 1650 | Andevanne |

### REINHOLD, Kurt    Uffz

| J15 | | – | | J24s | 6 Jul 1917 – 10 Dec 1917 | 4 | KIAcc |

Born 4 January 1896, Callenberg. Volunteered 2 August 1914, assigned to Infantry Regiment No.14. Wounded in action at Becelaere in October 1914. Reassigned to Ersatz Regiment 40 in December 1914, and assigned to Fliegerei in July 1916; pilot training at Fliegerschule Schneidemühl. Served with FA42 from March 1917 to June 1917; Eastern Front. Assigned to Jasta 24 from AFP4. Forced to land at Jasta 36 airfield at Cuerne on 16 October 1917, after a combat with his plane shot up. Lightly wounded in action 31 October 1917. Crashed on Emerchicourt airfield after returning from a combat on 8 December 1917. Killed during a test flight at Emerchicourt airfield due to wing failure.

| Victories: | 1. | 31 Jul 1917 | Triplane | | Bailleul |
| | 2. | 14 Aug 1917 | RE8 | 1600 | S Kemmel |
| | – | 29 Oct 1917 | Spad | 0955 | N Ypres |
| | 3. | 15 Nov 1917 | SE5 | 1325 | E Zillebekesee |
| | 4. | 7 Dec 1917 | Martinsyde | 1130 | Mercatel |

### REINHOLD, Max    Oblt

| J15 | 10 Oct 1916 – 26 Apr 1917 | | – | KIA |

Born 23 March 1889, Strassburg. Commanded Jasta 15 from 8 November 1916. Killed at 1930 hours during combat with three Spads over Lierval.

### REISCH, Hermann    Vfw

| J41 | | – 25 Jan 1918 | 1 | KIA |

Born 24 January 1894, Freiburg. Killed during combat with an AR2 near Ammerzweiler.

| Victories: | 1. | 14 Jan 1918 | Sopwith 1 1/2 | 1540 | Gebweiler |

### REISMANN, Kurt    Uffz

| J55 | Jan 1918 – 3 Apr 1918 | | – | KIAcc |

Born Mühlberg, 2 April 1893. (Rissmann?) Killed at Rajak, Syria during a practice flight.

### REISS, Wilhelm    Vfw

| J3 | (Apr 1917) – 31 Aug 1917 | 3 | KIA |

Born 21 October 1889, Jetterborn. Killed at 2030 hours, near Westroosebeke.

| Victories: | 1. | 10 May 1917 | BE2e | | Bailleul | |
| | 2. | 5 Jun 1917 | Nieuport | 2135 | Lambres | (a) |
| | 3. | 18 Aug 1917 | BE | 2034 | Becelaere | |

(a) Probably B1548, No 40 Sqn, RFC, Capt W T Allcock.

**REISSMANN, Rudolf      Flg**
J24s      10 May 1918 – 15 May 1918   –   KIA
Born 23 March 1898, Plauen. Departed at 0805 hours; shot down by a Spad at 0930.

**REIZ,      Uffz**
J78b      10 Jul 1918 –                        –
Joined Jasta 78b from Jastaschule II.

**RENTSCH, Max      Uffz**
J69           – 23 Mar 1918   –   KIAcc
Born 5 March 1894, Gleina. Killed shortly after take-off at 1120 hours.

**REPPCHEN, Fritz      Ltn**
J48      5 Sep 1918 –                        –
Joined Jasta 48 from Jastaschule I.

**RETSCH, Paul      Ltn**
J32      (Mar 1917) – 18 Mar 1917   –   WIA
Flying a Roland DII.

**REUSS,      Uffz**
J7           – 24 Jul 1918   1   WIA
Wounded in action 29 May 1918. Severely wounded in action 24 July 1918. Awarded Eiserne Kreuz I
Klasse. Awarded Anhaltische Friedrich Kreuz. Wound Badge in Black.

| Victories: | 1. | 22 Jul 1918 | DH9 | 1000 | Ypern |

**REUTER, Gustav      Gefr**
J20      14 Jun 1917 – 18 Jun 1918   –   KIAcc
Born 4 November 1896, Bochum. Killed during a test flight near Menin.

**RHODE, Kurt      Flg**
J4      18 Aug 1918 – 11 Nov 1918   –
Joined Jasta 4 from Jastaschule II.

**RICHARD, Werner      Ltn**
ObOst/
J81      15 Jun 1917 – 11 Sep 1917   –   KIAcc
Born 14 February 1895, Spremberg. Killed during a test flight near Wathram-Riga.

**RICHLER,      Ltn**
J32b                                   –

**RICHTER,      Vfw**
J46      10 Feb 1918 – (May 1918)   –

**RICHTER,      Ltn**
J74           – 11 Nov 1918   1
Victories:      1.      17 Oct 1918

**RICHTER, Emil Alfred      OfStv**
J50           – 21 May 1918   –   POW
Came down in French territory after combat and was taken prisoner.

**RICHTER, Heinrich      Ltn**
J9           – 30 Nov 1917   –   INJ
Severely injured in a landing accident. Knight's Cross 2nd Class with Swords of the Württemberg
Friedrich Order, 8 March 1918.

**RICHTHOFEN, Lothar Siegfried Fr von      Oblt**
J11      6 Mar 1917 – 13 May 1917   24   WIA        J11      19 Jul 1918– 12 Aug 1918   11   WIA
J11      24 Sep 1917 – 13 Mar 1918   5   WIA
Biography & Victories: See *Above the Lines*.

**RICHTHOFEN, Manfred Albrecht Fr von     Rittm**

| | | | | | |
|---|---|---|---|---|---|
| FA69 | 1915 – | – | J11 | 14 Jan 1917 – 25 Jun 1917 | 37 |
| KG2 | Mar 1916 – 1 Sep 1916 | – | JGI | 25 Jun 1917 – 21 Apr 1918 | 27 KIA |
| J2 | 1 Sep 1916 – 14 Jan 1917 | 16 | | | |

Biography & Victories: See *Above the Lines*.

---

**RICHTHOFEN, Wolfram Fr von     Ltn**

J11     4 Apr 1918 – 11 Nov 1918     8
Biography & Victories: See *Above the Lines*.

---

**RIEDEL, Ernst     Ltn**

J19     16 May 1918 – 16 Aug 1918     – KIAcc
Born 29 August 1895, Niederwalde. Killed during a test flight of Fokker EV 107/18 at the Chery-les-Pouilly airfield.

---

**RIEDLE,     Vfw**

J23     –

---

**RIEDLE, Franz     Ltn d R**

J76b     5 Dec 1917 – 6 Dec 1917     –     J16b     6 Dec 1917 – 18 Mar 1918     – KIA
Born 5 June 1896, Kempten (Schwab.). Killed during combat with a Camel over Morlain.

---

**RIEGERT, Raymond     Vfw**

J73     11 Feb 1918 –     –

---

**RIEGER,     Vfw**

FA1     –     J17     11 Nov 1916 – 16 Apr 1917     – INJ
Severely injured in a crash-landing after combat near Pontavert.

---

**RIEHM, Karl     Ltn d R**

J27     12 Feb 1917 – 21 Sep 1918     –     JGI     4 Oct 1918 – 11 Nov 1918     –
Born 4 November 1892. Served in FA68. Served with FA282 A prior to joining Jasta 27. Was OzbV for the Jasta. Awarded EKI. JGI Technical Officer to end of war. Died 19 March 1975.

---

**RIEMER, Claus     Ltn d R**

J26     12 Mar 1918 – 11 Nov 1918     8
Biography & Victories: See *Above the Lines*.

---

**RIENEAU, Rudolf     Ltn d R**

J1     (Oct 1917) – 28 Oct 1917     –     J19     28 Oct 1917 – 11 Nov 1918     6
Biography & Victories: See *Above the Lines*.

---

**RIENSBERG, Hellmuth     Flg**

J10     (Oct 1917) – 18 Jan 1918     – KIA
Born 25 December 1890, Spandau. Wounded in action 8 November 1917. Killed at 1030 hours over Beaurevoir, while flying Pfalz DIII 4059/17.

---

**RIESSINGER, Robert     Vfw**

J12     17 Mar 1917 – 16 Jun 1917     4 KIA
Born 31 August 1892, Elberfeld. Killed in a collision with a Nieuport south of Buissy.

| Victories: | 1. | 11 May 1917 | Pup | 1535 | SE Haynecourt | (a) |
|---|---|---|---|---|---|---|
| | 2. | 6 Jun 1917 | Pup | 1310 | SE Inchy | |
| | 3. | 15 Jun 1917 | RE8 | 1415 | Quéant | |
| | 4. | 16 Jun 1917 | Nieuport | 2130 | Buissy | (b) |

(a) N6464, 3 Sqn, RNAS, Lt J B Daniell, POW.
(b) Nieuport 17 B1610, No 60 Sqn, RFC, Lt D R C Lloyd, KIA; collided with Riessinger during combat.

---

**RIETH,     Ltn d R**

J6     11 Oct 1918 – 11 Nov 1918     1
Joined Jasta 6 from Jastaschule II.

| Victories: | 1. | 29 Oct 1918 | Spad | 1630 | | |
|---|---|---|---|---|---|---|

**RIEZLER, Emanuel    Ltn**
J34b    18 May 1918 – 30 May 1918    –    WIA        J34b    17 Jun 1918 – 11 Nov 1918    –
Joined Jasta 34b from Jastaschule II. Wounded in combat flying Albatros DVa 7053/17 on 30 May 1918,
SE of Albert. Rejoined Jasta 34b from FEA2b on 17 June 1918.

**RINCKE, Wilhelm    Uffz**
J54s    19 Jan 1918 – 8 Mar 1918    –    KIA
Born 9 April 1892, Hannover. Killed near Fontaine Notre Dame.

**RINGELMAN, Ernst    Uffz**
J16b    29 Jun 1918 – 11 Nov 1918    –

**RINK,    Ltn**
J28w    (Jul 1918) –    –
Staff Jagdgruppe 7.

**RITSCHERLE, Karl Waldemar    Ltn d R**
SchSt8    16 Apr 1917 – 7 Jan 1918    3        J60    22 Jun 1918 – 11 Nov 1918    5
FEA1    7 Jan 1918 – 22 Jun 1918    –
Biography & Victories: See *Above the Lines*.

**RITTER, Ernst de    Vfw**
J27    (Jun 1918) – 15 Oct 1918    1    WIA
Joined Jasta 27 from Jastaschule I. Shot down in a Fokker by a SE5a on 15 September 1918; not harmed.
Wounded in action 15 October 1918, during combat with SE5s. Awarded Eiserne Kreuz II Klasse. Died
23 January 1968, Richmond, Virginia, USA.
Victories:    –    2 Sep 1918    Camel            St Quentin

**ROCHELL,    Ltn**
J71    1 Oct 1918 – 11 Nov 1918    –

**RODDE,    Ltn**
J18    1 Dec 1917 – 11 Nov 1918    –
OzbV for Jasta 18. Awarded Eiserne Kreuz I Klasse.

**RODY, Hans    Uffz**
J21    – 19 Jan 1917    –        J30    19 Jan 1917 – 17 Mar 1917    –    KIAcc
Born 7 July 1888, Köln. Killed in a collision over the airfield at Phalempin, Lille.

**RÖDIGER, Otto    Ltn d R**
J6    28 Oct 1918 – 11 Nov 1918    –
Born 29 June 1896. Joined Jasta 6 from Jastaschule II. Died 8 September 1969, Hamburg, Germany.

**RÖHR,    Ltn**
J12    8 Oct 1916 –    –

**RÖHR,    Ltn**
J22    Nov 1916 – May 1917    1
Victories:    1.    Date and unit unknown
    2.    23 Apr 1917    Farman            Leuilly

**RÖHR,    Gefr**
J50    (Sep 1918) – 11 Nov 1918    1
Victories:    1.    26 Sep 1918    Bréguet    0831    SE Perthes

**ROEMER, Max    Ltn**
FAA208    –        J10    21 Sep 1917 – 2 Oct 1917    –    KIA
Born 29 February 1896, Mönchsberg. Shot down in flames at 1030 hours near Westroosebeke.

**ROER, Hellmuth    Ltn d R**
J27    – 2 Jul 1918    1    KIA
Born 9 May 1897, Münster. Killed near Chery-les-Pouilly.
Victories:    1.    1 Jun 1918    EA (Fr)            Château-Thierry

## RÖSLER, Otto    Uffz
J37            – 5 Sep 1918    – KIA
Born 24 September 1895, Wiesenthal. Killed over Flesquières.

## RÖSSEL, Willi    Sgt
Kest 1b                    –
Victories:    1.    25 Jun 1918    DH9                    Karlsruhe            (a)
(a) C2170, No 104 Sqn, IAF.

## RÖSSLER, Otto    OfStv
J23b    25 Sep 1917 – 24 Oct 1917    – KIA
Born 15 December 1895, Sinatengrun. Joined Jasta 23 from Jastaschule I. Killed in action by Flak between Eix and Abancourt.

## RÖTH, Friedrich Ritter von    Oblt d R
FAA296    1 Apr 1917 – 10 Sep 1917    –            Oblt d R
J34b    17 Sep 1917 – 4 Oct 1917    –            J16b    24 Apr 1918 – 11 Nov 1918    18
J23b    4 Oct 1917 – 24 Apr 1918    10
Biography & Victories: See *Above the Lines*.

## RÖTTER,    Oblt
J19    26 Oct 1916 – 28 Nov 1916    –            J12    28 Nov 1916 –            –
Joined Jasta 19 from AFP1.

## RÖTTGEN, Karl    Uffz
J39            – 12 Jul 1918    – KIA
Born 9 November 1894, Waldbrol. Shot down in flames near Vaigny.

## ROGALLA v BIEBERSTEIN, Hans-Joachim    Ltn d R
J3            – 6 May 1918    – KIAcc
Born 23 March 1895, Schweidnitz. Served in Leib Hussar Regiment 1. Killed when his wing broke during flight at 1735 hours over Rumbeke.

## ROHDE,    Vfw
J28w                    –

## ROHMANN, Karl    Vfw
J56            – 15 Aug 1918    – DOI
Born 25 October 1891, Rybnik. Severely injured in a crash-landing at Rumbeke;
died of injuries.

## ROLFES, Hans Joachim    Ltn d R
KG2/11    5 Oct 1916 – 20 Feb 1917    –            J45    17 Dec 1917 – 11 Nov 1918    16
J32    20 Feb 1917 – 17 Dec 1917    1
Biography & Victories: See *Above the Lines*.

## ROLFF, Emil    Ltn d R
J6    2 Jul 1918 – 19 Aug 1918    3    KIAcc
Born 29 July 1896, Stade. Joined Jasta 6 from Jastaschule I. Killed test flying a Fokker E V at 0950 hours near Bernes.

| Victories: | 1. | 17 Jul 1918 | Bréguet | 1040 | Monthurd |
|---|---|---|---|---|---|
| | 2. | 31 Jul 1918 | Nieuport | 1840 | Fère-en-Tardenois |
| | 3. | 16 Aug 1918 | Camel | 1230 | Mesnil |

## ROLLE, Herbert    Ltn
FA67                    –        J9    2 Oct 1917 –            3
J24    1 Dec 1916 – 2 Oct 1917    –

| Victories: | 1. | 6 Mar 1918 | Nieuport | 1245 | Machault |
|---|---|---|---|---|---|
| | 2. | 21 Apr 1918 | Spad | 1725 | l'Ecouvillon |
| | 3. | 3 Sep 1918 | Spad | 1031 | S Fismes |

## ROMEIS, Karl    Ltn d R
J80b    16 Mar 1918 – 11 Nov 1918    2
Joined Jasta 80b from Jastaschule I. Lightly wounded in action 23 March 1918, returned from hospital on 2 April 1918.

| Victories: | 1. | 12 Aug 1918 | Balloon | | Laronxe |
| | 2. | 3 Nov 1918 | Camel | 1300 | Gerden |

## ROSA, Umberto Mario Antonio    Ltn d R

| | | | | | | | |
|---|---|---|---|---|---|---|---|
| FAA229 | 5 May 1916 – 8 Sep 1916 | – | | FEA2 | 16 Feb 1918 – 26 Apr 1918 | – |
| AFP10 | 6 Oct 1916 – 22 Dec 1916 | – | | FEA9 | 26 Apr 1918 – 27 Jun 1918 | – |
| AFP11 | 22 Dec 1916 – | – | | FAA290 | 27 Jun 1918 – 23 Aug 1918 | – | KIAcc |
| J38 | 11 Jan 1918 – 16 Feb 1918 | – | | | | |

Born 9 January 1890, Mannheim. Volunteered for military service 1 October 1911, assigned to the Baden Grenadier Regiment 110. Promoted Unteroffizier 30 September 1912. Promoted Vizefeldwebel 17 June 1913. Awarded EK II on 8 May 1915. Promoted to Leutnant d R 30 June 1915. Transferred to aviation in 1915. Awarded Baden Ritterkreuz II Klasse mit Schwerten des Ordens vom Zähringer Löwen on 20 July 1916, and the EK I on 1 August 1916. Severely injured during a test flight on 21 January 1918. Flying with FAA290 when killed in an accident with his observer, Sgt Alfons Solleder, near La Chapell. (See *OTF* Journal Vol 6, No 3, 1991, pg 238.)

## ROSE, Gustav    Ltn d R

| | | | | | | |
|---|---|---|---|---|---|---|
| J22 | 3 Dec 1916 – Apr 1917 | – | | Kest 4a | 13 Jul 1918 – 11 Nov 1918 | – |
| J25 | Apr 1917 – 13 Jul 1918 | 3 | | | | |

| Victories: | 1. | 20 Jun 1917 | Nieuport | 0730 | Rastani |
| | 2. | 2 Jul 1917 | Farman | | Puturos |
| | 3. | 20 Jun 1918 | Spad | | E Trojaci |

## ROSENAU,    Uffz

| J33 | (Aug 1918) – 11 Nov 1918 | 2 |
|---|---|---|

| Victories: | 1. | Date and unit unknown | | | |
| | 2. | 25 Aug 1918 | SE5a | | Pelves |
| | 3. | 29 Oct 1918 | | | |

## ROSENFELD, Otto    Vfw

| | | | | | | | |
|---|---|---|---|---|---|---|---|
| FAA263 | – 6 Apr 1917 | – | | J41 | (Jul 1917) – 29 Dec 1917 | 4 | POW |
| J12 | 10 May 1917 – 12 Jun 1917 | 4 | WIA | J41 | (Apr 1918) – 7 Jul 1918 | 5 | KIA |

Biography & Victories: See *Above the Lines*.

## ROSENSTEIN, Willi    Ltn d R

| | | | | | | | |
|---|---|---|---|---|---|---|---|
| FA19 | 6 Mar 1915 – 28 Apr 1916 | – | WIA | J27 | 15 Feb 1917 – | 2 |
| AOK3 | – 23 Sep 1916 | – | | Kest 1a | 8 Jan 1918 – 2 Jul 1918 | 1 |
| J9 | 23 Sep 1916 – 15 Feb 1917 | – | | J40s | 2 Jul 1918 – 11 Nov 1918 | 6 |

Biography & Victories: See *Above the Lines*.

## ROSS, Ernst    Ltn

| FAA252 | – | | J44 | | – |
|---|---|---|---|---|---|

## ROSSBACH,    Uffz

| J12 | 8 May 1918 – 11 Nov 1918 | 1 |
|---|---|---|

| Victories: | 1. | 3 Nov 1918 | Spad | 1625 | Sommauthe |

## ROST,    Uffz

| J19 | 15 Oct 1918 – 11 Nov 1918 | – |
|---|---|---|

## ROST,    Ltn

| FA16 | 10 Jul 1918 | – | | J65 | 10 Aug 1918 – 11 Nov 1918 | – |
|---|---|---|---|---|---|---|

OzbV for Jasta 65.

## ROSTOCK, Amandus    Oblt d R

| J77b | 3 May 1918 – 16 Jul 1918 | 2 | | CO J76b | 16 Jul 1918 – 27 May 1918 | – | WIA |
|---|---|---|---|---|---|---|---|

Joined Jasta 77b from AFP6. Acting CO Jasta 77b, 16 to 24 May 1918.

| Victories: | 1. | 19 May 1918 | Camel | | W Marcelcave |
| | 2. | 5 Jun 1918 | BF2b | 1145 | Plainville |

## ROSTOCK,    Flg

| J36 | 22 Jun 1918 – 11 Nov 1918 | – |
|---|---|---|

Joined Jasta 36 from Jastaschule I.

**ROTH Franz   Ltn**
J34b   7 Nov 1917 – 22 Oct 1918   –   FEA2b   22 Oct 1918 –   –
Joined Jasta 34b from AFP7. Was OzbV for Jasta 34b.

**ROTH, Friedrich   Ltn d R**
J12   21 Jan 1917 – 16 Jul 1917   2
Victories:   1.   5 Apr 1917   FE2b   1105   Gouzeaucourt
             2.   11 Apr 1917   BE2c   0845   NE Abancourt   (a)
(a) BE2c #2769, 2/Lt F Matthews, (P), No 4 Sqn, RFC, POW.

**ROTHE, Alfred   Ltn d R**
J27   – 25 Jun 1918   –   KIAcc
Born 15 May 1897, Diedenhofen. Served in Reserve Infantry Regiment 203. Killed in an accident during a test flight at Mont de Soissons Ferme airfield.

**ROTHE, Paul   Vfw**
FA62   Oct 1916 – Mar 1917   –   J14   Apr 1917 – 11 Nov 1918   5
Biography & Victories: See *Above the Lines*.

**ROTHE,   Vfw**
J61   28 Mar 1918 – 11 Nov 1918   2
Injured 23 August 1918, in a collision with Ltn d R Georg Vieth over St Gobain; he survived but Vieth was killed.
Victories:   1.   31 Jul 1918   AR2   2000   S Carlepont
             –   14 Aug 1918   EA   1930   S Tracy-le-Mont
             2.   21 Aug 1918   Balloon

**ROTHSTEIN,   Vfw**
J35b   21 May 1918 –   –
Joined Jasta 35b from Jastaschule I.

**ROTSCZINKA,   Vfw**
J7   – 11 Jul 1917   – WIA

**ROTTMANN, Oswald   Uffz**
J14   – 12 Dec 1917   – KIA
Born 2 May 1891, Plauen. Killed near Asch.

**ROUSSELLE, Oskar   Ltn d R**
J4   Jul 1917 – 10 Aug 1917   – WIA   J4   Feb 1918 – 11 Nov 1918   –
Born 28 January 1893. Wounded at 2000 hours, over Artoishoek.

**ROZMIAREK,   Uffz**
J28w   – 12 Aug 1918   –   J62   12 Aug 1918 – 11 Nov 1918   1
Victories:   1.   29 Oct 1918   DH4   W Sivry

**RUCKDESCHEL,   Vfw**
J13   (Mar 1917) – (Sep 1917)   1
Victories:   1.   11 Mar 1917   Caudron   SE Vendresse

**RUCKLE, Richard   Ltn d R**
FEA8   9 Oct 1916 – 6 Mar 1917   –   AFP4   14 Sep 1917 – 16 Sep 1917   –
FEA10   6 Mar 1917 – 5 Jun 1917   –   JsSchI   16 Sep 1917 – 24 Sep 1917   –
AFP4   5 Jun 1917 – 13 Jun 1917   –   J33   24 Sep 1917 –   2
FFA231   13 Jun 1917 – 14 Sep 1917   –
Awarded EK II on 9 July 1917. Awarded Pilot's Badge on 1 August 1917. Württemberg Silver Military Merit Medal on 26 October 1917. Promoted Leutnant 25 February 1918. Awarded EK I.
Victories:   1.   15 May 1918   DH9   2045   Beerst
             2.   27 Sep 1918   BF2b   1130   Busigny

**RUCKSER, Simon   Uffz**
J37   1917 – 13 Apr 1917   1 WIA
Victories:   1.   13 Apr 1917   Balloon
             –   24 Jun 1917   Spad

**RUDENBERG,      Ltn d R**
J10        9 Sep 1917 – Feb 1918        –
Joined Jasta 10 from Jastaschule I.

**RUDNO-RUDZINSKI, Fr von      Oblt**
J17        5 Oct 1917 – 5 Jan 1918        –        CO J60     5 Jan 1918 – 26 May 1918     –   POW
Joined Jasta 17 from AFP4.

**RÜBE, Richard      Vfw**
J67        15 May 1918 – 11 Nov 1918     5
Biography & Victories: See *Above the Lines*.

**RÜCKERT, Otto      Vfw**
J48        29 Dec 1917 – 11 Mar 1918     –   WIA
Joined Jasta 48 from Jastaschule I. Lightly wounded but hospitalised.

**RÜDIGER, Alfred      Flg**
J59        (Feb 1918) –                   1
Victories:      1.        17 Jun 1918        DH9            1025            Quéant

**RÜGGEBERG, Paul      Uffz**
FA257                                      –        J43     23 Mar 1918 – 11 Nov 1918     2
Victories:      1.        26 Oct 1918        SE5a                          Velennes
                2.        31 Oct 1918        Camel

**RÜRTER,      Vfw**
J46        (Sep 1918) –                   –

**RÜSCHE, Alfred      Vfw**
J39                  – 5 Dec 1917     1   KIAcc
Born 5 September 1893, Degerfelden-Loerrach. Killed at Aviano, Italy.
Victories:      1.        26 Oct 1917        Caproni         1035            Olizza

**RÜSCHE, II      Vfw**
J39                  – 5 Mar 1918     –        J74     5 Mar 1918 – 11 Nov 1918     –

**RÜTTGERS,      Vfw**
J20                  – 6 Feb 1918     –        J71     6 Feb 1918 – 11 Nov 1918     1
Victories:      1.        21 Aug 1918        Spad            1152            Obersulzbach

**RUESS,      Uffz**
J7                  – 29 May 1918     –   WIA

**RUMEY, Fritz      Ltn d R**
FAA19      Aug 1915 – 1917              –        J5     10 Jun 1918 – 27 Sep 1918     45 KIA
J2         May 1917 – 10 Jun 1918        –
Biography & Victories: See *Above the Lines*.

**RUMMELSPACHER, Karl      Oblt**
CO J10     23 Oct 1916 – 18 Jun 1917     –        Idflieg     18 Jun 1917 –                 –
Victories:      –        9 Mar 1917        Nieuport

**RUMPEL, Theodor      Ltn d R**
FAA280     Jan 1917 – 18 Mar 1917        –        J16b     22 Apr 1917 – 17 Sep 1917     2
J26        18 Mar 1917 – 22 Apr 1917     –        J23b     17 Sep 1917 – 13 Apr 1918     3
Biography & Victories: See *Above the Lines*.

**RUNGE, Richard      Ltn d R**
J18        15 May 1917 – 15 Nov 1917     8   KIA
Biography & Victories: See *Above the Lines*.

**RUPPEL,      Ltn d R**
J17        12 Jun 1918 – 11 Nov 1918     –

## RUPPERT, Vfw
J19      5 Mar 1917 – 10 Oct 1917    1   WIA
Joined Jasta 19 from AFP A.
Victories:    1.       10 May 1917        Spad                                 S Berry-au-Bac

## RUPPERT, Uffz
J39                – 11 Nov 1918    1
Victories:    1.       5 Sep 1918         Balloon            1910             S Dury

## RUPPRECHT, Wilhelm   Ltn
J31                – 1 Jun 1918     –   KIA
Born 23 March 1897, Neumarkt. Killed near Laon.

## RUSSEL, Heinrich   Ltn d R
J28      24 May 1917 – 21 Jun 1917    –   KIAcc
Born 2 August 1888, Gosidi (Harz). Killed when he crashed his plane at Gheluve, west of Menin.

## SACHSE, Oblt
J1                   –
OzbV for Jasta 1.

## SACHSENBERG, Heinz   Ltn d R
J17      9 Dec 1916 – 14 Jun 1917    –             Idflieg    14 Jun 1917 –        –
Reported to Jasta 17 from AFP C.

## SAGEBUEHL, Ltn
J28w

## SAINT MONT, Wilhelm   Ltn d R
JB                – 19 Jun 1917    1      J52      1 Apr 1918 – 1 Jun 1918    –   KIA
J5       19 Jun 1917 – (Jan 1918)    –
Born 2 February 1896, Jillich. Served in FA6 before reporting to Jasta 52. Downed in flames over
Mourmelon, near Lille, jumped in parachute which also burned, he fell to his death.
Victories:    1.       17 May 1918        SE5a               1147             Estaires

## SAKOWSKI, Hans   Ltn
J32      12 Feb 1917 – 31 Mar 1917    –      J14                – 13 Nov 1917    –   POW
Kest 2   31 Mar 1917 –    –
Shot down by 3rd Army AA while flying Albatros DVa 5253/17 (G.90).

## SAKOWSKY, Klaus   Flg
J29      10 May 1918 – 21 May 1918    –   KIA
Born 23 February 1893, Berlin. Joined Jasta 29 from Jastaschule II. Killed over La Gorgue, at 1203
hours; his 'chute failed to open after he was shot down.

## SALB, Fritz   Uffz
J80b     10 Jul 1918 – 31 Jul 1918    –   KIA
Born 19 October 1897, Oberkotzau. Killed N Saargemund, in combat with DH9s while flying an Albatros
DIII.

## SALZWEDEL, Gebhardt   Ltn
J24s     21 Dec 1916 – 20 Jan 1917    –      J24s     20 Feb 1917 – 11 Nov 1918    2
Joined Jasta 24 from AFP A. Jastaschule I from 20 January 1917 to 20 February 1917.
Victories:    1.       11 Apr 1917        Nieuport 17                          Xures            (a)
              2.       23 May 1917        Spad VII                             SW Fresnes
(a) #1955, MdL Preher, Escadrille N 68, POW.

## SANDEL, Jürgen   Ltn
FA39                –             FAA259    9 Jan 1917 –        –
JB       Oct 1916 – 9 Jan 1917    –

## SANDLEITNER, Georg   Uffz
J77b     30 Jan 1918 – 2 Apr 1918    1   KIAcc
Born 4 January 1891, Landshut. Joined Jasta 77b from Jastaschule II. Killed during a test flight at

Wasquehal airfield.

| Victories: | 1. | 5 Mar 1918 | AR2 | | Bütweiler |

### SANTJER, Jon    Uffz

| J26 | Nov 1917 – 9 Feb 1918 | 1 | | J63 | 9 Feb 1918 – 31 Mar 1918 | 1 | KIA |

Born 15 October 1894, Emden. Joined Jasta 26 from AFP4. Killed in combat with a Spad over Hainvillers.

| Victories: | 1. | 25 Jan 1918 | BF2b | | Stadenberge |
| | 2. | 24 Mar 1918 | RE8 | | SW Ham |

### SARNIGHAUSEN,    Ltn

| J13 | – 1 May 1918 | – | | J69 | 1 May 1918 – 11 Nov 1918 | 1 |
| Victories: | 1. | 31 Oct 1918 | Spad | | Niedersept |

### SAUERMANN,    Ltn d R

| J27 | 18 Jul 1917 – 11 Sep 1917 | – | | J70 | (Jul 1918) – (Aug 1918) | 2 |
| Kest 2 | 11 Sep 1917 – | | – | | |
| Victories: | 1. | 7 Jul 1918 | DH9 | 1730 | Rixingen |
| | 2. | 11 Aug 1918 | DH9 | | Artzweiler |

### SAUERWEIN, Friedrich    Vfw

| J7 | (Mar 1917) – 9 May 1917 | 2 | WIA | FA9 | | – |

Wounded in Roland DII 822/16.

| Victories: | 1. | 25 Mar 1917 | Spad | 1615 | Ft Marre |
| | 2. | 28 Mar 1917 | Nieuport | 1035 | NW Douaumont |

### SCHAACK,    Uffz

| J28w | (Mar 1918) – (Sep 1918) | 2 |
| Victories: | 1. | 25 Aug 1918 | SE5a | | Bapaume |
| | 2. | 1 Sep 1918 | DH4 | | Tilloy |

### SCHAARSCHMIDT, Erich    Ltn d R

| J9 | – 27 Oct 1918 | – | POW |

### SCHABBEL, Fritz    Ltn

| J18 | 12 Aug 1917 – 15 Aug 1917 | – | | J14 | 15 Aug 1917 – |

### SCHADE,    Flg

| J5 | – 7 Oct 1918 | – | INJ |

Severely injured during a test flight.

### SCHADE,    Ltn d R

| J24 | 2 Mar 1917 – 15 Sep 1917 | – |

Reported to Jasta 24 from AFP4.

### SCHADE, Wilhelm    Flg

| J41 | – 7 Jun 1918 | – | POW |

### SCHÄDEL, Karl    Ltn d R

| J50 | (Jun 1918) – 11 Nov 1918 | – |

Field Artillery Rgt 25.

### SCHÄDLICH, Wilhelm    Flg

| J53 | 9 Jun 1918 – 9 Jun 1918 | – | INJ |

Joined Jasta 53 from Jastaschule II. Injured in a landing accident.

### SCHÄFER, Emil    Vfw

| J33 | | – |

Served in a Flieger-Abteilung prior to joining Jasta 33.

### SCHÄFER, Hugo    Oblt

| J10 | 28 Jun 1918 – 11 Nov 1918 | – |

OzbV for Jasta 10.

## SCHÄFER, Hugo     Ltn d R

| | | | | | | |
|---|---|---|---|---|---|---|
| J18 | 5 Oct 1917 – 18 Mar 1918 | – | | J15 | 18 Mar 1918 – 11 Nov 1918 | 11 |

Joined Jasta 18 from Jastaschule I.
Biography & Victories: See *Above the Lines*.

## SCHÄFER, Johann     Ltn d R

| | | | |
|---|---|---|---|
| J16b | 11 Jan 1918 – 10 Oct 1918 | 3 | KIA |

Born 6 June 1895, Hoffstetten. Reported to Jastaschule I on 31 December 1917. Reported to Jasta 16b from Jastaschule I. Killed SW of Roulers, probably by Maj G H Bowman and Capt F O Soden, No 41 Sqn, RAF, on SE5a E4092 and F5545 respectively.

| Victories: | 1. | 12 Jun 1918 | SE5a | 2120 | SE Bailleul |
|---|---|---|---|---|---|
| | 2. | 2 Jul 1918 | BF2b | 0950 | Zandvoorde |
| | 3. | 10 Oct 1918 | RE8 | | W Ypern |

## SCHÄFER, Karl Emil     Ltn

| | | | | | | | |
|---|---|---|---|---|---|---|---|
| KG2/8 | 30 Jul 1916 – 1917 | – | | J11 | 5 Feb 1917 – 26 Apr 1917 | 22 | |
| KG3/11 | 1917 – 1917 | 1 | | CO J28 | 26 Apr 1917 – 5 Jun 1917 | 7 | KIA |

Biography & Victories: See *Above the Lines*.

## SCHÄFER, Walter     Vfw

| | | | | | | | |
|---|---|---|---|---|---|---|---|
| FAA278 | | 1 | | J66 | 12 Feb 1918 – 28 Mar 1918 | 1 | KIA |
| J50 | 27 Jan 1918 – 12 Feb 1918 | – | | | | | |

Born 26 September 1890, Leipzig. Other crew member for first victory, Ltn Muhs (1). Killed by a Spad NW Charmes.

| Victories: | 1. | 5 Feb 1917 | Nieuport | | Chevreux |
|---|---|---|---|---|---|
| | 2. | 23 Mar 1918 | Spad XI | | Verneuil |

## SCHÄFFER, Wilhelm     Vfw

| | | | |
|---|---|---|---|
| J27 | – 17 Jun 1918 | – | KIAcc |

Born 12 May 1892, Zuffenhausen-Ludwigsburg. Flying a two-seater with Oblt Maximilian von Förster as a passenger when both were killed in an accident at Mont de Soissons Ferme airfield.

## SCHÄFER,     Ltn

| | | |
|---|---|---|
| J7 | | 1 |

| Victories: | 1. | 15 Jul 1917 | Farman | 1840 | Essen-Vladslov |
|---|---|---|---|---|---|

## SCHÄFER,     Uffz

| | | | | | |
|---|---|---|---|---|---|
| J77b | 20 Jun 1918 – 9 Oct 1918 | – | | AFP19 | 9 Oct 1918 – |

Reported to Jasta 77b from Jastaschule I.

## SCHÄFLIN,     Vfw

| | | |
|---|---|---|
| J77b | 14 Aug 1918 – 11 Nov 1918 | 1 |

Joined Jasta 77b from AFP B.

| Victories: | 1. | 26 Sep 1918 | DH9 | 1730 | Pullingen |
|---|---|---|---|---|---|

## SCHÄPE, Emil     Vfw

| | | | | | | |
|---|---|---|---|---|---|---|
| KG5/25 | – 2 Oct 1916 | – | | J5 | 15 Feb 1917 – 1 Mar 1917 | – |
| KG5/26 | 2 Oct 1916 – 1 Jan 1917 | 1 | | J33 | 1 Mar 1917 – 11 Nov 1918 | 17 |
| Schusta8 | 1 Jan 1917 – 15 Feb 1917 | – | | | | |

Biography & Victories: See *Above the Lines*.

## SCHÄTZLE, Ernst     Uffz

| | | | | | |
|---|---|---|---|---|---|
| SS12 | – | | J19 | 21 Jul 1917 – 11 Sep 1917 | – KIA |

Born Waldenburg, 8 September 1894. Hit by AA fire over St Loup.

## SCHAFFEN,     Vfw

| | | | | | | |
|---|---|---|---|---|---|---|
| J10 | 10 Jul 1918 – 20 Aug 1918 | – | | AFP4 | 20 Aug 1918 – | – |

Joined Jasta 10 from Jastaschule II.

## SCHALK, Georg     Vfw

| | | | | | | |
|---|---|---|---|---|---|---|
| J37 | 22 Apr 1918 – 24 Apr 1918 | – | | J34b | 24 Apr 1918 – 1 Jul 1918 | 2 KIA |

Born 7 October 1890, Schattenbach. Joined Jasta 37 from Jastaschule I. Killed near Albert, by Lt J S Griffith, No 60 Sqn, RAF.

| Victories: | 1. | 1 Jun 1918 | SE5a | | SE Roye |
| | 2. | 16 Jun 1918 | Camel | 2100 | Proyart |

## SCHALLERT,    Ltn
J51        (Jun 1918) –                –

## SCHARRENBROICH, Karl Fritz    Flg
J39              – 21 Aug 1918    – KIAcc
Born 9 June 1893, Bonn. Killed in a crash-landing after a combat near Bapaume.

## SCHARL, Heinrich    Uffz
J79b              – 28 Oct 1918    – KIA
Born 7 November 1896, München. Killed at Floyon.

## SCHATTAUER, Karl    Ltn
| KG6/34 | Mar 1916 – 27 Dec 1916 | – | | J16b | 22 Sep 1917 – 27 May 1918 | 8 | WIA |
| J23b | 27 Dec 1916 – 22 Sep 1917 | 1 | | | | | |

Biography & Victories: See *Above the Lines*.

## SCHAUMBERG,    Ltn
J5        Dec 1917 – 11 Nov 1918    –
Awarded EK II and EK I. OzbV for Jasta 5.

## SCHECK, Alhard    Ltn
J5        Aug 1917 – 19 Sep 1917    1  KIA
Born 8 March 1894, Neustettin. Killed over Nauroy-Le Cateau.

| Victories: | 1. | 6 Sep 1917 | Sopwith | 1405 | N St Quentin |

## SCHEEL, von    Ltn
J52        6 Jun 1918 – 29 Jun 1918    –        J14        29 Jun 1918 –        –
Joined Jasta 52 from Jastaschule I. Wound badge in black. Eiserne Kreuz II Klasse. Sächsische Albrechts-Orden Ritterkreuz 2 Klasse mit Schwerten.

## SCHEELE, Christian von    Ltn
JB 27        Jan 1917 – 4 Feb 1917    – KIA
Born 23 January 1895, Schwerin. Served with KG 2/11 before joining Jasta B. Killed near Le Mesnil, at 1500 hours, during combat with FE2bs and DH2s.

## SCHEERER, Wilhelm    Ltn d R
| SS13 | 5 Apr 1917 – | – | | AFP5 | – 9 Feb 1918 | – |
| AFP4 | – 20 Sep 1917 | – | | J64w | 10 Feb 1918 – 7 May 1918 | – WIA |
| J24s | 21 Sep 1917 – | – | | | | |

Born 15 May 1893, Tuttlingen, Württemberg. Reported for pilot's training at FEA 9 on 4 May 1916. Served with FA67, Kagohl 1/4 and Kogohl 7/37; wounded in action 11 July 1916. Severely wounded 7 November 1916. Awarded EK I on 12 December 1917. Awarded EK II on 22 Jan 1918. Awarded Württemberg Gold Military Merit Medal, 8 March 1918. Severely wounded in action while flying a Pfalz DIII during combat with an American Nieuport over Vieville-en-Haye. Died of wounds that night. Probably the victim of 1/Lt E V Rickenbacker, 94th Aero Sqn, USAS.

## SCHEFFELS, Otto    Gefr
J48        29 Dec 1917 –        –
Joined Jasta 48 from Jastaschule I.

## SCHEFFER, Kurt    Oblt
J11        12 Jul 1917 – 18 Dec 1917    –        FEA6        18 Dec 1917 –        –
Joined Jasta 11 from Flieger-Beobachter Schule, Köln. OzbV for Jasta 11.

## SCHEFFLER, August    Vfw
J81              – 27 Oct 1918    – KIA
Born 25 April 1897, Goitost. Killed near Fontaines.

## SCHEFFOLD,    Uffz
Kest 8        (Sep 1918) –

## SCHEICHER, Alfons    Ltn d R
SS2      1916 – 1916      –      J34b      17 Jul 1918 – 11 Nov 1918    6
Biography & Victories: See *Above the Lines*.

## SCHELL, Hans von    Ltn
FA1      –      J37      3 Oct 1917 – 11 Nov 1918    –
J30      16 Jan 1917 – 3 Oct 1917
Joined Jasta 30 from Jastaschule I. Was OzbV for Jasta 30 and Jasta 37. Crashed on airfield at Phalempin, on 21 May 1917, hospitalised.

| Victories: | 1. | 14 Apr 1917 | Sopwith 2 | | Douai |
|---|---|---|---|---|---|

## SCHELLENBERG,    Ltn d R
J27      20 Aug 1918 –      –

## SCHELLER,    Ltn
SchuSta2      –      J19      30 Mar 1917 – 11 Nov 1918    4
Known to have flown Albatros DII 1729/16.

| Victories: | 1. | 23 Aug 1917 | Caudron | | SW Loivre |
|---|---|---|---|---|---|
| | 2. | 15 Dec 1917 | Spad | | Brimon |
| | 3. | 13 Sep 1918 | Bréguet | 1720 | Rembercourt |
| | 4. | 15 Sep 1918 | Spad | | Pagny |

## SCHELLHAUS,    Sgt
J62      19 Jul 1918 – 23 Jul 1918      –
Joined Jasta 62 from Jastaschule II. Hospitalised 23 July 1918.

## SCHENDEL,    Vfw
J7      (Mar 1917) –      1      Kest 1a    (Sep 1918) – 11 Nov 1918    –
Known to have flown Albatros DVa 6775/17 and Fokker DVII 776/18 and Fokker DVII 229/18 in Kest 1a.

| Victories: | 1. | 11 Mar 1917 | Balloon | 1140 | Belrupt |
|---|---|---|---|---|---|

## SCHENK,    Ltn
J5      –
Lightly wounded in action 5 September 1918.

## SCHERF, Oskar    Ltn
J59      Sep 1918 – 11 Nov 1918    1
Served in Mountain Machine-gun Section 225, in Macedonia. Flight training at FEA6, Brieg. Joined Jasta 59 from Jastaschule I. Held rank of Major in Luftwaffe during WWII. Died 3 February 1974, Dortmund.

| Victories: | 1. | 27 Oct 1918 | Dolphin | | Douai |
|---|---|---|---|---|---|
| | – | 27 Oct 1918 | Dolphin | | |

## SCHEUREN,    Vfw
J69      1

| Victories: | 1. | 23 Mar 1918 | BF2b | 1157 | Roye-Nesle |
|---|---|---|---|---|---|

## SCHEUTZEL,    Gefr
J65      12 Jul 1918 – 11 Nov 1918    1

| Victories: | 1. | 13 Aug 1918 | DH4 | 1400 | Armaville |
|---|---|---|---|---|---|

## SCHEY,    Ltn
JB      – 17 Jun 1917      –      AFP2    17 Jun 1917 –

## SCHIBILSKY, Kurt    Ltn d R
FAA281      1      J10    15 Aug 1918 – 4 Oct 1918    –   POW
Born 26 October 1897. Joined Jasta 10 from Jastaschule II. POW #432 A.

| Victories: | 1. | 12 Jun 1918 | Spad | | |
|---|---|---|---|---|---|

## SCHICK, Max    Ltn
J76b    6 May 1918 – 23 Jun 1918    1   POW
Joined Jasta 76b from Jastaschule I. Shot down at 2015 hours flying Albatros DVa 5765/17.

| Victories: | 1. | 7 Jun 1918 | Spad | | Millencourt |
|---|---|---|---|---|---|

## SCHICKE,     Ltn d R
J24s      14 May 1918 – 11 Nov 1918     –
Reported to Jasta 24s from Idflieg. Served as OzbV for Jasta 24.

## SCHICKFUSS und NEUDORFF, Oskar von     Ltn
J3        (Apr 1917) – 5 Jun 1917     – KIA
Killed at 0938 hours, near Monchy, in an Albatros D III (G.43), by Major A J Scott, No 60 Sqn, RFC, Nieuport Scout B1575. Cousin to the von Richthofen brothers.

## SCHICKLER, Hilmar     Ltn
J19       6 Aug 1918 – 13 Aug 1918     – KIA
Born 29 September 1886, Stuttgart. Killed near Roye in Fokker DVII.

## SCHIEBLER, Artur     Vfw
J30       19 Apr 1918 – 27 May 1918     – KIA
Born 22 May 1892, Pirna. Joined Jasta 30 from Jastaschule II. Killed over Douvrin, in flames.

## SCHIEMANN, Fritz     Ltn
J6        15 Aug 1918 – 11 Nov 1918     2
Joined Jasta 6 from Jastaschule I.

| Victories: | 1. | 3 Sep 1918 | Balloon | 1525 | Croiselles |
|---|---|---|---|---|---|
|  | 2. | 29 Oct 1918 | Spad | 1625 |  |

## SCHIENER, Heinrich     Uffz
J27       5 Feb 1917 – 15 Feb 1917     – POW
Shot down by AA fire near Ploegsteert, flying Halberstadt DV 1108/16 (G.12).

## SCHILGEN,     Uffz
J26       (Jan 1918) – 11 Nov 1918     –

## SCHILLE,     Gefr
J24s      23 Sep 1917 – 19 Oct 1917     –          AFPB      19 Oct 1917 –          –
Joined Jasta 24s from AFP4.

## SCHILLER, Christian     Gefr
J19              – 20 Jan 1918     – KIAcc
Born 28 January 1891, Heidenheim. Killed near Ecly; collision on practice flight.

## SCHILLER,     FwLtn
Kest 1a          – 7 Sep 1918     – WIA

## SCHILLI,     Uffz
Kest 5    27 Oct 1917 – 25 Dec 1917     –          AFP4          – 17 Jun 1918     –
J47w      25 Dec 1917 – 9 Feb 1918     –          J47w      17 Jun 1918 –          –
J47w             – 31 May 1918     – WIA
Joined Kest 5 from AFP B. Injured during a test flight 9 February 1918. Lightly wounded in action 31 May 1918.

## SCHINDLER, Gustav     Vfw
J35b      20 Feb 1917 – 20 Jan 1918     2 KIAcc
Born 24 May 1894, Weigwitz. Joined Jasta 35 from FEA6. Lightly wounded in action 18 June 1917, over Galsingen, during combat with two two-seaters. Injured in an accident on 11 November 1917. Killed during a test flight of Albatros DV 5625/17 at 1450 hours SE Elincourt. Awarded Bavarian Militär-Verdeinstkreuz 2 Klass mit Schwerten, 4 April 1918.

| Victories: | 1. | 14 Apr 1917 | Sopwith 2 |  | Schlettstadt | (a) |
|---|---|---|---|---|---|---|
|  | 2. | 20 Oct 1917 | Camel | 1500 | Houthulstwald |  |

(a) Probably N5171, No 3 Wing, RNAS, W/Cdr C E H Rathbone (POW) Gunner Turner (KIA).

## SCHLACK,     Ltn
JB        (Oct 1918) – 11 Nov 1918     1

| Victories: | 1. | 30 Oct 1918 | DH9 |  | Blaton |
|---|---|---|---|---|---|

**SCHLEGEL, Karl Paul    Vfw**

| | | | | | | |
|---|---|---|---|---|---|---|
| FA39 | – 1917 | – | | J45 | (May 1918) – 27 Oct 1918 | 22 KIA |
| Kest 1b | May 1918 – May 1918 | – | | | | |

Biography & Victories: See *Above the Lines*.

---

**SCHLEGELMILCH, Erich    Ltn**

J29       6 Jun 1917 – 12 Aug 1917    –  KIA
Born 19 June 1896, Magdeburg. Joined Jasta 29 from AFP1. Wounded in action 15 July 1917. Killed at 1055 hours near Staden-Houthulster Wald.

---

**SCHLEICH, Eduard Ritter von    Hptm**       Oblt CO

| | | | | |
|---|---|---|---|---|
| FA2b | 24 Oct 1915 – 1916 | – WIA | J21 | 21 May 1917 – 23 Oct 1917 | 26 |
| CO | | | CO J32b | | |
| FlgSchI | 9 Sep 1916 – 12 Feb 1917 | – | | 23 Oct 1917 – 12 Jan 1918 | – |
| SchSt28 | 12 Feb 1917 – 21 May 1917 | – | Hptm CO | | |
| | | | JGr8 | 15 Mar 1918 – 11 Nov 1918 | 9 |

Biography & Victories: See *Above the Lines*.

---

**SCHLEICHARDT, Richard    OfStv**

| | | | | |
|---|---|---|---|---|
| J15 | – 20 Mar 1918 | 3 | J18 | 20 Mar 1918 – | – |

Awarded EKI. Served with FAA224.

| Victories: | 1. | 11 May 1918 | SE5 | 1821 | Dranoutre |
|---|---|---|---|---|---|
| | 2. | 12 Aug 1918 | DH9 | | Maursmünster |
| | 3. | 21 Sep 1918 | Spad | 1900 | Facqwald |

---

**SCHLEIFF, Franz    Oblt**

| | | | | | |
|---|---|---|---|---|---|
| FA54 | 1915 – 1916 | – | J41 | (Oct 1917) – 9 Jan 1918 | 1 |
| FA300 | (Aug 1916) – (Oct 1917) | 2 | CO J56 | 9 Jan 1918 – 27 Mar 1918 | 9 WIA |

Biography & Victories: See *Above the Lines*.

---

**SCHLENKER, George    Ltn d R**

| | | | | | |
|---|---|---|---|---|---|
| KG4 | 28 Dec 1915 – | | J41 | 6 Sep 1917 – 30 Sep 1918 | 7 WIA |
| J3 | 1 Sep 1916 – 6 Sep 1917 | 7 | | | |

Biography & Victories: See *Above the Lines*.

---

**SCHLETH, Heinrich    Ltn**

| | | | | |
|---|---|---|---|---|
| J37 | – 7 Nov 1917 | – | J29 | (Mar 1918) – 11 Nov 1918 | – |
| J29 | 7 Nov 1917 – 6 Feb 1918 | – | | | |

Admitted to hospital sick on 6 February 1918. Acting CO Jasta 29: 28 May 1918 – 21 June 1918.

---

**SCHLICHT,    Gefr**

J78b       6 Sep 1918 –    –
Joined Jasta 78b from Jastaschule II.

---

**SCHLIETER, Hans    Oblt**

| | | | | |
|---|---|---|---|---|
| J30 | 5 Jun 1917 – 20 Aug 1917 | – | CO J70 | 6 Feb 1918 – 11 Nov 1918 | 3 |
| J30 | 1 Nov 1917 – 6 Feb 1918 | – | | | |

Joined Jasta 30 from Jastaschule I. Transferred to AFP6 on 20 August 1917. Reported to Jasta 30 from FAA215, 1 November 1917. Lightly wounded in action with a DH9 on 16 September 1918.

| Victories: | 1. | 2 May 1918 | Spad | | W Badonviller |
|---|---|---|---|---|---|
| | 2. | 26 Jun 1918 | DH9 | 1305 | Schirmek |
| | 3. | 12 Jul 1918 | Spad | 1055 | SW Blamont |

---

**SCHLEMMEL,    Vfw**

J9       (Aug 1918) – 11 Nov 1918    2

| Victories: | 1. | 9 Aug 1918 | AWFK8 | 1725 | Harbonnières |
|---|---|---|---|---|---|
| | 2. | 28 Oct 1918 | SE5a | 1515 | SE Vervine |

---

**SCHLIEBEN, Richard von    Hptm**

| | | | | |
|---|---|---|---|---|
| KG7 | | – | Idflieg | 26 May 1917 – | – |
| CO J21 | 15 Nov 1916 – 26 May 1917 | – | | | |

## SCHLIMPEN, Johann    Gefr
J45                     – 20 Aug 1918    5   WIA
Biography & Victories: See *Above the Lines*.

## SCHLÖMER, Hans    Ltn d R
J5        (Nov 1917) – 31 May 1918    4   KIA
Born 14 November 1895, Achim. Awarded EK I. Killed near Morlancourt.

| Victories: | | | | | |
|---|---|---|---|---|---|
| 1. | 10 Dec 1917 | RE8 | 1045 | Hendecourt | |
| 2. | 13 Jan 1918 | AWFK8 | 1328 | Lempire | |
| 3. | 17 May 1918 | SE5a | 0715 | Achiet-le-Grand | |
| zlgzw | 20 May 1918 | DH4 | | | |
| 4. | 30 May 1918 | Camel | | Heilly | |

## SCHLÖTZER, Friedrich    Flg
J76b            – 12 Apr 1918    –   KIA
Born 10 February 1899, Hof. Killed at Cappy.

## SCHLOLAUT, Wilhelm    Ltn
J9        23 Sep 1916 – 17 Nov 1916    –   KIA
Born 8 July 1888, Breslau. Killed near Monthois.

## SCHLUCKEBIER, Werner    OfStv
J31        (Dec 1917) – 5 Mar 1918    –           J73    5 Mar 1918 – 11 Nov 1918    3
On leave from 10 Aug 1918 to 6 Sept 1918.

| Victories: | | | | | |
|---|---|---|---|---|---|
| 1. | 1 Jun 1918 | Spad | | SW Silléry | |
| 2. | 20 Sep 1918 | Voisin | | | |
| 3. | 27 Oct 1918 | Bréguet | 14B2 | Aisnetel | |

## SCHMELCHER, Karl    Vfw
J18        14 Jan 1917 – 29 Apr 1917    –           J71          – 19 Jul 1918    2   KIA
J4        29 Apr 1917 –
Born 3 February 1894, Frankfurt. Killed over Gebweiler.

| Victories: | | | | | |
|---|---|---|---|---|---|
| 1. | 7 Jun 1918 | | | | |
| 2. | 7 Jun 1918 | Balloon | 1900 | St Ulrich | (a) |

(a) French 84th Balloon Cié, Lt Ternyck made a safe jump by parachute.

## SCHMELTER, Willy    Gefr
J42        (Jun 1918) – 11 Nov 1918    3

| Victories: | | | | |
|---|---|---|---|---|
| 1. | 11 Jun 1918 | AR2 | | Méry |
| 2. | 30 Sep 1918 | SE5a | 0940 | Bohain |
| 3. | 1 Oct 1918 | RE8 | 0900 | N St Quentin |

## SCHMID, Ludwig    Ltn
J34b    20 Nov 1917 – 23 Jun 1918    2           JB          – 9 Oct 1918    –
CO                                                CO
J76b    24 Jun 1918 – 16 Jul 1918    –   WIA     J78b    9 Oct 1918 – 11 Nov 1918    –
Joined Jasta 34b from Jastaschule II. Wounded during a balloon attack. While with Jasta 34b his plane
carried two blue bands just back of the cockpit on the fuselage, and a blue prop spinner.

| Victories: | | | | |
|---|---|---|---|---|
| 1. | 23 Mar 1918 | DH4 | 1315 | E Péronne |
| 2. | 24 Mar 1918 | SE5 | 1315 | Brie |

## SCHMID, Mathais    Uffz
J80b    12 Mar 1918 – 22 May 1918    –   INJ
Born 3 November 1897. Joined Jasta 80b from Jastaschule I. Severely injured in an accident while
landing at Mörchingen airfield.

## SCHMID,    Uffz
J24s    26 Jul 1918 – 11 Nov 1918    –
Reported to Jasta 24s from AFP18.

## SCHMID zur NEDDEN,    Ltn
J1              – 8 Mar 1918    –           AFPF    16 Jun 1918 –
J72s    8 Mar 1918 – 16 Jun 1918    1

| Victories: | | | | |
|---|---|---|---|---|
| 1. | 11 Jun 1918 | Camel | | Faverolles |

## SCHMIDT, Adolf    Flg
J22s                    – 28 Mar 1918   –  KIA
Born Tuttlingen, 12 August 1896. Killed near Forestete-le-Château.

## SCHMIDT, Caspar    Gefr
J35b      29 Jun 1918 – 31 Oct 1918    2
Joined Jasta 35b from Jastaschule I. Transferred 31 October 1918.

| Victories: | 1. | 12 Sep 1918 | RE8 | | NW Quéant |
| | 2. | 15 Sep 1918 | Camel | | |

## SCHMIDT, Erich    Ltn d R
J7              1917 –                          J8              – 2 May 1918   –  KIAcc
Born 25 December 1890, Heilbronn. Killed during a test flight between Champien and Roiglise. Served with FA3 prior to joining Jasta 7.

## SCHMIDT, Franz    Ltn d R
J32b     24 Aug 1917 – (Sep 1917)    1

| Victories: | 1. | 30 Sep 1917 | Spad | 1130 | Höhe 304 |

## SCHMIDT, Heinrich    Ltn
J62      30 Jun 1918 – 11 Nov 1918   –
Joined Jasta 62 from Jastaschule I.

## SCHMIDT, Hermann    Ltn d R
J13      Sep 1917 – 1 May 1918    1          J69      1 May 1918 –                 1

| Victories: | zlgzw | 5 Mar 1918 | Caudron | | Verneuil |
| | 1. | 28 Mar 1918 | BF2b | | Proyart |
| | 2. | 22 May 1918 | Spad | | Noyon |

## SCHMIDT, Johann    Uffz
J79b           – 8 Aug 1918    2  WIA

| Victories: | 1. | 18 Jul 1918 | SE5a | 1820 | Soissons |
| | 2. | 8 Aug 1918 | DH9 | 1720 | S Caix |

## SCHMIDT, Julius    Ltn d R
KG4            – 1917                1          J6       9 Sep 1918 – 11 Nov 1918   –
J3       (Apr 1917) – 24 Sep 1917   14  WIA
Biography & Victories: See *Above the Lines*.

## SCHMIDT, Ludwig    Ltn d R
J23b     21 Oct 1917 – 26 Dec 1917   –         J78b     30 Dec 1917 –               –
AFPC     26 Dec 1917 – 30 Dec 1917   –
Joined Jasta 23b from Jastaschule I.

## SCHMIDT, Otto    Oblt
FA25     10 Apr 1916 – 23 Oct 1916   2         J29      19 Aug 1917 – 18 Oct 1917   4  WIA
J7       16 Mar 1917 – 30 Jun 1917   2         J5       3 Jul 1918 – 11 Nov 1918   10
J32      30 Jun 1917 – 19 Aug 1917   2
Biography & Victories: See *Above the Lines*.

## SCHMIDT, R.    Ltn d R
J81                                  –
Possibly two victories in Jasta 81.

## SCHMIDT, Richard    Ltn
J77b     10 Apr 1918 – 4 May 1918    –  INJ   J78b            – 11 Nov 1918     1
Joined Jasta 77b from Jastaschule I. Severely injured in a landing accident at Foucaucourt airfield.

| Victories: | 1. | 25 Sep 1918 | DH4 | 1430 | Zabern | (a) |
| (a) No 110 Sqn, IAF. | | | | | | |

## SCHMIDT, Robert    Ltn d R
J43      19 Jul 1918 – 11 Nov 1918    1  WIA
Shot down in flames at 2040 hours on 12 August 1918, during combat with SE5as of No 29 Sqn, RAF, took to his parachute and landed safely. His probable victor was Lt C J Venter.

| Victories: | 1. | 12 Aug 1918 | DH9 | 1130 | Lacouture |

## SCHMIDT, Willy    OfStv
J39                                                    1
Victories:    1.        26 Oct 1917        Caproni            1035            NE Tolmein

## SCHMIDT,    Ltn d R
J24s        9 Dec 1917 – 28 Jan 1918    –            Idflieg    28 Jan 1918 –                    –
Reported to Jasta 24s from Jastaschule I. Crash-landed Pfalz DIII 4107/17 on 11 December 1917, unharmed. Severely injured during a test flight of Pfalz DIII 4291/17 on 19 January 1918.

## SCHMIDT,    Vfw
J27                – 24 Sep 1918    – WIA

## SCHMIDT,    Vfw
J36        9 Sep 1918 – 11 Nov 1918    –

## SCHMIDT,    Uffz
J37            1918 –                –

## SCHMILINSKI,    Vfw
J61                            –
Wounded in action.

## SCHMITT, Franz    Ltn d R
FFA224            – 9 Apr 17        1            J29        6 Sep 1917 – 31 May 1918    1
JsSch        9 Apr 1917 –            –            Idflieg    31 May 1918 –                    –
J7        26 May 1917 – 6 Sep 1917    1
Promoted to Leutnant 26 October 1917. Awarded EKII on 8 Oct 1916. Ehrenbecher for first victory on 16 Dec 1916. Promoted Vizefeldwebel on 16 Dec 1916. Awarded EKI on 7 Feb 1917. Württemberg Gold Military Merit Medal, 16 March 1917. Promoted Leutnant 26 October 1917.
Victories:    1.        18 Nov 1916        Voisin                                            (a)
        2.        27 Jun 1917        Balloon                Elverdinghe
        3.        20 Sep 1917        Nieuport                Blankaartsee
(a) With his observer Ltn Walter Telge.

## SCHMITT,    Ltn
J27                            –
Lightly wounded in combat 24 September 1918, remained with Jasta.

## SCHMITZ, Eduard    Ltn
J52        1 Oct 1918 – 11 Nov 1918    –
Served as OzbV for Jasta 52.

## SCHMÜCKLE, Karl    Fw
J21s        (May 1918) – 21 Aug 1918    4            J15        22 Aug 1918 – 11 Nov 1918    2
Biography & Victories: See *Above the Lines*.

## SCHMUTZLER, Otto    Sgt
J4        (Dec 1917) – 16 May 1918    1 KIA
Born 14 June 1889, Zimmritz. Killed at 2000 hours, over Proyart.
Victories:    1.        15 May 1918        Camel            1210            SW Marcelcave

## SCHNECK,    Vfw
J9        (Jul 1918) – 11 Nov 1918    3
Victories:    1.        16 Jul 1918        Nieuport
        2.        15 Sep 1918        Spad            1940            E Vailly
        3.        24 Oct 1918        Bréguet            1210            Asfeld-la-Ville

## SCHNEEVOGEL,    Vfw
J46                                    1
Victories:    1.        16 Jul 1918        Dolphin                        SE Grandcourt

## SCHNEIDER, Adolf    Uffz
J1                – 2 Jun 1918    – KIA
Born 8 December 1894, Hamburg. Killed over Reims.

## SCHNEIDER, Georg　　Gefr
J16b　　28 Jul 1918 – 11 Nov 1918　　–

## SCHNEIDER, Heinrich　　Gefr
J21　　　　– 19 Jan 1917　　　–　　　　　　J30　　19 Jan 1917 – 15 Feb 1917　　– POW
Hit by Flak and forced to land near Ploegsteertwald, and taken prisoner while flying Halberstadt DIII
234/16.

## SCHNEIDER, Johann　　Ltn
J80b　　25 Feb 1918 – 17 Jul 1918　　–　　　　　　FAA292　17 Jul 1918 –　　　　　　　–
Joined Jasta 80b from Jastaschule I. Was OzbV for Jasta 80b.

## SCHNEIDER, Karl　　Uffz
J23b　　16 May 1918 – 11 Nov 1918　　–
Joined Jasta 23b from Jastaschule I. Injured in a landing accident near Haynecourt, on 5 June 1918,
returned to unit 14 June.

## SCHNEIDER, Kurt　　Ltn
J5　　25 Aug 1916 – 5 Jun 1917　　15 WIA
Biography & Victories: See *Above the Lines*.

## SCHNEIDER, Richard　　Vfw
FA6　　4 Jan 1917 – 5 Sep 1917　　–　　　　　　J19　　19 Oct 1917 – 11 Nov 1918　4
Born 22 September 1896, Frahnau. Volunteered for military service 5 March 1915. Trained at FEA6,
Grossenhain. Joined Jasta 19 from Jastaschule I.

| Victories: | 1. | 8 Jul 1918 | Spad | | Fismes |
|---|---|---|---|---|---|
| | 2. | 16 Jul 1918 | Spad | | Suippes |
| | 3. | 29 Oct 1918 | Bréguet | 1250 | Barricourt |
| | 4. | 6 Nov 1918 | Spad | 1625 | Stenay |

## SCHNEIDER, Roman　　Ltn
J79　　9 Feb 1918 – 11 Nov 1918　　5
Biography & Victories: See *Above the Lines*.

## SCHNEIDER, Uffz
J1　　(Oct 1918) – 11 Nov 1918　　2

| Victories: | 1. | 1 Oct 1918 | Camel | 1300 | Proville |
|---|---|---|---|---|---|
| | 2. | 1 Oct 1918 | RE8 | 1730 | Haynecourt |

## SCHNEIDER,　　Uffz
KG4　　　　　　　　　　–　　　　　　J20　　4 Feb 1917 –　　　　　　　–

## SCHNEIDER,　　Ltn
J26　　(Oct 1918) – 11 Nov 1918　　–

## SCHNEIDER,　　Ltn
J79b　　　　　　　　　　–

## SCHNEIDER,
J27　　　　　　　　　　–

## SCHNEIDEWIND, Gustav　　Vfw
FA29　　3 May 1917 – 4 Jun 1917　　–　　　　　　J1F　　7 Jan 1918 – 23 May 1918　3 WIA
J17　　17 Jun 1917 – 7 Jan 1918　　4　　　　　　FA305　　1918 –　　　　　　　–
Biography & Victories: See *Above the Lines*.

## SCHNELL, Max　　Vfw
J58　　20 Aug 1918 – 28 Oct 1918　　1 KIA
Born 20 February 1896, Krefeld. Shot down in flames at 1230 hours; jumped in parachute but landed
on a house near Wasmeul.

| Victories: | 1. | 8 Oct 1918 | SE5a | 0840 | Cambrai |
|---|---|---|---|---|---|

## SCHNORR, Douglas　　Ltn
J30　　20 Jan 1917 – 15 Feb 1918　　–　　　　　　J38　　15 Feb 1918 –　　　　　　　–
Served in FA24 prior to joining Jasta 30.

**SCHNULL,    Gefr**
J10      21 Sep 1916 –                         –

**SCHOBER, Otto    Ltn**
J18      13 Jun 1917 – 26 Oct 1917    1   KIA
Born 12 Mar 1890, Johannesburg, SA. Killed at 2020 hours near Sleyhage.

| Victories: | 1. | 11 Sep 1917 | DH4 | 1338 | S Terhand |
|---|---|---|---|---|---|

**SCHOBINGER, Guido    Ltn**
J43      22 Jul 1918 – 11 Nov 1918    1
Joined Jasta 43 from Jastaschule I. Acting CO Jasta 43 from 2 Nov 1918.

| Victories: | 1. | 14 Oct 1918 | SE5a | | Ypres |
|---|---|---|---|---|---|

**SCHOBINGER, Viktor    Ltn d R**
FA12     Apr 1917 – 1917                    J12    (Aug 1917) – 15 Nov 1917    8   WIA
Biography & Victories: See *Above the Lines.*

**SCHÖCK, Karl    Ltn d R**
J12      28 Nov 1916 – 19 May 1917    2   KIA
Born 12 April 1889, Neuenstadt. Killed at 0740 hours near Dury-St Quentin, by AA fire.

| Victories: | 1. | 23 Apr 1917 | Sopwith | 1205 | Dainville |
|---|---|---|---|---|---|
| | 2. | 5 May 1917 | Spad | 1205 | E Chérisy |

**SCHOEN, Martin    Ltn d R**
ObOst/J81          – 14 Oct 1917    1   KIA
Born 16 June 1888, Selbelang. Killed near Hustatin, Russia.

| Victories: | 1. | 8 Jul 1917 | Balloon | | Jezierna |
|---|---|---|---|---|---|

**SCHÖLLER, Heinrich    Ltn**
J23b     3 Aug 1918 – 11 Nov 1918    –
Joined Jasta 23b from Jastaschule II. Demobilised 11 February 1919.

**SCHÖNBERGER, Fritz    Ltn d R**
J16b     18 Dec 1917 – 21 May 1918    –          FEA2b   21 May 1918 –              –
Assigned to Jastaschule I on 6 December 1917. Joined Jasta 16b from Jastaschule I. Wounded in action 20 January 1918.

**SCHÖNE, Karl    Vfw**
FA279A          – 4 Mar 1917    –          J23    4 Mar 1917 – 18 Mar 1917    –   KIAcc
Born 20 September 1891, Leipzig. Killed in an accident during a test flight between Chambley and Pusieux.

**SCHÖNE,    Sgt**
J24s     14 Dec 1917 – 18 Dec 1917    –          J42    18 Dec 1917 –              –
Joined Jasta 24s from Jastaschule I.

**SCHÖNEBECK, Karl August von    Ltn**
FAA203     1917 – 1917              –          J59    26 Jan 1918 – 11 Jul 1918    1
J11      7 Jul 1917 – 26 Jan 1918    3          CO J33   11 Jul 1918 – 11 Nov 1918    4
Biography & Victories: See *Above the Lines.*

**SCHÖNFELDER, Kurt    Obflgmstr**
J7       23 Aug 1916 – 26 Jun 1918    13   KIA
Biography & Victories: See *Above the Lines.*

**SCHÖNFELDER, Paul    Uffz**
J29      6 Jul 1918 – 4 Nov 1918    1   KIA
Born 4 July 1896, Seidenberg. Joined Jasta 29 from Jastaschule 1. Received his Flugzeugfuhrer-Abzeichen on 25 August 1918. Killed near Oosterzeele.

| Victories: | 1. | 3 Sep 1918 | SE5a | 2000 | Agny |
|---|---|---|---|---|---|

**SCHÖNFELDT,    Vfw**
Kest 2   (Aug 1917) – Jan 1918    1          J66    12 Feb 1918 –              –
J50      Jan 1918 – 12 Feb 1918    –

| Victories: | 1. | 12 Aug 1917 | Sopwith | | Saargemund |
|---|---|---|---|---|---|

## SCHÖNHÖFER,    Uffz
J35b      25 Sep 1917 – 9 Oct 1917      –              AFP4      9 Oct 1917 –              –

## SCHÖNMANN, Friedrich    Vfw
SS23b                                –        FEA1b      18 Jul 1918 –              –
J77b      7 Apr 1918 – 18 Jul 1918      –        Jasta
                                                 Schonger 29 Oct 1918 – 11 Nov 1918
Awarded Bavarian Military Merit Cross, 3rd Class with Crown and Swords on 29 September 1917. Held Iron Cross 2nd Class. Joined Jasta 77b from Jastaschule I.

## SCHOLL, Hermann Ludwig    Ltn
J34b      6 Sep 1917 – 30 Oct 1917      –   KIA
Born 19 February 1897, Nürnberg. 5th Chev Rgt. Joined Jasta 34b from Jastaschule I. Killed near Filain-Reims, during a combat with a French two-seater. Down in flames; probably by Sgt Lignereux (P) & Lt Mangematin (O), Sop 24.

## SCHOLTZ, Edgar    Ltn d R
Kest 10                             1        J11      (Jan 1918) – 2 May 1918      5   KIAcc
Biography & Victories: See *Above the Lines*.

## SCHONEBECK, von    Ltn
J28w                                –
Member of Jagdgruppe 7 staff.

## SCHONGER, Rudolf    Oblt
J23b      19 Oct 1917 – 16 Jan 1918      –        FEA2b      2 Apr 1918 – 27 Jun 1918      –
FEA2b     16 Jan 1918 – 25 Feb 1918      –        FEA1b      27 Jun 1918 – 29 Oct 1918      –
J23b      25 Feb 1918 – 2 Apr 1918      –        JSchonger 29 Oct 1918 – 11 Nov 1918      –
Born 31 March 1891. Wounded in action 6 March 1918. During periods with Jasta 23b served as OzbV.

## SCHORISCH, Arthur    Vfw
J12       5 Mar 1917 –                4        Kest 1a      1 Sep 1918 –              –
Kest 4a        – 1 Sep 1918      –
Known to have flown Albatros DVa 7484/17, Fokker DVII 776/18 and Pfalz DVIII 101/18 while in Kest 1a.
Victories:    1.       17 Mar 1917    FE2b                        Vreucourt
              2.       12 Apr 1917    FE2b           1035         SE Eterpigny        (a)
              3.       20 Apr 1917    BE2e           0940         Ecoust-St Mei       (b)
              4.       23 Apr 1917    Sopwith        1200         Wancourt
(a) 4984, No 18 Sqn, RFC, Lt O D Maxted (P) & Lt A Todd, MC, (O), POWs.
(b) BE2f 2553, No 16 Sqn, RFC, Sgt J Dangerfield (P) & 2 A/M E D Harvey (AG) POWs.

## SCHORN, Hans    Vfw
J16b      4 Apr 1918 – 21 May 1918      1   KIA
Born 19 February 1896, Hartkirchen. Killed over Wytschaete.
Victories:    1.       25 Apr 1918    RE8            1115         Dickebuschsee

## SCHOTT, Heinrich    Vfw
J25             – 25 Apr 1918      1   KIA
Born 27 May 1891, Gitra. Injured in a landing accident 21 September 1917. Killed during a balloon attack at Opticar.
Victories:    1.       25 Apr 1918    Balloon                     Opticar

## SCHRADER, Anton    Vfw
J31             – 16 Aug 1917      1   KIA
Born 10 June 1883, Osttrich. Killed near Ypres.
Victories:    1.       28 Jul 1917    Nieuport 17                                      (a)
(a) A6783, No 40 Sqn, RFC, Lt D Godfrey, POW.

## SCHRAMM, Arno    Vfw
J7              – 23 Apr 1917      3   KIA
Born 21 September 1896, Statt. Killed near Linselles-Montfaucon.

| Victories: | 1. | 24 Nov 1916 | Nieuport | 1140 | Vaux-Teich |
|---|---|---|---|---|---|
| | 2. | 4 Dec 1916 | Nieuport | 1600 | Bouville |
| | 3. | 25 Mar 1917 | Nieuport | 1550 | E Consenvoye |

## SCHRAMM, Karl    Oblt
J52    24 Sep 1918 – 1 Oct 1918    –
Served as OzbV for Jasta 52.

## SCHRAMM,    Ltn d R
J56    19 Jul 1918 – 11 Nov 1918    3
Joined Jasta 56 from Jastaschule I.

| Victories: | 1. | 14 Aug 1918 | BF2b | 1915 | Dadizeele | |
|---|---|---|---|---|---|---|
| | 2. | 15 Aug 1918 | Camel | 0935 | S Langemarck | |
| | – | 15 Aug 1918 | Camel | | St Julien | (a) |
| | 3. | 3 Sep 1918 | BF2b | 1015 | Moorseele | |

(a) Also claimed by Ltn Ernst Baumgärtel who was given the victory.

## SCHRAMMER,    Uffz
J43                – 26 Feb 1918    –
Transferred to Stofl Heimat.

## SCHREDER, Adolf    OfStv
J17    18 Aug 1917 – 17 Mar 1918    1    KIA
Born 14 December 1888, Wascheta. Joined Jasta 17 from Jastaschule I. Killed at 1150, between Busigny and Bohain.

| Victories: | 1. | 5 Mar 1918 | SE5a | 1500 | S Vendheuille |
|---|---|---|---|---|---|

## SCHRIEBER, Arthur    Oblt
J40s    27 Jul 1917 – 11 Nov 1918    –
Joined Jasta 40 from FEA7. Served as OzbV for Jasta 40s.

## SCHREIBER, Gerhard    Ltn
J37                – 2 Jun 1918    –    KIA
Born 10 February 1894, Zerbst. Killed over Herbecourt.

## SCHREYECK,    Ltn
J18    8 Nov 1916 – (Dec 1917)    –

## SCHRÖDER, Bartholmäus    Oblt
CO J32    1 Apr 1917 – 28 Jun 1917    –        AFP1    28 Jun 1917 –        –
Reported to Jasta 32 from AFP A.

## SCHRÖDER, Fritz    Vfw
J39                – 9 Dec 1917    1    KIA
Born 5 May 1890, Benningsen. Killed near San Michele.

| Victories: | 1. | 2 Nov 1917 | Hanriot | 1600 | SW San Vito |
|---|---|---|---|---|---|

## SCHRÖDER, G    Ltn
J39                – 5 Mar 1918    –        J74    5 Mar 1918 – 11 Nov 1918    –
Served as OzbV for Jasta 74.

## SCHRÖDER, Herbert    Ltn d R
FAA206                –        AFP1            1917            –
J1    26 Jan 1917 – Nov 1917    5        J17        1917 – May 1918    –    WIA
Biography & Victories: See *Above the Lines*.

## SCHRÖDER, Paul    Ltn d R
KG5/30                        JB    2 Nov 1917 – (Feb 1918)    1
Awarded Württemberg Gold Military Merit Medal on 22 Dec 1916. Awarded Württemberg Knight's Cross of the Military Merit Order on 20 Feb 1918.

| Victories: | 1. | 3 Feb 1918 | Camel | 1510 | E Moorslede |
|---|---|---|---|---|---|

## SCHRÖDER,    Ltn d R
J10    6 May 1918 – 7 Jun 1918    –        FFA206    7 Jun 1918 –        –

## SCHRÖDER, Ltn
J13                                    I
Victories:    1.    20 Aug 1917    Spad                                    SE Malancourt

## SCHRÖDER, Ltn
J28w                                   –

## SCHROTH, Günther    Ltn d R
AFP5              – 26 May 1915    –         FA303    9 Nov 1917 – 3 Jan 1918    –
FA42    27 May 1915 – 23 Nov 1916    –       J2F      4 Jan 1918 – 30 Nov 1918    –
J19     24 Nov 1916 – 08 Nov 1917    –
Born 8 April 1894, Glunbowitz/Schleisen. Entered Army 26 November 1913, as a Fahrenjunker in Grenadier Rgt 9. Wounded in action 19 October 1914. Entered aviation 21 January 1915. Promoted Unteroffizier 23 June 1916. Offizierstellvertreter on 6 August 1914. Promoted Leutnant d R 9 September 1915. Eiserne Kreuz I Klasse. Hohenzollernsches Ehrenkreuz 3 Klasse. Türkische Eiserner Halbmond. Wound Badge in Black. Attained rank of Major General in Luftwaffe during WWII. Died 2 June 1945, Bloemendaal/Holland.

## SCHROTH, Johann    Vfw
SS23                              –         J35b    18 Mar 1917 – 22 Jul 1917    I
Injured in an accident 22 May 1917, and hospitalised.
Victories:    1.    2 May 1917    Nieuport                      W Delle        (a)
              –    19 May 1917    Caudron                       W Herzweiler
(a) Probably Sergent Segund of Escadrille N88.

## SCHUBART, Alfred    Ltn d R
ObOst/J81         – 21 Apr 1918    – KIAcc
Born 30 September 1887, Cottbus. Killed during a test flight near Liesse.

## SCHUBERT, Fritz    FwLtn
J6        (Mar 1917) – 25 Aug 1918    3
Joined JG I Staff as Technical Officer on 6 September 1918. Promoted from Feldwebelleutnant to Leutnant 10 October 1918.
Victories:    1.       16 Mar 1917    Balloon      1645    SW Roye
              zlgzw    16 Jun 1917    Sopwith      1906    Warneton
              2.       21 Jul 1917    Spad         2020    W Roubaix
              3.       29 Nov 1917    SE5          0945    Wambaix        (a)
(a) Probably B4890, Lt Dodds, No 56 Sqn, RFC.

## SCHUBERT, Gefr
J69               – 11 Nov 1918    I
Victories:    1.    27 Oct 1918    Spad                                    Velescot

## SCHÜRZ, Ltn
J13               –                I
Victories    1.    20 Apr 1917    Farman                                   Landricourt

## SCHÜSCHKE, OfStv
J64w    8 Feb 1918 – 27 Mar 1918    – POW
Joined Jasta 64w from AFP5. Shot down by AA fire and taken prisoner flying Pfalz DIIIa 8078/17 (G.157).

## SCHÜSSLER, Ltn
J18    (Aug 1917) – (Oct 1917)    –

## SCHÜTT, Lambert    Ltn d R
J66    (May 1918) – 15 Jul 1918    I KIA
Born 10 October 1896, Bassum. Acting CO Jasta 66, 26 June to 15 July 1918. Killed over the Marne.
Victories:    1.    28 Jun 1918    Spad

## SCHÜTZE, Erich    OfStv
FA201    (May 1917) –         I         J25    27 Apr 1918 – 11 Nov 1918    2
Rbz9    (Sep 1917) –         3
Biography & Victories: See *Above the Lines*.

## SCHUHMANN, Kurt Reinhold    Ltn d R

J5        May 1917 – 20 Aug 1917    2    KIA

Born 10 December 1893, Gera. Served in Field Artillery Regiment 55. Killed at 0900 hours, near Escarpelle-Douai.

| Victories: | 1. | 28 May 1917 | Nieuport | 1310 | NE Lens | (a) |
|---|---|---|---|---|---|---|
| | 2. | 18 Aug 1917 | BF2b | 0727 | S Brebières | (b) |

(a) Nieuport 23, B1624, No 60 Sqn, RFC, 2/Lt R U Phalen, KIA.
(b) No 11 Sqn, RFC.

## SCHUHMANN,    Vfw

J14        (Nov 1916) –                    1

| Victories: | 1. | 11 Nov 1916 | Scout (Fr) | | Champenoux |
|---|---|---|---|---|---|

## SCHULER,    Ltn

J19                        –

## SCHULTE, Gerhard    Ltn d R

J50        (Jan 1918) – 31 May 1918    3    POW

Served in Field Artillery Regiment 16. Served as OzbV for Jasta 50.

| Victories: | 1. | 17 Feb 1918 | Balloon | 1515 | Roucy |
|---|---|---|---|---|---|
| | 2. | 26 Feb 1918 | Balloon | 1540 | Bouvancourt |
| | 3. | 29 May 1918 | Spad | | E Marchais |

## SCHULTE, Adolf    Ltn d R

J12        23 Nov 1916 – 12 Apr 1917    9    KIA

Biography & Victories: See *Above the Lines*.

## SCHULTE, Joseph    Ltn d R

J14        (Jun 1918) – 23 Aug 1918    4            CO J21s 27 Aug 1918 – 11 Nov 1918    –

| Victories: | 1. | 27 Jun 1918 | Camel | 1120 | Rouge Croix |
|---|---|---|---|---|---|
| | 2. | 8 Jul 1918 | Camel | 2045 | Annouellin |
| | 3. | 19 Jul 1918 | SE5a | 0930 | Wattignies |
| | 4. | date unknown | | | |

## SCHULTE, Joseph    Ltn

J55        Feb 1918 – 11 Nov 1918    –

## SCHULTE,    Ltn

J5        (May 1917) –                    –

## SCHULTE,    Oblt

J5        (Oct 1918) – 11 Nov 1918    –

## SCHULTE-FROHLINDE, Julius    Ltn d R

J41                    – Aug 1918    –            J11    28 Aug 1918 – 11 Nov 1918    4

Born 26 May 1894. Transferred to Jastaschule I during August 1918. Joined Jasta 11 from Jastaschule I. Shot down and wounded during WWII (25 May 1940) while flying with a Kampfgeschwader. Died 20 November 1968, Düsseldorf.

| Victories: | 1. | 31 Aug 1918 | Camel | 1945 | Péronne |
|---|---|---|---|---|---|
| | 2. | 7 Sep 1918 | SE5 | 1300 | N Havrincourtwald |
| | 3. | 19 Sep 1918 | BF2b | 1600 | Bellenglise |
| | 4. | 4 Nov 1918 | DH4 | 1700 | |

## SCHULTE-SCHLUTIUS,    Ltn

J3        (Sep 1918) – 11 Nov 1918    –

## SCHULTZ, Hans    Ltn d R

J15                    – 20 Mar 1918    –            J18    20 Mar 1918 – 6 Jun 1918    1    POW

Shot down and crash-landed in British bombarded area on 22 March 1918, but eventually returned to his own lines 24 March 1918. Shot down and taken prisoner at 1905 hours north of Hazebrouck, after combat with SE5s while flying Fokker DVII 2455/18 (G/2Bde/14). Shot down by Lt C H R Lagesse, No 29 Sqn, RAF, in SE5a D5969.

| Victories: | 1. | 4 May 1918 | Camel | 1850 | Vieux Berquin |
|---|---|---|---|---|---|

## SCHULTZ von DRATZIG,     Ltn
J73        22 Jun 1918 – 11 Nov 1918     –

## SCHULTZE, Wilhelm      Ltn
J4         1 Sep 1916 – 30 Nov 1917    1  KIA
Born 4 June 1896, Berlin. Flew with KEK Vaux before it became Jasta 4. On 30 November 1917, he collided at 1135 hours with Ltn Rudolf Wendelmuth of Jasta 20 over Fontaine-Notre Dame, W Cambrai, while flying a Pfalz DIII. Both pilots were killed.

| Victories: | 1. | 18 Aug 1918 | RE8 | 1205 | Boesinghe |
|---|---|---|---|---|---|

## SCHULZ, Albin     Vfw
J5         1916 –                        –

## SCHULZ, Ernst      Ltn d R
J72s       Jun 1918 – 11 Nov 1918    4

| Victories: | 1. | 26 Sep 1918 | EA | | |
|---|---|---|---|---|---|
| | 2. | 28 Sep 1918 | Spad | Ardeuil | |
| | 3. | 28 Oct 1918 | Spad | 1510 | Château-Porcien |
| | 4. | 28 Oct 1918 | Spad | 1510 | Château-Porcien |

## SCHULZ, Hansjörg von     Ltn
Kest 7          – 11 Jul 1918     –  KIAcc
Born 23 January 1897.

## SCHULZ, Hugo     Ltn d R
J12        15 Apr 1918 – 12 Jun 1918    –  KIA
Born 30 May 1893, Boglab. Killed near Forêt de Laigne.

## SCHULZ, Kurt     Ltn
J37             – 25 Jun 1918     1  KIA
Born 22 May 1897, Strassburg. Killed over Dormans.

| Victories: | – | 4 Jan 1918 | Camel | 1140 | S Westroosebeke |
|---|---|---|---|---|---|
| | 1. | 29 Mar 1918 | AWFK8 | | |

## SCHULZ, Otto     Vfw
J20        11 Aug 1917 – 17 Mar 1918     –  KIAcc
Born 19 November 1895, Berlin. Killed during a test flight near Douai.

## SCHULZ, Wilhelm      Ltn
| FFA48 | 14 Oct 1916 – 20 Oct 1916 | – | J41 | 7 Jan 1918 – 28 May 1918 | 3 |
|---|---|---|---|---|---|
| J15 | 20 Oct 1916 – 31 Oct 1916 | – | J66 | 28 May 1918 – 25 Jun 1918 | 2  KIA |
| J16 | 31 Oct 1916 – 7 Jan 1918 | 1 | | | |

Biography & Victories: See *Above the Lines*.

## SCHULZE, August     Flg
J53        23 Jan 1918 – 22 Mar 1918     –  POW
Joined Jasta 53 from Jastaschule I. Force-landed inside Allied lines.

## SCHULZE, Ernest      Ltn d R
J48        16 Feb 1918 – 9 May 1918     –  KIA
Born 11 September 1895, Hannau. Served in Infantry Regiment 183. Joined Jasta 48 from Jastaschule I. Killed during combat with a Spad over Montdidier.

## SCHULZE, Gerhard     Ltn
J12        (Mar 1917) – 3 Mar 1918     –        MFJ1    3 Mar 1918 – 12 Jun 1918     –  KIA
Killed flying Albatros DVa 7337/17 at 1640 hours near Nieuport Mole.

## SCHULZE,     Ltn d R
J51        (Jul 1918) – 4 Oct 1918    1  WIA

| Victories: | 1. | 8 Jun 1918 | Camel |
|---|---|---|---|

## SCHUMACHER, Friedrich     Vfw
J10        (Mar 1918) – 8 Aug 1918    5
Biography & Victories: See *Above the Lines*.

## SCHUMANN, Kurt　　Flg
J47w　　10 Jan 1918 – 23 Apr 1918　　　–　　　　　AFP6　　23 Apr 1918 –　　　　　　　–
Joined Jasta 47w from Jastaschule I.

## SCHUMANN,　　Vfw
J17　　　28 Sep 1918 –　　　　　　　I
OzbV for Jasta 17.
Victories:　　　1.　　　3 Nov 1918　　　2-seater

## SCHUMM, Marat　　Uffz
Schusta26　　　　– 1917　　　　　2　　　　J52　　　10 Jan 1918 – 11 Nov 1918　　5
Biography & Victories: See *Above the Lines.*

## SCHUNKE, Willi　　Ltn
J20　　　13 Feb 1917 – 24 May 1917　　1　KIA
Born 27 January 1894, Wersdorf. Previously served with Schusta 18. Killed over Le Catelet.
Victories:　　　1.　　　23 Apr 1917　　　Morane　　　　　1400　　　　　SW St Quentin　　　(a)
(a) R W Hoskier (P) & J Dressy (O), N124.

## SCHUSTER, Günther　　Ltn d R
J17　　　23 Dec 1916 – 10 Sep 1917　　2　　　　J17　　　10 Jun 1918 – 1 Aug 1918　　1　WIA
J29　　　10 Sep 1917 – 10 Jun 1918　　3
Biography & Victories: See *Above the Lines.*

## SCHUSTER, Willi　　Ltn
J5　　　　　– 22 Jul 1918　　　– KIAcc
Born 4 November 1893, Lonnig. Served in Field Artillery Regiment 185. Killed during a test flight at Cappy.

## SCHWAB,　　Ltn
J15　　　　　　　　　　　　　–
Crashed Pfalz D III 4058/17, was not harmed.

## SCHWAGER,　　Ltn d R
J60　　　Oct 1918 – 11 Nov 1918　　　–

## SCHWANDNER, Heinrich　　Oblt
CO J32　23 Feb 1917 – 16 Mar 1917　　– KIA
Born 9 April 1889, Springhardt. Served in Infantry Regiment 5. Previously commanded Schutzstaffel 27. Shot down in flames at 1030 hours over Athienville, probably by Lt Albert Deullin, Escadrille N73.

## SCHWARTZ, Konrad　　Ltn
J22　　　　1918　　　　　　　4　　　　J66　　　15 Jul 1918 – 18 Jul 1918　　1　POW
Biography & Victories: See *Above the Lines.*

## SCHWARTZ, Wilhelm　　Ltn d R
J20　　　(Nov) 1917 – 22 Jan 1918　　1　　　　J13　　　1 May 1918 – 15 Jun 1918　　4　WIA
J43　　　22 Jan 1918 – 1 Feb 1918　　　–　　　　J73　　18 Oct 1918 – 11 Nov 1918　　2
J69　　　1 Feb 1918 – 1 May 1918　　　1
Biography & Victories: See *Above the Lines.*

## SCHWARTZKOPFF,　　Ltn
J12　　　1 Nov 1916 –　　　　　　　–

## SCHWARZ, Fritz　　Vfw
J33　　　Mar 1918 – 15 Aug 1918　　2　KIAcc
Born 5 April 1895, Bromberg. Killed near St Loup, Schusta 35's airfield.
Victories:　　1.　　　24 Mar 1918　　　DH4　　　　　　　　　　　Monhofen
　　　　　　　2.　　　26 May 1918　　　Spad　　　　　1600　　　　　E Dranoutre

## SCHWARZ, Hans　　Ltn d L
FAA233　15 Jan 1917 – 19 Mar 1918　　–　　　　J75　　　6 Apr 1918 – 31 Mar 1919　　–
Born 13 June 1986, Hamburg. Entered military service 1 May 1915, assigned to FEA5, Hannover. Gefreiter on 6 May 1916. Pilot at the Observer School, from 1 June 1916 to 9 December 1916. Promoted Unteroffizier 10 July 1917; Vizefeldwebel on 1 October 1917; Leutnant der Landwehr II on 7 April 1918.

Jastaschule Nivelle 20 Mar 1918 – 5 April 1918. Pilot and Technical Officer for Jasta 75. Attained the rank of General-Ingenieur in the Luftwaffe during WWII. Died 20 May 1968, Hamburg.

## SCHWARZ, Robert    Ltn d R
J52    12 Jun 1918 – 6 Jul 1918    1    WIA
Joined Jasta 52 from Jastaschule I. Wounded over Lestrem.

| Victories: | 1. | 27 Jun 1918 | Camel | 1030 | E Aubers |
|---|---|---|---|---|---|

## SCHWARZ, Robert    Uffz
J77b    17 Feb 1918 – 6 Apr 1918    1    KIA
Born 24 January 1897, Regensburg. Joined Jasta 77b from Jastaschule II. Killed at 1130 hours near Fouilloy.

| Victories: | 1. | 17 Mar 1918 | Spad | | Hagenbach |
|---|---|---|---|---|---|

## SCHWARZE,    Gefr
J40    27 Oct 1918 – 11 Nov 1918    –

## SCHWARZER, Felix    Ltn d R
J35b    –    J56    9 Jan 1918 – 24 Oct 1918    –    Hosp
Born 22 February 1888, Neisze. Served as OzbV for Jasta 56. Died of the 'flu' 2 Nov 1918.

## SCHWEITZER,    Flg
J50    (Oct 1918) – 11 Nov 1918    –

## SCHWEINITZ, Traugott von    Ltn
J11    27 Nov 1917 – 27 Dec 1917    –    KIA
Born 19 December 1897, Goldberg. Served in Hussar Regiment 6. Killed at 1435 hours near Avesnes-le-Sec, flying Albatros DVa 5313/17.

## SCHWENDEMANN, Josef    Vfw
SchSt14    Feb 1917 – 1917    –    J41    Sep 1917 – 1918    17
Biography & Victories: See *Above the Lines*.

## SCHWEPPE,    Uffz
J35b    18 Mar 1917 – 19 Mar 1918    1    JGr4    19 Mar 1918 –    –
Awarded EKI on 1 March 1918. Transferred to Jagdgruppe 4 on 19 March 1918. Awarded Bavarien Militär-Verdeinstkreuz 3 Klass mit Kröne und Schwarten on 4 April 1918.

| Victories: | 1. | 17 Feb 1918 | SE5 | 1340 | N Beaumetz | (a) |
|---|---|---|---|---|---|---|

(a) Lt D N Ross, No 24 Sqn, RFC, (KIA).

## SCHWIND, August    Gefr
J54s    19 Jan 1918 – 29 Apr 1918    3    INJ
Severely injured in a landing accident. Awarded the Baden Silberne Karl-Friedrich Militär-Verdeinstmedaille on 5 August 1918.

| Victories: | 1. | 18 Mar 1918 | Camel | 1100 | Busigny |
|---|---|---|---|---|---|
| | 2. | 24 Mar 1918 | SE5a | 1045 | Péronne |
| | 3. | 1 Apr 1918 | BF2b | | Villers-Bretonneux |

## SCHWIRTZKE, Paul    Ltn
J68    5 Apr 1918 – 11 Nov 1918    4
Acting CO Jasta 68 from 22 June to 14 July, and 16 July to 9 August 1918.

| Victories: | 1. | 5 Jul 1918 | Balloon | 1330 | Montigny | (a) |
|---|---|---|---|---|---|---|
| | 2. | 10 Oct 1918 | Balloon | | Maasknie | |
| | 3. | 4 Nov 1918 | Balloon | | Dannevoux | (b) |
| | 4. | 10 Nov 1918 | Balloon | | Verdun | (c) |

(a) French 67th Balloon Cié.
(b) French 61st Balloon Cié.
(c) USAS 3rd Balloon Co, 1/Lts G C Carroll and F D Cummings made safe descents by parachute.

## SCHYMIK, Alfons    Vfw
J24s    8 Jul 1918 – 28 Oct 1918    1    KIA
Born 1 July 1895, Aitchcchlau. Reported to Jasta 24s from AFP18. Killed at 0925 hours over Pommereuil,

during combat with a Dolphin, while flying Fokker DVII 329/18. Probably fell to Captain J W Pearson of No 23 Sqn, RAF.

| Victories: | 1. | 23 Aug 1918 | Spad | 1005 | Blérancourt |
|---|---|---|---|---|---|

## SEEL, Eberhard von    Hptm d R

| JB | – 10 May 1917 – | CO J17 | 10 May 1917 – 12 Jun 1917 | – KIA |
|---|---|---|---|---|

Born 24 January 1885, Wallmerrod. Served in Infantry Regiment 176. Shot down in flames during combat with a Spad near Montigny.

## SEELÄNDER,    Ltn

J62      6 Sep 1918 – 11 Nov 1918   –

## SEELÄNDER,    Ltn

J37             – 9 May 1918   – INJ

Severely injured during a forced landing after combat.

## SEELEN, Kurt von    Ltn

Kest 3

Lightly wounded in combat with DH4s on 13 June 1918.

## SEEWALD,    Ltn d R

J30      14 Dec 1917 – 28 Dec 1917   –      J54s      28 Dec 1917 –                3

Joined Jasta 30 from Jastaschule I.

| Victories: | 1. | 18 Mar 1918 | SE5a | | Le Cateau |
|---|---|---|---|---|---|
| | 2. | 30 May 1918 | SE5a | 2050 | N Ypern |
| | 3. | 16 Jun 1918 | SE5a | 0905 | Villers-Bretonneux |

## SEFFZIG, Theodor    Uffz

J14             – 16 Sep 1917   –      J34b      16 Sep 1917 – 13 Nov 1917   – POW

Shot down during combat with two Spads.

## SEIDEL,    Uffz

J3      (Sep 1918) – 11 Nov 1918   –

## SEIDEL, Hermann    Fw

J26      22 Nov 1917 – 5 Dec 1917   – KIA

Born 30 March 1890, Neudorf. Joined Jasta 26 from Jastaschule II. Killed over Passchendaele.

Victories:      see below

NB. There was a Gefr Seidel (pilot) in SS10 who scored two victories. If this is the same person, his kills were:

| | 1. | 27 May 1917 | Spad | | SW Craonne |
|---|---|---|---|---|---|
| | 2. | 16 Jun 1917 | Spad | | Jumigny |

## SEIFERT,    Ltn d R

J17      12 Jun 1918 – 11 Nov 1918   1

| Victories: | 1. | 4 Sep 1918 | Spad | 1230 | Soilly |
|---|---|---|---|---|---|

## SEIFERT, Karl Adolf    Ltn

J24s      1 Dec 1916 – 25 Apr 1918   1 KIAcc

Born 11 December 1893, Dresden. Served in FA12 prior to joining Jasta 24. Awarded Iron Cross II Class. Albert Order, Knight 2nd Class with Swords, 8 August 1917. Merit Order, Knight 2nd Class with Swords on 4 Mar 1918. Killed during a test flight flying Albatros DV 7253/17.

| Victories: | 1. | 27 Oct 1917 | Spad VII | 0830 | N Wervicq | (a) |
|---|---|---|---|---|---|---|

(a) B6776, 19 Sqn, RFC, Lt L Whitehouse, POW.

## SEIT, Kurt    Ltn

FA199            –      J80b      4 Jun 1918 – 11 Nov 1918   5

Biography & Victories: See *Above the Lines*.

## SEITZ, Hans    Ltn

J34b      30 Oct 1918 – 11 Nov 1918   –

Joined Jasta 34b from AFP17.

## SEITZ, Oskar    Ltn

| FAA292 | | – | | AFP6 | 20 Jul 1917 – | | – |
| J30 | 16 Apr 1917 – 20 Jul 1917 | – | | | | | |

Collided with Ltn Gustav Nernst (killed) near Arras, 21 April 1917, but as not harmed.

## SEITZ, Wilhelm Anton    Vfw

| J8 | 10 Nov 1916 – (Oct 1918) | 11 | J68 | (Oct 1918) – 11 Nov 1918 | 5 |

Biography & Victories: See *Above the Lines*.

## SELDNER, Eduard    Oblt

| KG3/14 | 3 Aug 1916 – 29 Dec 1916 | – | | J17 | 24 Apr 1918 – 27 May 1918 | – |
| KG3/13 | 30 Dec 1916 – 29 Jan 1917 | – | | Hptm | | |
| SchSt1 | 30 Jan 1917 – 20 Dec 1917 | – | | J57 | 28 May 1918 – 6 Oct 1918 | – |
| FEA1 | 21 Dec 1917 – 11 Apr 1918 | – | | CO | | |
| AFP6 | 12 Apr 1918 – 23 Apr 1918 | – | | J31 | 6 Oct 1918 – 30 Nov 1918 | – |

Born 15 September 1890, Karlsruhe. Entered military service 1 October 1909, Infantry Regiment 109. Fähnrich on 16 November 1910; Leutnant on 18 August 1911; Oberleutnant 18 August 1915. Assigned to FEA7 on 23 April 1916 for pilot training, completed various schools and assigned to Kampfgeschwader III, Staffel 14, in Obersten Heresleitung. Promoted to Hauptmann on 18 August 1918. Awarded Eiserne Kreuz I Klasse Badische Orden vom Zähringer Löwen, Ritterkreuz 2 Klasse mit Schwerten. Attained rank of Major-General in the Luftwaffe during WWII. Died 6 January 1951, Karlsruhe.

## SELZER,    Ltn d R

| J74 | Jun 1918 – 11 Nov 1918 | 1 |

Shot down and taken prisoner on 3 August 1918, however he escaped and returned to his unit.

| Victories: | 2LG | 3 Aug 1918 | Spad XI | 1930 | S Hourges |
| | 1. | 29 Oct 1918 | EA | | |

## SENF, Fritz    Uffz

| J20 | 31 Dec 1917 – 1 Mar 1918 | – | J59 | 1 Mar 1918 – 11 Nov 1918 | 2 |

Joined Jasta 20 from Jastaschule I.

| Victories: | 1. | 27 Sep 1918 | DH9 | Goeulzin |
| | 2. | 27 Oct 1918 | Dolphin | |

## SENFF, Otto    Vfw

| J48 | 14 Jun 1918 – 16 Aug 1918 | – KIA |

Born 4 June 1894, Darmstadt. Killed over Catigny.

## SENGER und ETTERLIN Johann-Gustav von    Ltn

| J12 | 29 Jul 1917 – 30 Nov 1917 | – KIA |

Born 12 December 1894, Engen. Enlisted on 8 August 1914, assigned to Feld-Artillerie Rgt Nr.76. Wounded in action 8 October 1914. Officer Cadet on 6 February 1915, promoted to Unteroffizier 10 February 1915, after school returned to his unit and was promoted to Feldwebel on 21 June 1915 and to Leutnant on 28 October 1915. Transferred to AFP8 on 15 October 1916 for pilot training, then on 9 November 1916, was sent to FEA 10 from here assigned to Feld-Flieger-Abteilung 12, later being assigned to Jasta 12. Killed in combat with SE5s at 1700 hours near Moeuvres-Bourlon Wald. Possibly collided with 2/Lt R E Dungate, No.46 Sqn, RFC, POW this date.

## SEVE,    Ltn

| J13 | | 1 |

| Victories: | 1. | 18 Mar 1917 | Caudron | Cerny-Beaurieux |

## SEYWALD, Heinrich    Ltn

| FA274 | Feb 1916 – | – | J23b | 30 Sep 1917 – 11 Nov 1918 | 6 |
| FA18 | | – | | | |

Biography & Victories: See *Above the Lines*.

## SICHO,    Uffz

| J7 | – 28 May 1918 | – WIA |

## SIEBENKAES,    Uffz

| J79b | – 6 Jul 1918 | – | AFP19 | 8 Aug 1918 – | – |
| J80b | 6 Jul 1918 – 8 Aug 1918 | – | | | |

**SIEBERT,      Ltn**
J15        (Aug 1918) – 11 Nov 1918     –

**SIEBOLD, Theodor      Ltn d R**
J38                  – 1 Oct 1917      – KIA
Born 23 December 1891, Gütersloh. Served in Infantry Regiment 32. Killed near Matnica, Macedonia.

**SIEG, Walter      Vfw**
J71                  – 16 Sep 1918     – KIAcc
Born 16 April 1895, Kuehn. Killed during a test flight of a Pfalz DXII at Habsheim.

**SIELEMANN,      Gefr**
J57        20 Feb 1918 – 27 Mar 1918    1   POW
During combat with Bristol Fighters he was shot down and taken prisoner near Bapaume, while flying
Pfalz DIII.
Victories:        1.        11 Mar 1918        RE8                1620              N Fresnoy

**SIEMPELKAMP, Eugen      Ltn d R**
J4         2 Mar 1918 – 10 Apr 1918    1               J64w      25 Jul 1918 – 14 Sep 1918    2   WIA
J29        10 Apr 1918 – 25 Jul 1918   2
Biography & Victories: See *Above the Lines*.

**SIEMPELKAMP, Ewald      Ltn**
J15                  – 20 Feb 1917     – INJ       J30       11 May 1918 – 23 Aug 1918    –   Hosp
Severely injured in a crash with Jasta 15. OzbV for Jasta 30 May 1918 – 23 Aug.

**SIENZ,      Ltn**
J10        14 Oct 1918 – 11 Nov 1918    –
Joined Jasta 10 from Jastaschule II.

**SIERLEN,**
Kest 4b    (Nov 1917) –                –

**SIEWERT,      Ltn**
J10                                    –

**SIGMANN, Michael      Vfw**
FEA1b                – 22 Aug 1917      –               JsSchII   12 Feb 1918 – 21 Feb 1918    –
FlgSch     22 Aug 1917 – 11 Feb 1918    –               J78b      21 Feb 1918 – 27 Aug 1918    – WIA
Born 25 October 1895. Wounded in the upper arm during combat near Luneville; was able to land safely.

**SILBERSCHMIDT, Hermann      Ltn**
J22                  – 4 Oct 1918      – KIA
Born 1 March 1897, Berlin-Lichtenberg. Served in Infantry Regiment 18. Killed near Flavigny-le-Grand.

**SIMON, Georg      Ltn**
J11        7 Nov 1916 – 29 Jan 1917    1  WIA      J11       13 Mar 1917 – 4 Jun 1917     – POW
Born 4 January 1885. Shot down at 1925 hours between Fontaine and Heniel, while flying Albatros DIII
2015/16 (G.42), by Capt C Chapman, No 29 Sqn, RFC, in Nieuport B1517. Died 5 November 1963.
Victories:        1.        5 Apr 1917        BF2b               1120              N Monchecourt        (a)
(a) BF2b #A3330, No 48 Sqn, RAF, Lt H A Cooper (P) & 2/Lt A Boldison (O), POWs.

**SIMON, Heinrich      Uffz**
J64w       8 Feb 1918 – 14 Apr 1918    – POW
Joined Jasta 64w from AFP5. Shot down at Toul airfield, at 0951 hours by Lt Alan Winslow 94th Pursuit
Sqn, USAS.

**SIMON,      Gefr**
J8ob       4 Jun 1918 – 11 Nov 1918    –
Joined Jasta 8ob from Jastaschule II.

**SIMONS,      Ltn d R**
J43        5 Jun 1918 – 4 Sep 1918     –               Idflieg   4 Sep 1918

## SKAURADZUN, Ltn d R

J4        (Dec 1917) – 8 Mar 1918   – WIA
Severely wounded flying Pfalz DIII 4042/17.

## SKOWRONSKI, Martin    Ltn

J6        24 Apr 1918 – 1 Jul 1918     3        AFP3     1 Jul 1918 –        –
Joined military service in August 1914, assigned to 11th Dragoon Regiment. Promoted Leutnant in July 1916. Started pilot's training in January 1917. Transferred to AFP5 in April 1918. Died 18 October 1969, Cali, Colombia, S America.

| Victories: | 1. | 31 May 1918 | Bréguet | 1940 | Marizy St Mard |
|---|---|---|---|---|---|
| | 2. | 3 Jun 1918 | Spad | 1250 | SE Neuilly |
| | 3. | 5 Jun 1918 | Bréguet | 1735 | Montigny l'Engarin |

## SKWORZ, Wilhelm    Vfw

J36       25 Jun 1918 – 3 Sep 1918   2 KIA
Born 23 December 1893, Zabrze. Joined Jasta 36 from Jastaschule I. Killed over Abancourt, during combat with SE5s.

| Victories: | 1. | 8 Aug 1918 | DH9 | | |
|---|---|---|---|---|---|
| | 2. | 1 Sep 1918 | DH4 | | Brunemont |

## SÖBECK,    Ltn

J22       Aug 1917 – (May 1918)   –        J67       19 Jul 1918 – 11 Nov 1918   –
Transferred to FBS Jüterborg in May 1918. Joined Jasta 67 from Flieger/Beobachterschule, Jüterborg.

## SOKOLOWSKI,    Vfw

J60       – 1 Jun 1918   – POW

## SOLTAU, Emil    Vfw

J20       14 Jun 1918 – 22 Jul 1918   2 KIA
Born 3 January 1892, Barsbuettel. Served in FAA242 before joining Jasta 20. Killed near Gheluvelt.

| Victories: | 1. | 12 Jun 1917 | Nieuport | | Olchowiec |
|---|---|---|---|---|---|
| | 2. | 15 Jul 1918 | SE5a | 0950 | NW Dadizeele |

## SOMMER, Wilhelm    Ltn

J39       (Jul 1918) – (Sep 1918)   5
Biography & Victories: See *Above the Lines.*

## SONNABEND,    Uffz

Kest 7       – 31 Aug 1918   –        Kest 1a   31 Aug 1918 –        –
Known to have flown Albatros DVa 7519/17 and Fokker D VII 666/18 with Kest 1a.

## SONNECK, Erich    Vfw

J66       27 Jan 1918 – 11 Nov 1918   6
Biography & Victories: See *Above the Lines.*

## SONNTAG, Karl    Ltn

J37       – 24 May 1917   – IIc
Severely injured in a crash at his airfield.

## SOWA, Otto    Vfw

J7        (May 1917) – 28 Dec 1917   2        J52       9 Jan 1918 – 11 Nov 1918   1

| Victories: | 1. | 12 Aug 1917 | Camel | 1150 | Pervyse |
|---|---|---|---|---|---|
| | 2. | 15 Aug 1917 | Sopwith 2 | 0920 | NW Leke |
| | 3. | 28 May 1918 | SE5a | 0900 | Neuf Berquin |
| | – | 18 Sep 1918 | DH9 | 1135 | Lomme |

## SPADINGER,    Vfw

J28w      (Mar 1918) –        1

| Victories: | 1. | 24 Aug 1918 | SE5a | | Tilloy |
|---|---|---|---|---|---|

## SPANNKUPT, Johann    Uffz

J79b       – 14 Oct 1918   – WIA
Severely wounded north of Wassigny.

## SPEIDEL, Max     Oblt
J8ob     8 Feb 1918 – 11 Nov 1918     –
Joined Jasta 8ob from FEA2. Was OzbV from 16 July 1918.

## SPERLING, Ernst     Vfw
J69          – 12 Jun 1918     – KIA
Born 28 December 1890, Griefenhagen. Killed near Noyon.

## SPILLE,     Ltn d R
J4                – 9 Feb 1918     –          J58        9 Feb 1918 – 11 Nov 1918    3

| Victories: | | | | | | |
|---|---|---|---|---|---|---|
| | 1. | 11 Apr 1918 | Camel | 1450 | Sailly-sur-Lys | (a) |
| | 2. | 4 Sep 1918 | DH9 | 1040 | Helesmes | |
| | 3. | 7 Oct 1918 | Camel | 1035 | Saucourt | |

(a) B5750, 210 Sqn, RAF, Lt M T McKelvey.

## SPINDLER, Erich     Ltn d R
J15              – 20 Mar 1918     –          J18        20 Mar 1918 – 11 Nov 1918    2
Awarded EK I.

| Victories: | | | | | |
|---|---|---|---|---|---|
| | 1. | 1 Jul 1918 | DH9 | 0820 | W Avning |
| | 2. | 21 Sep 1918 | Spad | 1905 | Combresholen |

## SPINDLER,     Ltn d R
J17     12 Dec 1917 – 11 Nov 1918     1
Joined Jasta 17 from Jastaschule II.

## SPITZHOFF, Karl     Ltn
J5        (Feb 1917) – (Aug 1917)     –
Joined Jasta 5 from Jastaschule I.

## SPLITGERBER, Otto     Ltn d L
J12     8 Oct 1916 – 6 Apr 1917     3  WIA     J38     (Jul 1917) – 13 Mar 1918     3  KIA
Biography & Victories: See *Above the Lines.*

## SPORBERT, Otto     OfStv
Kest 8          – 31 Dec 1917     –          J62     7 Feb 1918 – 11 Nov 1918     4
J27     31 Dec 1917 – 7 Feb 1918     –
Awarded EKI on 12 February 1918, for service with Kest 8. Awarded the Saxon Silver St Henry Medal on 13 October 1918.

| Victories: | | | | | |
|---|---|---|---|---|---|
| | 1. | 6 Apr 1918 | Spad | | Montdidier |
| | 2. | 20 Apr 1918 | SE5a | 1100 | NW Thennes |
| | 3. | 22 Apr 1918 | Spad | 2020 | Mezières |
| | 4. | 28 Jul 1918 | Spad | 1252 | Marfaux |

## SPUDICH, Willi     Vfw
J21          – 21 Aug 1917     – KIAcc
Born 26 November 1896, Osterode. Killed when he collided in the air with Vfw Zachmann over Vauquois, who made a safe landing.

## STAATS, Hans     Ltn
FAA225  28 Jan 1917 –          –          J12     11 Aug 1917 – 6 Mar 1918     1  KIA
Born 30 March 1896, Breslau. Joined Jasta 12 from Jastaschule I. Killed in a collision with a SE5a over Rony, flying an Albatros DVa 1788/16 (G.145), SE5a pilot 2/Lt D M Clemens, No 24 Sqn, RFC, in SE5 C9535.

| Victories: | | | | | |
|---|---|---|---|---|---|
| | 1. | 13 Oct 1917 | DH5 | 1100 | Quéant |

## STADLEY,     Vfw
AFP18   5 May 1918 – 18 May 1918     –          J62     6 Jun 1918 – 27 Jun 1918     1  POW
JsSch   18 May 1918 – 6 Jun 1918     –
Born 29 July 1898, Flottbeck. Enlisted February 1915, 76th Infantry Rgt. Transferred to 150th Infantry Rgt in May 1915, Russia, July 1916 to 146th Infantry Regiment, Macedonia; wounded in July 1917. Transferred to aviation in September 1917, FEA8. Observation School in February 1918. Shot down wounded by AA fire near La Neuville during a balloon attack and taken prisoner, flying Albatros DVa 7285/17; died of wounds.

| Victories: | | | | | |
|---|---|---|---|---|---|
| | 1. | 27 Jun 1918 | Balloon | 1515 | Montiers |

(See French III° Armée POW Interrogation Report.)

## STADTER, Otto     Uffz

J32b     (Sep 1917) – 11 Nov 1918     4
Severely injured on 28 March 1918, hospitalised, returned to unit 12 June 1918.

| Victories: | 1. | 18 Sep 1917 | Spad | 1607 | NW Douaumont |
|---|---|---|---|---|---|
| | 2. | 26 Sep 1917 | Spad | 1700 | Esnes |
| | 3. | 3 Jan 1918 | Spad | | Pontavert |
| | 4. | 1 Nov 1918 | EA | | |

## STAHL, Erich     Ltn

| | | | | | | |
|---|---|---|---|---|---|---|
| FA4 | 18 Sep 1916 – 7 Dec 1916 | – | J79b | 30 Jan 1918 – 27 Aug 1918 | 1 |
| FA252 | 18 Dec 1916 – 28 Jul 1917 | – | FEA1 | 28 Aug 1918 – | – |
| FEA1 | 29 Jul 1917 – 29 Jan 1918 | – | | | |

Born 29 March 1893, Munich. Entered military service 22 August 1914, 18th Bavarian Infantry Rgt. Fahrenjunker/Unteroffizier 1 December 1914. Fähnrich 15 February 1915; Leutnant 9 April 1915. Observer training FEA1b from 20 Nov 1915 to 25 Jan 1916. AFP6 from 26 Jan 1916 to 1 May 1916. Pilot's training FEA1b 2 May 1916 to 16 Sep 1916. OzbV for Jasta 79b. Attained rank of Major-General in Luftwaffe during WII. Died 15 January 1954, Gröppingen.

| Victories: | 1. | 15 Jul 1918 | Spad | 0940 | Berseuil |
|---|---|---|---|---|---|

## STAPENHÖRST, Eberhard     Ltn

J11     30 Jun 1917 – 13 Jan 1918     4  POW
Joined Jasta 11 from AFP4. Shot down by AA fire and taken prisoner after a balloon attack on 13 January 1918, while flying Fokker Dr1 144/17 (G.125).

| Victories: | 1. | 12 Aug 1917 | Sopwith | 0900 | NW Bixschoote |
|---|---|---|---|---|---|
| | 2. | 3 Sep 1917 | Triplane | 1030 | Wytschaete |
| | 3. | 4 Sep 1917 | Camel | 0840 | S Becelaere |
| | 4. | 9 Sep 1917 | Spad | 1247 | SW Zonnebeke |

## STARCK, Kurt     Vfw

| | | | | | | |
|---|---|---|---|---|---|---|
| J32b | (Jul 1917) – 30 Aug 1917 | 2 | Idflieg | 14 Aug 1918 – | – |
| J29 | 30 Aug 1917 – 14 Aug 1918 | – | | | |

| Victories: | 1. | 6 Jul 1917 | Farman | 1330 | Keilberg |
|---|---|---|---|---|---|
| | 2. | 12 Jul 1917 | Sopwith 2 | | SW Reims |

## STARCK, Walter     Vfw

J32b     – 11 Dec 1917     –  INJ

## STARK, Rudolf     Ltn d R

| | | | | | | |
|---|---|---|---|---|---|---|
| FAA296 | 15 Nov 1917 – 1917 | – | J77b | 24 May 1918 – 7 Jun 1918 | 1 |
| J34b | 18 Jan 1918 – 24 May 1918 | 5 | J35b | 7 Jun 1918 – 11 Nov 1918 | 5 |

Biography & Victories: See *Above the Lines*.

## STAROST,     Sgt

J61     21 Jul 1918 – 22 Aug 1918     –  POW
Served in infantry at beginning of war. Transferred to aviation as a mechanic in 1915, served in Russia with FA31. Reassigned to FEA5 as a mechanic. Started pilot's training in September 1916 at FEA 5. Remained as an instructor until 13 July 1918. Joined Jasta 61 from Jastaschule I. Hit by AA fire and forced to land near Ribécourt. (See French III° Armée POW Interrogation Report.)

## STAUDACHER, Georg     Vfw

J1     (May 1918) – (Sep 1918)     6
Biography & Victories: See *Above the Lines*.

## STECHELE,     Ltn

J80b     19 Mar 1918 – 11 Nov 1918     –
Joined Jasta 80b from Jastaschule II.

## STEGE,     Ltn

J21s     (May 1917) –     –

## STEGER, Otto     Ltn d R

| | | | | | |
|---|---|---|---|---|---|
| J53 | 8 May 1918 – 18 Sep 1918 | 1 | J36 | 18 Sep 1918 – 11 Nov 1918 | 1 |

Joined Jasta 53 from Jastaschule II.

| Victories: | 1. | 31 Aug 1918 | Spad | | Fresnes |
| | 2. | 4 Nov 1918 | BF2b | | Tournai |

## STEHLE, Karl     Ltn d R

| KEK 4 | | | | AFS | 21 Sep 1917 – 28 Feb 1918 | – |
| J4 | 25 Aug 1916 – 31 Mar 1917 | – | | AFP18 | 28 Feb 1918 – 4 Jul 1918 | – |
| CO | | | | Idflieg | 4 Jul 1918 – | – |
| Kest 6 | 31 Mar 1916 – 3 Sep 1917 | | | | | |
| CO | | | | | | |
| Kest 4b | 3 Sep 1917 – 21 Sep 1917 | – | | | | |

Born 24 October 1892, Teningen-Freiburg. Qualified for German Pilot's Licence #627 on 11 December 1913. Enlisted 3 August 1914, assigned to Fliegerschule as an instructor. Promoted Gefreiter on 1 December 1914; Unteroffizier on 20 January 1915. On 5 February 1915, transferred and on 24 February reported to FAA59. Qualified for Flugzeugführer-Abzeichen on 12 March 1915. Promoted Vizefeldwebel 7 April 1915. Awarded EK II Klasse on 13 May 1915, and the Baden Silberne Verdeinstmedaille. Promoted to Leutnant der Reserve 12 July 1915. Awarded the Bavarian Militär Verdeinstkreuz II Klasse mit Schwerten on 19 August 1915, and the Austrian Silber-Verdeinstkreuz mit Kröne, Bande der Tapferkeitsmedaille on 27 August 1915. Hospitalised 5 September 1915, returned to duty 8 April 1916, and assigned to Kampfeinsitzer-Abteilung 1, on 23 May 1916 reassigned to FFA23. Awarded the EKI. Awarded the Baden Ritterkreuz II Klasse Zähringer Löwen Orden mit Schwerten on 9 February 1917. Demobilised 23 January 1919.

## STEHLING,     Uffz

| J69 | | | 1 | | |
| Victories: | 1. | 4 Oct 1918 | Caudron R9 | | S Montreux |

## STEINGEN,     Flg

| J50 | – 11 Nov 1918 | – |

## STEILING,     Ltn d R

| J19 | 23 Sep 1918 – 27 Sep 1918 | – | INJ |

Joined Jasta 19 from Jastaschule I.

## STEIN, Joachim von     Uffz

| J35b | 25 Sep 1917 – 18 Feb 1918 | 1 | WIA | J35b | | – 11 Nov 1918 | – |

Promoted to Unteroffizier on 31 October 1917. Crash-landed on 2 December 1917, aircraft completely destroyed, pilot unharmed. Severely wounded and forced to land near Douai. Hospitalised and returned to Jasta 35b on 15 March 1918. Awarded Eiserne Kreuz I Klass on 23 April 1918.

| Victories: | 1. | 21 Oct 1917 | Camel | | W Roselaere |

## STEIN Wilhelm     Vfw

| J27 | 14 Feb 1917 – 8 Jul 1917 | – | | J27 | 31 Dec 1917 – 1 Jun 1918 | – | KIA |
| AFP4 | 8 Jul 1917 – | – | | | | | |

Born 3 November 1894, Düsseldorf. Killed near Soissons.

## STEIN,     Uffz

| J5 | 1918 – | – |

## STEIN,     Ltn

| J72s | (Jun 1918) – 11 Nov 1918 | – |

## STEIN,     Vfw

| J14 | | | 2 | | J45 | 25 Dec 1917 – 13 Aug 1918 | – | WIA |
| Victories: | 1. | 12 Apr 1918 | Balloon | | | | Epagny | |
| | 2. | 19 Jul 1918 | Balloon | | | 0850 | Creuves | |

## STEIN,     Ltn

| J45 | – 18 Oct 1918 | – | KIA |

## STEIN,     OfStv

| J61 | 28 Mar 1918 – | – |

**STEINBACH, Ltn**
J1              – 11 Nov 1918    –
Last OzbV for Jasta 1.

---

**STEINBACHER, Paul    OfStv**
J81        (Jun 1918) – 11 Aug 1918    – KIA
Born 15 February 1891, Lensburg. Killed over Reims.

---

**STEINBRECHER, Helmut    Ltn d R**
FA17          1917 – 1917          –          J46      12 Mar 1918 – 11 Nov 1918      5
FAA274        1917 – 1917
Biography & Victories: See *Above the Lines*.

---

**STEINER, Philip    Flg**
J30        17 Sep 1918 – 11 Nov 1918    –
Joined Jasta 30 from AFP6.

---

**STEINGEN, Flg**
J50              – 11 Nov 1918    –

---

**STEINHAÜER, Oblt**
J1        23 Aug 1916 –                  –
Served with FA32 before joining Jasta 1. First OzbV for Jasta 1.

---

**STEINHÄUSER, Werner    Ltn**
FA261    (Aug 1917) –              –          J11      (Dec 1917) – 26 Jun 1918      10 KIA
Biography & Victories: See *Above the Lines*.

---

**STEINSTRÄTER, Vfw**
J50        (Jun 1918) – 31 Aug 1918    1          FEA4    31 Aug 1918 –              –
Victories:      1.        5 Jun 1918        Spad                      Chelles

---

**STELZER, Hans    Ltn**
J26              – 19 Jul 1918    – KIA
Born 21 November 1898, Dt-Krone. Served in Field Artillery Regiment 15. Killed in action over Coeuvres.

---

**STEMM, von    Flg**
J58        5 Oct 1918 – 11 Nov 1918    –

---

**STEMMLER, Gottfried    Vfw**
J9              – 16 Jun 1917    – INJ    J76b    29 Mar 1918 – 11 Apr 1918      – KIA
Born 20 November 1892, Lautzkirchen. Involved in air collision with Ltn Friedrich von Hartmann on 16 June 1917, who was killed. Died in combat with SE5s at 1825 hours NE Albert, flying Albatros DVa 7249/17.

---

**STENGEL, Vfw**
J80b        26 Sep 1918 – 11 Nov 1918    –
Joined Jasta 80b from Jastaschule II.

---

**STENGLIN, Ernst Fr von    Ltn**
J1        19 Jan 1917 – Jan 1918        2
Victories:      1.        15 Feb 1917        Pup          1430        Lapignies        (a)
                2.        11 Mar 1917        Vickers                    Le Sars
                3.        8 Dec 1917
                4.        30 Dec 1917
                5.        30 Dec 1917        Caproni
                6.        1 Jan 1918        Camel          1109        S Vittorio        (a)
(a) These victories definitely confirmed, but it is not known if the other claims were confirmed.

---

**STENZEL, Gustav    Hptm**
FA66                          2          CO    J8 23 Sep 1916 – 28 Jul 1917      2 KIA
Born 2 October 1888, Hoefen. May 1905 joined Pommerschen Infantry Rgt 42. Transferred to aviation in 1912. Assigned to FA15 at outbreak of war. November 1914, transferred to Brief-Tablen Abt-Ostende. February 1915, transferred to BAO Eastern Front. June 1915, assigned to FA66 in Balkans; two kills.

Commanded Abwehrstaffel Vardar. Awarded Kroneorden IV Klasse – May 1914; Eiserne Kreuz II Klasse – August 1914; Eiserne Kreuz I Klasse – January 1915; Oosterische Verdeinstkreuz mit der Kriegserat III Klasse – March 1916; Bulgarische Verdeinstkreuz – 1916; Oosterische Flieger Abzeichen – 1916; Ehrenbecher 'Sieger im Luftkampf' on 15 April 1916. Killed near Rumbeke.

Victories:

| | | | | | |
|---|---|---|---|---|---|
| 1. | 23 Mar 1916 | 2-seater | | Lake Dorian | |
| 2. | 24 Mar 1916 | 2-seater | | Lake Dorian | |
| 3. | 24 Mar 1917 | Nieuport | | NW Dixmuiden | |
| 4. | 7 Jun 1917 | Nieuport | 1445 | W Gheluvelt | (a) |

(a) Probably B3674, No 40 Sqn, RFC, Lt J W Shaw, POW.

## STENZEL, Peter    Vfw

J14        (May 1918) – 24 Sep 1918    1   KIA
Born 26 June 1889, Piess. Killed over Fort d'Englos.

Victories:

| | | | | |
|---|---|---|---|---|
| 1. | 22 May 1918 | SE5a | 1225 | Neuf Berquin |

## STEPHEN, Anton    Ltn

JB        30 Aug 1917 – 8 Oct 1918    2        J70        – 11 Nov 1918    –
OzbV for Jasta B.

Victories:

| | | | | |
|---|---|---|---|---|
| 1. | 16 Sep 1918 | DH9a | | Germersheim |
| 2. | 25 Sep 1918 | DH4 | | S Alberschweiler |

## STEUDEL, Karl Theodor    Uffz

SS4                    1        J3        Jul 1917 – 2 Oct 1917    3   KIA
Born 9 March 1892, Gunnersdorf. Shot down in flames near Houthulst Wald.

Victories:

| | | | | | |
|---|---|---|---|---|---|
| 1. | 16 Apr 1917 | Sopwith 2 | 0910 | Douai | (a) |
| 2. | 10 Aug 1917 | RE8 | 1437 | Poelkapelle | |
| 3. | 14 Aug 1917 | Sop Tripe | 1720 | Langemarck | |
| 4. | 5 Sep 1917 | Camel | 0906 | S Armentières | (b) |
| – | 11 Sep 1917 | Sopwith | 0945 | Moorslede | |

(a) With his observer, Ltn Figulla.
(b) Probably B3777, No 70 Sqn, RFC, 2/Lt T C Huggard.

## STICKFORTH,    Ltn

Kest 2        – 12 Apr 1917    –        J42        8 Jul 1918 – 29 Jul 1918    –
J24s    12 Apr 1917 – 8 Jul 1918    2        J24s        29 Jul 1918 – 11 Nov 1918    –
Awarded Saxon Ritterkreuz II Klasse mit Schwerten des Albrechts-Orden on 20 June 1918. Temporarily commanded Jasta 42 from 8 July to 29 July 1918.

Victories:

| | | | | | |
|---|---|---|---|---|---|
| – | 13 Jul 1917 | Sopwith 2 | 1135 | Pilkem | (a) |
| – | 5 Oct 1917 | BF2b | 0815 | Dadizeele | (b) |
| – | 12 Oct 1917 | Spad | 1410 | Ketzelberg | (c) |
| 1. | 6 Apr 1918 | AR2 | 1420 | E Evcecourt | |
| 2. | 4 May 1918 | Spad | 2010 | Thiescourt Wald | |

(a) Credited to Jasta 6.
(b) Credited to Ltn Böhme, Jasta B.
(c) Credited to Ltn Vallendor, Jasta B.

## STILLER, Karl    OfStv

J1        – 9 May 1917    1   KIA
Born 6 October 1891, Scheidewitz. Killed at 1800 hours over Barisis-au-Bois.

Victories:

| | | | | |
|---|---|---|---|---|
| 1. | 6 May 1917 | Spad | 1845 | Aizy |

## STIMMEL, Manfred    Vfw

J32        – 6 Jul 1917    – POW
Shot down and taken prisoner at 1150 hours between Courcy and Thil, near Reims, by Lt Armand de Turenne of Escadrille N12 (3), and Capitaine Georges Matton, N48 (8).

## STOBEL,    Ltn

J3        (Mar 1917) – 19 May 1917    1   KIA

Victories:

| | | | | |
|---|---|---|---|---|
| 1. | 13 Apr 1917 | BE2g | | SW Oppy |

## STOCK,    Uffz

Kest 3    –
Forced to land in a burning aircraft on 12 June 1917; unharmed.

## STOCK, Heinz Vfw
J34b     12 Dec 1917 – 18 Dec 1917     1          J42     18 Dec 1917 –          –
Joined Jasta 34b from AFP5.

| Victories: | 1. | 4 May 1918 | AR2 | 1810 | NW Ricquebourg |
|---|---|---|---|---|---|

## STOCK, Karl Ltn
FFA3                                   –          J6      13 Jul 1917 – 5 Jan 1918     2
J22                    – 13 Jul 1917    –          J48     5 Jan 1918 – 3 Feb 1918     – KIA
Born 8 January 1894, Lemgo. Joined Jasta 22 from Jastaschule I. Awarded EK II and EK I. Killed near Villers-Outreaux, possibly by Captain H Maddocks of No 54 Sqn, RFC.

| Victories: | 1. | 20 Sep 1917 | Triplane | 0950 | Kemmel | |
|---|---|---|---|---|---|---|
| | 2. | 26 Sep 1917 | Spad | 0720 | NW Dadizeele | (a) |

(a) Probably B3490, No 23 Sqn, RFC, 2/Lt E Taylor.

## STOCK, Max Ltn
J48     24 Mar 1918 – 11 Nov 1918     –
Joined Jasta 48 from Jastaschule II.

## STOCK, Walter Ltn d R
FA3                                    –          J6      13 Jul 1917 – 5 Jan 1918     3
J22                    – 8 Jul 1917     –          J48     5 Jan 1918 – 11 Nov 1918     –
Commanded Jasta 48 from 23 August 1918.

| Victories: | 1. | 20 Jul 1917 | RE8 | 0840 | Armentières |
|---|---|---|---|---|---|
| | 2. | 28 Jul 1917 | DH4 | 1900 | Bahnof Kruis |
| | 3. | 10 Aug 1917 | SE5 | 1530 | Dadizeele |

## STOCKMANN, Otto Uffz
J66     – 9 Aug 1918     2 POW
Flying Fokker DVII 771/18 when shot down near de la Cuche, French Vème Armée Sector.

| Victories: | 1. | 31 Jul 1918 | Spad XI | | S Braisne |
|---|---|---|---|---|---|
| | 2. | 6 Aug 1918 | Spad XI | | S Braisne |

## STÖBER, Hugo Vfw
FA8                                    2          J16b    1 Nov 1916 – 10 Aug 1917     1 WIA
Awarded EKII & EKI.

| Victories: | 1. | 22 Jul 1916 | Farman | | Muhlhausen |
|---|---|---|---|---|---|
| | 2. | 30 Jul 1916 | Farman | | Sennheim |
| | 3. | 4 May 1917 | Sopwith 2 | | Altkirch |

## STÖR, Heinrich Ltn d R
J34b     17 Nov 1917 – 4 Mar 1918     –          J77b    18 Apr 1918 – 15 Jun 1918     –
FEA1b    4 Mar 1918 – 10 Apr 1918     –          J35b    15 Jun 1918 – 11 Nov 1918     1
J34b     10 Apr 1918 – 18 Apr 1918     –
Joined Jasta 34b from Jastaschule II. Awarded Bavarian Militär-Verdeinstkreuz 4 Klasse on 21 July 1918.

| Victories: | – | 5 Jul 1918 | Balloon | 1725 | NW Arras | |
|---|---|---|---|---|---|---|
| | 1. | 15 Sep 1918 | SE5a | 1908 | N Marquion | (a) |

(a) Thought to have been #D5314, No 19 Sqn, RAF, Lt G F Anderson (POW).

## STÖR, Wilhelm Vfw
J68     7 Apr 1918 – 11 Nov 1918     5
Biography & Victories: See *Above the Lines*.

## STÖLTING, Günther Ltn
J12     (Jul 1918) – 11 Nov 1918     –
Previously served with FAA242.

## STOLTENHOFF, Ltn d R
J27     5 Jul 1917 – 7 May 1918     –          J50     28 May 1918 – 17 Jun 1918     –
J58     7 May 1918 – 28 May 1918     –          J27     17 Jun 1918 – 11 Nov 1918     3
Joined Jasta 27 from Jastaschule I. Acting CO Jasta 58 from 7 May to 20 May 1918. Acting CO Jasta 50 from 28 May to 17 June 1918. Acting CO Jasta 27 from 6 July to 27 July 1918.

| Victories: | 1. | 16 Jul 1918 | Spad | 0640 | Chaumizy |
|---|---|---|---|---|---|
| | 2. | 2 Sep 1918 | | | |
| | – | 1 Oct 1918 | | | |
| | 3. | 14 Oct 1918 | | | |

## STORR, Georg    Uffz
J60              – 11 Apr 1918    – KIA
Born 17 May 1897, Ravensburg. Killed near Mortier-Laon.

## STOY,    Ltn d R
J31    (Dec 1917) – 31 Mar 1918    –            J10    31 Mar 1918 – 16 Jun 1918    –
Lightly wounded in action 2 May 1918, W of Péronne and forced to land. Transferred to Idflieg on 16 June 1918.

## STRÄHLE, Paul    Ltn d R
FAA213   15 Jul 1916 – 5 Sep 1916    –        J57    1 Jan 1918 – 11 Nov 1918    8
J18      27 Oct 1916 – 1 Jan 1918   7
Biography & Victories: See *Above the Lines*.

## STRASSER, Georg    Vfw
FA44           – 1916    –            FEA5    19 May 1918 –            –
J17    11 Nov 1916 – 19 May 1918   7
Biography & Victories: See *Above the Lines*.

## STRATMANN, Edouard    Ltn d R
J9              – 31 May 1918    – POW
Shot down wounded and taken prisoner about 10 km SW Villers-Cotterets, French VI Armée.

## STRAUBE, Kurt    Uffz
J66              – 18 Mar 1918   1 KIA
Born 16 December 1897, Zichopau. Shot down in flames over Aquilcourt, during combat with a Spad.

| Victories: | 1. | 17 Mar 1918 | Balloon | Nanteuil |
|---|---|---|---|---|

## STRAUBE,    Ltn
J70              – 11 Aug 1918    – WIA
Wounded in combat with a DH9 near Hagenau.

## STRAUCH, Josef    Ltn
J41                                1

| Victories: | 1. | 17 Mar 1918 | Sopwith 2 | W Rossberg |
|---|---|---|---|---|

## STRAUCH, Leo    Ltn
J4    Nov 1916 –            –        J31    (Sep 1917) – 5 Dec 1917    – WIA
J33            – (Sep 1917)    –        J31    (Mar 1918) – Jul 1918    –
Flew with FA16 prior to joining Jasta 4. Transferred in July 1918. Died 2 April 1972, Saarbrucken, Germany.

## STRECKER,    Uffz
J10    29 Jul 1918 – 30 Aug 1918    –        Idflieg    30 Aug 1918 –            –
Injured in an accident during a test flight on 4 August 1918.

## STREHL, Gerhard    Ltn
J12    28 Apr 1917 – 1 May 1917    – KIA
Born 9 April 1893, Poppelau. Shot down in flames and killed during combat with Pups and FE2bs over Epinoy.

## STREICHER, Anton    Flg
J48    5 Aug 1918 – 23 Sep 1918    –        AFP7    23 Sep 1918 –            –
Joined Jasta 48 from Jastaschule I.

## STREN,    Ltn
JB    (Jun 1917) – Aug 1917)    –

## STREY,     Uffz
J25                                                  2
Victories:        1.        11 Mar 1917       Caudron                              NW Kenali
                  2.        18 Mar 1917       EA                                   Monastir

---

## STREY,     Ltn
J31        (Apr 1917) –                        –

---

## STROBEL,     Ltn
J5         (Apr 1917) –                        –
Known to have flown Albatros D II 1798/16 with Jasta 5.

---

## STROBL,     Ltn
J40        27 Jul 1917 – Sep 1917             –

---

## STRÜNKLENBERG, Karl     Vfw
J9                1918 – 1918                  4(5)
Biography & Victories: See *Above the Lines*.

---

## STUDENT, Kurt     Oblt
FFA17    2 Aug 1914 – 9 Feb 1916      –               Hosp    2 May 1917 – 11 Jul 1917     –
KG4/19   10 Feb 1916 – 16 May 1916    – CO            FEA3    25 Feb 1918 – 13 Jun 1918    –
AOK3     17 May 1916 – 6 Oct 1916     3               Staff   14 Jun 1918 – 11 Nov 1918    –
CO J9    7 Oct 1916 – 2 May 1917      3    WIA
Biography & Victories: See *Above the Lines*.

---

## STÜMPERT, Heinrich     Uffz
J35b     25 Sep 1917 – (Feb 1918)      2
Born 6 February 1897. Awarded Eiserne Kreuz I Klasse on 26 January 1918.
Victories:        1.        12 Oct 1917       Camel                 1215           NW Courtrai       (a)
                  2.        Possibly one of the below was confirmed?
                  –         16 Oct 1917        Camel                                Allied Lines
                  –         5 Nov 1917    .    Camel                                Allied Lines
(a) Probably 2/Lt K H Willard, No 45 Sqn, RFC, (KIA).

---

## STUMPF, Gottfried     Ltn
J6       4 Aug 1917 – 18 Dec 1917     1               Jasta
J77b     18 Dec 1917 – 9 Jan 1918     –               Schonger 29 Oct 1918 – 11 Nov 1918    –
FEA1b    9 Jan 1918 –                 –
Joined Jasta 6 from AFP4. Lightly injured in a landing accident on 30 September 1917.
Victories:        1.        6 Nov 1917        Nieuport              0845           Zonnebeke

---

## STURM, Alfred     OfStv
FEA4     1 Jun 1915 – 28 Feb 1917     –               Kest9   1 Jan 1918 – 11 Nov 1918     –
J5       1 Mar 1917 – 31 Dec 1917     1
Born 23 Aug 1888, Saarbrücken. Entered military service 17 Oct 1905, student in NCO school. Infantry
Regiment 144, 30 Sep 1908 to 27 Jan 1915 WIA; hospitalised until 31 May 1915. Promoted Vizefeldwebel
1 Aug 1913; Offizierstellvertreter on 1 Jan 1915. Pilot's training at FEA4 from 1 June 1915–28 Feb 1917.
Known to have flown Albatros DII 914/16 and Albatros DII 1752/16 while with Jasta 5. Attained rank
of Lieutenant-General in the Luftwaffe during WWII, and awarded Ritterkreuz. Died 8 March 1962,
Detmold.
Victories:        1.        26 Apr 1917       FE2b                  2000           Brancourt

---

## STURMKEIT,     Flg
ObOst/
J81               – 5 Jul 1918             – WIA

---

## STUTZ, Erich     Vfw
J71                                            –

---

## STUTZ, Hermann     Ltn d R
KG4/22            1916 – 1917              –          J71     6 Feb 1918 – 11 Nov 1918     4
J20      25 Jan 1917 – 6 Feb 1918     2
Biography & Victories: See *Above the Lines*.

**SUCK, Hans     Ltn**
J4        14 Oct 1918 – 11 Nov 1918    –
Born 7 August 1897. Joined Jasta 4 from Jastaschule II. Died 1976, Wilhelmshaven, Germany.

**SUER, Wilhelm     Ltn d R**
JB        (May 1918) – (Aug 1918)    1
Victories:      1.      16 Jun 1918        DH9                    S Roye

**SUESS,     Uffz**
J64w      5 May 1918 – 11 Nov 1918    –
Reported from Jastaschule Valenciennes.

**SURMANN,     Ltn d R**
J27       22 Jul 1917 – 24 Dec 1917    –            FA19      24 Dec 1917 –              –

**SWOBODA,     Vfw**
J7        23 Aug 1916 – (Jun 1917)    –

**TABAKA, Franz     Vfw**
J32b             – 20 Sep 1917    1            FEA9      14 Nov 1917 –              –
J23b      20 Sep 1917 – 14 Nov 1917    –
Victories:      1.      16 Jul 1917        Farman         1940       Cornilette

**TAMMANN, Heinrich     Ltn d R**
J23b      29 Dec 1916 – 30 Jul 1917    1            FEA1b     30 Jul 1917 –              –
Previously served with KG 6/34.
Victories:      1.       5 May 1917        Nieuport        1945       Cerny

**TANN, Askan Fr von und zu der     Ltn**
FFA65          1916 –                    –            J24s      15 Jan 1918 – 2 Feb 1918    – KIA
Born 5 November 1896, Stargard. Served in Baden Lieb Gren Regiment 109. Awarded RK II
Z.L.O.m.S. on 26 May 1916. Killed in combat with Camels S Nauroy, near Bellenglise, at 1140 hours
while flying Albatros DV 4575/17.

**TANNEBERGER,     Ltn d R**
J50       (Jun 1918) – 5 Sep 1918    –            FEA9      5 Sep 1918 –              –
Served in Field Artillery Regiment 45.

**TAUCHER, Max     Vfw**
J34b      22 Sep 1917 – 16 Oct 1917    1 POW
Joined Jasta 34b from Jastaschule I. Shot down over the Forêt de Hesse.
Victories:      1.      16 Oct 1917        Spad           1350       Bethelainville

**TECHOW, Adolf     Vfw**
J18       21 Jul 1917 – 21 Jul 1917    –            J7        21 Jul 1917 – 22 Oct 1917    – KIA
Born 5 May 1893, Hamburg. Killed near Dixmuiden, during combat with a Camel.

**TEGTMEIER,     Uffz**
J57       (Jul 1918) – 4 Sep 1918    – WIA
Shot down on 30 August 1918, over Seranvillers, returned to unit OK. Severely wounded during combat
with Camels over Aniche; hospitalised.

**TEIGELER,     Vfw**
J22       Dec 1917 – Jan 1918    1
Victories:      1.       1 Jan 1918        Spad           1220       Terny-Sorny

**TEKA,     OfStv**
J1 23     Aug 1916 –                    –
Joined Jasta 1 from FAA210.

**TELGE,     Ltn**
J12       (Sep 1918) – 11 Nov 1918    1
Victories:      1.       3 Nov 1918        Spad           1620       Beaumont

**TENGE, Friedrich Carl    Vfw**
J81        (Jun 1918) – 11 Nov 1918    1
Victories:    1.        11 Aug 1918        Spad                        Magneux

**TETZLER,    Gefr**
J7                    –

**THÄSSLER, Frederich    Uffz**
J27        26 Feb 1917 – 7 Mar 1917        –            J35b    9 Mar 1917 – 28 Jul 1917    – KIA
Born 23 July 1896, Spandau. Reported to Jasta 27 from Unbungspark Ost. Reported to Jasta 35b from
AFP B. Killed at 2000 hours between Oostnieuwkerke and Westroosebeke.

**THEILLER, Renatus    Ltn d R**
FFA44            – 1916        1        J5        (Oct 1916) – 24 Mar 1917    10 KIA
FFA25        1916 – 1916        1
Biography & Victories: See *Above the Lines*.

**THEURER,    Uffz**
J38            – 23 Aug 1918    – WIA

**THEURICH Herbert    Oblt**
CO    J35 4 Mar 1917 – 14 Apr 1917    – KIA
Shot down in flames and killed over Neubreisach, flying Albatros DIII 2097/16.

**THIEDE, Fritz    Ltn d R**
BG2/5    Feb 1916 – 1917        –        J38    23 Jun 1918 – 11 Nov 1918    3
J24    21 Feb 1918 – 23 Jun 1918    5
Biography & Victories: See *Above the Lines*.

**THIEL,    Ltn**
KG3/15                        J28w    1 Sep 1917 – 15 Dec 1917    –
JB        (Feb 1917) – 1 Sep 1917        –        J49    15 Dec 1917 – 11 Nov 1918    1
Awarded Silberne Militär-Verdeinstmedaille on 22 Oct 1918. Awarded EK I, and EK II. Lightly
wounded in action 5 February 1917.
Victories:    1.        3 Oct 1918        Bréguet            0830            Orfeuil

**THIEME,    Uffz**
J71                    –

**THOM, Karl    Ltn**
FFA216        1915 – 16 May 1916    – INJ        FA234        1917 – 24 Apr 1917    –
FA48    Oct 1916 –            –        J21s    15 May 1917 – 11 Aug 1918    27 WIA
Biography & Victories: See *Above the Lines*.

**THOMAS, Alex    Oblt**
J13        – 1 May 1918    1        CO J69    1 May 1918 – 11 Nov 1918    –
Commanded Jasta 13 from 21 Feb to 1 May 1918.
Victories:    1.        Date and unit unknown
            2.        17 Feb 1918        Balloon            1450            W La Fère

**THOMAS, Erich    Ltn d R**
J9        Dec 1917 – 17 Mar 1918    8        J22    17 Mar 1918 – 23 Mar 1918    2 POW
Biography & Victories: See *Above the Lines*.

**THOMAS, Josef    Uffz**
J23b    23 Jun 1918 – 12 Jul 1918    – INJ
Joined Jasta 23b from Jastaschule I. Injured in a landing accident.

**THOMAS, Max    Flg**
J73    Sep 1918 – 14 Oct 1918    – KIA
Born 12 May 1899, Breslau. Killed over Liart.

**THOMAS,    Ltn**
J21        (May 1917) –            –

**THORMÄLEN, Adolf    Ltn**
J22s                    – 21 Apr 1918    –    POW
Shot down and taken prisoner after a balloon attack in an Albatros DVa near Sains-en-Amienois (G/2Bde/2).

---

**THUIR, Wilhelm    Uffz**
J35        (Jul 1917) –  11 Aug 1917    –   KIAcc
Born 8 June 1890, Lendersdorf. Killed at 1910 hours near Ichteghem, flying Albatros DV 2240/17.

---

**THUN, Erich    Ltn**
J7        Sep 1917 – 28 Dec 1917    1              J52      14 Jan 1918 –                    –
Victories:      zlg      3 Sep 1917       Spad              0825          Pervyse

---

**THURM, Alwin    Ltn d R**
J24        6 Jul 1917 – 4 Aug 1917    1              J31      4 Aug 1917 – 31 Dec 1917    4    KIA
Biography & Victories: See *Above the Lines*.

---

**THURN und TAXIS, Prinz von    Ltn**
J9        5 Oct 1916 – (Dec 1916)    –

---

**THUY, Emil    Ltn d R**
FFA53      10 Jul 1915  1 Nov 1916    1              J28w      26 Sep 1917 – 11 Nov 1918    21
J21        28 Jan 1917 – 26 Sep 1917    13
Biography & Victories: See *Above the Lines*.

---

**THIEDE,    Ltn**
J19        4 Apr 1918 –                    –

---

**TIEDJE,    OfStv**
J25                                        –

---

**TIEDJE,    OfStv**
J65        23 May 1918 – 11 Nov 1918    3
Joined Jasta 65 from Jastaschule II.

| Victories: | 1. | 27 May 1918 | Spad | | Montsec |
|---|---|---|---|---|---|
| | 2. | 30 May 1918 | Nieuport | 0900 | S Euvezin |
| | – | 31 Jul 1918 | DH4 | | |
| | – | 30 Aug 1918 | DH4 | | Latour |
| | 3. | 4 Oct 1918 | Spad | 1710 | Oussel |

---

**TILING,    Ltn d R**
J35b        30 Mar 1918 – 27 May 1918    –
Joined Jasta 35b from Jastaschule II. Hospitalised from 2 April to 16 April 1918. Awarded the Bavarian Militär-Verdeinstkreuz 4 Klasse on 19 May 1918.

---

**TISCHNER, Jakob    Gefr**
J35b        16 Jun 1918 –                    –
On 17 June 1918, while landing Roland DVIa 1205/18 he crashed into Pfalz DIIIa 1732/17 and demolished both aircraft.

---

**TODT,    Ltn d R**
J40        (Dec 1917) –                    –              FA46                            –

---

**TÖLKE, Hermann    Ltn**
J79b        16 Oct 1918 – 11 Nov 1918    –
Wounded in action at 1045 hours 4 October 1918; remained with unit.

---

**TÖNGES,    Uffz**
J3        (Aug 1917) – (Sep 1917)    1
Victories:      1.      25 Sep 1917       DH4                            Oekene

---

**TÖNJES,    Ltn**
J62        27 Jan 1918 – 11 Nov 1918    1
Acting CO Jasta 62, 22 May to 1 July 1918, and 21 August to 6 September 1918.
Victories:      1.      31 Mar 1918       SE5a                            Montdidier

**TÖPERT, Ltn**
J38 (Jul 1918) – –

---

**TOLISCHUSS, Uffz**
Kest 3 – 23 May 1917 – POW
After a balloon attack was shot down by two Nieuports and taken prisoner.

| Victories: | – | 23 May 1917 | Balloon | | Croismare |
|---|---|---|---|---|---|

---

**TOLLMANN, Flg**
J20 14 Jun 1918 – 13 Jul 1918 – KIA

---

**TRACINSKI, Uffz**
SS1 – J57 14 May 1918 – 14 Oct 1918 2 Inj
Shot down behind German lines on 29 June 1918; not harmed. Severely injured in a landing accident; hospitalised.

| Victories: | 1. | 3 Oct 1918 | Camel | | |
|---|---|---|---|---|---|
| | 2. | 9 Oct 1918 | BF2b | | Beuvry |

---

**TRÄGER, Alfred Ltn d R**
J8 10 Sep 1916 – 8 Feb 1917 2 WIA J8 1 Mar 1917 – 8 Apr 1917 – WIA
J27 14 Feb 1917 – 1 Mar 1917 – J8 – 21 Aug 1917 1 WIA
Severely wounded in action 8 April 1917.

| Victories: | 1. | 22 Oct 1916 | DH2 | | Polygonwald | |
|---|---|---|---|---|---|---|
| | 2. | 6 Feb 1917 | FE2d | 1630 | E Moorslede | (a) |
| | 3. | 16 Aug 1917 | RE8 | 0725 | St Julien | |

(a) #A3.

---

**TRÄGER, Alfred Ltn**
KG4 – Idflieg 25 Jun 1918 – –
J17 30 Jan 1917 – 25 Jun 1918 –

---

**TRAUTMANN, Vfw**
J64w 3 Sep 1918 – 11 Nov 1918 2
Joined Jasta 64w from Jastaschule II.

| Victories: | zlg | 12 Sep 1918 | Salmson | | Broussey | |
|---|---|---|---|---|---|---|
| | 1. | 10 Oct 1918 | DH4 | | Montauville | (a) |
| | 2. | 23 Oct 1918 | DH9 | 1305 | Frescaty | (b) |

(a) 20th Aero Sqn, USAS.
(b) D2932, No 104 Sqn, IAF, Lt B S Case & 2/Lt H Bridges.

---

**TREIBER, Karl Uffz**
J5 (Sep 1918) – 11 Nov 1918 7
Biography & Victories: See *Above the Lines*.

---

**TRENTPOHL, Ltn**
FA23 – J4 1 Oct 1916 – –

---

**TREPTOW, Reinhard OfStv**
FAA207 25 Oct 1915 – Apr 1917 – Kest 4a 13 Jul 1918 – 11 Nov 1918 –
J25 Apr 1917 – 13 Jul 1918 6
Biography & Victories: See *Above the Lines*.

---

**TRESENREUTER, Erwin Uffz**
J68 6 Mar 1918 – 15 May 1918 1 WIA
Joined Jasta 68 from Jastaschule I. Flying an Albatros DVa when attacked and wounded by a Fokker Dr I on 15 May 1918; forced to land near Hangest.

| Victories: | 1. | 22 Mar 1918 | Camel N | | St Quentin |
|---|---|---|---|---|---|

---

**TREUTZSCH, Wilhelm Uffz**
J29 28 Aug 1918 – 11 Nov 1918 –
Joined Jasta 29 from Jastaschule I.

---

**TRIEBNER, Ltn**
J51 – 3 Aug 1918 – POW

**TRIEBSWETTER, Andreas    Vfw**
J16b        9 Jan 1918 – 19 May 1918    4  KIA
Born 19 January 1891, Schliersee. Shot down in flames south of Furnes, during combat with Camels flown by Lt Jan Olieslagers, Belgian Esc 9ème and 213 Squadron RAF.

| Victories: | 1. | 8 Mar 1918 | Balloon | 1710 | NE Ypern |
|---|---|---|---|---|---|
| | 2. | 30 Mar 1918 | SE5 | | Tronville |
| | 3. | 1 Apr 1918 | AWFK8 | | Villers-Bretonneux |
| | 4. | 17 May 1918 | DH9 | 1825 | SW Zillebekesee |

**TROTZKY, Julius    OfStv**
J43        22 Jan 1918 – 17 May 1918    1  KIA
Born 14 July 1890, Angerburg. Served with FA34 prior to joining Jasta 43. Killed at 1945 hours flying Albatros DVa 7450/17, during combat with SE5s of No 40 Sqn, RAF over Carvin. Possibly by Lt C O Rusden.

| Victories: | 1. | Date and unit unknown, possibly FA34 | | | |
|---|---|---|---|---|---|
| | 2. | 8 May 1918 | Camel | 1230 | S Auchy |

**TSCHENTSCHEL, Gerold    Ltn d R**
FA37        1917 – 1918    1            J72s    26 Mar 1918 – 29 Sep 1918    4  WIA
J1          – 26 Mar 1918    –
Biography & Victories: See *Above the Lines.*

**TSCHIERSCHKE,    Vfw**
J24s        11 Jul 1918 – 10 Oct 1918    –  WIA

**TUCZEK, Heinrich    Vfw**
J9          5 Oct 1916 –            J21        – 10 Feb 1917    – KIA
Born 18 January 1894, Marburg. Shot down in flames at 1600 hours during a combat with a Caudron over Berru.

**TÜRCK,    Flg**
J43        22 Jan 1918 –            –

**TÜRCKHEIM zu ALTDORF, Otto Fr von    Ltn**
FAA266        –            Kest 4b    26 Nov 1917 – 23 Dec 1917    – KIA
FAA213        –
Born 2 June 1893, Heilbronn. Served in a machine gun company before transferring to Fliegertruppe in 1916. Awarded EKII & EKI. Killed at Waldkirche.

**TÜXEN, Robert    Ltn d R**
J6        (Jun 1917) – (Mar 1918)    2
Crashed while testing Fokker DV 2642/16 at 1400 on 11 November 1917; not harmed.

| Victories: | 1. | 17 Jul 1917 | Pup | 2105 | Comines |
|---|---|---|---|---|---|
| | 2. | 28 Jul 1917 | DH4 | 1835 | E Ingelmünster |

**TURCK, Ernst Wilhelm    Oblt**
J7          – 21 Jul 1917    –            CO J15    20 Mar 1918 – 18 May 1918    –
J18        21 Jul 1917 – 20 Mar 1918    1            CO J54    18 May 1918 –            –
Commanded Jasta 18, 13 October 1917 to 20 March 1918.

| Victories: | 1. | 16 Sep 1917 | DH4 | | Houthulsterwald |
|---|---|---|---|---|---|

**TURCK, Paul    Ltn d R**
J66        27 Jan 1918 – (Jul 1918)    5            J21s    (Jul 1918) – 3 Sep 1918    5
Biography & Victories: See *Above the Lines.*

**TUTSCHEK, Adolf Ritter von    Hptm**
FA6b        Oct 1916 – 1917    –            Hptm
J2          25 Jan 1917 – 28 Apr 1917    3            CO J12    28 Apr 1917 – 11 Aug 1917    20 WIA
                                                    CO JGII    1 Feb 1918 – 15 Mar 1918    4 KIA
Biography & Victories: See *Above the Lines.*

**TYBELSKY, Albert    Uffz**
FAA221        –            J19    27 Apr 1917 – 10 Apr 1918    1
Transferred to AFP18 on 10 April 1918.

| Victories: | 1. | 3 Sep 1917 | Balloon | | Pontavert |
|---|---|---|---|---|---|

**UDET, Ernst    Oblt**

| | | | | | | |
|---|---|---|---|---|---|---|
| FAA206 | 4 Sep 1915 – 24 Sep 1915 | – | J37 | 19 Jun 1917 – 18 Mar 1918 | 19 | |
| FA68 | 29 Nov 1915 – 7 Oct 1916 | 1 | Oblt | | | |
| Lt d R | | | J11 | 18 Mar 1918 – 20 May 1918 | 3 | |
| J15 | 8 Oct 1916 – 19 Jun 1917 | 5 | CO J4 | 20 May 1918 – 26 Sep 1918 | 34 | WIA |

Biography & Victories: See *Above the Lines*.

**ÜBERSCHAER, Karl    Uffz**

J39        – 23 Nov 1917    2    KIA
Born 7 January 1895, Breslau. Killed near the Paive, Italy, at 1500 hours.

| Victories: | 1. | 25 Oct 1917 | Voisin | | Roechin |
|---|---|---|---|---|---|
| | zlg | 25 Oct 1917 | Voisin | | Roechin |
| | 2. | 1 Nov 1917 | Savoia Pom | 1645 | Montegliano |

**ULBRICHT, Arno    Uffz**

J9        – 13 Aug 1917    1    WIA
Born 4 January 1896, Lichtenwalde. Severely wounded at 1015 hours S of Medeah Ferme, during combat with a Spad. Died of wounds 17 Aug 1917.

| Victories: | 1. | 13 Aug 1917 | Balloon | 1020 | Suippes |
|---|---|---|---|---|---|

**ULBRICH,    Fw**

| J7 | (Mar 1917) – | 2 | J27 | (Jul 1918) – (Aug 1918) | – |
|---|---|---|---|---|---|

| Victories: | 1. | 25 Mar 1917 | Nieuport | 1610 | SE Avocourt |
|---|---|---|---|---|---|
| | 2. | 28 Mar 1917 | Balloon | 0910 | Belleville |

**ULM, Franz    Uffz**

J34b    21 Aug 1918 – 11 Nov 1918    1
Joined Jasta 34b from Jastaschule I.

| Victories: | 1. | 9 Oct 1918 | Dolphin | 0800 | N Maretz |
|---|---|---|---|---|---|

**ULMER, Alfred    Ltn d R**

J31        –

**ULMER, Alfred    Ltn**

J8        10 Sep 1916 – 29 Jun 1917    5    KIA
Biography & Victories: See *Above the Lines*.

**ULMER, Werner    Ltn d R**

| J32 | 5 Jun 1917 – 16 Aug 1917 | – | J17 | (Mar 1918) – 11 Nov 1918 | – |
|---|---|---|---|---|---|
| J41 | 16 Aug 1917 – (Mar 1918) | – | | | |

OzbV for Jasta 17.

**ULTSCH, Bernhard    OfStv**

| SchSt29 | (Mar 1917) – 9 Sep 1917 | 3 | J77b | 9 Feb 1918 – 11 Nov 1918 | 4 |
|---|---|---|---|---|---|
| J39 | 9 Sep 1917 – 9 Feb 1918 | 5 | | | |

Biography & Victories: See *Above the Lines*.

**UNGER, Hans    Ltn**

J22s        Aug 1917 – 23 Mar 1918    –    POW
Shot down by Lt Chaput of Spa 57, after a balloon attack near Bohain.

**UNGEWITTER, Gerhard    Ltn d R**

J78b    22 Apr 1918 –        1
Joined Jasta 78b from Jastaschule I. Acting CO Jasta 78b, 13 August to 14 September 1918.

| Victories: | 1. | 13 Aug 1918 | DH4 | 1400 | Migneville | (a) |
|---|---|---|---|---|---|---|

(a) No 55 Sqn, IAF.

**UNGEWITTER, Kurt    Vfw**

| SS5 | 1917 – | 2 | J24s | 6 Jun 1918 – 11 Nov 1918 | 5 |
|---|---|---|---|---|---|

Biography & Victories: See *Above the Lines*.

**UNVERSEHRT,    Ltn**

J12        23 Oct 1916 –        –

## VAHLDIECK,     Uffz
J50       (Aug 1918) – 11 Nov 1918    1
Victories:       1.          17 Aug 1918        Spad                1715              Ormes

## VALENTIN,     Ltn
J78b                                    –

## VALLENDOR, Hermann     Ltn d R
FA23      May 1917 – 24 Jun 1917      –          J2        24 Aug 1917 – 11 Nov 1918    6
JsSch     24 Jun 1917 –
Biography & Victories: See *Above the Lines*.

## VEITH,     Ltn
J76b      17 Jun 1918 –               –
Joined Jasta 76b from Jastaschule I.

## VELTJENS, Josef     Ltn d R
FA23      10 May 1916 – Oct 1916      –          J18       15 Aug 1917 – 20 Mar 1918    5
J4        Oct 1916 – Nov 1916         –          CO J18    20 Mar 1918 – 11 Nov 1918    25
J14       Nov 1916 – 15 Aug 1917      5
Biography & Victories: See *Above the Lines*.

## VETTER,     Ltn
Kest 3                                  –
Lightly wounded in combat on 5 February 1918, forced to land near Landorf.

## VETTER,     Sgt
J21s                – 11 Nov 1918      1
Victories:       1.          5 Oct 1918         Spad                1810              S Orainville

## VIEBIG, Hans     Ltn
J20       1 Oct 1917 – 26 Oct 1917     1          J57       25 Jan 1917 – 30 Jun 1918    4    WIA
J18       26 Oct 1917 – 25 Jan 1918    –
Biography & Victories: See *Above the Lines*.

## VIEHWEGER, Günther     Oblt
JB        8 Sep 1916 – (Dec 1916)      –          CO J31    15 May 1917 – 6 Sep 1917     –
J17       5 Apr 1917 – 14 May 1917      –
Served in KG2 before reporting to Jasta 2. Joined Jasta 17 from AFP7.

## VIERECK, Wilhelm     OfStv
FA5b                                    –          J10       21 Sep 1916 – 22 Oct 1916    2    WIA
KekIII                                  –
Wounded over Provin, near Lille.
Victories:       zlg         8 Sep 1916         BE2c                                 Douai
                 1.          Date not known
                 2.          Date not known

## VIETH, Georg     Ltn d R
J61       28 Mar 1918 – 23 Aug 1918    – KIAcc
Born 8 August 1897, Nordhausen. Killed in a collision with Vfw Rothe near St Gobain.

## VIETZEN, Hans     Vfw
J12       16 Jun 1918 – 3 Jul 1918     – KIA
Born 30 December 1892, Hamburg. Killed near Corbie.

## VIKTOR,     Gefr
J71       Oct 1918 – 11 Nov 1918       1
Victories:       1.          3 Nov 1918         Balloon             St Cosman         (a)
(a) French 33rd Balloon Cié, Lt Van Hache and Adj Chevallier made safe parachute jumps.

## VILLINGER, Hans     Ltn d R
J18       23 Nov 1917 – 22 Dec 1917    – KIA
Born 17 June 1898, Reichenbach. Killed at 1530 hours near Le Mesnil-en-Vespres.

## VITZTHUM, Emil    Sgt
J16b     22 Jul 1918 – 15 Aug 1918    – WIA
Born 12 December 1893, Marstbreit. Severely wounded near Ypern; died of wounds next day.

## VÖLKER, Julius    Ltn
J31     (Apr 1917) – 30 May 1917    – INJ
Severely injured in a crash-landing.

## VÖLKER, Paul    Vfw
J60     – 11 Aug 1918    1   WIA
Born 8 December 1896, Geestemunde. Died of wounds 13 August 1918.

| Victories: | 1. | 16 Jul 1918 | Nieuport |
|---|---|---|---|

## VOGEL, Paul    Ltn d R
J23b     4 May 1918 – 15 Sep 1918    – POW
Born 8 October 1894, Roda. Served in Infantry Regiment 9. WIA 12 July 1918. Shot down in flames on 25 July 1918, but parachuted to safety. Again shot down in flames on 30 July 1918, and parachuted safely. Awarded EKI. Severely wounded when shot down and taken prisoner near Marquion, died of his wounds. Flying Pfalz D XII 2486/18 (G/HQ/6), downed by 2/Lt D E Cameron, No 1 Sqn, RAF, and Capt W E Staton and Lt L E Mitchell, No 62 Sqn, RAF.

| Victories: | – | J23b | 25 Jul 1918 | SE5a |
|---|---|---|---|---|

## VOGEL,    Ltn d R
J69                           1

| Victories: | 1. | 19 Jul 1918 | Sopwith | 1000 | Mourmelon-le-Grand |
|---|---|---|---|---|---|

## VOGEL,    Ltn
J29     21 Mar 1918 –     –
OzbV for Jagdgruppe 7.

## VOGT,    Uffz
J5     Dec 1917 – (May 1918)    –

## VOGT,    Ltn
J54s                   1

| Victories: | 1. | 16 Jun 1918 | SE5a | Romerstrasse |
|---|---|---|---|---|

## VOIGT, Bruno von    Oblt
| J8 | (Jun 1917) – (Aug 1917) | 3 | J66 | 3 Sep 1918 – 19 Sep 1918 | – |
|---|---|---|---|---|---|
| Hptm | | | | | |
| CO J1 | 18 Aug 1918 – 3 Sep 1918 | – | | | |

Joined Jasta 1 from FEA6. Commanded Jasta 66 from 9 Sep to 19 Sep 1918.

| Victories: | 1. | 8 Jun 1917 | Nieuport | 1415 | W Dadizeele | (a) |
|---|---|---|---|---|---|---|
| | 2. | 27 Jun 1917 | Spad | 2000 | N Bixschoote | (b) |
| | 3. | 19 Aug 1917 | RE8 | 1715 | Passchendaele | |

(a) Probably B1644, 1 Sqn, RFC, 2/Lt R L Boote, POW.
(b) Probably B1663, 19 Sqn, RFC, Lt M Lowe, KIA.

## VOIGT,    Ltn
J1     Dec 1916 – Feb 1917    –

## VOLKMANN, Hellmuth    Hptm
| FA25 | 3 Sep 1914 – 16 Nov 1914 | – | J6 | 25 Aug 1916 – 5 Nov 1916 | – |
|---|---|---|---|---|---|
| FAMetz | 17 Nov 1914 – 20 Jan 1915 | – | CO J10 | 6 Nov 1916 – 13 Dec 1916 | – |
| Oblt | | | Hptm | | |
| FA25 | 21 Jan 1915 – 8 Aug 1915 | – | KestSch | 14 Dec 1916 – | – |
| FlgSch | 9 Aug 1915 – 18 Oct 1915 | – | AFPA | 31 Dec 1917 – 27 May 1918 | – |
| FA71 | 19 Oct 1915 – 29 Jul 1916 | – | CO | | |
| AFP5 | 30 Jul 1916 – 24 Aug 1916 | – | FAA211 | 22 Oct 1918 – 11 Nov 1918 | – |

Born 28 February 1889, Diedenhofen, Lothringer. 18 March 1907 – Fahrenjunker in Pionier Bataillon 4; Fähnrich 18 November 1907; Leutnant 18 August 1908. Transferred to Fliegertruppe 20 June 1914, Flieger Battalion 4. Promoted Oberleutnant 25 February 1915. Commanded Kampfeinsitzer Schule Köln, Paderborn, and Warschau from 14 December 1916 to 18 July 1917. Commanded Jastaschule II 19 Jul 1917 to 9 September 1917. Staff of Kommandeurs der Flieger Heimat 10 to 19 September 1917.

Commanded Kampfeinsitzer Schule Sta II from 18 September 1917 to 30 December 1917. Promoted Hauptmann 28 November 1917. Reverted to the Infantry 28 May 1918 to 17 October 1918. Awarded the Knight's Cross with Swords of the Royal Hohenzollern House Order. Commanded the Legion Condor in Spain, late 1930s. Attained rank of General der Flieger in WWII. Commanded the Luftkreigsakademie until 16 April 1940, when he was dismissed from the Luftwaffe and became a General of the Infantry. Died 21 August 1940, Berlin-Gatow.

**VOLLBRACHT,    Ltn**

| J5 | (Aug 1918) – (Sep 1918) | 2 | | | |
|---|---|---|---|---|---|
| Victories: | 1. | 29 Aug 1918 | Bf2b | 1000 | Ligny |
| | 2. | 3 Sep 1918 | BF2b | 1840 | W Havrincourt |

**VOLLERS, Bernhard    Uffz**

J20      14 Jun 1918 – 11 Aug 1918   – KIAcc
Born 14 September 1897, Spaden. Killed during a test flight at Menin airfield.

**VOLLERT,    Ltn**

J76b    18 Nov 1917 –                    –
Served as OzbV for Jasta 76b.

**VOLLERTSEN, Heinrich    Ltn d R**

J20      8 Nov 1916 – 21 Feb 1917   –        J36      21 Feb 1917 – 3 Sep 1917      – KIA
Born 3 August 1890, Fiensburg. Lieb Infantry Regiment 83. Killed near Tenbrielen, possibly by AA fire.

**VONSCHOTT, Friedrich    Ltn d R**

J14      (Apr 1917) – 27 Apr 1917   – WIA
Born 23 December 1891, Wolfhagen. Severely wounded over Montchalons, died of wounds on 14 May 1917.

**VONSCHOTT,    Ltn**

| J46 | (Jun 1918) – 11 Nov 1918 | – | | | |
|---|---|---|---|---|---|
| Victories: | – | 4 Jul 1918 | Dolphin | 1845 | S Morlancourt |

**VORLÄNDER,    Ltn**

J5      Mar 1917 – (May 1917)   –
Known to have flown Albatros D II 1777/16 while with Jasta 5. Awarded Iron Cross I Class.

**VORTMANN, Ludwig    Ltn d R**

JB      (Jan 1918) – 29 Apr 1918   – KIA
Born 1 February 1896, Reckling. Killed in combat with SE5s NW Kemmelberg, down in flames, probably by Capt E A Mannock, No 74 Sqn, RAF.

**VOSS, Eberhard    Ltn d R**

| J20 | 8 Nov 1916 – 2 Jan 1917 | – | J20 | 28 Feb 1917 – 20 May 1917 | 1 | KIAcc |
|---|---|---|---|---|---|---|
| FAA267 | 2 Jan 1917 – 28 Feb 1917 | – | | | | |

Born 10 July 1885, Wieren. Killed during take-off at Guise.

| Victories: | 1. | 5 Apr 1917 | Nieuport | | Omissy |
|---|---|---|---|---|---|

**VOSS, Werner    Ltn d R**

| KG4/20 | 10 Mar 1916 – 21 Nov 1916 | – | J29 | 28 Jun 1917 – 3 Jul 1917 | – |
|---|---|---|---|---|---|
| J2 | 21 Nov 1916 – 20 May 1917 | 28 | J14 | 3 Jul 1917 – 30 Jul 1917 | – |
| J5 | 20 May 1917 – 28 Jun 1917 | 6 | J10 | 30 Jul 1917 – 23 Sep 1917 | 14 KIA |

Biography & Victories: See *Above the Lines*.

**VOSSEN, Fritz    Ltn d R**

J33                 – 27 Jul 1917   2 KIA
Born 24 September 1891, Berlin. Killed at 0900 hours over Moorslede, probably by Capitaine Georges Guynemer, N3; 50th claim.

| Victories: | 1. | 8 Jul 1917 | Balloon | 2105 | SE Arras |
|---|---|---|---|---|---|
| | 2. | 12 Jul 1917 | Sopwith 2 | 1050 | W St Quentin |

**VOTHKNECHT, Gottlieb    OfStv**

| J14 | – 4 Dec 1916 | – | J14 | 10 Apr 1917 – | – |
|---|---|---|---|---|---|
| J24 | 4 Dec 1916 – 10 Apr 1917 | 2 | | | |

| Victories: | 1. | 25 Feb 1917 | Sopwith 2 | | Saargemünd | (a) |
|---|---|---|---|---|---|---|
| | 2. | 9 Mar 1917 | Martinsyde | 1330 | Dombasel | |

(a) #9739, 3 Wing, RNAS.

## WACHHORST de WENTE, Otto    Ltn d R
J46          – 17 Mar 1918   –  KIA
Born 7 December 1889, Gr Mimmelage. Killed near Cambrai.

## WACKER, Hans    Ltn d R

| KG4/23 | 16 Jan 1916 – | | 1 | Kest 7 | 10 Oct 1917 – 17 Oct 1917 | – |
|---|---|---|---|---|---|---|
| J3 | 22 Aug 1916 – 30 Oct 1916 | – | WIA | FEA 10 | 17 Oct 1917 – 22 Dec 1917 | – † |
| Kest 1 | 26 Dec 1916 – 15 Apr 1917 | – | | FEA 10 | 9 Sep 1918 – 31 Dec 1918 | – |
| Kest 1b | 15 Apr 1917 – 2 Aug 1917 | – | | | | |

Born 16 April 1894, Karlsruhe. Volunteered 1 October 1913, assigned to Baden Infantry Rgt Nr.114.
Promoted to Unteroffizier on 9 July 1914. Awarded EKII on 11 October 1914. Promoted Vizefeldwebel
on 10 February 1915. Transferred to aviation and assigned to FEA3 on 1 July 1915. Flugzeugführer-
Abzeichen on 5 May 1916. Promoted to Leutnant d R on 30 May 1916. Ehrenbecker on 7 August 1916.
Awarded the Baden RK II Z.L.O.m.S. on 18 September 1916 and the EKI on 7 October 1916.
† Released temporarily from active duty.
(For further information see *OTF* Journal Vol 4, No 4, winter 1989, pg 338.)

| Victories: | 1. | 1 Aug 1916 |
|---|---|---|

## WACKWITZ, Gustav    Vfw
J29          9 Jun 1918 – 16 Jul 1918      1   KIAcc
Born 30 September 1895, Primsenau. Joined Jasta 29 from Jastaschule I. Killed during a test flight.

| Victories: | 1. | 11 Jul 1918 | DH9 | 0920 | Pecq |
|---|---|---|---|---|---|

## WACKWITZ, Max    Vfw

| FA65 | Apr 1916 – Nov 1916 | – | J24 | 10 Dec 1916 – 7 Dec 1917 | 4 | POW |
|---|---|---|---|---|---|---|
| J14 | 25 Oct 1916 – 1 Dec 1916 | – | | | | |

Born 19 December 1890, Dittersdorf. Reported to the 111th Infantry Regiment 11 October 1910. With
181st Infantry Regiment on 3 August 1914. September 1914 to January 1915 with 197th Reserve Infantry
Regiment. Transferred to Fliegerei on 11 July 1915. Learned to fly at DFW schule at Leipzig-Lindenthal.
Forced to land near Bignicourt, on 24 April 1917, due to damage to his aircraft. Shot down and forced
to land near Lavannes, on 27 May 1917; not harmed. Shot down and taken prisoner near Bethune by
ground fire at 1130 hours while flying Albatros DV 4545/17 (G.97). Awarded Iron Cross 1st and 2nd
Class; Saxon Silbern Friedrich-August Medal on 1 December 1916. Saxon Silbern Medaille des St
Heinrichs-Orden on 31 December 1917.

| Victories: | 1. | 10 May 1917 | Spad | | Fichtelberg |
|---|---|---|---|---|---|
| | 2. | 11 Sep 1917 | Sopwith | 1005 | Roulers-Ypern |
| | 3. | 26 Sep 1917 | Triplane | | Comines |
| | – | 7 Oct 1917 | RE8 | 0810 | Pilkem |
| | – | 8 Nov 1917 | Sopwith | 0850 | Bellevarde-Teich |
| | 4. | 5 Dec 1917 | RE8 | 1130 | Athies |

## WADOWSKI, Anton    Gefr
52          6 May 1918 – 8 Jul 1918      2   KIA
Born 10 June 1897, Oppein. Joined Jasta 52 from Jastaschule I. Killed near Armentières-Allenes, on a
Fokker DrI.

| Victories: | 1. | 29 Jun 1918 | Camel | 2010 | W La Bassée |
|---|---|---|---|---|---|
| | 2. | 2 Jul 1918 | SE5a | | Caestre |

## WAGENER, Werner    Ltn d R

| Kasta 38 | 24 Jul 1916 – 25 Feb 1917 | 1 | Kest 1a | – 1918 | – |
|---|---|---|---|---|---|
| J21 | 25 Feb 1917 – 19 Aug 1917 | 1 | Kest 5 | – 1918 | – |
| J39 | 19 Aug 1917 – 25 Nov 1917 | 3 | WIA | | |

Biography & Victories: See *Above the Lines.*

## WAGNER, August    Vfw
J58          3 Feb 1918 – 15 Mar 1918   –  KIA
Born 30 April 1895, Sondershausen. Joined Jasta 58 from Jastaschule II. Killed near Ecourt-St Quentin,
in flames, possibly by 2/Lt G T Travers, No 84 Sqn, RFC.

**WAGNER, Franz    Gefr**
J79b                    – 25 Sep 1918    –  KIA
Born 31 December 1897, Waldthurn. Killed near Preselles Ferme.

---

**WAGNER, Gilbert    Vfw**
J29        8 Jan 1918 – 12 Apr 1918    3  KIA
Born 27 July 1893, Mittersheim. Joined Jasta 29 from Jastaschule II. Killed over Armentières, possibly by Major K L Caldwell, No 74 Sqn, RAF.

| Victories: | 1. | Date and unit unknown | | | | |
|---|---|---|---|---|---|---|
| | 2. | 16 Feb 1918 | RE8 | 1215 | Pont-à-Vendin | |
| | 3. | 16 Mar 1918 | Camel | 1000 | SE Sainghin | (a) |
| | 4. | 1 Apr 1918 | Balloon | 1515 | Grénay | |

(a) Probably B5208, No 4 Sqn, AFC, 2/Lt W H Nicholls, POW.

---

**WAGNER, Hans    Uffz**
J80b    15 Mar 1918 – 3 May 1918    –  KIA
Born 12 February 1895, Kunchberg. Killed in flames near Juvrecourt, after combat with a Spad at 2015 hours. Probably by Adjutant Lucien Gasser, Escadrille Spa 87.

---

**WAGNER, Otto    Flg**
J79b                    – 4 Sep 1918    –  POW
Flying Fokker DVII 4503/18 G/3Bde/19, by Lt D J Hughes, No 3 Sqn, RAF, in Camel F1972.

---

**WAGNER, Paul    Vfw**
J28w    1 Jun 1917 – 8 Nov 1917    –            J76b    15 Nov 1917 – 4 Feb 1918    –  KIAcc
Born 8 February 1895, Augsburg. Killed in an accident at 1046 hours over Colmar Nord airfield.

---

**WAGNER, Richard    Ltn d R**
J26        Aug 1917 – 9 Oct 1917    –  KIA
Born 27 July 1890, Naumberg. Joined Jasta 26 from Jastaschule I. Shot down in flames and killed at 1615 hours SE Zonnebeke, after combat with an RE8.

---

**WAGNER, Wilhelm    Vfw**
J30        7 Apr 1918 – 27 Sep 1918    –            AFP6    27 Sep 1918 –            –
Joined Jasta 30 from AFP18.

---

**WAGNER,    Ltn**
J38                                    –

---

**WAGNER,    Gefr**
J78b        1 Sep 1918 –                            –
Joined Jasta 78b from Jastaschule I.

---

**WALDBERER,    Ltn d R**
J35b    19 Oct 1918 – 11 Nov 1918    –
Joined Jasta 35b from Jastaschule II.

---

**WALDHAUSEN, Hans    Oblt**
FFA53        1915 –        –        Oblt
FA9b        1916 –        –        J37    1 Aug 1917 – 27 Sep 1917    6  POW
Biography & Victories: See *Above the Lines*.

---

**WALDHELM, Kurt    Ltn d R**
J36    13 Jun 1918 – 4 Sep 1918    –  KIA
Born 17 April 1897, Hirschberg. Joined Jasta 36 from Jastaschule II. Killed over Abancourt.

---

**WALDHERR, Karl    Uffz**
J53        23 Jan 1918 – 11 Nov 1918    1
Joined Jasta 53 from Jastaschule II.

| Victories: | 1. | 22 Mar 1918 | BF2b | | Croix |
|---|---|---|---|---|---|

---

**WALDOW, Claus von    Ltn**
J15                    – 20 Mar 1918    –            J18    20 Mar 1918 –            –

## WALDVOGEL, Vfw

J25 —
Victories: 1. 16 Aug 1918

## WALGENBACH, Vfw

J42 – 8 Aug 1918 – POW

## WALK, Ludwig Vfw

| | | | | | | | |
|---|---|---|---|---|---|---|---|
| FAA286 | 3 Jan 1918 – 17 Apr 1918 | – | | 79b | 2 May 1918 – 12 Jul 1918 | – | |
| JsSch | 17 Apr 1918 – 2 May 1918 | – | | 77b | 12 Jul 1918 – 11 Nov 1918 | – | |

Born 20 July 1895, Munich. Assigned to Bavarian Reserve Infantry Rgt Nr.1 on 28 August 1914, later assigned to 24th Infantry Regiment. Gassed 13 January 1916, returned to the Front in May. Assigned to Fliegertruppe, FEA 1 on 18 May 1917. Joined Jasta 79b from Jastaschule I. Awarded EKI.

## WALLNER, Herbert Ltn d R

J3 – 10 Dec 1917 – KIA
Born 24 May 1892, Wirsitz. Reserve Infantry Regiment 34. Killed over Wynghene.

## WALTER, Johannes Vfw

| | | | | | | | |
|---|---|---|---|---|---|---|---|
| J36 | 22 Feb 1917 – 28 May 1917 | – | WIA | J53 | 13 Jan 1918 – 11 Nov 1918 | 1 | |
| J36 | Dec 1917 – 13 Jan 1918 | 1 | | | | | |

Severely wounded in upper thigh on 28 May 1917.

| Victories: | | | | | |
|---|---|---|---|---|---|
| | 1. | 8 Nov 1917 | SE5 | 1010 | Houthem |
| | 2. | 22 Mar 1918 | BF2b | 1600 | Croix |

## WALTHER, Siegfried Vfw

J55 – 25 Aug 1918 – KIA
KIA over Tulkern.

## WALTHER, Uffz

| | | | | | |
|---|---|---|---|---|---|
| J76b | 18 Nov 1917 – 20 Apr 1918 | 2 | AFP2 | 20 Apr 1918 – | – |

Joined Jasta 76b from Jastaschule II.

| Victories: | | | | | |
|---|---|---|---|---|---|
| | 1. | 7 Dec 1917 | Caudron R11 | 1550 | Gewenheim |
| | 2. | 11 Feb 1918 | AR2 | 1650 | Carspach |

## WALZ, Franz Josef Hptm

| | | | | | | | |
|---|---|---|---|---|---|---|---|
| FFA3b | 2 Aug 1914 – 23 Jul 1915 | – | | CO | | | |
| CO | | | | KGl/2 | 11 Oct 1916 – 2 Nov 1916 | – | |
| BAO | 24 Jul 1915 – 29 Dec 1915 | – | | CO J19 | 3 Nov 1916 – 29 Nov 1916 | – | |
| CO | | | | Hptm J2 | 29 Nov 1916 – 9 Jun 1917 | 1 | |
| Kasta 2 | 30 Dec 1915 – 30 Jul 1916 | 6 | WIA | J34 | 9 Jun 1917 – 7 Jul 1917 | – | |
| Hosp | 30 Jul 1916 – | | | FA304b | 7 Jul 1917 – | – | |
| FEA1 | – 10 Oct 1916 | | | | | | |

Biography & Victories: See *Above the Lines*.

## WANDELT, Gustav Ltn d R

J36 31 Dec 1917 – 23 Jan 1918 2 KIA
Born 6 December 1891, Poppen. Infantry Regiment 47. Promoted Leutnant 22 March 1915. Joined Jasta 36 from Jastaschule I. Collided with a Sopwith Camel during combat over Staden.

| Victories | | | | | |
|---|---|---|---|---|---|
| | 1. | 23 Jan 1918 | Camel | 1545 | Staden |
| | 2. | 23 Jan 1918 | Camel | 1550 | Zarrenlinde |

## WANDELT, Otto Gustav Vfw

J43 3 Feb 1918 – 6 May 1918 3 KIA
Born 27 December 1893, Friedrichsgrund. Killed at 1115 hours, during combat with an AWFK8 north of Bethune. Down in flames, probably by 2/Lt F H Baguley and Lt C A Horn of 2 Sqn, RAF.

| Victories: | | | | | |
|---|---|---|---|---|---|
| | 1. | 18 Mar 1918 | Balloon | | Champenoux |
| | 2. | 21 Apr 1918 | RE8 | 0840 | N Neuve Eglise |
| | 3. | 25 Apr 1918 | RE8 | 0940 | Fletre |

## WANJEK, Ltn

J81 (Jun 1918) – 11 Nov 1918
Temporarily commanded Jasta 81 from 25 August to 1 September 1918.

## WARMUTH, Anton    Ltn
J34b      18 Sep 1917 – 30 Oct 1917    – KIA
Born 15 January 1897, Freising. 17th Infantry Regiment. Joined Jasta 34b from Jastaschule I. Killed over Filain.

## WARSCHAUER, David    Ltn d R
| | | | | | | |
|---|---|---|---|---|---|---|
| FEA2 | 30 Oct 1917 – | | – | JsSchI | 18 Sep 1918 – 4 Oct 1918 | – |
| ΛFP6 | 14 Sep 1918 – 18 Sep 1918 | | – | J77b | 5 Oct 1918 – 11 Nov 1918 | – |

Born 4 October 1897, Gunzenhausen. Volkswehrkamp, 1 May 1919. Sicherheitskamp, 11 June 1919.

## WARSCHUN, Rudolf    Vfw
J51          – 15 May 1918    – KIA
Born 16 July 1893, Putzig. Killed near Zillebekesee.

## WASSERMANN, Friedrich    Uffz
J27      27 Jul 1917 – 12 Aug 1917    – KIA
Born 1 March 1894, Luckenwaide. Reported to Jasta 27 from AFP4. Killed over Ypern, flying an Albatros D III (G.61) probably by Lts F M Green and R M D Fairweather, No 7 Sqn, RFC, in A3695.

## WAWZIN,    Vfw
J10      1 Sep 1917 – Feb 1918      2

| Victories: | 1. | 18 Nov 1917 | Spad | 0925 | N Ypern |
|---|---|---|---|---|---|
| | 2. | 24 Apr 1918 | SE5 | | |

## WEBBER,    Ltn
J65      20 Jun 1918 – 10 Jul 1918    –      AFP C    10 Jul 1918 –      –
Joined Jasta 65 from AFP C. Served as OzbV for Jasta 65.

## WEBER, Alois    Ltn d R
J46          – 19 May 1918    – POW
Shot down over Villers-Bretonneux.

## WEBER, Artur    Vfw
J5      (Dec 1917) – 10 Feb 1918    1      J46    10 Feb 1918 – 21 Feb 1918    – KIA
Born 18 March 1891, Langenbielau. Killed in action during combat with four Camels at 1140 hours, near Carvin-Ascq.

| Victories: | 1. | 19 Dec 1917 | SE5a | 1430 | Havrincourtwald |
|---|---|---|---|---|---|

## WEBER, Eugen    Ltn
Kest 4b
Knight's Cross 2nd Class with Swords of the Württemberg Friedrich Order 20 February 1918.

## WEBER, Friedrich    Ltn
J21          – 21 Sep 1917    – KIA
Born 16 May 1896, Darmstadt. Killed at 1830 hours over Louvemont.

## WEBER, Friedrich-Karl    Ltn d R
SS8          – 1917      2      J29    9 Jun 1918 – 11 Nov 1918    2
Ltn d R
CO Kest    4b 1917 – 1918      –
Reported to Jasta 29 from Jastaschule I. Injured during à forced landing on 16 July 1918. Awarded Iron Cross 1st Class on 6 August 1918.

| Victories: | 1. | 3 May 1917 | Spad | | Ville-au-Bois | (a) |
|---|---|---|---|---|---|---|
| | 2. | 8 Nov 1917 | Spad | | | (b) |
| | 3. | 27 Jun 1918 | Camel | 1110 | Hantay | |
| | 4. | 3 Sep 1918 | SE5a | 2000 | Pelves | |

(a) With observer, Ltn Karl Ritscherle.
(b) Obs, Uffz Eisenberger.

## WEBER, Karl    Oblt
J28      25 Jan 1917 – (Jul 1917)    –
Previously served in Kampfstaffel Paderborn.

## WEBER, Ludwig    Vfw
J3      (Jan 1917) – 6 Apr 1917    1  WIA      J3      (Sep 1917) –      1
Wounded near Biache, in Albatros DII 510/16, hospitalised, but returned to unit later.

| Victories: | 1. | 3 Apr 1917 | BE2e | 1450 | NE Brebières |
|---|---|---|---|---|---|
| | 2. | 27 Sep 1917 | Camel | 1600 | Benkenberg |

## WEBER, Willy    Hptm
Kest 1b    (Apr 1918) – (Jun 1918)    –

## WEBER,    Vfw
J8    (Aug 1917) – (Mar 1918)    2

| Victories: | 1. | 10 Aug 1917 | Pup | 1630 | Slypshoek |
|---|---|---|---|---|---|
| | 2. | 28 Mar 1918 | Bréguet | | |

## WEBER,    Ltn
| FA13 | | – | J10 | 21 Sep 1916 – | – |
|---|---|---|---|---|---|

## WEBER,    Ltn
| J13 | – 1 May 1918 | – | J69 | 1 May 1918 – | – |
|---|---|---|---|---|---|

## WEBER,    Uffz
J25    – 24 Feb 1917    – INJ

## WECKBRODT, Rudolf    OfStv
| FFA58 | 1915 – | | J26 | 18 Jan 1917 – 26 Apr 1917 | 2 | WIA |
|---|---|---|---|---|---|---|
| FAA284 | | – | J26 | 9 Sep 1917 – 14 Oct 1917 | – | KIA |

Born 12 June 1890, Mannheim. Awarded both EKII and EKI. Wounded in action with FE2bs on 24 April 1917. Rejoined Jasta 26 from FEA1 on 9 September 1917. Killed at 1715 hours flying an Albatros DV 636/17 (G.79),W of Poelcapelle, during an attack on a RE8; by Lt Jones, No 32 Sqn, RFC. A9269, and No 22 Sqn, RFC, BF2b A7268.

| Victories | 1. | 23 Apr 1917 | DH4 | 1800 | SW Itancourt |
|---|---|---|---|---|---|
| | 2. | 21 Sep 1917 | 2-seater | 1745 | Wervicq |

## WECKERLE, Josef    Ltn d R
J79b    12 May 1918 – 7 Jun 1918    – POW
Born 12 May 1896, Munich. Served in Fuss Artillery Battalion 49. Transferred to aviation in September 1917, FEA1. Motor of his Pfalz DIII hit during combat, forced to land N Bois de Cossu. (See French III° Armée Prisoner Interrogation Report.)

## WEDEL, Erich Rudiger von    Oblt
J11    23 Apr 1918 – 11 Nov 1918    13
Biography & Victories: See *Above the Lines*.

## WEDEL, Hasso von    Oblt
| FFA17 | Nov 1915 – | – | JsSch | Oct 1917 – | – |
|---|---|---|---|---|---|
| FAA53 | | – | J14 | Feb 1918 – 21 Feb 1918 | – |
| FA206 | | – | J75 | 21 Feb 1918 – 21 Aug 1918 | 1 |
| FA39 | | – | J24s | 21 Aug 1918 – 11 Nov 1918 | 3 |
| FA59 | Oct 1917 | – | | | |

Unit in which first victory scored unknown.
Biography & Victories: See *Above the Lines*.

## WEDEL, Vivgenz von    Ltn
J1    (May 1918) – 20 May 1918    – KIAcc
Born 24 November 1893, Landsberg. OzbV for Jasta 1. Killed in a crash near Vouziers.

## WEIBELZAHL, Hermann    Vfw
J29    5 Oct 1918 – 11 Nov 1918    –
Joined Jasta 29 from Jastaschule I.

## WEICHEL, Robert    Uffz
J23b    10 Jun 1918 – 7 Sep 1918    –
Joined Jasta 23b from Jastaschule I.

## WEICHEL,    Vfw
| FA40 | | – | J18 | 27 Oct 1916 – 29 Apr 1917 | – |
|---|---|---|---|---|---|
| J8 | 10 Sep 1916 – 27 Oct 1916 | 1 | AFP4 | 29 Apr 1917 – | – |

| Victories: | 1. | 21 Oct 1916 | Balloon | 1620 | Nieppe |
|---|---|---|---|---|---|

**WEICHHOLD, Hans      Ltn d R**
J51          Jan 1918 – Jan 1918        –            FA19        Jan 1918 –                   –

**WEIDEMANN,      Uffz**
J1         (Aug 1918) –                 1
Victories        1.          21 Aug 1918       SE5a                    1645              Longavesnes

**WEIDEMAUER,      Sgt**
J28w      21 Feb 1918 –                 –

**WEIDNER,      Ltn**
J12       17 Jul 1917 –                –

**WEIDNER,      Gefr**
J81                 – 22 May 1918       –            J74         22 May 1918 – 11 Nov 1918    1
Victories:       1.          29 Oct 1918

**WEIG, Moritz      Ltn**
J76b       22 Apr 1918 – 2 May 1918     – POW
Joined Jasta 76b from Jastaschule I.

**WEIGAND, Ernst      Oblt**
J10        11 Jul 1917 – 25 Sep 1917    3  KIA
Born 10 April 1893, Munich. Joined Jasta 10 from AFP4. Lightly wounded in action at 1730 hours 14
September 1917, remained with Jasta. Probably by Capt J T B McCudden, No 56 Sqn, RFC. Acting
CO Jasta 10 from 23 to 25 September 1917. Shot down in flames during combat with SE5s of 56 Sqn,
RFC, at 1740 hours, near Nachtegaal.
Victories:       1.          28 Jul 1917       Sopwith                 2100              Beythem
                 2.          14 Aug 1917       Sopwith                 1045              Nieuwkapelle
                 3.          11 Sep 1917       Spad                    1020              Bixschoote

**WEIGEL, Otto      Ltn d R**
J14              – 14 Apr 1917            – KIA
Born 7 September 1891, Strassburg. Killed at 1215 hours near Craonelle.

**WEIGOLD, Hans      Flg**
J49              – 1 Apr 1918            – KIAcc
Born 13 September 1895, Warmensteinach. Killed in an accident by Aniche airfield.

**WEIMAR,      Vfw**
J41              – 9 Jan 1918            1            J56         9 Jan 1918 – 1 Apr 1918      2  POW
Forced to land his Albatros DVa 5734/17 (G.159) during combat on 1 April 1918, in Allied lines near
Gontelles, and taken prisoner, the victim of Lt W J A Duncan, No 60 Sqn, RFC, who landed nearby.
Victories:       1.          6 Nov 1917        Salmson                                   SW Eglingen
                 2.          17 Mar 1918       SE5a                    1030              Maissemy
                 3.          24 Mar 1918       Camel                                     Barleux

**WEINER, Georg      Ltn**
SS15             – 1916                  –            Kest 3      3 May 1917 – 4 Sep 1918      3
J20        25 Jan 1917 – May 1917        1            CO J3       4 Sep 1918 – 11 Nov 1918     5
Biography & Victories: See *Above the Lines*.

**WEINER,      Vfw**
J55        (May 1918) – 11 Nov 1918      1
Victories:       1.          6 May 1918        Balloon

**WEINGÄRTNER, Karl      Uffz**
J15        10 Oct 1916 –                 –            FAA287                                    –

**WEINGARTEN,      Ltn**
J1         (Jul 1917) – 16 Nov 1917      1            J31         16 Nov 1917 –                 –
Victories:       1.          29 Jul 1917       Paul Schmitt            0750              La Ferté Bois     (a)
(a) Probably Cpl C Desmaison (P) and Cpl F Ferrieux (O) Esc PS 126, both missing.

## WEINGARTH, Hugo    Hptm

| | | | |
|---|---|---|---|
| FAA256 | | JGII | 31 Jul 1917 – 11 Nov 1918   – |

Staff of JGII.

## WEINMANN, Karl    Vfw

| | | |
|---|---|---|
| J50 | – 26 Sep 1918 | –   POW |

Came down in French territory after a combat and was taken prisoner.

## WEINSCHENK, Albrecht    Ltn d R

| | | | |
|---|---|---|---|
| J18 | 13 Jul 1917 – 16 May 1918   – | J16b | 4 Oct 1918 – 11 Nov 1918   – |
| J16b | 16 May 1918 – 27 Sep 1918   1 | | |

Lightly wounded in combat 18 August 1917. Temporarily assigned to Kofl 7b from 27 September 1918 to 4 October 1918.

| Victories: | 1. | 25 Jul 1918 | BF2b | 0915 | Zonnebeke |
|---|---|---|---|---|---|

## WEISCHER, Theodor    Vfw

| | | | |
|---|---|---|---|
| J18 | – 23 Mar 1918   – | J15 | 23 Mar 1918 – 11 Nov 1918   4 |

Awarded Iron Cross 1st Class.

| Victories: | 1. | 16 Jun 1918 | DH4 | 1150 | Grivesnes |
|---|---|---|---|---|---|
| | 2. | 14 Sep 1918 | DH4 | 0900 | Boyonville |
| | 3. | 15 Sep 1918 | DH4 | 1215 | S Metz |
| | 4. | 5 Oct 1918 | Spad | 1605 | Montfaucon |

## WEISE, Wilhelm    Vfw

| | | | |
|---|---|---|---|
| J35b | 22 Jun 1917 – 4 Sep 1917   – | AFP4 | 4 Sep 1917 –   – |

Lightly wounded during combat with a Sopwith two-seater on 27 July 1917.

## WEISS, Erich    Ltn

| | | | |
|---|---|---|---|
| J28w | May 1917 – Dec 1917   1 | J33 | – 14 May 1918   1   KIA |

Born 4 January 1894, Ouedlinburg. Collided in the air with Leutnant Josef Jacobs, Jasta 7, on 18 December 1917, but was able to bring his plane down safely. Neither harmed. Awarded EKI. Killed near Dickebusch, on an Albatros DVa (G/2Bde/8) probably by 2/Lt W M Thomson & Lt G H Kemp (O), No 20 Sqn, RAF.

| Victories: | 1. | 21 Aug 1917 | Sopwith | 1930 | E Ypern |
|---|---|---|---|---|---|
| | 2. | 26 Feb 1918 | Nieuport | 1250 | NE Blamont |

## WEISS, Eugen    Vfw

| | | | |
|---|---|---|---|
| Kest 5 | 7 Apr 1917   1 | J29 | 28 Nov 1917 – 9 Apr 1918   1 |
| J29 | 7 Apr 1917 – 6 Aug 1917   – | Idflieg | 9 Apr 1918 –   – |
| FEA5 | 6 Aug 1917 – 28 Nov 1917   – | | |

Born 24 November 1893, Freiburg. Awarded EKII on 27 January 1916, and EKI on 30 June 1916. Wounded in action 16 June 1917. Awarded the Baden Silberne Karl-Friedrich-Militär-Verdeinstmedaille on 7 February 1918. Transferred to Idflieg on 9 April 1918.

| Victories: | 1. | 20 Jun 1916 | Nieuport | | Bois de Ville | |
|---|---|---|---|---|---|---|
| | 2. | 17 Dec 1917 | Nieuport | 1600 | Armentières | (a) |
| | 2. | 17 Dec 1917 | RE8 | 1610 | Hazebrouck | (a) |

(a) These victories are questionable as to whom they were awarded. (See *OTF* Journal, Vol 4, No 4, 1989, pgs 339-340.)

## WEISS, Georg    Gefr

| | |
|---|---|
| J77b | 5 Aug 1918 – 11 Nov 1918   – |

Joined Jasta 77b from Jastaschule I.

## WEISS, Hans    Vfw

| | | | |
|---|---|---|---|
| FA68 | Sep 1916 – 1917   – | Ltn d R | |
| FAA282 | – 14 Jul 1917   – | J41 | (Sep 1917) – 27 Mar 1918   10 |
| FAA289 | 14 Jul 1917 – 1 Aug 1917   – | J10 | 27 Mar 1918 – 18 Apr 1918   1 |
| JsSch | 1 Aug 1917 – | J11 | 18 Apr 1918 – 2 May 1918   5   KIA |

Biography & Victories: See *Above the Lines*.

## WEISS, Jakob    Uffz

| | |
|---|---|
| J5 | (Mar 1917) – (May 1917)   – |

Known to have flown Albatros D III 2225/16 while with Jasta 5.

**WEISS,     Ltn**
J18                                          –

---

**WEISS,     Ltn**
J26     (May 1918) –                         –
OzbV for Jasta 26.

---

**WEISSHAAR,     Ltn**
J65        1 Jul 1918 – 11 Nov 1918     2
Reported to Jasta 65 from Jastaschule II.

| Victories: | | | | | |
|---|---|---|---|---|---|
| 1. | 28 Aug 1918 | Balloon | 1110 | Raulecourt | (a) |
| 2. | 28 Aug 1918 | Balloon | 1112 | Gironville | (b) |

(a) USAS 9th Balloon Co, Lt S V Clark & Cpl L S Balay jumped safely.
(b) USAS 5th Balloon Co, 2/Lts J W Lake and J S Burrell jumped safely.

---

**WEIST,     Vfw**
J32b     (May 1918) –                        1

| Victories: | | | | |
|---|---|---|---|---|
| 1. | 18 May 1918 | DH4 | | Boiry |

---

**WEITZ, Friedrich     Ltn d R**
KEK Habs          – 10 Oct 1916     –          J26     18 Jan 1917 – 11 Mar 1917    2  WIA
J15       10 Oct 1916 – 18 Jan 1917    1
Born 1 November 1894, Luneberg. Served in Jdg Bat 10. Severely wounded near Iseghem, died of wounds
12 March 1917.

| Victories: | | | | | |
|---|---|---|---|---|---|
| 1. | 18 Dec 1916 | Nieuport | | Niederaspach | |
| 2. | 25 Feb 1917 | Nieuport | | SE Lutterbech | (a) |
| 3. | 11 Mar 1917 | Nieuport | 1020 | S Ammerzweiler | (b) |

(a) Probably #2409 Brigadier Rivière, N 81.
(b) Probably #2341/17 Lt Maus, N 49.

---

**WELLHAUSEN, Adolf     Vfw**
J17       11 Nov 1916 – 9 Feb 1917      – WIA
Born 12 February 1894, Essen. Previously served with FA25. Died of wounds 11 February.

---

**WELSS, Erich     Ltn**
J28w                                         –
OzbV for Jasta 28w. Knight's Cross 2nd Class with Swords of the Württemberg Friedrich Order on
25 July 1918.

---

**WELTZ, Karl     Ltn**
KG1/5                                        Oblt
J30       24 Jun 1917 – 15 Dec 1917     –     Kest 1a                – 1 Sep 1918     –
                                              Kest 9    1 Sep 1918 –
Transferred 15 December 1917 to B L Abt.

---

**WELTZ,     Ltn**
J25                                          1

| Victories: | | | | |
|---|---|---|---|---|
| 1. | 25 Apr 1917 | BE12 | | Paljorka | (a) |

(a) #7177, Lt G A Radcliffe, No 17 Sqn, RFC, KIA.

---

**WEMBER, Gustav     Ltn d R**
J61                  – 11 Nov 1918     4

| Victories: | | | | | |
|---|---|---|---|---|---|
| 1. | 3 Sep 1918 | Balloon | 1700 | Rueckkehn | |
| 2. | 24 Sep 1918 | Balloon | 0905 | | |
| 3. | 5 Oct 1918 | Balloon | 1100 | | (a) |
| 4. | 6 Oct 1918 | Spad | | | |

(a) French 51st Balloon Co.

---

**WENA,     Ltn**
J10                                          –

---

**WENDEL, Hellmuth     Ltn**
J15     (Dec 1916) – (May 1917)     1

| Victories: | | | | |
|---|---|---|---|---|
| 1. | 16 Apr 1917 | Nieuport | | Prouvais |

## WENDEL, Hewarth    Ltn
J15        (Dec 1916) – (May 1917)        –

## WENDELMUTH, Rudolf        Oblt d R
FA5                                    1            J20        19 Oct 1917 – 30 Nov 1917        3    KIA
Oblt d R J8   Apr 1917 – 19 Oct 1917        10
Biography & Victories: See *Above the Lines*.

## WENDLAND,    Ltn
J12        13 Oct 1917 – 29 Jan 1918        –            J58        28 Jan 1918 – 11 Nov 1918        –
Acting CO Jasta 58 from 12 April to 17 April; 24 April to 7 May; and 10 June to 22 July 1918.
Victories:        1.        Date and unit unknown

## WENDLAND, Friedrich        Ltn d R
FA25                – 1917                –            J24s        7 Jun 1918 – 29 Oct 1918        –
J35b        9 Mar 1917 – 21 Nov 1917        2            FEA6        29 Oct 1918 –
Kest 7        21 Nov 1917 – 7 Jun 1918        –
Born 1 June 1894, Magingen. Volunteered at mobilisation, assigned to Pioneer Battalion 7. Trained at
Fliegerschule 3 Darmstadt. Promoted Leutnant 2 February 1917. Reported to Jasta 35 from AFP B.
13 August 1917, forced to land after combat; unharmed. Iron Cross II & I Class. Awarded Bavarian
Militär-Verdeinst Orden 4 Klasse Mit Schwerten on 3 November 1917.

| Victories: | 1. | 3 Jun 1916, unit unknown | | | | |
|---|---|---|---|---|---|---|
| | 2. | Date and unit unknown | | | | |
| | 3. | 11 Aug 1917 | Nieuport | 1930 | Couckelaere | (a) |
| | 4. | 16 Aug 1917 | RE8 | 1805 | Langemarck | |

(a) B1518, 29 Sqn, RFC, Lt C G Guy, POW.

## WENDLER, Ernst        Ltn d R
KSt14        25 Jan 1916 – 1 Jul 1916        – WIA        J17        19 Jun 1917 – 1 Oct 1917        – WIA
FEA10        4 Sep 1916 – 25 May 1917        –            Kest 1b        27 Oct 1917 – 31 Jan 1918        –
JsSchI        25 May 1917 –                –            Kest 4b        31 Jan 1918 – 1 Apr 1918        –
JB        – 19 Jun 1917        –            FEA10        1 Apr 1918 – 11 Nov 1918        –
Pilot's Badge on 17 March 1916. Württemberg Gold Military Merit Medal, 29 June 1916. He was
wounded and his observer, Leutnant Erich Zimmermann, was killed, on 1 July 1916, by Major L.W.B.
Rees of No 32 Sqn, RFC. Awarded EKI. Württemberg Knight's Cross of the Military Merit Order. Shot
down on 16 September 1917, his plane was destroyed but he was not harmed. Transferred to Stoflg on
8 October 1917. Commanded Kest 1b from 31 Dec 1917 to 31 Jan 1918.

## WENDT, Albert        Gefr
J63        – 17 May 1918        – KIA
Born 19 April 1899, Berlin. Killed durng combat with a Camel near Villers Bretonneux, Albatros DVa
(G/5Bde/10); Capt L E Whitehead, No 65 Sqn, RAF, in Camel D1876.

## WENGER,    Gefr
FA17                –            FA254        12 May 1917 –                –
J29        20 Mar 1917 – 12 May 1917        –

## WENIG, Erwin        Oblt
J16        1 Nov 1916 – 6 Jan 1917        –            J28        20 Apr 1917 – 31 Oct 1917        1 WIA
FA9b        6 Jan 1917 – 27 Feb 1917        –            J65        23 Jan 1918 – 25 Jan 1918        –
JsSch I        27 Feb 1917 – 20 Apr 1917        –            CO J80b 25 Jan 1918 – 11 Nov 1918        3
Born 7 July 1893. Joined military service in 1912, assigned to 13th Bavarian Infantry Rgt. Promoted to
Leutnant 1 August 1914. Became an observer 21 September 1914. Served with FA8b from September
1915; his pilot was Uffz Otto Kissenberth. Served with KEK Ensisheim from August 1916. Shot down
in combat on both 5 and 6 June 1918, not harmed either time. Lightly wounded in action 18 June.
Awarded Eiserne Kreuz II and I Klasse, the Bavarian Militär-Verdeinst-Orden, and Saxon Ritterkreuz.

| Victories: | 1. | 2 Jun 1917 | Pup | 1910 | NE Ypern | (a) |
|---|---|---|---|---|---|---|
| | 2. | 3 May 1918 | Nieuport | 1205 | Remoncourt | (b) |
| | 3. | 17 May 1918 | AR2 | 1210 | Arracourt | |
| | 4. | 12 Sep 1918 | DH4 | | Phlyn | |

(a) Probably A6204, No 46 Sqn, RFC, Lt D R Cameron, POW.
(b) Probably 2/Lt C W Chapman, 94th Pursuit Sqn, USAS.

**WENN, Peter      Uffz**
J57        22 Feb 1918 – 2 Apr 1918      –  WIA
Born 13 October 1888, Merode. Severely wounded during combat with Camels, between Quesnoy and Wambrechies, died of wounds. Possibly by Capt S T Edwards of No 209 Sqn, RAF.

**WENSE, Bodo von der      Ltn**
J8            – Jul 1918        –            J6        6 Aug 1918 – 11 Aug 1918    –  KIA
JsSch      Jul 1918 – 6 Aug 1918    –
Born 31 May 1895, Ostindien. Transferred to Jastaschule I from Jasta 8. Killed near Péronne-Herbecourt.

**WENZ, Alfred      Ltn**
J11        26 Jul 1918 – 20 Oct 1918    –            J4        20 Oct 1918 – 11 Nov 1918    –
Born 4 December 1897. Served in the infantry from 1914 to early 1918. Joined Jasta 4 from Jastaschule I. Collided with Oblt Erich Löwenhardt during a combat on 10 August 1918, but made a safe parachute descent; Löwenhardt was killed. Died 12 February 1969, Garmisch, Germany.

**WENZEL, Paul      Ltn d R**
FA23        1916 – 1917        –            J6        Feb 1918 – 11 Aug 1918    10 WIA
J41          1917 – (Feb 1918)    –
Biography & Victories: See *Above the Lines*.

**WENZL, Richard      Ltn d R**
FAA236                                 –            J11        27 Mar 1918 – 17 May 1918    1
KeKOst          – 1917            –            J6        17 May 1918 – 20 Oct 1918    5
J31          (Apr 1917 – 27 Mar 1918    2            J4        20 Oct 1918 – 11 Nov 1918    4
Biography & Victories: See *Above the Lines*.

**WEPPEN, Waldemar von der      OfStv**
J27        15 Dec 1917 – 7 May 1918    –  KIA
Born 9 August 1894, Meiswich. Killed over Ypern.

**WERKMEISTER, August      Uffz**
J10        23 Sep 1917 – 25 Sep 1917    –  KIA
Born 23 January 1893, Werste. Shot down in flames at 1742 hours over Houthulsterwald; probably by No 56 Sqn, RFC.

**WERNEBURG,      Uffz**
J35b        18 Aug 1918 – 11 Nov 1918    –
Joined Jasta 35b from Jastaschule I.

**WERNER, Adolf      Vfw**
J17        10 Jul 1917 – 29 May 1918    2            FEA9    29 May 1918 –            –
Joined Jasta 17 from AFP4.
Victories:      1.        17 Jul 1917        BF2b            0930        Middelkerke        (a)
              2.        27 Jul 1917        2-seater        1515        S Dixmuiden
(a) BF2b A7166, Lt R B Hay, MC, (P) KIA & Lt O J Partington (O) POW.

**WERNER, Hans      Ltn d R**
J19        26 Oct 1916 – 16 Dec 1916    –            J1        16 Dec 1916 –            –
Previously served with Kagohl 1.

**WERNER, Herbert      Vfw**
J26            – 25 Jan 1918    1  KIA
Born 4 February 1894, Annaburg. Killed between Stadenberghe and Staden.
Victories:      1.        18 Dec 1917        Camel            1245        N Zillebekesee

**WERNER, Johannes      Ltn d R**
Unknown                    1            J14        5 Sep 1917 – 11 Nov 1918    6
Biography & Victories: See *Above the Lines*.

**WERNER,      Ltn d R**
J45        22 Aug 1918 – 18 Oct 1918    –
Hospitalised on 18 October 1918.

## WERNICKE, Karl    Ltn d R
J43        13 Jun 1918 – 16 Jul 1918     –   KIAcc
Born 14 January 1897, Vleicherode. Shortly after take-off his phosphorus ammo self-ignited causing him to crash where he died in his burning aircraft.

## WESTARP, von     Ltn
J15                                    –

## WESTPHAL, Siegfried     Uffz
J29        28 Jul 1918 – 11 Nov 1918   6
Biography & Victories: See *Above the Lines*.

## WEVER, Ernst     Ltn
J6        10 Sep 1916 – 16 Nov 1916    –   KIA
Born 19 December 1895, Petropolis. Shot down in flames over Pressoire Wald, near St Quentin.

## WEWER, Karl     Ltn
J26        18 Jan 1917 – 23 Dec 1917   3        FEA10    23 Dec 1917 –
Wounded in action 29 November 1917.

| Victories: | 1. | 21 Jun 1917 | Nieuport | 1145 | NE Becelaere | (a) |
|---|---|---|---|---|---|---|
| | 2. | 27 Jul 1917 | Camel | 2040 | Zonnebeke | |
| | 3. | 17 Oct 1917 | Camel | 1630 | SW Nieuport | |

(a) Probably B3495, No 1 Sqn, RFC, 2/Lt T M McFerren, POW.

## WICHARD, Friedrich-Wilhelm     Ltn d R
FEA8        13 Oct 1915 – 12 May 1916    –        FAA257    28 Sep 1916 – 28 Jan 1917    –
FA58        13 May 1916 – 27 Sep 1916    –        J24        28 Jan 1917 – 21 Apr 1917    – POW
Born 21 May 1894, Kassel. Entered military service 17 August 1914, with Infantry Regiment 83. Promoted Leutnant d R 20 March 1915. Wounded in action 13 June 1915. Assigned to aviation 13 October 1915. OzbV for Jasta 24. Shot down and taken prisoner during combat with some Spads flying Albatros DIII 2096/16 ('Vera'). Took off at 1810 hours. Possibly downed by Lieutenant Armand Pinsard of Escadrille N78 at 1830 hours. Attained rank of Major-General in Luftwaffe during WWII. Died 6 May 1968, Dortmund.

## WIEBE,     Oblt
J45        20 Aug 1918 –                –

## WIEDENMANN, Johann     Ltn d R
Kest 8        – 17 Oct 1917     – KIA
Born 11 September 1894, Heidenheim, Württemberg. Killed by Ostende-Zevecote.

## WIEHLE, Adolf     Ltn d R
J24        5 Jul 1917 – 18 Jul 1917     –        J20        18 Jul 1917 – 15 Sep 1917    – KIA
Born 16 February 1892, Debeleben. Served in Reserve Infantry Regiment 72. Joined Jasta 24 from AFP4. Killed in action over Nieuport, his plane exploded in the air.

## WIEHLE, Ernst     Vfw
SS3        7 Feb 1917 – 1918        1        J43        5 Jun 1918 – 11 Nov 1918   5
JsSch        – 5 Jun 1918        –
Biography & Victories: See *Above the Lines*.

## WIELAND, Philipp     Ltn d R
| FEA3 | 12 May 1915 – 13 Jul 1915 | – | CO J27 | 22 Feb 1917 – 5 May 1917 | – WIA |
|---|---|---|---|---|---|
| AFP4 | 13 Jul 1915 – 19 Jul 1915 | – | CO J27 | 17 May 1917 – 20 May 1917 | – |
| FFA3 | 19 Jul 1915 – 15 Apr 1916 | – | J8 | 20 May 1917 – 13 Jun 1917 | – WIA |
| KshI | 15 Apr 1916 – 15 May 1916 | – | J1 | 18 Jan 1918 – 7 Mar 1918 | – |
| FFA57 | 15 May 1916 – 25 Jun 1916 | – | J72 | 7 Mar 1918 – 27 Mar 1918 | – |
| FFA6 | 26 Jun 1916 – 14 Sep 1916 | 1 | AFP3 | 27 Mar 1918 – 3 Apr 1918 | – |
| J8 | 14 Sep 1916 – 20 Jan 1917 | – | Kofl3 | 3 Apr 1918 – 3 Jun 1918 | – |
| JsSchI | 20 Jan 1917 – 20 Feb 1917 | – | AFP3 | 3 Jun 1918 – 11 Nov 1918 | – |

Awarded EKII on 19 October 1914, with a Field Artillery Regiment, Nr.13 König Karl (1.W). Pilot's Badge on 1 August 1915. Württemberg Gold Military Merit Medal on 20 Sept 1915. Awarded EKI 26 March 1916. Wounded in combat 5 May 1917. Knight's Cross of the Württemberg Military Merit Order.

Württemberg Knight 2nd Class with Swords of the Friedrich Order on 8 November 1918.
Victories:        1.        6 Sep 1916        BE2                #7070

## WIELAND, Johann        Vfw
J68        6 Mar 1918 – 11 Apr 1918        1    KIA
Born 2 July 1894, Bonn. Killed in a bombing attack on his airfield at Balâtre.
Victories:        1.        2 Apr 1918        Sopwith 2        0720        Broyes

## WIEPRICH, Otto        Vfw
FAA250 (Gefr)                1                Vfw J57    22 Feb 1918 – 11 Nov 1918        3
Nicknamed 'Piple'. Other crew member on first victory, Ltn Reuschle. 27 June 1918 shot down during
combat with Camels, between Albert and Bapaume, fuel tank hit and forced to land, unharmed.
Victories:        1.        29 Nov 1917        DH5                        Dunkirk-Furnes
                 2.        17 Apr 1918        SE5                1510        N Hazebrouck
                 3.        19 May 1918        SE5                2030        Moorslede
                 4.        29 Aug 1918        DH9                        W Epinoy

## WIESNER, Rudolf        Vfw
J39                – 4 Feb 1918        –    KIA
Born 15 November 1893, Breslau. Killed at 1300 hours, near Vittorio, Italy.

## WIESSNER, Ernst        Ltn d R
FFA250        Jan 1917 – 10 Feb 1917        –                J18        10 Feb 1917 – 7 Jun 1917        5    KIA
Biography & Victories: See *Above the Lines*.

## WIGAN,        Ltn
J12                – 3 Jan 1918        –    POW

## WIGAND, Paul        Ltn d R
J3                – 10 Dec 1917        –    KIAcc
Born 26 September 1895, Göttengen. Field Artillery Regiment 102. Killed in an accident during a test
flight near Waterdammhoek.

## WILDE,        Ltn d R
J4        Sep 1917 – 6 Apr 1918        1                J73        6 Apr 1918 – 11 Nov 1918        –
Served as OzbV for Jasta 73, 25 April 1918 to end of war.
Victories:        1.        5 Oct 1917        Triplane        0750        E Dadizeele

## WILHELM, Alfred        Ltn
J77b        8 Oct 1918 – 14 Oct 1918        –                J34b        14 Oct 1918 – 11 Nov 1918        –
Joined Jasta 77b from Jastaschule I.

## WILHELM, Leo        Uffz
J34        6 Jun 1917 – 2 Jul 1917        –                Kest 7        2 Jul 1917 –        –
Joined Jasta 34 from AFP C.

## WILHELM, Wilhelm        Ltn d R
J64w        30 Jan 1918 – 11 Nov 1918        –
Served as OzbV for Jasta 64w.

## WILKE,        Flg
J12        (Sep 1918) – 11 Nov 1918        1
Victories:        1.        18 Sep 1918        Bréguet        1730        SW Conflans

## WILLISCH,        Ltn
J27                – 14 Oct 1918        1    WIA
Victories:        1.        8 Oct 1918

## WILLMANN, Max        Vfw
J30        18 Jul 1917 – 21 Sep 1917        –                AFP6        21 Sep 1917 –        –
Victories:        1.        Date and unit unknown

## WILPERT, von        Ltn
J36        11 Aug 1918 – 11 Nov 1918        –

## WIMMER, Max    Vfw
J28        27 Apr 1917 – 12 May 1917    –  WIA
Served in Schusta 22 before joining Jasta 28. Severely wounded over Ypern.

## WIMMER,    Vfw
J80b        18 Jun 1918 – 11 Nov 1918    –
Joined Jasta 80b from Jastaschule I.

## WINDISCH, Rudolf    Vfw / Ltn d R

| | | | | | | |
|---|---|---|---|---|---|---|
| FA62 | 1 May 1916 – 24 Nov 1916 | 1 | | J50 | 10 Jan 1918 – 24 Jan 1918 | – |
| KG2 | 24 Nov 1916 – 20 Feb 1917 | – | | J66 | 24 Jan 1918 – 27 May 1918 | 14 POW |
| J32 | 20 Feb 1917 – 10 Jan 1918 | 7 | | | | |

Biography & Victories: See *Above the Lines*.

## WINDMÜLLER, Erich    Vfw
J9            – 19 Feb 1918    –  KIA
Born 14 June 1887, Berlin. Killed in action with two Spads at 1145 hours over Tahure.

## WINKELMANN, Max    Vzflgmstr
J5            – 26 Jan 1917    –  POW
Shot down by AA fire in British lines.

## WINKLER,    Gefr
J36        22 Sep 1918 – 5 Nov 1918    –          FEA11    5 Nov 1918 –                    –

## WINTER,    Uffz
J68        24 Jun 1918 – 12 Aug 1918    –  WIA
Hit by AA fire.

## WINTERFELD, Joachim von    Ltn
J4        24 Apr 1918 – 5 Sep 1918    2  KIA
Born 16 September 1896, Wiesendorf-Cottbus. Killed at 1900 hours, between Avesnes-le-Sec and St
Amand, during combat with SE5s. Parachute failed to open. Fokker DVII (G/3Bde/17); claimed by Capt
G M Duncan, No 60 Sqn, RAF.

| Victories: | 1. | 3 May 1918 | AWFK8 | 2005 | S Blangy-Tronville |
|---|---|---|---|---|---|
| | 2. | 10 May 1918 | Camel | 2030 | N Hamel |

## WINTGENS, Kurt    Ltn

| | | | | | | |
|---|---|---|---|---|---|---|
| FFA67 | 1915 – 1915 | – | | FA6b | 1916 – 1916 | 5 |
| FA6b | 1915 – 1915 | – | | KeKV | 1916 – 25 Aug 1916 | 5 |
| FA48 | 5 Jul 1915 – 1916 | 3 | | J1 | 25 Aug 1916 – 25 Sep 1916 | 6  KIA |

Biography & Victories: See *Above the Lines*.

## WINTRATH, Johannes    Ltn d R
JB        20 Feb 1917 – 25 Sep 1917    1  KIA
Born 13 September 1893, Dortmund. Served in FAA221 from 27 Nov 1916 to 20 Feb 1917. Shot down
in flames and killed at 1230 hours, near Westende-Bad.

| Victories: | 1. | 17 Aug 1917 | Camel | 0815 | Spermelle |
|---|---|---|---|---|---|
| | – | 19 Aug 1917 | Camel | 1745 | Oostdunkerke |

## WIRTH, Hermann    Flg
J32b            – 3 Sep 1918    –  KIA
Born 23 April 1895, Heimbrechts. Killed over Douai.

## WIRTH, Max    Ltn d R
J34        15 Aug 1917 – 21 Aug 1917    –  KIA
Born 6 November 1890, Bad Reichenhall. Killed NW Etain.

## WIRTH, Robert    Gefr

| | | | | | | | |
|---|---|---|---|---|---|---|---|
| SS10 | | | 2 | Vfw | J37 – 26 Sep 1918 | 2  WIA | |
| Victories: | 1. | 22 Sep 1917 | Sopwith | | Boesinghe | | (a) |
| | 2. | 22 Sep 1917 | Sopwith | | Pypegaale | | (a) |
| | 3. | 8 Aug 1918 | Camel | | Warfussée | | |
| | 4. | 24 Sep 1918 | BF2b | 0830 | S Beauvois | | |

(a) Observer, Uffz Noethen.

**WIRTH,    Ltn**
J7       (May 1918) – (Jul 1918)        –

**WIRTZ,    Ltn**
J3                      – 1917          –        J7        14 Jun 1918 – 11 Nov 1918    –

**WIRTZ,    Ltn**
J15            1917 –                   –

**WISSEMANN, Kurt    Ltn d R**
J3       28 May 1917 – 28 Sep 1917    5   KIA
(Also flew with FA250; WIA 30 Apr 1917, as an observer.)
Biography & Victories: See *Above the Lines*.

**WISTERMANN, Fritz    Uffz**
J1                      – 22 Jun 1917        –   WIA

**WITT, Hans    Oblt d R**
J46       (Apr 1918) – 19 May 1918     –   KIA
Born 19 July 1891, Graudenz. Killed over Cachy, N Amiens, flying an Albatros DV: credited to Captain
A F W Beauchamp Proctor, No 84 Sqn, RAF, in SE5a C1772.

**WITTCHEN,    Vfw**
J12       12 Jun 1918 – 11 Nov 1918    2
Victories:        1.       30 Oct 1918       Spad XI             1230           Verpel
                  2.        3 Nov 1918       Spad                1625           Sommauthe

**WITTEKIND, Kurt    Ltn d R**
J8                      –                          Idflieg    20 Jun 1918 –                    –
J28w      25 Jan 1917 – 20 Jun 1918    2
Awarded EKI. Awarded Silberne Militär-Verdeinstmedaille, 3 May 1918. Knight's Cross 2nd Class with
Swords of the Württemberg Friedrich Order on 6 June 1918. Died 26 November 1918.
Victories:         –        9 May 1917       Sopwith             1900           Wytschaetebogen
                  1.        4 Jun 1917       SE5                 0840           NE Ypern              (a)
                  2.       12 Jun 1917       SE5                 1100           Wytschaete
(a) A8920, No 56 Sqn, RFC, Lt T M Dickinson.

**WITTENFELD,    Vfw**
SchSt14                    –                          FEA4       19 Aug 1918 –                    –
J50                     – 19 Aug 1918     –

**WITTENHAGEN,    Ltn**
J26                     – 9 Oct 1917        –        J31                     – 5 Mar 1918      1
J39        9 Oct 1917 –                    –        J73        5 Mar 1918 – 11 Nov 1918    –
Victories:        1.       20 Feb 1918       Camel                              Marco

**WITTKE, Alexander    Sgt**
J9                      – 1 Aug 1918        –   KIAcc
Born 1 August 1894, Koblenz. Killed in an accident at 1700 hours near the Maizy airfield while flying
a two-seater; the passenger, Ltn Böving, was also killed.

**WITTMANN, Ludwig    Uffz**
J78b      12 Jun 1918 – 25 Jun 1918     –        J8ob       25 Jun 1918 – 14 Aug 1918    – POW
Born 2 August 1898, Wolnzach-Markt, Bavaria. Joined military service in January 1917. Joined Jasta
78b from Jastaschule I. Flying Albatros DV 6831 when shot down near Mandray, south of St Die, at
1700 hours. Shot down by a RAF pilot (see French II Armée Prisoner Interrogation Report).

**WOHLGEMUTH,    Ltn**
J26                     – 11 Nov 1918     –

**WOITALLA,    Uffz**
J12                     – 28 Jun 1918     –

**WOLF, Werner    Ltn**
J51                     –

## WOLF,      Ltn
J5          (Jun 1917) – (Jul 1917)    1
Victories:      1.          Date and unit unknown
                2.          27 Jul 1917        Sopwith           2103              Esquerchin

## WOLFF, Erich      Ltn d R
J55                 – 9 May 1918   –  KIA
Born 10 December 1892, Nieder-Gutsdorf. Killed over Djenin.

## WOLFF, Fritz      Uffz
J17         12 Jun 1918 – 11 Nov 1918    1
Victories:      1.          2 Sep 1918         Spad              1930              Savigny

## WOLFF, Hans Joachim      Ltn
FAA216              – 6 Jul 1917        –              J11        6 Jul 1917 – 16 May 1918    10 KIA
Biography & Victories: See *Above the Lines*.

## WOLFF, Jakob      Ltn d L
J17         11 Nov 1916 – 27 Jul 1917    4  WIA
Joined Jasta 17 from AFP5. Promoted to Leutnant on 6 May 1917. Awarded Iron Cross 1st Class and
Rettungsmedaille. Died 4 December 1926.
Victories:      –           2 Feb 1917         Voisin                              S Regineville
                1.          9 Feb 1917         Voisin                              E Martincourt
                2.          28 Apr 1917        Caudron           0830              Brimont
                3.          30 May 1917        Balloon           1415              Berry-au-Bac
                4.          27 Jul 1917        Farman            1635              SW Dixmuiden

## WOLFF, Kurt      Oblt
J11         12 Oct 1916 – 2 May 1917     29             CO J11     28 Jun 1917 – 11 Jul 1917    2  WIA
CO J29      2 May 1917 – 28 Jun 1917     2              CO J11     11 Sep 1917 – 15 Sep 1917    –  KIA
Biography & Victories: See *Above the Lines*.

## WOLFF, Paul      Ltn d R
J13                 – 14 Sep 1918   –  POW
Shot down over Lake Lachaussée, at 1510 hours in a Fokker DVII; POW #627 A.

## WOLFF, Walter      Vfw
J55         Jan 1918 – 11 Nov 1918    –
Joined Jasta 55 from Jastaschule II.

## WOLFF,      Ltn d R
J6          Jan 1918 – 19 Apr 1918    –  WIA       Idflieg    20 Sep 1918 –                     –
J6          10 Aug 1918 – 27 Aug 1918    –  INJ
Wounded in action on 12 April 1918. Severely injured during a forced landing near Nesle.

## WOLFF,      Ltn d R
J45         27 Aug 1918 – 4 Sep 1918    1              J60        4 Sep 1918 – 11 Nov 1918    –
Joined Jasta 45 from Jastaschule II.
Victories:      1.          28 Sep 1918        Spad              1315              Vienne-le-Château

## WOLFSKEEL, Hans-Karl Fr von      Oblt
J34b        18 Feb 1918 – 19 Feb 1918    –  KIA
Born 27 March 1892, Reichenberg. Served in 11th Field Artillery Regiment. Joined Jasta 34b from
Jastaschule II. Killed in action during combat with Spads over Mort Homme near Verdun.

## WOLLSKI, Josef      OfStv
J51                 – 15 May 1918   –  KIA
Born 1 January 1888, Scheuri. Killed over Zillebeke See.

## WORTMANN, Hans      Ltn d R
JB          Nov 1916 – 2 Apr 1917    2  KIA
Born 19 July 1895, Loschwitz. Killed at 0950 hours, during combat with FE2ds over Vitry-en-Artois.
Victories:      1.          9 Nov 1916         Nieuport          1055              SW Le Transloy
                2.          20 Dec 1916        FE2b              1405              Sapignies

**WOSSANDLO,    Vfw**
J65        30 Oct 1918 – 11 Nov 1918    –

---

**WREGE, Theodor     Ltn d R**
J39                  – 14 Jan 1918    – KIA
Born 13 March 1897, Rubersdorf. Killed near Conegliano.

---

**WRONIECKI, Anton     Vfw**
J64w      21 Feb 1918 – 14 Apr 1918    – POW
Reported to Jasta 64w from AFP5. Shot down wounded and taken prisoner by 1/Lt Douglas Campbell, 94th Aero Sqn, USAS, over Toul airfield at 0952 hours.

---

**WÜBBEN,     Ltn**
J14                                  –
Lightly wounded in action 2 July 1918.

---

**WÜNSCHE,     Ltn**
J58        5 Oct 1918 – 11 Nov 1918    –

---

**WÜST, August     Ltn d R**
J42                  – 15 Aug 1918    – KIA
Born 22 December 1892, Karlsruhe. Killed over the Forest of Thiescourt.

---

**WÜSTHOFF, Kurt     Vfw / Ltn d R**
KG1          1915 –                         JGI      16 Mar 1918 – 16 Jun 1918    – (Staff)
J4       Jul 1917 – 16 Mar 1918    27       J15      16 Jun 1918 – 17 Jun 1918    – POW
Biography & Victories: See *Above the Lines*.

---

**WULFF, Josef     Rittm**
KG5/29              – 25 Aug 1916    1       Ober-
CO J6   25 Aug 1916 – 1 May 1917    2       Ost      30 Jun 1917 – 8 Apr 1918     –
                                            AFP7     8 Apr 1918 –                 –
Transferred to Stofl Heimat 1 May 1917. Commanded Jagdflieger Ober-Ost, 30 June 1917 to 8 April 1918. Awarded Ritterkreuz des Hausorden von Hohenzollern mit Schwerten on 10 December 1917.
Victories:       1.        Date and unit unknown, probably with Kasta 29
                 2.        3 Nov 1916        2-seater
                 3.        9 Nov 1916        Caudron

---

**WULFFEN, von     Ltn**
J52      6 Jun 1918 – 29 Jun 1918    –       J14      29 Jun 1918 – (Jul 1918)    1
Joined Jasta 52 from Jastaschule I.
Victories:       1.        8 Jul 1918        Camel        2030        Pont-à-Vendin

---

**WUNDERLICH, Leonard     Uffz**
J48        7 Aug 1918 –                –
Joined Jasta 48 from Jastaschule II.

---

**WUNNENBURG,     Vfw**
J60                  – 30 Jun 1918    – WIA    J60                  – 11 Nov 1918    –

---

**WUNSCH, Alfred     Ltn d R**
FAA220  16 Sep 1916 – 12 Jan 1917    –       J22s     22 Feb 1917 – 28 Jan 1918    –
FAA278  14 Jan 1917 –                –       J67      28 Jan 1918 – 1
Born 6 August 1892, Offenberg. Awarded EK II on 23 December 1914. Promoted Unteroffizier 10 February 1915, and Vizefeldwebel 30 March 1915. Transferred to aviation and reported to FEA7 on 14 June 1916. Flugzeugführer-Abzeichen on 19 November 1916. Promoted Leutnant d R on 26 June 1917. Awarded EKI on 14 September 1917. Awarded the Baden Ritterkreuz II Klasse Zähringer Löwen Orden mit Schwerten on 8 December 1917. Wounded in action 13 May 1918; remained with Jasta. Demobilised 7 December 1918.
Victories:       –        22 Dec 1916        Sopwith 2        1530        Vivaise
                 1.        30 Jun 1918        Salmson
(See *OTF* Journal, Vol 4, No 4, winter 1989, pg 340.)

**WURL,    Ltn**
J19        26 Oct 1916 – 11 Mar 1917    –              Idflieg    11 Mar 1917 –                    –
Previously served with Kampfstaffel 1.

---

**WURMB, Georg von      Ltn d R**
J12        (Sep 1918) – 11 Nov 1918    –
OzbV for Jasta 12.

---

**WURZMANN, Reinhold      Vfw**
J20        8 Nov 1916 – 23 Jan 1917    –              J20        28 Feb 1917 – 6 Apr 1917      – KIA
FA267A     23 Jan 1917 – 28 Feb 1917    –
Born 16 November 1893, Frankfurt. Killed near Maray, down in flames.

---

**ZACHER, Ludwig      Vfw**
J79b                    – 19 Oct 1918    – KIA
Born 23 May 1886, Pleinting. Killed near Chimay.

---

**ZACHMANN, Max      Vfw**
J21        (Apr 1917) –                            1
Collided with Vfw Spudich over Vauquois, on 21 August 1917, but managed to land safely with a damaged aircraft. Spudich was killed.

Victories:        1.        15 Apr 1917        Spad 7                1030            Sery            (a)
(a) Probably 1059, N 15, Lt Bergeron, POW.

---

**ZAHLER, Heinrich      Ltn**
J16b       5 Oct 1917 – 1 Dec 1917    –              J78b       17 Dec 1917 –                    –
AFP7       1 Dec 1917 – 17 Dec 1917    –
Served as OzbV for Jasta 78b.

---

**ZANDER, Martin      Hptm**
FFA90                                –              J1         22 Aug 1916 – 10 Nov 1916    3
CO KeKN                 – 22 Aug 1916    2
Biography & Victories: See *Above the Lines*.

---

**ZANDER,    Oblt**
J11        29 Sep 1918 – 11 Nov 1918    –
OzbV for Jasta 11.

---

**ZANY,**
J28        (May 1917) –                    –

---

**ZASTROW, Hellmuth von      Ltn**
FA60       May 1915 –                    –              Idflieg    4 Nov 1916 –                    –
J2         10 Sep 1916 – 4 Nov 1916    –
Born 15 November 1890, Berlin. Assigned to Flieger-Bataillon Nr.1, 1 Sep 1914. Obtained pilot's certificate on 23 Oct 1914. Assigned to Festungsfliegerabteilung at Graudenz, on 15 December 1914. Promoted Leutnant in February 1915. Awarded EKII. Promoted to Oberleutnant and from early 1917 served in the Office of the Inspector General for Air in Berlin. OzbV for Jasta 2.

---

**ZECH, Arthur      Ltn d R**
J36        7 Sep 1917 – 12 Oct 1917    –              FA19       12 Oct 1917 –                    –
Infantry Regiment 70. Promoted Leutnant 7 August 1915. Joined Jasta 36 from Jastaschule I.

---

**ZECH, Werner      Oblt**
FEA1                    – 14 Jun 1915    –              J1         7 Apr 1917 – 9 Sep 1917      3
FA12       14 Jun 1915 – 1 Jan 1916    –              CO J31     6 Sep 1917 – 2 Jun 1918      –
FA42       30 Jun 1916 – 9 Jul 1916    –              FEA8       2 Jun 1918 – Aug 1918        –
J14        6 Oct 1916 – 6 Apr 1917    –              FEA1       Aug 1918 – 11 Nov 1918       –
Born 25 February 1895, Stuttgart. Entered military service 25 June 1913, as Fahrenjunker in Infantry Regiment 125. Fähnrich on 11 February 1914. Promoted Leutnant 7 August 1914. Awarded EK II on 8 January 1915. Transferred to aviation 21 February 1915, for observer training. Württemberg Friedrich Order Knight 2nd Class on 22 Feb 1915. Served as an observer from 14 June 1915 to 9 July 1916. Awarded EKI on 20 June 1916. Pilot's training at Fokker-Kampfflieger-Abteilung A 10 July to 5 October 1916. Austrian Military Merit Cross 3rd Class with War Decoration on 22 Dec 1917. Württemberg

Knight's Cross of the Military Merit Order on 20 February 1918. Promoted to Oberleutnant on 22 March 1918. Transferred to Idflieg on 30 May 1918. Commanded Fliegerschule Graudenz/FEA8, 31 May 1918 to 15 August 1918. Commanded Fliegerschule Altenburg/FEA1, 16 August 1918 to 9 November 1918. Attained rank of Major-General in the Luftwaffe during WWII. Died 6 October 1981, Stuttgart.

| Victories: | 1. | 2 May 1917 | Balloon | 1900 | Vauxtin |
|---|---|---|---|---|---|
| | 2. | 5 May 1917 | Nieuport | 1105 | Aizy |
| | 3. | 7 May 1917 | Spad | 1600 | Martigny |

## ZECH,    Ltn
J31        (Apr 1917) – (Mar 1918)    –

## ZECH,    Ltn d R
J43        30 Jun 1918 –              –

## ZECHLIN,    Ltn
J1         (Sep 1916) – (Dec 1916)    –

## ZELL,    Gefr
J42                                   2
| Victories: | 1. | 10 Mar 1918 | AR2 | | Les Paroches |
|---|---|---|---|---|---|
| | 2. | 10 May 1918 | AR2 | | |

## ZELLNER, Ludwig    Gefr
J32b           – 31 Jul 1918      – KIA
Born 20 May 1892, Freising. Shot down in flames at 2056 hours over Hendecourt-les-Cagnicourt.

## ZEMPEL, Heinrich    Ltn d R
J37        – 15 May 1918 –        J65    15 May 1918 –                    1
17 July 1918, parachuted from his burning aircraft and was slightly injured.
| Victories: | 1. | 13 Jun 1918 | DH4 | 1245 | Uekingen |
|---|---|---|---|---|---|

## ZENCOMINIERSKI, Lothar    Ltn d R
Kest 2           – 4 Apr 1917    –        J45    22 Dec 1917 – 11 Nov 1918    3
J32b       4 Apr 1917 – 22 Dec 1917    –
Born 12 May 1896, Haidau/Liegnitz. Volunteered 2 August 1914, assigned to Jägerbattln 5. 1915 served in Infantry Regiment 36. Promoted Leutnant 22 March 1915. Wounded in left hand 1915. Transferred to Fliegerei in April 1916. From October 1916 to November 1918 he served with Kest 2, Kest 4, Kest 8, FA276, Jasta 32b, and Jasta 45. Acting CO Jasta 45 at various times in 1918. Awarded Iron Cross 2nd and 1st Class. Awarded Schleisischen Adler I & II Klasse.

| Victories: | zlg | 30 Oct 1917 | AR2 | | Oulchews |
|---|---|---|---|---|---|
| | 1. | 4 Jul 1918 | Bréguet | 2000 | Villers-Cotterets |
| | 2. | 5 Jul 1918 | Bréguet | 1000 | Neuilly |
| | 3. | 30 Jul 1918 | Spad | 1150 | Coincy |

## ZENTZYTZKI, Stanislaus    Ltn
J17        5 Jul 1917 – 18 Dec 1917    – INJ
Born 5 April 1896. Field Artillery Regiment 20. OzbV for Jasta 17. Severely injured at Bohain, while flying as a passenger in a two-seater; died of injuries.

## ZETTLEMAYER,    Oblt
J29                          –         J5    21 Mar 1918 – 11 Nov 1918    –
Awarded EK I. Adjutant for Jagdgruppe 11, 24 Aug 1917 to 21 Mar 1918. Adjutant for Jagdgruppe 2, 21 Mar 1918 to EOW.

## ZEUMER, Georg    Oblt
FA4        1914 –               JB    Apr 1917 – 17 Jun 1917    – KIA
KG2            –            4
Born 7 March 1890, Nikolei. Awarded the Knight's Cross of the Military St Henry Order on 17 November 1914, for service with FA4. Flew as Manfred von Richthofen's pilot while he served with FA69 on the Eastern front. Served with KG2 before going to Jasta B. Killed at 1000 hours, after combat with an RE8 SE Honnecourt and La Ferrière.

| Victories: | 1. | Date and unit unknown |
|---|---|---|
| | 2. | Date and unit unknown |
| | 3. | Date and unit unknown |
| | 4. | Date and unit unknown |

## ZICKE,
J8          –

## ZIEGESAR, Joachim von    Ltn

| | | | | | |
|---|---|---|---|---|---|
| FA23 | | – | J18 | 15 Mar 1918 – 18 Mar 1918 | – |
| J4 | 1 Oct 1916 – 16 Oct 1916 | – | J15 | 18 Mar 1918 – 11 Nov 1918 | 3 |
| J14 | 16 Oct 1916 – 15 Mar 1918 | – | | | |

Acting CO Jasta 15 from 13 Aug 1918 to 18 Aug 1918.

| Victories: | 1. | 6 Jun 1918 | DH9 | 1140 | Maignelay |
|---|---|---|---|---|---|
| | – | 9 Aug 1918 | Sopwith | 1830 | W Le Quesnel |
| | 2. | 26 Sep 1918 | Spad XIII | 1740 | Pont-à-Mousson |
| | 3. | 29 Oct 1918 | Bréguet | | Champigneulle |

## ZIEGLER, Günther    Uffz

| | | | | | | |
|---|---|---|---|---|---|---|
| FEA3 | 11 Aug 1914 – 9 Dec 1914 | – | | J26 | 18 Jan 1917 – 27 Aug 1917 | – |
| OfStv | | | | AFP4 | 28 Aug 1917 – 30 Oct 1917 | – |
| FAGaede | 10 Dec 1914 – 4 Feb 1915 | – | WIA | CO | | |
| Ltn d R | | | | Kest7 | 31 Oct 1917 – 31 Mar 1918 | – |
| FA65 | 4 Nov 1915 – 17 Jan 1917 | – | | FEA10 | 1 Apr 1918 – 11 Nov 1918 | – |

Born 9 February 1892, Deutsch-Lissa/Schleisen. Entered military service 1 October 1912, assigned to Luftshiffer-Bataillon I. Promoted Gefreiter 1 June 1913; Unteroffizier 1 September 1913; Vizefeldwebel 20 November 1914; Offizierstellvertreter 24 December 1914. Pilot's training FEA3 from 11 August 1914 to 9 December 1914. Wounded in action 4 February 1915, hospitalised until 4 May 1915. Pilot's training at FEA3 and 6, and Fliegerschule Mockau, from 5 May 1915 to 4 November 1915. Promoted Leutnant d R on 13 December 1915. Attained rank of Lieutenant General in the Luftwaffe during WWII. Died 31 December 1945.

## ZIEGLER gen STEGE, Maximilian    Oblt

| | | | | | | | |
|---|---|---|---|---|---|---|---|
| J26 | 18 Jan 1917 – 1 Aug 1917 | 2 | | CO J41 | 1 Aug 1917 – 3 Sep 1917 | – | KIAcc |

Born 2 June 1889, Bonn. Killed at Flugplatz Ensisheim.

| Victories: | 1. | 27 Jul 1917 | Martinsyde | 0800 | SW Langemarck | |
|---|---|---|---|---|---|---|
| | 2. | 27 Jul 1917 | SE5 | 0805 | W Moorslede | (a) |

(a) Probably SE5a 8911, 2/Lt T W White, No 56 Sqn, RFC, MIA.

## ZIESKE,    Gefr
J73    21 May 1918 –          –

## ZIETLOW, Walter    Oblt
J9    5 Oct 1916 – 10 Feb 1917    –   KIA
Born 4 December 1891, Alt Werder. Killed at 1030 hours near Hauvine-Leffincourt, during combat with two Nieuports, probably by Lt Georges Guynemer, N3, but unconfirmed.

## ZIFFER, Erich    Ltn
J69          – 12 Apr 1918    –   POW

## ZILCHER,    Ltn
J1    Jan 1917 – (May 1917)    1

| Victories: | 1. | 1 May 1917 | EA | 1300 | Révillon-Vailly |
|---|---|---|---|---|---|

## ZILLIG, Georg    Uffz
J79b          – 26 Jun 1918    –   INJ
Born 26 June 1895, Lichtenfels. Severely injured during a test flight; died of wounds 28 June.

## ZIMMERMANN,    Gefr
J35b          – 11 Oct 1917    –   INJ

## ZIMMERMANN,    Vfw
J60          – 11 Nov 1918    1

| Victories: | 1. | 27 Sep 1918 | Spad | 1820 | Tahure |
|---|---|---|---|---|---|

## ZOGMANN,    Ltn
J26    (Dec 1917) – (Mar 1918)    –

### ZOGMANN, Fritz    Uffz

| | | | | | |
|---|---|---|---|---|---|
| J39 | | – 15 Nov 1917 | 1 | J26 | 15 Nov 1917 – 26 Oct 1918   – KIA |

Born 9 April 1893, Berlin. Shot down in flames over Soultain.

| Victories: | 1. | 2 Nov 1917 | Hanriot | 1608 | W San Giovanni |
|---|---|---|---|---|---|

### ZOPF, Fritz    Uffz

J8ob      8 May 1918 – 10 May 1918   –  KIAcc

Born 4 June 1892, Nürnberg. Joined Jasta 8ob from Jastaschule I. Killed in an accident during a test flight over Morsberg.

### ZORN, Wilhelm    Uffz

J6o                          – 23 Apr 1918     8   POW

Biography & Victories: See *Above the Lines*.

### ZSCHUNKE, Erich      Ltn d R

| | | | | | |
|---|---|---|---|---|---|
| J6 | (Nov 1916) – 22 Nov 1916 | – WIA | J17 | 19 Dec 1917 – 29 May 1918 | – |
| J17 | 21 Mar 1917 – 26 Oct 1917 | – | Idflieg | 29 May 1918 – | – |
| Idflieg | 26 Oct 1917 – | | | | |

Joined Jasta 17 from AFP7. OzbV for Jasta 17. Awarded Saxon Knight's Cross 2nd Class with Swords of the Albert Order 5 January 1917.

### ZÜRN, Heinrich      Ltn d R

J62      24 Apr 1918 – 17 May 1918   –  KIA

Born 1 December 1892, Callenberg. Joined Jasta 62 from Jastaschule I. Killed between Gratibus and Montdidier.

### ZWITZERS,    Ltn

| | | | | | |
|---|---|---|---|---|---|
| J4 | 23 Oct 1917 – Feb 1918 | – | J62 | 12 Feb 1918 – 22 Mar 1918 | – POW |
| FBSchW† | Feb 1918 – 12 Feb 1918 | – | | | |

† Fliegerbeobachterschule West. Hit by ground fire and forced to land in Allied territory NW of Ham, flying an Albatros DVa (G.153).

# The Marine Jasta Pilots

### ACHILLES, Paul    Ltn z S
SFSI        2 Jan 1918 – 1 Sep 1918        2            MFJV        1 Sep 1918 – 11 Nov 1918        6
Some sources credit him with nine victories.
Biography & Victories: See *Above the Lines*.

### ANGERMEYER, Karl    Vfw
SFSI        Jan 1918 – 2 Feb 1918        –            MFJII        7 Feb 1918 – 3 May 1918        –    KIAcc
MFJI        2 Feb 1918 – 7 Feb 1918        –
Born 5 January 1896, Hamburg. Killed during a landing at Neumünster.

### ARNDS,    Flgmstr
MFA2        – Nov 1916        –            MFJI        Nov 1916 –            –

### BACHMANN,    Lt d R
SFSII    1
Victories:    1.        19 Jun 1917        Sopwith

### BARGMANN, Hermann    Ltn d R
Kusta 3        – 3 Aug 1918        –            MFJII        3 Aug 1918 – 28 Oct 1918        1    KIA
Born 25 October 1896, Bremerhaven.
Victories:    1.        28 Sep 1918        DH9            1815            Beerst

### BASTIAN, Werner    Ltn z S
MFJI        31 Jul 1918 – 31 Aug 1918        1    KIA
Born 2 October 1894, Spandau. Killed near Thourout.
Victories:    1.        14 Aug 1918        Camel            Oostkamp

### BAUM,    Flgmt
MFJV        – 15 Oct 1918        –    INT
Interned in Holland on 15 October 1918.

### BECHT, Phillip    Ltn z S
SFSZ        (1917) – 1918                    CO
SFSI        1918 – 2 Sep 1918        1            MFJI        2 Sep 1918 – 11 Nov 1918        3
Entered military service 15 June 1904. Held Iron Cross 2nd and 1st Class. Commanded 'C' Staffel, Zeebrugge Seaplane Station. Took part in a fight with several destroyers and torpedo boats on 5 June 1917, saving one officer and seven men from the enemy. Risked his life to save his squadron mates, Blume and Schindler, on 30 March 1918. With his flight severely damaged British submarine C51 on 6 June 1918. Served in Jagdgeschwader 5 Mölders during WWII. Died 13 September 1965. (Photo in *C&C US*, Vol 10, No 2, pg 119.)
Victories:    1.        21 Aug 1918        DH4            Zeebrugge
            2.        20 Sep 1918        Camel            Beerst
            3.        26 Oct 1918        Balloon            W Deinze
            4.        1 Nov 1918        2-seater            N Deinze

### BERNDT,    Flgomt
Kusta 4        – 15 Jun 1918        –            MFJI        15 Jun 1918 – 1 Oct 1918        –    WIA

### BIEBER,    Flgmt
SFSII        (Jun 1917) –        1            MFJV        1 Sep 1918 – 11 Nov 1918        –
SFSI        – 1 Sep 1918        2
On 19 June 1917, at great risk to himself, he landed and picked up squadron mate Dycke, who had been shot through the stomach, to bring him to an aid station, but Dycke died on the way.
Victories:    1.        19 Jun 1917        Sopwith
            2.        24 May 1918        DH
            3.        28 May 1918        DH9            0620            Stalhille

### BISCHOFF,
Kusta 4        – 23 Feb 1918        –            Kusta 4    28 Feb 1918 –            –
MFJI        23 Feb 1918 – 28 Feb 1918        –

## BLAAS, Eduard    Flgmstr
MFJII                           I        MFJIII      Jul 1918 – Oct 1918          4
Biography & Victories: See *Above the Lines*.

## BOEDICKER,    Flgmstr
MFAII              – Nov 1916      –        MFJI      Nov 1916 –                  –

## BORCHERT,    Flgmt
SS11               – 21 May 1918    –        MFJI      21 May 1918 –               1
Victories:       1.       30 Jun 1918      DH9                          Blankenberghe

## BOTTLER, Vzflgmstr
MFJI      5 Jun 1917 – 14 Jun 1917    I  WIA      MFJII      6 Nov 1917 – 9 Mar 1918      2  WIA
MFJI      6 Oct 1917 – 6 Nov 1917      –
During combat with Nieuports on 14 June 1917, was wounded in arm and hand but landed safely at Ghistelles.
Victories:       1.       2 Jun 1917      Sop Tripe                    N Warneford
                 2.       27 Jun 1918     DH4                          Wenduyne, at sea
                 3.       20 Jul 1918     Camel            1025        N Nieuport
                 –        30 Jul 1918     2-seater                     Pervyse

## BRANDT, Otto    Vzflgmstr
MFJI      3 Jun 1917 – 27 Jul 1917    – KIA
Born 1 Jan 1895, Berlin. Shot down on 11 July 1917 near Raversyde, he was not harmed. Shot down and killed at 1820 hours between Middelkerke and Westende.

## BRENNER, Flgmstr
MFJI              1917 – 14 Jun 1918    4        LFN      14 Jun 1918 –               –
Wounded in combat 3 September 1917, in the left upper thigh.
Victories:       1.       28 Sep 1917     RE8                          Wenduyne
                 2.       21 Oct 1917     Spad                         Ramskapelle
                 3.       19 Feb 1918     BF2b                         N Ypern
                 4.       23 Apr 1918     Camel            1430        Middelkerke

## BROCKHOFF, Ltn d R
MFJI      30 May 1917 – 23 Jun 1918    I        CO
                                                MFJIII      23 Jun 1918 – 11 Nov 1918      2
Entered military service 1 April 1913. Awarded Bavarian Militär-Verdeinstorden 4 Klasse mit Schwerten. Landed at Ghistelles, after a combat on 22 March 1918, during which the aircraft had been hit several times, he was not harmed.
Victories:       1.       8 May 1918      Sopwith                      Pervyse
                 2.       12 Jun 1918     DH4/9            1640        Oostdunkerque-Bad
                 3.       3 Sep 1918      Bréguet          2050        E Furnes
                 4.       26 Oct 1918     Balloon                      Deinze

## BRUNS, Flgmt
MFJI      28 May 1918 – 14 Jun 1918    –        LFN      14 Jun 1918 –               –

## BUHL, Albin    Obflgmstr
SFSII      14 Oct 1917 –                3        MFJIII      23 Jun 1918 – 1 Sep 1918      –
MFJII              – 23 Jun 1918        –        MFJIV      1 Sep 1918 – 11 Nov 1918      3
Some sources credit him with 12 victories.
Biography & Victories: See *Above the Lines*.

## BURGSTALLER, Flgomt
SFSII              1917    –            2
Victories:       1.       14 Apr 1917     Flying Boat
                 2.       26 May 1917     Flying Boat

## CRÜGER, Kurt    Ltn z S
MFJI      13 Apr 1917 – 3 Jul 1917    I  KIA
Born 19 June 1894, Kiel. Killed during combat with Sopwiths NE of Nieuport.
Victories:       1.       4 Jun 1917      Martinsyde       1450        Aeltre

## DREWS, Wilhelm   Flgmstr

MFJI      11 Mar 1918 –          –          MFJI      16 May 1918 – 22 Jun 1918      –
SFSI                 – 16 May 1918      –          MFJIII   22 Jun 1918 – 13 Aug 1918      – KIA
Born 26 December 1897, Burdelsdorf. Killed at Jabbeke, during an Allied bombing raid.

## DYCKE, Walter   Ltn d R

SFSII                – 19 Jun 1917      – WIA
Born 23 August 1887, Thiergart. Wounded in stomach, Vzflgmstr Bieber, risking his own life, landed and picked up Dycke in his one-seater aircraft, but Dycke died on the way home.

| Victories: | 1. | 19 Jun 1917 | Sopwith |
|---|---|---|---|

## ENGELFRIED, Karl   Flgmt

SFSI                 – 1 Sep 1918      1          MFJV      1 Sep 1918 – 11 Nov 1918      5
Some sources credit him with five victories.
Biography & Victories: See *Above the Lines*.

## ETZDORFF, Johannes   Ltn z S

SFSI      Mar 1918 – 28 May 1918      – KIA
Born 12 April 1894, Kustrin. Awarded Iron Cross 2nd Class. Killed at 0615 hours between Wenduyne and De Haan, during combat with a DH9.

## FAMMEN,   Flgmt

MFJI                 – 23 Apr 1918      – WIA

## FIETZMANN, Bruno   Flgomt

MFJII                – 25 Apr 1918      – KIA
Born 24 December 1895, Rothenberg. Flying Pfalz DIIIa 5942/17 when killed near Coxyde.

## FISCHER,   Ltn z S

MFJIII                            1

| Victories: | 1. | 1 Oct 1918 | Camel | | Clerkem |
|---|---|---|---|---|---|

## FREYMADL,   Ltn z S

SFSI      (Aug 1918) – 15 Sep 1918      –          MFJI      15 Sep 1918 – 1 Oct 1918      3 WIA
Awarded the Bavarian Militär-Verdeinstorden 4 Klasse mit Schwerten. Also awarded Iron Cross 2nd and 1st Class.

| Victories: | 1. | 15 Sep 1918 | DH9 | 1720 | Middleberg |
|---|---|---|---|---|---|
| | 2. | 26 Sep 1918 | DH4 | 1115 | Ostende |
| | 3. | 29 Sep 1918 | Camel | 0820 | SW Oostkamp |

## GOERTH, Hans   Vzflgmstr

Kusta 3                – 26 Feb 1918      –          MFJIII   22 Jun 1918 –
MFJI      26 Feb 1918 – 22 Jun 1918      –                                                            7
Biography & Victories: See *Above the Lines*.

## GÖTZ, Friedrich von   Ltn z S

MFJI      15 Aug 1917 – 11 Sep 1917      1 KIA
Born 8 January 1897, Hoyerswerde. Held Iron Cross 2nd and 1st Class. Shot down at 1900 hours near Schoore.

| Victories: | 1. | 11 Sep 1917 | BF2b | 1210 | Wynendaele |
|---|---|---|---|---|---|

## GOLDENSTEDT, Karl   Flgmt

MFJI      23 May 1918 – 14 Aug 1918      – KIA
Born 20 June 1897, Bremen. Killed over Oostkerke.

## GRABOWSKI, Wilhelm   Flgmt

MFJI      8 Mar 1918 – 11 Jun 1918      – WIA      MFJIV                – 13 Aug 1918      – WIA
Born 26 April 1897, Bielefeld. Wounded in the right hand 11 June 1918. Wounded at Jabbeke, during a bombing attack.

## GRÖSCHKE, Friedrich   Flgobmatr

SFSII      Aug 1918 – 21 Aug 1918      – KIA
Born 30 December 1897, Oldenberg. Wounded in the hand during combat 15 August 1918, at 2000 hours. Flying Fokker DVII 885/18 when killed over Blankenberghe.

## GROSCH,    Flgmstr
MFJI                    – 20 Aug 1917    –  WIA

## GROTH, Hans    Obflgmt
MFJI        Feb 1917 – 8 Jan 1918      –              MFJII      8 Jan 1918 – 26 Mar 1918   –  POW
Flying Pfalz DIII 5923/17 when shot down during a balloon attack.

## HACKBUSCH, Hermann    Vzflgmstr
LFN              – 17 Jun 1918      –          MFJI      17 Jun 1918 –                          3
Died 14 October 1933.

| Victories: | 1. | Date and unit unknown | | | |
|---|---|---|---|---|---|
| | 2. | 14 Aug 1918 | Camel | 1240 | Oostkamp-Zeebrugge |
| | 3. | 15 Sep 1918 | Dolphin | 1705 | Kokelaere |
| | 4. | 29 Sep 1918 | Camel | 0820 | SW Oostkamp |

## HAGEN, Walter    Flgmt
SFSI              – 1 Sep 1918      –          MFJIV     1 Sep 1918 – 11 Nov 1918    –

## HAGGENMÜLLER, Ottomar    Flgmstr
MFA2                         –             MFJII      6 Nov 1917 – 5 Dec 1917    –  KIA
MFJI              – 6 Nov 1917      2
Born 20 July 1888, Kempten. Killed N of Dixmuiden.

| Victories: | 1. | 4 Jun 1917 | Sopwith 2 | 1010 | N Frezenberg |
|---|---|---|---|---|---|
| | 2. | 7 Jun 1917 | Nieuport | 1205 | Bixschoote |

## HAHN,    Flgmt
MFJI    19 Apr 1917 –                     –

## HAHN, Heinrich    Obmt
MFJI      1 Mar 1918 – 16 May 1918    –  WIA
Landed near Ghistelles, after being wounded.

## HASSLER, Franz    Obmt
MFJI     11 Mar 1918 – 9 May 1918    –  KIAcc
Born 3 December 1887, Hadelschwendt. Killed turing a training flight.

## HECHNER,    Vzflgmstr
FA33              – 5 May 1917      –          MFJI     5 May 1917 –

## HEINRICH, Bertram    Ltn z S
MFJI        Feb 1917 – 31 Aug 1918     12 KIA
Biography & Victories: See *Above the Lines*.

## HEINZE, Friedrich    Obmt
MFA2              – Nov 1916      –          MFJII              – 13 Nov 1917    –  POW
MFJI
Flying an Albatros DIII when shot down wounded and taken prisoner, near Schoorbakke. Credited to
Captain B P G Beanlands, No 24 Sqn, RFC, in DH5 A9304 (G.89).

## HELD,    Flgmt
MFJII     (May 1918) –               1          MFJIII    (Jul 1918) –                   1

| Victories: | 1. | 21 May 1918 | Camel | | Ramskapelle |
|---|---|---|---|---|---|
| | 2. | 14 Jul 1918 | Spad | | |

## HILDEMANN, Herrmann    Flgomt
MFJI              – 19 Feb 1918    –  KIAcc
Born 5 May 1896, Teltow. Flying Albatros DV 2076/17 when he crashed shortly after take-off.

## HIRTH,    Vzflgmstr
MFJII              – 28 Jan 1918    –  INJ
Flying Pfalz DIIIa 5941/17 when injured in an accident during a test flight.

## HOFFKNECHT,    Ltn z S
SFSI              – 1 Sep 1918      –          MFJIV     1 Sep 1918 – 11 Nov 1918    1

| Victories: | 1. | 14 Oct 1918 | Camel | | Iseghem |
|---|---|---|---|---|---|

**HUBRICH, Gerhard      Flgmt**
SFSI              – 15 Sep 1918      4              MFJIV    15 Sep 1918 – 11 Nov 1918      8
Biography & Victories: See *Above the Lines*.

---

**ILLIG,      Flgmt**
MFJII              – 16 May 1918      – WIA        MFJII    4 Jun 1918 –                    1
Hosp    16 May 1918 – 4 Jun 1918      –
Victories:      1.        30 Aug 1918          DH9                    1440            Ostende

---

**JANNSEN,      Flgmt**
MFJI              – 23 Apr 1918      – INJ
Crash-landed near his airfield after the motor of his aircraft failed.

---

**JASTRAM,**
MFJI              – 3 Mar 1918      –             MFJI    12 Mar 1918 – 13 Mar 1918      –
AFP4    3 Mar 1918 – 12 Mar 1918      –           MFAII   13 Mar 1918 –

---

**KÄHLER, Clements      Oblt d R**
SFSI    2 Jan 1918 – 1 Sep 1918      2             MFJV    1 Sep 1918 – 11 Nov 1918      –
Crash-landed near Thourout, after his aircraft was hit during combat, he was not harmed.
Victories:      1.        29 Jun 1918          DH9                                    Varsenaere
                2.        12 Aug 1918          Camel                  1129            Wenduyne

---

**KAIRIES, Christian      Obflugmstr**
SFSI    1 Oct 1917 – 1 Sep 1918      6             MFJV    1 Sep 1918 – 1 Oct 1918      1 POW
Biography & Victories: See *Above the Lines*.

---

**KIESSLING,      Flgmt**
MFJI    8 Mar 1918 – 22 Jun 1918      –            MFJIV              – 13 Aug 1918      – WIA
MFJIII    22 Jun 1918 –                –
Wounded during a bombing attack on Jabbeke.

---

**KLOTZSCH,      Flgobmatr**
MFJII              – 10 Jul 1918      –            MFJI    10 Jul 1918 – 13 Aug 1918      – WIA
Wounded by a bomb splinter during a bombing attack on his airfield at Jabbeke.

---

**KNIE, Günther      Vzflgmstr**
Kusta 3              – 3 Aug 1918      –            MFJII    3 Aug 1918 – 13 Aug 1918      – KIA
Born 13 February 1896, Halle. Killed during a bombing attack on the airfield at Jabbeke.

---

**KRANTZ, Eberhard      Ltn z S**
SFSI    6 May 1918 – 1 Sep 1918      1             MFJIV    15 Sep 1918 – 11 Nov 1918      –
Commanded Seefrontstaffel 1 from 1 September until disbanded 15 September 1918. Attained rank of
Major d R in the Luftwaffe during WWII. Died 8 February 1969.
Victories:      1.        Unit unknown
                2.        21 Aug 1918          DH4                                    Ichteghem

---

**KRIEGER,      Flgmt**
MFJI    3 Jun 1917 –                  –

---

**KÜHN, Fritz      Flgobmt**
MFA2              – Nov 1916      –               MFJI    Nov 1916 – 7 Jun 1917      1 WIA
Born 25 January 1895, Berlin. Shot down and taken prisoner over Staden, later died of wounds.
Victories:      1.        3 Jun 1917          Sopwith 1              1010            W Zonnebeke

---

**KÜNSTLER,      Flgmt**
MFJI    30 Apr 1917 –                  3
Victories:      1.        3 Jun 1917          Nieuport                              N Ypern
                2.        7 Jun 1917          Nieuport                              Gheluvelt
                3.        11 Sep 1917          Camel                  1910            SW Schoors

---

**KULBE,      Flgmt**
MFJI    3 Jun 1917 –                  –           SFSI    10 Jul 1918 – 31 Jul 1918      – POW
MFJII              – 10 Jul 1918      3
Victories:      1.        9 Mar 1918          Camel                                Boitschoucke
                zlg        9 Mar 1918          Camel                                Boitschoucke

|   |   |   |   |   |   |
|---|---|---|---|---|---|
| 2. | 29 Jun 1918 | Balloon | | W Ostende | |
| 3. | 5 Jul 1918 | DH4 | 1920 | Ostende, at sea | |

## KURING, Carl     Vzflgmstr
MFJI          – 6 Nov 1917       –                    MFJII    6 Nov 1917 – 11 Nov 1918    4
Crash-landed Fokker DVII 612/18 after a hard combat, he was not harmed.

| Victories: | 1. | 15 May 1918 | Pup | | NW Oostkerke |
| | 2. | 1 Jun 1918 | DH9 | . | Ruidenberg |
| | 3. | 1 Aug 1918 | 2-seater | 2045 | |
| | 4. | 3 Oct 1918 | DH9 | | Roulers |

## KUTSCHKE, Karl     Flgmt
SFSI        Apr 1918 – 1 Sep 1918      1                 MFJV    1 Sep 1918 – 11 Nov 1918    4
Some sources credit him with seven victories.

| Victories: | 1. | 27 Jun 1918 | DH4 | | |
| | 2. | 15 Sep 1918 | DH9 | 1705 | Walcheren |
| | 3. | 1 Oct 1918 | DH9 | | Roulers |
| | 4. | 6 Oct 1918 | DH9 | | Blankenberghe |
| | 5. | 14 Oct 1918 | Camel | | Dixmuiden |

## LEDY,     Flgmstr
MFJII     Jul 1918 –                       –

## LICHTHERZ, Kurt     Vzflgmstr
MFJI          – 14 Jun 1917       –   KIA
Born 21 March 1895, Sulzbach. Killed over Middelkerke, at 2100 hours.

## LODEMANN, Theodor     Ltn z S
MFJI          – Mar 1918       –                    SFSI     Mar 1918 – 4 Jul 1918     3   KIA
Born 23 July 1894, Hamelin. Held Iron Cross 2nd and 1st Class. Killed near Ypern, during combat with an enemy scout.

| Victories: | 1. | 9 May 1918 | Camel | | At sea |
| | 2. | 21 May 1918 | BF2b | 0825 | Mariakerke |
| | 3. | 29 Jun 1918 | DH4 | | |

## LOHMANN,     Flgomt
MFJI     27 Apr 1917 –                   –

## LUDEWIG,     Flgmt
MFJI     2 Jan 1918 – 22 Jun 1918      –          MFJIII   22 Jun 1918 –                    1
Victories:          1.          13 Jul 1918 DH9

## LUITJENS, Luitjen     Flgomt
MFJI     3 Jun 1917 – 22 Aug 1917      –   KIA
Born 16 March 1891, Eckel. Shot down and killed between St Pierre Capelle and Spermalie.

## MAJEWSKI, Bruno     Ltn
MFJI                                           –
Received the Knight's Cross with Swords of the Royal Hohenzollern House Order on 16 July 1917. Also awarded Iron Cross 2nd and 1st Class.

## MATTHEUS, Wilhelm     Ltn d R
MFJI     6 Jun 1917 – 28 Dec 1917      1   WIA
Received the Knight's Cross with Swords of the Royal Hohenzollern House Order on 22 January 1917. Severely wounded in the chest during combat with three Sopwiths near Clerkem; believed to have died of wounds.

| Victories: | 1. | Date and unit unknown | | | |
| | 2. | 29 Jul 1917 | RE8 | 0640 | Nieuport Mole |

## MAYER,     Vzflgmstr
MFJI          – 1 May 1918      1          MFJIII   Sep 1918 –                    1
MFJII     1 May 1918 –                   1

| Victories: | 1. | Date and unit unknown | | | |
| | 2. | 9 Mar 1918 | Camel | | Boitschoucke |
| | 3. | 31 May 1918 | DH9 | 1433 | Aertrycke |
| | 4. | 5 Sep 1918 | Camel | 1525 | Stahlhille |

**MEINEL-TANNEBERG,     Flgmt**

| | | | | | |
|---|---|---|---|---|---|
| MFJII | – 4 Jul 1918 | – | MFJIII | 10 Jul 1918 – | – |
| MFJI | 4 Jul 1918 – 10 Jul 1918 | – | | | |

---

**MELCHER, Emil     Ltn**

| | | |
|---|---|---|
| MFJI | (Sep 1918) – | – |

---

**MERZ, Horst     Ltn z S**

| | | |
|---|---|---|
| MFJII | – 11 Nov 1918 | 1 |

Born 2 December 1891, Lehma (Saxony). Flew with Feldflieger-Abteilung 36 on Eastern Front. Served with Seeflieger-Abteilung I in Flanders prior to joining MFJII. Attained rank of Oberst (Colonel) in Luftwaffe, during WWII. Died 24 August 1979, Munich.

| Victories: | 1. | 23 Oct 1918 | Camel |
|---|---|---|---|

---

**METTLICH, Konrad     Oblt z S**

| | | | | | |
|---|---|---|---|---|---|
| MFA2 | – Nov 1916 | – | J8 | 1917 – 13 Mar 1918 | 6   KIA |
| MFJI | Nov 1916 – | – | | | |

Biography & Victories: See *Above the Lines*.

---

**MEYER, Franz     Vzflgmt**

| | | | | |
|---|---|---|---|---|
| MFJIV | | – | MFJV | – |

Credited with four victories in some sources.

---

**MEYER, Hermann     Ltn z S**

| | | | |
|---|---|---|---|
| MFJIV | – 3 Oct 1918 | – | KIA |

Born 30 March 1897, Ouackenbruch. Shot down in flames.

---

**MEYER, Karl     Obflgmt**

| | | | | | | |
|---|---|---|---|---|---|---|
| SFSII | 1916 – | 7 | SFSI | 16 Oct 1917 – 28 Dec 1917 | – | INJ |
| MFJI | – 16 Oct 1917 | 1 | | | | |

Biography & Victories: See *Above the Lines*.

---

**MÜLLER,     Vzflgmstr**

| | | | | | | |
|---|---|---|---|---|---|---|
| SFSII | (Apr 1917) – | 3 | SFSI | 3 Dec 1917 – 19 Jan 1918 | 1 | INJ |

Severely injured in a crash-landing of Albatros DIII 6588/17; hospitalised.

| Victories: | 1. | 14 Apr 1917 | Flying Boat | | |
|---|---|---|---|---|---|
| | 2. | 26 Apr 1917 | HP | 0400 | |
| | 3. | 26 May 1917 | Flying Boat | | |
| | 4. | 4 Jan 1918 | Caudron | | Coxyde |

---

**NAEKE,     Flgmt**

| | | | |
|---|---|---|---|
| MFJI | – 16 Sep 1918 | 1 | WIA |

| Victories: | 1. | 28 Sep 1918 | DH9 | 1430 | Leke |
|---|---|---|---|---|---|

---

**NAPP, Otto     Vzflgmt**

| | | | |
|---|---|---|---|
| MFJI | 5 Oct 1917 – 30 Nov 1917 | – | KIAcc |

Born 12 February 1888, Hoha a. d. Weser. Killed during a test flight of Albatros DV 4680/17 at the airfield of Coolkerke.

---

**NIEMEYER,     Oblt z S**

| | | |
|---|---|---|
| SFSII | 19 Dec 1917 – | 2 |

| Victories: | 1. | 31 Aug 1916 | Short |
|---|---|---|---|
| | 2. | 23 Oct 1916 | Flying Boat |

---

**NITZSCHE, Alfons     Flgmstr**

| | | | |
|---|---|---|---|
| MFJII | – 20 Jul 1918 | 1 | KIA |

Born 29 March 1897, Grottau. Killed in action at 1020 hours near Leffinghe flying Fokker DVII 506/18.

| Victories: | 1. | 13 Mar 1918 | DH4 | 1315 | NW Nieuport |
|---|---|---|---|---|---|

---

**OSTERKAMP, Theodor     Oblt z S**

| | | | | | |
|---|---|---|---|---|---|
| MFAII | Jun 1915 – Sep 1915 | – | MFJI | 13 Apr 1917 – 6 Nov 1917 | 5 |
| MFAI | Sep 1915 – 9 Mar 1917 | 1 | CO | | |
| CO | | | MFJII | 15 Jun 1917 – 11 Nov 1918 | 26 |
| MLA | 10 Mar 1917 – 12 Apr 1917 | – | | | |

Born 15 April 1892. Held rank of Lieutenant General in Luftwaffe, WWII. Awarded Knight's Cross of the Iron Cross, WWII. Died 2 January 1975, Baden-Baden.
Biography & Victories: See *Above the Lines*.

---

**PFEIFFER,　　Flgmt**
MFJIII　　　　　　　　　　　　　　　I
Victories:　　　1.　　　28 Sep 1918　　　Camel　　　　　1815　　　　　Woumen

---

**POSS, Reinhold　　Ltn z S**
SFSI　　May 1918 – 1 Sep 1918　　5　　　　MFJIV　1 Sep 1918 – 15 Oct 1918　　6　POW
Biography & Victories: See *Above the Lines*.

---

**RAHLER,**
MFJI　　2 Jan 1918 – 11 Jan 1918　　–　　　　SFSII　11 Jan 1918 –　　　　　　–

---

**RATH, Otto　　Ltn d R**
MFJI　　　　　– 17 Aug 1917　　– KIA
Born 2 September 1892, Stuttgart. Attacked a balloon over Furnes, and afterward, at 2030 hours, was killed in combat over Manekeusvere.

---

**REUSCH,　　Oblt d R**
MFJII　19 Oct 1917 – 21 Mar 1918　　–　　　　CO
　　　　　　　　　　　　　　　　　　　　　　Schusta 1 21 Mar 1918 –　　　　　–
Commanded MFJII.

---

**RIESS,　　Flgomt**
SS1　　　– 10 Sep 1918　　–　　　　MFJI　10 Sep 1918 – 11 Nov 1918　　1
Victories:　　　1.　　　29 Sep 1918　　　Camel　　　　　0820　　　　　SW Oostkamp

---

**RITTER,　　Ltn z S**
SFSI　　23 Oct 1917 – 11 Jan 1918　　–　　　　SFSII　11 Jan 1918 –　　　　　　–
Shot down W Dunkerque, 8 November 1917; unharmed.

---

**ROHE,　　Ltn**
FA33　　　– 20 May 1917　　–　　　　MFJI　20 May 1917 –　　　　　　2
Entered military service 1 April 1914. Awarded Iron Cross 2nd and 1st Class.
Victories:　　　1.　　　25 May 1917　　　FE2d　　　　　　　　　　　W Ypern
　　　　　　　2.　　　4 Jun 1917　　　Sopwith 2　　　1015　　　　　Polygonwald

---

**ROLSHOVEN, Hans　　Ltn z S**
SFSII　(Sep 1916) –　　　　　　1　　　CO SFSI　1 Oct 1917 – 6 May 1918　　2　KIAcc
Born 23 December 1894, Straifund. Crashed Brandenburg LW #571 during a test flight; not injured. Awarded the Hohenzollern Hausorden mit Schwerten on 2 October 1916, and the Iron Cross 2nd and 1st Class. Killed in an accident at 1830 hours at Zeebrugge, flying Pfalz DIII 6B1 #751.
Victories:　　　1.　　　7 Sep 1916　　　Caudron　　　1545　　　N Ostende
　　　　　　　2.　　　28 Nov 1917　　　DH5　　　　　　　　　Brugge
　　　　　　　3.　　　27 Apr 1918　　　Sopwith

---

**RUTSCHKE,　　Flgmt**
MFJI　21 Mar 1918 –　　　　　　–

---

**SACHSENBERG, Gotthard　　Oblt z S**
MLAII　　　　　　　　　　　　　–　　　　CO
MFJI　　Nov 1916 – 2 Sep 1918　　25　　　MJGI　2 Sep 1918 – 11 Nov 1918　　6
Biography & Victories: See *Above the Lines*.

---

**SANTEN, von　　Oblt z S**
MFA2　　　　　　　　　　　　　–　　　　MFJ1　Nov 1916 – 1 Feb 1917　　　　–
Awarded Iron Cross 2nd and 1st Class.

---

**SATTLER, Heinrich　　Ltn**
MFJII　　　　　– 9 Jun 1918　　– KIA
Born 19 December 1895, Lippstadt. Awarded Iron Cross 2nd Class. Killed near Wladsloo in Albatros DVa 7265/17.

**SAWATZKI, Horst    Flgmt**

| Kusta 3 | – | MFJI | 16 May 1918 – | | 1 WIA |

Wounded during combat at 2100 on 2 June 1918, between Middelkerke and Nieuport, while flying Albatros DV 4635/17, made a safe landing at Ghistelles. Lightly wounded in action 16 September 1918. Some sources credit him with four victories.

Victories:    1.    26 Sep 1918    Camel    1115    Ostende

**SCHACT,**

| LFN | – | MFJI | 16 Jul 1918 – | – |

**SCHARON, Karl    Vzflgmt**

| MFJII    14 Aug 1918 – 11 Nov 1918 | 8 |

Biography & Victories: See *Above the Lines*.

**SCHEDE,    Ltn R**

| MFJ2 | – 13 Apr 1918 | – | MFJ3 | 26 Aug 1918 – | – |
| MFJ2 | 13 Apr 1918 – 26 Aug 1918 | – |

**SCHIFFMANN, Karl    Flgomt**

| MFJIV | – 23 Sep 1918 | – KIA |

Born 2 July 1899, Stettin. Killed during combat with a Camel over Ichteghem.

**SCHMIDT,    Ltn**

| MFJII | – 10 Jul 1918 | – | SFSI | 10 Jul 1918 – 21 Jul 1918 | – POW |

**SCHNELL,    Vzflgmstr**

| LFA | – 5 May 1917 | – | MFA1 | 12 May 1917 – | – |
| MFJI | 5 May 1917 – 12 May 1917 | – |

**SCHÖNBAUM,    Flgobmatr**

| MFJV | – 15 Oct 1918 | – WIA |

**SCHÖNROCK,    Ltn z S**

| SFSI | Mar 1918 – 1 Sep 1918 | – | MFJIV | 1 Sep 1918 – 11 Nov 1918 | – |

**SCHRÖDER,    Flgobmatr**

| MFJI | – |

Promoted to Flugobermeister on 5 May 1917.

**SCHULER,    Ltn z S**

| SFSII | | 1 |

Victories:    1.    10 Oct 1916    EA (Br)

**SCHULTZE,    Ltn z S**

| MFJI | 3 Mar 1918 – 26 Jun 1918 | 2 | MFJIII | 26 Jun 1918 – | – |

Victories:    1.    27 May 1918    DH9    La Panne
             2.    25 Jun 1918    Spad    1215    Breedene

**SCHULZE, Gerhard    Ltn d R**

| MFJI | 3 Mar 1918 – 12 Jun 1918 | – KIA |

Born 6 October 1897, Wilhelmshagen. Shot down in flames at 1640 hours during combat with four Sopwiths near Nieuport-Mole, flying Albatros DVa 7337/17. Previously with Jasta 12.

**SCHUSTER,    Ltn d R**

| MFJ I | | 1 |

Victories:    1.    15 Oct 1918    Dolphin    Roulers

**SCHWARZ, Eduard    Flgmstr**

| SFSII | – 14 Jul 1918 | – KIAcc |

Born 5 May 1886, Minden. Departed at 1125 hours, last seen going down over the water about four km from Blankenberghe in Albatros D Va 7322/17.

## SCHWEISGUT,      Ltn z S
SFSI      21 Oct 1917 –                    –
Held Iron Cross 2nd and 1st Class.

| Victories: | – | 19 Dec 1917 | Handley Page | | Nieuport |
|---|---|---|---|---|---|

## SIEBEL,      Oblt z S
SFSI      10 Dec 1917 – 12 Mar 1918    –              SFSII      12 Mar 1918 –                    –
Entered military service 1 October 1902. Shot down 15 November 1917, flying a Pfalz DIII.

## SOEHL,      Flgomt
MFJI                                      –
Promoted to Flugobermeister on 5 May 1917.

## SPIES, Rudolf      Ltn z S
Borkum    5 Aug 1916 – 1 Jun 1917        –              SFSI      2 Jul 1917 – 13 Aug 1918      3    WIA
Born 2 December 1895, Moskau. Entered military service 1 October 1914, Uhlanen Regiment 17 (Lancer
Regiment). Pilot's training 11 February 1916 to 4 August 1916, at II Seeflieger-Abteilung,
Wilhelmshaven. Promoted Gefreiter 2 May 1915; Unteroffizier 31 July 1915; Vizewachtmeister 9 October
1915; Vizeflugmeister 1 December 1916; Leutnant d R 16 November 1917. Wounded during combat with
DH9s, hospitalised for rest of war. Awarded Iron Cross 2nd and 1st Class. Attained rank of General-
Ingenieur in the Luftwaffe during WWII. Died 2 February 1978.

| Victories: | 1. | 4 May 1918 | Seaplane | 1910 | Nieuport |
|---|---|---|---|---|---|
| | 2. | 4 May 1918 | Camel | 1915 | Westende |
| | 3. | 12 Aug 1918 | Camel | 1140 | Middelkerke |

## STRANG,      Ltn d R
SFSII 2

| Victories: | 1. | 26 May 1917 | Flying Boat | | |
|---|---|---|---|---|---|
| | 2. | Date unknown | | | |

## STIER,      Ltn z S
MFJV                     – 11 Nov 1918      –
Shot down in flames on 1 November 1918, took to his parachute and landed safely.

## STINSKY, Max      Ltn z S
MFJI                     – 6 May 1918      –              MFJII      5 Sep 1918 – 15 Sep 1918      1
SFSI      6 May 1918 – 5 Sep 1918      1              MFJIV      15 Sep 1918 – 14 Oct 1918      –    KIA
Born 27 May 1895, Konigsberg. Assigned as Deputy to Osterkamp from 5 September to 15 September
1918. Awarded Iron Cross 2nd and 1st Class. Last seen over Snelleghem.

| Victories: | 1. | 12 Aug 1918 | Camel | 2000 | Middelkerke |
|---|---|---|---|---|---|
| | 2. | 20 Sep 1918 | Camel | 1005 | SE Pervyse |

## STUCKE, Flgomt
KoflN                     – 14 Apr 1918      –              MFJII      14 Apr 1918 –                    2

| Victories: | 1. | 25 Apr 1918 | Camel | | Steenkerke |
|---|---|---|---|---|---|
| | 2. | 16 May 1918 | Spad | | Middelkerke |
| | – | 9 Jun 1918 | DH4 | | S Nieuport |
| | zlg | 27 Jun 1918 | Camel | | Wenduyne |

## THÖNE, Willy      Ltn z S
MFJI      17 May 1918 – 5
Biography & Victories: See *Above the Lines*.

## TINSCHERT,      Ltn d R
MFJI                     – 28 Sep 1917      –    WIA      LFN      14 Jun 1918 –                    –
MFJI      Mar 1918 – 14 Jun 1918      –
Entered military service 1 October 1907. Held Iron Cross 2nd & 1st Class. Wounded and forced to land
after combat with five Spads near Schoorebacke.

| Victories: | – | 29 Jan 1918 | DH4 | | Leffinghe |
|---|---|---|---|---|---|
| | – | 16 Mar 1918 | Bréguet | | Wielsle |
| | – | 21 May 1918 | BF2b | | At sea |

**UNDIENER, Armin    Flgmt**
MFJII              – 28 Jan 1918    – KIA
Born 8 December 1895, Munich. Killed between Middelkerke and Mariakerke flying Pfalz DIIIa 4169/17.

---

**VOIGT, Gottfried    Flgmstr**
MFJI              – 5 May 1917    –              SFSI    22 Jan 1918 –              –
MFA1    5 May 1917 –              –

---

**VOSS, Karl-Heinrich    Ltn d R**
MFJI              – 17 Dec 1917    1 KIA
Born 7 May 1895, Usedom. Shot down in flames during combat with four EA over Houthulster Wald, flying Albatros DV 2356/17 (G.100), by 2/Lt Kelsey, No 1 Sqn, RFC.
Victories:    1.        12 Dec 1917        Camel                              Leke              (a)
(a) F/S/Lt J C Clark, No 10 Sqn, RNAS, in Sopwith N6330, POW.

---

**WACKER,    Flgmstr**
MFJII    14 Aug 1918 –              –

---

**WAGNER,    Flgmstr**
MFJI    13 Jan 1918 –              3
Victories:    1.        21 May 1918        DH9                              Uitkerke
              2.        25 Jun 1918        DH9              1215              Ostende
              3.        29 Jun 1918        Camel                            S Leke

---

**WANGEMANN, Franz    Flgmt**
MFAII              –              LFA    26 May 1917 –              –
MFJI    Nov 1916 – 26 May 1917    –
Wounded in action 13 March 1917.

---

**WASSERTHAL, Otto    Flgomt**
MFJIV              – 31 Jul 1918    – KIA
Born 23 March 1895, Salzwedel. Killed over Nordholz.

---

**WASSERTHAL,    Flgomt**
MFJIV              – 11 Nov 1918    2
Victories:    1.        30 Oct 1918        DH9                              Deinze
              2.        1 Nov 1918        Camel                            SW Deinze

---

**WEIGEL,    Flgmt**
LFN              – 17 Jun 1918    –              MFJIII    23 Jun 1918 – 16 Jul 1918    – WIA
MFJI    17 Jun 1918 – 23 Jun 1918    –
Wounded during combat with DH4s, hospitalised at Brugge.

---

**WEINERT, Ltn d R**
MFJII    (May 1918) – 27 Aug 1918    1              LFA    27 Aug 1918 –
Wounded in action 9 June 1918.
Victories:    1.        8 May 1918        DH9                              Oostkerke
              2.        28 Sep 1918        DH                              Zande-Moere

---

**WESSELS, Heinrich    Ltn z S**
MFJI    2 Jan 1918 – 16 Sep 1918    6 KIA
Biography & Victories: See *Above the Lines*.

---

**WIELAND,    Ltn z S**
SFSI              – 30 Jul 1918    – WIA
Wounded during combat with Camels.

---

**WILHELM, Curt    Ltn z S**
MFJIV    1 Sep 1918 – 11 Nov 1918    2
Awarded Iron Cross 2nd Class. Comanded MFJIV from 15 October 1918.
Victories:    1.        16 Sep 1918        Camel                              Zeebrugge
              2.        24 Sep 1918        Camel              1415              Pervyse

**WIRTZ, Josef    Vzflgmstr**
MFJI        Nov 1916 – 24 Apr 1917    3   KIA
Born 3 March 1898, Oldenkirchen. Killed during combat when he collided in mid-air with a FE2d near Becelaere, while flying Albatros D III 2281/16, victims possibly 2/Lt A R Johnston (P) & Lt H R Nicholson (O) of No 20 Sqn, RFC, on FE2d A6385.

| Victories: | 1. | 7 Feb 1917 | Sopwith 2 | Roxem | (a) |
|---|---|---|---|---|---|
| | 2. | 24 Apr 1917 | FE2d | E Ypern | |
| | 3. | 24 Apr 1917 | FE2d | Becelaere | |

(a) F/Lt C R Blagrove & 2/AM Milne, 5 Wing, RNAS.

**ZENSES, Alexandre    Vzflgmt**
MFJII                  –11 Nov 1918    19
Biography & Victories: See *Above the Lines*.

**ZIMMERMANN, Fähnr z S**
SFSII      2 Jan 1918 –                  –

**ZWANG,    Vzflgmstr**
MFJIII

# Jagdgeschwader (JG) and Jagdgruppe (JGr) Formations

During the late summer of 1917, with the initial success of the first Jagdgeschwader (JGI) it became accepted that other formations of Jasta groupings would be beneficial, not only by increasing the number of fighters as a flying unit, but also for administration. However, it was obviously not deemed important to create further Jagdgeschwadern, at least not until early 1918. Therefore Jagdgruppen started to be formed which were to be non-permanent groupings of certain units. These were usually created for a specific purpose; to defend an area or to support a coming offensive. Although these Jagdgruppen (JGr) were often led by successful fighter pilots, several were commanded by experienced unit commanders who were not necessarily in the 'ace' class.

As will be seen below, the Jasta affiliations to these Jagdgruppen often changed and interchanged, as did the leaders, whereas the four Jagdgeschwadern kept its Jastas from formation until the war's end.

Also listed below is the very first example of forming Jastas into a fighting unit, that created towards the end of April 1917, Jastas 3, 4, 11 and 33 under Manfred von Richthofen's leadership which led directly to the forming of JGI in June. However, this first grouping, like JGI, did not necessarily operate together. This, like everything else, had to be learnt.

### Royal Prussian Jagdgeschwader Nr.I (Richthofen), formed 26 June 1917.

| | |
|---|---|
| Jastas 4, 6, 10, 11 | Commanded by Rittm Manfred von Richthofen |
| | 26 June 1917 – 21 April 1918 |
| | Commanded by Hptm Wilhelm Reinhard |
| | 22 April 1918 – 3 July 1918 |
| | Commanded by Oblt Hermann Göring |
| | 6 July 1918 – EOW |

### Royal Prussian Jagdgeschwader Nr.II, formed 2 February 1918.

| | |
|---|---|
| Jastas 12, 13, 15, 19 | Commanded by Hptm Adolf von Tutschek |
| | 6 February 1918 – 15 March 1918 |
| | Commanded by Hptm Rudolf Berthold |
| | 18 March 1918 – 10 August 1918 |
| | Commanded by Oblt Oskar von Boenigk |
| | 31 August 1918 – EOW |

### Royal Prussian Jagdgeschwader Nr.III, formed 2 February 1918.

| | |
|---|---|
| Jastas 2, 26, 27, 36 | Commanded by Oblt Bruno Loerzer |
| | 21 February 1918 – EOW |

### Royal Bavarian Jagdgeschwader Nr.IV, formed 3 October 1918.

| | |
|---|---|
| Jastas 23b, 32b, 34b, 35b | Commanded by Hptm Eduard von Schleich |
| | 3 October 1918 – EOW |

### Royal Prussian Marine Jagdgeschwader (4 Armee), formed 2 September 1918.

| | |
|---|---|
| Marine Feld Jastas I, II, III, IV, V | Commanded by Oblt z S Gotthard Sachsenberg |
| | 2 September 1918 – EOW |

| JAGDGRUPPEN | | Armee |
|---|---|---|
| **6 Armee Jagdgruppe** | | |
| Jastas 3, 4, 11, 33 | Commanded by Oblt Manfred von Richthofen | |
| | 30 April 1917 – 1 June 1917 | 6 |
| **Jagdgruppe 'Bethge'** | | |
| Jastas 12, 30, 37 | Commanded by Oblt Hans Bethge | |
| | 18 August 1917 – 5 November 1917 | 6 |
| **Jagdgruppe 'von Braun'** | | |
| Jastas 13, 14, 16b, 21s, 22s, 23b, 32b, 34b | Commanded by Oblt Konstantin von Braun | |
| | August 1917 – November 1917 | 5 |

## Jagdgruppe 'Dixmuiden'

| | | |
|---|---|---|
| Jastas 7, 29, 33, 35b | Commanded by Oblt Harald Auffahrt | |
| | 20 October 1917 – 28 November 1917 | 4 |
| Jastas 7, 16b, 51 | Commanded by Oblt Hans Gandert | |
| | 7 February 1918 – 1 March 1918 | 4 |

## Jagdgruppe 'Etreux' (which later became JGr 1)

| | | |
|---|---|---|
| Jastas 8, 35b | Commanded by Hptm Constantin von Bentheim | |
| | 9 December 1917 – 15 December 1917 | 2 |

## Jagdgruppe 'von Greim' (which was also known as and became JGr 10)

| | | |
|---|---|---|
| Jastas 34b, 37, 77b | Commanded by Oblt Robert von Greim | |
| | 18 April 1918 – 6 June 1918 | 2 |
| Jastas 34b, 37b | 9 June 1918 – 31 July 1918 | 18 |

## Jagdgruppe 'Houthulst'

| | | |
|---|---|---|
| Jastas 12, 17 | Commanded by Hptm Rudolf von Esebeck | |
| | 6 November 1917 – 16 November 1917 | 4 |

## Jagdgruppe 'Lille'

| | | |
|---|---|---|
| Jastas 28w, 37 | Commanded by Hptm Otto Hartmann | |
| | 20 July 1917 – 27 August 1917 | 4 |

which became:

## Jagdruppe 4 'Armee Nord'

| | | |
|---|---|---|
| Jastas 2, 17, 20, 28w & Kest 8w | Commanded by Hpt Otto Hartmann | |
| | 27 August 1917 – 3 September 1917 | 4 |
| Jastas 8, 20 | Commanded by Hpt Constantin von Bentheim | |
| | 30 September 1917 – 20 November 1917 | 4 |

## Jagdgruppe 6 Armee Nord

| | | |
|---|---|---|
| Jastas 18, 30 | Commanded by Oblt Hans Bethge | |
| | 23 November 1917 – 14 December 1917 | 6 |
| Jastas 18, 29, 30 | 14 December 1917 – 7 February 1918 | 6 |
| Jastas 18, 46, 57 | Commanded by Oblt Rudolf Berthold | |
| | 7 February 1918 – 18 March 1918 | 6 |

## Jagdgruppe 6 Armee Sud

| | | |
|---|---|---|
| Jastas 12, 20, 24s | Commanded by Oblt Paul Blumenbach | |
| | 23 November 1917 – 28 December 1917 | 6 |

## Jagdgruppe 18 Armee Sud

| | | |
|---|---|---|
| Jastas 24s, 48 | Commanded by Ltn Kurt Küppers | |
| | 15 February 1918 – 4 March 1918 | 18 |

## Jagdgruppe 'Tutschek'

| | | |
|---|---|---|
| Jastas 12, 30, 37 | Commanded by Oblt Adolf von Tutschek | |
| | 4 August 1917 – 11 August 1917 | 6 |

## Jagdgruppe Nr.1 (formally JGr Etreux)

| | | |
|---|---|---|
| | Commanded by Hptm Constantin von Bentheim | |
| Jastas 8, 17, 24s, 48 | 28 December 1917 – 15 February 1918 | 18 |
| Jastas 8, 17 | 15 February 1918 – 20 March 1918 | 18 |
| Jastas 8, 62, 68 | 21 March 1918 – 1 April 1918 | 18 |
| Jastas 8, 62, 68, 72 | 1 April 1918 – 11 July 1918 | 18 |
| Jastas 8, 31, 62, 68, 72s, 73, 74 | 11 July 1918 – 14 September 1918 | 1 |
| Jastas 8, 62, 68, 74 | 15 September 1918 – 2 October 1918 | 5 |
| Jastas 8, 62, 68, 74 | Commanded by Oblt Paul Blumenbach | |
| | 2 October 1918 – EOW | 5 |

## Jagdgruppe Nr.2

| | | |
|---|---|---|
| Jastas 8, 17 | Commanded by Hptm Constantin von Bentheim | |
| | 20 November 1917 – 7 December 1917 | 2 |
| Jastas 8, 17, 35b | 15 December 1917 – 28 December 1917 | 2 |
| Jastas 5, 46 | Commanded by Oblt Richard Flashar | |
| | 12 March 1918 – 17 June 1918 | 2 |
| | Commanded by Oblt Otto Schmidt | |
| | 17 June 1918 – 8 August 1918 | 2 |
| Jastas 5, 34b, 37, 46 | 8 August 1918 – 7 October 1918 | 2 |
| Jastas 5, 37, 46 | 7 October 1918 – EOW | 2 |

## Jagdgruppe Nr.3

| | | |
|---|---|---|
| Jastas 14, 20, 40s, 49 | Commanded by Oblt Hermann Martini | |
| | 19 March 1918 – 3 April 1918 | 17 |
| Jastas 40s, 47w, 49, 57, 58 | 4 April – 25 April 1918 | 6 |
| Jastas 20, 33, 40s, 49, 57, 58 | Commanded by Oblt Heinrich Lorenz | |
| | 25 April 1918 – 6 June 1918 | 4 |
| Jastas 14, 29, 30, 43, 52 | Commanded by Ltn Hans-Georg von der Marwitz | |
| | 6 June 1918 – 17 June 1918 | 6 |
| | Commanded by Oblt Richard Flashar | |
| | 17 June 1918 – 8 August 1918 | 6 |
| Jastas 29, 30, 43, 52 | Commanded by Oblt Harald Auffahrt | |
| | 8 August 1918 – 19 August 1918 | 2 |
| Jastas 14, 29, 30, 43, 52, 63 | Commanded by Oblt Richard Flashar | |
| | 19 August 1918 – 30 September 1918 | 6 |
| Jastas 14, 16b, 29, 56 | Commanded by Oblt Harald Auffahrt | |
| | 30 September 1918 – EOW | 4 |

## Jagdgruppe Nr.4

| | | |
|---|---|---|
| Jastas 2, 26, 27, 37, 47w | Commanded by Hptm Bruno Loerzer | |
| | 29 December 1917 – 2 February 1918 | 4 |
| Jastas 23b, 35b, 58, 59 | Commanded by Oblt Kurt von Döring | |
| | 2 February 1918 – 16 March 1918 | 17 |
| Jastas 14, 20, 40s, 49 | 16 March 1918 – 24 March 1918 | 17 |
| Jastas 9, 21s, 45, 60 | Commanded by Oblt Oskar von Boenigk | |
| | 24 March 1918 – 6 June 1918 | 7 |
| Jastas 21s, 60, 81 | 6 June 1918 – 27 June 1918 | 7 |
| Jastas 21s, 39, 60, 81 | 27 June 1918 – 5 August 1918 | 7 |
| Jastas 21s, 60, 81 | 5 August 1918 – 27 August 1918 | 7 |
| Jastas 21s, 60, 81 | Commanded by ?† | |
| | 27 August 1918 – 24 September 1918 | 7 |
| Jastas 1, 57, 58, 59 | Commanded by Rittm Kurt von Döring | |
| | 18 October 1918 – EOW | 17 |

## Jagdgruppe Nr.5

| | | |
|---|---|---|
| Jastas 48, 53, 69 | Commanded by Rittm Konstantin von Braun | |
| | 8 March 1918 – 16 Mar 1918 | 18 |
| Jastas 22s, 63, 69 | 23 March 1918 – 18 April 1918 | 18 |
| Jastas 22s, 61, 63, 69 | 18 April 1918 – 12 May 1918 | 18 |
| Jastas 22s, 50, 63, 66, 81 | 30 May 1918 – 6 June 1918 | 7 |
| Jastas 1, 9, 41, 45, 50, 66 | 6 June 1918 – 12 August 1918 | 7 |
| Jastas 9, 41, 45, 50, 66 | 12 August 1918 – 23 September 1918 | 7 |
| Jastas 41, 47w, 49, 50, 60, 81 | 24 September 1918 – 22 October 1918 | 3 |

## Jagdgruppe Nr.6 (previously JGr Dixmuiden)

| | | |
|---|---|---|
| Jastas 7, 16b, 28w, 51 | Commanded by Oblt Hans Gandert | |
| | 1 March 1918 – 9 March 1918 | 4 |
| Jastas 7, 28w, 47, 51 | 9 March 1918 – 29 March 1918 | 4 |
| Jastas 7, 28w, 51 | 29 March 1918 – 12 April 1918 | 4 |

† Possibly Oblt Wilhelm Pritsch CO Jasta 81 on 3 September, who was the senior Commanding Officer.

| Jastas 7, 28w, 51, 56 | 12 April 1918 – 5 May 1918 | 4 |
| Jastas 7, 40s, 51, 56 | 5 May 1918 – 11 May 1918 | 4 |
| Jastas 7, 16b, 40s, 51, 56 | 11 May 1918 – 6 June 1918 | 4 |
| Jastas 7, 16b, 20, 40s, 51, 56 | 6 June 1918 – 1 October 1918 | 4 |
| | (Gandert POW 29 September 1918) | |
| Jastas 7, 20, 40s, 51 | Commanded by Hptm Erhard Milch | |
| | 1 October 1918 – EOW | 4 |

## Jagdgruppe Nr.7

| Jastas 18, 24s, 31, 36 | Commanded by Oblt Rudolf Berthold | |
| | 16 August 1917 – 1 September 1917 | 4 |
| Jastas 18, 24s, 36 | 1 September 1917 – 23 November 1917 | 4 |
| Jastas 18, 58 | Commanded by Oblt Hermann Martini | |
| | 15 March 1918 – 24 March 1918 | 17 |
| Jastas 29, 30, 41, 52, 57 | Commanded by Oblt Otto Schmidt | |
| | 24 March 1918 – 31 March 1918 | 6 |
| Jastas 29, 30, 41, 47w, 52, 57 | Commanded by Oblt Harald Auffahrt | |
| | 31 March 1918 – 9 April 1918 | 6 |
| Jastas 29, 30, 41, 43, 52 | 13 April 1918 – 18 May 1918 | 6 |
| | Commanded by Oblt Richard Flashar | |
| | 18 May 1918 – 6 June 1918 | 6 |
| Jastas 28w, 33, 57, 58 | Commanded by Ltn Emil Thuy | |
| | 6 June 1918 – 8 July 1918 | 2 |
| | 8 July 1918 – 11 August 1918 | 1 |
| | 11 August 1918 – 13 August 1918 | 2 |
| | 13 August 1918 – 25 August 1918 | 1 |
| | 25 August 1918 – 13 October 1918 | 17 |
| Jastas 28w, 30, 33, 43, 52, 63 | 13 October 1918 – EOW | 6 |

## Jagdgruppe Nr.8

| Jastas 23b, 32b, 35b, 59 | Commanded by Oblt Eduard von Schleich | |
| | 15 March 1918 – 8 August 1918 | 17 |
| Jastas 23b, 32b, 35b | 8 August 1918 – 29 September 1918 | 17 |
| | Became Bavarian JG IV | |

## Jagdgruppe Nr.9

| Jastas 3, 28w, 37 | Commanded by Oblt Hermann Kohze | |
| | 5 February 1918 – 13 March 1918 | 4 |
| Jastas 3, 37, 54s, 56 | 13 March 1918 – 11 April 1918 | 2 |
| Jastas 3, 16 (or 37), 54s, 56 | 11 April 1918 – 4 May 1918 | 4 |
| Jastas 3, 54s, 56 (or 16b) | 4 May 1918 – 6 June 1918 | 4 |
| Jastas 3, 47w, 49, 54s, 77b | 6 June 1918 – 9 July 1918 | 2 |
| Jastas 3, 47w, 49, 54s, 77b | 9 July 1918 – 4 September 1918 | 3 |
| Jastas 3, 18, 54s, 77b, 80b & Kest 3 | Commanded by Ltn August Raben | |
| | 8 September 1918 – EOW | 19 |

## Jagdgruppe Nr.10 (also known as JGr von Greim till 11 August 1918)

| Jastas 16b, 34b, 37 | Commanded by Oblt Robert von Greim | |
| | 16 March 1918 – 18 April 1918 | 2 |
| Jastas 34b, 37, 77b | 18 April 1918 – 6 June 1918 | 2 |
| Jastas 34b, 37 | 9 June 1918 – 31 July 1918 | 18 |
| Jastas 1, 39, 59 | Commanded by Oblt Hans von Boddien | |
| | 13 August 1918 – 1 September 1918 | 17 |
| | Commanded by Rittm Kurt von Döring | |
| | 2 September 1918 – 26 September 1918 | 17 |
| Jastas 1, 59 | 27 September 1918 – 17 October 1918 | 17 |
| (became JGr 4) | | |

**Jagdgruppe Nr.11**

| Jastas 7, 29, 33, 35b | Commanded by Oblt Otto Schmidt | |
| | 26 August 1917 – 28 November 1917 | 4 |
| Jastas 17, 22s, 63 | Commanded by Hptm Rudolf von Esebeck | |
| | 16 March 1918 – 23 March 1918 | 18 |
| Jastas 17, 48, 53, 61 | Commanded by Rittm Heinz von Brederlow | |
| | 19 May 1918 – 10 July 1918 | 18 |
| | 10 July 1918 – 25 July 1918 | 3 |
| | 25 July 1918 – 18 September 1918 | 9 |
| | 18 September 1918 – 25 September 1918 | 7 |
| | 25 September 1918 – EOW | 3 |

**Jagdgruppe Nr.12**

| Jastas 24s, 44s, 79b | Commanded by Ltn Heinrich Kroll | |
| | 4 March 1918 – 18 April 1918 | 18 |
| Jastas 24s, 42, 44s, 79b | 18 April 1918 – 14 August 1918 | 18 |
| | Commanded by Oblt Hasso von Wedel | |
| | 23 August 1918 – EOW | 18 |

**Jagdgruppe Nr.14**

| Jastas 1, 31, 39 | Commanded by Oblt Hans Kummetz | |
| | 20 September – 11 January 1918 | 14 |
| | Commanded by Oblt Walter Korte | |
| | 11 January 1918 – 13 March 1918 | 14 |

**Jagdgruppe Nr.15**

| Jastas 3, 8, 26, 27 | Commanded by Hptm Constantin von Bentheim | |
| | 26 August 1917 – 30 September 1917 | 4 |

**Jagdgruppe 'A'**

| Jastas 41, 47w, 49, 50, 60 | Commanded by Rittm Konstantin von Braun? | |
| | 22 October 1918 – EOW | 18 |

**Jagdgruppe 'Habsheim'**

| Jastas 71, 75, 76b | Commanded by Oblt Walther Karjus | |
| | 23 August 1918 – 18 September 1918 | 'B' |
| Jastas 69, 71, 75, 76b | Commanded by Oblt Alex Thomas | |
| | 18 September – EOW | 'B' |

**Jagdgruppe 'Lenz'**

| Jastas 22s, 63, 69, 76b | Commanded by Ltn Alfred Lenz | |
| | 7 July 1918 – 19 August 1918 | 1 |

**Jagdgruppe 'Marville'**

| Jastas 65, 67 | Commanded by Ltn Julius Fichter | |
| | 16 September 1918 – 7 October 1918 | 5 |

**Jagdruppe 7 Armee Ost**

| Jastas 9, 21s, 45, 66 | Commanded by Ltn Hans Joachim Rolfes | |
| | 29 September 1918 – EOW | 7 |

**Jagdgruppe 'Siempelkamp'**

| Jastas 64w, 65 | Commanded by Ltn Eugen Siempelkamp | |
| | 18 July 1918 – 14 September 1918 | 'C' |

**Marine Jagdgruppe**

| MFJs I, II | Commanded by Ltn z S Gotthard Sachsenberg | |
| | 19 October 1917 – 23 June 1918 | 4 |
| MFJs I, II, III | 23 June 1918 – 1 September 1918 | 4 |

# Jasta Colours

As is well known, the German fighter pilots of WWI began to decorate their aeroplanes in late 1916, and by 1917 they were becoming more and more colourful. Initially this was for in-flight identification, so that pilots could easily and quickly recognise one another, especially the Staffelführers and Kette leaders.

Whereas the Allied aircraft were almost always in drab camouflage to help them blend in with the terrain, the Germans went out of their way to have the most garish colour schemes. This probably had much to do with the Allied airmen flying offensively over the German side of the lines where they often had to fight their way back. With drying fuel tanks and perhaps low on ammunition, the pilots needed every bit of help available to get home.

As time went on, many Jastas started to enhance personal colour schemes and emblems with something like a standard Jasta identification colour or marking. While these were sometimes made standard, it did not seem to be obligatory in all cases. What follows is an attempt to make some sense of the various colour schemes as they pertained to certain Jastas, together with some personal schemes that either complemented the main scheme, or had some definite reason for going against it.

Aircraft arrived on the Jastas in basic factory finish, doped with either the manufacturers' basic 'colouring' or, in the case of Albatros machines, varnished plywood fuselages, which gave them a yellowish look. For instance, Fokker DrI Triplanes arrived in a streaked dark green, and the Pfalz in a silver dope colour. Upper wing surfaces and sometimes upper decking of the fuselage in 1917 were often painted in a camouflaged effect, with lilac/mauve and dark green. By 1918 the standard lozenge printed fabric had been designed as a camouflage, which was used on wings and fuselages. Lozenge fabric was carried on the undersides of wings and fuselages too, in a slightly lighter pattern. All of course could be overpainted on the units in the field.

## JASTA 1

Little is known, although aircraft had distinctive personal colour schemes on Albatros DIII fighters in Italy in late 1917. From October 1917 to January 1918 these personal markings were of various black and white designs.

## JASTA 2

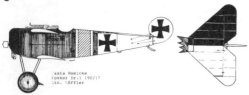

Jasta Boelcke
Fokker Dr.1 190/17
Ltn. Löffler

In the autumn of 1916, some Albatros DI and DII fighters were marked with a pilot's initials or part name, such as 'Bu' for Ltn Büttner, marked on the fuselage side. There is also some suggestion that some machines had some form of red colouring (which may have influenced one of its pilots, Manfred von Richthofen). Certainly there are RFC combat reports noting red aircraft, long before von Richthofen brought this colour into prominence. However, the actual shade of red has always been a problem for historians and probably the initial 'red' was little more than the reddish-brown colour used as camouflage in the autumn of 1916, which is probably what Jasta 2's machines sported.

By the summer of 1917 Jasta 2 (Boelcke) had a unit marking of white tails on Albatros DIIIs. Individual markings were in vogue; for instance

Leutnant Noth's machine was recorded as green with yellow spots by Lt W M Fry of 60 Squadron, who brought him down in May 1917. In March 1918 its Fokker DrI Triplanes had its Prussian colours of half white, half black tails and elevators, black engine cowlings with white faceplates. Personal fuselage markings varied, such as Hermann Vallendor's large white 'V' between cockpit and fuselage cross, or Otto Löffler's lemon yellow fuselage band, edged in white — his former 10th Grenadier Regt colours. Karl Bolle had a similar marking, a broad yellow band edged black and white (Kurassier Regt Nr.7) between the rear of the cockpit and the fuselage cross. The later Fokker DVIIs continued the half and half tail marking. This varied; it may have been used as a Kette identification, for upper surfaces have been seen as white/black and black/white. The Fokkers also carried white fronts on their engine cowling. Fuselages streaky green/brown or lozenge fabric later and wings lozenge fabric too.

## JASTA 4

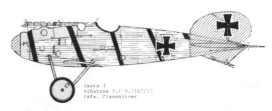

Jasta 4
Albatros D.V D.1162/17
Vzfw. Clausnitzer

Halberstadt DVs in the autumn of 1916 were

reddish-brown and olive green in colour with blue undersides. Hans Buddecke's machine also had blue struts and narrow yellow fuselage bands either side of the fuselage cross. In the summer of 1917, Albatros DIIIs and DVs had a single black spiral band which encircled (wrapped around) the fuselage from nose to tail. This was continued on the Pfalz DIII, DIIIa and Albatros DV machines until April 1918. Then its Fokker DrI Triplanes carried 'off white' cowlings, struts and wheel covers until June, as it was deemed not possible to continue its former marking on the DrIs. Fokker DVIIs had black noses, struts and wheel covers.

## JASTA 5

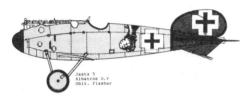

Jasta 5
Albatros D.V
Oblt. Flashar

Early Albatros DII and DIII machines were marked with large numbers or initials on fuselages, repeated under the lower wing, to identify pilots. By January 1918, its Albatros DVs were often, but not always, marked with a white chevron on the upper wing. Basic unit markings on their machines were green tails with a thin red outline and red spinners. Von Hippel flew a green-tailed Albatros DV, with a white fuselage band aft of the cockpit and a large letter 'H' on the port underside of the lower wing. In 1918 Oblt Flashar had a large mailed gauntlet insignia painted on the fuselage sides forward of the cross, with the white upper wing chevron marked over lozenge fabric. Fokker DrI Triplanes received from JGI in May generally stayed in old markings. Purely personal markings were in evidence on a few Fokker DVIIs.

## JASTA 6

By the late summer of 1917, Albatros DIII and DV machines had black and white chordwise stripes on upper and lower tailplane surfaces; occasionally black noses too. Fokker Triplanes had black and white stripes on the tailplane (top and bottom) and black engine cowlings. On Fokker DVIIs and Fokker EVs, the black and white tails continued, with black and white cowlings (or black and white petal pattern on EVs) and black and white wheel covers. Lozenge wing and fuselages.

## JASTA 7

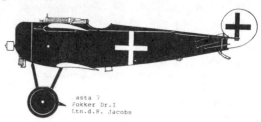

Jasta 7
Fokker Dr.I
Ltn.d.R. Jacobs

By 1918 this unit's aircraft had predominantly black fuselages and tails on their Albatros DV and Pfalz DIIIa machines. Josef Jacobs preferred to fly the Fokker Triplane, even when his unit was completely equipped with Fokker DVIIs, and his personal machine was almost entirely black, fuselage, tail and upper wings surfaces.

## JASTA 8

Albatros Scouts carried narrow stripes on rudder, fin and tailplane surfaces across the span and vertically up the rudder. This appears to be black on white, the white extending to cover the tail skid support. Walter Göttsch when he was with Jasta 8 over the winter of 1917 used white as his Kette marking.

## JASTA 9

Fokker DVIIs had black fuselages, white radiators and white wings. Walter Blume's aircraft carried the letter 'B' on its fuselage sides.

## JASTA 10

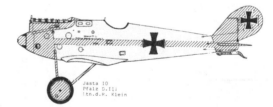

Jasta 10
Pfalz D.III
Ltn.d.R. Klein

Yellow noses on their Albatros DIIs and DVs in late summer of 1917. This was retained and supplemented (often) by yellow struts and wheel covers on Pfalz DIIIs and Fokker DVIIs. Pfalz 1370/17 had a green tail. Werner Voss's famous Fokker Triplane had a chrome yellow cowling (with face marking). Fokker DVIIs also had yellow noses, struts and wheel covers.

## JASTA 11

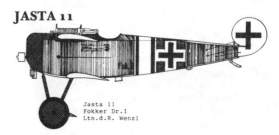

Jasta 11
Fokker Dr.I
Ltn.d.R. Wenzl

Influenced by Manfred von Richthofen's choice of
red, Jasta aircraft largely followed with red fuselages, tail struts and wheel covers on Albatros
DIIIs in the early summer of 1917. However,
neither Richthofen's nor other aircraft were usually
completely red, usually just the wings, fuselage and
tailplane, the undersides of wings being pale blue.
Von Richthofen occasionally had all red aircraft
during major offensives, not only as a recognition
sign for his pilots but for ground observers. Like
all air leaders, it was necessary to be instantly
spotted by his men when they were re-forming after
combat over a predetermined location. Similar
markings carried on Fokker Triplanes, the red
extending to the engine cowlings, struts and
wheels. This was continued on Fokker DVIIs.
Personal identification tended to be by an alternate
colour on the tails, such as yellow for Lothar von
Richthofen (from his 4th Dragoon Regt colour),
black on Schäfer's, white for Allmenröder, green
for Kurt Wolff. Often individual colours in any
Jasta were chosen from a pilot's former army unit
colour. Red was difficult to come by and the shade
varied depending on the source of supply. On
Richthofen's last Triplane, a red was mixed with
black to darken it, but it was still a rich colour,
and not the shade of maroon sometimes referred to.

## JASTA 12

Jasta 12
Fokker Dr.I
Vzfw. Neckel

Black tails, extending to midway along the fuselages, white spinners with a black cowling ring on
Albatros DIIIs and DVs, late 1917. Paul Billik's
personal marking was the well-photographed large
swastika emblem on a white square aft of the
cockpit on his DV. Black tails, including rudder,
and white cowlings on Fokker Triplanes. Otherwise the rest of the fuselage and upper wing
surfaces were either camouflaged mauve and green
on Albatros Scouts, or streaked dark green on
Triplanes. Undersides were pale blue. Von
Tutschek's well-photographed Triplane shows
these markings off very well, including the black
and white streamers from his lower wingtips to
denote the leader. The Triplanes seemed to sport
large white individual markings on their fuselages;
Blumenbach's 217/17 had a large white band
marked from just behind the cockpit to the fuselage
cross, while Ulrich Neckel had a large white
chevron, again from the cross to cockpit. The unit
also reverted to white rudders as directed by
Kogenluft in March. Fokker DVIIs had dark blue
fuselages and tailplanes with white noses.

## JASTA 13

Jasta 13
Fokker D.VII (OAW)
Ltn. Franz Büchner

Albatros Scouts had white tails and Fokker Dr1
Triplanes carried white cowlings and tails in
March 1918. Personal markings were marked on
the fuselage sides; Hans Pippart carried a white
vertical wavy band around the fuselage just aft of
the cockpit. Fokker DVIIs had green noses, dark
blue fuselages with a thin white line as the dividing
line. Wheel covers green and tailplanes blue, with
white stabiliser and rudder. Wings were lozenge
fabric while undersurfaces were pale blue. Franz
Büchner's DVII had a white and green (three
squares wide) checkerboard band aft of the cockpit
(Saxon colours), and in place of the fuselage cross
he had the head of a werewolf on a green
background.

## JASTA 14

Jasta 14
Albatros D.Va D.5253/17
Ltn. Sakowsky

In late 1917 a horizontal black and white fuselage
line was marked from nose to tail on Albatros DVs,
which was continued on its Fokker Triplanes in the
spring and early summer of 1918. Other aircraft
carried individual fuselage markings such as one
large white fuselage band, a black and white
angled fuselage band, and a 'barber's pole' white
band around the fuselage.

## JASTA 15

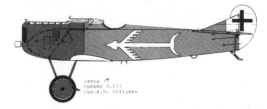

Jasta 15
Fokker D.VII
Ltn.d.R. Veltjens

One of its Pfalz DIIIs (the captured 4184/17) had
doped aluminium fuselage and fuselage motif in
black. In March 1918 its Fokker Triplanes had
white engine cowlings, and possibly brown
rudders. Ltn von Budde's tailplane was marked
with chevrons to denote the leader, winter/spring
1917-18. Under Rudolf Berthold in JGII, they had

Prussian blue fuselages and tails, red noses and white fins on SSW DIIIs and Fokker DVIIs. Berthold himself flew a DVII with blue wings and fuselage, red nose and cowling back to the cockpit, red wheel covers, white fin and white upper wing centre section. On the fuselage sides he carried a winged sword in white.

## JASTA 16b

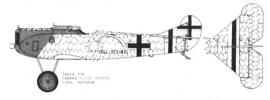

In January and February 1918 it had Albatros DVs and Pfalz DIIIs with black tails. Max Holtzem had an aluminium doped Pfalz with ten narrow black fuselage stripes between cockpit and tail. Painted over these was an eight-pointed black and white comet/star with arcing black and white tail. By late summer its Fokker DVIIs sported blue noses and a white-black-white band wrapped vertically around the tail.

## JASTA 17

Fokker DVIIs carried dark painted fuselages with white radiators by late 1918.

## JASTA 18

Under Berthold in early 1918, this unit had red noses and dark (Prussian?) blue fuselages on its Albatros D IIIs, DVs and Pfalz Scouts. Under August Raben they had vermilion red noses, white radiators and white rear fuselages. On the fuselage sides a black raven on Pfalz DIIIa, Triplanes and Fokker DVIIs. Individual DVII fuselage markings ranged from a three-pointed star (Kustner) which also carried inverted stripes on the upper surfaces of the tailplane, two narrow red bands around the fuselage forward of the tailplane (Glatz), four raven chicks below the main raven (von Buren), while Raben himself had the red nose paint extended back midway down the fuselage, his raven being shown in white.

## JASTA 19

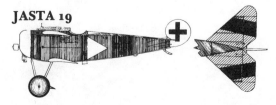

In the summer of 1917, Albatros DII, DIII and DVs were marked with stylistic (3-D effect) black and white pilot's initial(s), e.g. 'O' for Oertelt. Fokker Triplanes, in the spring of 1918, carried slightly inverted black bands on yellow tailplanes, and white cowlings. Early Triplanes also had a yellow number on the fuselage sides, repeated on the top fuselage decking. Walter Göttsch carried the number '2' on his 202/17, while 167/17 had a yellow '3'. Göttsch also brought with him the white marking of his Kette in Jasta 8, by painting the top surface of his upper wing of a second Triplane white. He also carried a white swastika marking on the fuselage but no fuselage cross. Rudolf Reinau's Triplane (504/17) had a white band wrapped about his DrI, seven white sections being evident, and again no fuselage cross. Undersurfaces were light blue. Fokker DVIIs had yellow noses, dark blue fuselages and tailplanes with white rudders and fins.

## JASTA 20

In the late summer of 1918 its aircraft had brown fuselages, white noses, white horizontal stabiliser/ rudders and elevators with dark outline.

## JASTA 21s

Late summer 1917 onwards, its Albatros Scouts had green and mauve fuselage and top wing surfaces, light blue undersurfaces. Some had olive green top decking only, with the rest of the fuselage left in natural varnished plywood. Behind the cockpit aircraft had a broad black and white band as a unit marking. Individual personal fuselage markings carried between this band and the cross. Eduard von Schleich's well-photographed Albatros DV showed off these markings well, with a green nose. His personal insignia was the brown crowned Bavarian lion rampant on a circle of light blue and white diamonds, forward of the cross, a small eight-pointed black and brown star beyond the cross. Fritz Höhn flew an aluminium doped Pfalz DIII which carried red zigzag markings to both fuselage sides which joined on the fuselage top. Also two broad red bands chordwise across the silver rudder area, while narrow red bands encircled the tailplane and elevators. Narrow black horizontal lines were painted on the forward fuselage, back to the cockpit, while a black 'H' was marked beneath the cockpit. Similar schemes were applied to Fokker DVIIs in 1918. Karl Thom's DVII carried a much larger black and white fuselage band from cockpit to fuselage cross. A large 'T' edged in white was marked below the cockpit. Fin and rudder white, lozenge fabric wings.

## JASTA 22s

Only personal markings are known. Its Pfalz DIIIs were generally aluminium doped completely. Alfred Lenz carried two large black horizontal bars either side of the fuselage cross, the outward ends being pointed. Lenz also had two straight black lines (marked for and aft) just outboard of the upper wing centre section, and two inverted black lines over tailplane and elevators. Albert Wünsch surrounded his fuselage cross with two black diamond-shape lines which met above and beneath the fuselage with the marking from the opposite side.

## JASTA 23b

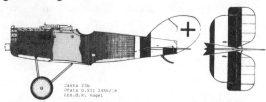

Jasta 23b
Pfalz D.XII 2486/18
Ltn.d.R. Vogel

In early 1917 some of its Albatros Scouts had dark (black?) fuselages but by the summer its machines were marked with a black swastika (an ancient good luck symbol) aft of the cockpit. In March 1918 a broad white band was painted vertically around tailplane, fin and fuselage, often supplemented by black bands fore and aft of this white band. These appeared on Albatros DVs, Roland DVIs and Pfalz DXIIs eventually. Ltn Vogel's Pfalz DXII brought down inside Allied lines on 15 September 1918 (2486/18) had lozenge wing surfaces, camouflaged fuselage in mauve, pale grey, dark green and light green, with broad white and black bands forward of the tail. Stabiliser and rudder were white, wheel covers dark green.

## JASTA 24s

Only personal markings known. In late 1918 Friedrich Altemeier's Fokker EV carried three interlocking rings on the fuselage, below the cockpit, probably black, edged white, just as he had done with his earlier Albatros DII and DIII. Stabiliser and rudders were white.

## JASTA 25

Had personal initials in black or white on Roland DIIa and Albatros DIIIs in Macedonia, also on Halberstadt DIIs.

## JASTA 26

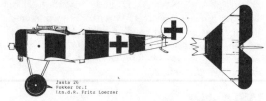

Jasta 26
Fokker Dr.I
Ltn.d.R. Fritz Loerzer

In the autumn of 1917, broad black and white bands encircled the entire fuselage and tail on Albatros DIIIs and DVs. The Fokker DrIs continued this, with black engine cowlings; the same with Fokker DVIIs. Fritz Loerzer's DrI, as a leader's identification, had its top wing centre section and the front third of the upper wing surface painted black. Otto Esswein had a large letter 'E' painted on the white band immediately behind the cockpit, repeated on a white band across the upper wing's centre section. The tailplanes had one broad white and two black bands across the upper surfaces.

## JASTA 27

In the summer of 1917, Albatros Scouts had black rear fuselages and tail units (later all fuselage was black), with a broad white band just aft of the cockpit, with a large black numeral for individual identification. Hermann Göring's DV had an all-black fuselage, white spinner and white band immediately behind it, all-white tail and rudder and white wheel covers; standard green and mauve upper wing surfaces and pale blue undersides. He had carried two double inverted white bands (chevrons?) on the upper wing of his earlier DIII with a single black chevron on the underside of the lower wing. Fokker Triplanes, in the spring of 1918, had yellow cowlings, struts and tail units, the rest left in natural streaked olive green upper surfaces, light blue underneath. The number on fuselage was withdrawn, pilots now using personal markings; Göring for instance had his struts, tail unit, rear fuselage, engine cowling and wheel covers in white on his DrI, much the same as his Albatros earlier. Fokker DVIIs continued with the general theme.

## JASTA 28w

Jasta 28w
Albatros D.V 1154/17
Ltn. Max von Müller

In August 1917, Albatros DIII and DV aircraft had yellow tailplanes with one chordwise black band overpainted on each side of the tailplane and elevator. Max Müller had a varnished plywood fuselage with white rudder and wheel covers. D1154/17 also carried a large black comet style fuselage marking edged white, red spinner and the letter 'M' beneath both lower wings.

## JASTA 29

Jasta 29
Fokker D.VII 387/18
Oblt. Auffarth

Albatros DIIIs had black and white numerals or letters on the fuselage. Brown and green upper wing surfaces, pale blue underneath. Fokker DVIIs, in the summer of 1918, carried yellow noses and green fuselages. A comet marking appeared on Harald Auffahrt's DVII's green fuselage, in the shape of an eight-pointed star with three curling trail lines in white. Stabiliser and rudder white, wings lozenge fabric.

## JASTA 30

During February to May 1918, Pfalz DIIIa machines were aluminium doped, marked with an orange diamond shape outlined in black on both sides of the fuselage, and a large diamond covering both surfaces of the tailplane and elevators. At least one machine had dark horizontal lines painted on the forward part of the nose and engine cowling. Ltn von der Marwitz's machine (4203/17) had his tail painted orange.

## JASTA 31

Its OAW-built Albatros Scouts had natural varnish finish on its fuselages with various personal emblems. Mauve and green camouflage to upper wing surfaces, light blue underneath. Richard Wenzl of this unit carried a personal marking of a broad white band edged black and white, midway down and around the fuselage of his 1917 fighter, a marking he later carried on his Jasta 11 Fokker Dr1 and again with Jasta 6 in 1918.

## JASTA 32b

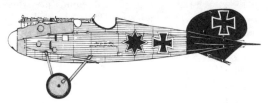

In September and October 1917, Albatros DVs had black tail units.

## JASTA 33

Under von Schönebeck in the summer of 1918, Fokker DVIIs had yellow noses and individual white numerals on the noses. (Possibly yellow tailplanes too.)

## JASTA 34b

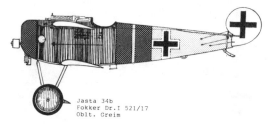

Jasta 34b
Fokker Dr.I 521/17
Oblt. Greim

From early 1918, silver-white fuselaged Albatros DVs and Pfalz DIIIs. Pilots identified by coloured bands around the fuselage. Rudolf Stark's colour was lilac; a photograph of his Pfalz DIII shows the spinner was lilac too. Fokker Triplanes and Fokker DVIIs had silver-white rear fuselages and tailplanes still with coloured bands for pilot identification. Robert Greim flew a silver-tailed Triplane (521/17) in June 1918; his personal marking comprised a red engine cowling and two broad red fuselage bands between cockpit and cross, divided by a thin silver gap. Johann Pütz carried a green engine cowling and two green fuselage bands, plus the Jasta's silver-white rear fuselage and tail.

## JASTA 35b

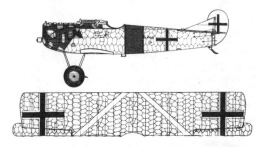

From May 1918 onwards, aircraft were marked with a (usually) white inverted chevron on the top wing (its apex facing forward in line of flight). However, this might have merely been two white bands, angled inwards from the edge of the aileron to the edge of the centre section. Sometimes this was repeated on the underside of the lower wing in black or white. Pilots were identified by coloured bands on the fuselage, sometimes coloured noses and tails too. Seen on Pfalz DIIIs, Roland DVIs, Pfalz DXIIs and Fokker DVIIs. Max Kämmerer had a yellow band behind the cockpit of his DXII (2454/18) but this did not extend to below the fuselage. He also carried a large yellow letter 'K' beneath the cockpit. Both wings lozenge fabric. Fuselage camouflaged in mauve (nose area), grey (to rear of cockpit), dark green (cross area) and pale green (rear fuselage) and dark grey on the fuselage back from a line starting from the stabiliser. The stabiliser and rudder were white, interplane struts pale grey, wheel covers dark green.

## JASTA 36

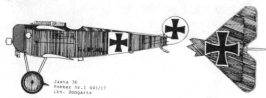

Jasta 36
Fokker Dr.I 441/17
Ltn. Bongartz

Blue noses and Albatros Scouts, Fokker Triplanes, Fokker DVIIs and Fokker EVs. Its Triplanes had normal green streaked camouflage and for a period they carried an unusual extra Patee cross on the upper decking of the tailplane, forward of the rudder. Other DrIs had a white line midway across the elevator. Fokker EVs in late 1918 had lozenge fabric, olive/brown wings and white rudder fin and cowling. Struts were light grey.

## JASTA 37

Jasta 37
Albatros D.Va
Ltn. Schreiber

In late 1917, early 1918, Albatros DIIIs and DVs had tailplanes diagonally striped in narrow black and white bands. Wheel covers also black and white striped and black spinners. Under Ernst Udet's command, summer 1917–March 1918, this was supplemented by all-black fuselages with white numerals on the nose and white symbols on fuselages. Udet himself carried a white chevron on the nose of his DV with a white 'LO' on the fuselage forward of the cross. Later, Fokker DVIIs mainly had diagonal black and white stripes only on the tailplane and elevators. Ltn Albert Hets also had his Fokker's fuselage painted black with a red band around it (712/18).

## JASTA 39

While this unit served in Italy, its pilots nevertheless still adorned their machines in similar fashion to their brethren in France. Only personal markings are known, such as August Raben having a similarly marked Albatros DIII as he later flew with Jasta 18 in France, with a black raven marking forward of the fuselage cross. Another carried fuselage stripes much like Jasta 26, while yet another had horizontal white lines marked along its fuselage and top decking.

## JASTA 40s

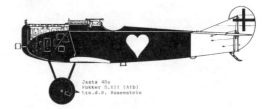

Jasta 40s
Fokker D.VII (Alb)
Ltn.d.R. Rosenstein

Saxon colours of white and green applied. Helmut Dilthey, leader in the early summer of 1918, flew a green and white striped Albatros DV. In the summer of 1918 this changed, Fokker DVIIs, and a few Albatros and Pfalz Scouts, having black fuselages, struts and wheel covers, with white tail units. Pilot's emblems on the fuselage sides in white. Some time after August the white tails were modified with many narrow chordwise stripes in black or very dark blue. Carl Degelow, who commanded from July 1918 to the Armistice, carried a large painting of a white stag on the side of his Pfalz DIIIa and Fokker DVII.

## JASTA 41

In early 1917 its Albatros Scouts had lozenge wing surfaces and natural varnished plywood fuselages. Ltn Albert Dietlen's machine carried a large sweeping dark (black?) band from the cockpit to the underneath of the lower fuselage side, probably repeated on the starboard side.

## JASTA 43

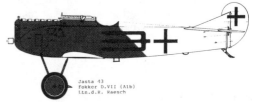

Jasta 43
Fokker D.VII (Alb)
Ltn.d.R. Raesch

In the spring of 1918, Albatros DIII and DVa machines had white tail units. In the summer their Fokker DVIIs all had white tails with a small black number on the fin. Noses and forward fuselages were in various individual colours and markings. Josef Raesch's DVII was white back from a diagonal line aft of the cockpit and carried what appears to be a three-pronged trident head facing forward. An example of its Pfalz DXIIs was silver doped fuselage, totally white tail and rudder, black number on the stabiliser and lozenge wing surfaces.

## JASTA 45

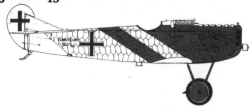

In the summer of 1918, Fokker DVIIs had dark-coloured noses and light-coloured rear fuselages with diagonal demarcations. Wings and remaining area of fuselage were in lozenge fabric. Any personal markings were carried on the fuselage sides.

## JASTA 46

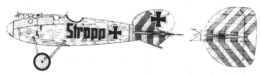

In April and May 1918, Albatros DVa and Pfalz DIIIa machines were marked with dark green and yellow chevron stripes on the tailplane and stabiliser, as shown in the National Air and Space Museum's example of the 'Stropp' Albatros. In the summer of 1918, and later, its Fokker DVIIs had white fuselages and tails aft of the cockpit with dark coloured noses. Other surfaces had lozenge fabric. Oskar Hennrich carried a large letter black 'H' aft of the cockpit as his personal marking.

## JASTA 47w

From Friedrich Ehmann's combat report (4 Nov 1918) we see that his Fokker DVII had a red nose and brown fuselage, Ehmann also noting a yellow band round the fuselage (4058/18). The earlier Pfalz DIIIa machines may have had red noses, factory-finish silver wings and dark brown fuselages too, which Mannock could have interpreted as 'black' in his combat report (11 May 1918) when he shot down Otto Äckerle.

## JASTA 49

An example of the unit's Albatros DIII (OAW) shows varnished plywood fuselage, dark red rear fuselage and stabiliser, lozenge wings, rudder and wheel covers. Either side of the fuselage cross, two broad zigzag fuselage bands, white centre, two blue edges. These were personal markings: colours highly speculative. Aircraft had pale blue noses and grey struts. Staffelführer Franz Ray seems to have flown an all-black Albatros DIII with white stabiliser and tail, off-white wheel covers and lozenge wing fabric.

## JASTA 50

OAW-built Albatros DIIIs had chevron-style stripes on their tailplanes, in April–May 1918. The dark line also appeared on the rear fuselage sides beneath the rear tailplane. Colouring is unclear, sky blue and red being suggested, or more likely black (or red) and white. Fokker DVIIs in the summer of 1918 had similar markings on a white tail unit.

## JASTA 51

Late 1918, its aircraft had tailplanes divided into right half black, left half green on upper surfaces.

## JASTA 52

Under Paul Billik's command, Fokker DVIIs in the summer of 1918 had all-black fuselages and tailplanes with pilot's personal markings in white on fuselage sides aft of the cockpit.

## JASTA 53

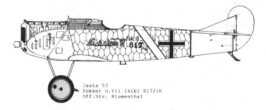

Jasta 53
Fokker D.VII (Alb) 817/18
Off.Stv. Blumenthal

In the summer of 1918, Fokker DVIIs had white, or off-white, noses and tails, as per Fritz Blumenthal's captured 817/18 'Nickchen IV' (12 Aug 1918).

## JASTA 56

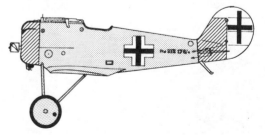

Summer 1918, under Lutz Beckmann, Fokker DVIIs had light blue-grey fuselages and yellow noses and tail units. Beckmann's own DVII had a red nose, the colour extending on the upper engine area back to the cockpit. Red fuselage band midway along the fuselage which had a white 'S-shape' marking (no cross), red rear fuselage starting at the tailplane. Stabiliser and rudder were white. Wing surfaces were lozenge fabric.

## JASTA 57

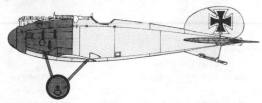

From formation, OAW Albatros DIII, DVs and Fokker DVIIs had pale blue fuselages and (usually) tailplanes, white stabiliser and fin, with different coloured noses painted back to the cockpit to identify the pilot. Paul Strähle's nose colour was red and he also had a broad red fuselage band aft of the cockpit on his DV and DVII and red wheel covers. Lozenge upper wing surfaces, pale blue underneath.

## JASTA 58

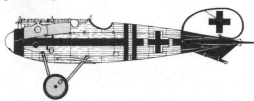

In the early summer of 1918, Albatros DVs apparently had white spinners with a black band immediately behind it, and black tailplanes. Stabiliser and fin was white, edged in black. Fokker DVIIs followed suit, with white radiator shells and black tail units.

## JASTA 59

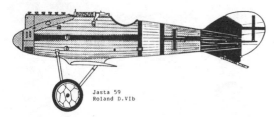

Jasta 59
Roland D.VIb

Personal markings only known. Ltn Lehmann's Albatros DV in 1918 probably had grey spinner, nose panel, struts and wheel covers. White rudder and a broad white fuselage stripe edged black (upon which Lehmann had a black cat with arched back marking). Pale coloured broad band forward of the tailplane.

## JASTA 60

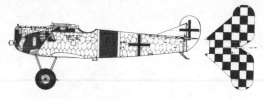

Fokker DVIIs in 1918 had black and white checkerboard tailplanes.

## JASTA 62

Jasta 62
Albatros D.Va
Ltn.d.R. Näther

According to the interrogation of Vfw Stadley (POW 27 June 1918), Albatros DVa fighters had black fuselages with red spinners, camouflaged upper surfaces on wings and presumably tailplanes. The picture of Max Näther's DVa would seem to confirm this.

## JASTA 63

Jasta 63
Albatros D.Va
Ltn. Leptien

Again, according to the aforementioned interrogation, 1918 Albatros DVa aircraft were all yellow except for camouflaged wings and tail. Jasta marking was black diamonds all over the fuselage, with natural varnish ply between them (which may refer to the 'yellow') and white tails. In fact, the location of the black tended to depict the varnished areas as 'full' diamond shapes. Lozenge wing surfaces.

## JASTA 64w

According to a POW interrogation report in April 1918, this unit had broad black and red bands on their tailplanes, these being Württemberg colours.

## JASTA 65

Judging from colours of Fokker DVII 'U.10' in the National Air and Space Museum, the unit had grey fuselages with chocolate brown noses and tailplanes. Lozenge fabric on wings and fuselage, white stabiliser and fin.

## JASTA 66

Oddly enough, Rudolf Windisch, the Staffelführer, carried a very similar personal marking of a leaping stag on his Fokker DVII, as that used by Carl Degelow of Jasta 40. Windisch's Fokker also carried lozenge fabric wings and fuselage. Apparently the stag emblem came from the symbol of a hospital in Windisch's native Dresden where he recuperated after being wounded in 1914. (Carl Degelow (Jasta 40) also spent time there.)

## JASTA 68

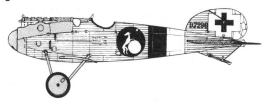

In April–May 1918, Albatros DVa machines were marked with a broad black (forward) and white (aft) band just forward of the tail. Fokker DVIIs flown later may have been similarly marked. Personal markings were placed forward of these bands.

## JASTA 71

Albatros DVa aircraft in the summer of 1918, and later Fokker DVIIs, had three chordwise white and red (?) stripes on the tailplanes, one in line with rudder and two across either wing surface. Large Balken crosses edged with varying degrees of white.

## JASTA 72s

Lozenge fabric wings and tailplane on Fokker DVIIs. Carl Menckhoff, the Staffelführer, carried a large white letter 'M' on the fuselage sides, repeated over the whole of the top wing centre section. Other pilots carried personal markings on fuselage sides. Rudder and the rear half of stabiliser white.

## JASTA 73

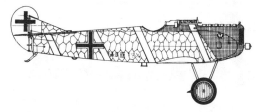

In May 1918, OAW-built Albatros DVa machines had a unit marking of a black spiral stripe or band around the fuselage from nose to tail. Personal markings included black horizontal stripes on the stabiliser (but not rudder) and also on tailplane. On Fokker DVIIs the spiral band was replaced by a white spiral stripe, with a narrow black edge, encircling the whole fuselage.

## JASTA 74

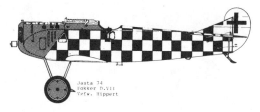

Supposedly their Fokker DVIIs had dark blue noses. The black and white checks on Willy Hippert's DVII 'Mimmi' are presumed to be a personal marking.

## JASTA 75

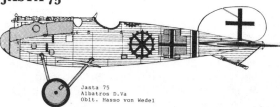

In June–July 1918, under Hasso von Wedel, Albatros DVa machines carried a narrow white-edged black (?) band vertically around the fuselage just forward of the tail, and chordwise black and white stripes over the tailplane.

## JASTA 76b

Believed to have blue and white striped tailplanes according to an Allied intelligence report. Vfw

Karl Koller's Albatros DVa 7221/17 (POW 25 May 1918) seems to confirm this description. Another machine brought down in April, flown by Ltn Richard Emmerich, had a white fuselage band and a large 'R' on the fuselage.

## JASTA 77b

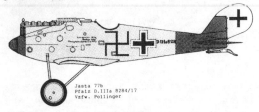

Jasta 77b
Pfalz D.IIIa 8284/17
Vzfw. Pollinger

Had 'Bavarian blue' tails and rear fuselages on Pfalz DIIIa and Albatros DV machines. Jakob Pollinger's Pfalz Scout 8284/17 (G/3/15) carried a large black swastika marking below and just aft of the cockpit.

## JASTA 78b

Jasta 78b
Fokker D.VII (OAW) 4464/18
Ltn. Jungwirth

In late summer 1918 its Fokker DVIIs had blue fuselages, tailplanes and wheel covers, with two vertical white fuselage bands just ahead of the tail. Stabiliser and fin white. Noses remained in factory finish.

## JASTA 79b

Believed to have carried crossed blue and white bars on the upper surface of the top wing on its Fokker DVIIs. Fuselages were a bluish-grey (also applied to tailplane, struts and wheel covers), with white noses, engine cowlings, fins and rudders. Pilot's had individual personal markings on the fuselage sides, e.g. an Ace of Spades 'card' (von Böhning), a chevron, a circle, 'Rudi', and 'Lot' (F Wagner).

## JASTA 80b

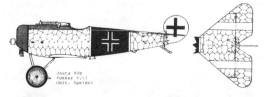

Jasta 80b
Fokker D.VI
Objt. Speidel

According to US intelligence, aircraft had 'tails' painted in black and white stripes. Ltn Spiedel's Fokker DVI had two chordwise white stripes only on a lozenge fabric tailplane, and a black rear fuselage.

## Seefrontstaffel I

The unit markings, dark, possibly red, noses, tails and elevators but with white fins. Fuselages believed to be grey. Personal markings were geometric designs on the fuselages aft of the cockpit. Lozenge fabric on Albatros DIII(OAW), DV and DVa aircraft.

## MFJ I

Marine Jasta 2
Pfalz D.III 4169/17
Flgmt. Undiener

This unit's Albatros Scouts had pale Brunswick green, bronze green and dark Venetian red camouflaged wings and tailplanes, changed to lozenge in 1918. Aircraft were generally marked with a dark spinner and cowling ring which in fact may have been chrome yellow. Mostly the aircraft seemed to carry personal markings, such as a stylised 'K' beneath a crown on a dark fuselage band, edged white, for Flgmt Künstler. Another machine carried an eight-point star on fuselage sides and top decking, or two fuselage bands. It is believed most personal markings were in black and white. Some Albatros DVs also had their fuselages stippled with dark green paint. The Staffelführer, Ltn z S Sachsenberg, flew Albatros DVa 5426/17, marked with a black and white chequered fuselage band. Flgmstr Haggenmüller had a white-outlined black 'H' on the fuselage of his Albatros DV 2078/17, which also bore a small number '31' on the fin above the serial number.

## MFJ II

Marine Jasta 1
Albatros D.V 2078/17
Flgmstr. Haggenmüller

Albatros Scouts carried personal markings, such as an 'H' for Flgmstr Haggenmüller's machine (the same as he used with MFJ I), 'V' for Karl Voss, a form of swastika on Vzflgmst Hechner's machine and a four-square (Polish) insignia on Ltn Heinrich's. Its Pfalz DIIIs were aluminium doped with an all-white tail assembly. Unit marking was yellow (or possibly red) on spinner and nose cowling. Vzflgmstr Kuring's machine carried a large yellow fuselage band marked back from midway to just aft of the cockpit. Interplane struts were also yellow. Flgmstr Arnim Undiener's Pfalz (169/17) had a double chequered band of black and white around the fuselage, midway between cockpit and the white tail. Another machine carried black lattice markings around its fuselage. Yellow certainly seems to be the predominant colour and all personal markings were either initials or geometric designs aft of the cockpit, although in the summer of 1917 large numbers were also carried on fuselage sides. There also seems to be a large coloured (yellow?) band around the fuselage of the unit's Siemens DIVs in 1918.

## MFJ III

The unit markings were white spinner, nose cowling and tailplane on their aluminium doped Pfalz DIII and DIIIa machines. Personal markings were black or white geometric designs aft of the cockpit or chrome yellow banding on fuselages or wings. With many transfers of pilots between the Marine units, and pilots taking their aircraft or markings with them, it is difficult to ascribe any particular individual markings to any of the Marine Jastas.

# Fighter 'G' Numbers

Towards the end of 1916 it was decided for Intelligence purposes to allocate a 'G' serial number to those German aircraft which came down on the British side of the lines. Despite the main volume of air action being fought on the German side, there was a surprising number of aircraft which did come down on the British side. Not all were in any condition to be deemed a captured machine, many were no more than smouldering wrecks, but once the system was in place, 'all' such machines, whether wreckage or an intact aeroplane, were generally given a 'G' number. There is evidence, however, that when aircraft came down in an active battle front, there was not always time to salvage anything from the machines and so a 'G' number was not allocated. There are also known to be some 'G' numbers that were not allocated at all. As the war progressed, allocation of these numbers was broken down into Brigade; thus from early April numbers will show individual Brigade allocations, e.g. G/1/2 is the 1st Brigade's No.2.

Some captured aircraft became quite famous photographically, or were shown at wartime exhibitions in Britain, while others were test-flown, etc. Where little more than wreckage resulted, just bits and pieces were sometimes salvaged, perhaps guns or the engine. Because there seems to be no definitive G-list, the following has been made up from several sources, both official and unofficial. There are too some aircraft noted as being brought down inside British lines but where no 'G' number seems either relevant or allocated. Sometimes the answer is that the date of the 'capture' and the date of the 'G' number allocation is different, and therefore it is difficult to tie the two together. Therefore the apparent non-G numbered aircraft are noted for future reference, or at least to show other aircraft that were brought down or were forced down inside British lines. For the fates of the German pilots, refer to the master A–Z pilot list.

| No. | Date | A/C Type | Serial | Where brought down | Pilot | Jasta | Remarks |
|---|---|---|---|---|---|---|---|
| | 1916 | | | | | | |
| G1† | 16 Nov | Albatros DI 'Bu' | 391/16 | Nr Pommier, Arras | Ltn K H O Büttner | J2 | BE2c 8 Sqn / Capt G A Parker / Lt H E Hervey |
| | 1917 | | | | | | |
| G5 | 25 Jan | Albatros DIII 'K' | 1982/16 | Moislains, SE Bapaume | Flgmt G Kinkel | J2 | DH2 7884 / 24 Sqn / Lt A E McKay |
| G8‡ | 23 Jan | Albatros DII | | Grandcourt | Vfw P Ostrop | J2 | DH2 7930 / 24 Sqn / Lt E C Pashley |
| ? | 26 Jan | Albatros?? | | | Vzflgmstr M Winkelmann | J5 | BE2e 9 Sqn 6274 |
| G10 | 13 Feb | Albatros DIII | 1990/16 | nr Sailly-Saillisel | Ltn G v Carlowitz | J1 | Lt L C Burcher, / Lt L H N Stroud |
| G11 | 15 Feb | Albatros DIII | 2017/16 | nr Vlamertinghe, Ypres | Ltn H von Keudell | J27 | Nieuport 2/Str / A229 46 Sqn / 2/Lt S Pratt / Lt G Bryers; / Nieuport Sct / A6610 1 Sqn, / 2Lt V H Collins |
| G12 | 15 Feb | Halberstadt DV | 420/16 | nr Ploegsteert | Uffz H Schiener | J27 | AA fire |
| ? | 15 Feb | Halberstadt DIII | 234/16 | nr Ploegsteert Wood | Gefr H Schneider | J30 | AA fire |
| G13 | 16 Feb | Albatros DIII | | nr Hebuterne | Ltn H Gutermuth | J5 | BE2c 5 Sqn / Sgt Smith / Lt Aldred |
| ? | 16 Feb | Scout | | | | | FC J A Glen / 8 Naval Sqn |
| G14 | 4 Mar | Albatros DII '8' | 910/16 | nr Tilloy | Ltn M Böhme | J5 | DH2 29 Sqn / Lt A J Pearson; / 11 Sqn, Lts / Graham and Boddy |
| G15 | 25 Mar | Albatros DIII | | Mercatel | POW/KIA | | Nieuport A311 / 60 Sqn / Lt F Bower |
| G16 | 25 Mar | Albatros DIII | | Mercatel | POW | | Nieuport A6772 / 60 Sqn / Lt A Binnie |
| G17 | 21 Mar | Albatros DII | 410/16 | nr Lagnicourt–Bois de Vaux | Prince Frederic Charles of Prussia | FA258 | DH2 7938 / 32 Sqn RFC / Lt C Pickthorn |

† Also noted as XG6.  ‡ G8 may not have been used.

| No. | Date | A/C Type | Serial | Where brought down | Pilot | Jasta | Remarks |
|---|---|---|---|---|---|---|---|
| G18 | 1 Apr | Albatros DIII | 2012/16 | Arras | Ltn A Mohr | J3 | BE2c 12 Sqn Lt D Gordon Lt H D Baker |
| G20 | 5 Apr | Albatros DIII | 1942/16 | nr Neuve Eglise | Ltn J Flink | J18 | FE2d A6385 20 Sqn RFC Lt H G White Pvt T Allum |
| G21 | 8 Apr | Albatros DIII | 2234/16 | Villeveque, N St Quentin | Ltn R Nauck | J6 | Nieuport Sct Esc N 124 Lt A de Laage de Meux |
| G22 | 21 Apr | Albatros DIII | 2147/16 | Nr Arras (Oppy) | Ltn G Nernst | J30 | Triplane 8 Sqn RNAS N5458; FL A R Arnold; FE2b A6375 20 Sqn RFC Lt R G Malcolm 2Lt J B Weir |
| G26 | 25 Apr | Albatros DIII | 2251/16 | NW Gavrelle | Vfw S Festner | J11 | Strutter A8232 43 Sqn RFC Lt C R O'Brien 2Lt J L Dickson |
| G30 | 1 May | Albatros DIII 'K' | 771/17 | Poperinghe, nr Elverdinghe | Ltn A Kutscher | J28w | Nieuport Sct B1508, B1550, 1 Sqn, Lt E S T Cole, Lt F Sharpe |
| G32 | 3 May | Albatros DII | 473/16 | FTL Fampoux | Gefr A Lehmke | J10 | out of petrol; flown to UK |
| G33 | 5 May | Albatros DIII | 1963/16 | Betheniville/ Pt Faverger | OfStv A Dierle | J24s | in flames; AA 4th Army Front burned (poss 3rd Army AA?) |
| G34 | 5 May | Albatros DV | | | | | |
| G39 | 19 May | Albatros DIII | 796/17 | nr Gouy-en-Ternois 51C.B.2.1. | Ltn G H P Noth | J2 | Nieuport Sct B1602 60 Sqn Lt W M Fry |
| G42 | 4 Jun | Albatros DIII | 2015/16 | Fontaine/Heninel, NE Arras | Ltn G Simon | J11 | Nieuport Sct B1517 29 Sqn, Capt C Chapman |
| G43 | 5 Jun | Albatros DIII | | nr Athies (Monchy) | Ltn O v Schickfuss und Neudorff | J3 | Nieuport Sct B1575, 60 Sqn Capt A J Scott |
| G49 | 24 Jun | Albatros DIII | | St Julian, W Ypres | Ltn E Reiher | J6 | AA/Spads? |

| No. | Date | A/C Type | Serial | Where brought down | Pilot | Jasta | Remarks |
|---|---|---|---|---|---|---|---|
| G50 | 2 Jul | Albatros DIII | 1162/17 | nr Hendecourt | Ltn H Hellinger | J5 | 12 KBS AA fire |
| G56 | 16 Jul | Albatros DV | 2129/17 | SE Poperinghe | Vfw E Clausnitzer | J4 | Spad 23 Sqn Lt D Langlands |
| ? | 15 Jul | Albatros DV | | POW | | | 60 Sqn, Capt K Caldwell Lts Jenkins, Sherwood and G A H Parkes; to UK intact |
| G60 | 12 Aug | Albatros DV | | nr Farbus Wood, Vimy | Ltn J v Bertrab | J30 | Nieuport Sct B3554, 40 Sqn Lt E Mannock |
| G61 | 12 Aug | Albatros DIII | | Pilkem-Boesinghe, nr Ypres | Uffz F Wassermann | J27 | RE8 7 Sqn A3695 Lt F M Green and Lt R M D Fairweather |
| G64 | 21 Aug | Albatros DVa | | Frenzenberg, Ypres | Oblt E v Dostler | J6 | RE8 A4381 7 Sqn Lts N Sharples M A O'Callaghan |
| G70 | 14 Sep | Albatros DVa | | N Dixmude | Ltn M v Chelius | J2 | BF2b A7227 48 Sqn Capt K R Park 2Lt H Owen |
| G71 | 16 Sep | Albatros DIII | | Menin/Houthem; nr Jean Capelle | Ltn A Bauer | J17 | 60 Sqn SE5s |
| G72 | 23 Sep | Fokker F1 | F103/17 | St Julien, N Frezenberg | Ltn W Voss | J10 | 3 claims/1 loss SE5 B525 56 Sqn, Lt A P Rhys Davids |
| G75 | 27 Sep | Albatros DV | 2284/17 | nr Souchez | Oblt H Waldhausen | J37 | Nieuport Sct B3617, 40 Sqn Lt J H Tudhope; Camel B6227 8(N) Sqn, Capt C D Booker |
| G78 | 1 Oct | Albatros DV | | Hooge | Ltn F Cleiss | J33 | Camel 45 Sqn Capt W A Wright RE8 A3405 53 Sqn Lt R Reeder & Cpl G Holmes |
| G79 | 14 Oct | Albatros DV | 636/17 | Poelcapelle-Zonnebeke | OfStv R Weckbrodt | J26 | RE8 or DH5 32 Sqn A9269 Lt W R Jones 1715(G) |

| No. | Date | A/C Type | Serial | Where brought down | Pilot | Jasta | Remarks |
|---|---|---|---|---|---|---|---|
| G80 | 17 Oct | Albatros DIII | | Ypres/Polygon Wood | Ltn J Wiedenmann? | K8? | BF2b A7268 22 Sqn, Capt R Stuart-Wortley, Lt H D McGrath |
| G89 | 13 Nov | Albatros DIII | | Schoorbakke M.36.a central | Obmt F Heinze | MFJII | DH5 A9304 24 Sqn; Capt B P G Beanlands |
| G90 | 13 Nov | Albatros DVa | 5253/17 | Vth Army area | Ltn H Sakowsky | J14 | 3 Army AA AW 10 Sqn B324 |
| G92 | 29 Nov | Albatros DVa | | Zonnebeke D.23.c | Oblt E Böhme | J2 | Lt J A Pattern and Lt P W Leycester |
| ? | 29 Nov | Albatros DIII | | Armesvelde/Zarren | ? | ? | BF2b A7170 48 Sqn; Capt B E Baker & 2AM B Jackman |
| G93 | 30 Nov | Pfalz DIIIa | 4116/17 | nr Flesquières | Ltn F Demandt | J10 | Camel B3514, 46 Sqn Capt G E Thomson POW/DOW 1 Dec |
| ? | 30 Nov | ? | | Havrincourt | Ltn H Hofacker | J33 | 1130(G); |
| G97 | 7 Dec | Albatros DV | 4545/17 | Mercatel, nr Bethune | Vfw M Wackwitz | J24s | MG fire; to UK |
| G98 | 12 Dec | Albatros DV | | nr Ferdinand Farm, Boesinghe | Ltn W Börner | J27 | Camel B2416 65 Sqn |
| G100 | 17 Dec | Albatros DV | 2356/17 | N of Ypres | Ltn K-H Voss | MFJI | Lt V Wigg wreck. 1 Sqn, 2/Lt Kelsey |
| G101 | 17 Dec | Albatros DVa | 5390/17 | nr Armentières | Ltn Clauss | J29 | RE8, 3 AFC Lt J L M Sandy Sgt H F Hughes |
| G103 | 18 Dec | Albatros DVa | | St Julien | Uffz W Jumpelt | J27 | 2nd Army AA |
| G110 | 27 Dec | Pfalz DIII | 1370/17 | Estrées-en-Chaussée airfield; FTL 1½ miles W of Vermand | Vfw Hecht | J10 | m/c taken to 35 Sqn a'field; brought down by 2/Lts Hanna and Burnard, 35 Sqn; AWFK8 B256 |
| G116 | 28 Dec | Pfalz DIII | 4020/17 | nr Le Transloy | Vfw M Brandenburg | J29 | AA fire |
| | 1918 | | | | | | |
| G123 | 6 Jan | Albatros DV | 2080/17 | E Passchendaele | Ltn W v Bülow | J2 | Spad B3640 23 Sqn Capt W M Fry AA fire; to UK |
| G125 | 13 Jan | Fokker Dr1 | 144/17 | 5th Brigade area | Ltn E Stapenhörst | J11 | AWFK8 C3537, 82 Sqn; |
| G129 | 29 Jan | Albatros DIII | 2370/17 | NE La Fère/St Gobain | Vfw J Kettel | J50 | |

| No. | Date | A/C Type | Serial | Where brought down | Pilot | Jasta | Remarks |
|---|---|---|---|---|---|---|---|
| G131 | 4 Feb | Albatros DVa | | E Ypres | Ltn B Langer | J3 | Lt R J Fagan 2/Lt A O Matt SE5s 60 Sqn, two claims |
| G134 | 16 Feb | Albatros DVa | 4422/17 | 28.D14.a SE Bailleul | Ltn Bastgen | J30 | SE5A B4881 1 Sqn, Lt P J Clayson |
| G138 | 19 Feb | Albatros DVa | 4495/17 | nr Hollebeke | Ltn H v Puttkammer | J3 | SE5A B4860 60 Sqn |
| G141 | 26 Feb | Pfalz DIII | 4184/17 | Nr Bonneuil | Vfw Hegeler | J15 | Lt W M Kent SE5A B664, 24 Sqn – UK, Lt A K Cowper, flown to UK |
| G144 | 6 Mar | Albatros DVa | 2359/17 | S of Feuchy | Ltn O Hohmuth | J23b | RE8, 13 Sqn 2/Lt F Bellway, 1 AM F Rose; UK. |
| G145 | 6 Mar | Albatros DVa | 1788/16 | nr Rony | Ltn H Staats | J12 | collision with SE5a 2/Lt D M Clementz, C9535 24 Sqn |
| G146 | 6 Mar | Pfalz DIII | 4236/17 | Lens | Gefr W Conderert | J52 | SE5A 40 Sqn One by Capt R J Tipton in C5934 |
| G151 | 18 Mar | Albatros DVa | 6691/17 | nr Essigny-le-Grand | Uffz Brinkmann | J44s | Spads 23 Sqn Lt E R Varley B6835, and B6845 Lt H A F Goodison |
| G152 | 22 Mar | Fokker Dr1 | 509/17 | NE Champion | Ltn H G v Haebler | J36 | AA fire |
| G153 | 22 Mar | Albatros DVa | | NW Ham | Ltn Zwitzers | J62 | AA fire |
| G154 | 22 Mar | Albatros DVa | | W Ham | Vfw Dettmering | J68 | MG fire |
| G155 | 22 Mar | Albatros DVa | | | | | gnd fire |

(on 22 March Gefr E Diehl and Flg A Schulze of Jasta 53 were both taken prisoner?
(and Capt A T Whealy, 203 Sqn credited with Alb DV captured/Br side, Marquion, 1230 hrs)

| No. | Date | A/C Type | Serial | Where brought down | Pilot | Jasta | Remarks |
|---|---|---|---|---|---|---|---|
| G157 | 27 Mar | Pfalz DIII | 8078/17 | | OfStv Schüschke | J64w | gnd fire? French lines |
| ? | 27 Mar | Pfalz DIII | 8178/17 | Meault, W Bapaume | Gefr Sielemann | J57 | gnd fire; to UK a Jasta 11 m/c 60 Sqn, SE5a |
| G158 | 24 Mar | Fokker Dr1 | 147/17 | | Ltn Keseling | J10 | |
| G159 | 1 Apr | Albatros DVa | 5734/17 | FTL nr Gontelles | Vfw Weimer | J56 | C9536, 60 Sqn, Lt W J A Duncan |

| No. | Date | A/C Type | Serial | Where brought down | Pilot | Jasta | Remarks |
|---|---|---|---|---|---|---|---|
| G163 | 10 Apr | Fokker Dr1 | 419/17 | Gentelles Wood | Ltn W Göttsch | J19 | landed nearby; a/c to UK 21st RE8 B6641 52 Sqn, Lt H L Taylor and Lt W I E Lane |
| G/3/1 | 11 Apr | Albatros DVa 'R' and white fuselage band | 5726/17 | Millencourt, Albert | Ltn R Emmerich | J76b | RE8 B844 15 Sqn 2/Lts R G Hart & L F Handford |
| XG14 | 12 Apr | Albatros DVa |  | Peronne-Chauny | Ltn E Ziffer | J69 | gnd fire? |
| G/2/2 | 21 Apr | Albatros DVa |  | Sains-en-Amienois | Ltn A Thormälen | J22s | 209 Sqn/ground fire |
| G/5/2 | 21 Apr | Fokker Dr1 | 425/17 | Corbie | Rittm M v Richthofen | JG1 |  |
| G/2/4 | 22 Apr | Albatros DVa | 8282/17 | E Hazebrouck | Uffz Müller | J43 | Salv by French gnd fire |
| G/3/4 | 25 Apr | Pfalz DIIIa | 8151/17 | Vimy-Combles | Flg A Köhler | J35b | Eng/trouble |
| G/1/2 | 3 May | Pfalz DIIIa |  | N Gonnelieu | Ltn E König | J23b | BF2b C859 |
| G/2/8 | 14 May | Albatros DVa |  | Dickebusch | Ltn E Weiss | J33 | 20 Sqn, Lt W M Thomson, Lt G H Kemp |
| G/2/9 | 14 May | Albatros DV | 5161/17 | nr Peselhoek | Uffz F-K Florian | J51 | BF2b C856 20 Sqn Lt D Latimer Lt T C Noel |
| G/5/8 | 16 May | Fokker Dr1 | 546/17 | nr Corbie | Ltn F Hübner | J4 | Camels 209 Sqn; B7199, D3329, B6398; Capt S T Edwards, Lt M S Taylor, Lt W R May. |
| G/5/10 | 17 May | Albatros DVa |  | Villers-Bretonneux | Gefr A Wendt | J63 | Camel D1876 65 Sqn, Capt L E Whitehead |
| ? | 19 May | Albatros DV |  | Cachy, N Amiens | Oblt H Witt | J46 | SE5A C1772 84 Sqn, Capt A F W Beauchamp Proctor |
| G/2/10 | 19 May | Fokker Dr1 | 546/17 | SE Ypres | Ltn R Plange | J36 | AWFK8 B3315 10 Sqn, Lt W Hughes and Lt F C Peacock |
| G/3/7 | 25 May | Albatros DVa | 7221/17 | nr Hedauville | Vfw K Koller | J76b | Camel D1903 65 Sqn |

| No. | Date | A/C Type | Serial | Where brought down | Pilot | Jasta | Remarks |
|---|---|---|---|---|---|---|---|
| G/5/12 | 27 May | Fokker DVII | 2184/18 | Achiet-le-Grand | | | Capt A A Leitch 3 Sqn Camel |
| G/2/12 | 29 May | Albatros DVa | | Merville-Neuf Berquin | Ltn G Keitsch | J74 | Lt G R Riley? wreckage; SE5a C1114 1 Sqn, Capt P J Clayson FL, fuel – UK |
| G/5/13 | 30 May | Pfalz DIIIa (swastika on fuselage) | 8284/17 | nr Bourney | Vfw J Pollinger | J77b | |
| G/2/13 | 31 May | Albatros D | 7296/17 | Montdidier | Ltn Rademacher | J10 | French? |
| ? | 5 Jun | Albatros DVa | | | Ltn F Ree | J68 | SE5A D5969 29 Sqn, Lt C H R Lagesse |
| G/2/14 | 6 Jun | Fokker DVII | 368/18 | N Hazebrouck (Nieppe) | Ltn H Schultz | J18 | Ten SE5s 1 Sqn led by Capt P J Clayson in C1114 |
| G/2/15 | 9 Jun | Fokker Dr1 | 583/17 | Dickebusch/Ouderdon | Gefr R Preiss | J14 | |
| ? | 12 Jun | Fokker DVII | 2062/18 | Mery | Ltn R Croissant | J68 | Camel D1794 73 Sqn, Capt M LeB-Smith |
| ? | 12 Jun | Albatros DV | | Tricot | Ltn A Erich | J63 | ditto |
| ? | 12 Jun | Fokker DVII | | Goumay | Ltn F Loerzer | J26 | SE5A D6860 2 AFC, Capt R C Phillips |
| G/5/17 | 17 Jun | Fokker DVII | 382/18 | nr Cachy | Ltn K Wüsthoff | J15 | SE5s, 24 Sqn C1084, D3444, C6481; Capt G O Johnson, Capt I D R McDonald & Lt H D Barton |
| G/2/16 | 19 Jun | Pfalz DIIIa | | Nieppe Forest/ Bailleul | Uffz M Mertens | J7 | Camel D1929 4 AFC, Capt A H Cobby |
| ? | 27 Jun | Albatros DVa | 7285/17 | Montiers/Compiègne | Vfw Stadley | J62 | Fr?/AA fire |
| ? | 28 Jun | Albatros DVa | 5255/17 | Montigny | Vfw E Busch | J62 | |
| G/1/10 | 9 Jul | Albatros DVa | 7265/17 | Steenwerck (Langenhoek) | Ltn H Sattler | MFJII | BF2b D7896 22 Sqn Lt T W Martin Sgt Hall |
| ? | 8 Aug | 2/Fokker DVIIs | | Proyart | | | Camels, 65 Sqn |
| ? | 10 Aug | Fokker DVII | | Cuvilly, E Bouchier French III Armée | Ltn Muhs | J12 | Camels D9637 & D9657, 209 Sqn |

| No. | Date | A/C Type | Serial | Where brought down | Pilot | Jasta | Remarks |
|---|---|---|---|---|---|---|---|
| G/5/20 | 12 Aug | Fokker DVII 'Nickchen IV' | 817/18 | SW Proyart | OfStv F Blumenthal | J53 | Capt J Summers Lt K B Watson; Camel C61 209 Sqn, Capt R M Foster and SE5A E4018, Capt F R McCall |
| G/5/24 | 12 Aug | Fokker DVII | | Fontaine | Gefr J Janizewski | J75 | Spad; 171o hrs |
| G/3/12 | 21 Aug | Fokker DVII | 2184/18 | Montigny | Vfw A Bernhörster | J61 | Camel F5938 3 Sqn |
| G/3/13 | 23 Aug | Fokker DVII | 4284/18 | St Martin-sur-Cojeul | Flg L Kormann | J79b | Lt G R Riley |
| G/3/14 | 27 Aug | Pfalz DIIIa | | | | | RE8 12 Sqn Lt C Pithey Lt H Rhodes |
| G/3/19 | 4 Sep | Fokker DVII | 4503/18 | Cambrai-Bapaume | Flg O Wagner | J79b | Camel F1972 3 Sqn |
| G/3/17 | 5 Sep | Fokker DVII | | Avesnes-le-Sec | Ltn J v Winterfeld | J4 | Lt D J Hughes SE5A D6960 ? 60 Sqn, Capt G M Duncan |
| G/3/18 | 5 Sep | Albatros DVa | | nr Ervillers | | | Wreckage found |
| ? | 5 Sep | Fokker DVII | | nr Bourlon Wood | flames | | Camel D3417 203 Sqn Maj R Collishaw salvaged, to UK |
| G/5/26 | 10 Sep | Fokker DVII | | | No losses? | | |
| G/HQ/6 | 15 Sep | Pfalz DXII | 2486/18 | Marquion | Ltn P Vogel | J23b | SE5A 1 Sqn Lt D E Cameron |
| G/1/16 | 16 Sep | Fokker DVII | | Houplines (Nieppe) nr Quesnoy | Ltn F Kresse | J7 | BF2b 62 Sqn Capt W E Staton Lt L E Mitchell |
| G/10/5 | 16 Sep | Fokker DVII | | | Gefr K Brandt | J51 | Camel 209 Sqn |
| ? | 16 Sep | Fokker DVII | | Somme area | Gefr J Katzner | J43 | SE5A, C1948 2 AFC Sqn Capt R L Manuel shot down on 5 Sept, but not located till the 16th |
| G/2/22 | 17 Sep | Fokker DVII 'K' | 4522/18 | Warville-Eply | Fw H Popp | J77b | SE5A 74 Sqn Maj K L Caldwell |
| ? | 24 Sep | Fokker DVII | | Suippes | Ltn W Meyer | J47 | AA fire |
| G/1/17 | 2 Oct | Fokker DVII | 5301/18 | E Tilloy | Vfw Belz | J1 | Camels, 54 Sqn to UK |

| No. | Date | A/C Type | Serial | Where brought down | Pilot | Jasta | Remarks |
|---|---|---|---|---|---|---|---|
| ? | 5 Oct | Pfalz DXII | 2600/18 | | | | |
| G/2/24 | 6 Oct | Albatros D | | nr Bailleul | | | |
| ? | 9 Oct | Fokker DVII | | W Mayerneine | | | |
| ? | 10 Oct | Fokker DVII | | SW Roulers | Ltn J Schäfer | J16b | wrecked Camels, 70 Sqn SE5As 41 Sqn E4092, Maj G H Bowman and F5545 Capt S O Soden |
| G/2/32 | 14 Oct | Fokker DVII | | | | | |
| G/2/13 | ? | Fokker DVII | | Wervicq | KIA | J? | |
| ? | 22 Oct | Fokker DVII | | Ooteghem, nr Sterhoek | Ltn A Auer | J40s | |
| G/2/27 | 28 Oct | Fokker DVII | 4043/18 | | | | SE5A F5545 41 Sqn F O Soden |
| G/2/28 | 28 Oct | Fokker DVII | | S Tournai | OfStv A Jäschke | J30 | SE5A E4084 29 Sqn, Capt C H R Lagesse |
| G/2/31 | 14 Oct | Fokker DVII | | W Roulers | | | |

# Jasta Pilot Casualties
## 1916

| Date | Pilot Jasta Casualty | Unit | |
|---|---|---|---|
| 5 Aug | Gefr Helmut Krause | Kest 4a | KIAcc |
| 8 Aug | Ltn Benno Berneis | 9 | KIA |
| 28 Aug | Ltn Joachim von Arnim | 2 | KIA |
| 1 Sep | Vfw Hans Miesegades | 3 | KIAcc |
| 12 Sep | Ltn Ewald von Mellenthin | 3 | KIA |
| 22 Sep | Ltn Winand Grafe | 2 | KIA |
| 22 Sep | Ltn Eberhard Fügner | 4 | WIA |
| 23 Sep | Ltn Hans Reimann | 2 | KIA |
| 23 Sep | Ltn Werner Lehmann | 9 | KIAcc |
| 25 Sep | Ltn Kurt Wintgens | 1 | KIA |
| 30 Sep | Ltn Ernst Diener | 2 | KIA |
| 1 Oct | Ltn Herwarth Philipps | 2 | KIA |
| 10 Oct | Uffz Julius Heck | Kest 5 | KIA |
| 16 Oct | Gefr Gustav Beerendonk | 10 | WIA |
| 20 Oct | Ltn Hans Wacker | 3 | WIA |
| 20 Oct | Vfw Paul Piechl | 5 | KIA |
| 21 Oct | Ltn Hans Petersson | 3 | KIA |
| 22 Oct | OfStv Leopold Rudolf Reimann | 2 | WIA |
| 22 Oct | Oblt Ludwig Linck | 10 | KIA |
| 22 Oct | OfStv Wilhelm Viereck | 10 | WIA |
| 28 Oct | Hptm Oswald Boelcke | 2 | KIA |
| 30 Oct | Ltn Hans Wacker | 3 | WIA |
| 2 Nov | Ltn Hermann Göring | 5 | WIA |
| 10 Nov | Vfw Christian Kress | 6 | KIA |
| 13 Nov | Ltn Bodo Fr von Lyncker | 2 | INJ |
| 16 Nov | Ltn Karl Heinrich Otto Büttner | 2 | POW |
| 16 Nov | Ltn Albert Krönig | 3 | INJ |
| 16 Nov | Ltn Ernst Wever | 6 | KIA |
| 16 Nov | Vfw Otto Augst | 12 | WIA |
| 17 Nov | Ltn Wilhelm Schlolaut | 9 | KIA |
| 22 Nov | Oblt Stefan Kirmaier | 2 | KIA |
| 22 Nov | Ltn Erich Zschunke | 6 | WIA |
| 22 Nov | Flg Robert Michaelis | 12 | KIA |
| 24 Nov | Uffz Otto Krönert | 14 | KIA |
| 1 Dec | Ltn Amann | 2 | POW |
| 4 Dec | OfStv Karl Ernthaller | 1 | KIA |
| 4 Dec | Vfw Wilhelm Hennebeil | 12 | KIA |
| 6 Dec | Ltn Hansen | 3 | WIA |
| 20 Dec | Ltn Kurt Haber | 3 | KIA |
| 24 Dec | Ltn Lothar Erdmann | 20 | KIA |
| 26 Dec | OfStv Hans Karl Müller | 5 | WIA |
| 27 Dec | Ltn Gustav Leffers | 1 | KIA |

## 1917

| Date | Pilot Jasta Casualty | Unit | |
|---|---|---|---|
| 5 Jan | Vfw Erwin Kernchen | 25 | KIAcc |
| 10 Jan | Ltn Otto Walter Höhne | 2 | WIA |
| 22 Jan | Ltn Karl Pertz | 23 | KIA |
| 23 Jan | Ltn Hans Imelmann | 2 | KIA |
| 23 Jan | Vfw Paul Ostrop | 2 | KIA |
| 24 Jan | OfStv Leopold Rudolf Reimann | 2 | KIAcc |
| 25 Jan | Flgmt Gustav Kinkel | 2 | POW |
| 26 Jan | Vzflgmstr Max Winkelmann | 5 | POW |
| 26 Jan | Ltn Karl Groterjahn | 22 | KIA |
| 27 Jan | Ltn Bruno Kalff | 20 | KIA |
| 29 Jan | Ltn Georg Simon | 11 | WIA |
| 29 Jan | Ltn Walter Lautz | 20 | WIA/DOW |
| 3 Feb | Vfw Walter Göttsch | 8 | WIA |
| 3 Feb | Uffz Heinrich Leiendecker | 9 | WIA |
| 4 Feb | Ltn Franz Christian von Scheele | 2 | KIA |
| 5 Feb | Vfw Thiel | 2 | WIA |
| 5 Feb | Vfw Alfred Ulmer | 8 | WIA |
| 6 Feb | Ltn Georg Ferner | 24 | WIA |
| 8 Feb | Ltn Alfred Träger | 8 | WIA |
| 8 Feb | Vfw Konrad Hess | 1 | KIAcc |
| 9 Feb | Vfw Adolf Wellhausen | 17 | WIA/DOW |
| 10 Feb | Oblt Walter Zeitlow | 9 | KIA |
| 10 Feb | Vfw Heinrich Tuczek | 21 | KIA |
| 11 Feb | Ltn Erwin Böhme | 2 | WIA |
| 13 Feb | Ltn Jürgen Georg von Carlowitz | 1 | KIA |
| 15 Feb | Ltn Hans von Keudell | 27 | KIA |
| 15 Feb | Uffz Heinrich Schiener | 27 | POW |
| 15 Feb | Ltn Hermann Klein | 29 | INJ |
| 15 Feb | Gefr Heinrich Schneider | 30 | POW |
| 16 Feb | Ltn Hans Gutermuth | 5 | KIA |
| 18 Feb | Oblt Bodo Fr von Lyncker | 25 | KIA |
| 20 Feb | Ltn Ewald Siempelkamp | 15 | INJ |
| 24 Feb | Uffz Weber | 25 | KIAcc |
| 25 Feb | Ltn Werner Junge | 9 | WIA/DOW |
| 4 Mar | Oblt Ernst Fr von Althaus | 4 | WIA |
| 4 Mar | Ltn Max Böhme | 5 | POW |
| 6 Mar | Ltn Hans-Georg Eduard Lübbert | 11 | WIA |
| 11 Mar | OfStv Alfred Behling | 1 | KIA |
| 11 Mar | Ltn Erkenbrecht | 12 | WIA |
| 12 Mar | Ltn Friedrich Weitz | 26 | WIA/DOW |
| 13 Mar | Flgmt Franz Wangemann | MFJI | WIA |
| 16 Mar | Vfw Friedrich Manschott | 7 | KIA |
| 16 Mar | Ltn Lothar von Hausen | 32 | POW |
| 16 Mar | Oblt Heinrich Schwandner | 32 | KIA |
| 17 Mar | Uffz Hans Rody | 30 | KIAcc |
| 18 Mar | Vfw Karl Schöne | 23 | KIAcc |
| 18 Mar | Ltn Paul Retsch | 32 | WIA |
| 21 Mar | Oblt Erich Marx | Kest 1a | KIA |
| 22 Mar | Vfw Georg Hentze | 34 | POW |
| 23 Mar | Ltn Ernst Ritter und Edler von Loessl | 18 | WIA/DOW |
| 24 Mar | Ltn Renatus Theiller | 5 | KIA |
| 25 Mar | Ltn Friedrich Mallinckrodt | 20 | WIA |
| 25 Mar | Gefr Berkling | 22 | WIA |
| 30 Mar | Ltn Hans-Georg Eduard Lübbert | 11 | KIA |
| Mar | Vfw Thomas Reichart | 12 | WIA |
| 1 Apr | Ltn Alfred Mohr | 3 | KIA |
| 2 Apr | Ltn Erich König | 2 | KIA |

| Date | Pilot Jasta Casualty | Unit | | Date | Pilot Jasta Casualty | Unit | |
|------|----------------------|------|---|------|----------------------|------|---|
| 2 Apr | Ltn Hans Wortmann | 2 | KIA | 4 May | Vfw Albert Franz | 33 | WIA/ |
| 2 Apr | Vfw Rudolf Nebel | 35 | POW | | | | DOW |
| 5 Apr | Ltn Josef Flink | 18 | POW | 5 May | Vfw Peter Glasmacher | 8 | KIA |
| 6 Apr | Uffz Ludwig Weber | 3 | WIA | 5 May | OfStv Anton Dierle | 24 | KIA |
| 6 Apr | Oblt Hans Berr | 5 | KIA | 5 May | Ltn Philipp Wieland | 27 | WIA |
| 6 Apr | Vfw Paul Hoppe | 5 | KIA | 6 May | Vfw Jäger | 20 | INJ |
| 6 Apr | Ltn Otto Splitgerber | 12 | WIA | 7 May | Vfw Wilhelm Dietrich | 1 | KIA |
| 6 Apr | Vfw Reinhold Wurzmann | 20 | KIA | 7 May | Ltn Wolfgang Plüschow | 11 | WIA |
| 8 Apr | Ltn Wilhelm Frankl | 4 | KIA | 9 May | OfStv Wilhelm Cymera | 1 | KIA |
| 8 Apr | Ltn Roland Nauck | 6 | KIA | 9 May | OfStv Karl Stiller | 1 | KIA |
| 8 Apr | Ltn Alfred Träger | 8 | WIA | 9 May | Ltn Hans Klein | 4 | WIA |
| 11 Apr | Vfw Karl Möwe | 29 | KIA | 9 May | Vfw Friedrich Saurwein | 7 | WIA |
| 12 Apr | Ltn Adolf Schulte | 12 | KIA | 9 May | Vfw Kairis | 13 | INJ |
| 13 Apr | Uffz Simon Ruckser | 37 | WIA | 10 May | Ltn Werner Albert | 31 | KIA |
| 14 Apr | Ltn Hartmuth Baldamus | 9 | KIA | 11 May | OfStv Edmund Nathanael | 5 | KIA |
| 14 Apr | Ltn Otto Weigel | 14 | KIA | 12 May | Ltn Kreutzer | 19 | WIA |
| 14 Apr | Ltn Friedrich Grünzweig | 16 | KIA | 12 May | Vfw Max Wimmer | 28 | WIA |
| 14 Apr | Ltn Gerhard Anders | 35 | WIA | 13 May | Ltn Lothar Fr von Richthofen | 11 | WIA |
| 14 Apr | Ltn Margraf | 35 | WIA | 13 May | Ltn Oskar Lang | Kest 1b | KIA |
| 14 Apr | Oblt Herbert Theurigh | 35 | KIA | 15 May | Ltn Karl Pokrantz | 29 | KIA |
| 14 Apr | Uffz Hermann Jopp | 37 | KIA | 18 May | Vfw Eduard Ey | 6 | KIAcc |
| 16 Apr | Ltn Hans-Olaf Esser | 15 | KIA | 18 May | OfStv Ernst Kleimenhagen | Kest 8w | KIAcc |
| 16 Apr | Vfw Rieger | 17 | WIA | 19 May | Ltn Georg Hermann Paul Noth | 2 | WIA/ |
| 19 Apr | Ltn Paul Herrmann | 31 | KIA | | | | POW/DOW |
| 20 Apr | OfStv Viktor Hebben | 10 | WIA | 19 May | Ltn Karl Emil Baur | 3 | KIA |
| 21 Apr | Ltn Günther von der Heyde | 9 | KIA | 19 May | Ltn Stobel | 3 | KIA |
| 21 Apr | Ltn Friedrich-Wilhelm Wichard | 24s | POW | 19 May | Ltn Eberhard Fügner | 4 | KIA |
| 21 Apr | Ltn Gustav Nernst | 30 | KIA | 19 May | Ltn Karl Schöck | 12 | KIA |
| 23 Apr | Vfw Arno Schramm | 7 | KIA | 20 May | Ltn Albert Münz | 2 | KIA |
| 23 Apr | Hptm Paul Henning von | | | 20 May | Ltn Kurt Franke | 2 | WIA/ |
| | Osterroht | 12 | KIA | | | | DOW |
| 23 Apr | Uffz Nauczak | 33 | WIA | 20 May | Ltn Hermann Pfeiffer | 9 | KIAcc |
| 24 Apr | Oblt Rudolf Berthold | 14 | WIA | 20 May | Ltn Eberhard Voss | 20 | KIAcc |
| 24 Apr | Ltn Fritz Kleindienst | 18 | KIA | 21 May | Fw Paul Markwirth | 7 | KIAcc |
| 24 Apr | Rttm Karl von Grieffenhagen | 18 | INJ | 21 May | Ltn Wolfgang Günther | 17 | INJ |
| 24 Apr | Vfw Rudolf Rath | 35 | KIA | 21 May | Ltn Hans von Schell | 30 | INJ |
| 24 Apr | Vzflgmstr Josef Wirtz | MFJI | KIA | 22 May | Vfw Johann Schroth | 35 | INJ |
| 25 Apr | Vfw Sebastian Festner | 11 | KIA | 23 May | Oblt Rudolf Berthold | 14 | WIA |
| 26 Apr | Vfw Emil Eisenhuth | 3 | KIA | 23 May | Ltn Ernst Ritter und Edler | | WIA/ |
| 26 Apr | Oblt Max Reinhold | 15 | KIA | | von Loesel | 18 | DOW |
| 26 Apr | OfStv Rudolf Weckbrodt | 26 | WIA | 23 May | Uffz Tolischuss | Kest 3 | POW |
| 27 Apr | Ltn Hans Eissfeldt | 10 | WIA | 24 May | Ltn Ernst Bauer | 3 | KIA |
| 27 Apr | Ltn Friedrich Vonschott | 14 | WIA/ | 24 May | Ltn Hans Hintsch | 11 | KIA |
| | | | DOW | 24 May | Ltn Wilhelm Allmenröder | 11 | WIA |
| 29 Apr | Ltn Peckmann | 15 | WIA | 24 May | Ltn Willi Schunke | 20 | KIA |
| 29 Apr | Ltn Ludwig Dornheim | 29 | KIA | 24 May | Ltn Karl Sonntag | 37 | IIC |
| 30 Apr | Ltn Adolf Frey | 9 | KIA | 25 May | Vfw Heinrich Müller | 15 | KIAcc |
| 30 Apr | Ltn Werner Marwitz | 9 | KIA | 25 May | Ltn Alfons Paulus | 21 | KIA |
| 30 Apr | Ltn Friedrich Mallinckrodt | 20 | WIA | 26 May | OfStv Grigo | 12 | WIA |
| Apr | Ltn Fritz Pütter | 9 | WIA | 26 May | Ltn Eberhard Hänisch | 15 | KIA |
| 1 May | Ltn Hermann Frommherz | 2 | INJ | 26 May | Uffz Erich Leyh | 29 | KIA |
| 1 May | Ltn Gerhard Strehl | 12 | KIA | 27 May | Ltn Jansen | Kest 8w | INJ |
| 1 May | Ltn Alexander Kutscher | 28 | KIA | 28 May | Vfw Johannes Walter | 36 | WIA |
| 2 May | Oblt Kurt Student | 9 | WIA | 29 May | Vfw Willy Glinkermann | 15 | KIA |
| 2 May | OfStv Franz Hilger | 27 | INJ | 30 May | Ltn Julius Völker | 31 | INJ |
| 2 May | Ltn Albert Dossenbach | 36 | WIA | 31 May | Uffz Christoph Hertel | 10 | INJ |
| 2 May | Vfw Richard Piez | Kest 3 | KIA | May | Ltn Brudel | 15 | KIA |
| 3 May | Ltn Kleemann | 5 | WIA | 1 Jun | Vfw Ernst Dahlmann | 5 | KIA |
| 3 May | Gefr Alfred Lemke | 10 | POW | 2 Jun | Ltn Paul Jaenicke | 22 | KIA |
| 3 May | Ltn Fritz Mönnich | 23 | WIA | 4 Jun | Ltn Georg Simon | 11 | POW |
| 3 May | Ltn Gottlieb Görne | 31 | KIA | 4 Jun | Vfw Wilhelm Eichenauer | 15 | KIA |
| 3 May | Ltn Albrecht von Kobilinski | 36 | WIA | 4 Jun | Vfw Matthias Dennecke | 18 | KIA |
| 4 May | Hptm Hans von Hünerbein | 5 | KIAcc | 5 Jun | Ltn Oskar von Schickfuss | | |
| 4 May | Ltn Gerlt | 19 | WIA | | und Neudorff | 3 | KIA |
| 4 May | Vfw Hans Brinkmann | 21 | KIA | 5 Jun | Ltn Kurt Schneider | 5 | WIA |
| 4 May | Vfw Eduard Horn | 21 | KIA | 5 Jun | Vfw Heinrich Küllmer | 6 | WIA |

| Date | Pilot Jasta Casualty | Unit | | Date | Pilot Jasta Casualty | Unit | |
|---|---|---|---|---|---|---|---|
| 5 Jun | Ltn Karl-Emil Schäfer | 28 | KIA | 21 Jul | Oblt Fritz von Bronsart und Schellendorf | 7 | KIA |
| 6 Jun | Vfw Paul Bona | 1 | KIA | 22 Jul | Vfw Georg Oefele | 12 | KIA |
| 6 Jun | Ltn Werner Voss | 5 | WIA | 22 Jul | Uffz Heinrichs | 18 | WIA |
| 7 Jun | Ltn P. Lohmann | 14 | WIA | 22 Jul | Vfw Willi Kempe | 34b | POW |
| 7 Jun | Ltn Ernst Wiessner | 18 | KIA | 24 Jul | Ltn Oskar Dänkert | 9 | KIA |
| 7 Jun | Vfw Franz Eberlein | 33 | WIA | 24 Jul | Ltn Bernhard Knake | 12 | KIAcc |
| 7 Jun | Flgomt Fritz Kühn | MFJ I | POW/ DOW | 25 Jul | Uffz Walter Reichenbach | 5 | INJ/ DOW |
| 8 Jun | Vfw Grigo | 12 | WIA | 26 Jul | Ltn Otto Brauneck | 11 | KIA |
| 8 Jun | Vfw Franz Bucher | 30 | KIA | 27 Jul | Ltn Jakob Wolff | 17 | WIA |
| 12 Jun | Vfw Otto Rosenfeld | 12 | WIA | 27 Jul | Ltn Erich Limpert | 21 | KIA |
| 12 Jun | Hptm Eberhardt von Seel | 17 | KIA | 27 Jul | OfStv Karl Gregor | 29 | WIA |
| 12 Jun | OfStv Martin Altmaier | 33 | KIA | 27 Jul | Ltn Werner Kathol | 29 | WIA |
| 13 Jun | Ltn Phillip Wieland | 8 | WIA | 27 Jul | Ltn Fritz Vossen | 33 | KIA |
| 14 Jun | Vzflgmstr Kurt Lichtherz | MFJ I | KIA | 27 Jul | Vfw Wilhelm Weise | 35b | WIA |
| 14 Jun | Vzflgmstr Bottler | MFJ I | WIA | 27 Jul | Vzflgmstr Otto Brandt | MFJ I | KIA |
| 15 Jun | Gefr Paul Laukandt | 13 | KIA | 28 Jul | Hptm Gustav Stenzel | 8 | KIA |
| 15 Jun | Oblt Heinrich Lorenz | 33 | WIA | 28 Jul | Ltn Alfred Niederhoff | 11 | KIA |
| 16 Jun | Vfw Leopold von Raffay | 6 | WIA | 28 Jul | Ltn Albrecht Crüsemann | 17 | KIA |
| 16 Jun | Ltn Friedrich von Hartmann | 9 | KIAcc | 28 Jul | Ltn Gustav Nolte | 18 | KIA |
| 16 Jun | Vfw Gottfried Stemmler | 9 | INJ | 28 Jul | Uffz Friedrich Thäsler | 35b | KIA |
| 16 Jun | Vfw Robert Riessinger | 12 | KIA | 30 Jul | Ltn Leopold von Raffay | 6 | INJ |
| 16 Jun | Ltn Hermann Becker | 12 | WIA | 5 Aug | Ltn Burkhardt Lehmann | 12 | KIA |
| 16 Jun | Vfw Eugen Weiss | 29 | WIA | 10 Aug | Ltn Oskar Rousselle | 4 | WIA |
| 17 Jun | Oblt Georg Zeumer | 2 | KIA | 10 Aug | Vfw Hugo Stöber | 16b | WIA |
| 17 Jun | Uffz Fritz Pohlmann | 31 | KIAcc | 10 Aug | Ltn Erwin Böhme | 29 | WIA |
| 18 Jun | Vfw Walter Dittrich | 1 | WIA | 11 Aug | Oblt Adolf von Tutschek | 12 | WIA |
| 18 Jun | Ltn Walter Bordfeld | 11 | KIA | 11 Aug | Uffz Wilhelm Thuir | 35b | KIAcc |
| 18 Jun | Vfw Gustav Schindler | 35 | WIA | 12 Aug | Vfw Julius Buckler | 17 | WIA |
| 21 Jun | Oblt Eduard Dostler | 6 | INJ | 12 Aug | Uffz Friedrich Wassermann | 27 | KIA |
| 21 Jun | Ltn Otto Maashoff | 11 | WIA | 12 Aug | Ltn Erich Schlegelmilch | 29 | KIA |
| 21 Jun | Ltn Heinrich Russell | 28 | KIA | 12 Aug | Ltn Joachim von Bertrab | 30 | POW |
| 22 Jun | Uffz Fritz Wistermann | 1 | WIA | 13 Aug | Uffz Arno Ulbircht | 9 | WIA/ DOW |
| 24 Jun | Ltn Erich Reiher | 6 | KIA | 14 Aug | Ltn Alfred Hübner | 4 | KIA |
| 24 Jun | Ltn Georg Weiner | 20 | INJ | 14 Aug | Ltn Hans Joachim Wolff | 11 | WIA |
| 27 Jun | Ltn Karl Allmenröder | 11 | KIA | 14 Aug | Ltn Haass | 29 | WIA |
| 27 Jun | Vfw Moritz Förster | 32 | KIA | 15 Aug | Uffz Hermann Brettel | 10 | WIA |
| 29 Jun | Ltn Alfred Ulmer | 8 | KIA | 15 Aug | Ltn Heinrich Brügmann | 30 | WIA/ DOW |
| 2 Jul | Ltn Horst Hellinger | 5 | KIA | 16 Aug | Ltn Ehlers | 17 | WIA |
| 2 Jul | Ltn Hans Forstmann | 30 | KIA | 16 Aug | Vfw Anton Schrader | 31 | KIA |
| 3 Jul | Ltn Albert Dossenbach | 10 | KIA | 16 Aug | Vfw Walter Hoffmann | 36 | KIA |
| 3 Jul | Lt.z.S. Kurt Crüger | MFJ I | WIA | 17 Aug | Ltn Franz Götte | 20 | WIA |
| 4 Jul | Ltn Walter Kirchbach | 35 | KIAcc | 17 Aug | Ltn Otto Rath | MFJ I | KIA |
| 6 Jul | Vfw Hermann Denkhaus | 7 | KIA | 18 Aug | Oblt Fritz Otto Bernert | 2 | WIA |
| 6 Jul | Vfw Manfred Stimmel | 32 | POW | 18 Aug | Ltn Albrecht Weinschenk | 18 | WIA |
| 6 Jul | Rttm Manfred Fr von Richthofen | JG I | WIA | 18 Aug | Vfw Otto Gerbig | 18 | KIA |
| 7 Jul | Ltn Reinhold Oertelt | 19 | KIA | 18 Aug | Ltn Edwin Kreuzer | 36 | WIAcc |
| 11 Jul | Vfw Rotsczinka | 7 | WIA | 19 Aug | Uffz Paul Felix | 15 | KIA |
| 11 Jul | Ltn Kurt Wolff | 11 | WIA | 20 Aug | Ltn Reinhold Schuhmann | 5 | KIA |
| 12 Jul | Vfw Linus Patermann | 4 | KIA | 20 Aug | Ltn Heinrich Geigl | 16b | WIA |
| 12 Jul | Ltn Günther Pastor | 29 | WIA | 20 Aug | Ltn Albert Dietlen | 23b | WIA |
| 12 Jul | Vfw Maier | 36 | WIA | 20 Aug | Vfw Josef Oehler | 24 | KIA |
| 13 Jul | Ltn Hans Klein | 4 | WIA | 20 Aug | Flgmstr Grosch | MFJ I | WIA |
| 13 Jul | Ltn Heinrich Bongartz | 36 | WIA | 21 Aug | Oblt Eduard Ritter von Dostler | 6 | KIA |
| 15 Jul | Ltn Erich Schlegelmilch | 29 | WIA | 21 Aug | Ltn Alfred Träger | 8 | WIA |
| 16 Jul | Vfw Ernst Clausnitzer | 4 | POW | 21 Aug | Vfw Willi Spudich | 21 | KIAcc |
| 16 Jul | Vfw Fritz Krebs | 6 | KIA | 21 Aug | Ltn Hugo Geiger | 34b | KIA |
| 16 Jul | Ltn Heinrich Geist | 9 | KIAcc | 21 Aug | Ltn Max Wirth | 34b | KIA |
| 17 Jul | Ltn Richard Krüger | 4 | WIA/ DOW | 22 Aug | Ltn Egon Könemann | 2 | KIA |
| 17 Jul | Ltn Karl Meyer | 11 | WIA | 22 Aug | Ltn Wilhelm Gros | 17 | KIA |
| 17 Jul | Vfw Julius Buckler | 17 | WIA | 22 Aug | Vfw Jahnke | 21 | WIA |
| 17 Jul | Ltn Hans Böhning | 36 | INJ | 22 Aug | Flgomt Luitjen Luitjens | MFJ I | KIA |
| 17 Jul | Vfw Debus | 36 | WIA | 23 Aug | Vfw Konrad Poralla | 32b | WIA |
| 18 Jul | Vfw Kunze | OberOst | POW | | | | |

| Date | Pilot Jasta Casualty | Unit | Casualty |
|---|---|---|---|
| 25 Aug | Vfw Fritz Rumey | 5 | WIA |
| 26 Aug | Uffz Carl Conradt | 17 | KIA |
| 31 Aug | Vfw Wilhelm Reiss | 3 | KIA |
| 3 Sep | Ltn Wilhelm Bockelmann | 11 | WIA |
| 3 Sep | Vfw Hans Bowski | 14 | WIA |
| 3 Sep | OfStv Hans Malz | 20 | KIA/GND |
| 3 Sep | Vfw Friedrich Matthies† | 20 | WIA/DOW/GND |
| 3 Sep | Vfw Gustav Beerendonk† | 20 | WIA/GND |
| 3 Sep | Hptm Otto Hartmann | 28 | KIA |
| 3 Sep | Vfw Kurt Petzinna | 29 | KIAcc |
| 3 Sep | Uffz Walter König | 31 | KIA |
| 3 Sep | Ltn Heinrich Vollertsen | 36 | KIA |
| 3 Sep | Ltn Josef Klever | 39 | KIA |
| 3 Sep | Oblt Maximilian Ziegler gen Stege | 41 | KIA |
| 3 Sep | Flgmt Brenner | MFJ I | WIA |
| 4 Sep | Oblt Wilhelm Reinhard | 11 | WIA |
| 4 Sep | Oblt Erich Hahn | 19 | KIA |
| 4 Sep | Ltn Lutz | 28 | WIA |
| 4 Sep | Ltn Gebhard Emberger | 29 | KIA |
| 4 Sep | Ltn Siegfried von Lieres und Wilkau | 29 | WIA |
| 4 Sep | Vfw Heinrich Mertens | 35b | WIA |
| 5 Sep | Ltn Franz Pernet | 2 | KIA |
| 5 Sep | Ltn Walter Höhndorf | 14 | KIAcc |
| 5 Sep | Vfw Alfred Muth | 27 | KIA |
| 6 Sep | Ltn Diether Collin | 22 | WIA |
| 7 Sep | Ltn Karl Odebrett | 16b | WIA |
| 7 Sep | Ltn Walter Entz | 38 | INJ/DOW |
| 8 Sep | Ltn Wilhelm Neumann | 40 | KIAcc |
| 9 Sep | Ltn Karl Hammes | 35b | WIA |
| 11 Sep | Uffz Ernst Schätzle | 19 | KIA |
| 11 Sep | Ltn Werner Richard | OberOst | KIAcc |
| 11 Sep | Ltn Friedrich von Götz | MFJ I | KIA |
| 13 Sep | Ltn Wilhelm Finhold | 34b | KIA |
| 14 Sep | Ltn Maximilian von Chelius | 2 | KIA |
| 14 Sep | Oblt Ernst Weigand | 10 | WIA |
| 14 Sep | Ltn Gisbert-Wilhelm Groos | 11 | WIA |
| 15 Nov | Ltn Hans Ritter von Adam | 6 | KIA |
| 15 Sep | Oblt Kurt Wolff | 11 | KIA |
| 15 Sep | Ltn Adolf Wiehle | 20 | KIA |
| 16 Sep | Ltn Alfred Bauer | 17 | KIA |
| 19 Sep | Ltn Alhard Scheck | 5 | KIA |
| 19 Sep | OfStv Paul Aue | 10 | WIA |
| 19 Sep | Gefr Becker | 20 | POW |
| 20 Sep | Ltn Erich Löwenhardt | 10 | WIA |
| 21 Sep | Ltn Richard Plange | 2 | WIA |
| 21 Sep | Ltn Friedrich-Karl Weber | 21 | KIA |
| 21 Sep | Vfw Heinrich Schott | 25 | INJ |
| 22 Sep | Vfw Fritz Kosmahl | 26 | WIA/DOW |
| 23 Sep | Ltn Werner Voss | 10 | KIA |
| 23 Sep | Ltn Hugo Jöns | 20 | KIA |
| 24 Sep | Ltn Julius Schmidt | 3 | WIA |
| 24 Sep | Vfw Fritz Rumey | 5 | WIA |
| 24 Sep | Oblt Werner Jahns | 28w | KIA |
| 25 Sep | Ltn Johannes Wintrath | 2 | KIA |
| 25 Sep | Ltn Walter Göttsch | 8 | WIA |
| 25 Sep | Oblt Ernst Weigand | 10 | KIA |
| 25 Sep | Uffz August Werkmeister | 10 | KIA |
| 25 Sep | Vfw Ludwig Hilz | 40 | WIA |
| 27 Sep | Oblt Hans Waldhausen | 37 | POW |
| 28 Sep | Ltn Kurt Wissemann | 3 | KIA |
| 28 Sep | Ltn Herbert Pastor | 29 | KIA |
| 28 Sep | Ltn Tinschert | MFJ I | WIA |
| 29 Sep | Ltn Ewald Gläser | 31 | KIAcc |
| 30 Sep | Vfw Gottfried Stumpf | 6 | INJ |
| 30 Sep | Uffz Bolkenius | Kest 7 | INJ |
| 1 Oct | Ltn Ernst Wendler | 17 | WIA |
| 1 Oct | Ltn Friedrich Cleiss | 33 | KIA |
| 1 Oct | Ltn Theodor Siebold | 38 | KIA |
| 2 Oct | Uffz Karl Theodor Steudel | 3 | KIA |
| 2 Oct | Ltn Max Roemer | 10 | KIA |
| 2 Oct | Ltn Walther Kleffel | 18 | WIA |
| 7 Oct | Ltn Paul Billik | 7 | WIA |
| 8 Oct | Vfw Walter Reichenbach | 2 | INJ |
| 9 Oct | Ltn Richard Wagner | 26 | KIA |
| 10 Oct | Oblt Rudolf Berthold | 18 | WIA |
| 10 Oct | Vfw Ruppert | 19 | WIA |
| 10 Oct | Ltn Johann Raithel | 34b | WIA |
| 11 Oct | Ltn Gustav Bellen | 10 | WIA |
| 11 Oct | Gefr Zimmermann | 35b | INJ |
| 14 Oct | Ltn Martin Schoen | 81 | KIA |
| 14 Oct | OfStv Rudolf Weckbrodt | 26 | KIA |
| 16 Oct | Vfw Max Taucher | 34b | POW |
| 17 Oct | Ltn Johann Wiedenmann | Kest 8w | KIA |
| 18 Oct | Ltn Xaver Dannhuber | 26 | WIA |
| 18 Oct | Oblt Otto Schmidt | 29 | WIA |
| 19 Oct | Ltn Franz Josef Karg | 23b | KIAcc |
| 20 Oct | Ltn Walter Lange | 2 | KIA |
| 20 Oct | Uffz Hardel | 10 | WIA |
| 20 Oct | Ltn Alfred Gerstenberg | 11 | WIA |
| 20 Oct | Uffz Emil Barheine | 35b | WIA |
| 21 Oct | Vfw Fritz Bachmann | 6 | KIA |
| 22 Oct | Vfw Adolf Techow | 7 | KIA |
| 24 Oct | Ltn Heinrich Breidt | 13 | KIA |
| 24 Oct | Vfw Otto Rösler | 23b | KIA |
| 26 Oct | Ltn Otto Schober | 18 | KIA |
| 26 Oct | Ltn Addix | 31 | WIA |
| 27 Oct | Ltn Franz Müller | 11 | KIAcc |
| 29 Oct | Vfw Josef Lautenschlager | 11 | KIA |
| 29 Oct | Ltn Fritz Berkemeyer | 27 | KIA |
| 30 Oct | Ltn d R Hans Wacker | 3 | WIA |
| 30 Oct | Ltn Heinrich Gontermann | 15 | KIAcc |
| 30 Oct | Ltn Anton Warmuth | 34b | KIA |
| 30 Oct | Ltn Hermann Scholl | 34b | KIA |
| 31 Oct | Ltn Günther Pastor | 11 | KIA |
| 31 Oct | Uffz Kurt Reinhold | 24s | WIA |
| 31 Oct | Oblt Erwin Wenig | 28 | WIA |
| 3 Nov | Vfw Gillardoni | 81 | POW |
| 4 Nov | Ltn Fritz Kieckhäfer | 29 | WIA |
| 4 Nov | Flg Anton Huchler | 39 | KIA |
| 4 Nov | Vfw Fleischmann | 81 | KIAcc |
| 6 Nov | Ltn Gerhard Bassenge | 2 | WIA |
| 7 Nov | Flg Karl Jäger | 31 | KIA |
| 8 Nov | Flg Hellmuth Riensberg | 10 | WIA |
| 10 Nov | Ltn d R Tuxen | 6 | IIC |
| 11 Nov | Vfw Gustav Schindler | 35b | IIC |
| 13 Nov | Ltn Hans Sakowski | 14 | POW |
| 13 Nov | Uffz Theodor Seffzig | 34b | POW |
| 13 Nov | Maat Friedrich Heinze | MFJ II | POW |
| 15 Nov | Ltn Hans Ritter von Adam | 6 | KIA |
| 15 Nov | Ltn Viktor Schobinger | 12 | WIA |
| 15 Nov | Ltn Richard Runge | 18 | KIA |
| 15 Nov | Ltn Hans Hoyer | 36 | KIA |
| 17 Nov | Ltn August Raben | 39 | WIA |
| 18 Nov | Oblt Otto Diendl | 1 | WIA |
| 18 Nov | Ltn Fritz Kuke | 33 | KIAcc |
| 18 Nov | Ltn Günther Lüdecke | 36 | INJ |

| Date | Pilot Jasta Casualty | Unit | | Date | Pilot Jasta Casualty | Unit | |
|------|----------------------|------|---|------|----------------------|------|---|
| 19 Nov | Vfw Kasper Rahier | 31 | KIA | 9 Dec | Ltn Bernhard Kilian | 21s | KIA |
| 20 Nov | Vfw Josef Heiligers | 30 | KIA | 9 Dec | Vfw Fritz Schröder | 39 | KIA |
| 23 Nov | Vfw Karl Bey | 5 | KIA | 10 Dec | Ltn Herbert Wallner | 3 | KIA |
| 23 Nov | Ltn Hans Joachim Wolff | 11 | WIA | 10 Dec | Ltn Paul Wigand | 3 | KIAcc |
| 23 Nov | Vfw Karl Überschaer | 39 | KIA | 10 Dec | Vfw Gustav Beerendonk | 20 | KIAcc |
| 23 Nov | Uffz Eduard Feig | 76b | KIAcc | 10 Dec | Uffz Friedrich Becker | 20 | KIAcc |
| 25 Nov | Ltn Werner Wagener | 39 | WIA | 10 Dec | Uffz Kurt Reinhold | 24s | KIA |
| 27 Nov | Ltn Erwin Haertl | 1 | WIA | 11 Dec | Vfw Walter Starck | 32b | INJ |
| 27 Nov | Vfw Otto Esswein | 26 | WIA | 12 Dec | Uffz Oswald Rottmann | 14 | KIA |
| 28 Nov | Vfw Ernst Oppermann | 31 | WIA/ DOW | 12 Dec | Ltn Walter Börner | 27 | KIA |
| | | | | 12 Dec | Uffz Kählert | 27 | POW |
| 29 Nov | Ltn Erwin Böhme | 2 | KIA | 12 Dec | Ltn Wilhelm Kolb | 76b | KIA |
| 29 Nov | Ltn Karl Wewer | 26 | WIA | 13 Dec | Ltn Paul Erichson | Kest 7 | WIA |
| 29 Nov | Ltn Walter Blume | 26 | WIA | 15 Dec | Uffz Bockstegers | 10 | INJ/ DOW |
| 30 Nov | Ltn Wilhelm Schultze | 4 | KIA | | | | |
| 30 Nov | Ltn Walter Göttsch | 8 | WIA | 17 Dec | Ltn Clauss | 29 | POW |
| 30 Nov | Ltn Heinrich Richter | 9 | INJ | 17 Dec | Ltn Karl-Heinrich Voss | MFJ I | KIA |
| 30 Nov | Ltn Friedrich Demandt | 10 | KIA | 18 Dec | Ltn Stanislaus Zentzytzki | 17 | KIAcc |
| 30 Nov | Ltn Johann Gustav von Senger und Etterlin | 12 | KIA | 19 Dec | Ltn Walter Braun | 20 | WIA/ DOW |
| 30 Nov | Ltn Julius Buckler | 17 | WIA | 22 Dec | Ltn Massmann | 14 | WIA |
| 30 Nov | Ltn Rudolf Wendelmuth | 20 | KIA | 22 Dec | Ltn Hans Villinger | 18 | KIA |
| 30 Nov | Ltn Hans Hofacker | 33 | WIA/ DOW | 22 Dec | Uffz Wilhelm Föge | 30 | WIA/ DOW |
| 30 Nov | Ltn Otto Napp | MFJ I | KIAcc | 23 Dec | Ltn Ernst Hess | 19 | KIA |
| 1 Dec | Ltn Walter Brachwitz | 17 | WIA/ DOW | 23 Dec | OfStv Karl Thom | 21s | WIA |
| | | | | 23 Dec | Ltn Otto Fr von Türckheim zu Altdorf | Kest 4b | KIA |
| 3 Dec | Vfw Otto Pelz | 32b | KIA | | | | |
| 3 Dec | Ltn Franz von Kerssenbrock | 39 | KIA | 27 Dec | Vfw Hecht | 10 | POW |
| 4 Dec | Vfw Max Kämmerer | 35b | INJ | 27 Dec | Ltn Traugott von Schweinitz | 11 | KIA |
| 4 Dec | Vfw Walter Horn | 37 | KIA | 28 Dec | Vfw Max Brandenburg | 29 | POW |
| 5 Dec | Vfw Hermann Seidel | 26 | KIA | 28 Dec | Flgmt Karl Meyer | SFS | WIA/ DOW |
| 5 Dec | Ltn Leo Strauch | 31 | WIA | | | | |
| 5 Dec | Vfw Alfred Rüsche | 39 | KIA | 28 Dec | Ltn Wilhelm Mattheus | MFJI | WIA |
| 5 Dec | Flgmstr Ottomar Haggenmuller | MFJ II | KIA | 29 Dec | Vfw Otto Rosenfeld | 41 | POW |
| 7 Dec | Vfw Max Wackwitz | 24s | POW | 30 Dec | Vfw Ludwig Gaim | 39 | WIA |
| 7 Dec | Ltn Prasse | 26 | INJ | 30 Dec | Vfw Karl Eisele | 43 | KIAcc |
| 8 Dec | Ltn Erich Daube | 2 | KIA | 31 Dec | Ltn Alwin Thurm | 31 | KIA |
| 8 Dec | Ltn Rudolf Bertelsmeier | 39 | POW | | | | |

† Bombing attack on his airfield.

# 1918

| Date | Pilot Jasta Casualty | Unit | | Date | Pilot Jasta Casualty | Unit | |
|------|----------------------|------|---|------|----------------------|------|---|
| 1 Jan | OfStv Karl Lang | 1 | KIA | 19 Jan | Uffz Richard Kade | 50 | KIAcc |
| 1 Jan | Uffz Albert Meinhardt | 21s | KIA | 19 Jan | Vzflgmstr Müller | SFS | INJ |
| 2 Jan | Ltn Günther Auffahrt | 29 | KIA | 20 Jan | Ltn Fritz Schönberger | 16b | WIA |
| 3 Jan | Ltn Wigan | 12 | POW | 20 Jan | Vfw Johannes Dikhaus | 19 | KIAcc |
| 3 Jan | Uffz Emil Liebert | 30 | KIA | 20 Jan | Gefr Christian Schiller | 19 | KIAcc |
| 4 Jan | Ltn Friedrich Gräpel | 28w | KIA | 20 Jan | Vfw Karl Knocke | 35b | INJ |
| 6 Jan | Ltn Walter von Bülow-Bothkamp | 2 | KIA | 20 Jan | Vfw Gustav Schindler | 35b | KIAcc |
| 6 Jan | Uffz Paul Proske | 7 | WIA | 21 Jan | Gefr Josef Mayer | 32b | KIA |
| 6 Jan | Lt Emil Thuy | 28w | WIA | 21 Jan | Ltn Umberto Mario Antonio Rosa | 38 | INJ |
| 9 Jan | Ltn Max Ritter von Müller | 2 | KIA | 21 Jan | Ltn Günther Gellenthin | 40s | KIA |
| 9 Jan | Ltn Hans Kiessling | 34b | WIA | 21 Jan | Flgmt Müller | SFS | INJ |
| 11 Jan | Oblt Hans Kummetz | 1 | KIA | 22 Jan | Ltn Günter | 8 | INJ |
| 13 Jan | Ltn Eberhard Stapenhörst | 11 | POW | 23 Jan | Ltn Gustav Wandelt | 36 | KIA |
| 14 Jan | Ltn Theodor Wrege | 39 | KIA | 24 Jan | Ltn Martin Möbius | 7 | KIA |
| 16 Jan | Vfw Otto Klüpfel | 77b | INJ | 24 Jan | Ltn Hans-Karl von Linsingen | 11 | WIA |
| 18 Jan | Flg Hellmuth Riensberg | 10 | KIA | 24 Jan | Uffz Fritz Jacob | 12 | KIA |
| 19 Jan | Vfw Martin Mallmann | 19 | KIA | 24 Jan | Uffz Heinrich Nägele | 38 | KIA |
| 19 Jan | Ltn Schmidt | 24s | INJ | 24 Jan | Flg Friedrich Maute | 47w | KIA |
| 19 Jan | Vfw Max Krauss | 27 | KIA | 25 Jan | Ltn Ernst Paland | 20 | WIA |

| Date | Pilot Jasta Casualty | Unit | | Date | Pilot Jasta Casualty | Unit | |
|------|----------------------|------|---|------|----------------------|------|---|
| 25 Jan | Vfw Herbert Werner | 26 | KIA | 1 Mar | Ltn Erich Just | 11 | WIA |
| 25 Jan | Vfw Hermann Reisch | 41 | KIA | 1 Mar | Flg Gustav Koriath | 19 | KIAcc |
| 27 Jan | Uffz Eugen Förtig | 16b | KIAcc | 5 Mar | Uffz Hellmuth Krätzschmer | 48 | INJ |
| 27 Jan | Uffz Karl Preuss | 31 | KIA | 5 Mar | Gefr Lothmann | 65 | POW |
| 28 Jan | Sgt Meyer | 8 | WIA | 6 Mar | Ltn Erich Bahr | 11 | KIA |
| 28 Jan | Ltn Reinhold Maier | 30 | WIA | 6 Mar | Gefr Walther Conderert | 52 | KIA |
| 28 Jan | Vzflgmstr Hirth | MFJ II | INJ | 6 Mar | Ltn Hans Staats | 12 | KIA |
| 28 Jan | Flgmt Armin Undiener | MFJ II | KIA | 6 Mar | Ltn Otto Hohmuth | 23b | POW |
| 29 Jan | Vfw Christian Brunnengräber | 13 | KIA | 6 Mar | Oblt Rudolf Schonger | 23b | WIA |
| 29 Jan | Gefr Hellmann | 27 | INJ | 6 Mar | Ltn Hellmuth Contag | 65 | KIA |
| 29 Jan | Ltn Kurt Brecht | 36 | KIA | 7 Mar | Ltn Niebecker | 43 | INJ |
| 29 Jan | Vfw Josef Kettel | 50 | KIA | 7 Mar | Vfw Krause | 80b | INJ |
| 30 Jan | Vfw Adam Barth | 10 | KIA | 8 Mar | Ltn Skauradzun | 4 | WIA |
| 30 Jan | Vfw Albert Hurrle | 13 | KIA | 8 Mar | OfStv Willi Kampe | 27 | KIA |
| 30 Jan | Oblt Bruno Justinus | 35b | KIA | 8 Mar | Vfw Heinrich Gockel | 33 | WIA |
| 2 Feb | Ltn Albert Krönig | 3 | KIAcc | 8 Mar | Flg Langenheim | 49 | INJ |
| 2 Feb | Ltn Askan Fr von und zu | | | 8 Mar | Ltn Heinrich Mindner | 51 | KIAcc |
| | der Tann | 24s | KIA | 8 Mar | Uffz Wilhelm Rincke | 54s | KIA |
| 2 Feb | Ltn Emil Thuy | 28w | WIA | 9 Mar | Ltn Max Naujock | 36 | KIA |
| 3 Feb | Ltn Erwin Klumpp | 2 | KIAcc | 9 Mar | Uffz Fritz Liese | 50 | KIA |
| 3 Feb | Ltn Karl Stock | 48 | KIA | 9 Mar | Ltn Joachim Nissen | 52 | WIA/ |
| 3 Feb | Ltn Max Kersting | 48 | KIA | | | | DOW |
| 4 Feb | Ltn Bruno Langer | 3 | KIA | 9 Mar | Vzflgmstr Bottler | MFJ II | WIA |
| 4 Feb | Ltn Konrad Bieler | 14 | WIA | 10 Mar | Ltn Wilhelm Gürke | 5 | KIA |
| 4 Feb | Oblt Josef Loeser | 39 | WIA | 10 Mar | Sgt Beschow | 6 | WIA |
| 4 Feb | Uffz Dierenfeld | 39 | WIA | 10 Mar | Oblt Hans-Joachim Buddecke | 18 | KIA |
| 4 Feb | Vfw Rudolf Wiesner | 39 | KIA | 10 Mar | Uffz Paul Nöckel | 28w | WIA |
| 4 Feb | Vfw Paul Wagner | 76b | KIA | 11 Mar | Vfw Otto Rückert | 48 | WIA |
| 5 Feb | Vfw Ernst Höfer | 42 | WIA | 11 Mar | Uffz Josef Henn | 53 | KIAcc |
| 5 Feb | Ltn Vetter | Kest 3 | WIA | 12 Mar | Ltn Karl Peveling | 46 | WIA |
| 8 Feb | Ltn Georg Michaelis | 41 | KIA | 12 Mar | Flg Georg Boit | 51 | KIA |
| 9 Feb | Uffz Schilli | 47w | INJ | 12 Mar | Vzflugmstr Bertram Heinrichs | MFJI | WIA |
| 10 Feb | Ltn Robert Denkhardt | 35b | KIAcc | 13 Mar | Lt.z.S. Konrad Mettlich | 8 | KIA |
| 10 Feb | Ltn Georg Ferner | 61 | KIAcc | 13 Mar | Vfw Adolf Besenmüller | 8 | WIA/ |
| 11 Feb | Ltn Xaver Dannhuber | 79b | INJ | | | | DOW |
| 14 Feb | Ltn Max Raspe | 44s | INJ | 13 Mar | Ltn Lothar Fr von Richthofen | 11 | WIA |
| 15 Feb | Uffz Paul Proske | 7 | WIA | 13 Mar | Ltn Heinrich Kämmerer | 20 | KIA |
| 15 Feb | Vfw Paul Hüttenrauch | 7 | INJ | 13 Mar | Ltn Otto Splitgerber | 38 | KIA |
| 16 Feb | Ltn Bastgen | 30 | POW | 13 Mar | Ltn Walter Bowein | 56 | KIA |
| 17 Feb | Ltn Friedrich-Wilhelm Lübbert | 11 | WIA | 13 Mar | Ltn Werner Hafner | 57 | KIA |
| 17 Feb | Ltn Fritz Poesch | 78b | KIAcc | 15 Mar | Hptm Adolf Ritter von Tutschek | JGII | KIA |
| 18 Feb | Vfw Martin Klein | 5 | KIA | 15 Mar | Vfw August Wagner | 58 | KIA |
| 18 Feb | Ltn Willi Etzold | 26 | KIA | 16 Mar | Ltn Paul Jäger | 9 | KIA |
| 18 Feb | Uffz Justus Kaiser | 35b | KIA | 16 Mar | Ltn Franz Bohlein | 10 | KIA |
| 18 Feb | Uffz Joachim von Stein | 35b | WIA | 17 Mar | Ltn Gotthilf Pleiss | 9 | POW |
| 19 Feb | Ltn Hans Fr von Puttkammer | 3 | POW | 17 Mar | Ltn Werner Steinhäuser | 11 | WIA |
| 19 Feb | Vfw Erich Windmüller | 9 | KIA | 17 Mar | OfStv Adolf Schreder | 17 | KIA |
| 19 Feb | Ltn Hans Klein | 10 | WIA | 17 Mar | Vfw Hans Kehr | 20 | KIA |
| 19 Feb | Ltn Heinrich Kütt | 23b | WIA | 17 Mar | Vfw Otto Schulz | 20 | KIAcc |
| 19 Feb | Oblt Hans-Karl Fr von | | | 17 Mar | Ltn Waldemar Janssen | 28w | KIA |
| | Wolfskeel-Reichenberg | 34b | KIA | 17 Mar | Oblt Hans Bethge | 30 | KIA |
| 19 Feb | Flgmt Hermann Hildemann | MFJ I | KIAcc | 17 Mar | Ltn Otto Wachhorst de Wente | 46 | KIA |
| 20 Feb | Ltn Wolfgang Güttler | 13 | KIAcc | 17 Mar | Vfw Jedwiel | 46 | WIA |
| 20 Feb | Vfw Paul Hiob | 13 | KIAcc | 17 Mar | Ltn Gerhard Laak | 61 | KIAcc |
| 20 Feb | Vfw Harling | 31 | WIA | 18 Mar | Flg Rudolf Ihde | 10 | KIA |
| 21 Feb | Uffz Rudolf Lingenfelder | 16b | KIAcc | 18 Mar | Ltn Franz Riedle | 16b | KIA |
| 21 Feb | Vfw Artur Weber | 46 | KIA | 18 Mar | Uffz Brinkmann | 44s | POW |
| 24 Feb | Uffz Weber | 25 | INJ | 18 Mar | Uffz Gustav Ecke | 54s | KIA |
| 26 Feb | Ltn Egon Koepsch | 4 | WIA | 18 Mar | Ltn Kurt Straube | 66 | KIA |
| 26 Feb | Ltn Max Hillmann | 7 | WIA | 18 Mar | Vfw Karl Arnold | 72s | INJ |
| 26 Feb | Uffz Hegeler | 15 | POW | 20 Mar | Ltn August Raben | 18 | INJ |
| 26 Feb | Uffz Fritz Classen | 26 | INJ | 21 Mar | Ltn Herbert Kohl | 34b | POW |
| 26 Feb | Uffz Paul Hess | 42 | KIA | 21 Mar | Ltn Ludwig Hanstein | 35b | KIA |
| 27 Feb | OfStv Jakob Landin | 32b | KIA | 21 Mar | Gefr Franz Matuszewsky | 73 | KIA |
| 27 Feb | Ltn Bernhard Benninghoff | 54s | KIAcc | 22 Mar | Ltn Hans Gottfried von Häbler | 36 | POW/ |
| 1 Mar | Ltn Eberhard Mohnicke | 11 | WIA | | | | DOW |

| Date | Pilot Jasta Casualty | Unit | |
|---|---|---|---|
| 22 Mar | Gefr Ernst Diehl | 53 | POW |
| 22 Mar | Flg August Schulze | 53 | POW |
| 22 Mar | Ltn Hermann Manger | 56 | KIA |
| 22 Mar | Ltn Zwitzers | 62 | POW |
| 22 Mar | Vzflgmstr Bertram Heinrich | MFJ I | WIA |
| 23 Mar | OfStv Dobberahn | 12 | WIA |
| 23 Mar | Ltn Joachim Huth | 14 | WIA |
| 23 Mar | Ltn Erich Thomas | 22s | POW |
| 23 Mar | Ltn Hans Unger | 22s | POW |
| 23 Mar | Uffz Max Rentsch | 69 | KIAcc |
| 23 Mar | Vfw Karl Behringer | 80b | WIA/DOW |
| 23 Mar | Ltn Karl Romeis | 80b | WIA |
| 24 Mar | Ltn Keseling | 11 | POW |
| 24 Mar | Oblt Ludwig Cordes | 16b | KIA |
| 24 Mar | Ltn Theodor Rumpel | 23b | WIA |
| 24 Mar | Vfw Walter Schäfer | 66 | KIA |
| 24 Mar | Gefr Linus Luger | 79b | WIA |
| 24 Mar | Flgobmatr Christian Kairies | SFS | WIA |
| 26 Mar | Flgomt Hans Groth | MFJ II | KIA |
| 27 Mar | Ltn Franz Schleiff | 56 | WIA |
| 27 Mar | Gefr Sielemann | 57 | POW |
| 27 Mar | OfStv Schüschke | 64w | POW |
| 28 Mar | Ltn Wilhelm Papenmeyer | 2 | KIA |
| 28 Mar | Ltn Hans-Georg von der Osten | 4 | WIA |
| 28 Mar | Flg Adolf Schmidt | 22s | KIA |
| 28 Mar | Vfw Otto Stadter | 32b | INJ |
| 28 Mar | Vfw Walter Schäfer | 66 | KIA |
| 29 Mar | Ltn Aloys Geistbeck | 32b | INJ |
| 30 Mar | Uffz Max Marczinke | 30 | POW |
| 30 Mar | Ltn Heinrich Bongartz | 36 | WIA |
| 30 Mar | Uffz Hellmuth Krätzschmer | 48 | POW |
| 31 Mar | Vfw Friedrich Neubauer | 63 | KIA |
| 31 Mar | Uffz Jan Santjer | 63 | KIA |
| 31 Mar | Uffz Ruppert Merkle | 63 | KIA |
| 1 Apr | Ltn Paul Hoffmann | 12 | WIA/DOW |
| 1 Apr | Ltn Richard Grüter | 17 | KIA |
| 1 Apr | Flg Hans Weigeld | 49 | KIA |
| 1 Apr | Ltn Rudolf Kommoss | 50 | KIA |
| 1 Apr | Vfw Weimar | 56 | POW |
| 1 Apr | Uffz Müller | 79b | WIA/POW |
| 2 Apr | Uffz Peter Wenn | 57 | WIA/DOW |
| 2 Apr | Uffz Georg Sandleitner | 77b | KIAcc |
| 3 Apr | Vfw Hurrle | 45 | POW |
| 3 Apr | Uffz Kurt Reismann | 55 | KIAcc |
| 3 Apr | Ltn Ernst Hensel | 62 | WIA/DOW |
| 3 Apr | Ltn Paul Quast | 63 | KIA |
| 4 Apr | Ltn Heinrich Geigl | 16b | KIA |
| 4 Apr | Uffz Erich Gürgenz | 46 | KIA |
| 5 Apr | Vfw Konrad Brendle | 45 | INJ |
| 6 Apr | Ltn Hans Lutteroth | 7 | KIAcc |
| 6 Apr | Vfw Willi Hampel | 55 | POW |
| 6 Apr | Sgt Pfänder | 69 | WIA |
| 6 Apr | Uffz Georg Erdmann | 73 | KIA |
| 6 Apr | Uffz Robert Schwarz | 77b | KIA |
| 7 Apr | Ltn Siegfried Gussmann | 11 | WIA |
| 10 Apr | Ltn Walter Göttsch | 19 | KIA |
| 11 Apr | Uffz Georg Storr | 60 | KIA |
| 11 Apr | Vfw Johann Wieland | 68 | KIA |
| 11 Apr | Ltn Ernst Braasch | 68 | KIA |
| 11 Apr | Ltn Richard Emmerich | 76b | KIA |
| 11 Apr | Uffz Gottfried Stemmler | 76b | KIA |
| 11 Apr | Ltn Wilhelm Buchstett | 79b | POW |
| 12 Apr | Ltn Wolff | 6 | WIA |
| 12 Apr | Uffz Robert Eiserbeck | 11 | KIA |
| 12 Apr | Vfw Gilbert Wagner | 29 | KIA |
| 12 Apr | Ltn Hövelhaus | 33 | WIA |
| 12 Apr | Ltn Karl Lupp | 46 | KIA |
| 12 Apr | Ltn Albert Dietlen | 58 | KIA |
| 12 Apr | Ltn Erich Ziffer | 69 | POW |
| 12 Apr | Flg Friedrich Schlötzer | 76b | KIA |
| 13 Apr | Ltn Daemrich | 29 | INJ |
| 14 Apr | Vfw Anton Wroniecki | 64w | POW |
| 14 Apr | Uffz Heinrich Simon | 64w | POW |
| 17 Apr | Ltn Fritz Danker | 32b | KIA |
| 17 Apr | Ltn Rudolf Matthaei | 46 | KIAcc |
| 19 Apr | Ltn Wolff | 6 | WIA |
| 20 Apr | Ltn Rudolf Eck | 16b | WIA |
| 20 Apr | Ltn Fritz Höhn | 21s | WIA |
| 20 Apr | Ltn John Färber | 22s | KIA |
| 21 Apr | Vfw Mäurer | 18 | WIA |
| 21 Apr | Rttm Manfred Fr von Richthofen | JGI | KIA |
| 21 Apr | Ltn Adolf Thormälen | 22s | POW |
| 21 Apr | Uffz Fritsche | 41 | WIA |
| 21 Apr | Uffz Müller | 43 | POW |
| 21 Apr | Ltn Waldemar Christensen | 46 | KIA |
| 21 Apr | Uffz Karl Heidelberg | 48 | KIA |
| 21 Apr | Ltn Aloys Brandenstein | 49 | WIA |
| 21 Apr | Ltn Rudolf Abt | 69 | POW |
| 21 Apr | Ltn Alfred Schubart | 81 | KIAcc |
| 22 Apr | Ltn August Handl | 16b | WIA/POW |
| 22 Apr | Vfw Erich Kauffmann | 47w | KIA |
| 23 Apr | Ltn Paul Lotz | 7 | WIA |
| 23 Apr | Uffz Emil Dassenies | 13 | KIA |
| 23 Apr | Uffz Wilhelm Zorn | 60 | POW |
| 23 Apr | Flgmt Fammen | MFJ I | WIA |
| 23 Apr | Flgmt Jannsen | MFJ I | INJ |
| 25 Apr | Vfw Heinrich Schott | 25 | KIA |
| 25 Apr | Ltn Karl Adolf Seifert | 24s | KIAcc |
| 25 Apr | Oblt Arthur Dieterle | 34b | WIA |
| 25 Apr | Uffz August Meyer | 34b | KIA |
| 25 Apr | Flg Andreas Köhler | 35b | POW |
| 25 Apr | Ltn Heinrich Bongartz | 36 | WIA |
| 25 Apr | Vfw Alfred Hübner | 36 | WIA |
| 25 Apr | Ltn Alfred King | 40s | WIA |
| 25 Apr | Flgomt Bruno Fictzmann | MFJ II | KIA |
| 26 Apr | Flg Franz Dürrwächter | 23b | KIAcc |
| 26 Apr | Uffz Fritz Demant | 52 | KIA |
| 27 Apr | Ltn Kurt Legel | 52 | KIAcc |
| 28 Apr | Vfw Kurt Kressner | 5 | INJ |
| 28 Apr | Ltn Fritz Bötzow | 55 | KIA |
| 29 Apr | Ltn Ludwig Vortmann | 2 | KIA |
| 29 Apr | Ltn Claus Riemer | 26 | INJ |
| 29 Apr | Ltn Heinrich Bongartz | 36 | WIA |
| 29 Apr | Uffz August Schwind | 54s | INJ |
| Apr | Ltn Karl Gallwitz | 2 | INJ |
| 2 May | Ltn Erich Schmidt | 8 | KIAcc |
| 2 May | Ltn Stoy | 10 | WIA |
| 2 May | Ltn Hans Weiss | 11 | KIA |
| 2 May | Ltn d R Edgar Scholtz | 11 | KIAcc |
| 2 May | Uffz Ernst Messtorf | 26 | KIA |
| 2 May | Ltn Josef Determeyer | 47w | WIA |
| 2 May | Vfw Friedrich Megerle | 70 | WIA |
| 2 May | Ltn Moritz Weig | 76b | POW |
| 2 May | Uffz Philipp Jopp | 79b | KIA |
| 2 May | Ltn Fritz Edler von Braun | 79b | WIA |
| 2 May | Vfw Konrad Poralla | 81 | INJ |

| Date | Pilot Jasta Casualty | Unit | | Date | Pilot Jasta Casualty | Unit | |
|------|----------------------|------|------|------|----------------------|------|------|
| 3 May | Ltn Erich Just | 11 | WIA | 19 May | Uffz Karl Pech | 29 | KIA |
| 3 May | Ltn Bigalk | 14 | INJ | 19 May | Ltn Karl Bauernfeind | 34b | WIA |
| 3 May | Ltn Ewald König | 23b | POW | 19 May | Ltn Richard Plange | 36 | KIA |
| 3 May | Uffz Paul Nöckel | 28w | INJ/ | 19 May | Ltn Alois Weber | 46 | POW |
| 3 May | Uffz Hans Wagner | 80b | KIA | 19 May | Oblt Hans Witt | 46 | KIA |
| 3 May | OfStv Karl Angermeyer | SFS | KIAcc | 20 May | Ltn Vivigenz von Wedel | 1 | KIAcc |
| 4 May | Ltn Fritz Kieckhäfer | 29 | WIA/ | 21 May | Vfw Hans Schorn | 16b | KIA |
| | | | DOW | 21 May | Flg Klaus Sakowski | 29 | KIA |
| 4 May | Ltn Karl Meierdirks | 55 | KIA | 21 May | Vfw Emil Alfred Richter | 50 | POW |
| 4 May | Ltn Richard Schmidt | 77b | INJ | 21 May | Vfw Friedrich Göthe | 52 | KIA |
| 5 May | Flg Mayer | 36 | WIA | 22 May | Ltn Breuer | 47w | WIA |
| 5 May | Uffz Meyer | 57 | INJ | 22 May | Uffz Mathias Schmid | 80b | INJ |
| 5 May | OfStv Bernhard Ultsch | 77b | INJ | 23 May | Ltn Hauffe | 9 | INJ |
| 6 May | Ltn Hans Joachim Rogalla | | | 23 May | Vfw Hans Oberländer | 30 | WIA |
| | von Bieberstein | 3 | KIAcc | 23 May | Ltn Erich Kayl | 32b | KIA |
| 6 May | Vfw Otto Gustav Wandelt | 43 | KIA | 23 May | Vfw Gustav Schniedewind | 55 | WIA |
| 6 May | Ltn Julius Buckler | 17 | WIA | 23 May | Uffz Richard Jentzsch | 71 | KIA |
| 6 May | Lt.z.S. Hans Rolshoven | SFS | KIA cc | 23 May | Oblt Walter Angermund | 76b | WIA |
| 7 May | Flg Heinrich Görzel | 19 | POW | 25 May | Vfw Karl Koller | 76b | POW |
| 7 May | OfStv Waldemar von der Weppen | 27 | KIA | 26 May | Oblt von Rudno-Rudzinski | 60 | POW |
| 7 May | Ltn Willi Scheerer | 64w | WIA/ | 27 May | Vfw Fritz Schattauer | 16b | WIA |
| | | | DOW | 27 May | Hptm Rudolf Freiherr von | | |
| 8 May | Ltn Heinz Müller | 27 | KIA | | Esebeck | 17 | KIA |
| 8 May | Uffz Johann Paul Meyer | 32b | KIA | 27 May | Ltn Franz Hausner | 23b | KIA |
| 8 May | Ltn Wolf Baron von | | | 27 May | Ltn Otto Hornfischer | 23b | KIA |
| | Manteuffel-Szöge | 35b | KIA | 27 May | Vfw Artur Schiebler | 30 | KIA |
| 8 May | Vfw Wilhelm Börlinghaus | 43 | KIA | 27 May | Ltn Johannes Lieberz | 35b | INJ |
| 8 May | Vfw Karl Käppeler | 55 | KIA | 27 May | Ltn Heinrich Arntzen | 50 | WIA |
| 8 May | Ltn Erich Wolff | 55 | KIA | 27 May | Ltn Walter Fritzsche | 65 | KIA |
| 9 May | Ltn Seeländer | 37 | INJ | 27 May | Ltn Rudolf Windisch | 66 | POW/ |
| 9 May | Uffz Höhne | 37 | INJ | | | | KILLED |
| 9 May | Ltn Ernst Schulze | 48 | KIA | 27 May | Oblt Amandus Rostock | 76b | WIA |
| 9 May | Uffz Otto Kutter | 48 | KIA | 27 May | Flg Haitsch | 79b | WIA |
| 9 May | Ltn Karl Hertz | 59 | KIA | 28 May | Gefr Peisker | 7 | INJ |
| 9 May | Flgomt Franz Hassler | MFJ I | KIAcc | 28 May | Uffz Sicho | 7 | WIA |
| 10 May | Uffz Fritz Zopf | 80b | KIAcc | 28 May | Ltn Bitsch | 9 | WIA |
| 10 May | Ltn Heinrich Büssing | Kest 4b | KIAcc | 28 May | Uffz Reuss | 7 | WIA |
| 11 May | Ltn Otto Äckerle | 47w | KIA | 28 May | Flg Wilhelm Dumbrowe | 12 | KIA |
| 11 May | Ltn Obermeier | 76b | WIA | 28 May | Oblt Harald Auffahrt | 29 | WIA |
| 13 May | Ltn Wilhelm Obsestadt | 56 | WIA | 28 May | Lt.z.S. Johannes Etzdorf | SFS | KIA |
| 13 May | Ltn Alfred Wunsch | 67 | WIA | 29 May | Ltn Paul Bäumer | 2 | INJ |
| 14 May | Uffz Paul Hüttenrauch | 7 | WIA | 29 May | Uffz Ruess | 7 | WIA |
| 14 May | Ltn Erich Weiss | 33 | KIA | 29 May | Ltn Rademacher | 10 | POW |
| 14 May | Uffz Friedrich-Karl Florian | 51 | POW | 29 May | Ltn Otto Kissenberth | 23b | INJ |
| 15 May | Flg Rudolf Reissmann | 24s | KIA | 29 May | Ltn Wilhelm Pannes | 46 | KIA |
| 15 May | OfStv Josef Wolski | 51 | KIA | 29 May | Ltn Günther Keitsch | 74 | KIA |
| 15 May | Vfw Rudolf Warschun | 51 | KIA | 29 May | Ltn Max Gebbert | 79b | INJ |
| 15 May | Ltn Walter Lütjohann | 63 | KIA | 30 May | Ltn Heidenreich | 6 | POW |
| 15 May | Uffz Erwin Tresenreuter | 68 | WIA | 30 May | Ltn Karl Köhler | 9 | KIA |
| 15 May | Oblt Walter Ewers | 77b | KIA | 30 May | Ltn Willibald Dehner | 32b | WIA/ |
| 16 May | Ltn Fedor Hübner | 4 | POW | | | | DOW |
| 16 May | Sgt Otto Schmutzler | 4 | KIA | 30 May | Vfw Hillerbrand | 32b | WIA |
| 16 May | Ltn Hans Joachim Wolff | 11 | KIA | 30 May | Ltn Emanuel Riezler | 34b | WIA |
| 16 May | Ltn Heinrich Küllmer | 23b | KIA | 30 May | Gefr Theodor Bauer | 34b | KIA |
| 16 May | Ltn Hans Nissen | 54s | KIA | 30 May | Ltn Bieck | 36 | POW |
| 16 May | Ltn Karl von Plessen | 59 | KIA | 30 May | Vfw Jakob Pollinger | 77b | POW |
| 16 May | Flgomt Heinrich Hahn | MFJ I | WIA | 31 May | Uffz Wilhelm Kutschera | 3 | KIA |
| 16 May | Flgmt Illig | MFJ II | WIA | 31 May | Ltn Viktor von Pressentin gen | | |
| 17 May | Vfw Julius Trotzky | 43 | KIA | | von Rautter | 4 | KIA |
| 17 May | Vfw Alfred Philipp | 57 | KIA | 31 May | Ltn Hans Schlömer | 5 | KIA |
| 17 May | Ltn Heinrich Zürn | 62 | KIA | 31 May | Ltn Edouard Stratmann | 9 | POW |
| 17 May | Gefr Albert Wendt | 63 | KIA | 31 May | Ltn Hans Grabe | 14 | WIA/ |
| 18 May | Sgt Fritz Broderek | 42 | KIA | | | | DOW |
| 18 May | Ltn Reinhold Klimsch | 51 | KIAcc | 31 May | Ltn Bucholz | 20 | WIA |
| 18 May | Ltn Feuereissen | 51 | WIA | 31 May | Ltn Erich Kaus | 30 | WIA |
| 19 May | Uffz Andreas Triebswetter | 16b | KIA | 31 May | Uffz Heinrich Koch | 36 | KIA |

| Date | Pilot Jasta Casualty | Unit | | Date | Pilot Jasta Casualty | Unit | |
|---|---|---|---|---|---|---|---|
| 31 May | Vfw Flatow | 45 | WIA | 12 Jun | Ltn Gerhard Schulze | MFJ I | KIA |
| 31 May | Uffz Schilli | 47w | WIA | 13 Jun | Uffz Dannemann | 56 | INJ |
| 31 May | Ltn Gerhard Schulte | 50 | POW | 13 Jun | Uffz Rudolf Kassner | 65 | KIA |
| 31 May | Ltn Walter Böning | 76b | WIA | 13 Jun | Ltn Kurt von Seelen | Kest 3 | WIA |
| 31 May | Vfw Georg Markert | 76b | KIA | 14 Jun | Vfw Josef Degen | 6 | POW |
| ? May | Ltn Herbert Schröder | 17 | WIA | 14 Jun | Ltn Busso von Alvensleben | 21s | POW/ |
| 1 Jun | Uffz Kroeger | 7 | WIA | | | | DOW |
| 1 Jun | Vfw Wilhelm Stein | 27 | KIA | 15 Jun | Ltn Wilhelm Schwartz | 13 | WIA |
| 1 Jun | Ltn Wilhelm Rupprecht | 31 | KIA | 16 Jun | Ltn Johannes Lieberz | 35b | INJ |
| 1 Jun | Uffz Graf | 31 | WIA | 16 Jun | Vfw Willy Peters | 66 | POW |
| 1 Jun | Uffz Friedrich Neumann | 37 | KIA | 16 Jun | Ltn Hansjörg von Dechend | 72s | KIA |
| 1 Jun | Ltn Wilhelm Saint Mont | 52 | KIA | 16 Jun | Gefr Flach | 81 | POW |
| 1 Jun | Vfw Sokolowski | 60 | POW | 16 Jun | Ltn Langenbach | 81 | POW |
| 1 Jun | Uffz Andreas Herold | 77b | KIA | 17 Jun | Ltn Kurt Wüsthoff | JG I | POW |
| 1 Jun | Uffz Alfred Dölger | 80b | WIA | 17 Jun | Uffz Kurt Meinel | 22s | KIAcc |
| 2 Jun | Uffz Adolf Schneider | 1 | KIA | 17 Jun | Flg Fritz Moser | 22s | KIAcc |
| 2 Jun | Ltn Heidenreich | 6 | POW | 17 Jun | Oblt Maximilian von Förster | 27 | KIAcc |
| 2 Jun | Ltn Gerhard Schreiber | 37 | KIA | 17 Jun | Vfw Wilhelm Schäffer | 27 | KIA |
| 2 Jun | Ltn Johann Dunkelberg | 58 | KIA | 17 Jun | Ltn Hans-Georg von der Marwitz | 30 | WIA |
| 2 Jun | Flgmt Horst Sawatzki | MFJ I | WIA | 17 Jun | Sgt Johann Braun | 69 | KIAcc |
| 3 Jun | Uffz Max Bauer | 23b | WIA | 18 Jun | Ltn Max Hillmann | 7 | KIAcc |
| 3 Jun | Oblt Josef Loeser | 46 | KIA | 18 Jun | Gefr Gustav Reuter | 20 | KIAcc |
| 3 Jun | Ltn Baum | 79b | POW | 18 Jun | Vfw Erich Dürre | 38 | KIA |
| 4 Jun | Ltn Emmerich Honig | 14 | KIAcc | 18 Jun | Ltn Rudolf Heins | 56 | WIA |
| 4 Jun | Ltn Bohnert | 43 | WIA | 18 Jun | Uffz Köhler | 56 | WIA |
| 5 Jun | Sgt Karl Schneider | 23b | INJ | 18 Jun | Oblt Erwin Wenig | 80b | WIA |
| 5 Jun | Ltn Friedrich Holthaus | 48 | KIA | 19 Jun | Uffz Max Mertens | 7 | KIA |
| 5 Jun | Vfw Paul Reimann | 52 | KIA | 20 Jun | Ltn Paul Piepiorka | 71 | KIA |
| 5 Jun | Ltn Fritz Ree | 68 | KIA | 20 Jun | Vfw Ludwig Bergmann | 79b | KIA |
| 6 Jun | Ltn Heinrich Otto | 10 | WIA | 20 Jun | Oblt Bruno Loerzer | JGIII | WIA |
| 6 Jun | Ltn Karl Albert Mendel | 18 | KIA | 21 Jun | Ltn Otto Maashoff | Kest 2 | WIA |
| 6 Jun | Ltn Hans Schultz | 18 | POW | 23 Jun | Vfw Ernst Bielefeld | 60 | KIA |
| 6 Jun | Ltn Günther Derlin | 20 | KIA | 23 Jun | Ltn Max Schick | 76b | POW |
| 6 Jun | Vfw Otto Heller | 40s | KIA | 25 Jun | Ltn Franz Hilberer | 13 | KIA |
| 6 Jun | Ltn Karl Becker | 61 | KIA | 25 Jun | Uffz Walter Hertzsch | 13 | KIA |
| 7 Jun | Vfw Fritz Maschinsky | 19 | POW | 25 Jun | Uffz Albin Peter | 14 | KIAcc |
| 7 Jun | Ltn Hans Friedrich | 34b | INJ | 25 Jun | Ltn Alfred Rothe | 27 | KIA |
| 7 Jun | Ltn Heinrich Kütt | 23b | WIA/ | 25 Jun | Ltn Kurt Schulz | 37 | KIA |
| | | | DOW | 25 Jun | Ltn Wilhelm Schulz | 66 | POW |
| 7 Jun | Flg Wilhelm Schade | 41 | POW | 26 Jun | Ltn Wilhelm Lehmann | 5 | KIA |
| 7 Jun | Oblt Maximilian Edler | | | 26 Jun | Obflgmstr Kurt Schönfelder | 7 | KIA |
| | von Daniels | 61 | KIA | 26 Jun | Ltn Werner Steinhäuser | 11 | KIA |
| 7 Jun | Ltn Josef Weckerle | 79b | POW | 26 Jun | Ltn von Decker | 20 | WIA |
| 8 Jun | Uffz Friedrich Heckel | 16b | WIA | 26 Jun | Uffz Georg Zillig | 79b | INJ |
| 8 Jun | Gefr Leonhard Horn | 16b | WIA | 27 Jun | Uffz Johann Meeder | 23b | WIA |
| 8 Jun | Ltn Wilhelm Erlewein | 47w | KIA | 27 Jun | Ltn Josef Müller | 29 | KIA |
| 8 Jun | Ltn Rüdiger Fr von Künsberg | 55 | KIA | 27 Jun | Gefr Eduard August Hellwig | 40s | WIA/ |
| 9 Jun | Ltn Johann Janzen | 6 | POW | | | | DOW |
| 9 Jun | Gefr Preis | 14 | POW | 27 Jun | Vfw Stadley | 62 | POW/ |
| 9 Jun | Ltn Heinrich Küffberger | 23b | KIA | | | | DOW |
| 9 Jun | Flg Wilhelm Schädlich | 53 | INJ | 28 Jun | Flg Hugo Jauch | 47w | KIAcc |
| 9 Jun | Ltn Heinrich Sattler | MFJ II | KIA | 28 Jun | Vfw Ernst Busch | 62 | KIA |
| 9 Jun | Ltn Weinert | MFJ II | WIA | 28 Jun | Oblt Hasso von Wedel | 75 | WIA |
| 10 Jun | Ltn Walter Balzer | 44s | KIA | 29 Jun | Uffz Heinrich Piel | 13 | KIA |
| 11 Jun | Gefr Heinz Kleineberg | 20 | POW | 29 Jun | Ltn Heinrich Seywald | 23b | WIA |
| 11 Jun | Ltn Fritz Imme | 42 | KIA | 29 Jun | Uffz Heinrich Reckendrees | 56 | KIA |
| 11 Jun | Flgmt Wilhelm Grabowski | MFJ I | WIA | 29 Jun | Gefr Friedrich Bär | 81 | KIA |
| 12 Jun | Ltn Hugo Schulz | 12 | KIA | 30 Jun | Ltn Lothar Feige | 10 | KIA |
| 12 Jun | Ltn Hubert Helten | 20 | KIA | 30 Jun | Ltn Friedrich Hofmann | 11 | KIA |
| 12 Jun | Ltn Fritz Loerzer | 26 | POW | 30 Jun | Ltn Ewald Carl | 51 | KIA |
| 12 Jun | Oblt Kurt Grasshoff | 38 | KIA | 30 Jun | Ltn Hans Viebig | 57 | WIA |
| 12 Jun | Ltn Arond Erich | 63 | KIA | 30 Jun | Vfw Wunnenberg | 60 | WIA |
| 12 Jun | Ltn Rudolf Croissant | 68 | KIA | 1 Jul | Vfw Georg Schalk | 34b | KIA |
| 12 Jun | Vfw Ernst Sperling | 69 | KIA | 1 Jul | Ltn Walter Reher | 48 | KIAcc |
| 12 Jun | Ltn Ernst | 69 | POW | 1 Jul | Ltn Kralewski | 63 | KIA |
| 12 Jun | Uffz Fritz Kühn | 79b | WIA | 1 Jul | Oblt Gottlieb Rasberger | 80b | WIA |

| Date | Pilot Jasta Casualty | Unit | |
|---|---|---|---|
| 2 Jul | Ltn Wuebben | 14 | WIA |
| 2 Jul | Ltn Hellmuth Roer | 27 | KIA |
| 2 Jul | Ltn Fruchtbar | 52 | WIA |
| 3 Jul | Flg Jakob Lux | 1 | KIA |
| 3 Jul | Vfw Hans Vietzen | 12 | KIA |
| 3 Jul | Hptm Wilhelm Reinhard | JGI | KIAcc |
| 4 Jul | Ltn Alfred Ponath | 68 | KIA |
| 4 Jul | Lt.z.S. Theodor Lodemann | SFS | KIA |
| 5 Jul | Oblt Wolfgang Plüschow | 31 | KIA |
| 5 Jul | Flg Stefan Meier | 79b | KIAcc |
| 5 Jul | Flg Sturmkeit | 81 | WIA |
| 6 Jul | Ltn Werner Junck | 8 | WIA |
| 6 Jul | Ltn Robert Schwarz | 52 | WIA |
| 7 Jul | Vfw Otto Rosenfeld | 41 | KIA |
| 8 Jul | Ltn Walter Noack | 29 | WIA |
| 8 Jul | Flg Anton Wadowski | 52 | KIA |
| 8 Jul | Gefr Rudolf Lang | 78b | WIA |
| 9 Jul | Ltn Helmut Dilthey | 40s | KIA |
| 9 Jul | Uffz Maier | 46 | WIA |
| 9 Jul | Ltn Hermann Munzert | 59 | KIA |
| 10 Jul | Ltn Eberhard Horn | 3 | INJ |
| 10 Jul | Gefr Paul Göhler | 3 | INJ |
| 10 Jul | Ltn August Hartmann | 30 | WIA |
| 10 Jul | Ltn Wilhelm Oberstadt | 56 | WIA |
| 11 Jul | Uffz Johannes Diebold | 71 | WIA |
| 11 Jul | Ltn Hansjörg von Schulz | Kest 7 | KIAcc |
| 12 Jul | Flg Josef Thomas | 23b | INJ |
| 12 Jul | Uffz Karl Röttgen | 39 | KIA |
| 12 Jul | Uffz Ludwig Artmann | 76b | KIA |
| 13 Jul | Ltn Karl Plauth | 20 | INJ |
| 13 Jul | Flg Tollmann | 20 | KIA |
| 13 Jul | Ltn von Decker | 20 | WIA |
| 13 Jul | Vfw Michael Lüderitz | 52 | KIA |
| 14 Jul | Flgmstr Eduard Schwarze | SFS | KIAcc |
| 15 Jul | Ltn Friedrich Friedrichs | 10 | KIA |
| 15 Jul | Vfw Alfred Hübner | 36 | WIA |
| 15 Jul | Ltn Lambert Schütt | 66 | KIA |
| 16 Jul | Lt Julius Bender | 4 | WIA |
| 16 Jul | Ltn Johannes Markgraf | 6 | KIAcc |
| 16 Jul | Ltn Hans Kirschstein | 6 | INJ/DOW |
| 16 Jul | Uffz Wilhelm Laabs | 13 | KIA |
| 16 Jul | Ltn Hilmar Glöcklen | 21s | WIA |
| 16 Jul | Vfw Gustav Wackwitz | 29 | KIAcc |
| 16 Jul | Ltn Friedrich Karl Weber | 29 | INJ |
| 16 Jul | Vfw Gustav Nolte | 36 | WIA |
| 16 Jul | Ltn Karl Wernicke | 43 | KIAcc |
| 16 Jul | Vfw Erich Meyer | 45 | INJ |
| 16 Jul | Ltn Fritz Pütter | 68 | WIA/DOW |
| 16 Jul | Vfw Friedrich Megerle | 70 | KIA |
| 16 Jul | Ltn Ludwig Schmid | 76b | WIA |
| 16 Jul | Ltn Karl Neu | 76b | WIA |
| 16 Jul | Flgmt Weigel | MFJ III | WIA |
| 17 Jul | Ltn Arthur Rahn | 19 | WIA |
| 17 Jul | Ltn Otto Franke | 30 | KIA |
| 17 Jul | Ltn Kurt Krüger | 55 | KIA |
| 17 Jul | Uffz Heinrich Pfaffenritter | 60 | WIA |
| 17 Jul | Ltn Heinrich Zempel | 65 | INJ |
| 18 Jul | Ltn Hermann Bolle | 2 | WIA |
| 18 Jul | Ltn Moritz Waldemar Bretschneider-Bodemer | 6 | KIA |
| 18 Jul | Gefr Ludwig Möller | 10 | KIA |
| 18 Jul | Ltn Kurt Jacob | 36 | WIA |
| 18 Jul | Ltn Konrad Schwartz | 66 | POW/DOW |
| 19 Jul | Ltn Hans Stelzer | 26 | KIA |
| 19 Jul | Vfw Karl Schmelcher | 71 | KIA |
| 19 Jul | Gefr Linus Luger | 79b | KIA |
| 20 Jul | Ltn Werner Meyer | 34b | WIA/DOW |
| 20 Jul | OfStv Paul Felsmann | Kest 4b | KIA |
| 20 Jul | Flgmstr Alfons Nitsche | MFJ II | KIA |
| 21 Jul | OfStv Otto Esswein | 26 | KIA |
| 21 Jul | Ltn Schmidt | SFS | POW |
| 22 Jul | Ltn Willi Schuster | 5 | KIAcc |
| 22 Jul | Vfw Emil Soltau | 20 | KIA |
| 22 Jul | Ltn Werner Nöldecke | 6 | INJ |
| 22 Jul | Uffz Paul Marszinski | 30 | KIA |
| 22 Jul | Gefr Bergmann | 66 | POW |
| 22 Jul | Flgmt Alexandre Zenses | MFJ II | WIA |
| 24 Jul | Uffz Ruess | 7 | WIA |
| 24 Jul | Vfw Friedrich Schumacher | 10 | WIA |
| 24 Jul | Ltn Höfig | 37 | KIA |
| 24 Jul | Ltn Friedrich Jakobs | 43 | WIA |
| 24 Jul | Uffz Kurt Hoffmann | 51 | KIA |
| 24 Jul | Vfw Kurt Beinecke | 51 | KIA |
| 25 Jul | Ltn Friedrich-Franz Fr von Hohenau | 11 | WIA/DOW |
| 25 Jul | Ltn von Dorrien | 11 | WIA |
| 25 Jul | Ltn Karl Menckhoff | 72s | POW |
| 29 Jul | Ltn Hermann Müller | 19 | INJ |
| 29 Jul | OfStv Johann Dierle | Kest 4b | KIA |
| 30 Jul | Ltn Heinz Drekmann | 4 | KIA |
| 30 Jul | Ltn Leopold von Raffay | 6 | INJ |
| 30 Jul | Uffz Wilhelm Meyer | 16b | WIA |
| 30 Jul | Ltn Ernst Kleinhempel | 46 | KIAcc |
| 30 Jul | Ltn Robert Dycke | 78b | WIA |
| 30 Jul | Ltn Hans Laurisch | Kest 4b | KIA |
| 30 Jul | Ltn Wieland | SFS | WIA |
| 31 Jul | Ltn Barth | 7 | WIA |
| 31 Jul | Gefr Ludwig Zellner | 32b | KIA |
| 31 Jul | Ltn Paul Erichson | 40s | WIA |
| 31 Jul | Uffz Fritz Salb | 80b | KIA |
| 31 Jul | Flgmt Kulbe | SFS | POW |
| 31 Jul | Flgomt Otto Wasserthal | MFJ IV | KIA |
| 1 Aug | Ltn Paul Wenzel | 6 | WIA |
| 1 Aug | Sgt Alexander Wittke | 9 | KIAcc |
| 1 Aug | Ltn Heinrich Böving | 9 | INJ/DOW |
| 1 Aug | Ltn Walter Lehmann | 10 | KIA |
| 1 Aug | Ltn Günther Schuster | 17 | WIA |
| 1 Aug | Ltn Joachim von Busse | 20 | WIA |
| 1 Aug | Ltn Waldemar von Dazur | 20 | INJ |
| 1 Aug | Vfw Dralle | 51 | POW |
| 1 Aug | Vzflgmstr Alexandre Zenses | MFJ II | WIA |
| 3 Aug | Vfw Drexler | 43 | WIA |
| 3 Aug | Ltn Triebner | 51 | POW |
| 3 Aug | Ltn Selzer | 74 | POW/ESCAPED |
| 4 Aug | Uffz Strecker | 10 | INJ |
| 7 Aug | OfStv Walter Hering | 17 | KIAcc |
| 7 Aug | Vfw Hermann Benzler | 30 | INJ |
| 7 Aug | Vfw Ernst David | 30 | KIAcc |
| 7 Aug | Vfw Prinz | 40s | IIC |
| 8 Aug | Vfw Walgenbach | 42 | POW |
| 8 Aug | Uffz Löhr | 44s | POW |
| 8 Aug | Ltn Rudolf Neitzer | 65 | KIA |
| 8 Aug | Ltn Hans Kiessling | 79b | WIA |
| 8 Aug | Uffz Johann Schmidt | 79b | WIA |
| 9 Aug | Ltn Reinhard | 4 | WIA |
| 9 Aug | Vfw Franz Hemer | 6 | WIA |

| Date | Pilot Jasta Casualty | Unit | |
|---|---|---|---|
| 9 Aug | Ltn Egon Patzer | 36 | KIA |
| 9 Aug | Uffz Otto Stockmann | 66 | POW |
| 10 Aug | Ltn Erich Löwenhardt | 10 | KIA |
| 10 Aug | Ltn Muhs | 12 | POW |
| 10 Aug | Ltn Paul Billik | 52 | POW |
| 10 Aug | Flg Georg Lindenberg | 52 | IIC |
| 10 Aug | Flg Herbert Koch | 64w | KIA |
| 10 Aug | Hptm Rudolf Berthold | JGII | WIA |
| 11 Aug | Ltn Paul Wenzel | 6 | WIA |
| 11 Aug | Ltn Bodo von der Wense | 6 | KIA |
| 11 Aug | Ltn Max Festler | 11 | KIA |
| 11 Aug | Ltn Hans Joachim Borck | 15 | KIA |
| 11 Aug | Ltn Hans Pippart | 19 | KIA |
| 11 Aug | Uffz Bernhard Vollers | 20 | KIAcc |
| 11 Aug | Ltn Karl Thom | 21s | WIA |
| 11 Aug | Gefr Max Bauer | 23b | WIA |
| 11 Aug | Oblt Josef Mühlfeldt | 23b | WIA/DOW |
| 11 Aug | Ltn Albert Hets | 37 | KIA |
| 11 Aug | Ltn Martin | 46 | WIA |
| 11 Aug | Vfw Paul Völker | 60 | WIA/DOW |
| 11 Aug | Ltn Straube | 70 | WIA |
| 11 Aug | OfStv Paul Steinbacher | 81 | KIA |
| 12 Aug | Vfw Hermann Benzier | 30 | INJ |
| 12 Aug | Ltn Robert Schmidt | 43 | WIA |
| 12 Aug | OfStv Fritz Blumenthal | 53 | POW |
| 12 Aug | Uffz Emil Possin | 53 | WIA |
| 12 Aug | Uffz Winter | 68 | WIA |
| 12 Aug | Vfw Heinrich Krüger | 70 | KIA |
| 12 Aug | Gefr Johann Janiszewski | 75 | KIA |
| 12 Aug | Vfw Karl Kallmünzer | 78b | KIA |
| 13 Aug | Ltn Lothar Freiherr von Richthofen | 11 | WIA |
| 13 Aug | Ltn Hilmar Schickler | 19 | KIA |
| 13 Aug | Ltn Erwin Häfner | 22s | KIAcc |
| 13 Aug | Flg Hermann Horstmann | 22s | KIAcc |
| 13 Aug | Flg Hoffmann | 24s | INJ |
| 13 Aug | Ltn Gutsche | 36 | WIA |
| 13 Aug | Vfw Stein | 45 | WIA |
| 13 Aug | Ltn Dieter Collin | 56 | WIA/DOW |
| 13 Aug | Oblt Reinhold Ritter von Benz | 78b | KIA |
| 13 Aug | Gefr Emil Estenfelder | 79b | WIA |
| 13 Aug | Flgobmatr Klotzsch† | MFJ I | WIA |
| 13 Aug | Vzflgmstr Günther Knie† | MFJ II | KIA |
| 13 Aug | Flgmt Wilhelm Drews† | MFJ III | KIA |
| 13 Aug | Flgmt Wilhelm Grabowski | MFJ I | WIA |
| 13 Aug | Flgmt Kiessling | MFJ IV | WIA |
| 13 Aug | Lt.z.S. Spies | SFS | WIA |
| 14 Aug | Flg Eickhoff | 17 | IIC |
| 14 Aug | Ltn Heinrich Kroll | 24s | WIA |
| 14 Aug | Ltn Kurt Brünninghaus | 31 | KIAcc |
| 14 Aug | Uffz Karl Klein | 37 | KIA |
| 14 Aug | Gefr Biehl | 59 | WIA |
| 14 Aug | OfStv Belitz | 69 | INJ |
| 14 Aug | Uffz Ludwig Wittmann | 80b | POW |
| 14 Aug | Flgmt Karl Goldenstedt | MFJ I | WIA |
| 15 Aug | Sgt Emil Vitzthum | 16b | WIA/DOW |
| 15 Aug | Vfw Fritz Schwarz | 33 | KIA |
| 15 Aug | Ltn August Wüst | 42 | KIA |
| 15 Aug | Vfw Karl Rohmann | 56 | INJ/DOW |
| 15 Aug | Flgobmatr Friedrich Gröschke | SFS | WIA |
| 16 Aug | Vfw Lechner | 6 | INJ |
| 16 Aug | Ltn Ernst Riedel | 19 | KIAcc |
| 16 Aug | Vfw Otto Senff | 48 | KIA |
| 17 Aug | Ltn Helmuth Fürstenau | 44s | KIA |
| 18 Aug | Ltn Wilhelm Gäckstatter | 51 | KIA |
| 19 Aug | Ltn Emil Rolff | 6 | KIAcc |
| 19 Aug | Uffz Paul Felix | 15 | KIA |
| 19 Aug | Flg Anders | 45 | INJ |
| 20 Aug | OfStv Jakob Ledermann | 13 | POW |
| 20 Aug | Ltn Erich Raabe | 41 | WIA |
| 20 Aug | Gefr Johann Schlimpen | 45 | KIA |
| 20 Aug | Vfw Thilo Boelcke | 67 | KIA |
| 21 Aug | Ltn Johannes Hentschel | 9 | INJ |
| 21 Aug | Uffz Rudolf Klamt | 10 | WIA |
| 21 Aug | Flg Karl Scharrenbroich | 39 | KIA |
| 21 Aug | Ltn Hans-Joachim Rolfes | 45 | WIA |
| 21 Aug | Vfw Eichhorn | 58 | INJ |
| 21 Aug | Vfw Anton Bernhörster | 61 | KIA |
| 21 Aug | Flgobmatr Friedrich Gröschke | SFS | KIA |
| 22 Aug | Vfw Kister | 1 | WIA |
| 22 Aug | Ltn Arthur Merz | 28w | WIA/DOW |
| 22 Aug | Ltn Hugo Krauss | 32b | KIA |
| 22 Aug | Uffz Walter Feibicke | 44s | KIAcc |
| 22 Aug | Uffz Bödinghaus | 61 | POW |
| 22 Aug | Sgt Starost | 61 | POW |
| 22 Aug | Oblt Theodor Cammann | 74 | WIA |
| 23 Aug | Ltn Raven Freiherr von Barnekow | 11 | WIA |
| 23 Aug | Vfw Emil Bergmann | 22s | KIAcc |
| 23 Aug | Flg Hermann Jander | 24s | KIA |
| 23 Aug | Uffz Theurer | 38 | WIA |
| 23 Aug | Vfw Rothe | 61 | INJ |
| 23 Aug | Ltn Georg Vieth | 61 | KIAcc |
| 23 Aug | Flg Leonard Kormann | 79b | KIA |
| 24 Aug | Oblt Walter Grosch | 4 | WIA |
| 24 Aug | Uffz Ernst Binkenstein | 51 | KIA |
| 24 Aug | Gefr Richard Probst | 79b | WIA/DOW |
| 24 Aug | Ltn Herbert Knappe | 81 | WIA |
| 25 Aug | Ltn Friedrich Wilhelm Dieves | 45 | POW |
| 25 Aug | Vfw Siegfried Walther | 55 | KIA |
| 25 Aug | Ltn Otto Fitzner | 65 | WIA |
| 26 Aug | Gefr Konrad Becker | 48 | KIA |
| 26 Aug | Vfw Ludwig Hilz | Kest 4b | KIA |
| 27 Aug | Ltn Wolff | 6 | INJ |
| 27 Aug | Vfw Michael Sigmann | 78b | WIA |
| 28 Aug | Ltn Franz Ruch | JG I | KIA |
| 29 Aug | Gefr Peter Peltzer | 5 | WIA/DOW |
| 29 Aug | Vfw Rudolf Lander | 52 | KIAcc |
| 29 Aug | Vfw Knobel | 57 | WIAcc |
| 30 Aug | OfStv Wilhelm Kühne | 18 | KIA |
| 30 Aug | Uffz Wilhelm Hofacker | 65 | KIA |
| 31 Aug | Ltn Hirschfeld | 81 | WIA |
| 31 Aug | Ltn Bertram Heinrich | MFJ I | KIA |
| 31 Aug | Ltn Werner Bastien | MFJ I | KIA |
| Aug | Ltn Johann Kopka | 61 | WIA |
| 2 Sep | Ltn Konrad Brendle | 45 | KIA |
| 2 Sep | Uffz Hennies | 49 | WIA |
| 2 Sep | Flg Karl Pabst | 50 | KIA |
| 2 Sep | Ltn Hans Quartier | 67 | POW |
| 2 Sep | Ltn Gottfried Clausnitzer | 72s | KIA |
| 2 Sep | Vfw Michael Sigmann | 78b | WIA |
| 2 Sep | Flg Ludwig Prillwitz | 81 | POW |
| 3 Sep | Flg Hermann Wirth | 32b | KIA |
| 3 Sep | Vfw Wilhelm Skworz | 36 | KIA |
| 3 Sep | Vfw Friedrich Engler | 62 | WIA |

| Date | Pilot Jasta Casualty | Unit | | Date | Pilot Jasta Casualty | Unit | |
|------|----------------------|------|------|------|----------------------|------|------|
| 4 Sep | Vfw Kurt Jentsch | 2 | WIA | 27 Sep | Ltn Fritz Heinz | 2 | KIA |
| 4 Sep | Vfw Hans Reimers | 6 | WIA/ | 27 Sep | Ltn Fritz Rumey | 5 | KIA |
| | | | DOW | 27 Sep | Ltn Steiling | 19 | INJ |
| 4 Sep | Ltn Bernhard Lauscher | 31 | INJ | 27 Sep | Ltn Holle | 31 | WIA |
| 4 Sep | Uffz Reinhold Neumann | 36 | WIA/ | 27 Sep | Ltn Paul Strähle | 57 | WIA |
| | | | DOW | 27 Sep | Ltn Hans Jebens | 59 | KIA |
| 4 Sep | Ltn Kurt Waldheim | 36 | KIA | 27 Sep | Oblt Hans Helmut von Boddien | 59 | WIA |
| 4 Sep | Gefr Tegtmeyer | 57 | WIA | 27 Sep | Ltn Max Näther | 62 | WIA |
| 4 Sep | Vfw Dünnhaupt | 58 | WIA | 28 Sep | Vfw Heinrich Brobowski | 53 | POW |
| 4 Sep | Flg Otto Wagner | 79b | POW | 28 Sep | Uffz Karl Hofmann | 60 | KIA |
| 5 Sep | Ltn Joachim von Winterfeld | 4 | WIA | 29 Sep | Ltn Fritz Paul Hoffmann | 2 | KIA |
| 5 Sep | Ltn Schenk | 5 | WIA | 29 Sep | Oblt Hans-Eberhardt Gandert | 51 | POW |
| 5 Sep | Ltn Heinrich Hager | 32b | WIA | 29 Sep | Ltn Gerold Tschentschel | 72s | WIA |
| 5 Sep | Uffz Otto Rösler | 37 | KIA | 30 Sep | Vfw Hermann Bernsmann | 29 | KIA |
| 5 Sep | Gefr Jakob Katzner | 43 | KIA | 30 Sep | Ltn Georg Schlenker | 41 | WIA |
| 6 Sep | Gefr Pägelow | 71 | MIA | 1 Oct | Flg Kurt Marocke | 5 | KIA |
| 7 Sep | FwLt Schiller | Kest 1a | WIA | 1 Oct | Vfw Friedrich Nüsch | 22s | WIA |
| 8 Sep | Gefr Kurt Blümener | 6 | KIA | 1 Oct | Flgmt Berndt | MFJ I | WIA |
| 13 Sep | Ltn Eugen Kelber | 12 | KIA | 1 Oct | Ltn Freymadl | MFJ I | WIA |
| 13 Sep | Ltn Kurt Hetze† | 13 | WIA | 1 Oct | Flgomt Christian Kairies | MFJ V | POW/ |
| 14 Sep | Gefr Anton Kempa | 3 | POW | | | | DOW |
| 14 Sep | Ltn Paul Wolff | 13 | POW | 2 Oct | Vfw Belz | 1 | POW |
| 14 Sep | Ltn Günther von Büren | 18 | WIA | 2 Oct | Ltn Raven Fr von Barnekow | 1 | WIA |
| 14 Sep | Ltn Eugen Siempelkamp | 64w | WIA | 2 Oct | Ltn Sylvester Garsztka | 31 | WIA |
| 15 Sep | Ltn Johannes Klein | 15 | WIA | 2 Oct | Ltn Bachem | 44s | WIA |
| 15 Sep | Ltn Paul Vogel | 23b | POW/ | 2 Oct | Vfw Josef Hohly | 65 | WIA |
| | | | DOW | 2 Oct | Flg Franz Neumann | 79b | WIA |
| 15 Sep | Vfw Ernst de Ritter | 27 | WIA | 3 Oct | Ltn Paul Hasselmann | 28w | KIA |
| 15 Sep | Ltn Hilmar Quittenbaum | 28w | KIA | 3 Oct | Ltn Fritz Höhn | 41 | KIA |
| 15 Sep | Uffz Ottowell | 33 | WIA | 3 Oct | Uffz Heinrich Marwede | 67 | POW |
| 15 Sep | Ltn Rudolf Stark | 35b | WIA | 3 Oct | Lt.z.S. Hermann Meyer | MFJ IV | KIA |
| 15 Sep | Vfw Kurt Pietzsch | 58 | WIA | 4 Oct | Ltn Kurt Schibilsky | 10 | POW |
| 16 Sep | Ltn Friedrich Kresse | 7 | KIA | 4 Oct | Ltn Hermann Silberschmidt | 22s | KIA |
| 16 Sep | Flg Siegfried Braun | 23b | KIA | 4 Oct | Ltn Oliver Fr von | | |
| 16 Sep | Gefr Kurt Brandt | 51 | KIA | | Beaulieu-Marconnay | 19 | WIA |
| 16 Sep | Oblt Hans Schlieter | 70 | WIA | 4 Oct | Uffz Paul Podbiel | 40s | KIA |
| 16 Sep | Vfw Walter Sieg | 71 | KIA | 4 Oct | Ltn Schulze | 51 | WIA |
| 16 Sep | Vzflgmstr Horst Sawatzki | MFJ I | WIA | 4 Oct | Ltn Ernst Baumgärtel | 56 | KIA |
| 16 Sep | Flgmt Naeke | MFJ I | WIA | 4 Oct | Ltn Hermann Tölke | 79b | WIA |
| 16 Sep | Lt z S Heinrich Wessels | MFJI | KIA | 5 Oct | Ltn Arno Benzler | 60 | WIA |
| 17 Sep | Sgt Hans Popp | 77b | KIA | 6 Oct | Vfw Hans Knaak | 9 | KIA |
| 18 Sep | Ltn Erich Kämpfe | 13 | WIA/ | 7 Oct | Flg Schade | 5 | INJ |
| | | | DOW | 7 Oct | Ltn Herbert Boy | 14 | POW |
| 20 Sep | Vfw Otto Fruhner | 26 | WIA | 7 Oct | Vfw Paul Groll | 40s | KIA |
| 20 Sep | Flg Friedrich Kinzig | 55 | KIA | 8 Oct | Uffz August Eigenbrodt | 7 | WIA |
| 20 Sep | Ltn Helmuth Gantz | 56 | WIA/ | 8 Oct | Flg Kurt Oertel | 20 | KIA |
| | | | DOW | 8 Oct | Ltn Karl Bers | 51 | WIA |
| 20 Sep | Ltn Hans Böhning | 79b | WIA | 9 Oct | Oblt Waldemar von Dazur | 20 | WIA |
| 21 Sep | Ltn Rudolf Klimke | 27 | WIA | 9 Oct | Ltn Hans Braun | 34b | KIA |
| 22 Sep | Ltn Karl Bauernfeind | 34b | KIA | 9 Oct | Ltn Gerhard Hoffmann | 68 | KIA |
| 23 Sep | Vfw Paul Färber | 22s | KIA | 10 Oct | Ltn Johann Schäfer | 16b | KIA |
| 23 Sep | Ltn Krayer | 45 | INJ | 10 Oct | Uffz Heinrich Haase | 21s | WIA |
| 23 Sep | Flgmt Karl Schiffmann | MFJ IV | KIA | 10 Oct | Vfw Tschierschke | 24s | WIA |
| 24 Sep | Vfw Peter Stenzel | 14 | KIA | 10 Oct | Vfw Heinrich Pfaffenritter | 60 | KIAcc |
| 24 Sep | Ltn Bruno Richard Hobein | 20 | WIA | 10 Oct | Sgt Karl Bohnenberger | 60 | KIAcc |
| 24 Sep | Vfw Schmitt | 27 | WIA | 10 Oct | Uffz Paul Dyrbusch | 68 | KIA |
| 24 Sep | Ltn Wilhelm Meyer | 47w | POW | 10 Oct | Vfw Heinrich Forstmann | Kest 1a | KIA |
| 24 Sep | Ltn Martin Demisch | 58 | WIA/ | 11 Oct | Ltn Josef Keller | 43 | INJ |
| | | | DOW | 11 Oct | Ltn Otto Hofmeister | 79b | KIAcc |
| 25 Sep | Uffz Janzen | 17 | INJ | 14 Oct | Oblt Fritz Ritter von Röth | 16b | WIA |
| 25 Sep | Gefr Franz Wagner | 79b | KIA | 14 Oct | Ltn Willisch | 27 | WIA |
| 26 Sep | Ltn Ernst Udet | 4 | WIA | 14 Oct | Ltn Mayer | 31 | WIA |
| 26 Sep | Vfw Robert Wirth | 37 | KIA | 14 Oct | Ltn Georg Meyer | 37 | WIA |
| 26 Sep | Ltn Mappes | 37 | WIA | 14 Oct | Uffz Tracinski | 57 | INJ |
| 26 Sep | Vfw Karl Weinmann | 50 | POW | 14 Oct | Flg Max Thomas | 73 | KIA |
| 26 Sep | Vfw Huar | 68 | WIA | 14 Oct | Flg Albert Müller | 75 | Died |

| Date | Pilot Jasta Casualty | Unit | | Date | Pilot Jasta Casualty | Unit | |
|------|---------------------|------|------|------|---------------------|------|------|
| 14 Oct | Uffz Johann Spannruft | 79b | WIA | 26 Oct | Uffz Fritz Zogmann | 26 | KIA |
| 14 Oct | Lt.z.S. Max Stinski | MFJ IV | KIA | 27 Oct | Ltn Erich Scharrschmidt | 9 | POW |
| 15 Oct | Vfw Ernst de Ritter | 27 | WIA | 27 Oct | Ltn Hinky | 44s | WIA |
| 15 Oct | Ltn Günther Dobberke | 60 | INJ | 27 Oct | Vfw Karl Paul Schlegel | 45 | KIA |
| 15 Oct | Ltn Reinhold Poss | MFJ IV | POW | 27 Oct | Vfw August Scheffler | 81 | KIA |
| 15 Oct | Flgobmatr Schönbaum | MFJ V | WIA | 28 Oct | Vfw Alfred Jaeschke | 30 | POW |
| 15 Oct | Flgmt Baum | MFJ V | INT | 28 Oct | Vfw Alfons Schymik | 24s | KIA |
| 16 Oct | Vfw Albert Haussmann | 13 | KIA | 28 Oct | Ltn Adolf Auer | 40s | WIA/ |
| 18 Oct | Ltn Gustav Böhren | 10 | KIA | | | | POW |
| 18 Oct | Ltn Oliver Fr von | | | 28 Oct | Vfw Hermann Kiep | 43 | KIA |
| | Beaulieu-Marconnay | 19 | WIA/ | 28 Oct | Vfw Max Schnell | 58 | KIA |
| | | | DOW | 28 Oct | Gefr Ludwig Hugel | 65 | KIA |
| 18 Oct | Ltn Stein | 45 | KIA | 28 Oct | Uffz Heinrich Scharl | 79b | KIA |
| 18 Oct | Sgt Albert Karsten | 48 | KIA | 28 Oct | Vfw Andreas Emele | 80b | KIA |
| 18 Oct | Ltn Erich Klink | 68 | KIA | 28 Oct | Ltn Hermann Bargmann | MFJ III | KIA |
| 19 Oct | Ltn Reinhold Maier | 30 | KIA | 29 Oct | Ltn Martin Fischer | 6 | KIA |
| 19 Oct | Vfw Ludwig Zacher | 79b | KIA | 29 Oct | Uffz Hans Haslbeck | 32b | KIA |
| 22 Oct | Ltn Willi Nebgen | 7 | KIA | 30 Oct | Uffz Josef Nebl | 23b | KIA |
| 23 Oct | Vfw Gustav Klaudat | 15 | WIA | 3 Nov | Ltn Heinz Maushake | 4 | WIA |
| 23 Oct | Ltn Paul Lotz | 44s | KIAcc | 4 Nov | Vfw Paul Keusen | 2 | KIA |
| 23 Oct | Vfw Emil Hanzog | 57 | KIA | 4 Nov | Uffz Paul Schönfelder | 29 | KIA |
| 23 Oct | Vfw Alfred Nauwerck | 57 | KIA | 4 Nov | Uffz Otto Hägele | 32b | KIA |
| 24 Oct | Ltn Emil Koch | 32b | WIA | 5 Nov | Ltn Richard Kirst | 10 | KIA |
| 24 Oct | Ltn Karl Jerratsch | Kest 7 | KIA | 5 Nov | Ltn Fritz Leicht | 31 | KIA |
| 25 Oct | Uffz Rudolf Praclik | 5 | WIA | 5 Nov | Sgt Gustav Otto Albrecht | 64w | KIA |
| 25 Oct | Ltn Otto Brandes | 24s | WIA | 9 Nov | Ltn Heinz Freiherr von | | |
| 26 Oct | Ltn Max Kliefoth | 19 | POW | | Beaulieu-Marconnay | 65 | POW |

† Killed on the ground in air raid.

# A–Z List of German Fighter Aces

| Name | | Rank | Units | Score |
|---|---|---|---|---|
| Achilles | Paul | Ltn z S | SFS, MFJV | 8 |
| Adam | Hans von | Ltn | J34b, 6 | 21 |
| Allmenröder | Karl | Ltn | J11 | 30 |
| Altemeier | Friedrich | Vfw | J14, 24s | 21 |
| Althaus | Ernst Fr von | Rittm | J4, 14, 10 | 9 |
| Anders | Fritz-Gerhard | Ltn | S8, J35b, 4, 73 | 7 |
| Anslinger | Leopold | Ltn | FA54, 24s | 10 |
| Arnold | Karl | Vfw | J72s | 6 |
| Arntzen | Heinrich | Ltn | J15, 20, 50 | 11 |
| Aue | Paul | OfStv | J10 | 10 |
| Auer | Hans | Ltn | J16b, 26, 32b | 5 |
| Auffarth | Harald | Oblt | J18, 29 | 29 |
| Averes | Dietrich | Vfw | J81 | 10 |
| | | | | |
| Baldamus | Hartmut | Ltn | J5, 9 | 18 |
| Barnekow | Raven Fr von | Ltn | J20, 1 | 11 |
| Bartels | Bernard | Uffz | J44s | 5 |
| Bassenge | Gerhard | Ltn | J5, 2 | 7 |
| Bäumer | Paul | Ltn | J5, 2 | 43 |
| Baur | Johann | Uffz | FA295 | 6 |
| Beaulieu-Marconnay | Oliver Fr von | Ltn | J18, 15, 19 | 25 |
| Becker | Hermann | Ltn | J12 | 23 |
| Beckmann | Ludwig | Ltn | J6, 48, 56 | 8 |
| Benzler | Arno | Ltn | J32b, 45, 65, 60 | 9 |
| Bernert | Otto (Fritz) | Oblt | J4, 2, 6 | 27 |
| Berr | Hans | Oblt | KekA, J5 | 10 |
| Berthold | Rudolf | Hptm | KekV, J4, 14, 18, JGII | 44 |
| Bertrab | Joachim von | Ltn | J30 | 5 |
| Besel | Rudolf | Uffz | S30 | 5 |
| Bethge | Hans | Oblt | J1, 30 | 20 |
| Bieleit | Otto | Vfw | J45, 66 | 5 |
| Billik | Paul | Ltn | J12, 7, 52 | 31 |
| Blaas | Eduard | Flgmt | MFJII, III | 5 |
| Blume | Walter | Ltn | J26, 9 | 28 |
| Boddien | Hans-Helmut von | Oblt | J11, 59 | 5 |
| Böhme | Erwin | Ltn | J2, 29 | 24 |
| Böhning | Hans | Ltn | J36, 79b, 32b | 17 |
| Boelcke | Oswald | Hptm | FA62, J2 | 40 |
| Boenigk | Oskar Fr von | Hptm | J4, 21s, JGII | 26 |
| Böning | Walter | Ltn | J19, 76b | 17 |
| Bönisch | Erich | Ltn z S | 1 Seaplane Stn | 5 |
| Bohnenkamp | Karl | Vfw | J22s | 15 |
| Bohny | Karl | Ltn | J17 | 8 |
| Bolle | Karl | Ltn | J28w, 2 | 35 |
| Bona | Paul | Vfw | J1 | 6 |
| Bongartz | Heinrich | Ltn | J36 | 33 |
| Borm | Gustav | Uffz | J1 | 5 |
| Bormann | Ernst | Ltn | J2 | 16 |
| Bowski | Hans | Vfw | J14, 51 | 5 |
| Boy | Herbert | Ltn | J14 | 5 |
| Brandenstein | Alois | Ltn | J49 | 8 |
| Brandt | Franz | Ltn | J19, 27, 26 | 10 |
| Brauneck | Otto | Ltn | J25, 11 | 10 |
| Breiten-Landenberg | Otto von | Ltn | J9, 6, 11 | 5 |
| Brendle | Konrad | Ltn | J17, 45 | 8 |
| Bretschneider-Bodemer | Moritz-Waldemar | Ltn | J6 | 6 |
| Brünig | Helmut | Ltn | J32b, 50, 41 | 7 |

| Name | | Rank | Units | Score |
|---|---|---|---|---|
| Buckler | Julius | Ltn | J17 | 36 |
| Buddecke | Hans-Joachim | Hptm | J4, 30, 18 | 13 |
| Buder | Erich | Vfw | J84, 26, K16 | 12 |
| Büchner | Franz | Ltn | J9, 13 | 40 |
| Bülow-Bothkamp | Harry von | Ltn | J36, 2 | 6 |
| Bülow-Bothkamp | Walter von | Ltn | J18, 36, 2 | 28 |
| Büttner | Siegfried | Ltn | J22, 61 | 13 |
| Buhl | Albin | Obflgmt | SFS, MFJIV | 6 |
| Burckhardt | Friedrich-Karl | Hptm | K4, J25 | 5 |
| Burkard | August | Ltn | J29 | 6 |
| Busse | Joachim von | Ltn | J3, 20 | 11 |
| Cammann | Theodor | Oblt | J2, 74 | 12 |
| Christ | Karl | Ltn | J28w | 5 |
| Christiansen | Friedrich | Oblt z S | SFL1 | 13 |
| Classen | Fritz | Vfw | J3, 26 | 11 |
| Collin | Dieter | Ltn | J2, 22s, 56 | 13 |
| Creutzmann | Otto | Ltn | J20, K4b, J43, 46 | 8 |
| Croneiss | Theodor Jakob | Oblt | FA6 | 5 |
| Cymera | Wilhelm | OfStv | J1 | 5 |
| Dahlmann | Hermann | Oblt | J29, 26, JGIII | 7 |
| Dannhuber | Xaver | Ltn | J26, 79b | 11 |
| Degelow | Carl | Ltn | J36b, 7, 40s | 30 |
| Demisch | Martin | Ltn | J58 | 10 |
| Deilmann | Karl | Ltn | J6 | 6 |
| Delling | August | Ltn | J34b | 5 |
| Dietlen | Albert | Ltn | J23b, 41, 58 | 9 |
| Dilthey | Helmut | Ltn | J27, 40 | 7 |
| Dobberke | Gunther | Ltn | J45, 60 | 8 |
| Döring | Kurt-Bertram von | Rittm | J4, JGr4, J66, 1 | 11 |
| Dörr | Gustav | Ltn | J45 | 35 |
| Donhauser | Hans Christian F | Ltn | J17 | 19 |
| Dossenbach | Albert | Ltn | J2, 36, 10 | 15 |
| Dostler | Eduard von | Oblt | J13, 34b, 6 | 26 |
| Drekmann | Heinz | Ltn | J26, 4 | 11 |
| Ehmann | Friedrich | Vfw | J47w | 8 |
| Ehmann | Gottfried | Vfw | S15 | 12 |
| Engelfried | Karl | Flgmt | SFS, MFJV | 6 |
| Eschwege | Rudolph von | Ltn | FA36, 66, 30 | 20 |
| Esswein | Otto | OfStv | J26 | 12 |
| Ewers | Walter | Oblt | J8, 12, 77b | 8 |
| Fahlbusch | Wilhelm | Ltn | K1 | 5 |
| Festner | Sebastian | Vfw | J11 | 12 |
| Fichter | Julius | Ltn | J22s, 67 | 7 |
| Fieseler | Gerhard | Ltn | J25 | 19 |
| Fitzner | Otto | Ltn | J17, 65 | 9 |
| Fleischer | Alfred | Ltn | J17 | 6 |
| Frädrich | Gustav | Ltn | J39, 1, 72s | 6 |
| Francke | Rudolf | Vfw | J2, 8 | 15 |
| Frankl | Wilhelm | Ltn | J4 | 20 |
| Freden | Hans von | Ltn | J1, 72s, 50 | 20 |
| Frickert | Wilhelm | Ltn | J64w, 65 | 12 |
| Friedrichs | Friedrich | Ltn | J10 | 21 |
| Frommherz | Hermann | Ltn | J2, 27 | 32 |
| Fruhner | Otto | Ltn | J26 | 27 |
| Gabriel | Willi | Vfw | J11 | 11 |
| Gaim | Ludwig | Vfw | J39 | 5 |
| Gallwitz | Karl | Ltn | J39, 2 | 10 |
| Gandert | Hans-Eberhardt | Oblt | J51 | 8 |
| Garsztka | Sylvester | Ltn | J31 | 6 |
| Geigl | Heinrich Georg | Ltn | J34b, 16b | 13 |
| Gildemeister | Johannes | Ltn | J20 | 5 |

| Name | | Rank | Units | Score |
|---|---|---|---|---|
| Gille | Friedrich | Uffz | J12 | 6 |
| Gilly | Hermann | Ltn | J40s, 29 | 7 |
| Göring | Hermann Wilhelm | Oblt | J27, 5, 26, 27, JGI | 22 |
| Goerth | Hans | Vzflgmst | MFJIII | 7 |
| Göttsch | Walter | Ltn | J8, 19 | 20 |
| Gontermann | Heinrich | Ltn | J5, 15 | 39 |
| Gossner | Max | Ltn | J23b, 16b, 77b | 8 |
| Grassmann | Justus | Ltn | J10 | 10 |
| Greim | Robert von | Oblt | J34b, JGr10, J9 | 28 |
| Groos | Gisbert-Wilhelm | Ltn | J4, 11 | 7 |
| Güttler | Wolfgang | Ltn | J24s, 13 | 8 |
| Gussmann | Siegfried | Ltn | J11 | 5 |
| Gutknecht | Adolf | Oblt | J43 | 8 |
| Haase | Heinrich | Uffz | J21s | 6 |
| Haber | Kurt | Ltn | J15, 3 | 5 |
| Habich | Hermann | Ltn | J49 | 7 |
| Haebler | Hans G von | Ltn | J36 | 8 |
| Hahn | Erich | Oblt | J1, 19 | 6 |
| Hanko | August | Ltn | J20, 28, 64w | 5 |
| Hanstein | Ludwig | Ltn | J16b, 35b | 16 |
| Hantelmann | Georg von | Ltn | J18, 15 | 25 |
| Hartmann | Otto | Hptm | J18, 28 | 7 |
| Haussmann | Albert | Vfw | J23b, 15, 13 | 15 |
| Heibert | Robert | OfStv | J33, 46 | 13 |
| Heinrich | Bertram | Ltn z S | MFJI | 12 |
| Heldmann | Alois | Ltn | J10 | 15 |
| Hemer | Franz | Ltn | J6 | 18 |
| Hengl | Georg von | Ltn | FA295 | 7 |
| Hengst | Friedrich | Ltn | J64w | 5 |
| Henkel | Heinrich | Ltn | J37 | 8 |
| Hennrich | Oskar | Vfw | J46 | 20 |
| Hess | Ernst | Ltn | J10, 28w, 19 | 17 |
| Hets | Albert | Ltn | J37 | 6 |
| Hetze | Kurt | Ltn | J13 | 5 |
| Hildebrandt | Robert | Ltn | J13, 12, 69, 53 | 6 |
| Hippert | Wilhelm | OfStv | J39, 74 | 8 |
| Höhn | Fritz | Ltn | J21s, 81, 60, 41 | 21 |
| Höhndorf | Walter | Ltn | J1, 4, 14 | 12 |
| Höhne | Otto Walter | Ltn | J1, 2, 59 | 6 |
| Hohly | Josef | Vfw | J29, 65 | 7 |
| Hoyer | Hans | Ltn | J36 | 8 |
| Hubrich | Gerhard | Flgmt | SFS, MFJIV | 12 |
| Hübner | Alfred | Vfw | J36 | 6 |
| Hüttenrauch | Paul | Uffz | J7 | 8 |
| Huffzky | Friedrich | Fw | SS15 | 9 |
| Hutterer | Michael | Uffz | J23b | 8 |
| Imelmann | Hans | Ltn | J2 | 6 |
| Immelmann | Max | Oblt | FA62 | 15 |
| Jacob | Kurt | Ltn | J33, 36 | 7 |
| Jacobs | Josef Carl Peter | Ltn | J12, 22s, 7 | 48 |
| Jacobsen | Fritz John | Vfw | J17, 9, 31, 73 | 8 |
| Janzen | Johann | Ltn | J23b, 4, 6 | 13 |
| Jensen | Johannes | Ltn | J57 | 6 |
| Jentsch | Karl Friedrich K | Vfw | J1, 5, 61, 2 | 7 |
| Johns | Martin | Ltn | J63 | 7 |
| Jorke | Reinhold | OfStv | J12, 13, 39 | 14 |
| Juhnke | Hermann | Vfw | J41, 52 | 5 |
| Junck | Werner | Ltn | J8 | 5 |
| Just | Erich | Ltn | J11 | 6 |
| Kahle | Willy | Fw | J27 | 6 |
| Kahlow | Max | Vfw | J34b | 6 |
| Kairies | Christian | Obflgmstr | SFS, MFJV | 7 |

| Name | | Rank | Units | Score |
|---|---|---|---|---|
| Kampe | Willi | OfStv | J8, 27 | 8 |
| Keudell | Hans von | Ltn | J1, 27 | 12 |
| Kieckhafer | Fritz | Ltn | J32b, 29 | 8 |
| Kirchfeld | Franz | Ltn | J73 | 8 |
| Kirmaier | Stefan | Oblt | J2 | 11 |
| Kirschstein | Hans | Ltn | J6 | 27 |
| Kissenberth | Otto | Oblt | J16b, 23b | 20 |
| Klaiber | Otto | Vfw | J12 | 6 |
| Klaudit | Gustav | Vfw | J15 | 6 |
| Klein | Hans | Oblt | J4, 10 | 22 |
| Klein | Johannes | Ltn | J29, 18, 15 | 16 |
| Klimke | Rudolf | Ltn | J27 | 17 |
| Knappe | Herbert Wilhelm F | Ltn | J73, 81 | 9 |
| Koch | Emil | Ltn | J12, 32b | 7 |
| König | Erich | Ltn | J2 | 6 |
| Könnecke | Otto | Ltn | J25, 5 | 35 |
| Koepsch | Egon | Ltn | J4, 11 | 9 |
| Körner | Hans | Ltn | J8, 27, 19 | 7 |
| Kohlbach | Wilhelm | Ltn | J50, 10 | 5 |
| Kopka | Johann | OfStv | J61 | 5 |
| Korff | Arthur | Ltn | J60 | 8 |
| Kosmahl | Fritz | OfStv | J26 | 9 |
| Krebs | Fritz | Vfw | J6 | 8 |
| Kroll | Heinrich Claudius | Oblt | J9, 24s | 33 |
| Kühne | Wilhelm | OfStv | J29, 15, 18 | 7 |
| Küppers | Kurt | Ltn | J6, 48 | 6 |
| Kuhn | Max | Vfw | J21s | 12 |
| Kummetz | Hans | Oblt | J1 | 7 |
| Kunz | Hermann | Ltn | J3, 7, 55 | 6 |
| Kutschke | Karl | Flgmt | SFS, MFJV | 5 |
| Kypke | Walter | Ltn | J14, 41, K5, J47w | 9 |
| Lange | Helmut | Ltn | J26 | 9 |
| Laumann | Arthur | Ltn | J66, 10 | 28 |
| Leffers | Gustav | Ltn | J1 | 9 |
| Lenz | Alfred | Ltn | J4, 14, 22s | 6 |
| Leptien | Hermann | Ltn | J21s, 63 | 7 |
| Leusch | Wilhelm | Ltn | J13, 19 | 5 |
| Lindenberger | Alfred | Ltn | J2 | 12 |
| Löffler | Otto | Ltn | J2 | 15 |
| Loerzer | Bruno | Hptm | J17, 26, JGIII | 44 |
| Loerzer | Fritz | Ltn | J6, 26, 63 | 11 |
| Löwenhardt | Erich | Ltn | J10 | 54 |
| Lorenz | Heinrich | Oblt | J1, 33 | 5 |
| Lotz | Paul | Ltn | J7, 44s | 10 |
| Luer | Ludwig | Ltn | J27, 62 | 6 |
| Lux | Albert | Vfw | J27 | 7 |
| Mahn | Herbert | Ltn | J72s | 9 |
| Mai | Josef | Ltn | J5 | 30 |
| Mallinckrodt | Friedrich | Ltn | J6, 20 | 6 |
| Manschott | Friedrich | Vfw | J7 | 12 |
| Marwede | Hans Heinrich | Uffz | J67 | 5 |
| Marwitz | Hans-Georg von der | Oblt | J30 | 15 |
| Matthaei | Rudolf | Ltn | J21s, 5, 46 | 10 |
| Maushake | Heinrich | Ltn | J4 | 6 |
| Meinecke | Emil | Ltn | FA6 | 6 |
| Menckhoff | Carl | Oblt | J3, 72s | 39 |
| Mendel | Karl Albert | Ltn | J15, 18 | 7 |
| Mesch | Christian | Vfw | J26 | 13 |
| Mettlich | Konrad | Oblt z S | MFJI, J8 | 6 |
| Meyer | Erich | Uffz | J45, K6, K8 | 5 |
| Meyer | Georg | Ltn | J22s, 7, 37 | 24 |
| Meyer | Karl | Obflgmstr | SFS, MFJI | 8 |
| Mohnicke | Eberhardt | Ltn | J11 | 9 |
| Mohr | Alfred | Ltn | J3 | 6 |
| Monnington | Kurt | Ltn | J15, 18 | 8 |

| Name | | Rank | Units | Score |
|---|---|---|---|---|
| Müller | Hans | Ltn | J12, 15, 18 | 12 |
| Müller | Hans Karl | Ltn | J5 | 9 |
| Müller | Max von | Ltn | J2, 28w | 36 |
| Mulzer | Max von | Ltn | FA62, 32b, KekN, B | 10 |
| | | | | |
| Näther | Max | Ltn | J62 | 26 |
| Nagler | Alfons | Vfw | J74, 81 | 10 |
| Nathanael | Edmund | OfStv | J22s, 5 | 15 |
| Neckel | Ulrich | Ltn | J12, 19, 6 | 30 |
| Neuenhofen | Wilhelm | Ltn | J27 | 15 |
| Niederhoff | Alfred | Ltn | J20, 11 | 7 |
| Niethammer | Werner | Ltn | J13 | 6 |
| Noltenius | Friedrich Theodor | Ltn | J27, 6, 11 | 21 |
| Nülle | Hans | Vfw | J39 | 11 |
| | | | | |
| Oberlander | Hans | Ltn | J30 | 6 |
| Odebrett | Karl | Ltn | J16b, 42 | 21 |
| Osten | Hans-Georg von der | Ltn | J11, 4 | 5 |
| Osterkamp | Theodor | Oblt z S | MFJI, II | 32 |
| Osterroht | Paul H A T von | Hptm | J12 | 7 |
| Otto | Rudolf | Ltn | J74, 68 | 6 |
| | | | | |
| Parschau | Otto | Ltn | KG1, FA32 | 8 |
| Pech | Karl | Vfw | J29 | 9 |
| Pfeiffer | Hermann | Ltn | J9 | 11 |
| Piechulek | Franz | Ltn | J41, 56 | 14 |
| Pippart | Hans Martin | Ltn | J13, 19 | 22 |
| Plange | Richard | Ltn | J2, 36 | 7 |
| Plauth | Karl | Ltn | J20, 51 | 17 |
| Poeschke | Friedrich | Vfw | J53 | 8 |
| Poss | Reinhold | Ltn z S | SFS, MFJIV | 11 |
| Pressentin von Rautter | Viktor von | Ltn | J59, 4 | 15 |
| Preuss | Werner | Ltn | J66 | 22 |
| Pütter | Fritz | Ltn | J9, 68 | 25 |
| Pütz | Johann | Vfw | J23b, 34b | 7 |
| | | | | |
| Quandt | Theodor | Ltn | J36, 53 | 15 |
| | | | | |
| Raesch | Josef | Ltn | J43 | 7 |
| Rahn | Arthur | Ltn | J19, 15, 18 | 6 |
| Ray | Franz | Ltn | J1, 28w, 49 | 17 |
| Reimann | Leopold Rudolf | OfStv | J1, 2 | 5 |
| Reinhard | Wilhelm | Hptm | J11, 6, JGI | 20 |
| Richthofen | Lothar S Fr von | Oblt | J11 | 40 |
| Richthofen | Manfred A Fr von | Rittm | J2, 11, JGI | 80 |
| Richthofen | Wolfram Fr von | Ltn | J11 | 8 |
| Riemer | Claus | Ltn | J26 | 8 |
| Rienau | Rudolf | Ltn | J1, 19 | 6 |
| Ritscherle | Karl Waldemar | Ltn | J60 | 8 |
| Röth | Friedrich von | Oblt | J34b, 23b, 16b | 28 |
| Rolfes | Hans Joachim | Ltn | J32b, 45 | 17 |
| Rosencrantz | Hans | Ltn | KG1 | 5 |
| Rosenfeld | Otto | Vfw | J12, 41 | 13 |
| Rosenstein | Willi | Ltn | J9, 27, K1b, J40s | 9 |
| Rothe | Paul | Vfw | J14 | 5 |
| Rübe | Richard | Vfw | J67 | 5 |
| Rumey | Fritz | Ltn | J2, 5 | 45 |
| Rumpel | Theodor | Ltn | J26, 16b, 23b | 5 |
| Runge | Richard | Ltn | J18 | 8 |
| | | | | |
| Sachsenberg | Gotthard | Oblt z S | MFJI, MFJGrI | 31 |
| Schäfer | Hugo | Ltn | J18, 15 | 11 |
| Schäfer | Karl Emil | Ltn | J11, 28w | 30 |
| Schäpe | Emil | Vfw | J5, 33 | 18 |
| Scharon | Karl | Vzflgmst | MFJII | 8 |
| Schattauer | Karl Fritz | Ltn | J23b, 16b | 9 |

| Name | | Rank | Units | Score |
|---|---|---|---|---|
| Scheicher | Alfons | Ltn | J34b | 6 |
| Schilling | Hans | Oblt | FA5, 22s | 8 |
| Schlegel | Karl Paul | Vfw | J45 | 22 |
| Schleich | Eduard von | Hptm | J21, 32b, JGr8 | 35 |
| Schleiff | Franz | Oblt | J41, 56 | 12 |
| Schlenker | Georg | Ltn | J3, 41 | 14 |
| Schlimpen | Johann | Gefr | J45 | 5 |
| Schmidt | Julius | Ltn | J3, 6 | 15 |
| Schmidt | Otto | Oblt | J7, 32b, 29, 5, JGr2, J2 | 20 |
| Schmückle | Karl | Fw | J21s, 15 | 6 |
| Schneider | Kurt | Ltn | J5 | 15 |
| Schneider | Roman | Ltn | J79b | 5 |
| Schneidewind | Gustav | Vfw | J17, 1F | 7 |
| Schobinger | Viktor | Ltn | J12 | 8 |
| Scholtz | Edgar | Ltn | J11 | 6 |
| Schönebeck | Karl August von | Ltn | J11, 59, 33 | 8 |
| Schönfelder | Kurt | Obflgmstr | J7 | 13 |
| Schröder | Herbert | Ltn | J1, 17 | 5 |
| Schulte | Adolf | Ltn | J12 | 9 |
| Schulz | Wilhelm | Ltn | J15, 16b, 41, 66 | 6 |
| Schumacher | Friedrich | Vfw | J10 | 5 |
| Schumm | Marat | Uffz | J52 | 7 |
| Schuster | Gunther | Ltn | J17, 29 | 6 |
| Schütze | Erich | OfStv | J25 | 6 |
| Schüz | Hans | Hptm | FA6, 2, 13 | 10 |
| Schwartz | Konrad | Ltn | J22s, 66 | 5 |
| Schwartz | Wilhelm | Ltn | J20, 43, 69, 13, 73 | 8 |
| Schwendemann | Josef | Vfw | J41 | 17 |
| Seit | Kurt | Ltn | J80b | 5 |
| Seitz | Wilhelm Anton | Ltn | J8, 68 | 16 |
| Seywald | Heinrich | Ltn | J23b | 6 |
| Siempelkamp | Eugen | Ltn | J4, 29, 64w | 5 |
| Sommer | Wilhelm | Ltn | J39 | 5 |
| Sonneck | Erich | Vfw | J66 | 6 |
| Splitgerber | Otto | Ltn | J12, 38 | 6 |
| Stark | Rudolf | Ltn | J34b, 77b, 35b | 11 |
| Staudacher | Georg | Vfw | J1 | 6 |
| Steinbrecher | Helmut | Ltn | J46 | 5 |
| Steinhauser | Werner | Ltn | J11 | 10 |
| Stör | Wilhelm | Vfw | J68 | 5 |
| Strähle | Paul | Ltn | J18, 57 | 15 |
| Strasser | Georg | Vfw | J17 | 7 |
| Strünklenberg | Karl | Vfw | J9 | 5 |
| Student | Kurt | Oblt | J9 | 6 |
| Stutz | Hermann | Ltn | J20, 71 | 6 |
| | | | | |
| Theiller | Renatus | Ltn | J5 | 12 |
| Thiede | Fritz | Ltn | J24s, 38 | 8 |
| Thöne | Willy | Ltn z S | MFJI | 5 |
| Thom | Karl | Ltn | J21s | 27 |
| Thomas | Erich | Ltn | J9, 22s | 10 |
| Thurm | Alwin | Ltn | J24s, 31 | 5 |
| Thuy | Emil | Ltn | J21s, 28, JGr7 | 35 |
| Tranker | Oswald | Vfw | S16 | 5 |
| Treiber | Karl | Uffz | J5 | 7 |
| Treptow | Reinhard | OfStv | J25, K4a | 6 |
| Tschentschel | Gerold | Ltn | J72s | 5 |
| Turck | Paul | Ltn | J66, 21s | 10 |
| Tutschek | Adolf von | Hptm | J2, 12, JGII | 27 |
| | | | | |
| Udet | Ernst | Oblt | J15, 37, 11, 4 | 62 |
| Ulmer | Alfred | Ltn | J8 | 5 |
| Ultsch | Bernard | OfStv | J39, 77b | 12 |
| Ungewitter | Kurt | Vfw | J24s | 7 |
| | | | | |
| Vallendor | Hermann | Ltn | J2 | 6 |

| Name | | Rank | Units | Score |
|---|---|---|---|---|
| Veltjens | Joseph | Ltn | J14, 18, 15 | 35 |
| Viebig | Hans | Ltn | J20, 18, 57 | 5 |
| Voss | Werner | Ltn | J2, 5, 29, 14, 10 | 48 |
| | | | | |
| Wagener | Werner | Ltn | J21s, 39 | 5 |
| Waldhausen | Hans | Oblt | J37 | 6 |
| Walz | Franz Josef | Hptm | J19, 2, 34b | 7 |
| Wedel | Erich Rudiger von | Oblt | J11 | 13 |
| Wedel | Hasso von | Oblt | J14, 75, 24s, JGr12 | 5 |
| Weiner | Georg | Ltn | J20, K3, J3 | 9 |
| Weiss | Hans | Ltn | J41, 10, 11 | 16 |
| Wendelmuth | Rudolf | Ltn | J8, 20 | 14 |
| Wenzel | Paul | Ltn | J41, 6 | 10 |
| Wenzl | Richard | Ltn | J31, 11, 6 | 12 |
| Werner | Johannes | Ltn | J14 | 7 |
| Wessels | Heinrich | Ltn z S | MFJI | 6 |
| Westphal | Siegfried | Uffz | J29 | 6 |
| Wiehle | Ernst | Vfw | J43 | 6 |
| Wiessner | Ernst | Ltn | J18 | 5 |
| Windisch | Rudolf | Ltn | J32b, 50, 66 | 22 |
| Wintgens | Kurt | Ltn | J4, 1 | 19 |
| Wissemann | Kurt | Ltn | J3 | 5 |
| Wolff | Hans Joachim | Ltn | J11 | 10 |
| Wolff | Kurt | Oblt | J11, 29 | 33 |
| Wüsthoff | Kurt | Ltn | J4, 15 | 27 |
| | | | | |
| Zander | Martin | Hptm | J1 | 5 |
| Zenses | Alexandre | Vzflgmst | MFJII | 19 |
| Zorn | Wilhelm | Uffz | J60 | 8 |